1 MONTH OF
FREE
READING

at

www.ForgottenBooks.com

By purchasing this book you are eligible for one month membership to ForgottenBooks.com, giving you unlimited access to our entire collection of over 1,000,000 titles via our web site and mobile apps.

To claim your free month visit:

www.forgottenbooks.com/free98372

ISBN 978-1-5284-7354-5
PIBN 10098372

and Germany; that of Spain was afterward added. This resolution of the Council almost discouraged Pope John; but he
now received a still more severe blow. An anonymous pamphlet suddenly appeared, charging him with the most revolting crimes(1). He admitted his guilt of some, denied others, and
would have thrown himself on the mercy of the Council, had
not the members refused to notice the anonymous accusations.
New courage, however, was infused into the hearts of the opposition; and on February 15, 1415, the French, English, and
German nations sent a deputation to the Pontiff to beg him
to resign. John affected to be willing, but none of the formulas which he offered were acceptable. Finally, the German
nation openly proclaimed that, in the circumstances, the
Council could invoke the secular arm against the Pope. On
February 28, the four nations drew up a formula couched in
these terms: "I, John XXIII., Pope, for the repose of the
entire Christian people, do declare, promise, agree, and swear
to God, to His Church, and to this Holy Council, that I will
freely and voluntarily give peace to the Church by my simple
renunciation of the Pontificate, and that I will effect this renunciation whenever the present Council deems proper, and
whenever Peter de Luna, styled Benedict XIII., and Angelo
Corrario, styled Gregory XII, give up their claims to the
Supreme Pontificate." The patriarch of Antioch conveyed
this document to Pope John, and in the presence of the Sacred College, the Council, and the emperor, the Pontiff declared
that he would sign it on the morrow, when the second session
of the Council was to be held.

SESS. II.—March 2, 1415, was the day that was to witness
the formal promise of John XXIII. to lay down the tiara
when the Council would demand that session. He celebrated
Mass, and then ascending his throne, he read aloud the formula we have given, and then kneeling at the foot of the altar,
he laid his hand over his heart, and said: "Thus do I promise."
The assembly fairly shouted its congratulations; the emper-
or arose, thanked the Pontiff, and laying aside his crown, pros-
trated himself and kissed the Apostolic feet. In the name of
all the nations, the patriarch of Antioch did the same, and

(1) NIEM: loc. cit., b. II., c. iii.

the *Te Deum* was chanted. Amid the joy caused by this event, the Council sent a message to the nuncios of Peter de Luna, accepting the offer of an interview between that claim- ant and Sigismund, and fixing the mouth of June as the time. On March 5, the nations demanded that the Pontiff should issue a Bull, confirmatory of his late promise; and after some hesitation he yielded. As, however, in the instrument given he had spoken only of a personal cession, the nations now in- sisted that the emperor and other delegates should be made procurators of Pope John in this matter, and that, if deemed advisable by the fathers, the said procuratory powers should be exercised at the imminent imperial colloquy with Peter de Luna. Pope John rejected this idea, and he was upheld by the whole Italian nation. Even many influential synodals of the other nations began to think that they were infringing on the necessary liberty of the head of the Church; and when there arose, on March 11, a debate on the propriety of choos- ing a new Pontiff, the archbishop of Mayence firmly an- nounced that if John XXIII. were not elected, he would obey no other. The opponents of Pope John now had recourse to the defamatory pamphlet above mentioned; and the Eng- lish and German nations held particular congregations for its examination, the French taking no part (1). Under the in- fluence of the emotions produced by this investigation, the two nations demanded of the Pope, on March 15, that he would promise not to dissolve the Council before the accomplish- ment of union; that he would not transfer the Council; that he would not depart from Constance; that he would appoint Sigismund as his procurator in the matter of the abdication; and that he would issue Bulls confirmatory of these pledges. This schedule was approved by the Italian and French nations, although the former protested against urging the last article. On March 16, the patriarch of Antioch presented these de- mands to Pope John, and Cardinal Zabarella replied in the Pontiff's name, that there was no intention of prematurely dissolving the Council, or of transferring it against its own will; that the Pope would accord no procuration, since he in- tended to take the more sure and honorable way of going to

(1) LENFANT: *History of the Council of Constance*, vol. I., p. 118.

STUDIES

IN

CHURCH HISTORY,

BY

REV. REUBEN PARSONS, D. D.

"That a theologian should be well versed in history, is shown by the fate of those who, through ignorance of history, have fallen into error . . . . . . Whenever we theologians preach. argue, or explain Holy Writ, we enter the domain of history.—"

MELCHIOR CANUS, *Loc Theol.*, B. XI., c. 2.

VOL. III.

CENTURIES XV.–XVI.

SECOND EDITION.

FR. PUSTET & CO.,

NEW YORK AND CINCINNATI

STUDIES IN CHURCH HISTORY.

CHAPTER I.

JOHN HUSS.

This heresiarch was a native of Bohemia, and probably he derived his name from the village in which he first saw the light. At the time when the election of Alexander V. (1409) gave new virulence to the Western Schism, Huss was rector of the University of Prague, and had become distinguished for eloquence, subtlety, and love of novelty (1). The famous Jerome of Prague was a disciple of Huss; and when he returned from a finishing term at Oxford, he brought some of the writings of Wycliffe, insisting that the English innovator's doctrines were the very kernel (all others were the mere shell) of knowledge. More works of Wycliffe were soon introduced into Bohemia by an English refugee named Peter Payne. Devoured with avidity, these books furnished democratic ideas to political malcontents, but Huss became enamored of the new theology; and when, in 1409, Alexander V. issued a Brief prohibiting preaching in the minor churches of Bohemia, "because of the great number of persons infected with the Wycliffite doctrines," the innovator disobeyed, and publicly defended those teachings. The Pope now commanded Cardinal Otho Colonna to investigate the case of Huss, and as the citation was ignored by the preacher, he was excommunicated (Feb., 1411); and the cardinal threatened to interdict any place which would tolerate his presence. Influenced by King Wenceslaus, who dreaded the effects of an interdict. Huss soon made a profession of the orthodox faith; but in 1412, when John XXIII. published a crusade against King Ladislas of Naples, and offered indulgences to its participants, Wenceslaus encouraged Huss and Jerome to declaim against the Pontifical action, and their

(1) BALBINUS: *Bohemian History,* b. IV., c. v.—ÆNEAS SYLVIUS; *Bohemian History,* c. XXXV

followers grossly outraged the publishers of the Indulgences (1). In the autumn of 1412, Huss was again excommunicated, and Wenceslaus allowed the publication of the decree. The heresiarch appealed to Christ; and retiring to Krakowec, composed his treatise on *The Church.* In the meantime his errors were being propagated throughout Poland by Jerome. The German throne was then occupied by Sigismund (2), a brother and heir of Wenceslaus, who, sincerely desirous of peace among his future subjects of Bohemia, agreed with the latter to have Huss tried at the coming Council of Constance. Huss made no objections to this project; and returning to Prague, he affixed placards on the city walls informing the citizens that he was ready to answer before the Council for all his teachings, and that if convicted of error, he was also ready to suffer merited punishment.

On Oct. 18, Sigismund signed a safe-conduct for Huss, guaranteeing him protection on his way to the Council (3). Abundantly supplied with money by his friends, accompanied by many of these, and protected by three Bohemian knights and their retinues, the heresiarch traversed Germany; and on Nov. 4, the Pontiff was informed that Huss demanded his protection. The Pope replied: "Even though Huss had murdered my own brother, I would not allow any injustice to be done to him in Constance." The Pontiff even modified the effects of the excommunication under which the innovator labored, so far as to permit communication with him. Huss, however, manifested anything but a proper spirit; in spite of his censures, he frequently celebrated Mass, and preached to his attendants. On Nov. 28 he was cited to appear before a congregation of cardinals, and after some hesitation he obeyed; protesting to their Eminences that he would abjure any error of which he would be convicted. He was then reconducted to his lodging; but from this date he no longer enjoyed his liberty, thanks

(1) Woksa, a knight, caused two prostitutes to carry the Bull to a stake, and it was publicly burnt.

(2) Sigismund became king of Hungary in 1386, of Germany in 1410, of Bohemia in 1420, and received the crown of the Holy Roman Empire in 1433 from Pope Eugenius IV.

(3) Palacky, in his *History of Bohemia*, vol. III., pt. 1, proves that this passport was not received by Huss until Nov. 5, after his arrival at Constance.

to an attempt at flight (1). A series of accusations against Huss was soon drawn up by the great Gerson and by Paletz, and the Pontiff appointed two commissions to examine them. These commissioners frequently visited Huss in the Dominican convent where he was confined; but their examinations were often interrupted by the negotiations then being held for the purpose of procuring the resignation of the three claimants of the Papacy, and their powers were finally annulled by the flight of John XXIII. from Constance on March 20, 1415. The Council, however, in its fifth session, held on April 1, designated a new commission, composed of the cardinals d'Ailly and of St. Mark, the bishop of Dole, and the abbot of Citeaux. These vainly tried to obtain from Huss a pure and simple submission to the decrees of the Council; and on June 5 he was called before a general congregation of that assembly. His writings were exhibited; and he avowed their authorship, declaring that he would retract whatever would be demonstrated to be wrong. By this attempt to draw the Council into a discussion with a subject whose duty it was to hear and to obey, Huss attacked the judiciary authority of the assembly. Naturally enough, therefore, he was ordered to answer simply whether he had taught such and such a doctrine. He replied so contemptuously that great excitement ensued, and the sitting terminated. A second interrogatory was held on June 7, in the presence of the emperor-elect, Sigismund. Cardinal d'Ailly and Michael de Causis insisted that Huss had erred in the Eucharistic doctrine; but the heresiarch firmly, and it would seem with reason, repelled the charge. When accused of propagating certain errors of Wycliffe, Huss protested that he regarded some of the condemned propositions as orthodox. As to the Englishman's doctrine that a priest in mortal sin could neither baptize nor consecrate, Huss qualified the assertion so as to signify that such a priest could not worthily officiate. When charged with declaring himself a saint, with advising recourse to arms against the "enemies of truth," with causing scandal, sedi-

(1) So say many olden writers, though Palacky discredits the assertion. As to his imprisonment, he was allowed to receive visitors and to write letters, and he himself did not regard his seclusion as very severe,—PALACKY, *loc. cit.*

tion, etc., he admitted some of the accusations and denied others.   D'Ailly and Sigismund then urged him to submit to the Council.   The words of the sovereign throw much light upon the subject of the safe-conduct, upon the alleged violation of which Protestant polemics are prone to dwell. Sigismund said that " Huss had come to Constance under the imperial safe-conduct, which secured to him a public interrogatory ; that he had been heard peaceably and publicly, and that *therefore the imperial promise had been kept ;* that if Huss would submit to the Council, he would receive kind treatment, but that if he obstinately persisted in heresy, the sovereign himself would be the first to lead him to the stake." Huss uttered no protest against this interpretation of the safe-conduct.   On June 8 were read twenty-six articles from the treatise of Huss on *The Church ;* also seven from his pamphlet against Paletz, and six from his diatribe against Stanislaus of Znaim.   The heresiarch avowed some, denied some, and modified others.   Then, in the name of the Council, d'Ailly demanded from Huss, firstly, an admission of his errors in the aforesaid articles ; secondly, a promise to teach them no more ; thirdly, a public retractation of them.   Huss refused to comply.

On June 9, Cardinal Viviers, president of the Council, laid before Huss a very moderate form of retractation ; and several synodals encouraged him by the example of the learned Origen, of Peter Lombard, and even of St. Augustine, to submit his judgment to that of the Church.   His obstinate refusal was met by a grant of a delay until July 6, that he might fully reflect on his position.   The interval was spent by Huss in writing epistles to the Bohemians, and in repelling the earnest endeavors of d'Ailly, and other eminent persons, to convert him.   On July 6 the Council of Constance celebrated its fifteenth session.   Huss was placed on a raised seat ; .and by his side were laid the sacerdotal vestments with which he was to be clothed, preparatory to a final deprivation of them, if it became necessary to proceed to his solemn degradation from the priestly office.   Then a detailed account of the previous proceedings was read.   When Huss tried again to draw the Council into a discussion of his views, he was ordered to merely declare whether he now abandoned them or not. Nevertheless the fathers entered on the record his protest that he did not deny Transubstantiation; that he had not proclaimed himself a divine person, and that he had not denied the validity of a baptism performed by a wicked priest. After these articles had been laid aside, there remained thirty, of which the Council decreed that "many of them were erroneous, some scandalous, some offensive to pious ears, some rash and seditious; others notoriously heretical, and already condemned by the holy fathers and General Councils."—As to the person of Huss, the Council declared him "a heretic, and wished him to be regarded as such; thus judging him and his appeal by the present decree—his appeal being scandalous and contrary to discipline, and he himself being a seducer of the Bohemians and a preacher of a false Gospel. Because of his obstinacy, the Council declares him fallen from the priestly dignity, condemns him to be degraded, and orders the archbishop of Milan, and five other archbishops to execute the sentence in presence of the Council" (1). Then Huss prayed God to forgive his enemies, and the ceremony of degradation was begun. When he had been fully vested with the sacerdotal habiliments, he was again entreated to have mercy on himself, and to bow to the decisions of Christ's Church. He remained immovable. Then, one by one, the sacred vestments were stripped from him, and he heard the words: "By the authority of Almighty God, Father, Son, and Holy Ghost, and by our own, we take the clerical habit from thee, and we depose, degrade, and deprive thee of every order, benefice, and clerical privilege." He was declared excluded from the Church, and on his head was placed a paper cap inscribed "heresiarch." Then were pronounced the words which decided the worldly fate of John Huss: "Since Holy Church has nothing more to perform in the case of John Huss, this Holy Synod of

(1) At this juncture, Huss cried: "Why do you condemn my writings, when you cannot even read those which are written in Bohemian?" Nevertheless, remarks Hefele, in one of his letters Huss says that he is "much pleased because his enemies read his books, and he doubts not that they notice them more that they do Holy Writ" (*Works of Huss*, vol. I., epist. 14). And among the fathers of Constance were Paletz, Michael de Causis, and other Bohemian bishops, besides many Germans who had studied at Prague, and must have understood Bohemian. Finally, the greater part of the innovator's works were in Latin.

Constance decrees that he be delivered to the secular judg-ment and to the secular power." Sigismund now placed the heresiarch in the custody of the elector-palatine, who, in his turn, consigned him to the magistrates of Constance, to be dealt with according to the laws of the empire. Huss was asked to receive the ministrations of a confessor ; but although he had never denied the necessity of sacramental confession, he refused the offer, and began to chant the *Miserere* and other prayers of the Church. When he had been fastened to the stake, the duke of Bavaria and the lord of Papenheim rode up to the pile, and besought him, for the last time, to recant. Their efforts were vain; the signal was given, the flames burst forth, and crying, "Jesus Christ, Son of the Living God, have mercy on me !", Huss went to judgment.

The doctrine of Huss—at least, as it was in the beginning of his vagaries—may be styled a revival of that of Wycliffe, although the Bohemian was the more systematic of the two. Huss seems to have conceived a plan of "reformation," which would have worked a revolution in the constitution of the Church. According to him, the Church of the pre-destined (that of Abel, Noah, Moses), was very distinct from that of the reprobate (that of Cain, Ham, Ishmael, etc.). The true Catholic Church, theologized the Bohemian, is formed by all the predestined of all times, and being the Mystic Body of Christ, she can contain only the pure. Reprobates, therefore, are in, but not of the Church ; they no more form a part of the Mystic Body than excrements do of the human body. Hence all priests, even the Pope, who do not lead virtuous lives, forfeit their pastoral authority. Christ is the sole head of the Church ; the Pope enjoys no headship, for we know not that he is in the grace of God. It was Con-stantine who instituted the primacy of the Roman Pontiff; hence the Holy Roman Emperor is the Pope's superior. We should obey God rather than men, and therefore we should always examine whether the edicts of our superiors conform to the law of God ; consequently no excommunication is to be feared, if it is found to be unjust. The Pope has no more power to bind and loose than any priest possesses, and his censures are acts of tyranny. Although Huss declaims against Indulgences, he does not formally attack the Catholic doctrine. His disciples attacked the sacred mystery of the Eucharist, auricular confession, purgatory, and the veneration of saints ; but we shall show that Huss left these dogmas intact. The favorite target of Huss is the Papacy ; for, weakened though this tremendous power was by the Western Schism, the Bohemian innovator saw that no changes, such as he contemplated, could be effected so long as a Roman Pontiff directed the affairs of the Church (1).

Those Protestants who would fain add somewhat to the antiquity of their position by claiming religious kinship with Huss, should inform themselves, firstly, concerning that heresiarch's opinions as to the Eucharist. It is true that in

(1) The following are the thirty propositions inculcated by Huss, and anathematized by the Council of Constance : I. The Church is the society of the predestined. II. Paul was never a member of the devil, although he performed actions similar to those of the wicked. III. The foreseen (*præsciti*) are not a part of the Church, since no member of the Church can be finally lost. IV. The two natures of our Lord form one Christ (this proposition is orthodox in itself, but in the context of Huss it presents a false sense.—See *The Church*, c. 4.) V. The foreseen (*præsciti*) are never members of the Church ; the predestined always are. VI. Inasmuch as the Church is the society of the predestined, it is an article of faith. VII. Peter was never the head of the Church. VIII. A priest who is in a state of sin has a false idea of the Sacraments. IX. The Pope and his prerogatives were instituted by the emperor. X. Without a special revelation, no one can say of himself or of another that he is the head of a particular church ; with much more reason this is true of the Roman Church. XI. The Pope cannot be head of a particular church unless he is one of the predestined. XII. No one can be vicar of Christ or of Peter unless he imitates their virtues. XIII. The Pope is not the successor of Peter when his habits are contrary to those of Peter ; the case of cardinals is the same. XIV. Those doctors who teach that a condemned and persistent heretic ought to be delivered to the secular power are like the Pharisees and the high-priests of the Jews. XV. Ecclesiastical obedience is an invention of the priests, and is contrary to the formal teaching of Scripture. XVI. When a man is virtuous, he always acts virtuously ; when he is vicious, he always acts viciously. XVII. and XVIII. A priest should always preach, even when excommunicated ; if the Pope or any other prohibits him, he should not obey. XIX. The clergy oppress the laity with ecclesiastical censures, which are of no other use than to encourage priestly avarice, and to cover priestly perversity. XX. When the Pope is wicked, he is a devil, like Judas, and is not the head of the Church, of which he is not even a member. XXI. The grace of predestination is the tie which unites and preserves the Church. XXII. When the Pope or any prelate is wicked, he cannot rightly be styled a shepherd ; he is rather a robber and a ravisher. XXIII. The Pope ought not to be styled " His Holiness," not even because of his dignity. XXIV. If the Pope acts in a manner contrary to the spirit of Christ, he enters the fold by another way than that of Christ, even though be be regularly elected. XXV. The condemnation of Wycliffe's forty-five propositions was unjust. XXVI. A unanimous choice of the electors, or the consent of a majority of them, does not legitimately elect one as a true successor of the Apostles. XXVII. It is untrue that the Church must have a visible spiritual head. XXVIII. If there were no such pretended head, Christ would direct His Church by means of His true disciples scattered throughout the world. XXIX. The Apostles and faithful priests directed the Church before the institution of the Papacy, and could do so until the end of the world. XXX. Whoever is in a state of sin cannot be a temporal superior, a prelate, etc., while he continues in that state.

the Council of Constance, many witnesses swore that " he
taught that after the consecration, the material bread or the
substance of bread remained on the altar," but Huss called
these witnesses liars, and to the charge by Broda he replied :
" I said and I say that there remains in the Host that Bread
who said : ' I am the Bread of Life,' ... and of which every
priest says in the Mass, ' I will take the Heavenly Bread,
and I will call upon the name of the Lord.' ... It is true
that bread remains in the Host, but no mortal bread."
Shortly before his death, certain of his alleged doctrines
were quoted to him ; and with his own hand he wrote replies to the charges, which replies were transcribed from the
original autograph by John Przibram, once a famous Hussite,
but afterward converted, and author of a work on the *Non-
Subsistence of the Bread.* John Cochlæus, a great adversary of Luther, had read this book ; and he gathered from it
that when Huss was charged with teaching that the bread
remained after consecration, he answered: "It is not true "(1).
In his treatise on *The Sacrament of the Body and Blood of
the Lord*, written in his prison at Constance, Huss says : " By
the power and institution of Christ, true God and true man,
there is in the venerable Sacrament, by means of His priest,
His true Body—that Body which was conceived and born of
the most chaste Virgin Mary by the power of the Holy
Ghost; that Body which lay in the tomb for three days ;
that Body which ascended into heaven, and sitteth at the right
hand of God the Father ; that, and no other, is in the same
venerable Sacrament without a new substantial inception of
itself. For Christ said: ' This is My Body, etc.' ... I
have delivered this doctrine in my sermons, and I have never
taught that the material substance of bread remains in the
Sacrament of the altar, as the enemies of truth have falsely
declared." In another treatise on *The Body of Christ*, Huss
says : " Great was the heresy of Berengarius, who held that,
before the consecration, the bread on the altar is unconsecrated bread, and after the consecration, merely consecrated
bread, and not the true Body of Christ."

Huss did not deny the necessity of sacramental confes-

(1) COCHLÆUS ; *History of the Hussites*, b. II.; Milan, 1549.

sion; nay, he expressly asserted it. In his treatise on Penance we read: "As the doctors say, there are three parts in
perfect penance ; namely, contrition, confession, and satisfaction. ... Confession is the avowal of our sins before God
and a priest, and it should be clear and entire—clear, that
the priest may understand ; and entire, lest the penitent
may knowingly conceal some sin." Commenting on *James
v.*, he concludes from the text: "Confess therefore your
sins one to another," that "it is evident that confession is of
precept. The Lord implicitly prescribed it in *Matt. iv.*,
'Do penance,' and the Apostles afterward explicitly commanded it."

Not one of the numerous sects which have resulted from
the Lutheran rebellion admits the Sacrament of Extreme
Unction. Huss admitted it as one of the seven Sacraments,
divinely instituted to confer grace. Explaining the words
of St. James: "Is any man sick among you?" he writes:
"This Sacrament was instituted for the relief of the sick,
and for the forgiveness of sin ; hence there is in it both an
anointing and prayer. Prayer, however, does not always
succeed, because what is sought is not always for the sick
person's good. ... Extreme Unction may be repeated, but
not so Baptism, Confirmation, and Orders, which impress a
character in the recipient."

Huss admitted the doctrine of purgatory, and held that
prayer, sacrifice, and alms aided the souls therein detained.
In a sermon on *Obsequies*, he says: "There are three good
reasons for funeral ceremonies. First, that we may think of
the most painful and disgraceful death of Christ, and of our
sins, the cause of that death. Second, that by noting the
miseries of the dead, we may improve our own condition.
Third, that by devoutly praying for the dead, we may assist
the sleeping Church, that is, the saints who are in purgatory.
... A second class of souls, although abounding in love of
Christ, have their love shared with temporal things, and
hence have venial sins to be expiated. ... St. Augustine says
that when sacrifices, either of the altar or of alms of any sort,
are offered for the baptized, such are actions of thanksgiving
for the very good ; when offered for the not very bad, they

are propitiations ; if for the very wicked, they are of no use to them, but are consolations for the living."

Huss also taught the doctrine of veneration of the saints. In the explanation of his faith, he said : " I know that Christ taught that all members are of help to each other, when He cured the centurion's servant. . . . If, therefore, a man who is yet mortal can obtain the favor of Christ God for another, yea, for the whole militant Church, what fool will dare to say that the same cannot be effected by one who dwells with Christ in glory ? . . . The Virgin Mary is our advocate, our mediatrix, and, in a certain sense, the cause of the Incarnation, Passion, and Resurrection of Jesus Christ, and consequently the cause of the salvation of all who are saved."

And nevertheless, the man who so strenuously taught Transubstantiation, the necessity of Confession, the seven Sacraments, the existence of purgatory and the duty of praying for the dead, the veneration of the saints, is styled by Luther a man " adorned by the great and excellent gifts of the Holy Ghost, who taught Christian doctrine with pen and tongue, and suffered death for so doing. . . . If he is to be called a heretic, scarcely any man upon whom the sun has shone can be regarded as a Christian "(1). This same Huss was regarded by the "Bohemian Brethren," who rejected all the above doctrines, as a martyr to truth, as their own leader, and as the apostle of Bohemia. Nor is this strange; for it accords with the genius of heresy to be inconsistent, and to destroy, with one hand, what it has constructed with the other.

After the condemnation and execution of Huss and of Jerome of Prague, the Council of Constance drew up a decree, the design of which was to compel the king of Bohemia to protect the freedom of the Church, to obtain the restitution of all property stolen by the Hussites from the orthodox, to exclude all heretics from the Faculty of the University of Prague, and to restrict the power of preaching to duly authorized persons. But Wenceslaus was not one upon whom the Church could rely in such emergencies. The vices which had entailed his loss of the imperial dignity caused him to

(1) At the end of the *Letters of John Huss*, edited in 1537.

neglect the most sacred duties of royalty. Violent and cruel, lecherous and a drunkard, he was utterly wanting in will (1). Again, the chief ecclesiastical authority in Bohemia was unfaithful to its mission. Archbishop Zbinko, who had resisted Huss from the beginning, had died while on a mission to urge Sigismund to come to the aid of the orthodox of Bohemia ; and the metropolitan see of Prague was occupied by Conrad of Westphalia, a monster of avarice and an incarnation of inconstancy, who finally deserted openly to the Hussites (2). Hussitism had begun as a reform, and in the course of time had acquired a violent and sombre character ; the extermination, not the conversion of sinners, was its object. The Church was to be rebuilt of new materials, rather than restored. Huss had contented himself with attacking the constitution of the Church : his disciples very soon made havoc with the Creed, and Bohemia presented as frightful a picture as religious discord has ever produced on the face of the earth. Churches and monasteries were pillaged ; the orthodox priests were expelled when not murdered outright ; and laymen pretended to administer the Sacraments. Cochlæus informs us that a shoemaker of Prague parodied the celebration of Mass ; and that in Guttenburg, a soldier snatched the chalice from the altar, and carried the Precious Blood to a tavern (3). The Hussites were addicted to pilgrimages to certain mountains, which they named Horeb and Thabor ; and from these places were derived their designations of Horebites and Thaborites. The Calixtines were those who differed from the Catholics only in the custom of communicating under both species ; although, being animated by much of the spirit of the others, they often made common cause with them (4). On the death of the ferocious John of Trocznow, better known as Ziska (5), the Thaborites were divided

(1) BALBINUS ; *Epitome*, b. IV., ch. i.—*Kings of Bohemia* ; sect. II., ch. iii.—COCHLÆUS ; b. IV.—DUBRAVIUS : *History of Bohemia*, b. XXIII.—ÆNEAS SYLVIUS ; *History of Bohemia*, ch. xxviii.

(2) DUBRAVIUS ; *loc. cit.*—DLUGOSS ; *History of Poland*, b. XI.

(3) B. IV.

(4) BALBINUS ; *loc. cit.*, b. V., ch. v.

(5) Bonnechose, more than partial to the Hussites, says of Ziska's character and exploits : " Bohemia, from one extremity to the other, became one vast field of carnage ; everywhere conflagrations displayed to view dreadful massacres. Woe to the towns, castles, and, above

into two factions, one retaining its old name, and led by
Procopius Rasa, called by Ziska the "Hercules of his country;" the other assuming the name of "Orphans," because
its members deemed no man worthy to succeed to their blind
hero. The Calixtines were finally admitted to communion
by the Council of Basel : being allowed to retain the use of
the chalice on condition that they would admit that their
practice was not of divine precept, and that they would not
molest the followers of the other discipline. The instrument of union, called *Compactata*, was rejected by the Thaborites and Orphans ; even the Calixtines soon violated its
provisions by insisting on the necessity of all following their
rite, and by depriving all who rejected it of Christian burial.
Their leader in the new rebellion was John Rockizany, archbishop of Prague. Some of the Calixtines soon came to the

all, to the monasteries that closed their gates—all the inhabitants were put to the sword.
... The sight of a monk or priest filled Ziska with a gloomy rage. ... He smote, burned, and
exterminated, coldly glutting his vengeance in the shock of combatants, the gleam of flames,
the shrieks of victims, 'punishing,' as Balbinus expresses it, 'one sacrilege by a thousand.'
Bohemia, Germany, all Europe, were soon filled with the name of this terrible man. Wenceslaus awoke from his shameful slumber at the noise of his falling palaces, the burning of
his churches, the slaughter of his senate ; he started up in a frightful fit of passion, which
was injurious to himself alone, for it suffocated him. ... In becoming blind, Ziska became
still more terrible ; his misfortune was a fresh stimulus to his rage as to his genius, and revealed almost incredible faculties in him. His memory of localities was prodigious ; it was
enough for him to have once passed through a land to be forever master of all its slightest
peculiarities. Bohemia, with her waters, woods, valleys, and plains, was now as present to
his thoughts as the reality had ever been to his sight. A spirit of fire in a body of iron, his
activity knew no fatigue, and became exasperated at rest. His soldiers used to mutter : 'All
seasons are alike to this blind man ; he goes by day as by night.' Wherever there was a
monastery to burn, a town to take, or an army to combat, he hurried to the spot, and was
soon accomplishing the deed of blood with a superhuman force, as if impelled by an exter-
minating God. ... He expired (of the plague) on Oct. 11, 1424, ordering his soldiers to make
a drum out of his skin, that its noise might fill his enemies with terror ; his body he left to
the birds of prey." *John Huss and the Council of Constance.*—Aventinus, whose pen
was one of the most unjust ever wielded against the Church, admits that the Hussites laid
waste more than 550 ecclesiastical foundations, that priests and religious were often massacred, and their bodies burnt. *Annals of the Bavarians*; b. VII., no. 4.—It was the misfortune of Bohemia that the principal author of these ravages was the best general of his
age. In 1420 Sigismund led 140,000 men against Ziska ; but beaten in every battle, he returned home with merely the sterile honor of having been crowned king of Bohemia. In
1421 Albert of Austria helped Sigismund to return to Bohemia, and Prague meditated submission, when the Hussites offered the crown, first to Vladislas of Poland, and then to the
duke of Lithuania. The latter prince accepted for his brother ; but this offer to a foreigner,
made without the consent of Ziska, embroiled the Thaborites with the Calixtines. Ziska
himself had aimed at the crown, and now commenced between the factions a pitiless struggle, the end of which was that Prague was about to succumb to the fiery fanatic when death
ended his ambition. So great had been the power of Ziska, that it is said that Sigismund
thought of making him imperial vicar in Bohemia with an annual subsidy, and that Ziska
contemplated an acceptance of the offer. SYLVIUS ; *loc. cit.*, c. xlvi.—DUBRAVIUS ; b.
XXVI.—BALBINUS ; c. viii.—COCHLÆUS ; b. V.

conclusion that their sect was entirely too Roman in its teach-ings, and therefore founded the " Bohemian Brethren," who, while affecting to be the sole real disciples of Huss, entered into communion with the Lutherans at the synod of San-domir in 1570.

Several points in the matter of John Huss and his con-demnation merit examination. Firstly, his death was os-tensibly that of a man thoroughly devoted to the idea which entailed his fate. Had we no other testimony than that of his friends, we might doubt the reality of his constancy and the sincerity of his piety during the dread ordeal. But Æneas Sylvius, speaking of the deaths of Huss and Jerome, says : " Both met their fate bravely, and they hastened to the stake as though invited to a banquet, emitting not one sound which would indicate a weak spirit. We read of no philosopher who met death so bravely as they endured the burning." Hefele feels himself compelled " not to deny that Huss sincerely meant well, for an impostor does not die as he died." This point we will not discuss ; but rather pass to a less problematical question—that of the safe-con-duct given by Sigismund to the heresiarch. There is no need of commenting on the fable which narrates that, when about to suffer, Huss cried : " To-day you burn a goose (such was the meaning of *hus*), but after a century will appear a swan (Luther) which you will not burn." Not one contemporary of Huss mentions this prophecy ; not until the time of Luther did it appear (1). So now to the safe-conduct. Mosheim insists that the condemnation of Huss was a violation of the public faith (2). Some Protestant authors have even asserted that the Council of Constance had given a safe-conduct to the heresiarch, and that it justi-fied its perfidy by decreeing that no faith was to be kept with heretics. Now there is not a shadow of proof that the Council gave any such assurance to Huss ; it did give one to Jerome, but it expressly stipulated that the due course of law was not to be frustrated (3). As for the Conciliary decree (Sess.19) which has been so maliciously interpreted, it mere-

---

(1) See PALACKY, *loc. cit.*—GIESELER. *Ecclesiastical Law*, vol. II., pt. 4.

(2) *Eccl. Hist.*, cent. XV., pt. 2, c. ii., 5.

(3) " *Salva justitia.*" Even Bonnechose admits this.

ly explains the safe-conduct of Sigismund in the same sense
in which, as we have seen, its royal author explained it;
that is, it was not intended to prevent the legal examination and conviction—if merited—of Huss. Bad faith would
scarcely have been justified by that Council which had ordered, immediately after the election of Martin V., all suspects of heresy to be interrogated as to whether they held
falsification to be allowable, in any circumstances whatsoever (1). But, confining ourselves to the nature of the safe-
conduct in question, we must observe that Sigismund, in the
face of Huss and his partisans, interpreted that document as
a mere passport to the Council which was to judge the innovator. The Bohemian knights who accompanied Huss accepted the royal interpretation; even while complaining of
their friend's imprisonment when as yet not convicted, they
disclaimed any desire of impunity for him: "Nor do we wish
him to go unpunished, if he is shown to have uttered false
doctrine" (2). And in the bitter letters which the Hussite
nobility addressed to the fathers of Constance after the burning of Huss, not a word is said of any violation of Sigismund's or of any other safe-conduct. But what better indication of the meaning of the document can be required
than that furnished by Huss himself? In the first place,
before his departure for Constance, he declared: "If they
convict me of any error, and show that I have thought anything against faith, I will not refuse any punishment due to
a heretic." Secondly, when Sigismund told the Council
that he would be the first to lead a persistent heretic to the
stake, Huss made no protest against such an interpretation
of the safe-conduct.

Protestant authors represent the terrible carnage committed by the Hussites as a retaliation for the cruelties of
the Council of Constance. But the Hussite excesses had
devastated Bohemia long before the trial of Huss; just as,
in the following century, the German Anabaptists committed

(1) Gieseler, *loc. cit.*, adduces two acts of the Council to sustain this hideous accusation,
but Hefele notes that he mutilates the first by omitting this very pertinent clause: "He
who gives a safe-conduct must do everything possible to insure its being respected;" and
the second act is not a decree, but a design of one which was not adopted.

(2) Van der Hardt; *Council of Constance*, vol. IV.

similar barbarities before the execution of their leaders. Mosheim is particularly strong in this assertion (1); but we may reply, with Bergier, that this author's own admissions militate against his theory of injustice at Constance. I. He admits that in 1408 Huss endeavored to withdraw the University of Prague from the jurisdiction of Pope Gregory XII. II. He concedes that Huss, an enthusiastic Realist, bitterly persecuted the Nominalists, who were very numerous in the University. III. He says that Huss aroused against himself the indignation of the entire German nation by depriving them of the two or three votes which they had hitherto cast in University matters; and thus caused the desertion of two (some say five) thousand students to Leipsic, where they founded a rival establishment. IV. He admits that Huss publicly declaimed most virulently against the clergy. V. He acknowledges the contempt evinced by Huss for the excommunication launched by John XXII. Such are Mosheim's admissions, but he utterly ignores the following facts: I. Huss appealed to the Council from the Papal excommunication, thus submitting himself to its judgment. II. He publicly offered to undergo the punishment decreed by the public law against heretics, if he were convicted of heresy. III. He abused his safe-conduct by celebrating Mass and by preaching in defiance of his excommunication. Mosheim also admits that the Hussites rebelled against Sigismund, who had become their sovereign, and that this rebellion occurred simply because they would not submit to the decrees of Constance. They conceded that heretics deserved death, but they denied that Huss had been a heretic. Was an army of ignorant men, well asks Bergier, to judge of the orthodoxy of a doctrine ?

We have seen that Hefele inclines to believe in the sincerity of John Huss. Whether or not the reader will admit that a learned and sane Catholic can "sincerely desire good" while resisting unto death the teaching authority of the Church, he will agree with the remarks with which this judicious author qualifies his opinion: " It is certain, however, that all the principles of reform (cherished by Huss) threat-

(1) *Loc. cit.*

ened ruin not only to the Church, but to the state and society;
and Sigismund rightly said that there had never been a more
dangerous heretic than Huss. Undoubtedly Huss hoped that
a reforming council like that of Constance would approve of
his efforts for reform, but while the reforms decreed by that
assembly were very numerous in matters of discipline, the
same fathers were rigorous in their maintenance of dogma ;
and the propositions of Huss appeared to the most enlightened of them—to Gerson, for instance—as so many rank and
intolerable heresies. The Council had met in order to procure for the Church a peace long departed, and precisely,
therefore, Huss, whose principles would again destroy that
desirable peace, was to be rigorously judged. At Constance
whoever troubled the peace of the Church was threatened
with death ; that enlightened personage, Gerson, even proposed
that death should be inflicted on the Pope, if he interfered
with that peace (1), and there were real fears for the life of
the Sovereign Pontiff. Could Huss expect more lenient treatment than the Pope ? "

Few authors have so extravagantly lauded Huss as Bonnechose (2). He seldom quotes any authority not openly Hussite, and—strange thing for one professing to write history—
he sometimes relies on John Fox, the Protestant " martyrologist." The reader will be interested by some of this writer's
admissions : " It was impossible not to acknowledge the moral
authority, the very serious ascendency, which John Huss had
acquired over the minds of men. ... The magistrates of Prague
blamed him, and joined with the heads of the University, the
court, and the clergy, against him. So many elements of discord portended fresh troubles of a more serious character
than those which had already caused the voluntary exile of
Huss, but no apprehension shook his resolution. ... On the
appointed day (of a public discussion to which the innovator
had challenged all priests and monks), the concourse was prodigious, and the alarmed rector endeavored vainly to dissolve
the assembly. A doctor of Canon Law defended the Pope and
the Bulls, and then turning to John Huss, he said : ' You are

(1) *Deponibility of the Pope—Methods of Union.*
(2) *John Huss and the Council of Constance.* Abp. Martin Spalding's valuable essay
is mainly directed against this work.

a priest, subordinate to the Pope, your spiritual father; only
filthy birds defile their own nests; Ham was accursed for having exposed his father's shame.' ... The magistrates deliberated (when Huss had led a mob against the prison wherein
some of their fellow-rioters were confined) in trouble and consternation, and the town council replied, in the name of all:
'Dear master, we are surprised at your kindling a fire in
which you run the risk of being burnt yourself. It is very
hard for us to pardon persons who do not spare even the
sanctuary, who fill the city with tumult, and who, if not pre·
vented, will stain our streets with slaughter.' ... The minds
of all men seemed in a blaze; the city was the theatre of
bloody scenes every day; in Prague there was no longer security for personal safety; even the king deemed it prudent to
depart. ... Huss had the powerful support of the nobility,
several of whom were sincerely touched by the elevation and
purity of his doctrines, while many adopted them either
through opposition to the court, or through jealousy of the
higher clergy, or through the hope of sharing the spoils. ...
Some of Huss's opinions, particularly those borrowed from
Wycliffe, concerning titles and Church property, were much
to the taste of Wenceslaus. 'Secular lords,' he was wont to
say, 'have the right to take away, when they please, the temporal possessions of those ecclesiastics who live in sin.' ...
Wenceslaus adopted these ideas, *which were those of most of
the reformers, and which rendered many princes favorable to
them.* He made himself the judge as to how Church property was to be used; and as he cared nothing for the poor,
the badly employed wealth of the clergy fell into his coffers,
and when he openly supported the new teachings, his severity and exactions increased the Hussite party. Several wealthy
ecclesiastics declared themselves Hussites; with the view of
saving their own property, they adopted the doctrines which
enjoined a good employment of it. ... In a paper affixed to
the palace gates, Huss announced that he was about to justify
himself before the Council, 'so that if any one suspects me of
heresy, he may proceed thither and prove, in presence of the
Pope and doctors, that I ever held or propagated false or
mistaken doctrine. If any man convicts me of having taught

anything contrary to the Christian faith, I consent to bear every penalty to which heretics are liable.'"

CHAPTER II.

THE COUNCIL OF PISA.

Rendered desolate by the Great Western Schism, the Church had long vainly sought to terminate it. Gregory XII., third successor of Urban VI., and Peter de Luna, who, under the name of Benedict XIII., had inherited the pretensions of the so-called Clement VII., were both obstinate, and the latter manifested very little good faith. In 1408, Charles VI. of France, tired of their broken promises of cession or of compromise, resolved to obey neither; and imitating him, many powers declared for neutrality. Some of the cardinals of both obediences now decided to meet at Leghorn, and there debate as to the best way of securing a way out of the great difficulty. Under date of June 30, 1408, thirteen cardinals published in Leghorn a document according to which they had sworn, firstly, to prosecute the work of union unto a happy end, and meanwhile to adhere to neither one of the competitors; secondly, in case of the death of one of these, to elect no successor until the Church had pronounced on the right of the survivor, and in case of the death of both, to proceed to no election without the consent of two-thirds of the cardinals of each obedience; thirdly, to approve of no election which might be made by those cardinals who then remained in the obedience of Gregory or of Benedict; and fourthly, to treat of no other business, until the consummation of union, unless all the cardinals consented. This agreement was afterward ratified, by special adhesions, by all the cardinals of both Colleges who were not present at its original signature. On July 1, the Roman cardinals announced to Christendom that they had abandoned Gregory, and exhorted all anti-schismatics to do likewise, and to pay no more revenues into the Apostolic Chamber. Both claimants vainly tried promises and threats to break the concord of the Leghorn cardinals; their Eminences seized the reins of government, confirmed

Balthassar Cossa as legate at Bologna, sent the cardinal of Bordeaux as legate to Paris and London, and Maramaur into Germany ; and finally, on July 14, they sent to all the prelates of Christendom a summons to a General Council to be held at Pisa on March 25, 1409. At the same time the cardinals of each obedience notified their respective Pontiffs of their intentions, praying them to consent, and either to come to the Council, or to send nuncios with full powers. Neither claimant paid any serious attention to the invitation.

But had the cardinals any right to convoke a General Council ? Perplexity soon agitated not only the outside world, but many of the cardinals themselves. The Faculties of Bologna, Florence, and Paris were consulted ; but they gave no complete solution of the question. At this juncture Gerson issued his famous treatise on the *Deponibility of the Pope*, in which there are some blunders unworthy of so great a theologian, but which, like many other extravagancies of the time, may be explained by the disturbed state of the Church. "In such perturbed times," remarks Christophe, "the wisest intelligences, involved in the tumult of disorder, lose some of their rectitude and precision" (1). Worldly policy also entered into the question. France, England, Castile, Genoa, and Florence were with the cardinals ; Venice affected neutrality ; Aragon, Naples (2), Hungary, Poland, Dalmatia, Croatia, Servia, Bulgaria, Russia, and Scotland declared against holding the Council. In the empire, although Cardinal Maramaur was received with extraordinary honors, and although he gained Austria, Bohemia, and the great princes to his cause, Robert of Bavaria, the king of the Romans, persisted in the obedience of Gregory.

On the appointed day, March 25, 1409, the Council was opened in the cathedral of Pisa. There were present twenty-four cardinals, four patriarchs (those of Jerusalem, Alexandria, Antioch, and Grad), ninety-two bishops, one hundred and seventy-five procurators of bishops, eighty-seven abbots, one

(1) *Papacy during the Fifteenth Century*, b. XVI.: Paris, 1863.

(2) Ladislas of Naples had everything to lose by the deposition of Gregory, who had given to him Rome, the March of Ancona, Bologna, Faenza, Perugia, Forli, nearly all the Patrimony, and the duchy of Spoleto—all for the petty annual sum of 25,000 florins. PIER€ M!NERBETI ; y. 1408, ch. xxii.—*Spec. Hist.*—SOZOM.; *Pistor.*, p. 1193.

hundred and eight procurators of abbots, more than three
hundred doctors in theology or Canon Law; deputies from the
Universities of Bologna, Florence, Paris, Oxford, Cambridge,
Orleans, Toulouse, Angers, Montpellier, Cracow, Vienna,
Prague, and Cologne; the orators of France, England, Poland,
Sicily, Bohemia, Portugal, Cyprus, Burgundy, Brabant, Cleves,
Lorraine, Brandenburg, and Thuringia; the grand-master of
Rhodes, and the procurator of the Teutonic knights. Guy de
Malésec, cardinal-bishop of Palestrina, a creation of Gregory
XI., and dean of both Colleges, was chosen president. On
the second day, by request of the president, two cardinals,
two bishops, the advocate of the Council, and two notaries
proceeded to the doors of the cathedral, opened them, and
called in a loud voice upon Angelo Corrario, Peter de Luna,
and the cardinals of Todi, Auch, Fieschi, and Chalant to appear. None of the cited answering, the assembly was asked
whether any one present was empowered to represent them.
Returning to their places, the accusers asked the Council for
a declaration *in contumaciam* against the delinquents. In the
next two sessions this ceremony was repeated, and on the
fourth, held on March 30, after due deliberation, the president
pronounced the cited persons contumacious; granting, however, a respite to the four cardinals until April 15. On that
day a further delay was granted, pending the arrival of some
important ambassadors. Toward the end of April there arrived at Pisa, as advocate of Gregory, Charles di Malatesta,
lord of Rimini, a man famous in literature, an eloquent orator,
and a renowned knight. In a series of fifty articles he urged
the postponement of the Council, and a change of place. Consideration for Malatesta caused the Council to confer with him;
but his requests were finally refused, and he was about to depart, when Thomas of Fermo made him an offer on the part
of the assembly. If Gregory would resign the tiara, he would
be made life-legate for Forli and the Trevesine March, and
would receive, also for life, the government of the March of Ancona; if he preferred a residence at court, he would be assured
the first place in the Sacred College, and the lordships of Montefiascone, Orvieto, Faenza, and other places would be settled
upon his nephews. When Malatesta, on the part of Gregory,

rejected this proposition, the Council yielded to his original demands so far as to promise to transfer its sessions to Pistoja or San Miniato. Malatesta now returned to his fief of Rimini, where Gregory was residing, and made every effort to induce the feeble old man to yield. Lamentations and tears ensued, but as yet Gregory remained resolute in his hold on the tiara.

On May 9, the Council declared itself œcumenical; and on the following day, at the instance of the bishop of Salisbury, the cardinals of the obedience of Peter de Luna dissolved what little of connection, in hopes of influencing him to resign, they had continued to hold with him. Until June the prelates were occupied in hearing testimony concerning the conduct of the rival Pontiffs; when all was ready, the fifth was fixed as the day for definitive sentence. This eventful day was that of the fifteenth session. Again two cardinals, Colonna and Sant' Angelo, accompanied by two bishops and many doctors and notaries, went to the doors and cited Angelo Corrario and Peter de Luna; then the procurators of the Council demanded definitive sentence. All the members consented to the demand, the doors were thrown open, and the patriarch of Alexandria declared that Angelo Corrario and Peter de Luna, styled by their followers Gregory XII. and Benedict XIII., having been shown to be schismatics and abettors of schism, and having been guilty of enormous crimes, notably, of violating their oaths and scandalizing the Church, were declared by the Council to be unworthy of the Supreme Pontificate, and were therefore deposed. This sentence, hitherto without example, was hailed with acclamations of joy, and a *Te Deum* was chanted.

A new Pontiff was now to be chosen. Some of the prelates wished the election to be made by the Council; but the majority, following the judgment of the patriarch of Alexandria, wished for no derogation from established usage, and that the cardinals should enter into Conclave, notwithstanding the doubtful source of many of their titles. While the Council was considering this point, three knights and a royal chancellor, ambassadors of the king of Aragon, informed the fathers that their master was now willing to assist them in the work

of union, and that nuncios of Benedict XIII. demanded an audience.   Certain cardinals were appointed to receive the nuncios in the church of St. Martin, and these latter, having run
the gauntlet of a hooting populace, entered the church, and
the doors were shut.   No honors were accorded to the messengers; and they were asked whether they came from Peter
de Luna.   When they replied that they were " nuncios of the
holy father, Pope Benedict XIII.," they were saluted with cries
of " nuncios of a schismatic and heretic."   When silence was
restored, the archbishop of Tarragona, the head of the embassy, asked whether he was free to speak his mind.   The cardinal of Aquileia replied that the nuncios knew of the sentence
launched against the two pretenders, and of the legal penalties incurred by those who attacked that sentence.   The nuncios consulted a moment with the Aragonese deputies, and
then retired, as they averred, for reflection.   The next morning revealed that they had secretly left the city (1).

On June 15, the guardianship of the Conclave was entrusted
to the grand-master of the Hospitalers; and amid the prayers
of nearly all Christendom the cardinals entered upon their
important task.   If we except the suspicious testimony of
Boniface Ferrier, there is no reason for believing that the
proceedings were influenced by extraordinary intrigue.   There
was one cardinal, Balthassar Cossa, who had acquired great
influence over his colleagues by his eminent services in the
cause of union, and whose election seemed probable from the
beginning; but he worked in the interest of Peter Filargo, and
by a unanimous vote that cardinal was proclaimed as Pontiff on
June 26, 1409.   He assumed the name of Alexander V.   On
July 7, the new Pontiff was crowned by the cardinal of Saluzzo; and the world flattered itself that the Great Schism was

---

(1) According to the Carthusian monk, Boniface Ferrier, one of the nuncios, who wrote
an account of this embassy (see *Thes. Anecd.*, v. II., c. lviii.), this flight was caused by the
threatening attitude of the Pisan mob. The nuncios would have been stoned, he says, on
their exit from St. Martin's, had they not been escorted by the marshal of the court and
many influential citizens. Boniface says (*ibid.*, c. lxiii.) that, wishing to confer with Gregory,
they applied for a safe-conduct to Balthassar Cossa, then legate at Bologna (afterward Pope
John XXIII.), and that he sent them word that if he met them with a safe-conduct or not,
he would burn them alive if he could seize them. Perhaps Cossa would have been capable
of such an action; but the passionate style of Ferrier merits little confidence. It was the
general impression among the synodals that the nuncios had come to Pisa, not to further
the cause of union, but as spies and intriguers for de Luna. NIEM; *Schism,* b. III., c. xlv.
—MONSTRELET; *Chronicle,* b. I., c. lv.

at an end. But Spain and Scotland persevered in the obedience of de Luna; Naples, Hungary, Bavaria, and the northern kingdoms remained faithful to Gregory XII.; and ere
long the election of Alexander V. was generally regarded as
a mistake.

When the Pisan prelates relied upon the Christian world
to rally around the banner of their new Pontiff, they ignored
the deep root that the schism had taken in the passions and
interests of peoples as well as of kings. Peter d'Ailly had
doubted the success of the proceedings at Pisa. Shortly before the opening of the Council, he had written a treatise in
which, while avowing the legitimacy of the proposed depositions, he said: "If the conduct of the two claimants permits
a new election, it should not be held unless it is clear that all
Christendom will accept it, or at least that there will be such
a majority for it that the pretenders will have but a few followers; otherwise a fresh schism will be added to the old
one" (1). Many other Catholic writers showed more repugnance for the acts of the Pisan assembly than that evinced by
d'Ailly. Theodoric de Vrie says that it is doubtful whether
the spirit which animated the Council was that of Moses and
Aaron, or rather that of Dathan and Abyron (2). Clemangis
is of opinion that if the synodals did not deceive the Church,
they deceived themselves (3). St. Antonine of Florence declares that, "according to common opinion," the assembly
was a *conciliabulum,* and could not make Alexander V. a legitimate Pontiff (4). In our day the facts may be discussed
with more impartiality; but, as Christophe says, "we may be
allowed to think that the attempt at Pisa to terminate the
schism was unhappy." It cannot be denied, however, that
the obedience of Alexander extended rapidly; and if, to use
the words of Bossuet, "the monster of the Great Schism was
not entirely crushed at Pisa, at least it there received a blow
which was the prelude to its total extinction, five years afterward, at Constance."

From the readiness with which Theodoric de Vrie, Clemangis, St. Antonine—and to them may be added the cardinals

(1) *Collection of Old Writers,* p. 916.   (2) In VAN DER HARDT, vol. I.
(3) *Disputation on the Matter of General Councils.*
(4) *Chronicle,* pt. III., tit. 22., c. v.

Cajetan, Turrecremata, and many other celebrated authors—
denied the authority of the Pisan Council, the reader will see
that the œcumenicity of that assembly was, from its very beginning, at least dubious. And since it is the custom of Rome
to style the Council of the Vatican the Nineteenth General Council, that of Trent the Eighteenth, the Fifth Lateran the Seventeenth, that of Florence the Sixteenth, and that of Vienne
(y. 1311) the Fifteenth, an additional argument is now furnished for the denial of the character of a General Council to
the assembly of Pisa. In the palmy days of Gallicanism, nearly
all French authors fought strenuously for the œcumenicity of
that assembly which first applied the great Gallican principle
of the superiority of a General Council over the Pope. Chief
among these writers are Alexandre, and his imitator, or rather
his abbreviator, Amat de Graveson. The learned Gerson, by
his work on the *Deponibility of the Pope*, and because of his
persistent exaltation of the Pisan Council, furnished the Gallican school with the authority of a truly great name; but no
one has better defended the œcumenicity of the Pisan assembly than the Dominican historian (1). It must be admitted that
the arguments of this school, whatever may be thought of
their general value, are exceedingly specious in this matter;
even Bellarmine, although he regarded Alexander V. and John
XXIII. as legitimate Pontiffs, was led to pronounce on the
œcumenical character of the Pisan Council that it was "neither approved nor rejected." We now proceed to lay before
the reader the arguments adduced on each side of the question.

1. *For the œcumenicity of the Pisan Council:* St. Antonine
and Cardinal Cajetan refused to recognize the legitimacy of
this assembly, firstly, because it was not convoked by a Supreme Pontiff; secondly, because it did not terminate the
schism, but rather intensified its bitterness. These authors
add that the Council of Constance could not have regarded
the Pisan fathers as possessing power to depose Gregory XII.
and Benedict XIII., since it allowed the resignation of the
former. Other writers add that many kingdoms and provinces did not recognize the Council of Pisa, since they continued

(1) Cent. XV., dissert. 2.

in obedience either to Gregory or to Benedict. Now, as to the necessity of convocation by Papal authority, such necessity can exist only when the Pontiff is undoubtedly a legitimate one. But when two or more rival Popes refuse to give peace to the Church by resignation, especially when they have already sworn to do so, if called upon; then to deny that the Church has remedial power in the premises is to assert that Christ did not provide sufficiently for the security of His mystic Body. As to the action of the Council of Constance in receiving the resignation of Corrario, it does not follow therefrom that the Council regarded his deposition at Pisa as invalid. The fathers of Constance merely deemed it more prudent to obtain as much security as possible from any future disturbance. As for the failure of the Pisan assembly to extinguish the schism, such an argument would militate against the œcumenicity of nearly every General Council, since the heresies against which they pronounced did not always immediately collapse. As to the refusal of many countries to recognize the Pisan decrees, the recalcitrants were comparatively a small portion of the Christian world, while the fathers of Pisa represented the universal Church.

2. *Against the œcumenicity of the Pisan Council:* Although unknown, one of the two claimants, Gregory XII. or Benedict XIII., was the legitimate Pope. Neither one convoked the Council of Pisa; nay, each firmly opposed it, and each convoked a Council of his own—Gregory at Friuli, and Benedict at Perpignan. But without Papal convocation, no Council, be it ever so well attended, can be œcumenical. Undoubtedly the cardinals of Leghorn were in good faith when they excogitated the Council of Pisa as a remedy for the tremendous evil of their day. But all the good faith in the world could not give to them a power which Christ gave only to the Roman Pontiff. Nor was the attendance at this Council of a very œcumenical character. There was no attendance from Spain, which, as the cardinal of St. Mark remarked at Constance, was then "as large a portion of Christendom as Christian Greece." All the bishops of Scotland were absent, and a great many Italians and Germans. Bossuet should not have contemned this fact; for when it suited him to do so, he denied

the œcumenicity of the Sixth General Council because of the absence of the Spanish bishops. It is true that in some of the General Councils celebrated in the East there was almost a total absence of Western prelates ; but then the confirmation by the Roman Pontiff supplied this defect. At Pisa, however, this confirmation was wanting ; for it cannot be said that the approval by Alexander V. effected it. When Alexander was elected, the Pisan Council enjoyed an authority at best uncertain; his own authority, therefore, was uncertain. Finally, the Council of Constance was careful not to style the Pisan assembly a General Council; it used the term "congregation," or "assemblage": "there was held a large assemblage, which they called a General Council of both obediences" (1). John XXIII., successor to Alexander V., endeavored to induce this Council to declare the Pisan œcumenical, lest his own title to the Papacy should be questioned. But he failed; chiefly because of the exertions of d'Ailly, who, although addicted to the super-exaltation of General Councils, admitted that the Pisan assembly had left as much difficulty as it had found, and that nothing certain accrued from its proceedings.

CHAPTER III.

THE COUNCIL OF CONSTANCE.

The Council of Pisa had decreed that another Synod should assemble within three years, for the purpose of considering measures of reform, and for the consummation of unity. Accordingly, John XXIII. convoked a Council to meet at Rome; and in April, 1412, its sessions were begun in the Basilica of the Apostles. There were present a small number of bishops from Italy, Hungary, Bohemia, England, Scotland, and from such parts of Germany as recognized John XXIII. as Pontiff; deputies of the clergy and of the king of France ; and representatives of the University of Paris. The doctrines of Wycliffe and Huss were condemned ; but it was evident that Pope John desired no discussion of the points for the treatment of which the Council had met. In a contemporary *Life of John*

(1) See the articles proposed by the Conciliar commissioners concerning Benedict XIII.

XXIII., published by Muratori, we are told that whenever a synodal would broach any such matter, Cardinal Zabarella would arise, and in a prolix discourse contrive to defeat the endeavor. Finally, the Pontiff prorogued the Council until December ; but indicated no place of reunion. The emperor Sigismund, however, was determined to put an end to the schism, in order that more energy might be employed against the innovators in the empire. Pope John was urged to resume the Council ; and he reluctantly appointed a commission to negotiate with Sigismund as to the place of meeting. To the great chagrin of the Pontiff, the legates agreed upon Constance, an imperial city, and for that very reason, thought Pope John, no favorable place for his future fortunes. Leonard of Arezzo, an eye-witness, tells us that John cursed his destiny (1) ; he even undertook a journey to Piacenza, where Sigismund was residing, hoping to persuade the emperor to a change of place. But after Sigismund had so remonstrated with the Pontiff that he must have foreseen the humiliations in store for him at the Council, it was finally agreed that the assembly should be held at Constance on November 1, 1414. The Papal letters of convocation were issued, and Sigismund wrote to Gregory XII. and Benedict XIII.; begging them to attend the Council, and satisfy their consciences. Neither of the claimants deemed it wise to accept the invitation ; Gregory empowered Cardinal John Dominick of Ragusa, and Contareno, patriarch of Constantinople, to represent him ; while Benedict sent a few prelates, who soon departed. The authors of the day inform us that the Council brought more than a hundred thousand strangers to Constance ; between bishops, doctors, and other clergymen, there were eighteen thousand directly or indirectly connected with the Council. The bishops numbered over three hundred.

John XXIII. presided over the first two sessions ; but, as we shall see, his fears led him to flee from Constance. The presidency then devolved on Cardinal d'Ailly for the third session ; on Giordano Orsini, cardinal-bishop of Albano, in the fourth ; on John de Brogny, cardinal-bishop of Ostia, during the fifth and all the other sessions held until the election

(1) *Commentary*. in Muratori, vol. XIX.

of Pope Martin V.; and for the final sessions, on the newly-elected Pontiff. We shall now give a succinct account of the forty-five sessions of this Council. Session I.—Pope John tried to procure from the Council a declaration that it was a continuation of the Council of Pisa; for as such he had formally announced it in his Bull of convocation, in his Bull of prorogation, and on the opening day. Had such a declaration been made by the Council, his position as legitimate Pontiff would have been strengthened. On December 7, the partisans of Pope John XXIII. having insisted on the above declaration, and on a proclamation of the canonicity of all that had been effected at Pisa, Cardinal d'Ailly objected, contending, in the first place, that the Council of Pisa needed no confirmation from that of Constance, and that such procedure would excite scruples as to the authority of the former; secondly, that no coercion should be used in regard to Gregory XII. or Benedict XIII., and that their causes should not be touched until their nuncios had arrived; thirdly, that while it was probable that the Council of Pisa had been œcumenical, it was not necessarily to be concluded that it had not erred in its decrees on the schism (1). Sigismund arrived on December 24, and at his suggestion particular congregations, over which Pope John could exert no influence, held meetings under the sovereign's immediate protection, and the Pontiff intrigued to thwart their efforts. Having gained over some of their members, he was informed, every day, of every proceeding; but the spies were detected, and ordered out of the Council (2). Meanwhile, the synodals learned that nuncios of Gregory and Benedict were approaching Constance. The Pontiff insisted that the cardinals among them should receive none of the honors of the purple; while the emperor, d'Ailly, and other sincere promoters of the union, declared that such honors ought to be accorded. The latter party carried its point. The first to arrive were the nuncios of Benedict; and they at once proposed an interview between the king of Aragon, Benedict's chief protector, and Sigismund. Answer to this proposal was indefinitely postponed. Then came the nuncios of Gregory; namely, the cardinal of Ragusa, the patriarch-elect

(1) Van der Hardt; vol. II., pt. 8.   (2) Niem; *Life of John XXIII.*, b. II., c. II..

of Constantinople, the duke Louis of Bavaria, the bishops of Verdun, Worms, and Spire, and representatives of the archbishop of Treves. A general congregation was held, the emperor assisting, and the nuncios were asked if their powers were full; if they recognized the Council; and if they would unite with it. The cardinal of Ragusa replied that their powers were plenary, and he exhibited a Bull whereby Gregory offered to abdicate, on condition that his rivals did the same, and that Balthassar Cossa (*sic*) did not preside over the Council. The duke of Bavaria further said that if Cossa would withdraw from the presidency, he himself would warrant that Gregory would either attend the Council or would send plenipotentiaries to assist in his name. The fathers replied that John XXIII. would preside over their sessions, but that they would gladly welcome the arrival of Gregory. The opinion was gaining adherents every day that the Pisan proceedings ought not to be ratified; that they should be studiously ignored. Such a view necessarily implied the resignation of John XXIII.; and as the liberalities of Pope John had gained over a large number of the bishops, d'Ailly hit upon an expedient whereby to neutralize the Pontiff's influence. He proposed to accord, in the matter at issue—not one, he said, of faith, Sacraments, or discipline, in which bishops alone could have a definitive voice—votes to the numerous doctors, as well as to the sovereigns, and even to their ambassadors. Cardinal Filastro followed in another memorial, advocating the same views, and the result was that the Council adopted them. This action was a severe blow to Pope John; but he still possessed a powerful resource in the vote *per capita*. The Italian synodals were nearly all devoted to him, and they were very numerous; his own household would wield fifty votes, on the part of so many chamberlains; and his gifts had secured the sympathies of many poor bishops of other nationalities. Owing to the late resolution of the Council, the number of voters, if the votes were to be taken *per capita*, was over eighteen thousand; hence to prevent confusion, and especially to deprive Pope John of a strong weapon, it was decided that the members should vote by nations. There were then present the four nationalities of Italy, France, England,

and Germany ; that of Spain was afterward added. This res.
olution of the Council almost discouraged Pope John ; but he
now received a still more severe blow. An anonymous pamphlet suddenly appeared, charging him with the most revolting crimes(1). He admitted his guilt of some, denied others, and
would have thrown himself on the mercy of the Council, had
not the members refused to notice the anonymous accusations.
New courage, however, was infused into the hearts of the opposition ; and on February 15, 1415, the French, English, and
German nations sent a deputation to the Pontiff to beg him
to resign. John affected to be willing, but none of the formulas which he offered were acceptable. Finally, the German
nation openly proclaimed that, in the circumstances, the
Council could invoke the secular arm against the Pope. On
February 28, the four nations drew up a formula couched in
these terms : " I, John XXIII., Pope, for the repose of the
entire Christian pecple do declare, promise, agree, and swear
to God, to His Church, and to this Holy Council, that I will
freely and voluntarily give peace to the Church by my simple
renunciation of the Pontificate, and that I will effect this renunciation whenever the present Council deems proper, and
whenever Peter de Luna, styled Benedict XIII., and Angelo
Corrario, styled Gregory XII , give up their claims to the
Supreme Pontificate." The patriarch of Antioch conveyed
this document to Pope John, and in the presence of the Sacred College, the Council, and the emperor, the Pontiff declared
that he would sign it on the morrow, when the second session
of the Council was to be held.

SESS. II.—March 2, 1415, was the day that was to witness
the formal promise of John XXIII. to lay down the tiara
when the Council would demand that session. He celebrated
Mass, and then ascending his throne, he read aloud the formula we have given, and then kneeling at the foot of the altar,
he laid his hand over his heart, and said : " Thus do I promise."
The assembly fairly shouted its congratulations ; the emper-
or arose, thanked the Pontiff, and laying aside his crown, pros-
trated himself and kissed the Apostolic feet. In the name of
all the nations, the patriarch of Antioch did the same, and

(1) NIEM : *loc. cit.*, b. II., c. iii.

the *Te Deum* was chanted. Amid the joy caused by this event, the Council sent a message to the nuncios of Peter de Luna, accepting the offer of an interview between that claimant and Sigismund, and fixing the month of June as the time. On March 5, the nations demanded that the Pontiff should issue a Bull, confirmatory of his late promise; and after some hesitation he yielded. As, however, in the instrument given he had spoken only of a personal cession, the nations now insisted that the emperor and other delegates should be made procurators of Pope John in this matter, and that, if deemed advisable by the fathers, the said procuratory powers should be exercised at the imminent imperial colloquy with Peter de Luna. Pope John rejected this idea, and he was upheld by the whole Italian nation. Even many influential synodals of the other nations began to think that they were infringing on the necessary liberty of the head of the Church; and when there arose, on March 11, a debate on the propriety of choosing a new Pontiff, the archbishop of Mayence firmly announced that if John XXIII. were not elected, he would obey no other. The opponents of Pope John now had recourse to the defamatory pamphlet above mentioned; and the English and German nations held particular congregations for its examination, the French taking no part (1). Under the influence of the emotions produced by this investigation, the two nations demanded of the Pope, on March 15, that he would promise not to dissolve the Council before the accomplishment of union; that he would not transfer the Council; that he would not depart from Constance; that he would appoint Sigismund as his procurator in the matter of the abdication; and that he would issue Bulls confirmatory of these pledges. This schedule was approved by the Italian and French nations, although the former protested against urging the last article. On March 16, the patriarch of Antioch presented these demands to Pope John, and Cardinal Zabarella replied in the Pontiff's name, that there was no intention of prematurely dissolving the Council, or of transferring it against its own will; that the Pope would accord no procuration, since he intended to take the more sure and honorable way of going to

(1) LENFANT: *History of the Council of Constance,* vol. I., p. 118.

Nice (1), and there abdicating in his own person. Meanwhile, Pope John had resolved to flee from Constance, trusting that so much confusion would ensue, that the Council would dissolve. But it was difficult to leave the city without the permission of Sigismund, as guards were at the gates, and already the cardinal of Sant' Angelo had been turned back. The Pope essayed flattery, sending to the emperor, on *Lœtare* Sunday, that prize so much coveted by princes—the golden rose. When this failed, he tried the power of money, knowing that Sigismund was in need. Succeeding no better, he loudly complained to the magistrates that their city was his prison. All was in vain; and his intentions transpiring, the English nation proposed to seize the pontifical person; and only the opposition of the French prevented the adoption of this course (2). Pope John now consulted with Frederick, duke of Austria, the intermediary being the archbishop of Mayence. Before the Council, in return for an annual pension of six thousand florins, and the title of Captain-general of the Roman Church, Frederick had already promised to aid the Pontiff in such an emergency (3). A solemn tournament was being held on March 21, and while the duke of Austria and the count of Cilley were breaking lances, Pope John, disguised as a groom, and mounted on a miserable jade, went out of the city. In a few hours he was safe in Schaffhaus, where he was joined by the duke. Many of the bishops, thinking the cause of union lost, prepared to return home; but Sigismund mounted his horse and scoured the city to detain them, giving his royal word that the Council should continue until its end was attained. Frederick of Austria was placed under the ban of both Council and empire. The courage of many of the synodals now became audacity, if no harsher name should be assigned to their sayings. Gerson went so far as to declare, in a discourse pronounced in full session, that the Pontiff could not change the decrees of a General Council; that a Council could regulate the use of the Apostolic power; and that in a General Council none of the faithful should be excluded (4).

(1) Nice had been chosen as the place for the interview between Sigismund and Peter de Luna.

(2) GERARD DE ROO: *Austrian Affairs*, b. IV.   (3) *Ibid.*

(4) In VAN DER HARDT, vol. II., pt. 11.

SESS. III.—This session was held on March 26, and was be-gun in the absence of all the members of the Sacred College, excepting d'Ailly, who presided, and Zabarella; some had gone to Schaffhaus, and the others insisted on the presence of their colleagues. The following decrees were published: I. That the Holy Council was properly and legally convoked and opened. II. That by the departure of the Pope, the Council had not been dissolved, but still retained all its authority, in spite of any ordinances to the contrary, either already issued or to be issued. III. That the Holy Synod could not be dissolved until the schism was healed, and the Church reformed in faith and morals, in head and members. IV. That the same Holy Synod could not be transferred to another place without its own consent. V. That those who ought to be present at the Council should not depart, unless for good reason—said reason to be examined by a commission deputed by the Council. A synodal who was allowed to depart should leave a procurator in his place. Scarcely had these decrees been issued, when three cardinals, who had been sent to the fugitive Pontiff, returned to Constance, reporting that Pope John still promised to be faithful to his pledges, and that he requested that nothing should be undertaken against the duke of Austria for some time. This message was regarded as a ruse to gain time, and to suspend the synodal deliberations; therefore instructions were issued to a particular congregation to prepare apposite decrees for the next session.

SESS. IV.—On March 30, Cardinal Zabarella read the following proposed decrees: I. The Synod held its power immediately from Jesus Christ, and every person—no matter how great his dignity, even the Pope—was obliged to obey it in all that concerned faith, the healing of the schism, and the reformation of the Church in head and members. II. The penalties by law established would be visited upon all—no matter what their dignity, even upon the Pope—who would disobey its decrees or those of any other General Council. III. Pope John XXIII. and all members of the Council had always been free. IV. The authority of the Holy Council being necessary for the unity of the Church, to faith and morals, the flight of the Pope should be regarded as scandalous, destructive to his promises, ruinous to the Council, and as redolent of schism and heresy (1). The cardinals discussed these articles outside the Council; and it was only when the nations withdrew the last one, that all but four entered the hall and accepted the three others. The Council now learned that on the previous day, March 29, Pope John had suddenly moved to Lauffemberg, and that he had declared that his promises at Constance were valueless, since they had been given under coercion.

Sess. V.—In this session, celebrated on April 6, the three decrees read in the preceding session were confirmed; and commissaries were appointed to examine the doctrines of John Huss. On April 10, Pope John removed from Lauffemberg to Fribourg, hoping to pass into the territories of Duke John of Burgundy, a bitter foe of the Council. Therefore the synodals drew up an act of procuration, to be sent to the Pontiff, and by which he was to declare that he voluntarily resigned the tiara, and to promise never to insinuate any doubt as to the validity of the present abdication.

Sess. VI.—On April 17, the Council approved the act of procuration drawn up in the previous session, and it was sent to the Pontiff. The nuncios found him at Brisach; but he made only promises until April 30, when he heard that Frederick of Austria, his mainstay and last hope, was about to go to Constance. He then signed the act of procuration; but with a proviso that it would be valid only in case that his full liberty and maintenance were secured for the rest of his life, and that Frederick found full grace with the emperor. The Council regarded this clause as another subterfuge, and resolved to cite him canonically in the next session.

Sess. VII.—On May 2, the Council decreed that: Seeing that Pope John XXIII., contrary to his promises to labor for the extinction of schism and for the reformation of the Church, had fled in a scandalous and clandestine manner, and in one injurious to the cause of union; seeing that he constantly moved further away from the Council; seeing that he

(1) The last article was added on motion of Gerson. In giving this decree we follow the printed editions of the synodal acts, but we shall see that it is very probable that Zabarella did not read the words " faith " and " head and members."

was charged with many grievous crimes ; he, with all his adherents, was cited to appear within nine days to answer for his flight, and to the accusations against his person.

Sess. VIII.—Ou May 4, the doctrines and memory of Wycliffe were condemned, his writings ordered to be burnt, and his remains to be removed from consecrated ground. Frederick of Austria was admitted to peace, and he promised to advise Pope John to submit. The cardinals Brancaccio, Colonna, and of Tricaric, who had hitherto clung to the fortunes of Pope John, joined the Council. On May 9, the Pontiff received the Conciliar citation; but he simply ordered the cardinals Zabarella, Filastro, and d'Ailly to plead his cause, and said that he would await the term of the summons.

Sess. IX.—On May 13, after the reading of the passage of Scripture : " There shall be signs in the sun and the moon," the promotor demanded that as the term of the Pontiff's citation had expired, he should now be pronounced contumacious, and be suspended from his functions. Cardinal Zabarella, in his own name, and in those of his colleagues, Filastro and d'Ailly, announced that the conduct of Pope John was indefensible. A commission of thirteen, at the head of which were the cardinals Orsini and Filastro, was then named to formulate the process of the accused.

Sess. X.—On May 14, the fathers published their sentence whereby Pope John XXIII. was suspended " from all administration, spiritual and temporal, of the Papacy," because it was evident from good sources that " to the notorious scandal of himself and of the Church, he had badly administered, ruled, and governed the popedom and the polity of the Church ; that he had furnished the peoples with bad example by his condemnable life and bad morals ; that he had been guilty of notorious simony in conferring cathedral churches, monasteries, and other ecclesiastical benefices for a stated price ; that he had wasted the goods and rights of the Roman and other churches ;" and that, when charitably admonished, he had persisted in his iniquity. On May 18, the bishops of Asti, Toulon, and Augsburg informed the Pontiff of this decree. The bishop of Toulon demanded the leaden seal, the ring of the fisherman, and the book of supplications. Pope John handed over these objects in silence.

Sess. XI.—For three weeks before this session, which occurred on May 25, an investigation had been going on into the charges against Pope John made in the anonymous pamphlet already mentioned; so bitter against him had the synodals become, that they now eagerly dragged into light a book which they had already rejected with just indignation. Many witnesses, mostly officials of the Roman court, had been heard, and the testimony had been arranged in seventy articles. The *Acts* give only fifty, but they tell us that the honor of the Holy See required the suppression of twenty. These articles were now read; and on the same day the Council sent a deputation with them to the Pontiff. On approaching the Pope, the messengers attempted to kiss his feet; but the guards not allowing that homage, the cardinals among them kissed his mouth and hands, and addressed him as "your Holiness." Having heard the charges, Pope John replied that he would not defend himself, but would submit to the decisions of the Council. He would receive the sentence, he said, with uncovered head; but he recommended his honor, as far as the good of the Church permitted, to the consideration of the fathers.

Sess. XII.—On May 29, after a formal citation of the Pontiff, the promotor announced that the moment of justice had arrived. Then the bishop of Arras read the following sentence: "In the name of the Holy Trinity, the Holy Council of Constance, having invoked the name of Jesus Christ, and having examined in the presence of the Living God, the charges presented against Pope John XXIII., and having heard the proofs of said charges; decrees and declares that the flight of said Pontiff, in disguise and indecent clothing, was culpable and scandalous to the Church of God and to the Holy Council, and was undertaken in order to interfere with the work of union, and to prolong the schism; that the said Pope John XXIII. is guilty of simony, and is a notorious squanderer of the goods of the Church; and that the scandal of his life and morals has dishonored the Church and the Christian people. Therefore, the Holy Council declares John

XXIII. deposed and deprived of the Sovereign Pontificate, frees all the faithful from their obligation of fidelity to him, and prohibits any recognition of him as Pope." This unprecedented sentence was heard amid the silence of death ; the cardinal Zabarella alone arose to speak, but he was not allowed to proceed. All the fathers uttered " placet," and then the Pontifical seal was broken. When the sentence was made known to its victim, he told the deputies that he had already removed the Pontifical cross from his apartments, and that if he had possessed other garments, he would have put off all those bearing any Papal insignia. Not only did he not wish to be Pope any longer, but he wished that he had never been elected, for he had not passed one happy day since his elevation. Laying his hand over his heart, he said : " I swear to never utter, publicly or privately, any complaint against this sentence, and now *I freely renounce any right I may possess to the Pontificate*." As we must here take leave of John XXIII., we shall briefly trace the later career of Balthassar Cossa. He was transferred to the fortress of Gotleben, whence he was sent to Heidelberg, to be guarded by the palatine of the Rhine ; after some time he was taken to Mannheim. After four years of confinement, he conquered the count-palatine with thirty thousand golden scudi, and regained his freedom. Then he showed the world a good example ; for he went at once to Florence, where his successor, Martin V., was residing ; and prostrate at the feet of his former subject, he besought the blessing of the true vicar of Jesus Christ. Pope Martin V. was moved to tears ; he made the humilitated Cossa bishop of Tusculum and dean of the Sacred College ; and ordered that his seat, placed next to the Papal throne, should be more elevated than those of his colleagues.

SESS. XIII.—On June 15, the Council issued a decree concerning the administration of the Holy Eucharist under one species. This was directed against the Calixtine Hussites, and it declared that the custom of giving only the species of bread to the laity was introduced solely for convenience, and that it is of faith that " the entire Body and Blood of Christ is truly contained both under the species of bread and under the species of wine. Hence, as this custom, reasonably in-

troduced by the Holy Church and by the fathers, has been
so long observed, it must be regarded as a law which ought
not to be despised, or be changed without the permission of
the Church."

Sess. XIV. This session, held on July 4, is famous on account of the voluntary abdication of him who, of the three claimants, had possessed—to put the matter very mildly—at least the
best titles to the Pontificate. On June 15, Charles Malatesta
of Rimini, the generous host of Gregory XII., arrived at Constance with the joyful information that Pope Gregory was
ready to resign the tiara, and that he, the lord of Rimini, had
received full powers to actuate the abdication. A conference
was held at once; and as Gregory did not recognize the legitimacy of the Council, Malatesta offered to do so for him, if he
were allowed to reconvoke the assembly in the name of Gregory XII., and if, at the moment of Gregory's resignation, all
persons of the late obedience of John XXIII. were excluded
from the presidency. All was readily granted, and everything
was arranged for the happiest session of the Council. For
the nonce, the cardinals of the obedience of the deposed Pontiff were regarded as non-existent. The emperor, assisted by
the cardinal of Ragusa and by Malatesta, took the presidential seat. The prothonotary of the duke of Bavaria read the
Bull of Gregory appointing a procurator, and another authorizing the Council of Constance. Then the cardinal of Ragusa
convoked, authorized, and confirmed the Council. The proceedings of the two obediences were reciprocally annulled, and
the cardinal of Ragusa having received the kiss of peace, the
cardinal de Brogny resumed the presidential chair, and Malatesta read Gregory's renunciation of the Papal tiara. A solemn *Te Deum* was then sung. When Gregory heard of the
action of Malatesta, he summoned his council, informed them
that he was now Cardinal Angelo Corrario, and to make things
more sure, again renounced the Pontificate, at once laying aside
all the Papal insignia. He was made cardinal-bishop of Porto
and perpetual legate in the March of Ancona; and two years
afterward he died at Recanati.

Sess. XV. On July 6, the matter of John Huss was again
resumed, and the heresiarch was delivered to the secular arm,

as we have already described. In this session the doctrine of John Petit concerning tyrannicide was also condemned. After the assassination of Louis, duke of Orleans, brother of King Charles VI. of France (1407), this Petit, a Norman priest and a doctor of Paris, had written a *Justification of the Duke of Burgundy*, in which he contended that it was licit for any one to kill such a tyrant as, according to him, Louis had been; and that if the duke of Burgundy—the instigator of the murder—had not caused the death of the prince, he would have been guilty of sin. The Council declared this doctrine "erroneous in faith and morals, heretical, scandalous, seditious, and calculated to lead to lies, perjury, and treason" (1).

SESS. XVI., XVII., XVIII. The deposition of John XXIII. and the abdication of Gregory XII. had greatly simplified the task of the fathers of Constance. But Benedict XIII. was still recognized by Spain, Scotland, Sardinia, Corsica, and Majorica and Minorica; and his own indomitable will gave but little hope that he would abandon his pretensions.

Cherishing, however, an infinitesimal spark of hope, the Council resolved to further the interview between Benedict and Sigismund which the Aragonese ambassadors had proposed. Accordingly, in the sixteenth session, held on July 11, fourteen legates were appointed to accompany the emperor to Perpignan, where both Benedict and Sigismund wished the meeting to be, instead of at Nice, as originally suggested. In the seventeenth session, celebrated on July 15, prayers were offered for the success of Sigismund's endeavor ; and with a numerous es-

(1) The following passage in Cantù surprises us : " Master John Petit, professor of theology in the university, showed in twelve arguments—according to the number of the Apostles—that the duke did what was right for God, for the king, and for the realm ; and that it is licit, even meritorious, to kill a tyrant in any manner whatever. Although Gerson, chancellor of the university, and the archbishop of Paris, refuted this proposition, they could not obtain the condemnation of John Petit by the Council of Constance—so powerful was the protection of the duke of Burgundy." *Univ. Hist.*, b. XIII., ch. vii. Here is an implication that the Council did not condemn the *doctrine* of tyrannicide. If the great historian alludes to the non-condemnation of the person of Petit, he must know that the foolish man was dead at the time, and that it was by no means the custom to exhume from consecrated ground *every* heretic's bones. The allusion to the influence of the duke of Burgundy is, for Cantù, far-fetched. This prince contended that John Petit, his protegee, was not the author of the obnoxious teaching ; that it was drawn from works forged by the prince's enemies ; and he begged the Council " not to dishonor the royal blood of Most Christian France which ran in his veins " by an inference that he would countenance heresy. The Council condemned the mischievous *doctrine*, and that was all that it was called upon to do.

cort of princes, and attended by four thousand horse, the imperial negotiator departed. On Sept. 19, Sigismund arrived at Perpignan, and immediately waited upon Benedict. The interview lasted two hours, and Benedict was very courteous, very warm in his protestations of a desire for unity, and he shed tears when speaking of the desolation of the Church; but nothing definite was arranged. In another interview Benedict had recourse to all kinds of subterfuges (1); and in a third he tried to exhaust the patience of Sigismund and the legates by a speech of seven hours' duration, at the end of which, in spite of his age, he appeared perfectly cool and fresh (2). After five weeks of similar proceedings, the legates proposed that Benedict should imitate Gregory by convoking the Council of Constance in his own name, and that then, having given to that assembly what authority he could, he should tender his abdication through a procurator. The obstinate old man promised to reply on Oct. 30, and when the day came, he pronounced one of his tedious discourses, finishing with this declaration: "I have fought the good fight, I have kept the faith, and a crown of justice awaits me. Now I alone am Pontiff. In present circumstances it is by the Council at Constance, not by me, that the schism is prolonged; let that assembly recognize me as Pope, and the schism is ended. Let no one expect me to ever desert the bark of Peter, at the helm of which God has placed me!" (3) From this day Sigismund saw Benedict no more, but the legates persevered until hope was exhausted. Meanwhile, Ferdinand of Aragon had resolved to withdraw from the obedience of Benedict, and the ambassadors of Castile and Navarre were entrusted with the same mission by their sovereigns. The act of withdrawal was drawn up on Jan. 6, 1416, and was published by St. Vincent Ferrer.

SESS. XIX., XX. While the negotiations above narrated were being held, the Council proceeded with its sessions. In the nineteenth, held on Sept. 23, Jerome of Prague abjured the errors of Wycliffe and Huss. The Council declared that a safe-conduct from a secular prince secured no person from

(1) RELIGIOUS OF ST. DENIS; vol. V., b. XXXVI., ch. xxxvi.
(2) MARIANA; *Spanish History*, b. XX., ch. vii.
(3) SURITA; b. XII.—Vat. MS. in MURATORI, vol. III., pt. 2.

punishment, if convicted of heresy and persisting obstinately in the crime. In the twentieth session, held on Nov. 21,
Frederick of Austria was admonished for having usurped
rights of the church of Trent.

SESS. XXI.—On May 30, 1416, Jerome of Prague, having
withdrawn his retractation, was adjudged a relapsed and
obstinate heretic, and was delivered to the secular arm.

SESS. XXIII.—On Nov. 5, 1416, a commission was appointed to examine the charges made against Peter de Luna. All
were found to turn on his obstinate pretensions to the tiara;
nothing was alleged against his character; the very abuses
in his administration were due to his want of power.

SESS. XXIV.—On Nov. 28, Benedict was cited, by means of
two deputies sent to him, to appear before the Council.

SESS. XXIX.—On March 8, 1417, the deputies sent to Benedict made their report, saying: "Peter de Luna gave us
audience (at Paniscola) on Jan. 21. We found him surrounded by three cardinals, and about three hundred prelates, clergymen, and laics. We honored him only with a
bow. Having procured silence, we read the synodal decree
in a loud voice. At first, the Pontiff appeared to listen peaceably enough, but when he heard himself styled a heretic and
a schismatic, impatience seized him, and he cried out: 'That
is false; they lie.' His trouble was so great, that although
he had announced four points in his reply, he touched only
three. However, he grew more calm, and discoursed at
length on the various ways of giving peace to the Church, declaring that he deemed the method of discussion and justice
to be the best, and that he would not adopt that of abdication until he had exhausted the other. Then he said: 'Because I do not yield to the demands made at Constance, it
does not follow that I am a heretic; the true Church is not
where those prelates are, but here at Paniscola, where I am.
Behold the ark of Noah!' he cried, striking his throne."
After hearing this report, the Council declared, for the first
time, the contumacy of Peter de Luna. This declaration was
repeated in the next two sessions, and in the thirty-sixth he
was summoned to hear his sentence. In the thirty-seventh
session, held on July 26, 1417, Cardinal Filastro pronounced,

in the name of the Council, the deposition and excommunication of Peter de Luna.

Taught by the evils following the precipitate election of Pisa, the fathers at Constance showed no haste in electing a Pontiff. They feared that Peter de Luna might recover the sympathies of the peoples who had so long obeyed him; but so many testimonies of the fidelity of Europe to the Council were received, that the prelates resolved to put an end to the widowhood of the Church. Thirty deputies, taken from each nation, were joined with the Sacred College to take part in the Conclave. These were the patriarch of Constantinople; the archbishops of Milan, Tours, Bourges, Riga, and Gniesen; the bishops of Meaux, Aix, Cuença, Feltri, Badajoz, Penna, Traw, London, Bath, Litchfield, Norwich, and Geneva; the abbots of Cluny and St. Mary's of York; the general of the Dominicans, the dean of York, the archdeacon of Boulogne, the prior of Rhodes, and six doctors from the different nations. These deputies, with the twenty-three cardinals then at Constance, entered into Conclave on Nov. 8. At first each nation manifested some inclination to prefer a Pontiff taken from itself, but the world had seen enough of cismontane Popes; the evils of the residence at Avignon were recent; and it was evidently proper that the Pope-King should be of the nationality of his immediate diocesans, and of his temporal subjects. The first to relinquish their pretensions were the Germans; then the English followed the good example; and after some hesitation the French and Spaniards resolved to elect an Italian. On Nov. 11, every vote was cast for Otho Colonna, cardinal-deacon of the Title of St. George of the Golden Veil; and the Great Western Schism was ended. The Council continued its sessions until the end of April, 1418, but its mission was accomplished when it had restored peace to the Church.

We now approach the once vexing question concerning the proper interpretation and the value of the famous decrees of the fourth and fifth sessions of this Council. It is well to know whether or not a *General* Council really decreed the supremacy of such bodies over the Roman Pontiff. One would vainly seek, before the fifteenth century, for any difference among Catholic polemics as to the infallibility of the Pontiff and his supreme authority over the whole body of the episcopate; before the fifteenth century, theologians, when treating of the Papal authority, knew no distinction between the bishops *collectively* considered, and the same *distinctively* regarded. Even though the contest between Pope Boniface VIII. and King Philip the Fair had greatly exasperated the French clergy—so extravagantly loyal to their imperious sovereign—we read in the document presented, in the name of the whole French nation, to Pope Clement V.: "There is no question of the heresy of the late Pope as Pope, but of his heresy as a private person; for *no Pope, as Pope, could ever be a heretic.* Hence when we inquire as to the heresy of the late Pontiff, a General Council need not be assembled. For it is you, Holy Father, who are the vicar of Jesus Christ, and who represent the entire body of the Church, and who possess the keys of the kingdom of heaven; nor can a General Council be congregated without you, *nor can it know anything unless through you."* Even Gerson admits the modern origin of his theory: "Before the celebration of this Holy Synod of Constance, this tradition (of the Papal supremacy over a Council) had so penetrated the minds of many, that the teacher of the contrary doctrine would have been either condemned or noted as a heretic " (1). After Gerson the most strenuous defender of the same theory was Peter d'Ailly, but—more moderate than his disciple—he regarded it as only a probable opinion, and one to be followed only in extreme cases. It is needless to remark that not only the Gallican school, but all the factious—Richer, the Jansenists, all court-theologians, Febronius, Eybel, etc.—patronized the seditious doctrine, and lauded to the skies the wisdom of the fathers of Constance as apparently illustrated in the decrees of their fourth and fifth sessions.

We have said that the opinion of Gerson dates only from his own time. Bossuet endeavored to prove the contrary, and was most diligent in his search among the monuments of the past. He was rewarded by the discovery that examinations of Pontifical definitions had been made by certain Coun-

(1) *Ecclesiastical Power*, consid. 12.

cils; but how little that fact militates for his theory we have
already shown when treating of the Fourth and Sixth General
Councils. The case of Pope Honorius, as we have seen, is
of no help to the cause of Conciliar supremacy; the very fact of
the famous anathema having been directed against him when
dead shows that the Sixth Council attempted no real jurisdiction in his regard, since it is certain that a Pope loses his
primacy with his life. It is well to note, with Peter Ballerini (1), the words of Pope Adrian II., which were read in the
Eighth Council: "We read that the Roman Pontiff has
judged the pontiffs of all churches, but we do not read that
any have judged him. For even though an anathema was
pronounced against Honorius after his death (when he was
no longer Pope), this was because he had been charged with
heresy, the only thing which justifies inferiors in resisting
their superiors or in rejecting corrupted doctrine. And even
in this case, not one of the patriarchs or bishops could pronounce any sentence whatever, until the authoritative consent
of the Pontiff of the first See had been obtained" (2). From
the early ages to the time of Gerson, the ecclesiastical records constantly furnish testimonies against his theory. We
lay no stress on the famous saying ascribed to the synod of
Sinuessa ("The first See is judged by no one"), because it
appears more than probable that the *Acts* of this synod are
apocryphal (3). But as far back as the Pontificate of St. Sylvester I., we read in the last Canon of a Roman Council that
"no one can judge the first See." We have seen how the
letters sent to the Council of Chalcedon all begin with the
address, "To Leo, the Most Holy and Most Blessed Universal Patriarch of great Rome, and to the Holy General Council met in the city of Chalcedon;" how that Council recog-

(1) *Roman Pontiff*, pt. 2, ch. v., § 1.　　　　(2) Session 10.

(3) The genuineness of these *Acts* is defended by Bellarmine, Labbe, Ciaconio, and Schelestrat. Baronio, in his first edition, hesitates; in his second, he favors them. The Bollan-
dists, in the Appendix to vol. III., defend them; but in treating of the saints of May they retract, and admit the validity of the adverse arguments of Papebroch. The *Acts* are rejected by Alexandre, Francis Pagi, Mansi, Graveson, and Basnage. Ruinart, Fleury, and Palma omit the subject. The critical Zaccaria appears to regard them as apocryphal; for in his
Collection of Dissertations on Ecclesiastical History, he receives the adverse dissertation
of De Marco. The chief importance of the question of the authenticity of these *Acts* is due
to their bearing on the controverted question of Pope Marcellinus and the idols. The best
dissertation on the subject is that by Galimberti (now Cardinal), entitled an *Apology for
Pope Marcellinus*, Rome, 1876.

nized Pope St. Leo I. as its head ; and how it anathematized
Dioscorus and his "Robber-Synod" because they had dared
to condemn the Pontiff. And yet Dioscorus was patriarch
of Alexandria, the first see after Rome, and he was at the
head of a Council claiming to be œcumenical. The fifth
Roman Council, under Symmachus, adopted as its own decree the book of the deacon Ennodius, in which we read :
"God wished the causes of other men to be settled by men ;
but He reserved, without question, the bishop of this See to
His own judgment." The reader will also remember the
large synod called by Charlemagne in reference to the charges
brought against Pope St. Leo III. (1). Even in the Council
of Constance there was edited a Bull of Pope Martin V., in
which it was decreed that all suspected heretics should be
asked whether they held that the Roman Pontiff possessed
supreme power in the Church. From innumerable testimonies by Popes, we select one from an epistle of Gelasius
I. (y. 492) : "Every church in the world knows that the Holy
Roman Church has the right to judge all, and that no one can
pass judgment on her decision " (2).

Coming now to an examination of the famous decrees of
Constance, we may observe, in the first place, that the words
which give so much comfort to our adversaries are not of certain authenticity. The learned Netherlander, Schelestrat (3),
contends that in the decree of the fourth session, the words
"the reformation of the Church in head and members " were
added by the prelates of Basel ; he also casts doubt on the
authenticity of the word "faith " in the same sentence, insisting that it is not found in the editions of the synodal *Acts*

(1) PLATINA ; *Life of Leo III.* PAULUS ÆMILIUS ; *History of the Franks.*

(2) *To the Bishops of Dardania.* In another part of this letter the Pontiff says that " appeals can be made to the Apostolic See from every part of the world, but no one is allowed
to appeal from it." Already Athanasius of Alexandria and Paul of Constantinople, synodi-
cally deposed, had appealed to Pope Julius and been restored (SOZOM., *Hist.,* b. III., c. vii.) ;
Flavian of Constantinople had appealed from the second Council of Ephesus to Pope St. Leo
I. (ST. LEO I.: *Epist. to Theodosius*) ; and St. Chrysostom to Pope St. Innocent I.

(3) Emanuel Schelestrat, born at Antwerp in 1648, died at Rome in 1692 while filling the
position of sub-librarian of the Vatican Library. Besides other valuable works, he published at Antwerp in 1683 the *Acts of the Council of Constance, in Explanation of the
Decrees of the Fourth and Fifth Sessions* ; and at Rome in 1683 a *Treatise on the Meaning and Authority of the Decrees on Ecclesiastical Power, Edited by the Council of Constance.* It was against this latter work that Anthony Arnauld wrote his *Light on the Authority of General Councils.*

published at Hagenow in 1500, at Milan in 1511, and at Paris in 1524, and charging the Franciscan, Peter Crabbe, with its first production, in his edition of the Councils issued at Cologne in 1551. If the opinions of Schelestrat are correct, the decree of the fourth session should read: "Every person, no matter how great his dignity, even the Pope, is obliged to obey the Council in all that concerns the extinction of the schism," and as we shall show that the clause, "even the Pope," must be applied only to a dubious Pontiff, it is evident, in the supposition of Schelestrat, that the Council of Constance did not assert the subjection of the Roman Pontiff to a General Council. Alexandre, Maimbourg, the Continuator of Fleury, Du Pin, and other Gallican authors affect to contemn the arguments of Schelestrat; but the famous Protestant theologian, Dr. Burnet, reflects Zaccaria (1), "tells us (2) that Schelestrat showed him some Vatican MSS., two of which were evidently of the time of the Council, and in which these words were not found." Burnet adds that these MSS. must have been as old as the Council, for he says that he knew the style and caligraphy of that century too well to be deceived. Besides these two codices, Schelestrat adduces three which were drawn up by notaries, and were used by the prelates at Basel; and in these three the questioned words are absent. He also speaks of two others, of which one was of about the time of the Council, and the other was written in old Italian characters; in both the disputed words are wanting. The Protestant historians of the Council, Van der Hardt and Lenfant, corroborate Schelestrat. The former cites two codices of Vienna, one of Wolfenbuttel (mentioned also in the *Greek Library* of Fabricius, vol. XL), one of Brunswick (which he believes to have been written in the Council), one of Gotha, and one of the Pauline Library of Leipsic. Lenfant adduces a Parisian codex of St. Victor. Hardouin declares that he met no writer who found the doubtful words in approved codices.

Alexandre endeavors to elude the force of Schelestrat's argument by recurring to many codices which contain the dis-

(1) *Anti-Febbronio*, pt. 2, b. IV., ch. iii., no. 8.
(2) *Journey in Switzerland and Italy.*

puted words ; certainly a more logical proceeding than that
of the author of the *Defence of the Gallican Clergy*, and that
of Cardinal La Luzerne, who would have us regard the codices
of Schelestrat as of no value in the premises, because of their
comparatively late introduction into the field of discussion.   It
frequently happens that long after works have been edited,
more authoritative MSS. of the same works are drawn from
their hiding-places, and the learned world is forced to accept
readings different from those to which it has been accustomed.
As to the superior value of the codices adduced by Schelestrat, it is recognized by such critics as Lenfant, Van der
Hardt, Hardouin, Burnet, Roncaglia, and Zaccaria.   Cardinal
Orsi confirms the argument of the Netherlander by proving
that Zabarella, whose province it was to read, in the fifth
session of Constance, the decree of the fourth, did not read
the famous words, because of the opposition already evinced
by the Sacred College to their insertion in the decree.   La
Luzerne accounts for the existence of the Schelestratian codices by the presumed fact that "a few years after the Council of Constance, the court of Rome exerted every nerve to
withdraw itself from the authority of that Council's decrees,"
and he concludes his attempted refutation of Orsi's defence of
the Schelestratian theory with these words : "These manuscripts, said to have been found by Schelestrat in the Vatican
Library, and cited so frequently and so emphatically by the
ultramontanes, are miserable writings without authenticity
or authority, fabricated by party interest, and they should
be returned to an oblivion from which they should never
have been drawn" (1).   La Luzerne smiles at Orsi's introduction of the Zabarella reading in the fifth session, and insists that "this anecdote proves that the decree was really
issued in the fourth session.   The nations reproached him
for his faithless omission, and thus attested that they had
worded the decree just as we possess it" (2).   The astute
bishop of Langres certainly presents the strongest of arguments against the Schelestratian theory, when he reminds
us that "the authenticity of the decree of the fourth session
alone is contested ; the decree of the fifth session is univer-

(1) *On the Declaration*, etc., c. xx., art. 1, no. 7.   (2) *Ibid.*, no. 6.

sally acknowledged as authentic. The question (raised by Schelestrat) is therefore useless, and the difficulty presented is without object. Even though we grant that the decree of the fourth session was falsified, it is still certain that in its fifth session the Council declared that every General Coun cil is superior to the Pope " (1). From this argument there is but one escape ; and that is by proving that our adversaries misinterpret the meaning of the decree of the fifth session.

Laying aside, therefore, the theory of vitiation, we shall nevertheless prove that the Council of Constance does not furnish an instance of a General Council asserting the supremacy of such assemblies over the Roman Pontiff. In the first place, the Council of Constance labored under many defects, so far as the famous decrees are concerned; and principally under that of want of Apostolic confirmation. Secondly, the decrees of the fourth and fifth sessions were issued, not as dogmas of faith, but as Synodal Constitutions. Thirdly, they were meant to apply, not to a certainly legiti- mate Pontiff, but to a dubious one. Fourthly, unity was fin- ally restored to the Church without any recourse to the theory of the supremacy of a General Council.

I. The asserters of the absolute œcumenicity of the Coun- cil of Constance ought to show that John XXIII., the convoker of the assembly, was possessed of a better right to the tiara than that of Gregory XII. or Benedict XIII.; also that during the fourth and fifth sessions, when the Council was composed only of prelates belonging to the obedience of John XXIII., the assembly was truly universal. They should also show the futility of the objections made by John XXIII.— the Pontiff recognized by the Council—complaining of the division of the Council into four unequal nations, and the con- sequent counting of votes, not *per capita*, as the Canons re- quired, but by said nations—a system which gave the same weight to the three votes of England as to the hundred of Italy or of France. But, above all, ere it can be concluded that a Gen- eral Council asserted the subjection of a Pontiff to itself, it should be proved that such a decree received the Apostolic approbation—not an ambiguous one, but one so clear and

(1) *Ibid.*, no. 4.

certain that said decree, otherwise of such uncertain authority, must necessarily be regarded as emanating from the Catholic Church. John XXIII. gave no such approbation, for he
fled from the Council before its third session; and so long as
he was free, he showed himself averse to all the synodal proceedings. At one time he appeared to respect the actions of
the Council, but then he was a captive. Nor was the necessary confirmation granted by the certainly legitimate Pontiff,
Martin V. This Pope expressly approved the proceedings
against Wycliffe, Huss, and Jerome of Prague; and in one
of his Constitutions given before the end of the Council, he
declared that he supplied, in these matters, all the defects of
the assembly. But there is not a trace of his approbation of
the decrees in question. On the contrary, he declared to the
Polish orators at the Council that, in no case whatever, could
an appeal be made from the Holy See to a General Council;
and he issued a special Bull to that effect, thus "entirely
destroying the very foundations" of the Conciliar decrees,
as Gerson complained (1). In the forty-fifth session, Martin
V. certainly declared that he "wished the inviolable observation of each and every thing synodally (*conciliariter*) determined, concluded, and decreed by the present Council in
matters of faith (*in materia fidei*), and that he approved and
ratified the said things *synodally* done, approving nothing
otherwise or in another way (*et non aliter, nec alio modo*)."
But this approbation can apply only to the decrees concerning Wycliffe, Huss, and Jerome of Prague; for, as we shall
now show, the decrees of the fourth and fifth sessions, read
them as we may, were not issued with the forms usual in
dogmatic definitions, but after the manner of Synodal Constitutions (2).

II. In the fifth session, according to the *Acts* of the Council, "by order of the entire Holy Synod, the reverend
Father Andrew, (bishop) elect of Poznania, arose and published certain chapters which had already been deliberated

(1) *Dialog. Apolog.*

(2) No argument for Conciliar supremacy can be deduced from the fact that Martin V., in
his Bull to the emperor Sigismund, designated as "canonical" the deposition of John XXIII.
This claimant had subjected himself to the judgment of the Council, and since he afterward
coincided with that judgment, as he had promised to do, he may be said to have freely abdicated, rather than to have been deposed by the Council.

and concluded by way of Synodal Constitutions." In some codices the word "Constitutions" is repeated after the decrees, and the use of this term shows that the Council did not intend to propose a dogma of faith. As Peter Ballerini and Melchior Canus remark, just as all the decrees of the Supreme Pontiffs, even when on dogmatic matters, do not constitute dogmas of faith, so neither do all the statutes of Councils. "When a matter is declared to be believed or condemned *ex fide*, an anathema or similar form of censure is pronounced against those who contradict. If no such note is found, then, even though the matter may pertain to faith, the decree is not a certain dogmatic definition. Among Catholics there are many questions which refer to faith; such, for example, as pertain to the form, matter, or minister of certain Sacraments; and which, so long as the Church gives no definition, form no dogma of faith. In these matters, so long as they are debated among Catholics, Pontiffs and Councils do not easily render dogmatic judgment; and until the subject is clearly decided, if something is decreed which circumstances appear to demand for the good of the Church, it is not always and at once to be numbered among dogmas and definitions" (1). When the Council of Constance, influenced by the necessity of finding and actuating a remedy for the direful schism, issued its decree enjoining compliance upon the rival Pontiffs, it used no such terminology as it adopted in condemning the errors of Wycliffe, etc. Even Gerson, whose audacity would have led him to condemn his opponents in this matter as heretics, admitted that the doctrine of Conciliar superiority was *openly* opposed by many who were not therefore regarded as heretics by the Council (2). And an event occurred in the Council, shortly after the publication of the famous decrees, which plainly shows that the fathers did not regard said decrees as other than remedial Constitutions. When the condemnation of Wycliffe's errors had been prepared, there was a debate concerning the name in which the decree should be pronounced; whether it should be that of the Pontiff or that

---

(1) Ibid., c. viii., no. 4.
(2) Ecclesiastical Power, consid. 12—Sermon for the Feast of St. Anthony.

of the Council. Cardinal d'Ailly strenuously urged, before the congregation of theologians called to consider the matter, the claims of the Council; but out of the forty doctors only twelve favored his view. How would the twenty-eight defenders of the Papal prerogative have dared to vote for its assertion, if the famous decrees had been proposed as decrees of faith? Is it not evident that, even after the publication of these constitutions, the synodals regarded their subject-matter as open to dispute? But Gerson himself, the very head and front of the cismontane host, admitted that the Constitutions were not of faith. In a lengthy treatise, issued during the Council, he does not accuse his adversaries of heresy, but concludes his advocacy of Synodal supremacy in these words : "However, these things are presented not as by one definitively determining, but as by one persuading doctrinally ; for I submit the matter to the consideration of the Holy Council."

III. In the General Council of Florence (y. 1438), Cardinal Turrecremata contended that the decrees of Constance were intended to be applied only in the case of a dubious Pontiff. In those decrees, said he, in his *Apology* for Pope Eugenius, "the Council does not speak of any schism whatever, but only of that schism which existed when the decrees were published." He then demonstrated that the Pope ought to enforce such decrees of reformation, not because the Council so ordained, but because of the natural fitness of things (1), for, said he, unless in case of heresy, an undoubted Pontiff cannot be subjected to a Council. When

(1) This idea is well expressed by Peter Ballerini (*loc. cit.*, nos. 10 and 11) as follows : "In the case of schism, in which the Supreme Pontiff, above all others, ought to use every means to extinguish it and to restore the unity of which his primacy makes him the guardian, should he not abdicate, because of that very law of charity which commands that private should yield to the public good? If he has bound himself by oath to do so, he is obliged, by natural and divine law, to yield. He is then obliged by a law superior to any Synod, by that natural and divine law to which even the Supreme Pontiffs are subject. For the same reason he would be obliged in the case of reformation in head and members. Who can doubt that the Supreme Pontiff is bound, by natural and divine law, to reform whatever needs reformation, either in himself or in the other members of the Church? If a General Council were to propose and demand this, he ought to do it, not because of the Council's right, but because of the natural and divine law urged in the Council's decree. Here the coercive force is not in the Council, but in the natural and divine law. And if the decree is issued in a truly General Council, where there is the assent or confirmation of the Pontiff, then by such assent he freely subjects himself to the same decree, and is voluntarily bound by it, all coercion excluded."

Turrecremata thus spoke, he was heard by many whose memory would have enabled them to contradict him, had his
interpretation of the decrees been wrong. Pope Eugenius
IV., in his Constitution beginning *Moses*, given at Florence in
1439, interpreted the decrees of Constance in the same manner. When the prelates of Basel declared that Conciliar
supremacy was a doctrine of faith defined at Constance, the
Pontiff, with the approbation of the Council of Florence,
condemned the proposition as "contrary to Scripture, to the
Fathers, and to the same Council of Constance." No Catholic, remarks Roncaglia (1), will hold that the subjection of
a dubious Pope cannot be numbered among the truths of
faith; therefore the doctrine of Basel, condemned by Eugenius IV., in the Council of Florence, was the one that subjected a certainly legitimate Pontiff to a Council—a teaching, defined Eugenius, which was foreign to the minds of
the fathers of Constance. Again, the very decrees of Constance show that they were meant to affect only a dubious
Pope. It is expressly stated that "in order to procure union and the reformation of the Church more easily, the
Council ordains, etc." Just before these words we read this
passage: "This Holy Synod, ... legitimately assembled for
the extinction of the present schism, and for the union and reformation of the Church of God in head and members," and,
remarks Zaccaria (2), the word "this" or "aforesaid" is evidently understood before "union," as Maimbourg himself
admitted when he translated the text thus: "In order to the
more easily procure *this* union, etc." But this union and this
reformation were nothing else than the extinction of the
schism. Finally, from a protest of the Italian, French, and
Spanish "nations," which is found in the *Acts* of the Council before the fortieth session, we learn that these nations
had a serious discussion with the German nation as to
which work should be first undertaken, the election of
a certainly legitimate Pontiff, or the task of reformation.
The Germans wished to give precedence to the latter work,
but the others carried their point. But the Germans in-

(1) *Animadversions on Alexandre's Dissert. iv.*, cent. XV., § 2.
(2) *Loc. cit.*, no. 9.

sisted that the Council should guarantee to begin the task
of reform before the coronation of the new Pope. Various decrees were composed, but "it was finally declared
that a Pope-elect could not be bound" (1). But if the Council, in its fourth and fifth sessions, had already attempted to
bind a certainly legitimate Pontiff, why did not the German
nation continue to press its demand, and quote the decrees as
a justification of the proceeding? It should also be observed
that on this same day, September 11, 1417, the Italian,
French, and Spanish nations, in their protest commencing
"Hear these things," insisted that nothing further should
be done until a Pontiff was chosen, for otherwise "it would
follow that the Church of God was without a head or law;
that the Church would remain in danger, for in the absence
of a head whose province it would be to convoke a Council,
an undoubted Council could scarcely be assembled." From
this fact also, therefore, we must conclude that the fathers
of Constance had not declared that, even when the Pontiff
was certainly legitimate, the Council possessed authority
immediately from God.

IV. Divine Providence so disposed that the Great Schism
was healed without any recourse to the theory which we combat. Gregory XII., whom we contend to have been the legitimate Pontiff, voluntarily abdicated the tiara. John XXIII.,
whom the partisans of the Pisan assembly regarded as
Pope, was indeed deposed, but with his own consent; and
if it be said that this consent was extorted by fear, and
that this fear was unjustly caused (which is false), then at
least it is certain that Balthassar Cossa afterward venerated
Martin V. as Pontiff. The obstinate Peter de Luna refused
to yield, and was deposed; but he had become a schismatic,
and hence was declared deposed rather than really deposed. By the very fact of his separation from the Church,
this prelate lost the Primacy, if he had ever possessed it.
Therefore he was amenable to the Council (2).

(1) "*Tandem fuit dictum quod Papa electus ligari non poterat.*"

(2) Peter Ballerini thus speaks of the situation of Peter de Luna: "Since it is certain
that a schismatic is not in the Catholic Church, it is equally certain that he cannot have any
primatial jurisdiction, for all jurisdiction is in the Church (See ANTONINUS, pt. II., tit. 3, c.
xi., § 7, conclus. 3). A schismatic is not only he who separates from the Roman Pontiff, the

CHAPTER IV.

JOAN OF ARC.

In the year 1411, in the little village of Domremy, on the confines of Champagne, Burgundy, and Lorraine, was born a peasant girl to whom, although until her womanhood "unable to handle a sword or to mount a horse," modern Frenchmen probably owe the fact that the sovereign of England does not now wear the crown of the United Kingdom of Great Britain, Ireland, and France. No purely secular heroine has attained to such celebrity as Jeanne, or, as she is styled in our language, Joan of Arc. At the commencement of this century, more than four hundred works, not counting, of course, the fly-sheets of prose and poetry circulated among the crowd during the solemn annual processions at Orleans, had treated of her career (1). Some of these works have aimed at the coronation of the Maid with the halo of canonized sanctity; others have been content with advocating her claim to the lasting gratitude of her countrymen, and to the admiration and sympathy of all humanity; a few have derided her memory.

King Charles VI. of France (1380–1422) was subject to attacks of insanity. His queen, Isabella of Bavaria, a shameless princess, an unfaithful wife, and a heartless mother, caused Henry V. of England to be named regent of the kingdom, with future succession, to the prejudice of the dauphin, her own son. The princes of the blood-royal and the great nobles of France, instead of supporting the tottering throne, warred upon each other. John of Burgundy caused the as-

head of the Church, but also he who is divided from the body and unity of the Church, and does not communicate with it. ... The body of the Church which, because of the schism, had been divided into three parts or obediences, was made one when the three obediences united in the Council of Constance. This did not occur at the commencement of the Council; but when, after the union of the obediences of Gregory XII. and John XXIII., the others, and principally the most obstinate, the Spaniards, returned to unity—all except a very few who continued to adhere to Benedict XIII. in Paniscola, a remote corner of Spain, and who certainly could not be called the Catholic Church. When, therefore, after the union of all the obediences and of the whole body, Benedict was disjoined from the body and unity of the Catholic Church, he became a real schismatic, even a heretic, pretending that the Church of Christ was to be found only in his partisans at Paniscola." *Loc. cit.*, no. 17.

(1) CHAUSSARD ; *Joan of Arc, an Historical and Complete Collection,* Orleans, 1806.

sassination of the duke d'Orleans, brother of the king; Tannegui du Chatel then slew the duke of Burgundy; and the whole kingdom became a prey to fire and sword. On the death of Henry V. in 1422, the duke of Bedford assumed the regency of France in the name of the infant Henry VI., while the legitimate king, Charles VI., died in the hands of the Burgundians. The armies of the young Charles VII. were everywhere defeated by his rebellious subjects and the English invaders; only the provinces south of the Loire remained in his power, and his insolent enemies styled him the "little king of Bourges." He had already thought of seeking refuge in Spain or in Scotland; and according to all human foresight, the throne of Charlemagne and of St. Louis was a thing of the past, when the Maid came to its succor. Joan always insisted that her mission was from heaven, and as no other human being participated in her visions, we must recur to her own testimony for an account of them (1).

Thus she testified before her judges: "Whatever good I have worked for France, I have performed by the grace and command of the King of Heaven, as He enjoined upon me by means of His angels and saints; and all that I know came to my knowledge only by the revelation and command of God. ... By His order I went to King Charles VII., son of King Charles VI.; I would have been torn to pieces, sooner than have gone to him without the divine command. All my deeds are in the hands of God; in Him, and in Him alone, all my trust has been placed. With all my strength I have executed whatever the voices of His saints enjoined upon me, if I rightly understood them. ... Were I to wish to narrate all that God revealed to me, eight entire days would not suffice; but I will tell you how the saints first appeared to me. One day about noon, in the summer of seven years ago, when I was about thirteen years old, I was in my father's garden; and then I heard for the first time, at my right hand, and toward the church, a voice; while there appeared to my eyes a figure surrounded by unearthly splendor, having the aspect

(1) QUICHERAT; *The Process of the Condemnation and of the Rehabilitation of Joan of Arc, Called the Maid; Published for the First Time from the MSS. of the National Library. Followed by All the Historical Documents Obtainable, and Accompanied by Notes and Explanations*; 5 vols., 8vo; Paris, 1849.

of a good and virtuous man, but with wings, and entirely im-
mersed in light. He was followed by heavenly angels; for
very often the angels come among Christians, who are not at
all aware of such a presence. I myself have often seen angels
in the company of Christians. The one who appeared to me
was St. Michael; his voice seemed very venerable to me, but
as I was then a little girl, I felt great fear because of the apparition, and I doubted whether it was really of an angel. ...
I saw him and the other angels with these my eyes as I now
see you, my judges; and I believe all that he said and did,
as I believe in the passion and death of our Lord and Saviour Jesus Christ. I am led to such faith by the aid he gave
me, and by his good counsels and lessons. ... That angel told
me that, above all, I must be a good girl, and go often to
church; that then God would help me. He told me of God's
great pity for France, and that I should fly to the aid of her
king. He also told me that SS. Catharine and Margaret
would visit me, and that I should do whatever they bade me
do. ... Afterward SS. Catharine and Margaret appeared to
me, and ordered me to go to Robert de Vaudricourt, an
officer of the king, at Vaucouleurs. They said that he would
repel me several times, but that finally he would do my will,
and would furnish me an escort to the king in the interior of
France; then I would raise the siege of Orleans. I replied
that I was only a poor girl, unable to mount a horse and to
lead in war. Then they said that I should carry my standard bravely; that God would help me, and my king would
receive his whole kingdom, in spite of his enemies. 'Be con-
soled,' they added, 'and when thou shalt be before thy king,
thou shalt give him a good sign, which will cause him to confide in thee, and to bid thee welcome.' These saints have
guided me during seven successive years, and have succored
me in all my fatigues and miseries; even now they visit me
every day. I have never asked them for any other thing than
protection in my undertakings in war, and for God's help for
the French; for myself I have asked only the salvation of my
soul. When I first heard their voices, I voluntarily promised
God that I would remain a virgin, pure in body and soul, if,
of course, such were His will; and then they promised to lead

me into paradise. ... These saints did not order me to keep
their appearance secret; but I feared to reveal it, thinking
that the Burgundians, and above all, my father, would prevent
my going to the king. I was allowed to speak of the apparitions to my father, but I would not have done so for the
world. As for other things, I have always been obedient
therein to my father and my mother; if I was not in this
matter, and if I departed without their knowledge, I believe
that I was not in fault; for I went in obedience to the command of God, and when such a command was issued, I would
have obeyed, though I had a hundred fathers and a hundred
mothers, and though I were the daughter of a king. ... From
the time that I knew that I was to journey into the interior
of France, I abstained, as much as I could, from the plays
and recreations under the tree of the Fates. In fact, I think
that I never danced under that tree after I reached the age
of reason (1). ... The saints generally appear to me surrounded by splendor; I see their faces, garments, hair, and
arms, but whether they have other members I know not. I
always see them under the same appearance, and I have
never noticed any contradiction in their remarks. I have
learned to distinguish them, one from another; I recognize
them by their tone of voice and by their salutation of me, for
they always call me by name when they begin to speak. SS.
Margaret and Catharine have rich and precious crowns on
their heads, as is but right. I understand all that they say
to me; for they speak French well, and have soft, tender, and

(1) Here Joan alludes to an old beech tree which grew near a medicinal spring in the
neighborhood of Domremy, and which was said to have sheltered the Fates in Druidical
times. Under this venerable tree many of the village feasts were held; and especially in
Spring, on the Sunday when the Church sings *Lœtare Jerusalem* at the Introit, the lord of
Domremy there met the festive villagers, and distributed refreshments to them. According
to the testimony of many who knew her, Joan preferred to sing rather than to dance on such
occasions; and if she sometimes helped to decorate the tree, most of her flowers went to a
little image of the Blessed Virgin near-by. The enemies of the Maid afterward charged her
with having practised magic under the tree of the Fates, and with having thus acquired the
ability to defeat the English. She thus repelled the accusation: "My brother has said that
in my native place some thought that I received my mission under the tree of the Fates.
But I protest that this is false. I do not know that any saint ever appeared to me under
that tree. When I stood before the king, some persons asked me if there was such a tree in
my native place, because various prophecies had announced that from such a one a virgin
would come and perform wonderful things. But I had no faith in this, and I never have had
any book on magic in my hands." At the time the Maid thus spoke, and for centuries afterward, very learned men believed in magic.

loving voices. ... Now and then SS. Catharine and Margaret order me to go to confession. ... They come to me without my calling them, and if they did not come often, I would pray God to send them to me. They have always come when I needed them. Great is my joy when St. Michael, the angels, and the two saints come to me, for then I know that I am not in mortal sin ; were I in such a state they would abandon me at once. ... I have embraced SS. Catharine and Margaret in my arms. Even now I hear their voices every day, and indeed I need to hear them ; were I not so encouraged, I would be dead. ... I believe in them as I do in the existence of God." This account of her mission to save France was never varied or denied by Joan, even when in the midst of devouring flames.

With great difficulty the Maid prevailed on one of her uncles to visit the governor of Vaucouleurs, and to unfold to him her design. The sturdy soldier advised the uncle to cure his niece with a good thrashing ; but Joan persisted, and after a few months of struggle she induced Vaudricourt to further her journey. Donning male attire, by the advice, as she declared, of her heavenly visitants, for her protection among a lascivious soldiery, and girding on the sword which Vaudricourt had given her, the Maid started on her perilous journey on Feb. 13, 1429. She had to travel for a hundred and fifty hours through districts occupied by the enemy, and infested by assassins ; but she comforted her dissuading friends with the assurance : "If the enemy holds the road, my Lord will clear it. For this task I was born." She was accompanied by one of her brothers, by two gentlemen and their pages, and by a royal messenger and a royal equerry.

At this time Talbot was besieging Orleans, and deputies from the suffering city had informed King Charles that its surrender was daily expected. When Joan arrived at Fierbois, then the residence of the French court, she sent a letter to Charles, telling him that she brought help by the command of God. After examinations by the royal counsellors, she was led to the audience-chamber, where the king had mingled with the courtiers, and was disguised in ordinary garments. Joan proceeded at once to Charles, and falling to her knees, embraced those of her sovereign, crying: "God grant you a happy life, my liege!" Charles replied: "I am not the king; he is beyond." Joan answered: "In the name of God, you are the king." Charles then led her apart, and conversed with her for some time. Then she gave to the young sovereign the sign which was to inspire him with confidence in her mission, and which her enemies vainly tried to force her to reveal. Joan afterward said that when she had answered many of the king's questions, she declared to him "in the name of the Lord, that he was the son of Charles VI., and the true heir to the French throne." In these words lies the whole secret. In the National Library of Paris is an autograph containing narratives of famous deeds of kings and emperors. The author was one Sala, and he lived shortly after the Maid. Charles VIII. having entrusted to him the education of his son, he heard the secret from an old knight, who himself had heard it from Charles VII., of whom he had been a favorite. Sala ingenuously says: "When Charles VII. had so fallen that he possessed only Bourges and a few other strong places, our Lord God sent to him a rude maiden; ... and as some may be disgusted with the king's attention to her words, know that she gave him a message from God upon a matter which he had mentioned only to God in his prayers. When, therefore, the Maid told him what she could have learned only from divine inspiration, he abandoned himself to her guidance." Owing to the wickedness of his mother, Isabella of Bavaria, Charles VII. had feared that perhaps he was illegitimate; and once he had prayed to God that if he was indeed the lawful heir to the French crown, it might be preserved to him. To this secret prayer corresponded the words of Joan, that he was the son of Charles VI. It was natural that Joan should conceal this secret, for if the English had learned that Charles himself doubted his own legitimacy, they would have used that doubt to destroy what little influence he still possessed over the French. In the *Chronicle of the Maid*, which is the document *par excellence* upon Joan, and which was first published by Denis Godefroy in his *History of Charles VII.*, we are told that "one day the Maid said to the king in private: 'Gentle dauphin (Joan

always thus addressed Charles until after his coronation),.
why do you not believe? I tell you that God pities you, your
kingdom, and your people. St. Louis and Charlemagne are
on their knees before Him, praying for you; and I can tell
you, if it pleases you to hear it, something which will make
you believe me.' Nevertheless, she was willing that a few
of the gentlemen of the king should be present, and at her
request the king caused an oath of secrecy to be taken by
the duke d'Alençon, the lord of Treves, the lord Christopher·
d'Harcourt, and his confessor, master Gerard Machet; and
in their presence she told the king of something important,.
though secret, which he had done." One of the most interesting documents concerning the Maid is a *Diary of the*
Siege of Orleans, printed in that city in 1576, but written by·
one Soubsdan in 1467 in illustration of a far older MS. In
this work we are told that Joan "declared to the king, in
presence of his confessor and a few of his privy counsellors,.
a vow which he had made, and which God alone had heard."
This revélation of the Maid is given in more detail by an Or-
leanese chronicler cited by Gorres, but whose work we do
not find among the " determinative pieces " edited by Quicherat in his edition of the *Process*. According to this writer,
Joan asked the monarch whether he would credit her mis--
sion if she revealed to him a secret known only to God and
himself. Charles replying in the affirmative, she said: " My·
lord, do you remember that on the last feast of All Saints,.
while you were alone in your bed-chamber in the castle of
Loches, you made a triple prayer to God? " Charles replied
that he had indeed done so; and then the Maid asked him
whether he had mentioned those prayers to any one, even to
his confessor. Receiving a negative response, Joan said :
" My lord, the first prayer you then made was that God
would take from you all desire for the crown, if you were not
its rightful heir. The second prayer was that if the misfortunes of France were due to your sins, God would free your·
people, and punish you alone, either with death or any chastisement He might select. The third prayer was that if the
people's own sins had brought their miseries on them, God
would avert His anger from them."

The deputies from Orleans now returned to the city, full of hope that the siege would soon be raised. But the royal advisers opined that the Maid should be entrusted with no military expedition before she had been examined by the most learned and authoritative prelates and by doctors well versed in Scripture and law. She was conducted to Poitiers, where a tribunal of examiners was convoked under the presidency of the archbishop of Rheims, as chancellor of the kingdom. One after the other, the learned doctors tried to show that Joan labored under hallucinations; Holy Writ and famous works were quoted, while the Maid patiently listened. At length she replied: "In the books of the Lord God there are more things than in yours." She predicted the defeat of the English, and the delivery of Orleans; the coronation of King Charles at Rheims; the restoration of Paris to his obedience; and the recovery of his liberty by the duke d'Orleans, then a prisoner in England. Christopher d'Harcourt, bishop of Castres, was the first to proclaim his belief in the heavenly mission of the Maid; finally, the assembly pronounced that the king could safely accept the offered service. The celebrated Æneas Sylvius, who ascended the Papal throne as Pius II., thirty years after the murder of Joan, speaks as follows of this examination: "Interrogated concerning matters of faith, she answered in accordance with Christian doctrine; her morals having been investigated, she was found to be most pure and honest. Nothing was found to be feigned, and nothing ascribable to malign art. When asked why she had donned a man's clothing, which was forbidden to a woman, she replied that she was a virgin, and that both dresses befitted virgins; furthermore, since she was to wield a man's weapons, God had ordered her to wear a man's garments."

It having been decided that the fortunes of the Lilies should be entrusted to the Maid, she now put on the insignia of a king's officer; her armor was a gift from Charles, but she claimed that her banner and sword came from God. She declared that her saints (thus she always styled her celestial visitants) had told her to use a sword which would be found buried near the altar of the church of St. Catharine in Fier-

bois.   She had a letter written to the priests of that church,
begging them to search for the weapon ; excavations were made,
and a sword inscribed with five crosses was found.   Cleared of
its rust, it was placed in a scabbard of red velvet embroidered
with lilies; but the citizens of Tours gave her another sheath,
made of cloth of gold.   However, Joan would use neither ; she
always carried one of common leather.   Her banner was white,
and covered with lilies, and on it our Lord was represented as
judging the world ; at the Lord's feet were two angels, one of
whom held a lily which He was blessing.   The motto on the
standard was " Jesus, Maria."   The retinue of the Maid consisted of the knight John d'Aulon, whom the noble Dunois
styled the first of his chevaliers, two pages, two heralds, two
footmen, and a master of the household.   Her confessor and
chaplain was an Augustinian friar.   Before setting out for
Orleans, Joan predicted that she would be wounded before
that city, but that nevertheless she would complete her task.
This prophecy is narrated by the lord de Rotslaer, writing
from Lyons to the court of Brabant on April 22; Joan did not
enter Orleans before the 29th, and she was wounded on May 7.
The Maid raised her standard on April 21; and followed by
the archbishop of Rheims, by the grandmaster of the royal
household, and by a small army, she marched on Blois.   Here
she dictated the following letter to the English commanders :
" King of England ; and thou, duke of Bedford, who stylest
thyself governor of the French kingdom ; thou, William de la
Poule, earl of Suffolk ; thou, John, lord Talbot ; Thomas, lord
Scales ; who all style yourselves governors for the duke of
Bedford : Give His due to the King of heaven, and restore
to the Maid who is sent by the King of heaven the keys of all
the faithful cities of France which you have taken and ruined.
She has come hither to vindicate the rights and privileges of
the royal blood of France.   She is disposed to peace if justice
influences you to depart from France, and to indemnify her
for your residence in her territories.   And you, nobles and
plebeians, archers and soldiers, who are now before Orleans,
return to your own country in the name of God; and do not
allow yourselves to be surprised by the Maid, who will soon
seek ye for your hurt.   King of England! if you do not obey

me, I, captain in this war, will disperse your troops, whether they like it or not, in whatever part of France I may find them. If they dare to resist, they shall all perish. God, the King of heaven, orders me to chase you from France, every one of you; only he who obeys will be admitted to my grace. And do not believe that God, the King of heaven, the Son of the Immaculate Mary, wishes you to possess this kingdom; it is reserved for the legitimate heir, King Charles. God has so declared to King Charles by the tongue of the Maid; and I tell you that the king will enter Paris with a good following. If you place no faith in the message of God and of the Maid, the edges of our swords will strike you, wherever we find you; and there will be such a noise of hunt as has not been heard in all France for a thousand years. And bear in mind that the King of heaven can send more troops to the Maid than you can oppose to her; and when the tempest of horrid sword-blows bursts forth, it will be plain on which side heaven knows justice to reside. Duke of Bedford! the Maid entreats thee not to be obstinate, to thy own harm. If thou deniest her right, thou shalt meet her in a place where the French will perform the most glorious feat of arms that was ever accomplished for the good of Christendom. If thou desirest peace, let the Maid have thy reply in Orleans; otherwise thou shalt soon realize thy immense loss. Written on this Tuesday of the Holy Week, 1429."

On April 27, Joan departed from Blois to the relief of Orleans. At the head of the little army of less than five thousand men, marched a number of priests chanting the *Veni Creator*, and other hymns. During the march of two days the Maid constantly exhorted the soldiers to persevere in the state of grace; most of them went to confession; as many temptations as possible were removed from the line of march. We refer the reader to secular history for the details of Joan's military career. Suffice it here to say that after many difficulties, even at the hands of the French generals, the Maid led the royal troops of France from victory to victory, and on July 17, Charles VII. was crowned at Rheims. When the archbishop had performed the function, the simple peasant girl, whose hand had led her king from the depths of misfortune to the height of power, bent her knee before her sovereign, and with tears of joy said to him: "Now, my king, is fulfilled the will of God, which demanded that I should deliver Orleans, and conduct you to the city of Rheims to receive the sacred unction which would show that you are the lawful sovereign of France." Joan considered her mission now terminated, and humbly begged the royal permission to return to her native village. But the king's advisers deemed it prudent to take advantage of the enthusiasm excited by the prestige of the Maid, and to compel her continued service with the army. She accompanied the king in his expedition against Paris, and on Sept. 8 she attacked the fortifications. After a day's fighting she was wounded; and though wishing to continue the combat, was dragged perforce from the scene, while Charles ordered a retreat. When her wound was healed, Joan hastened to the relief of Melun, saved the city, and on its very bastions, as she declared, her saints told her that she would fall into the hands of the enemy before the feast of St. John. She should not fear, said the saints, but should embrace the cross with gratitude, and God would give her grace to carry it. She then begged her heavenly friends to pray God to spare her a long captivity, and to call her soon to Himself. The saints simply exhorted her to be patient. In May of the next year, Joan defeated the enemy near Lagny, and then advanced on Compiegne, which the duke of Burgundy and the earl of Arundel had attacked with a numerous army. On the 22d, she made a sortie; and after a heroic combat, her followers were compelled to give way. While she was covering their retreat, she was taken prisoner. Lionel of Vendome conducted her to Marigny; and there she was sold to John of Luxembourg, who took her to the castle of Beaulieu. Removed to Beauvais, she learned that she had been sold to the English. Dread of the future now combined with her anxiety for Compiegne to make her captivity insupportable; and she cherished a design of jumping from the tower in which she was confined. Every day St. Catharine told her that God would deliver Compiegne, and that she would not be free before she had seen the king of England. "I wish not to see him," replied Joan; "I would sooner die than fall

into the hands of the English." In her anguish, she jumped
from the tower, and was found unconscious but unwounded
in the ditch. At first, influenced by his aunt, who pitied the
Maid, Luxembourg hesitated to deliver her to the English;
but these bitter enemies of Joan soon found a means of obtaining the person of her who had done so much to prevent
their conquest of her country. Joan had been captured in
the diocese of Beauvais; and therefore the bishop of Beauvais might be considered as her spiritual judge. This prelate, Peter Cauchon (1), was entirely devoted to the English,
principally because the inhabitants of Beauvais, on the approach of Joan to their city, had expelled him as a traitor to
his country. The English leaders requested Cauchon to preside at the trial of the Maid, but he hesitated to undertake
the terrible mission. He demanded permission to consult
the University of Paris, then entirely devoted to the English
invaders, for all the doctors who remained faithful to their
legitimate king had fled from the capital. On July 14th, to
its everlasting shame, the University sent to Cauchon two letters, one for the duke of Burgundy, and one for John of Luxembourg, requesting both to deliver the Maid to the bishop,
who would persecute her as guilty of "idolatry and other
crimes against faith." On the presentation of these letters,
only want of ready money prevented Cauchon from obtaining
immediate possession of the prisoner. On Aug. 4th, the
states of Normandy were taxed for the amount demanded by
Luxembourg, and on Oct. 20th, the money was paid. But
the trial was deferred until Jan. 9th, 1431, and the first ex-

(1) Quicherat gives the following account of this bishop: " Peter Cauchon ... arrived
at political distinction because of his university honors. George Chastellain calls him 'a
grand and solemn clerk,' a eulogy sufficiently justified by the suffrages of the University
of Paris, which called him to its rectorship, and employed him, during the reign of Charles
VI., in important negotiations. In time he became conservator of the privileges of this illustrious body. Duboulai, in his *Hist. Univ. Paris.*, vol. V., does not hesitate to represent
Cauchon as a 'magnificent and beneficent' man; the correspondence of Nicholas de Clemangis is full of his praises; in fine, Philip the Good, duke of Burgundy, thought so much of
him, that when he had procured for him the see of Beauvais, he accompanied him at his installation. After his retirement to Rouen, he became the *ame damnée* of the Lancastrian
princes, who profited by his inordinate ambition and his resentment against Charles VII.
They rewarded his complaisance in the matter of the Maid with the promise of the archbish-
opric of Rouen, then vacant. This promise is shown to have been made, in the recent publication of Sir Harris Nicholas, *Proceedings and Ordinances of the Privy Council of England*, London, 1835. ... In spite of this powerful recommendation, the favored prelate did
not obtain the coveted see." *Process, etc.*, vol. I., pt. 1.

amination of Joan was held on Feb. 21, in the city of Rouen.

During seventeen sessions, which lasted until March 17th, Joan was surrounded by snares; deafened with questions; tormented in every way. Without counsel or any assistance whatever; weakened and sore from the chains with which she was loaded, night and day; knowing that every sentence she uttered might be so interpreted as to send her to the stake ; the peasant girl remained firm and tranquil, and always returned calm and temperate answers. While constantly proclaiming the reality of her visions, none of her remarks betrayed any fanaticism or exaltation. He who reads the *Process* carefully will feel that there was no great extravagance on the part of John Fabry, one of the assessors at the trial, when he asserted that it was his deliberate judgment that the replies of Joan to her judges were the fruit of heavenly inspiration. We earnestly recommend the reader to study the *Process*, our limits allowing only a few extracts to be given. "My thoughts and my deeds," she said, "are in the hands of God, and I confide entirely in Him. I have done nothing without His command, and it was through His revelation that I received all that I know ; and the good I have worked was done because He wished it to be done. I went to the king by command of God and His angels; I put on the clothing of a man; and I would have been drawn by wild horses, sooner than disregard His or their wishes. If He chose me instead of another, it was because He wished to expel the king's enemies by the arm of a girl. ... I say to my lord, the bishop of Beauvais : You claim to be my judge, and I know not whether you are; but beware of pronouncing an unjust sentence, and of thus exposing yourself to extreme danger. I warn you, so that if the Lord punishes you, I will have done my duty. ... I demand to be taken before the Pope ; I will answer him as I ought to answer. ... If you doubt the truth of what I tell you about my saints, send to Poitiers, where I was first examined. My king believed in me, and after hearing the decision of the ecclesiastical authorities. ... My voices told me to answer you courageously, and with a joyful countenance. Therefore I shall readily tell you all that God allows me to reveal ; but I can tell you nothing which was revealed to me concerning the king of France, without the consent of my saints."

Joan had not surrendered herself as a prisoner of war; hence she regarded herself as free to take advantage of an opportunity to regain her liberty. When she heard that Cauchon had pronounced that any attempt to flee would indicate her guilt of magical practices, she said: "I do not recognize his right to prohibit my flight; were I to escape, no man could say that I broke my word." Three months before her death, the judges asked her what her saints had promised her concerning her fate. JOAN: "That has nothing to do with the trial." J.: "But have they given you any promise?" JOAN: "Yes, they made me one, but I shall not tell it, for it does not concern the trial. But I shall manifest it in three months." J.: "Have your saints told you that you will be freed from prison in three months?" JOAN: "That has nothing to do with the trial. Now I know not when I shall be free. Perhaps they who desire my death will take their time." On another occasion she said: "St. Catharine signified that help would come to me; my voices tell me that I shall be freed 'by means of a great victory'; and they tell me to bear everything with patience, and not to be sad because of my martyrdom, for through it I am to enter paradise. By martyrdom I understand my sufferings in prison; I know not whether greater pain awaits me. In every event I abandon myself to the will of the Lord." Regarding her visions, the judges demanded: "When did you last hear the voices?" JOAN: "Yesterday and to-day." J.: "At what hour yesterday?" JOAN: "Three times; first at Matins; then at Vespers, finally at the Ave Maria." J.: "What were you doing yesterday when you heard the voices?" JOAN: "I was sleeping, and the voices awakened me." J.: "Were you awakened by a call, or by a touch on the arm?" JOAN: "They aroused me without touching me." J.: "Was the voice in your room?" JOAN: "No; it seemed to come from over the castle." J.: "Did you thank that voice, and kneel before it?" JOAN: "I thanked it, remaining in bed. I joined my hands, and prayed it to assist me and to advise me as to what I should do. The voice answered that I should reply to you courageously." J.: " What did it say on the instant that you awoke?" JOAN : "I begged it to advise me as to what I should say to you ; and it told me to speak bravely, and God would help me." J.: " Had the voice said anything before you thus prayed?" JOAN: " Some words which I did not well understand. But it is true that when I was fully awake, it told me to answer you courageously." J.: " Did this voice ever vary in its counsels?" JOAN: "I have never found the least contradiction in its sayings. I believe that this voice comes from God and obeys God, as firmly as I believe the teachings of Jesus, and in the redemption of man by God." J.: "Is this voice that of an angel, or that of a saint, or does it proceed directly from God?" JOAN : "The voice comes from God. I do not tell you more clearly what I know concerning it, because I fear to err more seriously by telling what would displease you, than by allowing you to find your own answer." J.: " When you hear the voices, do you see anything?" JOAN · "I cannot tell you all, for I have not permission to do so ; but the voice is good." J.: " Has the voice eyes and face?" JOAN : "At present you shall not learn this from me. I do not forget that children are told that many persons have been hung for telling the whole truth." One day she was asked how she had felt for the last few days, and she replied: "You can see for yourselves that I am as well as I can be." On another occasion, being asked whether she saw St. Michael and other angels in body and in substance, she answered : "I see them with my bodily eyes as I see you." J.: " What sign have you that these revelations come from God, and that they who speak to you are SS. Catharine and Margaret?" JOAN : " I have told you that it is enough that they are SS. Catharine and Margaret. If you please, believe me once." J.: " Does St. Margaret speak English?" JOAN: "Why should she speak English, since she is not of the English party?" J.: " Was St. Michael naked?" JOAN: "Do you think that God cannot cover him?" J.: "Did he have long hair?" JOAN: "Why should he cut his hair?" J.: " When you were a little girl, did you wish to hurt the English?" JOAN: "I greatly desired that my king should recover his kingdom." J.: "Do SS. Catharine and

Margaret abhor the English?" JOAN: "They love whatever God loves, and hate what He hates." J.: "Does God hate the English?" JOAN: "I know nothing of God's love or hatred for the English, and nothing concerning His thoughts about their souls; but this I do know, that the English, save those who die, will be expelled from France, and that in the end, God will grant victory to us." J.: "Do you not believe that, so far as earthly prosperity is concerned, your angel deceived you, seeing that you are now a prisoner?" JOAN: "Since God has willed that I should be a prisoner, I believe that I have been captured for some good end." J.: "Do you believe that after your visions you can possibly fall into mortal sin?" JOAN: "God alone knows. I do not think I am in mortal sin, but if I ever committed such, it is for God to judge me; that is, God and His priests in the confessional." J.: "When jumping from the tower, did you intend killing yourself?" JOAN: "No; but I recommended myself to God, hoping to escape from the English." J.: "Why did you have that picture put on your banner?" JOAN: "I have told you often enough that I did everything by the command of God. In attacks on the enemy, I carried my banner, that I might avoid killing any one; indeed, *I never killed any one.*" J.: "Do you believe that your voices would still visit you if you were married?" JOAN: "God alone knows."

On March 24, the records of the examination were read to the Maid, and with a few unimportant exceptions, she found them correct. Thus far the proceedings had formed merely a preparatory information, for the purpose of finding whether the Maid could be a subject of accusation; but on the 27th, the *Process*, properly so called, commenced. The promotor formulated seventy-seven points of accusation, which infamously caricatured the life of Joan. Then she was asked to submit herself, purely and simply, to the judgment of the Church. Here, remarks Gorres, the directors of the unjust proceedings merely wished Joan to recognize the sentence of those who called themselves the Church. On the previous day she had been visited in her prison by John Delafontaine, accompanied by two Dominican friars, with the intention of advising her. Having exhorted her to believe and hold all

that the Church believes and holds, Delafontaine had told
her that the teaching Church was composed of the Pope and
the bishops, and not of Cauchon and his satellites; that she
should willingly submit to the decision of the Pope or of a
General Council. When, therefore, in the presence of Cauchon, Friar Isambert proposed that Joan should submit to the
General Council about to meet at Basel, she willingly assented: "I demand to be taken before the Holy Father; I will
not submit to the judgment of my enemies." As this appeal
simply nullified the whole process, Cauchon angrily shouted to Isambert to "be silent in the name of the devil" (1).
He then ordered the notary to set down nothing as to the
prisoner's appeal, and the servile assessors submitted to the
injustice. Twelve articles of accusation were now drawn up,
based upon the seventy-seven points, and they terminated
with the direct lie that Joan had refused to submit to the
judgment of the Church. So evident was the injustice of
these twelve articles, that the notary Manchon added to the
Acts an observation to the effect that said articles were not
drawn in good faith, and that they did not agree with the examinations. His note, however, was not registered; and he
wanted the courage to show his opposition openly, as he
afterward declared. Upon these twelve articles, composed
in secret, based on a falsification of the examinations, and
not communicated to the Maid, were founded the decisions
of the University of Paris and of the Chapter of Rouen, whereby Joan was condemned. On April 22, twenty-two doctors
and licentiates in theology, with many other men of learning,
declared that the works and visions of the Maid were lies and
inventions of the demon; and that they were redolent of superstition, enchantment, blasphemy, pride, temerity, and idol-

---

(1) *Process of Rehabilitation*, ch. 4.—When Cauchon found that Delafontaine and the
two Dominicans had suggested the appeal to the Pontiff, he uttered such horrible threats of
vengeance that had not the timid vice-inquisitor summoned a little courage, and threatened
to withdraw from the trial, the three good Samaritans would probably have lost their lives.
On the afternoon of the appeal, these friends appeared again before the cell of Joan, but
there they were met by the earl of Warwick, who declared that if they gave the Maid another word of advice, he would have them thrown into the Seine. See the testimony of the
Dominican, William Duval, in the *Preliminaries to the Process of Rehabilitation*. From
the day of the appeal, Cauchon alone was allowed by Warwick access to Joan's cell. Such
permission was not accorded even to the vice-inquisitor, who was a judge concurrent with
Cauchon.

atry. The bishop of Avranches, a venerable and honorable prelate, was asked by the judges for his opinion; and he declared that he opined with St. Thomas of Aquin that such a case as the present ought to be referred to the Pontiff or to a General Council.

In the meantime, Joan had fallen seriously ill. Fearful that the victim would escape from his hands, Warwick sent two physicians to her with injunctions to spare no expense or care to effect her cure. "The king of England (then only ten years old) would not have her die a natural death for the world; she has cost him dearly, and he wishes her to die at the stake." So insisted Warwick, and her physicians enabled her to receive the usual admonitions to avow her guilt. On May 9, when she was admonished for the third time, her enemies tried to terrify her by informing her that the torture awaited her. "If perchance," she said, "pain should draw a confession from me, I protest, from this moment, that it will be false. On the feast of the Holy Cross, May 3d, an angel came to me to give me strength, and my voices told me that he was the angel Gabriel. God has been the Author of all my deeds; the devil has had no power over me. Even though they tear me to pieces, I shall not speak otherwise." On the 12th a discussion took place as to the utility of applying torture to the Maid; but only two of the court were sufficiently cruel to advise the use of this method of discovering truth. The death of the heroine had been determined, but her enemies feared the people. An infamous fraud was therefore devised. Two sentences were prepared, and two declarations of submission were to be presented to Joan for her signature or mark. The first sentence condemned her to death, if she did not submit; the second was to be used in case she averred her guilt, and it ordered her perpetual imprisonment. On the 24th Joan was led to the cemetery of St. Ouen, where two platforms had been erected, one for the Maid, and the other for the curials, chief among whom was Cardinal Henry Beaufort, bishop of Winchester, ex-chancellor of England, and grand-uncle of King Henry VI. The presence of the executioner with his apparatus added to the impressiveness of the scene. The *Acts* of the trial were read;

Joan listening patiently, and at the end appealing again to
Rome, and firmly denying the charges in the twelve articles.
Cauchon then began to read the sentence of condemnation,
beginning with the downright lie that Joan had "obstinately and frequently refused to submit her case to our lord the
Pontiff." As Cauchon was proceeding, the immense crowd
was moved to something like compassion, and many were
begging the Maid to sign the paper tendered her. At first
she merely replied: "You take much trouble to influence
me," but finally she signified that she would obey her judges.
Cauchon ceased his reading, and the canon Erard (1) handed to the curial Massieu (2) a paper containing a promise
that Joan would never again wear masculine dress, carry
arms, or allow her hair to hang down over her shoulders (3).
Still Joan hesitated to sign this document, asking that it
should first be examined by the ecclesiastical authorities, to
whom, according to law, she ought then to have been consigned. But Erard insisted, saying: "Sign, or to-day your
life ends in the flames." She then was assisted by a secretary of King Henry to make her mark; but the paper she
signed, and which was inserted in the *Acts,* was not the one
which had been read by Massieu. It began with very different words, and it made Joan style herself impious, a fabrica-
tor of false visions, a thirster after human blood, a blasphemer of God, a profaner of the Sacraments, etc. Massieu himself afterward testified : "I know for certain that the paper
which I read is not the one given in the *Process.*" After the
signature of Joan had been obtained, Cauchon read the sentence of imprisonment ; whereupon the Maid demanded to
be sent to an ecclesiastical prison, since they said that she

(1) William Erard, or Evrard, was about to proceed as representative of France at the
Council of Basel, when the trial of Joan detained him. On the day of the false abjuration
he preached a violent diatribe against Charles VII. He was afterward rewarded by Henry
VI. with a royal chaplaincy, a manor in the county of Southampton, and an annual pension
of twenty pounds. DUBOULAI; *Hist. Univ. Paris,* vol. V. RYMER ; vol. X.

(2) John Massieu, "dean of Christianity" in Rouen (rural dean in that section of the diocese which was called the Deanery of Christianity), afterward testified in the *Process of
Rehabilitation.*

(3) Cauchon now asked Cardinal Henry what he thought should be done, and his Eminence
replied that the case was one which called simply for a condemnation to some penance.
The English became furious when they found that the Maid was not to be burnt; and it was
sworn in the second process that when Warwick complained of the court's lenity, one of
the judges replied : "Rest assured that we shall soon have her again."

was condemned by the Church. But Cauchon cried to the guards: "Take her to the prison from which you brought her!" On her return to her cell, Joan doffed her masculine attire, resuming that of her sex. Then she received a visit from John Le Maitre, the irresolute vice-inquisitor, who had yielded only to fear in assisting at the trial, and was exhorted by him not to resume the clothing of a man. If she did, he said, she was lost. Several others made similar exhortations; but so violent was the English hatred of the Maid, and so anxiously did they yearn for an excuse to put her to death, that these sympathizers were nearly clubbed to death by the mob. Very soon an opportunity and an excuse were afforded to Joan's enemies for her destruction. Her jailers had removed her feminine habiliments while she was in bed, but had replaced them with her masculine dress. Massieu afterward testified that on the morning of Trinity Sunday, as Joan had told him, she said to her jailers: " Leave the room, for I wish to arise." An Englishman then took up the masculine garments, and threw them at her, saying: "Very well; arise!" She replied: " Friends, you know that these clothes are forbidden to me." The dispute lasted until mid-day, when the necessities of nature forcing the unfortunate to leave the cell, she perforce put on the prohibited garments. On her return she prayed in vain for the restitution of her feminine dress. No sooner was it known that Joan had resumed the clothing of a man, than the English soldiers threatened Cauchon with death, unless he punished her for her "relapse." Warwick and the bishop visited her, and she complained bitterly of her treatment by the guards, insisting that she had been forced to don the masculine garments in order to protect her honor. " Had I been placed in an ecclesiastical prison," she said, " this would not have happened." Then Cauchon began to press her concerning her visions, and asked if she still received visits from SS. Catharine and Margaret. Just as when she stood in the square of St. Ouen, so now her fate depended upon her reply to an insidious question; but she resolutely answered: " Yes; both have appeared to me, and through them God has shown me how He pities me for having saved my life by that fatal abjuration. When I was on the platform they told me to answer the orator intrepidly, and now I say that he is a false orator, for he punished me for crimes which I never committed. Ever since Thursday (the day of the false abjuration), the two saints have told me that then I did grievously wrong. ... I shall do penance by suffering death, rather than by the torments of prison. ... I did not at all know what was written in the abjuration, and I never intended to retract." On leaving the prison, Cauchon cried to Warwick and to the English who filled the vestibule: "All goes well; be of good cheer! At last, the matter is finished." And the exultant English shouted: "She is caught!"

On the 29th the court met to deliberate concerning the final sentence, and the friar Martin L'Advenu was authorized to prepare Joan for death. When, in the early morning of the 30th, he informed her of her fate, nature gave way for a while, and the poor girl threw herself on the ground in her excess of misery. "Alas!" she cried, "are they so pitiless as to reduce to ashes this young and healthy body which has never been stained? Had they put me in an ecclesiastical prison, where churchmen would have been my jailers, this misfortune would not have overtaken me. But God is witness of this enormous injustice." However, she soon recovered her wonted serenity; and having made her confession, she prepared to receive her Sacramental Lord— a blessing which her cunningly merciless foes had long denied her. The authorities then had the Holy Eucharist brought toward the prison without any lights, chants, or any solemnity whatever; but the resolute Dominican insisted upon all the fitting observances, a procession of clerics was formed, and with the Litanies and the *Orate pro ea* sounding their encouragement, the Maid received her God. After a few hours the impious Cauchon visited his victim, and Joan addressed him: "Bishop, my death is due entirely to you." The wretch replied: "You die because you have not kept your promises; because you have repeated your former crimes." Joan answered: "Would that you had confided me to my legitimate custodian, an ecclesiastical tribunal! Then this would not have happened. But from you I appeal to God."

At nine in the morning of May 30, 1431, Joan of Arc ascended the judgment car to be carried to the place of her death. She was dressed in her feminine costume, and at one side of her was her confessor, Martin L'Advenu, while John Massieu was on the other. Eight hundred soldiers acted as escort, and allowed no one to approach near enough to speak to her. But in spite of the precautions, one individual succeeded in penetrating the serried ranks. This was a priest, by name Nicholas L'Oyseleur, who had often played traitor to the Maid (1). He was now stricken by remorse, and cried out for her forgiveness. Instantly the English seized him, and but for the interposition of Warwick, his repentance would have cost him his life. Meanwhile the cortege moved toward the market-place near the church of the Saviour, the resigned girl constantly recommending herself to God and her saints. Many were moved to tears, as they afterward attested; but the immense majority of the spectators were either English or partisans of the English cause. When the fatal spot had been reached, Nicholas Midy (2) preached a sermon, or rather a tissue of absurdities, finishing with these words: "Joan, go in peace; the Church can no longer defend thee, and she consigns thee to the arm of the secular power." When Midy had finished, Joan immediately, without waiting for Cauchon who would have addressed her, knelt down and fervently prayed God and her saints to aid her in that tremendous time. She begged pardon of all men, enemies as well as friends, for any evil she might peradventure have done them; and she forgave all who had ever injured her. She besought the priests, each one, to celebrate a Mass for the repose of her soul, and begged the people to pray for her. When she had

(1) Nicholas L'Oyseleur, or *Aucupis*, canon of the cathedral of Rouen, became a spy of Cauchon, and gained the confidence of Joan by representing himself as a prisoner of war, taken in arms for Charles VII. Gorres remarks that if there is any irrefragable testimony for the innocence of the Maid, it is that of this man. He had penetrated her inmost thoughts, had advised her to her own harm, and had suggested to her foes that torture would probably conquer her. And at the end of the tragedy his remorse proclaimed the rectitude of Joan. Following the suggestion of Warwick, the unfortunate man fled to Basel, where he met a sudden death.

(2) Nicholas Midy, doctor in theology, was an assessor at the trial, and one of the most hostile to Joan. He is supposed to have drawn up the twelve articles on which her condemnation was founded. During the second trial, a witness testified that Midy died of leprosy soon after the catastrophe, but Duboulai speaks of a Master Nicholas Midy as haranguing Charles VII., in the name of the University of Paris, when that monarch entered his capital in 1438.

prayed for half an hour, the English soldiers grew impatient, and shouted for the Maid to be put into their hands.
As Massieu was comforting her, they cried : "Master John,
what are you doing? Are we to stay here till dinner-time?"
Then Cauchon said to the executioner : "Do thy duty!" Two
assistants helped Joan to descend from the platform on which,
until then, she had been placed ; and then a few soldiers
savagely dragged her to the pyre, while she exclaimed :
"Rouen, Rouen! thou art my last abiding place!" When
she had been bound to the stake, there remained on the pile,
close to her side, resolved to encourage her to the last possible
moment, the noble Dominican friar, Martin L'Advenu. The
flames were already rising around them, and Joan's tunic was
blazing, when she turned to her last friend on earth, and bade
him look to his safety. At this instant, Cauchon approached
the pile. "Ah!" exclaimed the dying heroine, "you are the
cause of my death. Had you placed me in the prison of the
Church, I would not now be here. Rouen, I fear that my death
will cost you much." Just before the flames entirely enfolded
her, the Maid asked for some holy water ; then she was seen
to bend down her head, and from the midst of the devouring
fire were heard her last words : "Jesus! Jesus! Jesus!"

Thus died the Maid of Orleans ; faithful to the Church, although many churchmen were foully guilty of her death ; faithful to France, although French judges unjustly condemned
her ; faithful to her king, although he weakly abandoned
her. Very different was the end of her principal persecu-
tors. Cauchon soon found himself the object of general detestation, and that there was a probability of his being called
to account by the Holy See. He therefore obtained from the
English government letters of security, in which it was declared to be the intention of King Henry to impede any action
against Cauchon and his assistants in the trial of the Maid ;
and the English orators at Rome and at Basel were ordered
to ask every ally of Henry to do the same. The wretched
bishop was also guilty of another fraud, in his anxiety to
defend himself. He added to the *Acts* of the trial a lot of
forged testimony to the effect that Joan, before her death,
admitted that her visions were the work of the demon, and

that she begged pardon of the English for the injuries she had done them. This false examination is the only one of the *Acts* which is wanting in the signatures of the notaries; and in the second *Process* William Manchon testified that Cauchon tried to force him to subscribe to an examination at which he had not assisted. In 1442, Cauchon died suddenly, while under the hands of his barber. The vice-inquisitor disappeared, and no man ever learned what had become of him. The canon Estivet, promotor of the cause, and an intimate companion of Cauchon, was found dead in a sewer, soon after the tragedy of Rouen. The miserable Oyseleur fell dead in a church at Basel. Midy died of leprosy.

We have frequently cited the *Process of Rehabilitation*, whereby the honor of Joan was vindicated, and the judgment of the Bedford-Cauchon court reversed. We now proceed to give a succinct account of the second *Process*. Some might have thought it more prudent to trust to time for the vindication of the Maid; for it certainly was an ungracious task to stamp the note of infamy upon many great ones of the earth who were yet living, and to decry the motives, learning, or good judgment of such a body as the University of Paris. But King Charles became ashamed of his cowardly abandonment of his benefactress, and he it was who took the first steps for an impartial investigation of her career and of her condemnation. On Feb. 15, 1449, he ordered William Bouillé (1), one of his ministers, to undertake, in Rouen, an examination of certain persons who had been concerned in, or had at least witnessed, the first *Process* (2). The informations gathered by Bouillé and the *Acts* of the Bedford-Cauchon court were submitted to men learned in law and other sciences (3), and these decided that God alone could judge with

(1) William Bouillé, rector of the University of Paris, dean of its faculty of theology, dean of the cathedral of Noyon and of St. Florent de Roye, was a member of the royal grand council. At the time of Joan's condemnation, he was provost of the college of Beauvais in Paris.

(2) Their testimonies are given in full in the *Preliminaries* to the *Process of Rehabilitation*. The persons examined, at this stage of the proceedings, were John Toutmouillé, a Dominican, doctor in theology; Isambert de la Pierre, Martin L'Advenu, William Manchon, and John Massieu, whom the reader has already met; William Duval, a Dominican, and doctor in theology; and John Beaupaire, canon, and doctor in theology.

(3) One of these experts was Theodore de Leliis, an auditor of the Ruota for twenty-five years, and one of the best canonists of the fifteenth century. Another was John Brehal, inquisitor-general for the kingdom of France.

certainty of the reliability of Joan's visions ; that, however, human wisdom could affirm that, all the circumstances being considered, these visions were probable, since they involved no impossibility, or anything repugnant to the rules of sound criticism ; and that the *Process* of condemnation was most un. just and null for many reasons, both in form and substance. In June, 1455, Pope Calixtus III. issued a Brief whereby he charged John Orsini, archbishop of Rheims, the bish- ops of Paris and Coutances, and the inquisitor, John Bre- hal, with the examination of the *Process*, and with the duty of hearing both parties to the controversy. On Nov. 17th, Isabella d'Arc, mother of Joan, accompanied by her two sons and many relations, appeared before the commission, and having declared that Joan had ever been a devoted child of the Church ; that "she had never harbored a thought contrary to the faith ; but that her enemies, hating the king whom she served, instituted the said *Process* against her ;" they de- manded that a new trial should be undertaken. Then the commissioners publicly cited the relatives, successors, and heirs of Peter Cauchon, of Estivet, and of Le Maitre, to appear in Rouen on Dec. 12, to show reason why a new *Process* should not be initiated. These parties appeared, and made no opposition to a new trial. Then commenced the taking of testimony at Rouen, Paris, Lyons, Domremy, and Orleans, concerning the life and deeds of the Maid. These testimon- ies, together with those taken previously by Cardinal d'Es- touteville, pontifical legate and archbishop of Rouen, number one hundred and forty-four, and are from the most noble princes and knights of France, as well as from the most humble citizens of Domremy. First among them is the evidence of the valorous Dunois, the most glorious name in that glorious age. This old warrior frankly proclaimed that his greatest triumphs were due to the humble Joan, and he swore that he firmly believed that her mission was from God. Still more in- teresting is the testimony of the Duke d'Alençon, for he had joined the English, and had been condemned to death by the court of peers, his life being spared only by the mercy of the king. This prince also swore that he believed in Joan's divine mission ; and that, having examined the fortifications around Orleans, he was convinced that the Maid took them with her small army, only by the aid of a miracle. Then came the testimony of John d'Aulon, the squire of the Maid; of Louis des Contes, her page; of Friar John Pasquerel, her confessor; all of whom knew her most secret ways and actions. Many of the peasants of Domremy, among whom she had grown to womanhood, swore to the good repute she had always enjoyed. So also did the clergy, the nobles, and the military officers of the neighborhood. Even the executioner who burned her, and who threw her heart (which would not burn) and ashes into the Seine, testified to the evidences of her sanctity. From all these testimonies it became evident to the minds of the impartial judges that the whole *Process* of condemnation had been a hideous fraud. They heard what iniquitous means had been used to deceive the Maid; how, in spite of her ignorance and inexperience, no advocate had been allowed her; how she had been treated so cruelly in her prison; that it was strange that she retained any strength of endurance or any vigor of intellect. And above all, they heard the avowal of the notary, which manifested the fraud in the matter of the twelve articles, in which her replies had been falsified, and her justifications suppressed. In regard to the visions of the Maid, her irreprehensible life, her virginal purity so rigorously maintained, her predictions so wonderfully fulfilled; all seemed to indicate that they were, as she insisted, of divine origin. Hence it was that on July 7, 1456, the commission for the reversal of Joan's condemnation published the following decree:

"In the name of the Most Holy and Indivisible Trinity, the Father, Son, and Holy Ghost. Amen. Jesus Christ, God-Man, our Redeemer, in the wisdom of His eternal Majesty constituted the Blessed Peter and his Apostolic successors as Supreme heads of His militant Church, that they might manifest the light of truth, indicate the way of justice, protect the good, aid the oppressed, and lead the wandering to the right path. Hence we, John, archbishop of Rheims; William, bishop of Paris; Richard, bishop of Coutances; and John Brehal, of the Order of Preachers, professor of sacred theology, inquisitor into heretical depravity in the kingdom

of France; judges specially designated by our most holy lord
the Pope: Having considered the process which, by virtue of an
Apostolic Brief, was solemnly begun before us by the noble (1)
widow, Isabella d'Arc, Peter and John d'Arc, mother and
brothers of the defunct Joan d'Arc of happy memory, commonly
called the Maid, against the sub-inquisitor into heretical depravity in the diocese of Beauvais, against the promotor for criminal
affairs in the episcopal court of Beauvais, and against the
reverend father in Christ, William de Hellande, bishop of
Beauvais, and against all other parties interested in this matter.   Having considered the citation issued by the accusers
(the family of Arc) and by our promotor, and having seen
their proofs of the honor and innocence of the Maid, and of
the nullity, falsity, and injustice of the *Process* which was
instituted against the deceased Joan by Peter Cauchon, John
d'Estivet, and John Le Maitre.   Having repeatedly seen and
examined the original letters, documents, means of proof,
Acts, observations, and protocols of the said *Process*, which
were furnished to us by the notaries of the same, and of the
authenticity of which we are satisfied.   Having held mature
consultation with the notaries and others; having seen the
articles and interrogatories, and having weighed the depositions of the witnesses concerning the conduct of the deceased;
concerning her departure from her native place; concerning
the examinations she underwent for many days at Poitiers
and other places, in presence of many prelates, doctors, and
learned men, especially of Regnault, archbishop of Rheims
and metropolitan of the bishop of Beauvais; and having seen
the depositions of witnesses concerning the miraculous liberation of Orleans, and concerning the coronation at Rheims;
and having observed all the circumstances of the process, the
qualifications of the judges, and the manner in which the process itself was conducted.   Having closed the replies, and
having heard our promotor, we ended the *Process* in the
name of Christ, and fixed on this day for the publication of
our sentence.   Having seen, weighed, and considered all the
foregoing; and especially having considered those twelve articles which the preceding judges asserted to be taken from

(1) By a decree of Dec., 1429, King Charles VII. had ennobled the whole family of Arc.

the depositions of the deceased, and which they communicated to many distinguished men in order to obtain their opinion. That our sentence may be pronounced in the sight of
God, who alone can read souls, and knows His own revelations, of which He is the infallible judge; therefore, in the
presence of God, ... we judge and pronounce as justice demands: That the above-mentioned twelve articles are false,
fraudulent, calumnious, drawn from the aforesaid *Process* and
from the avowals of the deceased only by cunning and by
wickedness, repressing the truth and expressing falsehood in
many essential points; that the judges were led to pronounce
their sentence by the fact that these articles furnish, without
proof, certain aggravating circumstances which are not found
in the *Process* and avowals, and that they repress many miti-
gating circumstances and all the justifications, and change
and misinterpret the meaning of words. Therefore, we annul,
quash, and declare invalid these articles as false, fraudulent,
calumnious, and not conformable to the avowals; and we declare that justice demands their destruction. And having
given scrupulous attention to the other portions of the *Process*,
and especially to the two clauses entitled: 'Fallen' and 'Relapsed'; and having maturely considered the dispositions of
the judges and of those who held Joan in prison, and having
seen that she protested against her judges, that she often demanded that she and her career and her depositions should
be sent to the Apostolic See and to our holy Father the Supreme Pontiff, to whom she ever declared herself submissive;
having examined the false, fraudulent, and pretended abjuration, which was extorted from Joan in presence of the executioner and of the rack, and without her understanding it;
having weighed the reports of the prelates and doctors concerning the nullity and injustice of the *Process*; having considered, in fine, all these and many other things, specially and
collectively. By this our definitive sentence, having God
alone as our Guide, we recognize and declare that the said
Process and its sentences, the abjuration and all its consequences, are null and of no effect because of fraud, calumny,
wickedness, contradiction, and manifest defects in law and
substance; and that therefore they never had any efficacy or

vigor. We annul and quash them, and declare that the said
Joan, and her relatives, the accusers of to-day, are free from
every dishonor or stain accruing from the aforesaid *Process.*"

It might not prove uninteresting to the reader were we to
devote some space to a cursory review of the most important
of the almost innumerable works elicited by the career of the
Maid of Orleans. Our limits will not permit this; but we
cannot avoid noticing the manner in which the heroine has
been treated by one author of celebrity, from whom a much
more accurate account might have been expected. Catholic
students are accustomed to consult Lingard with respect; for
he is by far the best historian of his nation. But his fancied
prudence in a too frequent endeavor to placate the prejudices
of his Protestant countrymen often causes him to at least
minimize the truth. And so evident is this tendency when
he treats of the Maid of Orleans, that Gorres does not hesitate to say that while Hume is one of the most superficial
and most badly informed historians in the matter of Joan,
"Lingard shows himself to be no better informed." For instance, Lingard goes so far as to say that if the English had
killed the Maid, immediately after taking her prisoner, they
would have done only what she had done to Franquet d'Arras.
The enemies of Joan certainly insisted that she had put
Franquet, a prisoner of war, to death; but in her examination of March 14th she declared that this captain of freebooters was condemned, after a trial which lasted fifteen days,
as a traitor, murderer, and robber, and that the sentence was
pronounced by the magistrates of Lagny. "Let every one
think," says Gorres, "what he will concerning the vocation
of Joan; but we have a right to expect a historian to examine
documents before he pronounces judgment. Greater exactness and profundity are shown by Sharon Turner than by
Lingard in this matter, and doubtless because the former, in
his *History of England during the Middle Age,* had recourse
to the work of Lebrun" (1).

(1) The great work of Lebrun de Charmettes appeared in 1817, and it furnished more
material for a history of Joan of Arc than any other investigator had amassed, although, in
many respects, it was but a copy of the work by L'Averdy which had been issued in 1793, in
volume III. of the *Notices and Extracts from the Manuscripts of the Royal Library of
France.*

That Joan of Arc was one of the chief glories of France, is the conviction of every impartial mind which is familiar with a history which is redolent of glory. And yet 'even among Frenchmen there have not been wanting writers who would fain rob the Maid of some of her laurels to place them on the brow of a courtesan. Du Haillan, historiographer of France in the sixteenth century, informs the world that Agnes Sorel, the infamous mistress of Charles VII., was the real motive power by which the English were expelled from France (Calais excepted). He says that Agnes upbraided the king for his supineness, and having told him that an astrologer had predicted that she was to be loved by one of the most courageous monarchs in Christendom, she signified her intention of making the acquaintance of his foe, the king of England; that then Charles shook off his lethargy, and undertook his victorious campaigns (1). This fable was adopted in 1599 by Beroalde de Verville, in his *La Pucelle Restituée;* then by the licentious and license-loving Brantôme, and to a certain extent by the moderns, Villaret and Anquetil. Sismondi, Michelet, and Henri Martin laud "the good influence" of Agnes, but reject the story of Du Haillan. The reader will be surprised to learn that under the liberal government of Louis Philippe, the youth of France were asked to accept this yarn as cold history, in a work "designed especially for religious communities and female seminaries" (2). Among the authors who have exploded this detraction from the glory of the Maid may be mentioned Bréquigny, Clément, Le Roux de Lincy, Lelanne, and Beaucourt. Their arguments are many and conclusive, but we need furnish only one. Agnes Sorel did not appear at the court of France until 1444, and Joan of Arc had saved France in 1429. It may also be noted that at the time when the favorite is alleged to have threatened to desert Charles VII. for the caresses of Henry VI., the latter monarch was only eight years of age.

Certain polemics insist that Catholics, as such, have no right to glory in Joan of Arc. Did not the Church condemn her as a sorceress, and burn her at the stake? Well indeed,

---

(1) *History of France*; Paris, 1576.

(2) *Abridgment of a Course of History, especially Designed for Religious Communities and Female Seminaries,* by M. S. Lefranc; Paris, 1836.

we are told, did the dying Maid sternly rebuke the Church, when she addressed to Cauchon those pathetically bitter words : "Bishop, I die because of thee!" But was the bishop of Beauvais, or even the famous University of Paris, the Church? No more than Warwick, and her other English murderers were ; no more than Benedict Arnold, when he devastated the Connecticut shore, was the Continental army ; no more than Bazaine, the traitor of Metz, was the heart of France. Cauchon, Estivet, L'Oyseleur, and the Faculty of Paris, were undoubtedly churchmen ; and Lucifer was once an angel of light. If we wish to know the mind—we will not say of the Church, but of true churchmen—regarding the case of the Maid, we will not restrict our researches to the tribunal of Rouen. We will consider, in the first place, the course of the ecclesiastical questioners of Joan at Poitiers. Those clergymen were more numerous, and more distinguished, than were the sycophants of Rouen ; and after a minute investigation which lasted six weeks, they proclaimed that in Joan they had found : "Nought but good, humility, purity, devotion, and simplicity." Secondly, the opinions of the Catholic clergy can be evinced from the treatises in her honor composed by the "pious Gerson," the learned and cautious Chancellor of that same Faculty of Paris which trampled on justice to please the foreign invader ; also from the writings of Gelu, archbishop of Embrun. Thirdly, if we wish to know how the priests regarded the Maid, let us listen to the innumerable preachers who, like the Dominican, Helie Bodont, went from city to city proclaiming "the wondrous miracles accomplished in France by means of the Maid whom God has led to our lord the king." Observe, also, the many Masses and Offices offered, and the processions made in all the sanctuaries of France, in thanksgiving to heaven for the mission of Joan. Consider the thousands of medals struck in commemoration of the virgin of Domremy, and worn by so many persons of every rank, after they were blessed by the clergy. By observations such as these, and not by a contemplation of the mock tribunal of Rouen, is the mind of Catholic churchmen to be discerned. And we would ask whether the decision of Cauchon and his associates should be compared with the truly authoritative voice of the Holy See enjoining the rehabilitation of the memory of the holy victim. Certainly, Pope Calixtus III., issuing his Rescript dated June 2, 1454, ordering a new *Process* for the vindication of Joan, is to be considered a more authentic representative of ecclesiastical opinion than either the iniquitous prelate of Beauvais or the fawning University of Paris, when he says: "Although the said Joan besought the bishop (Cauchon) and John Le Maitre to consign her to the judgment of this Apostolic See, if they deemed her guilty of anything which breathed of heresy; and although she was ever willing to abide by that judgment; nevertheless, after depriving the said Joan of every means wherewith she might establish her innocence, after a contempt of every maxim of justice, and acting only in accordance with their own arbitrary desires, the said judges pronounced their wicked sentence, etc." And we know how firmly the Maid herself spurned the notion which Cauchon would have impressed in her simple mind, that the Church was judging her at Rouen. "Take me to the Pope of Rome!" she cried, again and again; justly penetrated by the thought that she was not being tried by the Church, but by an English, though ostensibly ecclesiastical tribunal. Richard de Grouchet, who attended at her ordeal in Rouen, testifies that: "One day they asked her whether she would submit to the decision of the bishop of Beauvais, and to that of the assessors named by that prelate; and she refused, demanding to be taken before the Pope. Then they told her that the *Process* would be forwarded to the Holy See; and she cried out: 'No; I cannot permit that; for I do not know what you will put in your report. I want to be questioned by the Pontiff.' I was present; and I can swear that Joan was ever submissive to the Church." It is evident, therefore, that the Church had no part in the condemnation of the Maid. Every monument of the time attests that the virgin of Domremy was the victim of secular politics. The agents of the crime were, on one side, pride; and on the other, thirst for gold or dignities. Well did Joan know the real authors of her misery. Every day they tried to worry her conscience by representing, that if she resisted her judges, she resisted the Church. She could not always evade their captious subtleties; she could not openly defy a bishop; but her faith and the facts before her gave to her an instinctive sentiment of the truth, and despite all sorts of sophisms, she appealed to that Church which she loved and trusted—that Church which she did not recognize in the Anglo-Burgundian tribunal. And when her condemnation was announced, she protested: "Had I been put in an ecclesiastical prison, as I so earnestly besought, this misfortune would not have befallen me."

It is a remarkable fact that many persons who fancy that they entertain an accurate idea of the career of Joan of Arc, possess a very incomplete knowledge of the most salient facts, to say nothing of the spirit, of that career. The histories upon which they have relied, even though otherwise meritorious, present only such of the grand lines of her personality as materialism recognizes; and consequently, the life which they contemplate is, to use a trite illustration, like the play of "Hamlet" without the character of the prince. Not a few Catholics, even persons of considerable erudition, are fairly surprised when they are asked to regard the Maid from a supernatural point of view; and the writer has been edified, more than once, on beholding a countenance illumined with joy because of the discovery, never anticipated, that the most interesting of heroines has claims to admiration much greater than the mundane spirit discerns. The materialist pronounces her a visionary, a victim of hysteria, or at best, an insane patriot. But hysteria or fanaticism could scarcely have surrounded Joan with an atmosphere of such angelic purity that it infused chaste thoughts into all who came near her; they could scarcely have transformed the utterly illiterate rustic into a graceful and heroic chevalier, an accomplished artillerist, and an able general; they could scarcely have changed, immediately after a terrific battle, the cool commander and intrepid knight into a sweet and anxious nurse for the wounded; they could scarcely have turned the commonplace peasant into an accurate prophet. As to the insane love of country which the materialist would ascribe to Joan as the moving spirit of her career, no fact of history stands out in greater relief than the sincere belief, on her part, at least, that she was, in all she did for France, merely the instrument of the Most High. It is vain to falsify history, in an endeavor to substitute a merely conventional personage for the true Maid of Orleans, to make of her a mere intrepid Amazon, a theatrical character like the Camilla chanted by Virgil (1).

That Joan was sent by God to deliver France, was firmly believed by her contemporary countrymen of every class. The famous Dunois, the foremost knight of his day, testified to his belief that " her deeds were due to divine inspiration." Similar testimony was given by the duke d'Alençon ; by John d'Aulon, her steward ; by Milet, registrar of the Estates of Paris ; by the licentiate, Viole ; by the Dominican professor of theology, Baignard ; and by innumerable other reliable persons who knew Joan well. The celebrated Gerson, writing eight days after the raising of the siege of Orleans, says, of the stupendous event : " This was the work of the Lord." And mark how the mission of the Maid was regarded by Gelu, archbishop of Embrun, the same counsellor who had warned the dauphin that " the claims of the girl should not be easily credited ; since her sex and training render her susceptible to illusion." M. Lanery d'Arc, in his interesting labor of love (2) adduces a treatise composed by this cautious prelate after the event of Orleans, in which he thus advises his sovereign : " You should not oppose the will of this divinely commissioned girl, but rather yield entire obedience to her. You must know that divine wisdom will instruct its agent better than any human prudence can do it." Another illustration of the opinion prevalent among the educated men of the time is found in the remark of St. Antoninus, then archbishop of Florence, to the effect that the deeds of Joan indicated that she was led by the Holy Spirit. And the erudite Pope Pius II. (Æneas Sylvius) uses the same language in his carefully prepared " Commentaries." The Sage of Fer-

(1) " Prælia Virgo
Dura pati, cursuque pedum prævertere ventos,
Lyciam ut gerat, ipsa pharetram,
Et pastoralem præfixa cuspide myrtum."
(2) *Memoirs and Consultations in Favor of Joan of Arc* ; Paris, 1890. This writer, a litterateur of merit, is a collateral descendant of Joan.

ney said that Joan would have been worshipped, had she lived in ancient times. Well, men did not adore the Maid; but they showed, even during her life, that they regarded her as a saint, as well as the deliverer of her country. In the examination held on March 3d, her judges asked her whether she was aware that her partisans had held religious services, preached sermons, and even offered Masses in her honor; and she replied: "I know nothing about such services. If they held them, it was not at my command. But if they prayed for me, I think that they did no harm." What she did not know on that point, we do know; for many of the prayers which were publicly offered for her, and in her honor—notably a Collect, a Secret, and a Post-communion—have come down to us, and are extremely touching (1). Contemporary medals are also extant, some of the many which were worn by the faithful as signs of their veneration for their benefactress. One, now in the Museum of Cluny, bears the date of 1430, and its authenticity is admitted by severe and competent experts in numismatics, such as Vallet de Viriville and Quicherat. Pictures of the Maid were found in the churches of France very soon after her murder; and some of them, like that in the chapel at Montargis, refute the theory that the original celebrations at Orleans were merely in memory of a brave woman; for the head of Joan is circled by a halo, a symbol adopted only in the case of a saint.

---

(1) The Collect is as follows: "O Almighty and Eternal God; who through Thy holy and ineffable clemency, and by the wonderful strength of Thy arm, hast raised up a young virgin for the glory and welfare of France, for the expulsion, confusion, and ruin of our enemies; and who hast permitted, in the fulfilment of the mission which Thou didst confide to her, that she should fall into the hands of those enemies; grant to our prayers that, through the intercession of the Blessed Mary ever Virgin, and of all the saints, we may behold her escape in safety from their power, that she may continue to execute Thy formal commands!" The Secret reads: "O Father of virtues and Almighty God; may Thy holy benediction descend on this oblation; may it excite Thy miraculous power; and through the intercession of the Blessed Virgin Mary and of all the saints, may it preserve and deliver the Maid now confined in the prison of our enemies; and may it enable her to perform effectively the work which Thou hast ordained!" The Post-communion is as follows: "O Almighty God; hearken to the prayers of Thy people; and through the sacraments which we have received, and through the intercession of the Blessed Virgin Mary and of all the saints, break the chains of the Maid who, while performing the deeds enjoined by Thee, has been shut up in the prison of our enemies! Through Thy divine compassion and mercy, grant that she may accomplish in safety the mission which Thou hast entrusted to her!" Making due allowance for their spirit of hatred, we can adduce the testimony of Joan's judges in proof of the veneration she inspired. The 52d article of the charges expressly mentions that throughout France she was regarded as more angel than woman.

The supernatural, observes the Angelic Doctor, "is a special intervention of God, outside the ordinary ways of His providence." In the physical order, this intervention is shown by miracles; and in the moral, it is demonstrated by sanctity. Now we contend that no candid person of average intelligence can read the Life of the Maid of Orleâns, without the conviction that the supernatural is prominent in nearly each one of its salient events. We behold a young girl passing two years amid the tumultuous disorders of a licentious soldiery, with no diminution of her angelic piety. She becomes the object of the choicest favors of Heaven, and she receives the veneration of bishops, princes, and people; nevertheless, her humility remains profound. She shares actively in the hereditary strife of powerful rivals, but her charity is never weakened. All this passes the limits of the natural; it is a miracle of sanctity. We can do no more than allude to the miracles which Joan performed, and which will form a prominent feature of the examination now being made by the Holy See, as to the value of her claims for canonization. But the reader will be interested if we make more than an allusion to the prophecies which were current in France, long before the birth of the Maid, relative to the coming of a virgin from the Bois-Chesnu—a wood near Domremy,—who was to be the deliverer of France from thraldom. We select for notice the prediction by the famous sage of the fifth century, Merlin, with whom the poems of Tennyson have probably familiarized the reader, and whose prophecies are not to be utterly despised. The learned Benedictine, Sigebert of Gemblours, who wrote in the twelfth century, says of Merlin: "He unveiled many obscure things, and predicted many events which were understood only after their accomplishment. The Holy Spirit reveals His secrets to whom He wills; now by a sybil, then by a Balaam." Now the Cymric Druid wrote: "A maiden shall come from the Bois-Chesnu to furnish remedy for all these evils. When she will have taken all the fortresses, she will dissipate all the sources of evil with her breath. Torrents of tears will flow from her eyes, and she will fill the island with fearful clamor. She will be killed by a stag with ten antlers, four of which will wear golden diadems, the other six being

changed to the horns of a buffalo.   The isles of Brittany will
resound with terrible noise ; and the Danish wood will rise, crying : 'Come, O Cambrian, and bring Cornwall to thy side!'" At
the time of the rehabilitation of the memory of the Maid, 1453,
the Grand-Inquisitor, John Brehal, took much notice of this
Merlinian prophecy, indicating quite clearly that it had been
fulfilled in all its details by the career of Joan.   Thus he ac-
commodated the prediction to her momentous life.   1. The
Bois-Chesnu, a wood near Domremy, the native village of
Joan, bore that name in her day.   2. The evils of the kingdom were remedied when the Maid underwent the severe examination by the theologians and lawyers at Poitiers ; or when
she took all the Anglo-Burgundian fortresses, and conducted
her king to Rheims, there to be crowned.   3. By her breath,
that is, by her vehement objurgations, she destroyed the
sources of evil when she rebuked the artisans for their treason.
4. Certainly Joan shed torrents of tears because of the miseries of her country, and because of her compassion for her
foes.   5. She filled all Britain with clamor, for no one knew
where her victories would end.   6. She was killed by a stag
with ten antlers, namely, the English monarch, Henry VI.,
who was ten years old when Joan was murdered.   The four
diadem-bearing antlers were the four years following the birth
of Henry during which the English exercised their power in
France with some degree of moderation ; but those antlers
were changed to buffalo's horns, when the islanders entered
upon a course of tyranny and rapine.   7. The rise of the
Danish wood is the revolt of all Normandy, the inhabitants of
which were originally Danes, against England.   They cried :
"Come, Cambria!" for the French crown originated in Clovis,
who was a Sicambrian (1).   They cried : "Conquer Cornwall!"
meaning, by a rhetorical figure, "England," of which Cornwall is a portion.

Joan was a tactician of the first order ; a strategist equal to
Talbot, who, until her advent, had been regarded as the best
commander of the time.   Whence came this knowledge on the
part of an untutored peasant girl who "knew not A, B, C, or

(1) "Mitis depone colla, Sicamber!" said St. Remigius, when Clovis stood before him for
baptism.   The Sicambri were the noblest tribe of the Frank nation.   See St. Greg. Tur.,
Hist. Eccl. Francorum, b. II., ch. xxxi.

'how to handle a sword, or how to mount a horse?" No historian has ventured to deny her wonderful military successes, and none has asserted that her campaigns were prosecuted under other human guidance than her own. The duke d'Alençon, one of the most illustrious soldiers of the day, and who served under Joan, testified as follows: "In all things outside the science of war, the Maid was simple, and like every young girl; but in military matters she excelled. Not only could she tilt well, but she knew the management of artillery, could arrange the lines of an army, and could plan a battle. We were all astonished when we saw her displaying in the field a foresight and ability which would have been creditable in a general of thirty years of experience; and in the employment of artillery, her talent was extraordinary." Reflect a little on the condition of France when Joan besought the dauphin to accept her services; and then remember that in five days she raised the siege of Orleans. In three days she reduced three cities, and defeated in pitched battle the hitherto invincible veterans of Suffolk and Talbot. Her campaign of the Loire, remarks M. Marius Sepet, was in no degree inferior in conception and execution to that lightning Italian campaign which was the tactical masterpiece of Napoleon (1). There have been published recently, four volumes of a work devoted entirely to an examination of the military abilities of the Maid; and the author, an eminent officer of artillery, finds proof of the consummate tactical science possessed by her, not only in her triumphant campaign of the Loire, but also in the unfortunate one of the Oise, which failed, not through any miscalculation on her part, but because of the foul treason of Bournel at Soisson (2). This critic follows the heroine into the region where, two centuries afterward, the grand Condè gained his greatest victory; and comparing the operations of Joan on the Oise with those preceding the battle of Rocroy, he discerns the palm of superior subtlety of strategy to the peasant girl. In fine, we may ask with Alain Chartier, a contemporary of Joan: "Was there wanting in the Maid any one quality which is necessary in a great and successful general? Her

(1) *Joan of Arc*; Paris, 1870.
(2) *Joan of Arc as Tactician and Strategist, by Paul Marin, Captain of Artillery*; Paris 1892.

prudence was wonderful; her courage has never been excelled; her activity was like that of a spirit; her justice and other virtues have been equalled by no warrior. Is the attack to be made? She heads her army, arranges her lines, fulfils her duties as commander, and then becomes a simple soldier. At a given signal, she balances her lance, spurs her steed, and like lightning she is in the midst of the foe. No; this girl is not of earth; she has come from heaven to sustain decaying France with her brain and her arm." In fact, the military career of Joan is so great a miracle, it so evidently proves that her mission was of God, that her enemies tried to account for her military training and successes by human means. But mark how futile was their argument. In Article VIII. of the accusation brought by Cauchon, it was alleged that: "In about her twentieth year, of her own accord, and without the permission of her parents, she went to Neufchâteau in Lorraine, and there passed some time in the service of an inn-keeper named La Rousse, whose hostelry was an habitual resort of depraved women, and at which soldiers were constantly lodging. Here she used to care for the cattle in the fields, and take the horses to pasture and water; and thus she learned how to ride and how to handle weapons." If a short apprenticeship in the duties of a groom suffices to form an accomplished knight and a consummate general, then this assertion is of some weight. Voltaire, in his anxiety to find some proof for his cruel aspersions on the purity of the Maid, seizes eagerly upon this charge, being attracted by the passage concerning the loose women with whom she must, according to Cauchon, have consorted. The Burgundian historian of the fifteenth century, Enguerran de Monstrelet, naturally credits the allegation of Cauchon; but on the margin of his MS. in the National Library of France, there is written a note, evidently made in the time of Charles VII. or of Louis XI., which warns us that: "During her entire life, until she was led to the king, she cared for lambs, and never mounted a horse." And this truth is evinced by the testimony of five witnesses who were thoroughly acquainted with the entire early career of Joan (1); and by that of Stephen de

(1) *Procès*, II., 411, 392, 428, 416, 421, Depositions of Lacloppe, Morel, Isabella Girardin, Guillemette, and Watte in.

Syone, dean of Neufchateau, who knew both the parish priest
of the Maid and the presumedly loose hostess, La Rousse. He
swore as follows: "From a great many persons I know that
little Joan, when she went to Neufchateau, dwelled with the
innkeeper named La Rousse, who was an exceedingly honest
woman; and furthermore, I know that during all the time
that Joan was at that inn she was in the company of her
father and of other people of Domremy who had fled thither
for fear of the advancing enemy" (1).

In the divine balance, a martyr weighs more than a hero.
It would seem that the baptism of blood is generally a concomitant of a divine mission; that the apostles of the Crucified
must continue the ineffable mysteries of His sufferings. And
does not history show us that the lives of nearly all inspired
persons have been dramas ending in tragedy? So it was
with the sweet Maid of Orleans. Not only in the market-place
of Rouen, amid devouring flames, did she suffer for her faith
in the words of her saints. When she first opened her mind
to Vaudricourt, the commander at Vaucouleurs, and demanded to be conveyed to her king, her treatment as a fool was
the beginning of her painful road to the stake. Even her
father, whom she so tenderly loved, added to her grief by
scouting her claims, and threatening to drown her as a witch
if she persisted in her design. Then, forsooth, the good pastor of Domremy must needs exorcise the innocent child, lest
perforce Satan had taken up his abode in her heart. Everywhere doubt and scorn, when she knew so well that God was
impelling her. And even when she had succeeded in bending
the dauphin to the will of her saints, and her victorious campaign began, another martyrdom beset her in the torpor of
the monarch and the tergiversations of his courtiers. Then
there were the tortures of body and mind, inseparable from
the military life, so different from the modesty and evenness
of her customary ways. Then, also, was the constant dread
of capture; for her saints had told her that she would be a
prisoner before the Feast of St. John would arrive. And
when she fell into the hands of the English, who can picture
the sufferings of the pure maiden, condemned to the constant

(1) *Ibid.* iii., 402, Deposition of Stephen de Syone.

company, by night as well as by day, of uncouth and licentious soldiers? Then she had to bear the charges of unchastity, heresy, witchcraft, barbarity, and mendacity, brought against her by a tribunal sold to her own and her country's foe. And her death? We much do doubt if there has ever lived a wretch so hardened as not to feel the tears mounting to his eyes, when he fancied the terrible scene as cold history portrays it. How daring was the lie inscribed on the mitre which the murderers placed on her serene and effulgent brow! "Heretic, Relapsed, Apostate, Idolatress." How our breasts heave with indignation, as we read the placard hung at the foot of the pyre: "Joan, who has styled herself 'the Maid.' A liar, pernicious woman, seducer of the people, sorceress, blasphemer of God, denier of the faith in Jesus Christ, braggart, idolatrous, cruel, dissolute, invoker of demons, schismatic, and heretic." But the hour of reparation has arrived; the signal given by Pope Calixtus III., when he ordered the rehabilitation of the martyr's memory, has been heeded; and France awaits with confidence the moment when her sons will use, with propriety, the words which the ascendency of truth compelled Shakespeare to put on the lips of Charles VII.: "Joan la Pucelle shall be France's saint."

CHAPTER V.

POPE EUGENIUS IV. AND THE COUNCIL OF BASEL.

Pope Martin V. having died on Feb. 20, 1431, fourteen cardinals entered into Conclave on March 2d, and raised to the Papacy the cardinal Gabriel Gondelmero, who assumed the name of Eugenius IV. He was a Venetian by birth, and came of patrician stock. His father was a distinguished soldier, and his mother, Beriola Corrario, had seen her brother elevated to the Chair of Peter as Gregory XII.; one of her grandsons was destined to be known as Pope Paul II. When quite young, Gabriel had given most of his patrimony to the poor, and having founded a house of regular canons, had retired to its seclusion; but when his uncle received the tiara, he was called to court and made Papal treasurer. In 1407, he was appointed to the diocese of Siena, and in 1408 was enrolled in the Sacred College. Being a friend of the Orsini princes, Gondelmero was not favored by Martin V., a Colonna; but that Pontiff so appreciated his administrative abilities, that he appointed him legate in the Marches, and afterward at Bologna. Eugenius IV. was forty-eight years of age when he donned the tiara; he was of majestic presence, but austerity had impressed its pallid mark on his countenance. He was exceedingly temperate, rarely drinking anything but sugared water, and never having more than one course at his table. Night and day he wore a hair-shirt; and that he might lose no time, he always studied when his sleep was interrupted (1). He was esteemed by all, but feared by many, and his severity frequently repelled affection.

One of the first acts of Eugenius was the reconstitution of the Sapienza, the great Roman University, and so extensive were the privileges he accorded to its professors and students, that he has been regarded as a precursor of the Renaissance. He was not a *litterato;* but he had the tastes of one, and he greatly sympathized with the "humanists" (2). Among his secretaries were enrolled the most celebrated humanists of his day: Leonardo Bruni (3), Poggio Bracciolini (4), Blondus Flavius, Aurispa, George of Trebizond, and Ambrose Traversari. So well did Eugenius know how to discern and to reward merit, that his successor, Nicholas V., found an easy task in inaugurating that golden age of the Renaissance which formed the glory of his reign. That glory would probably have belonged to Eugenius himself, had the contentions of Basel not distracted his attention. There is much in the political events of this reign to interest the student; but we must restrict our investigations to its salient features.

The fathers of Constance had decreed that another Council

---

(1) VESPASIANO; *Commentaries on the Life of Pope Eugenius IV.*; in MURATORI; *Italian Writers*, vol. XXV.

(2) Eugenius of Viterbo records this saying of Eugenius IV.: "We ought to fear the learned, as well as love them, for they are not men to quietly bear an offence, and they can avenge themselves with weapons, the thrusts of which we may find it hard to parry." *History of Twenty Centuries*, MS. in the Angelica Library.

(3) Often called Aretino, from Arezzo, his birthplace.

(4) The indefatigable researches of Poggio, his vast erudition, and the importance of his labors, have caused the first half of the fifteenth century to be known among the learned as the Age of Poggio.

should be held within five years; and accordingly Martin V. had ordered the bishops to assemble at Siena. But owing to the intrigues of the king of Aragon, who was active in perpetuating the line of Peter de Luna, and who therefore interdicted all communication with Pope Martin throughout his dominions, the Pontiff decided, firstly, not to preside in person over the assembly, and finally, to dissolve it (1). Before separating, however, the prelates resolved to meet after seven years in the city of Basel. When the day had arrived, March 3, 1431, on which this Council should have been opened, only one prelate, the abbot of Vezelay, was on hand (2); and not until July did two representatives of Cardinal Julian Cesarini, whom Pope Eugenius had delegated to preside, announce the opening. Cesarini himself did not arrive at Basel until September; and even then he was nearly alone, and only on Dec. 14 did he open the first session with an attendance of three bishops and seven abbots. Here we must remark that on Nov. 12, the Pontiff had issued a Bull, addressed to his legate, directing him to dissolve the Council of Basel; since the Greek emperor had signified to the Holy See the wish of the schismatics to unite with the Catholics in a Council to be held in Italy. The Pope added that the new Council would meet at Bologna, and that he himself would preside. Shortly after the sending of this Bull, Eugenius learned that the prelates at Basel had invited the Hussites to a discussion of their doctrines; and being justly offended at this want of respect for the Holy See, which had already anathematized those errors, he issued, on Dec. 18, another Bull in which he dissolved the Council of Basel. This action of the Pontiff caused much irritation among the members of the Council; Cesarini indeed abandoned his presidency, but he wrote a remonstrance to the Pope, begging him to reconsider his decree, as the prelates at Basel were determined to continue their sittings. In fact, this little body of three bishops and seven abbots now elected a new president, Phili-

---

(1) RAYNALD; y. 1423, nos. 10, 11, 12; y. 1424, no. 5 —MARIANA: b. XX., c. xiv.—ILLESCAS; *Pontiffs*, b. VI.—*Life of Martin V.*; in MURATORI, vol. III., pt. 2.—PLATINA; *Martin V*.

(2) This abbot entered the cathedral, called on the chapter to witness his presence, and caused a notary to draw up an instrument certifying to the opening of the Council. MARTENE and DURAND; *Collection of Old Writers*, vol. VIII, pt. 2.

·bert, bishop of Coutances ; and presumed to summon to their
·sessions, under the usual canonical penalties, all whose right
it was to participate in a General Council.   A second session
was held on Feb. 15, 1432, and the synodals decreed that the
·Council, actually convened in the name of the Holy Spirit,
·could be dissolved, transferred, or deferred, by no one, not
even by the Pope, without its own consent.   At this session
the number of the synodals was increased by four, and hence
this decree was signed by fourteen prelates.   From every
part of Europe there now came approbations which were well
calculated to confirm the recalcitrants in their exaggerated
notion of their own importance ; even several great universities sent them encouragement (1).   And the clergy of France,
convoked at Bourges by Charles VII., although they insisted
upon due respect to the head of the Church, contended that
the Council of Basel should be continued, and asked the king
to beg the Pontiff to withdraw his decree of dissolution (2).
Sympathetic messages were also sent to Basel by the duke
of Milan, the duke of Savoy, the duke of Burgundy, the king
of England, and the duke of Saxony (3).   But no one of these
sovereigns took such an interest in the Council of Basel as
·did the emperor Sigismund.   He had become convinced that
brute force could not subject the Bohemians to German domination ; it was to the interest of the Church to crush the
Hussite heresy, and to the interest of the empire to subject
the Bohemians to its sway.   It appeared to Sigismund that
their attachment to the Hussite doctrines was the chief cause
of the hatred of the Bohemians toward the German sceptre ;
·those teachings, he thought, could be suppressed only by the
Council of Basel.   Under date of Jan. 9, 1432, he sent a memorial, entitled, " Advice to the Pope," in which he earnestly
besought Eugenius to countenance the Council.   He con-
·tended that the abolition of the Greek schism was certainly
much to be desired, but that it was not of sufficient importance to justify the dissolution of the Council of Basel ; and
·again, it was very improbable that the reunion, so often at-
·tempted, would be effected at a time when the Catholic

(1) DUBOULAI ; *History of the University of Paris*, vol. V.
(2) LABBE ; vol. XII., *Advice of the Prelates*, etc., no. 8.
(3) MARTENE and DURAND ; *loc. cit.*, p. 60, 64, 67, 105, 108, 113.

Church was lacerated by heresy. If the Council of Basel now terminated its sessions, heresy would become more audacious. Finally, Sigismund more than insinuated that the Papal decree of dissolution would neither prevent the Council from sitting, and other prelates from going to it, nor would it cause the sovereigns to withdraw their protection from it. This not very respectful letter was followed by an embassy which was received by the Pontiff, on March 17, in full Consistory; but not until thirty-nine days had elapsed, was the following answer returned to the imperial meddler: "We entreat our dear son, and we ask you to join in our prayer, not to interfere in matters altogether out of his province; we request him not to trouble the Roman Church. The emperor has no right to concern himself either with the Council or with us. It is his duty to submit to our decisions, and to those of the Council; he must respect the Pontiff who sits in the Chair of Peter. If he touches ecclesiastical matters, let him know that there is a God above all kings, who defends His Church and His vicar" (1). Meanwhile, Sigismund was encouraging the revolt of the synodals of Basel; and having heard that it was rumored that he was about to withdraw his countenance from the assembly, he wrote to the recalcitrants: "If our letters do not induce His Holiness to withdraw his decree, our ambassadors have orders to declare to him that we will not receive the imperial crown at his hands" (2). As we learn from Æneas Sylvius (afterward Pope Pius II.), Eugenius IV. was well aware that Sigismund, whose policy was allied with that of the Visconti of Milan, thought to make use of the Council of Basel, in case of need, to intimidate the Holy See (3).

Six days after the imperial ambassadors had received the Papal reply to their master's officious advice, Pope Eugenius announced to Sigismund that he was about to send three nuncios to Basel, who would endeavor to arrange matters with the synodals. As these nuncios could not depart at once, the Pontiff immediately despatched one of his chamberlains,

(1) *Idem.*, vol. VII.
(2) *Epistle of Sigismund to the Council*, in MARTENE, vol. VIII.
(3) *Commentary on the Proceedings of the Council of Basel; edited by the Canon Michael Catalani, from the Vatican Codex*; Fermo, 1803.

John de Prato, to Basel. Cesarini was still residing in Basel; but he had exercised no office in connection with the assembly since he had received the Pontifical command to dissolve it. It is not unlikely that his great eloquence, his austere and authoritative character, and his well-known zeal, would have soon recalled the prelates of Basel to a sense of duty, had not Dominick Capranica (1), and the cardinals Branda de Castiglione, Carillo, Aleman of Arles, Cervantes, and Rochetaillée come upon the scene. These cardinals had become hostile to Pope Eugenius for some unknown reason; and they now commenced to attack his moral character, which was certainly beyond reproach. Their calumnies were seconded by a crowd of malcontents who flocked to Basel from all quarters, especially from the universities of Germany, to vomit their diatribes against the court of Rome. "These onslaughts," says Christophe, "added to the audacity of the crowd of doctors who had come from Paris, from Cologne, and other German universities—of those second-rate men who, since the Council of Pisa, were an encumbrance to the general assemblies of the Church, and who arrogated to themselves the right to trace the paths to be followed by the fathers. They were theologians of haughty but narrow minds who regarded as irrefragable dogmas, mere opinions raised amid the tumults of the schools. Orators without any practical knowledge, they measured everything according to the petty dimensions of a syllogism (2). Imprudent declaimers, they thought to serve the Church when they only fomented the passions disturbing her. With one voice, all these doctors extolled the voice of a General Council." It was under the empire of these influences that the prelates of Basel, in their

(1) Capranica, a man of great learning, a profound statesman, and almost ascetic in his habits, had been appointed to the cardinalate, *in petto*, by Martin V. in 1430. On the death of Martin, the cardinals refused to admit Capranica into the Conclave, and one of the first acts of Eugenius IV. was the issue of a decree declaring that a nomination *in petto* conferred no cardinalitial rights. Capranica then requested Eugenius to ratify the nomination, but in vain. He afterward went to Basel, and appealed from the Pope to the Council. The opposition of Eugenius to Capranica originated in the latter's devotion to the Colonna family —a devotion so thorough and notorious that when, in April, 1431, the Roman populace arose in arms to defend Eugenius from the armed attack of Anthony Colonna, the Capranica palace was sacked and gutted.

(2) Christophe might have omitted this remark. The Church fears no logic. The trouble with all assemblies like that of Basel is that they do not sufficiently regard the "petty dimensions of a syllogism."

third session on April 29, pronounced the nullity of the Bull of dissolution, and summoned Pope Eugenius to appear before them, personally or by plenipotentiaries, within three months. In the fourth session on June 20, the Council decreed that the Pope could appoint no new cardinals during the sittings of the assembly, and that in case of an *interpontificium* (1), the Conclave should be held in the place where the Council was deliberating. The Papal nuncios were now on their way to Basel; but hearing that the Council had imprisoned John de Prato, they paused at Constance, and sent on to Basel for safe-conducts (2). Having received these securities, they entered a general congregation of the Council on Aug. 25; and after some persuasive remarks, they announced that the Pontiff had entertained no design of breaking up the Council when he wished to transfer its sessions to some other place. He merely desired it to be nearer to himself; and the synodals were free to choose a place of meeting from among the cities subject to the Holy See. But the Council rejected these overtures in an illogical reply; and on Sept. 6 a motion was made to declare the contumacy of Pope Eugenius. The nuncios protested; a delay was accorded; and in the eighth session on Dec. 18, a further term of sixty days was assigned, within which Eugenius should present himself before the Council.

The Hussites of Bohemia had been invited, from its very beginning, to attend the Council of Basel. In this invitation the prelates assume the tone of superior authority—of a body subordinate to no jurisdiction on earth. "You have complained that you have never been allowed a fair hearing. Behold! This reason is now removed. We invite you to come! not before a commission, but into the presence of a general assembly, to explain as much as you wish. The Holy Ghost will preside, and He will be the judge as to what must be held and be done in the Church." Such words plainly signified a willingness to reopen a question which the Church had already settled, that is, the orthodoxy or heterodoxy of the Hussite tenets. It is no wonder that Pope Eugenius IV. resisted such impudent pretensions; and that one of the nuncios,

---

(1) Vacancy of the Holy See.   (2) See copy of their protest, in MARTENE, vol. VIII.

the archbishop of Tarento, said to the Council: "This call upon the Hussites to discuss again the question of their errors is an attack on the justice of the sentences pronounced by the Councils of Constance and Siena. It favors heretics, and will cause perplexity among the faithful." The prelates realized the force of this reasoning; and they disclaimed any intention of reopening the question of Hussite orthodoxy, protesting that they merely wished to lead the heretics back to the fold by means of an amicable discussion. The Hussites having agreed in a diet held at Egra on April 27, 1432, to come to the Council of Basel, their representatives, headed by Ziska's successor, the famous Procopius Rasa, and by John Rockizany, archbishop of Prague, arrived on Jan. 4, 1433. A general congregation of the Council was held; and Cesarini, presiding by permission of the Pontiff, addressed a learned and conciliatory discourse to the Hussites. On Jan. 16, discussions began on the Communion under both species, on correction for public sin, on free preaching, and on the civil domain of the clergy. During ten days the Hussites argued on their side; during eighteen, Catholic doctors defended the doctrines of the Church. No decision was reached; and the duke of Bavaria suggested that disputes should cease, and that there should be instituted a pacific conference of three cardinals, five bishops, several doctors, and an equal number of Hussite deputies. Accordingly, the conference decided that the Council should send into Bohemia an embassy which would devise some means of pacification on the spot. Philip, bishop of Coutances, was placed at the head of the embassy; and the conferences were resumed in Bohemia with the following final result. The Bohemians were allowed to communicate under both species, but the priests should always explain to the communicants that said manner was not of necessity; that in fact, the Body and Blood of Christ were equally under each species of the Eucharist. Secondly, the Bohemians were to admit that mortal sin, and especially if of a public nature, is to be punished according to the law of God and the regulations of the fathers; but only by those who exercise lawful authority in the Church. Thirdly, the Bohemians were to grant that the word of God is to be announced only by authorized preachers. Fourthly, the Bohemians were to admit that the clergy can licitly hold movable and immovable property. These four articles, sanctioned by the Council under the name of *compactata*, were promulgated on Jan. 2, 1434, in a solemn diet of the Bohemian nobles and deputies. All the orders of the state were reconciled to the Church, and swore obedience to the Apostolic See. The Taborites and Orphans alone refused to submit, and again took to arms; but they were finally defeated, and losing their martial and ferocious chief, Procopius Rasa, were soon things of the past.

When the Council of Basel had remitted the Hussite question to Bohemian soil, it was free to return to its hobby, the superiority of a General Council over the Roman Pontiff. The tenth session commenced on Feb. 19, 1433; and in it a commission was appointed to examine into the pretended contumacy of the Pope. In the twelfth session, celebrated on July 12, sixty days were accorded, within which Eugenius might send his adherence to the Council; if he failed therein, he would be deposed. Hitherto, the conduct of the Pontiff had been somewhat hesitating. After having sent four nuncios to preside over the Council, he had ordered them to allow Cesarini to resume that office; then he named to the presidency the cardinals Orsini, of Santa Croce, de Foix, and of St. Mark's; soon he reappointed the first four nuncios as his representatives; then almost immediately he restored Cesarini. But the decree of the twelfth session of Basel excited the Pontiff's energy; and on July 29 he issued a Bull annulling all the acts and decrees of the Baselean assembly which had not been contemplated by the Holy See at the commencement of the same. At this time the obstinate prelates received reproofs from many quarters. The kings of France, England, and Portugal; the doge of Venice; the dukes of Savoy and Burgundy; and five electors of the empire; all conjured them to put an end to their scandalous proceedings. Even Sigismund was tired of their rebellion, and on May 11 they had received from him a letter stating that he was about to receive the imperial crown from Pope Eugenius; and under date of June 4, they duly received information of his having been crowned in the Vatican Basilica. It certainly seemed that the prelates would now yield, were it only because of shame; for before Sigismund departed from· the Eternal City, the Pope had issued a Bull abolishing all his previous decrees against the Council, and declaring his willingness that the sessions should continue, providing that only those matters were touched, for the consideration of which the assembly had been convoked. But the prelates disliked the terminology used by the Pontiff; "We wish" and "We are willing" ought to be changed, as they asked Cesarini to inform the Pope, into "We decree" and "We declare." Hence when Sigismund arrived at Basel, instead of finding the concord for which he had hoped, he was assailed with complaints. He felt that, just then, he needed the friendship of the Council more than he did that of the Pope; and he forgot that when in Rome, he had been so touched by the generosity of Eugenius, that he had exclaimed that "the Pontiff had done more than he ought to have done; that the prelates of Basel ought to yield; that if they refused, he would do wonderful things against them" (1). Sigismund again took the part of the Council; but the Pope insisted that the apparently innocent change of phraseology covered an injury to the Holy See, and refused to countenance it. In the thirteenth session, held on Sept. 11, the prelates wished to act upon the alleged contumacy of Pope Eugenius; but to please the duke of Bavaria, a delay was granted until Nov. 7. On that day the fourteenth session was held, Sigismund assisting in full imperial state. From this moment the emperor assumed the role of mediator; and he soon obtained an important concession from the Council. All its preceding acts were revoked; and new legates, appointed by the Pontiff, were to preside over the deliberations. On his part, Eugenius consented to use the phrases "We decree", etc.; annulled his sentences against certain of the synodals; and withdrew his restrictions. Finally, in its sixteenth session, on Feb. 5, 1434, the Council, perhaps sincerely but certainly ungenerously, corresponded to the excessive meekness of the Pontiff by condescending to declare that since Pope Eugenius had fully

_____

(1) *Epistle of Eugenius IV. to Francis Foscari*, in Raynald, y. 1433, no. 19.

satisfied its citations and requisitions, it received his Bulls (1).
The Council enjoyed another apparent triumph when it
beheld the investiture of its champion, Capranica, with the
cardinalitial insignia.

From this time the majority of the Baselean prelates affected to believe that Pope Eugenius IV. had acknowledged
the subjection of the Pontifical to the Conciliar authority.
The Pontifical theologians vainly reminded them that Eugenius had merely yielded to circumstances in order to avoid
scandal; that the recognition of an assembly does not imply an
approbation of all its acts; and that the Pope had authorized a convocation of a new Council, rather than a continuation of the old one. Our attention must now be directed for
a moment to the political situation in Italy; for just at this
time, the temporal dominion of the Roman Pontiff, and therefore his independence, was in jeopardy. Giovanna II., queen
of Naples, had adopted as successor Alfonso V., king of Aragon and of Sicily; but her suspicions of his loyalty soon
caused her to choose that Louis of Anjou who had contested
the throne of Naples with her brother Ladislao. Pope Martin V. approved this selection, investing Louis with the kingdom; and Alfonso departed with his Aragonese. However,
Louis soon succumbing to the climate, and Giovanna feeling
herself near to death, she willed her crown to René, a brother of Louis. With this portion of the peninsula Eugenius
had no trouble. But in the north, the Florentines were anxious for revenge on the Lucchese, friends of the Visconti,
dukes of Milan. Visconti, aided by the Genoese, broke up
the Florentine siege of Lucca, but Pope Eugenius, indignant
at the intrigues of Visconti with the Colonna princes, and
averse to that sovereign because he had precipitated a war
which the Pontiff wished to spare his country (2), determined

(1) ÆNEAS SYLVIUS; *loc. cit.*, p. 65.—*Cedula Oblata*, in MARTENE.—AUGUST. PATRIC.,
History of the Council of Basel, in LABBE: vol. XIII.

(2) Three years before the death of Martin V. Cardinal Albergati had reconciled Venice,
Lombardy, and Florence in the name of the Holy See; but while laying down their arms,
these powers nourished their jealousies. When the Venetian Gondelmero was elected to
the Papacy, Venice and Florence expected a reversal of Pope Martin's policy, which had
been favorable to Milan. But Eugenius declared for neutrality, and that his neutrality
might weigh for good and peace, he said to the rival ambassadors in their first audience:
" I wish you to keep peace, for I shall be the implacable enemy of him who breaks it "
(FLAVIUS BLONDUS; *Three Decades*, b. IV.). Philip Mary Visconti suspected that these

to weaken the power of the duke. Aided by Eugenius, and
by a Venetian army under the famous general, the count of
Carmagnola, the Florentines began a campaign against Visconti. But the fortune of war declared for the rising star of
Francis Sforza, the Milanese commander. While Carmagnola was engaged with the forces of Sforza on land, the Milanese
defeated the Venetians on the Po; and thus threatened on
his front and flanks, the great leader was forced to retreat.
At length the Venetians and Visconti made peace; but this
peace was injurious to the States of the Church. Visconti
now had no use for his multitude of mercenaries; but instead
of disbanding them, he employed *condottieri* to lead them
against the Papal territories. The most distinguished of these
leaders was Francis Sforza (1), to whom the grandeur of the
Visconti was pre-eminently due. Sforza had some sense of
decency; and therefore he sought a pretext for crossing the
Papal frontier. He accordingly informed Eugenius that the
hereditary estates of the Sforzas in the kingdom of Naples
had been attacked by Caldora, and that he was about to res-
cue them; he therefore requested permission to march
through the Romagna and the Marches, promising to do no
harm to any of the vassals of the Holy See (2). Unsuspicious
of treachery, the Pope acquiesced; and as soon as Sforza
had entered the March of Ancona, he announced himself as
vicar of the Council of Basel, occupied Jesi, forced Osimo,
Fermo, Recanati, Ascoli, and Ancona to capitulate, and took
Montedelmo by storm (3). Other *condottieri* entered the
duchy of Spoleto, also proclaiming themselves vicars of the
Council. Fortebraccio penetrated into the Patrimony, stormed
Vetralla and Castelnuovo, ravaged the Campagna, captured

words indicated hatred of his person rather than a sincere desire for peace, and took his
measures accordingly. From its very beginning, Duke Philip Mary protected the Council
of Basel, and his states were a refuge for every enemy of the Roman Court. In a letter to
the Baselean recalcitrants he said: "I am ready not only to work for the consolidation and
maintenance of the Council, but to risk my states and my life for that object."

(1) In order to attach Sforza more strongly to his dynasty, Philip Mary promised him
his daughter Bianca in marriage, and this promise made the condottiero very influential
with the numerous adventurers whom he had educated to discipline, and who were entranced by his military genius.

(2) *Letter of Eugenius IV. to the doge Francis Foscari*, in RAYNALD, y. 1433, no. 26.

(3) SIMONETTA ; *Life of Sforza*, in MURATORI, vol. XXI. LEONARDO ARETINO; *Commentary*, in MURATORI, vol. XIX. *Chronicle of Bologna*, ibid., vol. XVIII.

Tivoli through treason, and knocked at the gates of Rome (1).
At this time the world certainly believed that the Baselean
prelates were at the bottom of all these troubles ; but am.
bassadors of the emperor, of the king of France, and of the
duke of Burgundy, went together to Rome, and declared to
the Pontiff, in full consistory, that Sigismund, on his arrival at
Basel, had investigated the matter, and that it seemed certain that the self-styled vicars had forged their pretended
Conciliar commissions (2). This assertion was certainly of
some consolation to the Pontiff, but his temporal dominion
was in no less danger. He suddenly conceived the idea of
gaining over his chief foes, and of setting them against the rest.
The plan succeeded to a certain extent. Sforza, perhaps remembering the devotion of his father, the celebrated constable, to the Holy See, and perhaps because he preferred reg-
ularity to irregularity, promised his aid to the Pope, and
was named *gonfaloniere* of the Roman Church, and marquis
of the March of Ancona during his life (3). He then turned
his arms against Fortebraccio, defeated him at Montefiascone,
and would have driven him over the frontier, had not Visconti sent him a powerful reinforcement under the famous Piccinino. With this aid Fortebraccio resumed the offensive, and
soon opened communications with the Ghibellines of Rome.
The Colonna princes of course headed the malcontents ; and
on May 29, 1434, Poncelleto di Pietro led a horde of armed
rebels against the capital. All the city gates were seized,
except the Cappena, which Sforza, warned in time, was able
to garrison. Poncelleto was made governer of the capital ;
and seven *conservatori*, among whom was John Somma di
Colonna, were set up as rulers of the city. The next day the
new magistrates demanded of Pope Eugenius his recognition
of the new order of affairs, possession of Castel San Angelo and
of Ostia, and the surrender of his nephew, Francis Gondel-
muro, as a hostage. The Pontiff yielded, and guards were
placed around his palace. In this revolution the rebels certainly believed that they were acting in a way to please both
Visconti and the Council of Basel ; Blondus Flavius declares

(1) SIMONETTA ; *loc. cit.*, b. III.
(2) BZOVIUS ; *Oration of J. B. Cigala,* at ʒ. 1433, no. 20.
(3) BLONDUS FLAVIUS; *loc. cit.*, b. V.—SIMONETTA ; *loc. cit.*—RAYNALD ; ʒ. 1434, no. 8.

that they intended to secure the person of the Pope until the Council and the duke had decided what to do with him. However this may be, Eugenius escaped from Rome, and·received a most hearty reception in Florence.

Pope Eugenius officially informed the Council of his calamities, which certainly were more those of the Church than his own; but although the prelates deemed it proper to blame the conduct of Visconti (1), they sent no sign of sympathy to the Pontiff. They merely despatched two representatives to the men in power at Rome, to demand the freedom of Cardinal Gondelmero; and Eugenius seized the opportunity to negotiate with his rebellious subjects. He found the Romans already tired of their new government, and on Oct. 26 they joyfully opened their gates to the Papal representatives. Visconti now called treachery to his aid; he sent a relative, the bishop of Novara, with proposals of peace to Eugenius, but with secret instructions to devise some means of kidnapping the Pontiff. The plot was discovered and avowed, and Eugenius pardoned the episcopal culprit (2). In the following year, 1435, the holy cardinal, Nicholas Albergati, who had been charged by the Council of Basel with the task of restoring peace in Italy, earnestly pressed the duke to seek a reconciliation with the Holy See. The marquis of Ferrara, Nicholas d' Este, offered his mediation; and the result was that on Aug. 10, Visconti evacuated the Papal States. While this negotiation was progressing, Vitelleschi cleared the Campagna of all rebels, and conquered all the strongholds of the Colonna and the Savelli. Fortebraccio lost his life in battle.

We now return to the Council of Basel. At this period one would have supposed that the assembly had convened merely for the purpose of despoiling the Holy See of all power. The most influential members appeared to have undertaken a crusade against the Papacy; the bishop of Tours dared to say: "This time we must either take the Apostolic See altogether away from the Italians, or we must so thoroughly pluck it, that we need not care where it resides " (3).

(1) SANUTO ; in MURATORI, vol. XXII.

(2) BLONDUS FLAVIUS; *Decade* III., b. 6. SCIPIONE AMMIRATO; *Hist. Flor.*, pt. II., b. 21.

(3) Aut Apostolicam Sedem ex manibus Italorum hac vice eripiemus, aut sic deplumatam relinquemus, ut ubi maneat nihil curandum sit. " ÆNEAS SYLVIUS; *loc. cit.*

In the twenty-first session, after the suppression of the *annates* (1), and every other revenue derived by Rome from benefices, Pope Eugenius was accused of not conforming to the
Conciliar decrees; and notwithstanding the protests of the legates, the prelates sent to him what they insultingly styled a
juridical admonition. In an interview with the Pontiff, accorded on July 14, 1435, the messengers insisted on a cate-
gorical declaration as to the readiness of the Pope to obey
the dictates of the Council; and one of the Papal secretaries, the
famous Poggio Bracciolini, replied that his Holiness would
consult with the Sacred College on such grave matters. Eugenius now despatched Ambrose Traversari and Anthony San
Vito to Basel; but while the great merit of these personages
secured for them a favorable reception, little respect was paid
to their legatine character. Even in their presence the prelates moved a new remonstrance against Eugenius; and on Jan.
20, 1436, a most arrogant document was delivered to the care
of Cardinal Aleman of Arles and two other prelates, to be
handed to him. But at this juncture a Bull was received from
Eugenius, announcing that he received the decrees of the
Council without reservation.

Now came the apparent triumph of the revolutionary doctrines. In a memoir which appeared at this time (2), it was
held that the Pope is not the head of the teaching Church;
that he is not even the directing head, when the Church is
united in General Council; that such an assembly has no
president but Jesus Christ. That such propositions could
have been put forward, may appear less surprising to the reader when he has weighed the following reflections made by
Christophe upon the conduct of Cardinal Aleman, archbishop
of Arles, one of the most zealous champions of the Council
of Basel: "No one had so enthusiastically received the doctrines drawn from the decrees of Constance as the cardinal
of Arles. In his youth, at that age when impressions are so
vivid, he had witnessed the unheard-of sight of a Council

(1) The *annates* were certain sums of money derived from the first year's revenue accruing from benefices conferred by the Pontiff. For an excellent history of the *annates*, and
a thorough vindication of the Pope's right to receive them, see the *Antifebbronio* of Zaccaria, pt. II., b. 5, ch. III.

(2) *An Inquiry into the Power of the Pope*, in MARTENE, *Ampl. Col.*, v. 8.

making and unmaking Popes ; of one disposing, so to say, of
the tiara ; and he had therefore concluded that the synodal
power had no superior and no equal. And since, in his mind,
everything swelled to the greatest possible dimensions, a Council was œcumenical, in his eyes, only when it rested on the
widest of foundations ; only when it included priests, as well as
bishops in its bosom—a democratic idea which Aleman pretended to find in tradition. With such subversive ideas, the
cardinal thought that the reform of the Church was to come
from a restoration of that state of things which he believed to
have been destroyed by Pontifical preponderance; and this
conclusion, rather than personal rancor, made him the bitter
antagonist of Eugenius IV. He regarded this Pontiff, defending the rights of the Holy See, as an obstacle to good ; any
other Pope, doing the same, would have been as destestable
to him. Hence it was that Aleman became the idol of the
multitude from his first appearance at Basel. ... Undoubtedly
Louis Aleman was not deceived as to the real worth of the
flock which blindly followed him—an ignoble mob of individuals without titles, without talents, yea, without morality—
but, like an able leader, he understood that in large assemblies, deeply agitated by new ideas, his is the power who knows
how to attract even the vilest crowd ; and he did not disdain
to employ this despicable instrument, for he thought that
good would accrue to the Church, and that the holiness of
the end excused the unworthiness of the means." The upright and solid mind of Traversari was disgusted with the
turbulence of the Baselean mob; in his oration to the emperor he styled the assembly a " funereal synod." Æneas
Sylvius was also sickened, and with imminent danger to his liberty he cried out that " the synagogue of Satan, not the Church
of God, was sitting at Basel. " And some time before this
period, while a degree of decency still reigned, the emperor
Sigismund, when leaving the Council, declared that " he left
behind him a stinking sink of iniquities."

In July, 1434, there arrived at Basel, as representatives of
the Greek schismatics and as ambassadors of the Greek emperor, the patriarch of Constantinople and three other ecclesiastical dignitaries. We shall treat of their negotiations for

union when we come to speak of the Council of Florence;
here we need show merely how this noble project became an
occasion of widening the breach between Pope Eugenius
IV. and the prelates of Basel. The discussions as to where
the union should be consummated were tedious and bitter;
the Council insisting upon Basel itself, and the Greeks declaring that they would accept any place in Italy, or, outside
of Italy, either Buda or Vienna, but on no consideration
would they hold a conference at Basel. The Council finally
yielded on condition that the emperor John Paleologus
should be requested to select Basel; if he did not, the Council would abide by his choice; the emperor himself was to
come to the conference, as also were all the oriental patriarchs, and a sufficient number of bishops to represent the
schismatic churches; the western churches were to advance
8,000 ducats to pay for the passage of the voyagers (1); a subsidy of 15,000 ducats was to be given to Paleologus, and a
fleet was to protect Constantinople during his absence. This
treaty was approved in the nineteenth session, and was sent
at once to Eugenius for his ratification. The Pontiff was
surprised at the presumption of the Council in thus acting
on its own authority. He replied that he would delay the
ratification until the arrival in Rome of Albergati and Cervantes, then on their journey from Basel; that he had already
sent one of his secretaries, the famous Hellenist Garatoni,
to Constantinople, with full powers to arrange for the proposed conference, and that it would probably be held in the
Greek capital; that, finally, he was displeased at the action
of the Council in making an arrangement without the knowledge of the Holy See, at the risk of placing the Latin Church
in a ridiculous position, if there should now be found in
existence two contradictory treaties. This inconvenient and
ridiculous situation foreseen by the Pope soon manifested itself; and in spite of a conciliatory and common-sense letter
of Eugenius, the Baseleans rejected the agreement made
by Garatoni, whereby Constantinople had been made the
place of conference. The Pontiff submitted; and after some

---

(1) According to Syropulos, the number of the Greeks was to be seven hundred. Gibbon
declares that this is a gross exaggeration, but Vespasiano (*Life of Nicholas V.* in MURA-
TORI, vol. XXV.) says that he counted five hundred at Florence.

hesitation, Paleologus, always firmly rejecting Basel, agreed that the reunion should be consummated at some place in Italy.

In its twenty-fourth session, held on April 14, 1436, the Council widened the breach between the Holy See and itself by insisting on a publication of indulgences to all who would contribute to the funds necessary for the coming conference with the schismatics. The Papal legates protested that the decree was a usurpation of the power of the keys; but the mob of inferior ecclesiastics carried the day by dint of shouting, and the prelates (merely twenty-three in number, of whom ten only were bishops) passed the resolution. Pope Eugenius now resolved to justify himself, if we may use the phrase, before Christendom; he sent nuncios to every sovereign, charging them to lay before the different courts a full history of the Council of Basel from the day of its opening. In the instructions given to the nuncios the Pontiff commences with a narrative of his own efforts to aid the Council in the work of reformation, of destruction of heresy, and of the reunion of the schismatics with the Catholic Church. Then after an account of what the Council has done, the Pope develops a formidable act of accusation against the synodals. He shows how they have pretended to subject the head of the Church to Conciliar decrees before said decrees have received his sovereign sanction; how they have imposed offensive conditions before recognizing the legates appointed to preside over their deliberations; how they have held, contrary to ancient tradition, that General Councils receive their powers immediately from God; how they have usurped the administration of the Church by naming legates *a latere*, by imposing tithes, by claiming the revenues of the Church, by calling to themselves causes which should be heard only by the Holy See, by quashing the judgments of the Roman Pontiff; how they have presumed to suppress *annates,* to publish Indulgences, and to regulate Conclaves. Nearly all the cardinals, adds the Pontiff, have fled from Basel; and he warns the sovereigns that they cannot tolerate these scandals any longer.

The twenty-fifth session, held on May 7, 1437, was, according to arrangement with the Greeks, to furnish a definite resolution as to the choice of place for the reunion of the schismatic Greeks with the Catholic Church. The members could not agree; and two factions were born amid scenes of violence almost unprecedented in ecclesiastical annals. The minority, composed mainly of the most distinguished prelates, and headed by the legates, sanctioned the choice of Florence or Udine, and decreed that no tithes should be levied before the arrival of the Greeks. The majority, led by the irrepressible Cardinal Aleman, declared for Avignon, and decreed that all tithes and receipts from Indulgences should go to its inhabitants. When the time arrived for sealing the decrees, each faction claimed the exclusive right to use the seal of the Council; and after a furious struggle it was agreed that three arbitrators should impress the seal upon the decree of their choice. Cardinal Cervantes, the archbishop of Palermo (Tudeschi), and the bishop of Burgos were selected for this office; and the decree of the minority was sealed, and sent to the Pope for his ratification. But the seal now disappeared, and the multitude began to suspect that the decree sent had not been properly authenticated. Then ensued a horrible tumult, amid which the archbishop of Tarento, suspected of the supposed chicanery, was excluded from the sessions, under pain of excommunication. The procurator of the archbishop protested in his favor, and was himself dragged by the hair toward the prison, when he was rescued by the firmness of Cesarini. Then the precious lot infuriated against the legate; he placed guards around his residence, and took the first opportunity to flee from Basel (1). This and similar scenes were witnessed by the Greek envoys; and realizing that little good could be expected from such an anarchical body, they departed for Bologna, where the Pontiff had been residing since April, 1436. In full Consistory, on May 24, 1437, they announced that they adhered to the terms of the decree received by his Holiness, and requested the Pontiff to confirm it. Eugenius issued a Bull of Confirmation on June 29.

When the recalcitrants of Basel heard that the Pope had

(1) *Bull of Convocation of the Council of Ferrara*, in LABBE, vol. XIII.

confirmed the decree of the minority, they resolved to effect immediately the deposition, or at least the suspension of Eugenius. Cesarini and Cervantes and all the ambassadors protested in vain; the followers of Aleman carried their point, and in the twenty-sixth session the Pontiff and his cardinals were cited to render an account of their conduct within sixty days. The reply of the Pope was a decree transferring the Council to Ferrara, but allowing the Baselean prelates to remain one month to attend exclusively to the Hussites. The rebels now endeavored to regain the friendship of the emperor Sigismund, who, under the influence of the learned and zealous Traversari, had become devoted to Eugenius; but he replied to the messengers: "You found the Church in peace; beware lest you introduce discord into the fold! You desire a union of Latins and Greeks, but look out lest you divide the Latins themselves!" On Oct. 1, in its twenty-eighth session, the Council declared the contumacy of the Pontiff; on the 13th, in its twenty-ninth session, the Bull of transfer was pronounced null, and four months were allowed to Eugenius to abrogate it, under pain of suspension. In case of his suspension, two additional months would be granted him within which to amend; when they elapsed, if he remained unrepentant, he would be deposed. At this juncture the emperor Sigismund died, and the Council of Basel rejoiced. When the legitimate Council opened at Ferrara, the few prelates of Basel who had not openly opposed the Pontiff prepared to join it; and this defection so enraged the faction of Aleman, that it resolved to precipitate matters. The term accorded to the Pope for consideration had not elapsed when, in the thirty-first session, held on Jan. 24, Eugenius IV. was declared suspended from the Papacy; and the Council declared that it undertook the spiritual and temporal administration of the Church.

The spectacle of two Councils, one at Ferrara, the other at Basel; of one devoted to the Roman Pontiff, the other only hesitating to anathematize him; was perplexing to the simple-minded. Meanwhile many thought that either the passions of the Baseleans would soon subside, and the true Catholic spirit resume its sway, or that some favorable incident would serve to bring about a compromise. Most of the ambassadors continued to remain at Basel, but whenever the decisive step was threatened against Eugenius, they demanded a prolongation of the period within which the Pope, according to the synodical decree, was to beg pardon for his alleged delinquencies; and they always obtained the prorogation of the term, for they threatened, in case of refusal, to withdraw from the Council. And here we must observe that the course of the Baselean prelates was not well defined, even in their own minds. How were they to effect the deposition of Eugenius with at least a semblance of right on their side? It was an established opinion that a deposition could be undertaken only in the case of manifest heresy on the part of a Supreme Pontiff; and how could it be proved that Eugenius was a heretic? Some of the Baseleans held that Eugenius was indeed a heretic; others contended that he was also a relapsed heretic; a third party—and though it was the smallest section, it included the most learned members—asserted his entire orthodoxy. The conclusions of the second faction, rigorously deduced from a principle that widely obtained at that time, were adopted, says Sylvius, by the great majority of the Baseleans. The archbishop of Palermo endeavored to combat them, denying that the great principle was clearly established as of Catholic faith, though he admitted that it was true. John of Segovia then insisted that even though Eugenius had not erred in pronouncing the dissolution of the Council, he had erred in maintaining his decree in defiance of the Conciliar remonstrance. This dispute degenerated into mere personalities, and finally the matter was adjourned until April 23, 1439. Then ensued a scene of wrangling such as even this Council had not yet presented; and the patriarch of Aquilea treated the more moderate archbishop of Palermo to this threat: "Do not flatter yourselves that this matter will end as you wish. You do not know the Germans. If you go on in this way, you will soon have no heads on your shoulders." However, the patriarch apologized for his outburst, and then the archbishop thus addressed the crowd of priests, consultors, etc., who, during the whole course of this Council, exercised a more than legitimate pressure on the prelates: "You despise prelates, kings, and princes. Beware lest you yourselves become the laughing-stock of the world. You wish to bring this matter to a conclusion, but that is not your business; we form the majority of the prelates, and the decision belongs to them. In the name of the prelates I move to adjourn the debate." The prelates now left their seats in a state of thorough demoralization.

At the thirty-third session, held on May 16, there were present, between bishops and abbots, twenty prelates; there was but one Italian bishop (of Grosseto), and none attended from Spain; but there were more of the inferior clergy than there had been at any other session. All of the opposition were absent, and hence it was unanimously defined that a General Council is superior to the Pontiff; that the Pontiff cannot dissolve, transfer, or prorogue a General Council without its consent; that these propositions are of Catholic faith. In the thirty-fourth session, held on June 25, in the presence of three hundred ecclesiastics of the second order, thirty-nine prelates declared Pope Eugenius deposed from the Supreme Pontificate; a rebel against the Church; a violator of the Canons; a disturber of unity; guilty of simony, perjury, schism, and heresy; and they absolved all the faithful from their obligation of obedience to him. The anger of heaven seemed to manifest itself immediately; the plague, then ravaging portions of Europe, suddenly appeared in Basel, and so extensive were its effects, that the cemeteries were soon filled, and new ones had to be opened. The arrogant patriarch of Aquilea was one of the first victims; many of the synodals succumbed; many took with them the seeds of disease, and expired ere they could reach home. The bishop of Burgos died in Switzerland; the bishop of Evora at Strasbourg; the abbot of Vezelay, he who for one day had fancied himself a whole Council, at Spire; the bishop of Lubeck at Buda.

The prelates of Basel had expected Pope Eugenius to sink at once under their blow; but, surrounded by the western and eastern episcopates at Ferrara, his voice was more powerful and more respected than ever, as he fulminated a Bull against the iniquitous decrees. Nor did much encouragement await the messengers despatched by the Baseleans to all parts of Europe to announce their final action. At Strasbourg, Worms,

and Spire; even at Mayence under the eyes of the Diet; the
placards announcing the deposition of Eugenius were torn
from the doors of the churches. The Diet refused to take
any action until a more numerous assembly could be convened;
and it even rejected the demands of the schismatic legates
that the Germans should, in the meantime, not give to Eugenius the title of "Holiness." Henry VI. of England remained
constant in his fidelity to the successor of St. Peter. Philip
of Burgundy would allow none of his subjects to hold any
communication with the Baseleans. In France, although the
assembly of Bourges had based its legislation upon Baselean
decrees, general opinion was more favorable to the Pontiff
than to the schismatics; the estates of Languedoc even besought the king to uphold the dignity of the Roman See.
Just before the culmination of the Baselean revolt, Charles
VII. had accused the faction of Aleman of wishing to divide,
when even laymen were working for the unity of the Church (1).
But the most energetic protests came from Italy, where
party interests and political rancor had often antagonized the
Pontiffs as temporal princes; but where their spiritual power
had been always revered. Notwithstanding this widespread
devotion to the legitimate Pontiff, the schismatics proceeded
to their pretended election of a new Pope. An electoral college was appointed, all the members of which were devoted
to Aleman, and he was named its chief. The cardinal had determined to give an influential head to the revolution, and his
choice was the duke Amadeo VIII. of Savoy, a prince who for
five years had been playing the part of an amateur hermit and
philosopher. His previous life had shown that he was possessed of a most fantastic imagination; nevertheless Amadeo
was a man of great piety, and when Aleman insisted that it
was "his duty to secure peace to the Church" he changed his
role of hermit for that of Pope with the same ease with which
he had laid aside the ermine and donned the cowl. Elected
on Nov. 5, 1439, Amadeo assumed the name of Felix V., immediately created four "cardinals", and announced to Christendom
that he had accepted the tiara because he could not resist the
Holy Spirit. No prince in Europe was so highly connected

(1) AUGUST. PATRIC., in LABBE, vol. XIII.

as Amadeo of Savoy ; he was a most able man, and he was probably the wealthiest sovereign of his time ; but he was immediately declared an anti-pope by Italy, Spain, Portugal, England, and Burgundy. As for France, the ambassadors of Charles VII. declared to the Baseleans that the French would obey Pope Eugenius IV. until a new General Council or an assembly of the French Church should otherwise command. As to the empire, Albert II., successor of Sigismund, decreed neutrality ; on the election of Frederick III., two Diets were held, at which the legates of Amadeo were recognized only as representatives of the assembly of Basel, and in which it was finally decided that Eugenius was the legitimate Pontiff, and that the Germans could hold no direct communication with the anti-pope (1). Frederick afterward visited Basel and called upon Amadeo in his palace ; but the courtesy was plainly that of the emperor to the ex-duke of Savoy, and in no respect was the latter treated as Pontiff. Nowhere, outside of his own Savoy and Piedmont, save in Switzerland, Poland, Bavaria, and in the universities of Paris, Cracow, Vienna, Cologne, and Erfurt, could " Felix V. " extend his obedience. One good reason for his failure had been predicted by Cardinal Cesarini. His partisans had made great calculations on the influence of his wealth ; but whenever money was demanded, the ex-duke replied : " I have children, and I must not reduce them to penury " (2). He even refused to lend Charles VII. the paltry sum of three thousand francs. Nor did the anti-pope succeed, in the face of the power which had elected him, in upholding his own dignity ; he allowed the signatures of the Baselean prelates to precede his own in the public documents ; he permitted an auditor of the Council to exercise a jurisdiction independent of his own. In the most important deliberations the Council scarcely consulted him.

While Amadeo was posing as Pope Felix V., the Council of Ferrara, menaced by the plague and by the enemies of Pope Eugenius, was transferred to Florence, where the schismatic Greeks were finally reconciled to the Catholic Church. The joy of the Pontiff was increased by the return of the

---

(1) GERARD ROO ; *Austrian History*, v. V.
(2) *Commentaries of Pius II.*, b. VII.

Armenians and the Jacobites to the fold. Returning to Rome, he also received the Syrian, Mesopotamian, Maronite, and Chaldean schismatics into the unity of the Church. We now approach the end of this eventful Pontificate. After eight years of neutrality, the German princes were forced, by the pronounced aversion of the various German peoples to the schism, to recognize Eugenius IV. as the true Pontiff. This recognition was effected at Frankfort on Sept. 1, 1446; but the emperor and princes insisted on the following conditions: The Pope was to convoke, within ten years, a General Council, and it was to be held either at Constance, Strasbourg, Mayence, Worms, or Treves; secondly, the Pope was to acknowledge the supremacy of a General Council; thirdly, the Holy See was to free the Germans from certain money obligations, especially the *annates*; fourthly, the archbishops of Treves and Cologne, who had been deposed as schismatics, were to be restored to their sees. A solemn embassy was sent to Rome to procure the Pontifical consent to these conditions. Æneas Sylvius, who had long espoused the Baselean cause in good faith, and had even acted as secretary to Amadeo, but had been converted by Cardinal Cesarini, was the mouthpiece of the ambassadors; and he has furnished us with a full and interesting account of the mission. Although the Pontiff complained bitterly of the long neutrality of the Germans, he was very affable in the main, and appointed a commission of six cardinals to consider the four conditions. At this juncture Eugenius was attacked by a violent fever, and his speedy death was regarded as certain; but on Feb. 6, 1447, he held a Consistory, and delivered a Bull approving the Frankfort conditions. But great prudence was observed in reference to the wording of the acceptance of the first and second articles. Eugenius did not promise to convoke another General Council; he merely declared that he would endeavor to influence the sovereigns of Christendom to correspond to the wishes of the emperor. He did not say that he recognized the supremacy of a General Council; he declared that he venerated the Council of Constance, the decree of that Council on the authority of such assemblies, as well as the decrees of other Councils, after the example of his predecessors (1). This was the last official act of Eugenius IV (2).

As we shall devote a chapter to the Pontificate of Nicholas V., we now mention only his efforts to terminate the schism of Basel. Many of the Germans still leaned toward perfect neutrality; but Cardinal Carvajal, the Papal legate, obtained from a Diet held at Aschaffenbourg, on July 14, 1447, the recognition of Nicholas as legitimate Pontiff. Frederick III. then ordered the few synodals who still pretended to form the Council of Basel to separate within a certain period. The emperor was obeyed; but the anti-pope continued to wear a tiara at Lausanne. However, King Charles VII of France had already proposed to Pope Nicholas certain conditions which he thought that Amadeo would probably accept and in a letter dated April 26, the Pontiff had signified his opinion that the conditions were moderate and acceptable to Rome. They were embodied in five articles. Firstly, Amadeo would abandon all his claims to the Papacy. Secondly, all censures hitherto launched by either party were to be withdrawn. Thirdly, the promotions made by Amadeo were to be confirmed. Fourthly, some suitable position was to be devised for the ex-duke and ex-anti-pope. Fifthly, a General Council was to assemble in France (3). In the last days of July there began to assemble at Lyons a number of representatives from all quarters to take measures to end the

(1) RAYNALD; y. 1447, no. 2-7.—COCHLÆUS; *Hussites*, b. IX.; Milan, 1549.

(2) "They who judge a sovereign's merits," says Christophe," by the success of his reign will not call Eugenius IV. a great Pope, for he was always unfortunate. They who regard the personal qualities of the man will not hesitate to say that no one has been more worthy of the tiara. He was regular in fulfilling the lightest duties of the Pontificate; he was mortified, even to maceration : he was disinterested, even to a contempt for riches; he was charitable, even to his own impoverishment, especially in a case of fallen grandeur. Toward his household he was royally magnificent, but an anchorite could not have been more stinting than he was to himself. A great lover of justice, he esteemed virtue alone; a zealous promoter of the Catholic faith, he desired no other glory than that of having procured the triumph of the Church. When successful, he was not inflated; under adverse fortune, he was not weak, but stood immovable amid all its vacillations. He was never carried out of himself by hope, nor saddened by doubt; he was ever equal to himself. He was inaccessible to anger, and he was utterly indifferent as to what was said or written about himself. The most rigid Puritanism cannot blame him for that nepotism with which it has reproached some Pontiffs. He did indeed raise one of his nephews to the cardinalate, but he never showed him any partiality. As for such of his relatives as were not ecclesiastics, he treated them the same as he did a number of poor gentlemen whom he entertained in his palace, out of charity." See also MURATORI, *Annals*, at y. 1447.

(3) *Acherian Spicilegium*, vol. III.

schism. On the part of Amadeo came many distinguished personages, and the Council of Basel was represented by Cardinal Aleman. The conference was prolonged until Oct. 18; and then the ambassadors of France, England, and the German princes went to Geneva, where Amadeo was holding his court. Here they found the anti-pope willing to abdicate on the following conditions. Firstly, he was to convoke a new Council, and abdicate in its presence. Secondly, before the renunciation, he was to issue three Bulls; the first reinstating all persons deposed by Eugenius IV. and Nicholas V.; the second withdrawing all censures launched by himself against those who had not recognized him; the third confirming his own administrative acts. Thirdly, after his abdication, the Council convoked by him would elect Nicholas V., and would reinstate, by a special decree, all persons who had sustained his own cause, or that of Eugenius or of Nicholas. Fourthly, by authority of this same Council he would receive the title of "perpetual legate of the Holy See," accompanied by extensive prerogatives, all of which Nicholas V. would be bound to confirm in due form (1). When the Pontiff heard these conditions, he refused to consent to them; but in April, 1448, he accorded the one concerning the treatment of Amadeo, and at length he yielded in the matter of the three Bulls. On April 7, 1449, the so-called Felix V. called to Lausanne what remained of the Council of Basel, and renounced his claims to the Pontificate. Twelve days afterward the Council terminated the schism by ratifying the abdication, and by proclaiming its obedience to Pope Nicholas V.

Such, then, in a few words, is the history of the Council of Basel, an assembly which most Protestant writers affect to praise, and to which Gallicans have ascribed the quality of œcumenicity. A mere cursory glance at the facts just narrated will convince the Catholic reader that this assembly, which Mosheim styles "a great Council, and worthy of eternal remembrance," was not a General Council, and that its decrees are of no binding authority on the Universal Church. Among the Gallican defenders of the Baseleans, the first place should

(1) GUICHERON; *Genealogical History of the Royal House of Savoy*, vol. II.

be assigned to Bossuet and La Luzerne; among their opponents, prominence is merited by Orsi, Roncaglia, and Zaccaria.
Commenting on the work of Orsi, La Luzerne is "surprised
at the violence with which the learned cardinal speaks of
the Council of Basel. He constantly treats its members as
criminals, rebels, schismatics, and sacrilegious persons. In
many places he gives the name of a new Dioscorus to Cardinal Aleman, the president of the Council, one of the most
virtuous persons of his age, whose holiness and miracles
merited from Clement VII. the title of Blessed." The reader can judge for himself whether or not the Council and its
president deserved the treatment accorded them by Orsi;
we shall merely remark with reference to the Baselean decrees which concern the relations between Pontiff and Council, that they are of no authority whatever; firstly, because
they were not the work of a General Council; secondly, because they did not receive the approbation of the Roman Pontiff. That the assembly of Basel was not œcumenical,
even in regard to the sole Western Patriarchate, when it issued these decrees, is evident. At the first session only three
bishops were present; at the second and third, only eight of
the fourteen signers were bishops. Italy was scarcely represented at all during the entire Council; Castile was not represented at first, and when some of its bishops did attend, they
directed their energies, not to a subjugation of the Pope to a
Council, but to the restoration of unity; England was faithful
to the Pontiff at the commencement of the Council. Such
was the condition of the Baselean assembly during the second
session, when the decrees of Constance were renewed and applied to the case of a certain, as well as of a dubious Pontiff.
And if it be replied that it is not necessary for every country to
be represented in a General Council, the non-œcumenicity of
the Baselean convention is evinced by the non-adherence of
the Papal legates to its decrees. For, says the Angelic Doctor: "The fathers assembled in Council can establish nothing unless through the intervention of the authority of the
Roman Pontiff; and as we read in *Glossa, dist. 17, General Councils,* 'That is universal which is established by the Pope or
by his legate, with all the bishops'" (1). The *Acts* of the Coun-

(1) *Against the Assailants of Religion,* c. **iv.**

·cil show that the legate Cesarini abdicated his presidency on
Feb. 8, and that the famous second session was held on Feb.
15, 1432. It is true that after the sixth session Cesarini yield-
·ed to the entreaties of the prelates, and resumed the presidency for a time, but then he was no longer a Papal legate.
And in the eighteenth session, when the decrees of the second
were renewed, no Pontifical legates were present as such ; some
were absent from the assembly, and those who attended did
so in their private capacity, not as legates (1).

It is sometimes said that Pope Eugenius IV. approved the
Conciliary decrees concerning the Papal subjection to a General Council when he revoked his Bull of dissolution, and declared his adverse Bulls and Diplomas "null and void." But
granting that this revocation was freely made by the Pontiff,
which may be denied (2), it does not follow that he thereby approved and confirmed all the Conciliary proceedings. The
Councils of Constantinople (first), Chalcedon, and Constance
are regarded as legitimate ; and nevertheless the Pontiffs St.
Leo I., Pelagius, Gregory, and Martin did not approve of all
their decrees. And we know that Eugenius revoked his Bull of
dissolution only on condition that the Baseleans would rescind
those decrees which attacked the Papal supremacy. Torquemada tells us that " the synod having promised, and the princes having become security for the fulfilment of the promise,
that the honor of his Holiness and of the Apostolic See
should be preserved, the Pontiff changed his mind, and willed
that the dissolution should become null " (3). And in the
Constitution beginning *Dudum*, issued for the revocation of
the dissolution, Pope Eugenius states that he restores the

(1) Torquemada, in his *Answer to the Baseleans*, recited in the Council of Florence,
says: " The legates did not consent; indeed, they contradicted, and protested as strongly
as they could ; however, some of them, when they saw that otherwise they would not be
admitted to the presidency, afterward consented, but only as private persons."

(2) Torquemada says: " It is said that Andrew, the Venetian ambassador, and certain
cardinals, then attending on Eugenius, fearing the great scandals threatening the Church,
declared to the Pontiff that they would leave him to himself if he did not issue a Bull of acceptance of the Council. Then, as it is said, the aforesaid lords expedited the Bulls, while
the Pope was lying in bed, and sent them to Basel." Alexandre, in *Cent. XV., Diss. 8., art.
3, no. 41*, makes light of this passage, because of the " it is said," and certainly mere
rumors, when presented by most men, are not to be credited ; but Torquemada was not a
man to record everything that he heard, and besides this fact, we must remember that the
circumstances of the time give probability to the story.

(3) *Summa*, b. II., c. 100.

Conciliary status to the Baselean assembly, providing that "each and every thing done against our authority by the said Council be first entirely abrogated, and things be restored to their pristine condition." The Pontiff also imposed as a condition of the revocation that his legates should be " *effectively* admitted to the presidency of the synod." Now these conditions were not fulfilled ; therefore the assembly did not recover its Conciliary status. But Eugenius tells us, with even more distinctness than in the above testimonies, that he did not approve the famous decrees. Torquemada was at the Council of Florence, and he heard the Pontiff say to the members: "We indeed willed that the Council (of Basel) should be resumed, and continue as it had begun ; but nevertheless we did not approve its decrees " (1). Writing to Francis Foscarini, doge of Venice, the Pontiff says: "Rather would we have laid down this Apostolic dignity, and our life itself, sooner than have permitted that the Pontifical dignity and the authority of the Apostolic See should be subjected, contrary to all Canons, to the Council. Such a thing was never done by any of our predecessors, nor indeed, was it ever asked of them " (2). In fine, so well understood was the mind of Eugenius IV. on this subject, that in the Council of Bourges the archbishop of Palermo did not hesitate to say : " It is notorious that Eugenius has constantly opposed the first two conclusions " (3).

CHAPTER VI.

THE COUNCIL OF FLORENCE (SIXTEENTH GENERAL).

Pope Eugenius IV. having decreed the transfer of the Sixteenth General Council from Basel to Ferrara, Cardinal Nicholas Albergati, legate of the Pontiff, declared the Council opened in the latter city on Jan. 8, 1438. On Jan. 27, Pope Eugenius arrived at Ferrara, and on Feb. 8, before a general congregation of the synodals, he explained his difference with the recalcitrants of Basel, and declared that he was ready to do all that a Supreme Pontiff could rightly perform in order to produce unity of thought and action among the pastors of the

(1) *Ibid.*   (2) RAYNALD; y. 1433, no. 19.
(3) AUGUST. PATRICIUS ; *History of the Council of Basel.*

Church.   In the Second Session, celebrated on Feb. 15, under·
the presidency of the Pope, seventy-two bishops were present; and the Synod pronounced the seditious decrees of Basel
null and void, and declared the excommunication and deposition of the obstinate prelates.   On March 4, the Greek emper-
or, John Paleologus, accompanied by twenty-two archbishops
and bishops, and eleven abbots, as also by a large number of
Greek senators and nobles—in all, over seven hundred persons, arrived at Ferrara for the purpose of effecting the long-
talked-of and now much-desired reconciliation of the schis-·
matics with the Holy See (1).   The patriarch Joseph of Constantinople was detained by sickness until the 7th, and on
his landing was received by four cardinals and twenty-four
Latin bishops, and by the marquis d'Este of Ferrara; then,
accompanied by two cardinal-deacons, the chief representative
of the Greek schism paid his respects to the Supreme Pontiff·
of Christendom.

Everything seemed to be ready for the consummation of
the great object of the Council, when the Greek emperor requested that the Western sovereigns should be present at
the reunion, either in person or through their envoys.   Seven
months of delay therefore ensued before the Latins and
Greeks could meet in full Council (2); but meanwhile there
were held many private conferences in which consideration
was to be given to the doctrines on the Procession of the

(1) The commissaries of the Council of Basel had vainly tried, by promises of great subsidies and of a grand army to combat the Turks, to induce the Greeks to accept Avignon as
the place wherein to effect the reunion. From the decks of their Avignonese galleys the
Baselean envoys beheld these other, but apparently repentant schismatics, embark on the
Venetian squadron of Anthony Gondelmero on Nov. 25, 1437. Arriving at Venice on Feb. 9,
1438, the Greeks were received with honors to which the imperial dignity in the East had
long been strange. Both emperor and patriarch made desperate efforts to impress the Latins
with an idea of their grandeur—efforts very much out of place in persons humbly begging
for aid against an enemy at their very gates. Thinking that the Western ' barbarians ''
would easily be affected by glitter, and that they did not know how really poor his'' Roman ''
empire was, Paleologus had made use of a large sum just received from Russia to cover his
throne and bedstead with plates of massive gold. The patriarch, in order to sustain his
dignity, had despoiled his cathedral of St. Sophia of many of its sacred vessels and most
precious ornaments. This affectation of wealth seems the more puerile when we reflect
that the Greeks had been obliged to travel in an Italian fleet, and at the expense of the
Papal treasury ; that on his arrival at Venice, the emperor received from Pope Eugenius
15,000 ducats ; and that during their stay in Italy the expenses of the entire cortege were
defrayed by the Pontiff. SYROPULOS ; *Hist. Conc. Flor.*, sect. III., c. xvii., xviii.; sect. IV.,
c. xxviii. VESPASIANO ; *Life of Nicholas V.*, in MURATORI, vol. XXV.

(2) Many of the Western bishops were also desirous of this delay, since they trusted that·
the Baselean prelates would come to their senses in the interval, and appear at Ferrara.

Holy Ghost, on Purgatory, on the Beatific Vision, on the supremacy of the Roman Pontiff, and on the "matter" of the Holy Eucharist. Sixteen theologians were appointed to conduct these debates; and the learned Camaldolese, Ambrose Traversari, acted as interpreter when necessary. When the conferences had been arranged, the Greeks obstinately refused to discuss the doctrine of the Procession; but they agreed to consider those on Purgatory and the Beatific Vision. When they had heard the exposition of the belief of the Roman Church on these points, they declared that it differed but little from their teaching, and they proposed to give their answer in writing. This document did not prove satisfactory to the Westerns; for while the Greeks admitted a middle state in which souls, not entirely purified from the stains of sin, are temporarily detained, and in which they are relieved by the prayers and sacrifices of the Church Militant; they excluded from this state of purgation the pain of fire, which they regarded as peculiar to the hell of the damned, and that only after the general resurrection. The conferences soon degenerated into altercations; but finally, on Oct. 8, was held what it regarded as the First Session of the Council, those already celebrated being considered as preliminary. Six doctors were now named to discuss the questions at issue. The Catholics selected Cardinal Julian Cesarini; Andrew, archbishop of Rhodes; Louis, bishop of Forli; Peter Perquiere, a Franciscan; John of Montenero, a Dominican; and John Torquemada, whom we have already met at the Council of Basel. The Greek historian, Michael Ducas, speaks of Cesarini as the most eminent of the Latin theologians (1). Torquemada had been among the principal defenders of the Holy See at Basel (2); of the three others we know little. The schismatics chose for their champions Mark, archbishop of Ephesus; Isidore, metropolitan of Kiew in Russia; Bessarion, archbishop of Nicea; Xanthopulus Siderophas, "high-guardian of the sacred vessels;" Balsamon the Librarian; and Gemisthes Pletho, a famous dialectician. A brief notice of some of these schismatic champions will not be uninteresting. Mark of Ephesus, the chief athlete of the Greek schism at this period, was an erudite theo-

_____

(1) *History*, c. xxxi.   (2) TIRABOSCHI; vol. VI., b. II.

logian, but was excessively addicted to subtleties and soph·
isms. He upheld the errors of his party as the palladium
of the Byzantine empire ; and while the hordes of Islam were
only awaiting the signal to enter St. Sophia's, he insisted that
the " Latin " doctrine was the sole enemy which his countrymen had to fear. Isidore of Kiew was a native of Thessalon-
ica ; and having become a monk of the Order of St. Basil,
was raised, in time, to the see of Kiew. As learned and eloquent as Mark of Ephesus, he was his superior in piety and
good sense. George Gemisthes Pletho, a Lacedemonian, was
in his ninetieth year when, though a layman, the influence
of Bessarion caused his appointment as consultor to the
Greek synodals of the Sixteenth Council. He was probably
the best philosopher in the East, and was so ardent a Platonist that he scoffed at Aristotle ; his Christianity was at best
problematical (1). By far the most interesting of the Greek
champions was Bessarion, a native of Trebizond, and, like
his quondam tutor Pletho, a zealous Platonist. He was a
man of elevated character, frank and noble in his manners,
and pre-eminently adapted to the role of pacificator, as he
demonstrated both during and after the Council of Florence.

In the discussions which began on Oct. 14, 1438, the schismatics immediately, and, as they thought, triumphantly, cited
the decrees of ancient Synods and Fathers prohibiting any
additions to the Creed (2). We have already given, in our
dissertation on the *Filioque* (3), the arguments by which the
Catholics proved that they had merely explained, not made

---

(1) Pletho taught that Christianity and Islamism would both soon perish, and give place
to a purer religion—a new form of paganism. In his *Conciliation of Discrepancies*, he
holds that "in every conjunction of Saturn and Jupiter, the entire world suffers such
changes that not only kingdoms, but new religions arise, as was seen in the advent of
Nabuchodonosor, Moses, Alexander, *the Nazarene*, and Mohammed."

(2) The Greeks having been allowed to either attack or defend, they preferred to attack,
and began by asking why the Roman Church had added the *Filioque*, "and from the Son,"
to the symbol. This manner of treating the controverted points had been combated by
Bessarion in the private conferences of the Greeks, as he deemed it disadvantageous to
their cause. He would have preferred to commence with an examination of the doctrine
expressed by the *Filioque* ; because, said he, it is better to make an attack which may
obviate any necessity for a second combat. "If we prove," he argued, "that the doctrine of
the *Filioque* is false, it will be unnecessary to show that the addition ought not to have
been made ; the dispute will be ended. But if, on the contrary, we begin by attacking
the legitimacy of the addition, then even if we gain the victory, we must still show that
the doctrine is false."

(3) Vol. II., ch. v.

any addition to the Creed. On the part of the schismatics, Bessarion took up these arguments, and insisted that 'a real addition had been made, since by the clause "and from the Son" a new dogma was expressed; that this act of the Roman Church was inadmissible, for the Roman Church was not the Universal Church; that finally, even the Universal Church could not make such an addition, since the prohibition of Ephesus was absolute. Shortly afterwards the learned archbishop admitted that this last assertion could not be upheld; and it is surprising that such a dialectician did not confine the debate, from the outset, to the authority or non-authority of the Roman Church. The Catholic theologians quickly perceived the false position of their opponents; and the bishop of Forli proved that the Universal Church must possess the right to add words to the Symbol, since she enjoys the essential right of determining what is, and what is not, of faith. The discussion was then confined to the capital point; the schismatics were compelled to show that after the Seventh Council, the Church had lost the right of defining matters of faith. Mark of Ephesus realized the difficulty and tried to evade it by exclaiming: "Erase the *Filioque* from the Creed; re-establish the primitive *Profession of Faith;* and union is consummated." But principle and truth were at stake, and Cesarini insisted: "Examine? If the addition is blasphemous, cut it out; if it is correct, receive it!" Then, as Bessarion had foreseen, the Greeks were forced to enter on an examination of the doctrine of the Procession; and the Byzantine emperor vainly besought the Pontiff that the discussion might take place in private session. This was the last act of the Sixteenth Council at Ferrara. The plague was desolating the city, and the horrors of war were approaching it; hence Pope Eugenius IV. decreed the transfer of the Council to Florence. The Greeks were very averse to the transfer, but the Pontiff declared that he could no longer pay them the promised subsidies at Ferrara; that he had been obliged to accept a loan from Cosmo dei Medici on condition that the synodals would meet in Florence (1). But

(1) During the entire sojourn of the Greeks in Italy, the Pope gave the emperor 30 golden florins per month ; to the patriarch, 25 ; to all others of rank, 4 ; to each attendant, 3. The golden florin of that day was equal to five dollars of our money.

he promised to furnish 12,000 florins, and two more galleys, for the defence of Constantinople; to satisfy all the wants of the visitors; and to allow them, united or schismatic, to depart in three or four months.   Cosmo dei Medici received the synodals with that magnificence which befitted the chief magistrate of Florence and the wealthiest individual in Europe.

The sessions were renewed at Florence on March 2, 1439. The schismatics now endeavored to show that the expression " and from the Son " was not orthodox, and the dispute was commenced by Mark of Ephesus and John of Montenero. When asked to prove that the Holy Ghost proceeds also from the Son, the Dominican cited testimonies from nearly all the Oriental fathers, thus showing what had been the olden tradition of the Greeks themselves.   Mark then accused the Latins of having corrupted these passages; but his wisest colleagues refused to credit the charge, for the Dominican introduced codices of indisputable authenticity, especially one of St. Basil, of a date anterior to the Photian schism.   Mark then raised the following difficulty : " In defending your doctrine on the Procession of the Holy Ghost, you must fall into one of two errors.   Either you suppose two divine Principles, and then you destroy the divine unity ; or, to maintain that unity, you make the Son and the Holy Ghost attributes of the Father, and then you destroy the Trinity."   To this objection Montenero replied that in the Catholic doctrine no double Principle was supposed; firstly, because the Holy Ghost, being the love of the Father and the Son, is produced by one unique power, that of love ; secondly, because as the Word has nothing that He does not receive from the Father, so the Holy Ghost, who is said to proceed from the Son, has, and can have only one original Principle.   After a few more objections, which elicited triumphant replies from Montenero, Mark of Ephesus retired, and took no further part in the sessions of the Council.   His retreat ended the combat.   The principal champions of the schismatics, such as Isidore of Kiew and Bessarion, were convinced of the orthodoxy of the Latins; the patriarch and the emperor visibly sympathized with them; but, although reduced to silence, the majority of the Greeks remained attached to their error. When the Pontiff wished to demand from each synodal, under oath, what were his views, the schismatics rejected this method of terminating the ques· tion. Then Bessarion arose, and put forth all his eloquence to influence his brethren to put an end to the schism. He showed that the fathers, Eastern and Western, were unanimous in admitting the Procession of the Holy Ghost through the Son; he contended that any obscurity, on the part of some fathers, should be dissipated by the light furnished by the clear passages of others; and he impressed upon the Greeks the need of union, were it only for the political existence of the Byzantine empire. In conclusion, the archbishop of Nicea declared that the Roman Church professed the right faith concerning the Holy Ghost; that the addition of the *Filioque* was proper; and that he was ready to defend in writing what he then sustained with his tongue, being willing to lose his see rather than abandon his convictions (1). These remarks of so influential a prelate as Bessarion produced a vivid sensation; and the senator, George Scholarius, followed in the same sense. However, the majority of the schismatics remained obstinate, and the unionists were becoming impatient. The private conferences had been going on for more than a month, when the Latins sent to the schismatics a *Profession of Faith* which was rejected. The Greeks admitted that the Holy Ghost proceeds from the Son; but they contended that the Procession is by emission or effusion. The Latins, in return, did not reject these words, but they required the Greeks to declare the precise significance which they attached to them; and to state clearly and definitively whether they understood said words in the sense of the fathers. The schismatics were now pushed to the wall. They could not refuse to give the statement required by the Catholics; and they could not give it without acknowledging the truth of the Roman doctrine, unless they again recurred to the sophisms already confuted. Therefore they procrastinated; and the more sincere among them now threatened to unite with the Catholics by individual abjurations of the schism.

Frightened at this decision, the Byzantine emperor called a

(1) TRAVERSARI; *Epistles*, b. II., no. 19.

meeting of his prelates and consultors at the residence of the patriarch. The teachings of the fathers were again examined, and finally, on May 30, the patriarch pronounced that the Holy Ghost proceeds from the Father through the Son, eternally and substantially, as from one Principle and one sole Cause ; and that the doctrine is orthodox which teaches that the Holy Ghost receives from the Father and the Son. When the patriarchal decision was first presented, thirteen of the Greek bishops received it, five protested against it, and one, the archbishop of Trebizond, was absent; but three days afterward only one, Mark of Ephesus, rejected it. On June 6, a solemn deputation of the Greeks waited upon Pope Eugenius IV., and declared : " *We agree with you that the addition to the Creed, that you recite, is derived from the holy fathers ; we approve it, and are united with you. We declare that the Holy Ghost proceeds from the Father and the Son, as from one Principle and Cause.*" The writing of his signature to this adhesion was the last public act of the patriarch Joseph, for he died on the following day. These lines were found in his writing, and duly signed : " Being come to the end of my life, and being about to pay the common debt, I wrote and sign, with the grace of God, my *Profession of Faith*, that all my children may know it. I declare that I receive and believe all that is held and taught by the Catholic and Apostolic Church of Jesus Christ, the Church of the elder Rome. I acknowledge that the Pope of the elder Rome is the blessed father of fathers, the Great Pontiff, and the Vicar of Jesus Christ, who assures the faith of Christians. I also believe in the Purgatory of souls."

On July 6, Pope Eugenius IV., all the synodals, and the emperor met in the church of Sta. Maria del Fiore. Cardinal Cesarini ascended the pulpit, and read, in Latin, the Apostolic Constitution which declared that the Easterns and Westerns alike acknowledged that the Holy Ghost proceeds from the Father and the Son ; that leavened and unleavened bread are equally valid matter of the Holy Eucharist; that the just, dying before their sins are entirely expiated, are purified in Purgatory, and are there assisted by the prayers of the living ; that the completely purified soul is received into heaven, to enjoy there the intuitive vision of God; that those who die in actual mortal sin, or simply in original sin, descend into hell *(in infernum)*, there to undergo *different* punishments; that the Roman Pontiff is the successor of the Blessed Peter, Prince of the Apostles; that he is the. true vicar of Jesus Christ, the head of the Universal Church, and the father and teacher of all Christians; that Christ has given to him, in the person of the Blessed Peter, the full power of feeding and governing the Universal Church. Then Bessarion mounted the pulpit, and read a Greek version of the same document. All the Greek bishops, Mark of Ephesus alone excepted, cried "Amen!"; and having signed the Constitution, they all (Mark excepted), together with the emperor, kissed the knees and right hand of the Pontiff.

Before the departure of the Greeks, there arrived at Florence representatives of the patriarch of the Armenians, who requested to be received into the communion of the Universal Church. Some time before the Photian schism, the Armenians, hitherto subjects of the Constantinopolitan patriarch, had formed a national church. While the Armenians were discussing their differences with the theologians appointed by the Council, the Greeks departed for home; and hence the Gallican theologians used to hold that the decree of union, afterward issued by Pope Eugenius IV., must not be regarded as the work of a General Council. We shall treat of this question when we shall have finished our historical sketch. The Council of Florence was also asked to accord communion to the Jacobites or Monophysites of Ethiopia, Egypt, and Lybia. This progeny of Eutyches was represented by Andrew, abbot of the monastery of St. Anthony in Egypt, as envoy of the Monophysite patriarch John, and in his suite of thirty-nine persons was an African king (1). Some have

(1) The following account of the reception of the Ethiopian embassy is taken from a MS. codex (No. XVII., class XXV., with title "Città di Firenze") in the Magliabecchi Library: "On Sunday, Aug. 26, there arrived in Florence about forty Indians, sent by Priest John of Greater India. Among them were three ambassadors of the said Priest John, and one of them was a king who carried in his hand a golden cross. Another was a cardinal, that is, one of their abbots, who are of the rank of our cardinals. There was also a knight. The said abbot had his head wrapped in a quantity of white linen. All of them were black, withered, and very deformed. They came to unite their faith with ours. ... On Sept. 2 they delivered their message to our holy father Eugenius, and when reduced to our language, it sounded thus . 'All men who approach your Holiness, most blessed father, should

thought that this Monophysite patriarch was the " Priest John," about whom so much has been written, and the search for whom was the occasion of the Portuguese discovery of the Cape of Good Hope. The Ethiopian deputies were received by Pope Eugenius IV. on Sept. 2, and the abbot Andrew acknowledged the supremacy of the Roman See, the legitimacy of the Council of Chalcedon, and the illegality of the " Robber-Synod, " the so-called Second Council of Ephesus. He also anathematized Ebion, Cerinthus, Marcion, Paul of Samosata, Manes, Valentine, Nestorius, Eutyches ; in fine, all the heresiarchs with whose errors his countrymen had become infected. Pope Eugenius then pronounced the Jacobites united with the Roman Church. Finally, on May 6, 1442, the Pontiff transferred the Council from Florence to Rome.

" In its second and third sessions, the Council of Basel declared that the Pope could not dissolve or transfer it without its own consent; and in its sixteenth session the Pontiff accepted this decree. In France, we regard the Council of Basel as œcumenical until its twenty-sixth session ; that of Florence, held in spite of the decrees of Basel, cannot be called General. The bishops of France were not there : the king had prohibited their attendance, and they had not been canonically called to it. Nevertheless, many French theologians have contended that this Council was really œcumenical." When Bergier wrote these words, the opinion expressed by

give great thanks to God, because He has allowed them to behold, in you, Christ again conversing on earth with sinners. But we, who were born in Ethiopia, have peculiar reasons for such gratitude to God for having been permitted to gaze upon your blessed features. No person comes to you from such a distance as we do, who are located at the end of the earth ; and with due respect to all others, we think that no people has more devotion to the Pope of Rome than we have. We have conquered every obstacle in order to arrive here, and when we return home, we will give great joy to our countrymen : for in our empire, whenever any one comes from the Roman Pontiff, the great and humble, men, women, and children, all run to kiss his feet, and blessed is the person who can procure a piece of his clothes. And our empire is indeed a great one ; our emperor has a hundred crowned kings in his obedience : to our country belonged the ancient glories of the queen of Sheba, who was attracted to Jerusalem by the fame of Solomon, just as we, who are inferior to her, are now drawn to you, who are greater than Solomon. To our land also belonged Queen Candace, and the royal eunuch whom Philip baptized. You, therefore, who are the greatest of the great, ought to behold us little ones with joy, on account of these our great associations, and also because of the care which God has had of us. For it is certain that other peoples who have left you, have fallen into decay : but we, although wandering from the Roman See, are still free and powerful. Our separation has been owing to our distance, to the dangers surrounding us, and to the neglect of previous pastors in our regard.' "

them was licit: and some members of the Gallican school were firmly persuaded that the Council of Florence was never, for one moment, œcumenical. At the time of the Council of Trent, the cardinal of Lorraine energetically defended this opinion: but, as Alexandre insists, the French church never rejected the Council of Florence. The French bishops were prohibited by the king to attend the Council, but they were present in spirit and in will. Many of the prelates of those provinces which had not yet been incorporated in the monarchy did attend at Florence, e. g., the bishops of Terouanne, Nevers, Digne, Bayeux, and Angers. Alexandre's Gallicanism does not prevent his showing that the Council of Florence was œcumenical in every sense, "until the departure of the Greeks," and such was the opinion of De Marca, of Bossuet, of the Faculty of Paris, and of the French clergy (1). Such of the Gallican school as refused, before the Vatican Council, to admit the œcumenicity of the assembly of Florence, were doubtless influenced by the difficulty of reconciling its doctrine on the Pontiff with certain Gallican opinions, especially with the three last articles of the *Declaration of 1682*. But this same reason should have caused them to reject the Councils of Constance and Basel; for these assemblies directly controverted the doctrine enunciated in the first article of the *Declaration* (2).

When theologians argue about the *materia* of the Sacraments, the decree issued by the Council of Florence in reference to the Armenians and Jacobites is often brought forward; and those who differ from the Florentine prelates in

---

(1) BERTHIER ; *History of the French Church*, vol. XVI., b. XLVIII.

(2) In this article it is asserted that " kings and sovereigns are not subject in temporal matters, by command of God, to any ecclesiastical power ; they cannot be deposed, either directly or indirectly, by the authority of the keys ; their subjects cannot be dispensed from the submission that they owe, nor can they be absolved from their oaths of allegiance. This doctrine, necessary for public tranquillity, and no less advantageous to the Church than to the State, should be held inviolate, as conformable to the will of God, to the tradition of the holy fathers, and to the example of the saints." How could the framers of this article revere the Council of Constance, when, in its seventeenth session, that assembly prohibited any and all persons, " whether kings, cardinals, patriarchs, archbishops, bishops, dukes, princes, marquises, counts, or of any other dignity, ecclesiastical or secular," from placing any obstacle to the extinction of the schism ; and declared all delinquents " *ipso facto* excommunicated, and deprived of every honor, dignity, office, and benefice"? And the Council of Basel, extolled to the skies by all ultra-Gallicans, decreed the same penalties against all who would interfere with the Papal legates. See the " safe-conduct," given in the General Congregation of July 18, 1432.

the question of the *materia* assert that this decree possesses
no Conciliar authority, since, as they contend, it was issued
after the departure of the Greeks had deprived the Council of
its quality of œcumenicity. Such was the opinion of Sirmond,
Alexandre, Habert, and Wittasse. Since the decisions of
the Council of the Vatican, this controversy has lost all of its
importance: for it is certain that when Pope Eugenius IV.
issued the decree in which the question of the *materia* is
treated, he spoke *ex cathedra*.

Basnage (1), Potter (2), Mosheim (3), and other Protestant
authors naturally manifest much hostility toward the Council of Florence. Here is a Council of the Universal Church,
attended by representatives of those who had separated from
the Roman See many centuries before, and all unite in a profession of belief in those dogmas which Luther, Calvin, and
the Anglicans will soon pronounce unscriptural and mere
human inventions. The Eastern separatists could not have
derived their doctrines from Rome, the presumed corrupter
of the deposit of faith, after their secession; therefore these
doctrines must have been held by the whole Church at the
time when unity was broken. And what are these dogmas,
as to the antiquity of which Roman Catholic, schismatic Greek,
and Ethiopian Monophysite agree? The doctrine of Purgatory, and of the efficacy of prayer for the dead; that of the
Seven Sacraments, and especially that of the Real Presence
of our Lord in the Holy Eucharist; and that of the Sacrifice
of the Mass. It is not strange then that the modern apologists of heresy should be displeased with the Council of Florence. Again, the recognition of the Papal supremacy and the
consummation of the union of Christendom—short-lived, certainly, but then unanimously desired—were irritating to Potter,
Mosheim, and others of that ilk, who were yet lamenting the recent Protestant failure in the matter of Cyril Lucar (4). They
insist that trickery and threats were used by the Catholics
to induce the schismatics to sign a common *Profession of
Faith*. They pretend to prove the truth of their assertion by
the history of the union written by the schismatic, Sylvester

(1) *History of the Church*, b. XXVII., c. xii., § 6.   (3) *History*, cent. 15, pt. 2, c. i., 13.

(2) *Spirit of the Church*, vol. IV., b. VII.   (4) See our vol. II., ch. ix., p. 131.

Syropulos, who, they say, clearly shows, firstly, that Pope Eugenius IV. prevailed by promises of aid against the Turks, and by bribes of money, in keeping the Greeks away from Basel, and in obtaining their recognition of the Conciliar character of his assembly, then at Ferrara. It is certain, secondly, they say, that Bessarion was the principal instrument used by the Pontiff, and that he was seduced by the promise of a cardinal's hat. Thirdly, they accuse the Catholics of cowardice and inconsistency, inasmuch as, in their intense desire to procure the recognition of the Papal supremacy, they were willing to tolerate, on the part of the Orientals, positive errors of doctrine. Thus they allowed them to depart, still clinging, as is evident from the reply of the archbishop of Mitylene, to the Catholic objections (1), to their doctrine that Christian and consummated matrimony can be dissolved on account of adultery.

To these objections Bergier makes the following reply: "It was the emperor John Paleologus who first proposed the union of the two churches, hoping to obtain from the Catho-

(1) After the *Definition of Faith* had been signed by all the synodals, Mark of Ephesus alone excepted, the Greeks were asked to give reasons for several peculiar customs. Why do they pour warm water into the chalice? Before the bread has become the Body of Christ, why do they recite the words of John XIX., "One of the soldiers with a spear opened His side, and immediately there came out blood and water"? Why do they say: "And behold the star ... stood over where the Child was"? Why do the Greek priests confer Confirmation? Why do they anoint corpses before burial? Why are they not content with the words of the Lord, "Receive and eat, etc.," but add: "And make this bread into the Precious Body of Thy Christ," and "Changing them by Thy Holy Spirit, Amen, Amen, Amen"? Why do they dissolve marriages, when the Lord said: "What God hath joined, etc."? And since the patriarch Joseph had died at Florence, why did not the Greeks proceed to elect a successor? The *Acts* of the Council inform us that the archbishop of Mitylene "replied to these questions properly and canonically, excepting as to the one of matrimony, and that concerning the patriarch; and about these the Pope spoke to the emperor." After a few days, the Pontiff summoned the Eastern bishops, and thus addressed them: "Brethren, by favor of God we are united in faith. Since, then, by the secret judgment of God, I am the head among you members, and I ought to instruct you in what contributes to piety and to the good of the Church, I have some things to say to you, as to brethren and teachers of the churches. And I say, firstly, that all complain about your dissolution of marriage; this must be corrected. Secondly, as to the bishop of Ephesus. He must account for his abandonment of our Synod; he is not wiser than all of us. ... Thirdly, since the holy patriarch of Constantinople has been received into the eternal tabernacles, another patriarch should be chosen, and here where I am present." The Greeks replied that the Pope's remarks were most wise, but that a satisfactory answer could not be given without previous consultation among themselves and with the emperor. On their own individual responsibility, however, they said that *when they dissolved marriages, they did so with good reasons*. As to Mark of Ephesus, he would answer for his conduct. Concerning the election of a new patriarch, they insisted that it was the custom of the Greeks to hold that election in Constantinople. When Paleologus heard of these reclamations, and of the replies thereto, he forbade any further notice of the matter.

lic powers aid against the Turks. The Pope could only promise to use his influence with the sovereigns. If he did not succeed, ought he be accused of deceiving the Greeks? Had he not heeded the propositions of the emperor, he would now be charged with having lost, either through avarice or through obstinacy, an opportunity of ending the schism. The Greeks were too poor to journey to Italy at their own expense; the emperor, reduced to the most humiliating straits, could not advance the money. It was but just, therefore, that the Pontiff should furnish the funds. To assert that this money was a bribe to the Greeks, to induce them to stifle the voices of their own consciences and to betray the interests of their church, is to gratuitously and malignantly calumniate. Bessarion was incontestably the wisest and most moderate man among the Greeks; he had desired the extinction of the schism long before he could have been tempted by any promise. At the Council of Florence he spoke with an erudition, a solidity, and a precision which excited the admiration of the Latins, and the Greeks could not contradict him. What is proved by the hatred which the latter conceived for him? Merely their own obstinacy. If the Pope had not recompensed Bessarion for his services, he would have been accused of black ingratitude. It is sufficient to read the *History* of Syropulos to realize the extent to which the Greeks carried their stupid obstinacy. They wished, before entering upon the question of the Procession of the Holy Ghost, that the first thing undertaken should be the removal of the *Filioque* from the Creed. The dogma was proved to them, not only by the Scriptures, but by the writings of the Greek fathers, and so forcibly that they could not reply. The same was done with regard to other points that they raised. If, therefore, they did not sign the *Profession* voluntarily, and in good faith; if they revoked their signatures when they had returned home; they, not the Latins, were deceivers. The Greeks brought four accusations against the Roman Church. ... The Catholics were bound to satisfy them. ... If, in 1638, the Greeks had been willing to unite with the Protestants, these latter, who were so ambitious of such union, would have pushed their spirit of concession much further than was done by the Council of Florence."

As to the accusation of excessive complaisance, on the part of the Catholics, in the matter of the Greek custom dissolving matrimony because of adultery, more than Bergier says (1) can be, and ought to be said in defence of the Council's action. The indissolubility of consummated Christian matrimony is certainly Catholic doctrine; and Pope Pius IX. condemned the proposition which teaches that matrimony is not indissoluble according to the natural law (2). But at the time of the Council of Florence, the indissolubility of matrimony, even in case of adultery, had not been proclaimed under pain of anathema. Even the Council of Trent, out of consideration for the Greek subjects of Venice, as we learn from Pallavicino (3), so tempered its Canon as to anathematize only those who declared that the Church erred in her teaching on this subject; and although, as Tournely well says, it

(1) The French apologist merely says : " Had the Greeks been attacked on other points of dogma or of discipline, our Protestants would say that the Catholics had foolishly confirmed them in their schism."

(2) *Syallabus*, prop. 67.

(3) *Council of Trent.*, b. XXII., c. iv., no. 27.—The following are the historian's words: " A Canon had been prepared, anathematizing any one who would say that consummated marriages could be dissolved on account of adultery. But when the final draft was shown to the Venetian ambassadors, they solemnly declared to the assembly, on Aug. 11 (1563), that the ancient republic had always been most faithful to the Apostolic See and to the General Councils celebrated under its authority, and that said republic had ever zealously received and venerated all the Apostolic and Conciliary decrees ; . . . but that unless what was being prepared in the 7th Canon were modified in some way, no slight offence might be given to the Eastern churches, especially those of the islands belonging to Venice, viz., Crete, Cyprus, Corfu, Zante, Cephalonia, and many others, to the sacrifice of public quiet and to the detriment of the Catholic Church. It was plain to the fathers, said the ambassadors, that although the Greeks partly differed from the Roman Church, yet things had not become so desperate that improvement might not be expected, especially since the Greek subjects of the republic, although they followed their own rite, obeyed bishops appointed by the Roman Pontiff. (From this passage the reader will perceive that the obnoxious practice was followed by the *united*, as well as by the *schismatics* of the Greek rite.) The duty of the ambassadors, and the very fitness of things, compelled them not to allow these peoples to be stricken with an anathema which might incite them to tumult, and to an entire withdrawal from the Roman communion. It was certain (continued the Venetian ambassadors) that the Greeks followed the most ancient custom of their forefathers in repudiating an adulterous spouse, and taking another : and that they had never been anathematized by any General Council, although this custom had been well known by the Roman Catholic Church. Therefore the ambassadors deemed it their duty to most earnestly beseech that the Canon might be so moderately worded that it would cause no harm to the Greeks, especially by any anathema. Doubtless it might be so couched as to offer no indignity to the Catholic Church, and to preserve due reverence to the doctors. They thought that the desire of the Council might be attained, and the republic be content, if the canon were drawn in some such terms as these: ' Let him be anathema who says that the Holy Roman and Apostolic Church, the mother and teacher of the others, has erred or errs when she has taught or teaches, etc. ' "

would seem that the doctrine is now of faith, even though the Council of Trent did not explicitly declare it such, it is nevertheless certain that Pope Eugenius IV. did not so regard it; since, in the twenty-fifth session of Florence, he addressed the Greeks as persons finally joined in faith with the Roman Church. No cowardice, therefore, was displayed, and no desire of domination at any cost of principle; but rather a prudent economy was exercised when the Greeks were allowed to depart from Florence without having promised, in this matter of matrimony, to follow the teaching of Rome (1).

Mark of Ephesus accused the Latins of having adduced, in defence of their doctrine on the Procession, falsified testimonies of the fathers. To this calumny Bessarion thus replied: "Finally, they (the Latins) laid before us testimonies of the fathers which clearly evinced the truth of this doctrine. And they brought forward passages, not only of the Western fathers, against which we could only say that they had been corrupted by the Latins, but also our Epiphanius, plainly declaring the Holy Ghost to be from the Father and the Son; and we replied that said testimony had been corrupted. They introduced Cyprian and others, and we gave the same answer. They adduced the authority of Western saints; we returned the same reply, and no other. And when we had debated among ourselves for many days as to what we ought to say, we could devise no other, though it seemed too trivial to allege. Firstly, because this doctrine (of the Latins) appeared to be in accord with the mind of the saints. Secondly, so many and so ancient were the volumes containing it, that they could not have been easily falsified; and we could show no copies, either in Latin or in Greek, which gave the quoted passages differently from the version of the Latins. Thirdly, we were

(1) It is uncertain when the practice of dissolving matrimony on account of adultery was introduced among the Greeks. Origen says (*Comment. on Matt.*) that some bishops allowed marriage to a second spouse, while the first was living, but he does not assign any reason for this permission, and expressly states that it was "against the law of Scripture." In his time, therefore, the practice could not have been fully established. But it is certain that a law of Justinian (6th cent.) allowed such marriages; nay, even in the days of St Chrysostom (4th cent.) there was a civil law permitting them, but the saint declared them contrary to the ecclesiastical law (*Hom. on I. Cor. vii.* 39). "We may well suspect," says Tournely (*Matrimony*, q. 5, art. 2), "that these civil laws strengthened a corrupt practice of the Greeks, and that the bishops, fearful of offending the sovereign, gradually came to tolerate, by their silence, an abuse which has, in the course of time, become so firmly established that we can scarcely hope that it will ever be abolished."

able to produce no doctors who asserted the contrary. When, therefore, we could find no worthy reply, we were silent, and for many days we held no session with the Latins" (1). But Bessarion was not satisfied with repelling this accusation against the Latins; he retorted it against the Greeks (2). Speaking of a passage of St. Basel (3), in which that father says that the Holy Ghost " is from the Son, having His being from Him, receiving from Him, and depending entirely from that Cause," the archbishop of Nicea tells us that out of six codices of St. Basel's works brought by his countrymen to Florence, five gave this passage in its entirety; while the one that wanted it "was defective in some parts, and had many additions, according to the pleasure of the corrupter." When he returned to Constantinople, Bessarion searched the libraries, and he found some new codices, written after the Council of Florence had terminated, and in which the above passage was wanting; whereas in other ancient MSS. which he consulted it was given.

Gemistes Pletho, the celebrated Platonist, who had manifested very little zeal for union during the Council of Florence, and who persisted in schism to the last, tried to evade the force of the argument drawn from the Greek subscriptions to the *Acts* of that Synod, by asserting that the patriarch Joseph, the metropolitan Isidore of Kiew, and Mark of Ephesus, did not sign the decrees; that those who did, retracted immediately on their return to Greece. This shows, he contends, that there was no freedom of action at Florence. But if there was no freedom of action, how did these three avoid subscribing? Again, it is false that Isidore of Kiew did not subscribe, for we read in the *Acts*: " I, Isidore, metropolitan of Kiew and of all Russia, and holding the place of the lord Dorotheus, the most holy patriarch of the Apostolic see of Antioch, being satisfied, have subscribed." As for the patriarch Joseph of Constantinople, he was most zealous for unity; and that he would have subscribed to the agreement of reunion, had death spared him until that document was prepared, is evident from the paper found in his desk, and which we have already given.

(1) *Epistle to Alexis Lascaris,* c. v.   (2) *Ibid.* c. i.   (3) *Against Eunomius,* b. III.

CHAPTER VII.

THE PONTIFICATE OF NICHOLAS V.

AFTER the obsequies of Pope Eugenius IV., eighteen cardinals entered into conclave, on March 4, 1447. Prosper Colonna had a majority of votes at the outset, but the cardinal Tagliacozzo of Taranto nominated Thomas Parentucelli, bishop of Bologna, who soon received eleven votes. On the 6th, Cardinal Turrecremata approached Parentucelli, and said: "It is I who make you Pope, Thomas; for to-day is the eve of your holy patron's feast." This accession gave the requisite two-thirds to the cardinal of Bologna, and he was at once proclaimed as Pope Nicholas V. Thomas Parentucelli was the son of a physician of Pisa, and was born in that city in 1398. His mother, Andreola Calendrini, was a Sarzannese, and, as much of her son's childhood was passed at her birthplace, he came to be styled "De Sarzanna." The death of his father and the cruelty of his step-father rendered his childhood a continual misery, and when he was twelve years old, his mother, relying upon a dream which seemed to prognosticate for him a great destiny, sent him into the world as a poor scholar. For six years, living meanwhile on charity, he attended the schools of Bologna, and with such success that, in his nineteenth year, he became tutor to the children of some wealthy Florentines. After four years of pedagogy, he devoted his savings to a resumption of his studies, returned to Bologna, and in due time received the doctorate in theology. His worth soon attracted the notice of the great cardinal Nicholas Albergati, bishop of Bologna, who had ordained him to the priesthood, and he was made master of the episcopal household. According to his contemporaries, the erudition of Thomas de Sarzanna was prodigious: he knew the entire Bible by heart, and there was no Latin or Greek author with whose works he was not familiar. In poetry, oratory, history, cosmography, he was as proficient as in theology and philosophy (1). After

(1) While Albergati was attending the Council of Florence, Thomas de Sarzanna became intimate with most of the learned men of the pontifical court. With such men as the celebrated Poggio, Leonardo Aretino, Mananetti, Aurispa, Marsuppini, and Caspar of Bologna.

the death of Albergati, and a service of twenty years in his house, Thomas was attached by Pope Eugenius IV. to his court, with the title of apostolic deacon, and in time he became vice-chamberlain, bishop of Bologna, and finally cardinal, of the title of St. Susanna. When raised to the Pontificate he had been a cardinal only two months.

At this time the political situation of Europe was quite complicated. France and England, as was usual with them, were at war; Hungary and Germany were embroiled in a dispute of succession; Bohemia was yet a prey to heresy; the Ottomans had been victorious at Varna, and the last ramparts of the Greek empire were tottering. The union of the schismatics with the Catholic Church—which, if it had lasted, would have saved the Greek empire from the Turk—was being broken by frivolous subtleties of the Greek theologians, and by the unfounded and contemptible arrogance of the Greek populations. Alfonso of Aragon, master of the Two Sicilies, and most powerful of the Iberian princes, was a menace to the independence of the Papal States. In these territories of the Church, the so-called "vicars" of the Pontiff-King were working for their independence. Sforza, Florence, Venice, and Visconti, were continuing a struggle for supremacy, the issue of which no one could foresee. The Roman treasury was only a record of debts. To cap the climax, the schism of Basel was as yet unhealed, and hence discipline was relaxed, and the conscience of Christendom troubled.

The new Pontiff thought that kindness might avail as a remedy for all these evils: he would make of the Papacy a power of conciliation. Personally, he was well fitted for this work. Gracious and amiable, he never uttered a harsh word. Prudent in the extreme, he never acted upon recent impressions. Moderate and impartial, he seemed to satisfy wrang-

he established an academy, which was wont to meet for debate in a retired nook of Albergati's palace while the prelates were at their Conciliary sessions. Thomas also, on several occasions, took part in the Conciliary debates on the Procession of the Holy Ghost. Vespasiano (*Commentary on Pope Eugenius*; in MURATORI, v. 25) tells us that Thomas was a thorough bibliomaniac, and that, despite his slender resources, he always kept a number of copyists employed in transcribing the rare MSS. which he frequently unearthed. His diligence restored to the world many a lost author. It was he who taught Cosmo dei Medici how to classify the precious collection of his library of St. Mark, and this instruction served as a criterion in the arrangement of the great libraries of the Abbey of Fiesole, of Montefeltro at Urbino, and of Alexander Sforza at Pesaro.

ling ambassadors and humble supplicants, even when their requests were necessarily refused. And this calmness of character was in Nicholas entirely the work of virtue; for nature had made him quick and impatient (1). One of his first acts was to attempt a restoration of concord between the allied republics of Venice and Florence, and the sovereigns of Milan and Naples (2). A Papal legate called a congress of the belligerents at Ferrara, but while the conditions of peace were being discussed, Philip Mary Visconti died, willing his states to Alfonso of Naples. The Venetians now became enemies to the Milanese, who, tired of tyranny, reasserted their liberty, and called upon Sforza to aid them in preserving it. Florence declared against Venice, while Alfonso found himself opposed by all. Sforza made peace with the Holy See, and his brother Alexander was confirmed in the lordship of Pesaro.

During the struggle that ensued between the Milanese patriots and Sforza, who claimed the duchy as son-in-law to Visconti, Pope Nicholas preserved the constant esteem of both parties. It was mainly owing to the efforts of Nicholas that the emperor Frederick III. yielded to the just complaints of the Hungarians, and restored to them their young king, Ladislas, whom a wicked and short-sighted policy had detained at the imperial court. By this means the Hungarians were left free to correspond with the efforts put forth by their heroic Hunjady to save Germany and all Christendom from the rapidly-advancing Osmanli. Had Hunjady and the valorous Albanian, George Castriot (better known by his Mahometan name of Scanderbeg, the " lord Alexander "), been even moderately aided by the Western powers, Mahomet II. would not have entered Constantinople. But the republics of Italy, which monopolized the commerce with the East, were at war among themselves. The king of Aragon could do nothing without the aid of the Italian fleets, and without loans from the Italian bankers. The Germans could see no

(1) ÆNEAS SYLVIUS, loc. cit. Vespasiano says that " by nature he was choleric, but he knew how to temper his anger with prudence."

(2) Toward the end of the Pontificate of Eugenius IV. these powers had changed their policies. The two republics had warred at first on the side of Sforza, and were only desirous of crushing Visconti ; now this prince was allied with Alfonso of Naples and Sforza himself.

sense in attacking a power which did not, as yet, directly attack themselves, and their emperor was feeble, indolent, and without the slightest military talent. France and England would not allow, just then, the religious sentiment to calm their political passions.

Therefore all that Scanderbeg and Hunjady could do was to defend, the former, the Epirote Mountains, and the latter, the line of the Danube. They did, indeed, in 1448, design to unite the Albanian, Wallachian, and Hungarian forces, and to attempt to revenge the disaster of Varna. But the celerity of Amurath's movements prevented the junction, and, alone, the resolute Hunjady fought the great battle of Kossovo, in which he resisted, for three days, an Ottoman army four times more numerous than his own, only leaving the field after half his enemies were killed.

In February, 1451, the greatest and most terrible of all the Turkish sultans, Mahomet II., ascended the Ottoman throne. He was ferocious, arrogant, implacable; and had often been heard to say that, once in power, he would have no other object than the extirpation of Christianity. This sultan was actuated by a powerful motive in his desire to distinguish himself in the eyes of his followers. He had been twice obliged to resign the supreme power, because his countrymen had no confidence in his ability; he would inaugurate his reign by no less an enterprise than the capture of Constantinople. The supine and voluptuous Greeks realized the intentions of their enemy when they beheld, only a few miles from their capital, the rising walls of a new Mahometan castle. But their emperor, Constantine Paleologus Dracosez, was, strange to say, a man of imperturbable courage. Provisioning the city as well as he could, and repairing the walls, he sent deputies to all the sovereigns of Europe, asking for aid. The West was not disposed to heed the request, for the Greeks had already, scores of times, appealed for a help which they could, and would not, have given to themselves; while their almost uninterrupted course of indifference —when it was not hostility and treachery—to the Crusades had won for them the contempt and detestation of Europe.

The Roman Pontiff had more reason than any other Western sovereign to be offended and disgusted with the Greeks. Twelve years had passed since they had sworn obedience to the Chair of Peter, and the decree of union had not yet been promulgated in the empire ; the great mass of the clergy and people cherished a virulent hatred toward the Catholics, or, as they ever styled the friends of unity, the Latins ; even Constantine Paleologus—so much superior to his predecessors—had suffered an assembly, held in St. Sophia's in 1450, to condemn the Council of Florence, and to depose and banish Gregory of Melissa. Notwithstanding these and other grievances, Pope Nicholas V. undertook to furnish the unfortunate empire with ships and money.

On April 6, 1453, Mahomet II. besieged Constantinople with 260,000 men and a fleet of 300 vessels. Despite the immense population of his capital, the emperor could rally to his standard only 4,970 Greeks; but an auxiliary corps of 2,000 foreigners, mostly Italians, came to his aid. With this small force, which he placed under the command of the Genoese Giustiniani, Paleologus awaited the assault of his enemy. The Greek historians Phrantza and Ducas highly eulogize the military genius, coolness, and intrepidity of Giustiniani; and it is very probable that if the fleet of Pope Nicholas had arrived in time to second his valor and his science, Mahomet II. would have abandoned his attempt. More than 10,000 Turks had perished in the assaults, and the sultan's counsellors had advised a retreat, when Mahomet conceived the idea of transporting by land a portion of his fleet to the inner harbor of the city. Eighty vessels were thus brought close to the walls, and the final assault was ordered. After two hours of desperate fighting, the result was yet dubious, when the noble Giustiniani received a dangerous wound, and was incapacitated from directing the defence. The enfeebled garrison now lost heart ; Constantine vainly strove to rally them, and fell amid a heap of his foes. Two days after the fall of the doomed city, a fleet of ten Roman, ten Neapolitan, and nine Venetian galleys appeared off Negropont.

Great was the terror of Europe when the ancient capital had succumbed to the power of the Crescent ; then, indeed, when it was almost too late for their own escape, did princes and peoples wish that during the previous centuries they had paid more attention to the warnings, prayers, and threats of the Popes, and had shown more energy, more perseverance, and more single-mindedness in the Crusades, which alone had postponed the present calamity, and alone had prevented its being visited, long ago, upon every capital in Christendom. Now again the Roman See raised its voice to bid Europe unite against the common foe. The cardinal Isidore addressed a graphic picture of the present danger to all the sovereigns, and a plan of action was soon matured. A general peace was to be proclaimed in Europe ; Milan, Florence, and Venice were to reinforce Scanderbeg with 20,000 cavalry, and thus threaten the Turk from the South ; Naples, Genoa, Florence, and Venice were to furnish a fleet to capture Gallipoli, occupy the Dardanelles, and thus obstruct the Ottoman advance into Europe ; the Hungarians were to form a coalition with the Bohemians and other Slavonic peoples, and attack the Osmanli from the North. Æneas Sylvius (Piccolomini) succeeded, for the moment, in infusing a little warlike vigor into the lazy Frederick III., and a Diet was convoked to meet at Ratisbon in May, 1454, to devise ways and means.

On September 30, 1453, four months after the fall of Constantinople, Pope Nicholas published a solemn appeal to all Christians, exhorting them to unite against the hordes of Mahomet, conceding indulgences to all who would take up arms for the Holy War, and ordering a levy of tithes on all ecclesiastical revenues, including his own. The cardinal Capranica was commissioned to re-establish concord at Genoa, and to make peace between that republic and the king of Aragon ; the cardinal d'Estouteville was sent to urge the king of France to be the first prince to take the Cross ; Capistrano was ordered to preach the Crusade in Austria, Bohemia, and Moravia. Capranica succeeded in his mission ; the king of France, however, made his movements depend on those of the emperor. Alfonso of Aragon declared that he would march against the Turk, even though he went alone. Philip the Good of Burgundy, was most enthusiastic in the cause, and Denmark, Sweden, and Norway manifested good dispositions.

Nothing, however, gave the Pontiff so much confidence of success in his enterprise as the reconciliation of Venice, Florence, Sforza, and Naples; effected by the exhortations of an humble anchorite, Simonetto of Camerino (1). A Diet was held at Ratisbon in May, 1454, and it was resolved that the Christian forces should set out in the following April.

Daring as he was, the news of these preparations disquieted Mahomet II.; and he endeavored to avert the threatened danger by writing to Pope Nicholas. This amusing letter and the answer of the Pontiff were found by Christophe in the great monastery of Montecassino (2). "The King of kings and Lord of lords, the High-Admiral Machabech, Sultan Begri, and son of the great Sultan Amurath, sends greeting to Nicholas, Vicar of Jesus Christ, crucified by the Jews," and informs the Pontiff that he does very wrong to oppose the conquests of the Turks; that he exposes himself and his children to great danger, and prepares an immense effusion of human blood. The Pope upholds an unjust cause, for Greece belongs of right to Mahomet II., as he is the avenger of Hector and the Trojans; Italy also is his, because he is the lineal descendant of Æneas. The Roman Pontiff should not be hostile to the Ottoman domination, because when that is established, Rome will recover her ancient glory. Again, it is the design of the sultan to accord to the Christian religion the most perfect liberty; nay, it is very probable that when he has conquered the world, the great Mahomet II. will embrace the religion of that Jesus, of whose sanctity and miracles he has heard so much. In his reply, Pope Nicholas ridicules the false compassion of a prince whose conscience is stained with the massacres and all kinds of outrages perpetrated, only the other day, at Constantinople; he declares the responsibility of Mahomet II. for every drop of blood that shall be shed. As to the hinted conversion, he begs the sultan to remember that Jesus was meek and hum-

(1) PLATINA; *Nicholas V*. ÆNEAS SYLVIUS; *Epist.* 127. GIANNOZZO MANETTI; *Life of Nicholas V.*, b. II.

(2) "They are so singular," says Christophe, "that one might doubt their authenticity. But singularity is no proof of fraud. There is nothing in the correspondence contrary to the known characters of the supposed writers. The MS. is certainly of the 15th century. These letters explain how it was that, ten years afterward, Pius II. dared to write to Mahomet II. exhorting him to become a Christian, a letter no less extraordinary than that of the sultan to Nicholas V.

ble, and suggests that he conform his life to that of this great model But there was no necessity for the letter of Mahomet II. to the Pontiff. The energetic resolutions of the Diet of Ratisbon produced no effect. Frederick III. could not shake off his indolence; and the enthusiasm of the other German princes was only sufficiently efficacious to promise a definitive organization in a future Diet, to be held in October. In this assembly, despite the eloquence of Æneas Sylvius (1), nothing definitive was effected. The lethargy of Germany was contagious; and the other Christian powers became, for a time, religiously and politically blind.

We must now notice one of the most important civil events of this pontificate—that is, a conspiracy which, like that of Cola di Rienzo, a century before, had for its object the substitution of a republican for the Papal *régime*. The author of this conspiracy, Stephen Porcaro, was a cavalier of talent, eloquence, and courage; he resembled "the last of the tribunes" in audacity and in the possession of a fantastic imagination. In reading the sonnets of Petrarch, he had become impressed with the idea that he was the knight upon whom the poet ordered his readers to gaze with admiration, since said hero was the hope of the Seven Hills (2). A number of learned men were then resuscitating the glorious memories of ancient Italy, and Porcaro felt that his was the task of renovating her political constitution. "He was," says Christophe, "a demagogue, but perhaps in good faith, because he was one of those Utopian politicians, who, in their schemes, consider neither the lessons of history nor the changes of ideas, but apply their systems indiscriminately to all generations and all peoples, obstinately believing that human happiness is linked with the triumph of their own principles." Shortly after the death of Pope Eugenius IV., Porcaro made his first attempt at revolution. The Roman people, under the presidency of the archbishop of Benevento, had assembled in the church of Ara Cœli, during the vacancy of the Holy See, in

(1) Oration on the "Fall of Constantinople," in Epistle 130.
(2) The ode "Spirito Gentil ":
      "Sopra 'l monte Tarpeo, canzon, vedrai
      Un cavalier, ch' Italia tutta onora
      .   .   .   .
      Ti chier merce da tutti setti i colli."

order to deliberate upon certain requests which were to be addressed to the cardinals. Porcaro seized his opportunity, and in a vehement discourse he reminded the Romans of the glory and freedom of their ancestors, and exhorted them to obtain, by arms if necessary, a constitution which, while not violating the sovereign rights of the Pontiff, would give to them the political power. A sedition would have occurred then and there, had not Lellio Vallegio, an influential citizen, caused moderate counsels to prevail. When Pope Nicholas heard of this event, he thought to gain Porcaro, and also to avoid inaugurating his reign with a sentence of banishment, by appointing the enthusiast to the office of Podestà of Anagni. But the demagogue used his office to promote sedition, and the Pontiff, still unwilling to adopt harsh measures, ordered him to reside in Bologna, and to report every day to the cardinal-legate Bessarion. The leniency of Nicholas was again abused, and having imbued his nephew Sciarra with his ideas, Porcaro sent him to Rome to prepare a revolt. Sciarra collected a body of four hundred men, some of whom were enthusiasts like his uncle, but the majority were of that stamp which any revolution will always find ready at the call of a leader. When all was prepared for the outbreak, Stephen Porcaro evaded the vigilance of Bessarion, arrived in Rome, and would probably have succeeded in overturning the government, had he not spent three days in haranguing his followers, convincing them that more than a million of scudi awaited them in the houses of the cardinals and in the government offices (1). This delay enabled the Papal government to learn of Porcaro's arrival in Rome, and the plot was discovered. The design of Porcaro was to introduce his band among the congregation at St. Peter's on the Feast of the Epiphany, 1453, and during the celebration of High Mass they were to kill the Pontiff and the cardinals, imprison the rest of the court, seize Castel San Angelo, convoke the people at the capitol, and proclaim the republic, or, rather, the dictatorship of the "liberator" (2). The greater number of the

(1) LEO ALBERTI ; *Conspiracy of Porcaro*, in MURATORI, v. XXV.
(2) VESPASIANO ; *Life of Nicholas V.* ZANTEFLIET ; in MARTENES' *Ampl. Collect.*, v. V. SABELLICUS ; *Venetian History*, dec. iii., b. VII.

conspirators were arrested in the house of their leader, and on January 13 many of them were hanged with him on the ramparts of San Angelo.

The conspiracy of Porcaro and the fall of Constantinople undermined the health of Pope Nicholas V. The former event rendered him diffident and morose toward the Romans, and he heard himself blamed for the latter. But he received one great consolation, just before his death, which happened on March 25, 1455. Moved by the exhortations of the Pontiff and by the influence of the anchorite Simonetto, King Alfonso had ratified the peace concluded at Lodi between Sforza, the new duke of Milan, and the Venetians, and had entered into an alliance with both Milan and Venice for twenty-five years. "We know no sovereign," says Christophe, "who in so short a period has had a more brilliant career than that of Nicholas V. The pacification of the Church, the extinction of discord in Italy, the embellishment of Rome, the foundation of the Vatican Library—the most powerful impulse ever given to the arts and to literature,—the inauguration of a new civilization by the resurrection of the ancient luminaries, are so many immortal deeds due to his wisdom and genius. We may ask ourselves: What glory would not have accrued to the tiara had Time—that great enemy of the projects of man—not been wanting for the execution of his vast designs? The Papacy, become through him the source of enlightenment, as it had already been the centre of all grandeur, would have recovered, by the ascendency of its regenerating activity, all the prestige of that moral influence which seventy years of religious dissension had caused it to lose. The premature death of Nicholas V. prevented the completion of this magnificent restoration. A little later Leo X. will take up the work of Thomas de Sarzanna, and will give his own name to the age which he will illumine. But Leo X. will be only the most effulgent figure of that period; he will have, in France and in Spain, rivals who will share with him the honor of putting the human race in the path of progress. Nicholas V. stood alone. In his day the great royalties of Europe were yet shrouded in darkness; the Papacy alone illumined the world."

CHAPTER VIII.

POPE CALIXTUS III.—THE EXCOMMUNICATED COMET.

It is related of St. Vincent Ferrer that after having preached one of his eloquent sermons in Valentia, he was asked for a special blessing by a young priest who had been one of his hearers ; and that regarding the suppliant with a fixed and inspired countenance, he said : " My son, I congratulate you ; for you are destined to be the ornament of your country and of your family. As for me, I shall be, after my death, an object of your veneration. Direct all your energies, my son, toward the acquisition of virtue " (1). This young priest was Alphonsus Borgia, a member of a family which had been illustrious for centuries in Spain, but which he was to make known to Italy and the Christian world, and on which one of his nephews, also a Pope, was to be the means of conferring, through the malice of would-be historians, a very malodorous reputation. Born in Xativa in 1378, the year which witnessed the birth of the Great Western Schism, Alphonsus made his studies at the University of Lerida, and became distinguished as a jurisconsult. Having acquired the confidence of King Alphonsus of Aragon, he succeeded in terminating a fearful war which that monarch had waged against Castile for seven years. By his skill and prudence he effected a reconciliation between Pope Eugenius IV. and his sovereign, and the Pontiff admitted him into the Sacred College. When the cardinals, fifteen in number, entered into Conclave on April 4, 1455, to choose a successor to Nicholas V., they found themselves unable to elect either Capranica, the candidate of the Italian party, or d'Estouteville, the favorite of the Frenchmen. They therefore meditated seriously on the propriety of elevating the celebrated archbishop of Nicea, the ex-schismatic Bessarion ; and they were deterred from so doing only by the protest of Cœtivi, the cardinal of Avignon, who depicted graphically the risk which might be entailed by placing the tiara on the

(1) MARINO SANUTO ; *Lives of the Doges of Venice,* vol. XXII., p. 1159.—BZOVIUS ; *An. ..ls,* at y. 1419, no. 24.

head of a Greek neophyte, one who had but lately abandoned the schismatic ranks (1). In this emergency the electors turned their thoughts toward Cardinal Borgia, who, although seventy-seven years of age, was possessed of great energy, and whose perspicacity was universally admired. Every vote was cast for this new candidate whom no person, previous to the Conclave, had regarded as such; and he assumed the name of Calixtus III.

To the generality of Protestant scholars, and perhaps to the average Catholic reader, this Pontiff is known principally as the alleged hero of a tale so rankly absurd that its discussion may appear to the student as an insult to his intelligence, or at least as an implication that he possesses no sense of humor. Among all the lies of history—and their name is legion—we have encountered none so utterly absurd as the one now claiming consideration. We are asked to believe that in the year 1456 a Roman Pontiff hurled the thunderbolts of the Vatican against a comet. Very little education is required for a knowledge that excommunication is a depriving one of the right of communion, or association, with the body to which he has been hitherto aggregated; and we have never understood that comets belong to any human corporation. We would ask certain American lecturers what would be their course if rumor should suddenly proclaim that our chief magistrate had declared a blockade of all the approaches, mental or physical, to the fifth satellite of Jupiter. Would they not search, or cause to be searched, the archives of the Secretariate of State in the capital, in order to determine whether our president had really attained to such a height of enterprise? Let them search the *Bullarium Romanum*, and then inform the world whether they have found any trace of the Pope's bull against the comet. Meanwhile we shall give, for the edification of the reader, some account of the alleged papal ebullition, as it was detailed fifty years ago by an Episcopalian minister, in a work destined for that praiseworthy object, the education of the people (2). "Pope Calixtus III. reported the comet as in league with the Turks;

(1) VESPASIANO; *Life of Cardinal Dominick Capranica* —SUMMONTE; b. V.—PLATINA; *Calixtus III.—Commentaries of Pius II.*, b. I.

(2) *Gallery of Nature*, by the Rev. Thomas Milman; London, 1846.

and ordered the *Ave Maria* to be repeated three times daily, instead of twice, and directed the church bells to be rung at noon. In the *Ave Maria* the prayer was added: 'Lord, deliver us from the devil, the Turks, and the comet!' Once each day these three obnoxious personages were regularly excommunicated. There was perhaps as much worldly policy as superstition in sounding this note of alarm; for fees accumulated to the priesthood from the increase of confessions. The comet, at length, after patiently enduring some months of daily excommunication and cursing, showed signs of retreat," etc., etc., *usque ad nauseam.* As there is scarcely a twelve-year-old Catholic child who will not detect as many misrepresentations in this lucubration as there are sentences, we shall confine our remarks to what is merely necessary in the premises.

When Cardinal Alphonsus Borgia donned the tiara in 1455, he was known throughout Christendom as a thorough scholar, a man of great sagacity and sound judgment, and as so accomplished a jurisconsult that it was said that only two of his predecessors had equalled him. Therefore, since Calixtus III. was no fool, why attempt to hold him up to ridicule? Perhaps because he was a Borgia, the founder of that family's grandeur,—of that family which is the bugbear of Protestant credulists, a choice target for the shafts of anti-Catholic sarcasm, and a fancied mine of wealth for every tenth-rate novelist. At the time of which we are speaking, Christendom was humiliated before the victorious insolence and aggressive ambition of Mahomet II., who from the towers of lately-conquered Constantinople was laying out the path of his lustful hordes, then panting to be led to the destruction of European civilization. Immediately after his election, while yet seated on the throne where he had received the first homage of the Sacred College, Calixtus, filled with a sense of his paternal responsibility for the welfare of the nations, had spontaneously and loudly pronounced this oath: "I, Pope Calixtus, third of that name, do here promise and swear, in the presence of the Blessed Trinity, of the ever-virgin Mother of God, of the Holy Apostles Peter and Paul, and of the entire heavenly host, that I shall use every effort, even unto the sacrifice of my life, in order to recover the city of Constantinople, lately captured and sacked by Mahomet, the enemy of Christ and the son of Satan." And had he not kept that oath—had he not, in order to sustain the heroic troops of Cardinal Scarampo, St. John Capistrano, and Hunjady, mortgaged the pontifical estates, melted down the sacred vessels of the Church, stripped his tiara of its jewels,—the ferocious Islamite would have been able to fulfil his vow to crush the religion of the West under the hoofs of his victorious cavalry (1). It was in order to secure the protection of the God of Armies that Calixtus III. commanded that everywhere, thrice a day, the bells of every parish church and of every religious institution should be rung to summon the faithful to the recitation of the *Angelus,* and not in order to scare away the comet, which had not yet appeared (2). When that dread visitant did show itself, the peoples of Europe were filled with consternation; and other portents simultaneously contributed to a fear that God was about to empty the vials of judgment over His wayward children. In the Terra di Lavoro, the Abruzzi, and the Puglia, according to the contemporary Florentine historian, St. Antonine, 30,000 persons were destroyed by an earthquake; and another contemporary, Æneas Sylvius, states that 30,000 others were engulfed in its fissures in the city of Naples alone. These and many other fearful phenomena greatly terrified the people ; and we would like to believe that if certain of our American astronomers were to witness such fearful manifestations—especially if they were to behold, outside the Golden Gate of San Francisco, a fiery island like that which then appeared in the Ægean (3), they also would feel like saying their prayers. At any rate,

(1) In the Basilica of St. Sophia, just turned into a mosque, Mahomet took this oath : " I, Mahomet, son of Amurath, sultan and governor of Baram and of Rachmael, raised up by the great God, placed in the circle of the Sun, more than all other emperors covered with glory, fortunate in everything, feared by all mortals, most potent through the prayers of the saints and of the Prophet Mahomet, emperor of all the emperors and prince of all the princes now existing in both West and East; I do promise to the One God, by this, my oath, that I shall accord no sleep to my eyes, eat no delicate food, touch nothing beautiful ... until I have banished the God of the West from the face of the earth, for the glory of the great God Sabaoth, and of Mahomet, his Prophet."

(2) St. Antonine ; b. XII., ch. xiv.—Æneas Sylvius ; *Epist.* 227.—Platina ; *Life of Calixtus III.*

(3) Gobelin, secretary to Æneas Sylvius, narrates that there arose in the Ægean Sea an island more than a hundred feet high, which was a mass of flame for many days.

Pope Calixtus availed himself of the opportunity afforded by the not unreasonable apprehensions of men, to detach them more from the perishable things of earth, and to induce them to use their energies for the greater glory of God. Upon this fact, and upon it alone, has been based the tale of the Pope's bull against the comet.

Calixtus III. needed no encouragement from the monarchs of Christendom to place himself at the head of a new Crusade; but he was filled with hope when he heard, in nearly all the congratulatory addresses which followed his elevation, royal promises and even vows to expel Mahomet II. from Constantinople. The emperor Frederick III. was especially profuse with his professions of zeal, which were delivered by means of Æneas Sylvius; but not a German did he send to the field. In vain did Cardinal Carvajal beseech the German princes to furnish the contingents which they and their emperor had grandiloquently promised in many Diets. Nor did the French king, the beneficiary of Joan of Arc, show any more readiness to correspond to the ardor of the Pontiff who wrote to him: "If the Most High grants the aid of France to this cause, the destruction of the Turks is assured" (1). Charles VII. even opposed the collection of the tithes which had been decreed in France in aid of the Holy War. The king of Naples, the king of England, and the duke of Burgundy also ignored their solemn engagements in the premises. This lethargy of the principal Christian powers could not but encourage Mahomet II.; and at the head of 150,000 veterans he laid siege to Belgrade, the vulnerable spot of Hungary and of European Christendom. Two hundred armed brigantines floated on the Save and the Danube, at the confluence of which rivers the devoted city was situated. Against the Turkish forces King Ladislaus of Hungary could dispose of a mere handful of troops; but the heroism and faith of a Neapolitan friar were to prove the salvation of Europe. St. John Capistrano, so-named after the Neapolitan village where he was born, at the age of sixty-eight had undertaken the conversion of the Hussites of Bohemia, and the excitation of the German peoples to

(1) RAYNALD; at y. 1456, no. 4.—ST. ANTONINE; ch. xiv., tit. 22. MARINO SANUTO; loc. cit.—PLATINA; loc. cit.—CHARTIER; Life of Charles VII., p. 288.

a crusade against the Islamites. His labors in the former task were so successful that over 16,000 Hussites were received by him into the fold of the Church (1). In the matter of the crusade, however, the saint failed to produce any effective enthusiasm in either the princes or people of Germany. In May, 1455, the humble and energetic Franciscan entered Hungary with the design of inciting the Magyars to an effort for the preservation of European Christianity; and his labors were blessed with success. For forty days Mahomet II. had bombarded Belgrade, and its fortifications were in ruins when a force of Hungarians and Poles, led by Capistrano and Hunjady, penetrated into the city (2), having previously burnt or dispersed the entire Mahometan fleet. But the Ottoman conqueror still hoped to conquer by force of numbers, and in person he conducted a general assault. His confidence seemed to be justified; for after several hours of desperate struggle, the Crescent floated over the ruined ramparts. The Hungarians were in full retreat, when Capistrano ran among them, crucifix raised on high, and crying "Jesus, Jesus!" encouraged them to turn and charge the foe. With Hunjady at their head, they renewed the fight, and the Turks were compelled to recoil, dragging with them the wounded and unconscious sultan. Belgrade and Europe were saved; for when he recovered his senses, Mahomet ordered an immediate raising of the siege, leaving behind him all his war material and 24,000 of his dead (3). Both Capistrano and Hunjady announced this victory to Pope Calixtus, sending to him sixteen of the enemy's tents, made of cloth of gold, one of which was that of the sultan.

(1) THWROCZ; *Hungarian Chronicles*, pt. 3, ch. lii.—WADDING; *Annals*, vol. VI., at y. 1455, no. 43.

(2) Historians differ as to the number of the troops whom Capistrano and Hunjady brought to the succor of Belgrade. A modern author of reliability, Camille Paganel, in his *Life of Scanderbeg*, makes them 60,000. But Ranzanus says that scarcely 500 Poles obeyed the summons of Capistrano; Thwrocz puts the number at 300; Dlugossi says 800. Of course, the Hungarians who followed Capistrano were more numerous; but, as Christophe observes, if 60,000 fresh combatants had entered Belgrade, after having destroyed his fleet, the sultan would scarcely have ordered the assault.

(3) The details of this victory may be found in the *Hungarian Chronicle* by Thwrocz; the *Epitome* by Rauzanus; the *Hungarian Affairs* by Bonfini; the *Bohemian History* by Æneas Sylvius; the *Bohemian History* by Dubraw; the *Polish History* by Dlugossi; and with more satisfaction, in the narratives of Capistrano and Taghacozzo, given by Rinaldi, at y. 1457, nos. 29-37.

Calixtus III. was too perspicacious to yield to feelings of security on account of the retreat of Mahomet II. from Belgrade; he had studied the character of the conqueror of Constantinople, and realized that the standard-bearer of Islam would not rest until he had washed away the stain of his discomfiture with Christian blood. The first care of the Pontiff was to provide for the security of Rhodes, where the Knights-Hospitalers—since the suppression of the Templars, the flower of military monasticism—were stationed as advanced pickets to watch over the safety of Europe. He immediately sent an abundance of provisions and war material to the soldier-monks, and prepared to double the pontifical fleet of sixteen vessels with which Cardinal Scarampo was cruising in the waters of the Levant. During three years this cardinalitial mariner patrolled the Archipelago, protecting the islands which had not succumbed to the power of the Crescent, and retaking from the Turks the isles of Lemnos, Mytilene, Stalimene, Imbros, and Naxos. In fact, with the exception of Hunjady and Alexander Castriota (better known by the Turkish form of his name, Scanderbeg, "the lord Alexander"), Cardinal Scarampo was the sole adversary to confront the Ottoman power between the years 1457 and 1460; and he so operated as to keep the Islamites of Asia and Africa in constant tremor (1). But Pope Calixtus did not despair of inducing at least the king of France to follow in the footsteps of Godfrey de Bouillon. "Would to God," he wrote to Charles VII., "that the other Catholic princes had our zeal for the defeat of the infidels!" And sending to that monarch the flattering gift of the Golden Rose, the Pontiff wrote : "Receive this present, dear son, as a pledge of our regard for your Serenity. Among all the flowers of earth there is none so sweet and beautiful as the rose. May heaven grant that a divine perfume may enthrall your senses, and cause you to display the generosity of your heart by an energetic defence of the faith!" It would appear that the continued appeals of the father of the faithful influenced Charles VII.; for we find the Pontiff menacing the doctors of the University of Paris, and the clergy of Normandy and Autun, for re-

(1) MARINO SANUTO ; loc. cit., vol. XXII., p. 1159.—PHILIP BERGOM., Chronicle, b. XV.

-sisting the collection of a tax which the king had destined to the equipment of thirty galleys for a crusade. The king even entered into alliance with Ladislaus of Hungary to fight the common enemy of the Christian nations, promising to give his daughter Magdalen to the Magyar sovereign in marriage as a pledge of his sincerity. But at this juncture Ladislaus died, and instead of equipping a fleet in the service of the Cross, Charles used some of the ships in a war against England, and the others to aid the son of René of Anjou in subduing the kingdom of Naples (1).

The incumbent of the Holy Roman Empire, Frederick III., continued to make brilliant offers of an army for a crusade; but instead of fulfilling their promises, he and all the other German princes preferred to indulge in the worn-out Germanic recriminations against the court of Rome, as an excuse for their laggardness. They accused the Pontiff of ignoring the decrees of Constance and of Basel; and in a *Memorandum*, which was drawn up by Martin Meyer, chancellor of the archbishop of Mayence, they inveighed against the "abuses of the *Curia*" in a style which would have warmed the heart of Wycliffe. Calixtus assigned the duty of refuting this insolent document to Æneas Sylvius, once secretary to Frederick III., and now a cardinal and prime minister of His Holiness. Æneas Sylvius does not deny the existence of abuses in the Roman court; he cheerfully admits that as men, the Popes often make mistakes or worse (2); and in regard to the real motive of the *Memorandum*, the "intolerable exactions" of the papal officials and the consequent miseries of "unfortunate Germany," the secretary admits that irregularities in the perception of tithes and donatives sometimes occur, but he plainly shows that the funds received are legitimate and worthily expended. The language of Æneas Sylvius was eminently frank and moderate, and his logic sound; but the German complaints continued, and Pope Calixtus wrote, with his own hand, an explanation to the emperor. He showed how the

(1) BONFINI; *loc. cit.*, decad. 3, *b*. VIII.—CHARTIER; *loc. cit.*, p. 295.—ST. ANTONINE; tit. 22, ch. xvi.

(2) "*Fatemur, aliquando in Romana Curia, quam regunt homines, aliqua fieri quæ digna essent emendatione ; nec dubitamus ipsos Romanæ urbis præsules, etiam in quantum homines, falli, errare, labi, aut decipi posse.*"

greater part of the revenues of the Holy See were devoted to the support of the valiant Scanderbeg in his position as a bulwark against Islam; to the maintenance of a powerful pontifical squadron in the Levant; to succoring the Christians in the territories of the fallen Lower Empire and in Asia. And the Pontiff added : " Remember that none of this money, no matter whence it may come, is ever taken by us for ourselves, never stowed in our coffers, never expended for jewels or other luxuries. It is all consecrated to the service of the faith " (1). The emperor is reminded that if any one has a right to complain, it is the Pope, to whom only a portion of his legitimate revenues from Germany and certain other countries ever come, because of the rapacity of the secular potentates who appropriate the funds to their own purposes.

The throne of Naples was at this period occupied by the House of Aragon; and as we have observed, the cardinal Alphonsus Borgia had been a devoted servant of King Alphonsus I. As chief pastor of Christendom, however, Calixtus III. found that his duties did not always accord with the designs of his former friend and protector. The monarch could not appreciate this necessary change of attitude; and his chagrin was unbounded when the Pontiff refused his request to be invested with the March of Ancona and other ecclesiastical territories as a feudatary of the Holy See. His rage was increased when, having nominated certain unworthy persons for the mitre, the Pope refused to confirm the act, saying: "Let his majesty of Aragon govern his kingdom, but let him leave to us the supreme apostolate!" (2). But these were not the sole causes of the refusal of Alphonsus of Aragon to fulfil his promise to aid in the war against Islam. The little republic of Siena was hostile to Alphonsus, and he encouraged Piccinino to invade its territory; whereupon Calixtus, Venice, and Sforza saved the Sienese autonomy, and Alphonsus rightly credited the Pope with the intervention. Again, Alphonsus and Sforza, hitherto enemies, suddenly entered into alliance, and agreed upon intermarriages in their families to cement the friendship. Like all.

(1) RAYNALD ; at y. 1456, no. 50 ; y. 1457, no. 40.
(2) ÆNEAS SYLVIUS ; *History of Europe*, ch. lviii.

Roman Pontiffs, Calixtus III. was ever alive in the preservation of a prudent balance of power in Italy ; therefore he endeavored to prevent these marriages.   Finally, and this was the most bitter grievance to Alphonsus, our Pontiff refused his request to invest the monarch's illegitimate son, Ferdinand, duke of Calabria, with the kingdom of the Two Sicilies. Serious consequences might have resulted from these disagreements, had not Alphonsus died in 1458.   When Calixtus heard of this demise, he immediately declared the Two Sicilies devolved upon the Holy See, they being fiefs of the Roman Pontiff, and there being no legitimate heir to their late sovereign.   When treating of the Deposing Power once enjoyed by the Popes, we showed that the vassalage of the Two Sicilies to the Holy See was always recognized by all parties concerned, from the days of Robert Guiscard to our own times ; and that the vassalage of the Neapolitan part of the kingdom dates from the eighth century (1).   But historians differ when they assign the motive which actuated Pope Calixtus III. when he availed himself of his undoubted right as suzerain of this kingdom.   Some contend that he wished to substitute for the royal House of Aragon the noble but not royal House of Borgia (2).   But this opinion is pure conjecture, and was probably conceived by men who witnessed the enterprising essays of the greatest of the Borgias, fifty years after the death of Calixtus.   This Pontiff certainly evinced much affection for his family; but his universally acknowledged piety and the disinterestedness of all his public actions cause us to believe that he cherished the desire of definitively annexing the most valuable fief of the Holy See to the States of the Church.   Whatever were his intentions in the matter, death prevented their actuation on Aug. 8, 1458, ten weeks after the demise of Alphonsus I.

(1) See our vol. II., page 214.

(2) Thus COSTANZO ; *History of Naples*, b. IX.—SIMONETTA ; *Life of Francis Sforza*, in MURATORI, vol. XXI., *b*. XXVI.—PIGNA ; *The Princes of Este*, b. VII.

CHAPTER IX.

THE PONTIFICATE OF PIUS II.—THE PRAGMATIC SANCTION OF CHARLES VII.

Æneas Sylvius Piccolomini was born at Corsigniano in 1405, of an old and noble, though reduced family. His scientific and literary studies were made at the University of Siena. He became distinguished for his legal acquirements, but his first reputation was made as a poet. After leaving the University he remained a layman, and passed some time in the service of Cardinal Capranica and of Bartholomew Visconti, bishop of Novara; but finally became a member of the household of Cardinal Albergati, who seems to have communicated to him the great art of managing men, for which both were famous. The Council of Basel made Æneas its secretary, and employed him in a great many nunciatures in various lands. After the pretended deposition of Pope Eugenius IV., Æneas became secretary of the Anti-Pope, Felix V., and in 1442 he was made a member of his council by the emperor Frederick III. He was now ordained priest, and he soon abandoned the schismatics of Basel. In 1456 Pope Calixtus III. enrolled him in the Sacred College. This Pope died on the 8th of August, 1458, and after a Conclave of four days the cardinals elected Æneas Sylvius Piccolomini, who assumed the name of Pius II. Long before the world heard of Pius II., it had resounded with the praises of Æneas Sylvius Piccolomini. For years, wherever there was a great assembly, religious or political, his figure had been familiar, and all had been entranced by his eloquence. But he was now weak in health; his mind was clear, but he had almost lost the use of his limbs. His iron will, however, was to sustain him through several years of an agitated pontificate.

In the mind of Pius II. one thought dominated every other earthly one—the necessity of curbing the power of the Osmanli. Both as layman and as cleric; as secretary to the Council of Basel, to Felix, and to Frederick; as bishop and as cardinal; he had seized every opportunity to unite Christen-

dom for its own defence.   As Supreme Pontiff, he possessed
an influence which a man of his calibre could not allow to lie
dormant.   To the realization of this one idea everything else
was made to tend; nothing could claim his attention which
did not march, in some way, with his great project.   Firstly,
the Papal States must give the Pontiff-King no cause of distraction.   Hence, since Piccinino has profited by a vacancy
of the Holy See to seize Assisi, Gualdo, and Nocera, he must
be dispossessed of his spoils, even though the Pontiff has to
make some minor sacrifice.   Ferdinand of Naples, successor
to Alphonsus, was refused the investiture of that kingdom by
the late Pontiff; but Pius II. will grant it, on condition, among
others, that the king will expel Piccinino from the usurped
territories.   When the French cardinals and the bishop of
Marseilles, ambassador of René of Anjou, protest against this
ignoring or denial of René's claims to Naples, Pius asks them:
"Can René expel Piccinino from our States?"   So the decree
of Calixtus is abrogated, Ferdinand becomes legitimate king
of Naples, and the ambitious *condottiere* abandons the usurped
districts.   Free from distraction at home, Pius now directs
every energy to the one object.

As discord among the Christian sovereigns had hitherto
been the sole reason why the Mahometans had succeeded in
gaining a foothold in Europe, Pope Pius II. decided to convoke a general congress of princes and peoples, and to personally attend it, there to plead the cause of Christ and of
civilization.   Mantua was designated as the place where the
sovereigns or their delegates were to meet the Supreme Pontiff on June 1, 1459.   In order to show the world how much
he had the crusade at heart, and in order to have time to interview many of the princes and nobles through whose territories he would pass, he departed from Rome in the latter
part of January.   This spectacle of a Pontiff, broken down by
infirmities and premature old age, leaving his capital to cross
the Apennines in the depth of winter in order to urge Christendom to protect itself from slavery and outrage, ought certainly to have inspired the most indifferent with zeal.   After
visiting the Liberian Basilica, and placing his enterprise
under the special protection of the Mother of God, Pope Pius

set out amid the lamentations of the entire population. He
was accompanied by six cardinals; the others remained in
Rome, the cardinal de Cusa representing the Pope as legate. Throughout his journey—which lasted four months—
the Pontiff was reverently and enthusiastically received; but
a special rivalry in magnificence was displayed by the Orsini at Campagnano, by Cosmo dei Medici at Florence, and
by Borso d'Este at Ferrara. But when, on May 27, Pius arrived at Mantua, he was grievously pained on finding that
only a few of the powers were represented in the assembly
from which he had expected so much good.

The month of September having arrived, with no signs of
the envoys of France and England, and as Sforza, upon whose
military skill the Pope chiefly relied, could not remain much
longer at Mantua, the serious business of the congress was
commenced. After a three hours' discourse by the Pontiff,
and a thoroughly soldierly speech by Sforza, a discussion
ensued as to a plan of campaign, and as to ways and means
for sustaining it. Before the final conference had closed, the
envoys of France and England appeared,—the former only to
complain, the latter to give mere vague promises of co-operation. The Frenchmen expressed their king's displeasure
because the Pontiff had preferred a bastard of Aragon to a
French prince for the Neapolitan throne, and they declared
that the Pope need not expect the French to join the crusade
while they were at war with England; they were not opposed
to the idea of a peace conference, under the presidency of a
Papal legate, but they had no definite instructions to arrange
one. Then the representatives of Venice gave another illustration of that republic's characteristic devotion to Mammon.
Most of the Venetian possessions lay on the Turkish frontiers, and the Senate could not break with the sultan until it
was certain that all Christendom was ready to take the
field (1). However, in spite of all these drawbacks to success,
Pope Pius secured from many of the powers represented at
Mantua substantial assurance of a determination to second
his efforts for the Holy Land. On his part, the Pontiff
decreed a tax of one-tenth on the clergy; all agreed that the

(1) SIMONETTA; *Life of Sforza*, b. XXVI.

faithful laity should pay a thirtieth, while the Jews should be assessed for a twentieth. The emperor promised to furnish, on the part of Germany, 32,000 foot and 10,000 horse; Hungary engaged to raise 40,000, half of whom should be cavalry; the duke of Burgundy agreed to send 6,000 men of all arms; the Italian States were to furnish and equip, at their own expense, a powerful fleet; Scanderbeg and his brave Albanians were always, to a man, in arms; and much was hoped from a league between the Asiatic Christians and the Mahometan enemies of the Turks.

But the Holy See was destined to be again disappointed. Charles VII. of France, malcontent with Pius II., held himself aloof from all the Pontiff's projects. England preferred to spill her best blood for York and Lancaster, rather than devote some of it to the ransom of Christ's sepulchre. A great part of Germany now revolted against the incapable Frederick III., and discussed the propriety of substituting in his place the king of Poland, George Podibraski. Cardinal Bessarion, whom Pope Pius had sent as legate into Germany to urge the feeble Frederick to ratify his engagements, vainly exerted all his eloquence: not one generous response did he obtain from monarch, princes, or people (1). Hungary, now under the rule of Matthias Corvinus, son of Hunjady, could only act on the defensive against the Turks; but that she did bravely and well. The reader will find in Raynald (y. 1461) the singular letter of Pope Pius II. to Máhomet II., in which the Pontiff demonstrates the divinity of Christianity, and exhorts this most fanatical of all Ottoman sultans to abjure Islam, concluding in these words: "Do not disregard our words, prince; do not neglect our counsel. Receive the baptism of Christ; be regenerated in the Holy Ghost; receive the Gospel. Thus you will save your soul, you will accomplish your grand designs, all Europe will admire you, and the glory of your name will be sung by posterity." The conqueror did not deign to answer this letter, and Pius soon realized that force alone could save Europe from the Turk.

The indefatigable Pontiff now took a resolution, of which

(1) See William Coxe's *History of the House of Austria*, v. I., c. xvii.

none of his predecessors had even dreamed—that of placing himself at the head of a crusade. At first he confided this project only to six cardinals, his intimate counsellors, and after some days of consultation they agreed that the idea was a sublime inspiration. Pius II. then made supreme efforts to incite the Christian powers to immediate action. But although Louis XI. had already promised 70,000 men for a crusade, he now refused to move, and accused the Pope of being an enemy of peace. Better success attended the Pope's application to Philip of Burgundy; this prince promised to march, at the first signal, with 6,000 men. Venice, at length awakened to a sense of her danger, also corresponded to the Pontiff's zeal, and with enthusiasm; Cardinal Bessarion blessed the standard of the admiral, Ursacio Giustiniani, and a powerful fleet departed for the coasts of the Peloponnesus. The Pontiff could now hope for aid also from Hungary and Germany, as Matthias Corvinus and Frederick III. had been lately reconciled by the papal nuncios; and in celebration of this peace, the gallant Hungarian had just attacked Mahomet II. at Iaïckza, and forced him to raise the siege of that place, and to flee in disgrace, leaving behind all his material of war. Assistance was also promised by Alexander Sforza and by Piccinino, who had lately completed the pacification of Italy by a treaty of mutual defence. It was with great confidence, therefore, that Pope Pius met the deputies of the above powers; and when he found that Venice alone was ready, he nevertheless called a consistory, and definitively committed himself to the crusade. In his address he reviewed the events of his pontificate, and justified his actions.

"You yourselves," he cried, "have often urged me to undertake this expedition! Now, then, the time has come for you to show whether your religion, faith, and zeal were sincere. I shall give you the example; you will only follow me. Just as Jesus Christ, the model of shepherds, gave His life for His sheep, so I have resolved to give mine, that the flock entrusted to my care may not be destroyed by the Mussulmans. We shall equip a fleet as powerful as our resources will permit; and then, despite our age and our infirmities, we shall embark, and, entrusting ourselves to the winds, shall go into Greece, and if necessary into Asia. Do not ask the use of the majesty of the supreme priesthood on the field of battle ; we declare that we can no longer defer the Holy War, unless we are willing to be dishonored in the face of the entire world. And what else can we do? All other means have been tried, and to no purpose. The earth has resounded with our exhortations ; they have been received with indifference. We have imposed a levy of tithes ; an appeal was made to a General Council; we have published indulgences. It has been said that we extorted money to enrich ourselves. The credit of our court is destroyed, and the supreme priesthood derided. Some extraordinary measure must be taken if confidence is to be restored, and that measure shall be the sacrifice of our own person. No longer shall we say to the sovereigns of the earth, ' Go !' ; for they do not hear us. But we shall cry, ' Follow us !' Perhaps, then, seeing the Roman Pontiff, the common father of the faithful, the Vicar of Jesus Christ, a weak old man, starting for the war, men will be somewhat ashamed to remain at home, and will finally rush to arms to revenge the outrages on oppressed religion. The cause we have marked out is undoubtedly perilous ; we do not shut our eyes to that fact. But we do not march alone against the enemy : we shall be seconded by the maritime power of Venice, by the armaments of other Italian States, and by the duke of Burgundy, with his valiant chivalry. The Poles and Hungarians will attack the Turk from the north, and revolted Greece will reach us her hand from the south ; the Albanians, Servians, and Epirotes impatiently await the hour to unfold the banner of independence. In Asia the khan of Caramania, and the many Mussulmans who with reason detest the Ottoman yoke, will come to our assistance."

Undoubtedly, Pope Pius II. had no intention of heading the crusaders, sword in hand : " We shall appear in your midst, surrounded by the venerable cardinals of the Roman Church, and by many bishops and priests, under the standard of the Cross, and carrying the Holy Eucharist and the relics of the saints. Jesus Christ will be with us, and we with Him." The Pope then appointed the rendezvous and the date,—namely, the port of Ancona, during June, 1464. From this moment, regarding himself as the very soul of the crusade, Pius II. took upon himself every detail of its organization. It was necessary, of course, to have a commander-in-chief, and for that office none seemed so fit as the veteran general, Alexander Sforza, duke of Milan. To induce Sforza to undertake the charge the Pontiff appealed to his religion, his military pride, and his personal record of valor; and when the warrior objected his sixty years, Pius exclaimed: "The old will follow the old; this war will be called the war of the old!" Under the impulse of the Vatican, Christian Europe seemed to have recovered its ancient enthusiasm, and with confidence in the success of the great design of his life, the Pontiff prepared to depart from Rome. But he was now attacked by a slow fever, which, while it left him his energy of will, consumed the little physical force remaining in his frame. The physicians were enjoined to say nothing of his condition, and they obeyed.

On June 18, 1464, the Pope visited St. Peter's for the last time, and set out for Ancona. Of all the princes and warriors who were to have met him on his arrival, not one had come; though he found an immense multitude of rash pilgrims, who, thinking that the Church would provide them with everything, were utterly without arms or resources of any kind. A powerful army might have been made of this eager crowd, but there was no general to command them; and the Genoese transports, which were to receive them, had not arrived. Impatient of delay, little by little most of them deserted, to make their way home as best they could. Nor had the Venetian fleet, the very backbone of the enterprise, made its appearance. These cruel disappointments so aggravated the Pontiff's illness, that the physicians declared he had but a few days to live. At length the Venetian sails appeared on the horizon, and the Pope desired his attendants to carry him to the window. The sight of the fleet gave him, for an instant, new life; but, falling back, he moaned: "Alas! yesterday the means of embarking were wanting, and to-day I myself am wanting!" He was then carried, almost dying, to his bed. After receiving the last consolations of

Holy Church, he peacefully expired on the 14th of August, 1464.

Christophe says of this Pontiff: "Pius II. was worthy of the eminent place that he occupied. In youth he had yielded to the storm of the passions; it is from his own ingenuous avowal, in his Fifteenth *Epistle*, that we know it. But the falls that deprave some natures served to give him knowledge of life, and to save him from the snares set by the world for weak humanity. On the throne he exhibited the virtues of a saint and the qualities of a great Pontiff. He was grave in his manners, simple in his habits, zealous for discipline, knowing only duty as a rule of action, devoted to the Church—as a son to his mother; disinterested, and perhaps too much so, for a prince. ... His conversation was brief and sententious. Many of his sayings have been handed down to us, and, in general, they are diplomatically profound. ... All the humanists expected protection when he mounted the pontifical throne : he himself had promised it. But his political embarrassments and his projects of crusade absorbed all his thoughts and resources, and he was only able to furnish some partial encouragements. If we regard Pius II. as a literary man, we are astonished at the variety and plenitude of his faculties. Without fear of contradiction, we may term him the foremost man of his epoch. As a humanist, he was superior even to the most illustrious of his contemporaries, in extent of acquirements, in the use of his erudition, in taste, and in elegance of style " (1).

The most important document issued by Pius II. was his *Bull of Retractations*, dated April 26, 1463. Alluding to the errors which he had professed in his early life, he called on Christendom to " reject Æneas, and receive Pius." In the Bull *Execrabilis*, dated Jan. 18, 1460, he condemned all appeals from a Pope to a General Council. It is not our province to show that such appeals are indefensible and illegitimate; it will be sufficient to say that as the Pontiff is superior to the Council, such an appeal would be absurd. Leaving to the dogmatic theologian the task of developing this point, we may be allowed to use our office of historian to show that

(1) *The Papacy in the Fifteenth Century* ; Paris, 1863.

the appeals in question were unknown to antiquity. Febronius asserts that "such appeals are most ancient" (1), while
De Marca, though almost as bitter an adversary of the Papal
supremacy as the coadjutor of Treves, admits that they are
"new" (2). Bossuet thinks that he discovers instances of
such appeals in England in the years 1256, 1264, and
1267 (3). Some Gallicans have contended that the first example of an appeal of this nature is found in the case of
Philip the Fair. But neither Febronius nor any other author
has been able to show the antiquity of such appeals. Heretics certainly have made them, e. g., the Pelagians and the
Nestorians, but we now have no question with those who are
sure to deny submission to any authority that contradicts
them. In the first centuries not one instance can be adduced
of a Catholic having appealed from a Papal decision to that
of a General Council. There are many cases of discontent,
many even of temporary resistance; but of appeals not one.
The Asiatics resisted Pope St. Victor in the Easter controversy; St. Cyprian and the Africans, Firmilian and the
Orientals, resisted Pope St. Stephen in the question of heretical baptism; St. Hilary resisted Pope St. Leo long and
firmly in the matter of Celidonius; but none of them appealed
to a Council. Even the Donatists, though they complained
of the Roman Synod, as St. Augustine frequently tells us,
are never spoken of as appealing from it, but from the Synod
of Arles. In fact, they bowed to no decision, but ever appealing to the emperor, were rightly called by St Augustine
more obstinate than the demon. "I think," said the saint,
"that if the devil were so often condemned by a judge of his
own selection as these heretics have been, he would not be
impudent enough to resist." Can we suppose then, asks
Sirmond, that these Donatists, who yielded to no condemnation, would have hesitated to appeal from the Pope to a
Council, if they could have done so in accordance with
law? (4) If the English appeals adduced by Bossuet are to
be received as matter of history, certainly they are of too

(1) *State of the Church*, etc.; c. vi., § 10.   (2) *Concord*, etc.; b. IV., c. xvii.
(3) *Defense of the Declaration*, etc.; pt. 2., b. XV., c. xxv.
(4) *Notes to the Council of Arles.*

modern a date to militate for our adversaries. Lingard, when speaking of the Papal " exactions " during the reign of Henry III., takes for granted that these appeals were made. but, like Bossuet, he relies on the authority of Matthew of Paris, who merits no confidence when he treats of subjects which afford him an opportunity of assailing the Roman Pontiffs. The example of Frederick II., brought forth by De Marca, is not so much an appeal from the Pope as of one from a General Council to another and more general assembly ; for Matthew of Paris himself, speaking of Frederick's procurator at the General Council of Lyons (1245), says : " He appealed for Frederick to a more general Council soon to be held, for then all the prelates or their procurators, and the orators of all the princes, were not present. The Pope replied : ' A General Council of many is sufficient ; with great inconvenience these patriarchs, archbishops, and bishops from all parts of the world, and many nobles or their procurators, have vainly awaited thy lord's humility. They who are absent have been kept away by the tricks of thy lord ' " (1). The instance of Philip the Fair proves nothing ; for in that case the king affected to regard Pope Boniface VIII. as an intruder, not as a legitimate Pontiff. The first instance of an undoubted appeal from Pope to Council is found in the last session of the Council of Constance (1418). The Polish orators had desired Pope Martin V. to condemn a certain book which had been already condemned by the prelates in their private congregations. When the orators found that the Pontiff had not complied, they appealed to a future Council ; but none of the synodals seconded their appeal, while Pope Martin reproved their rashness, and enjoined silence upon them, under pain of excommunication. If this appeal had been regarded as legitimate, the synodals would have sustained the Poles, for the former also desired the Papal condemnation of the book in question, as is shown by their own course in its regard. From the time of the Council of Constance, Gerson and his disciples continually

---

(1) Roncaglia observes that such an appeal as this cannot be seriously regarded. By such means every decision of the Church could be easily eluded, for a Council without some absentees is almost an impossibility.

exalted the authority of a General Council, and hence instances of appeal from the Pontiff became quite frequent, especially on the part of the Theological Faculty of Paris. Speaking of this Faculty's appeals, Melchior Canus says: " The doctors of Paris appealed from the Council of Lateran, and this appeal, made in the name of the Academy, is circulated. Whose it is, I do not here dispute; but I do insist that it is circulated to the scandal and detriment of the Church. There are extant anathemas of Pius II. against those who appeal to a future Council; and it is manifest, without any of the reasons given by Pius in his two letters, that this thing is of the greatest help to heretics, and that it opens a very wide window for the destruction of ecclesiastical obedience, and for the ruin of true piety " (1).

Our attention is now claimed by the struggle of Pope Pius II. against the famous *Pragmatic Sanction* of Charles VII. This term, presumably of Byzantine origin, is used to designate many imperial and royal decrees ; but in ecclesiastical history it is applied especially to the decree on Church matters said to have been issued by St. Louis in 1268 ; to that issued at the Council of Bourges by Charles VII. in 1438 ; and to that of the Germans issued in the Diet of Mentz in 1439, ordering the reception of the Baselean decrees.

The *Pragmatic Sanction* ascribed to St. Louis consists of the following articles: " I. The churches of our kingdom, the prelates, patrons, and ordinary bestowers of benefices, shall enjoy their full rights, and each one shall preserve the proper jurisdiction. II. The cathedral and other churches of our kingdom shall have freedom of election, and shall fully enjoy it. III. We will and ordain that simony, that sinful plague which contaminates the Church, be banished from our kingdom. IV. We will and ordain that all promotions, collations, provisions, and dispositions of prelacies, diguities, and of all other benefices whatsoever, and all ecclesiastical offices in our kingdom, be made according to the disposition, order, and determination of the common law, of the Holy Councils, and of the ancient fathers. V. We will that in no manner whatever there be levied or collected those pecuniary

(1) *Loc. Theol.*, b. V., c. ult., no. 9.

exactions and most heavy burdens which the Roman Church has imposed and may impose upon the church of France, and because of which our kingdom is miserably impoverished; saving, however, a reasonable, pious, and most urgent cause, and then with our free and express consent, and that of the church of France.   VI. Finally, we renew and approve all the liberties, franchises, immunities, rights, and privileges successively granted by the kings our predecessors, and by ourselves, to the churches, monasteries, holy places, and ecclesiastical persons." That St. Louis never issued the above document is evinced by the following arguments. The first allusion to it was made in the Council of Bourges in 1438, nearly two centuries after it is said to have been promulgated; and then that astute king, Louis XI., furnished the world, for the first time, with the precise text. And here it should be observed that this text, furnished by the not very honest Louis XI., commences with a peculiar Pontifical formula which is utterly foreign to the style of the French Chancery, viz., "For a perpetual remembrance of the thing." Again, the fifth article of this sanction, the only one which gives to the pseudo-decree any importance in the eyes of the enemies of Rome, alludes to abuses that were unknown in France at the time of St. Louis. The exactions of the Papal treasury became great, perhaps indeed oppressive, during the "captivity" of Avignon; and they caused wounds which festered even after the return of the Papacy to its legitimate and natural seat, and which furnished a pretext to parliaments and kings to interfere in Church temporalities. And it was just when complaints were at their loudest, that this pretended *Sanction* of St. Louis appeared. It would certainly seem that this document is the *Sanction* of Charles VII. developed; and when we find it appearing so mysteriously, without certain parentage, and with various readings, we are disposed to credit Charles VII. with its invention, and his crafty son with its embellishment. Both these monarchs were interested in producing a document which would appear to justify the *Sanction* issued by Charles himself. And how is it that none of the innumerable writers of those days, not even such acute chroniclers as Joinville and Nangis, or such violent partisans as Gerson, speak of so important a document? Long before the Council of Bourges the world had read the other decrees of the saintly monarch; but until that Council, or rather until the time of Louis XI., it did not read this one.

The *Pragmatic Sanction* of Charles VII., issued by the advice of nearly all the bishops and great nobles of France, is a royal proclamation and enforcement of a decree of the Council of Bourges, which at first sets forth how great a confusion has crept into ecclesiastical matters, and then states that as the Council of Basel has decreed some things which appear opportune for such an emergency, the assembly of Bourges has decided to receive said decrees, but with some modifications rendered necessary by the circumstances of the French church. The *Sanction* itself consists of twenty-three titles, the principal of which narrate the acceptance of the Baselean decrees (1). One of these decrees recognized the right of appeal from a Papal decision to that of a General Council; and it was against this decree that Pius II. issued the celebrated Bull *Execrabilis*, renewing the condemnation promulgated by Martin V. This *Sanction*, in spite of the reiterated reclamations of Eugenius IV., Nicholas V., and Calixtus III., had for twenty-one years formed the discipline of the French church, when Pius II. issued his Bull, declaring that to admit the right of appeal from Pope to Council would be both fatal and ridiculous; fatal, because it would open the door to impunity, would nourish a spirit of insubordination to the Holy See, and would subvert the hierarchy; ridiculous, since it would be absurd to invoke the authority of a tribunal that did not exist, and the future existence of which was problematical, and entirely dependent upon the will of him against whom appeal would be made. The first result of the Bull *Execrabilis* was a protest, in the name of Charles VII., on the part of Dauvet, procurator-general, charging Pope Pius II. with a desire to break with France, and appealing from his sentence to a General Council, to be as-

---

(1) This Pragmatic Sanction was, of course, registered in parliament, and although, after the time of Pius II., it was opposed by Innocent VII., Alexander VI., and Julius II., it possessed the force of law in France until the Concordat of 1516, concluded between Leo X. and Francis I., which abolished canonical elections, and gave the right of nomination to the king.

·sembled as soon as possible, in French territory. But this insult to the Pontifical authority produced no evil consequences, for the Pontiff wished to preserve at least some semblance of friendship with Charles, in order that he might yet be induced to join in a Crusade ; while the king did not carry out the programme of ·Dauvet, because just then he was in hopes of procuring a special favor from Rome—the transfer of the bishop of Coutances to the see of Tournay. The negotiations ended unfortunately for the monarch, and he indulged in bitter recriminations against the Holy See, although protesting his submission to its authority. The dispute was suddenly terminated by the death of Charles VII. in 1461. The celebrated Louis XI. succeeded to his father's throne, and his character did not promise a firm peace with the Holy See. Nevertheless, he abolished the *Pragmatic Sanction*. When yet dauphin he had sworn to do away with it, if he ever ascended the throne ; furthermore, having been accustomed to oppose his father's policy, he was not disposed to espouse his peculiar quarrels with Rome. Several times indeed, Louis XI. threatened to restore the obnoxious *Sanction*, unless Pope Pius II. would revoke his investiture of Ferdinand I. in the kingdom of Naples, and accord it to the grandson of René of Anjou, who had married a daughter of France; but the Pontiff triumphed over threats and promises.

CHAPTER X.

POPE PAUL II.

The mortal remains of Pope Pius II. having been consigned to their tomb in the church of Sant' Andrea della Valle, the Sacred College, to the number of twenty, entered into Conclave in the Vatican on Aug. 27, 1464. According to a custom practised in many preceding Conclaves, the first action of the cardinals was the drafting of a document which all were to sign, and by which, in this case, each one promised, in the event of his elevation to the Papacy : I. To prosecute the war against the Turks, and to devote to this end the profits of an alum mine recently opened at Tolfa. II. To reform the Sacred College. III. To not cause the Roman

Court to travel, even within the bounds of Italy, unless with the consent of a majority of the cardinals; and not to transfer said Court to a foreign land without the consent of all. IV. To call a General Council within three years. V. To limit the number of cardinals to twenty-four; to create none who were not over thirty years of age, and were not proficient in sacred learning; to create only one member of his own family; and finally, to create none without the approbation of the Sacred College. VI. To appoint bishops only in Consistory. VII. To depose no prelate on the demand of a prince, unless after juridical process. VIII. To alienate no portion of the Papal States, diminish their revenues, declare war or make alliances, without the consent of the cardinals. IX. To entrust the chief command of the Papal army to none of his relatives. X. To allow the cardinals to examine, twice a year, and by themselves, whether the Pontiff had been faithful to this compact. This final clause, odious and humiliating, to say the least, had been inserted in no preceding compromise. In the first balloting, twelve votes were cast for Peter Barbo, cardinal-priest of the title of St. Mark. Fourteen votes being necessary for an election, recourse was had to the *accesso*, and four cardinals simultaneously pronounced for Barbo; all then assented, and paid homage to the elect, who took the name of Paul II (1). The family of Barbo was of senatorial rank, and had already given two Pontiffs to the Church, Eugenius IV. and Gregory XII. On the election of his uncle, Eugenius IV., Peter Barbo was summoned to court, and in 1440, he was enrolled in the Sacred College. During the reigns of Eugenius IV., Calixtus III., and Pius II., he was held in such esteem that "it was generally believed at court that if any one wished to obtain any favor, he should refer it to the Venetian cardinal Peter" (2). It is not our purpose to detail the events of this Pontificate; our principal object

(1) Barbo had wished to assume the name of Formosus; but since he was remarkably handsome, his late brethren suggested that another name would be in better taste. He then chose the name of Mark; but " St. Mark " was the war-cry of Venice, and as Barbo was a Venetian, this selection might have been regarded as indicative of too much partiality for his country.

(2) CANENSIUS; *Life of Paul II.*, edited by Cardinal Quirini (Rome, 1740), with an erudite defence of Paul II against the attacks of Platina. Muratori highly extols this work of Quirini.

is to refute certain calumnies with which the name of Paul
II. has been aspersed. Concerning his reign we briefly note
that the greater part of his attention was devoted to the extirpation of Hussitism, then almost triumphant under the
patronage of George Podiebrad; that he purged the Roman
court of simoniacs, and would not allow even his civil officers
to receive presents (1); that he greatly remedied the abuse
of commendatory benefices; that he was most profuse in re-
lieving the poor with his own money. There are few Pontiffs concerning whom more contradictory judgments have
been pronounced than those formed regarding Paul II. Muratori says that it is perhaps undeniable that, as Philip of
Bergamo testifies, this Pontiff died " loved by few and hated
by nearly all, although this fact is justified by no good reason." According to some, Paul II. was effeminate and pee-
vish, while others regard him as a most resolute sovereign;
some call him a spendthrift, while others declare that he was
a miser; some discern in him the pitying father of the unfortunate, while again he is styled the harshest of despots.
Spondanus, in an evident determination to be impartial, can
say no more in favor of Paul II. than that " he is to be neither highly lauded nor severely condemned." De Mornay,
the " Protestant Pope " of the early French Calvinists, gravely
declares that our Pontiff was strangled by the devil while in
the act of sin. Roscoe is not quite so severe, but he presents
Paul as " an ostentatious, profligate, and illiterate priest " (2).

And now for the charges of ostentation, profligacy, and
illiteracy, which Roscoe—whom it is the fashion to regard as
reasonable and moderate—does not hesitate to make against
Paul II. Ginguené, Hallam, and Sismondi say nothing of this
Pontiff's profligacy, though they equal Roscoe in aversion
to his memory. Excepting De Mornay, no author of note
attacks his morals; not one of his contemporaries insinuates
any reflection upon them—not even Ammanati, so rigid in
his own life, and the leader of a *rigidist* school among the
cardinals; not even Platina, upon whose testimony all the
decriers of Pope Paul's memory are forced to rely almost
solely, and whose virulence would certainly have allowed no

(1) Constitution *Munera.*   (2) *Lorenzo dei Medici.*

error of the Pontiff, in the matter of morality, to pass unno-
ticed in his biography. The charge of ostentation, however,
is not so easily dismissed: but reflection will show that little
blame ought to accrue to our Pontiff because he spent his own
money in a royal manner. Pope Paul II. certainly loved display: the *cavalcata*, or procession, which followed his coronation exceeded in splendor all preceding ones: his tiara, made
by Giordano, the first goldsmith of the age, was valued at
200,000 scudi: he spent immense sums for jewels, etc.; he
wished the cardinals to present an appearance of dignified
splendor, and therefore gave them the white mitre, the red
hat, and prescribed red as the color of their dress, ornaments,
and equipages; near to what had been his own titular church
of St. Mark he built a magnificent palace (1), surrounded it
with extensive gardens, and adorned it with numerous ancient statues and costly furniture. The tastes of Paul II. were
artistic, and he had been used to profusion from his infancy;
when he ascended the Papal throne he injured no one, but
rather benefited many by expending his revenues in a lavish
manner. We learn from Platina, his bitter foe, that Paul
" took great care that all kinds of provisions should always
be plentiful, and be cheaper than they had ever been." Certainly Platina asserts that the Pope "was diligent in accumulating money," but he adds that " he spent this money freely;
he frequently aided poor cardinals, needy bishops and princes, noble persons deprived of their properties, and young
women, widows, and the infirm." Canensius relates several
instances of princely generosity on the part of Cardinal Barbo.

The most important charge brought against Paul II. is that
of his having been a foe to science, an enemy of letters. Roscoe asserts that " during the pontificate of Paul II., letters and
science experienced at Rome a cruel and unrelenting persecution; and their professors exhibited in their sufferings a degree
of constancy and resolution which, in another cause, might have
advanced them to the rank of martyrs." He then describes
the alleged tyranny and barbarism of our Pontiff, and cites, besides Platina, in corroboration of his charge, Tiraboschi; but

(1) Afterward given by Sixtus V. to the Republic of Venice, and hence still called the
Palazzo di Venezia.

he does not give the passage on which he relies. Now, if the reader will consult Tiraboschi, he will find that this author asserts the very contrary of what Roscoe would imply. However, Platina certainly fortifies Roscoe's position. He declares that Paul II. "so hated and despised profane studies, that he called their cultivators heretics." Let us try to discover how much credence is due to Platina in this matter. One of the first cares of the newly-elected Paul II. had been the removal of every cause of corruption from the Roman court; and among the many congregations and tribunals to which his reforming hand extended was the College of Abbreviators (1). This body, says Egidius of Viterbo (d. 1532), had become thoroughly corrupt; all its labors were sold for gold. Paul II. found that more than reformation was needed in this case: he decreed the abolition of the College. One of the prelates thus deprived of a lucrative post was Platina (2), and it is well to note his own account of what followed: "This College was filled with learned and worthy persons; there were men versed in both divine and human law; there were poets and orators, who gave no less honor to the court than they received from it. Paul cast all these aside, like so many strangers and worthless people; depriving them of their offices, although they had paid for them, and thus were guaranteed their possession (3). The greater sufferers tried to change the mind of the Pontiff; and I, who was one of these, earnestly besought that our cause should be referred to the auditors of the *Ruota*. Then he, regarding me with distorted eyes, said: 'What! You appeal to other judges concerning what I do? Know you not that all justice and law are in my breast? I wish it to be so. Go away, all of you, and whither you please; I am Pope, and

(1) The duty of an Abbreviator is to make a minute of any papal decision, or of any reply which the Pope wishes to be sent in answer to a letter, and to prepare the needed document in official form.

(2) His proper name was Sacchi, but he adopted the name Platina from the Latin designation of his native town, Piadena, near Cremona. After the accession of Sixtus IV. in 1471, Platina was made prefect of the Vatican Library, and from that time he probably enjoyed a sufficiency of this world's goods; for Jovius informs us that he bequeathed to Pomponius Lætus an elegant mansion with costly gardens, in which laurel crowns were to be bestowed on those members of the Academy whom their brethren should deem worthy of such honor.

(3) Platina omits to state that Paul II., before dismissing the Abbreviators, restored to them the sums which, in accordance with the detestable custom of the time, they had paid for their offices. Constitution "*Divina*" of Sixtus IV., "*Bullar.*," vol. I., const. 16.

can do or undo what I will.' Having heard this cruel sentence, we continued to labor day and night, begging every vile courtier to assist us in procuring another audience with the Pontiff. We were all outraged and dismissed, like so many outlaws and excommunicated persons. For twenty consecutive nights— because nearly all business was conducted at night—we labored in vain. Being unable to bear such ignominy, I resolved to do by writing what I and my companions could not effect by an audience. I therefore wrote a letter in almost these words: 'If it is just for you, without hearing us, to despoil us of what we have properly and legitimately bought, we ought to be allowed to complain of the injustice done to us. Since we have been so outrageously and contemptuously dismissed by you, we shall request the kings and princes to call a Council, before which you must answer for having deprived us of our legitimate possession.'" When the Pope had read this letter, he ordered that Platina should be arrested and imprisoned.

Perhaps it would have been better if the Pope had merely smiled at Platina's ridiculous menace ; for the friends of the discarded officials now affected to regard the insolent scribe as a martyr to learning. After four months Platina obtained his release through the intercession of Cardinal di Gonzaga ; and Paul seems to have soon forgiven the humanist's audacity, for we find the latter delivering an oration before the Pope and cardinals in 1468 (1). But the misfortunes of Platina were not at an end. At this time there flourished at Rome an academy composed mainly of those humanists whom the prodigal generosity of Pope Nicholas V. had attracted from all parts of Italy, and even from distant lands. The chief of this society was the famous Julius Pomponius Lætus, who had been a pupil of Lorenzo Valla. Most of the members had belonged to the College of the Abbreviators. The love of these academicians for antiquity was so fanatical that most of them had exchanged their family and baptismal names for fictitious ones taken from the ancient Romans and Greeks (2).

(1) This oration is given by Bzovius, y. 1468, no. 2.

(2) Pomponius was wont to genuflect before an altar dedicated to Romulus, although he used to lead his scholars to a sanctuary of the Madonna on the Quirinal, and certainly died an edifying death. While De Rossi was prosecuting his investigations in the Catacombs of St. Sebastian at Rome, he found among the names of those who had visited this holy spot in

The seditious letter of Platina had naturally rendered Pope Paul II. suspicious of all the humanist's companions in the Academy. Their sessions may have been innocent of any political or really heterodox intent, but many of the academicians bore an equivocal reputation for morality ; and all were almost pagan in their worship of antiquity. "Paul II. is accused," says Cantù, "of having persecuted the restorers of classic studies; but I am inclined to sympathize with him if he was dismayed on seeing paganism manifesting itself not only in the fine arts, but in doctrine and in the lives of men; on beholding these men, ashamed of their baptismal names, changing Pietro into Pierio, Giovanni into Jovianus, Marino into Glaucus ; on learning that they revived the feasts of antiquity, sacrificing a fig-pecker, and, under pretence of honoring Plato, giving forth impious or theurgic doctrines,—things which some may regard as trivial, but which may lead to more serious ones."

Our Pontiff would probably not have interfered directly with the academicians, had he not been led to believe that they contemplated his deposition. The carnival of 1469 was being celebrated with great splendor, and, as usual in this reign, at the expense of the Pope, when it was reported that, under the leadership of Callimachus (Philip Buonaccorsi), a revolution had been planned ; one Luke Tozzi, a notorious demagogue, who had been exiled, had been seen in the forests of Velletri at the head of a band of malcontents, and had avowed his intention of aiding the conspirators ; a letter of Pomponius Lætus to Platina had been intercepted, in which the latter was styled " Most Holy Father." Immediately many citizens and several of the court were arrested ; most of the academicians, among them Callimachus, fled in time ; but Platina and a few others were captured. Pomponius was at this time in Venice, and his extradition was demanded and granted. On the trial it was shown that the flattering epithet applied by Pomponius to Platina had been used only in play; it was

the fifteenth century that of Pomponius Lætus, expressed in this curious fashion, " In the reign of Pom., supreme Pontiff " ; and even thus, " Pomponius, supreme Pontiff, all-worthy priest (*pantagathos sacerdos*) of the Roman Academy " ; which titles, remarks Cantù (*Heretics of Italy*, disc. ix., note 33), would indicate an established hierarchy in the suspected society, and again draw suspicion on Pomponius.

proved that Tozzi had not left Naples; in fine, it appeared that no conspiracy had been formed. After a detention of one year the accused were liberated (1); but, in good or bad faith, the humanists called on posterity to pity them for their sufferings in the cause of learning. We have said that it would appear that no conspiracy had really been formed in the Roman Academy against Paul II. But it is almost, if not quite, certain that at least Callimachus was guilty of treasonable designs against the Pontiff. Palma cites a work entitled *Memorials of Cremonese Extant in Rome*, written by a learned Dominican, Vairani, in 1778, which contains all the letters written by Platina during his incarceration. Among these is one to a certain Lucidus, in which occur expressions which indicate that Callimachus had often uttered seditious sentiments in the Academy and that Platina had feared their consequences. If Palma judges correctly, we may easily account for the severity of Paul II. toward the academicians.

Impartial judges, such as the Cardinal of Pavia, certainly blamed Paul II. for having been too credulous in lending an ear to the accusations against the academicians; but the sole testimony of the aggrieved Platina is not sufficiently weighty to induce us to believe that this Pontiff was actuated by a hatred or contempt of letters. It was during this Pontificate that the art of printing was introduced into Rome, and its rapid development shows that Paul II. did not regard it with disfavor. Then appeared editions of Cicero's *Letters*, his " *Officia*," the *Paradoxes*, the books on *Friendship* and on *Old Age*, the *Bible*, the *Letters* of St. Jerome, the works of St. Cyprian, of St Leo I., the *Commentaries* of Cæsar, Livy, Virgil, Ovid, Annœus, Lucanus, Silius Italicus, Julius Calphurnius; the elder Pliny, Quintilian, Suetonius, Aulus Gallicus, Apuleus, Alcinous, Strabo, the *Cosmography* of Ptolemy, the *Antiquities* of Denis of Halicarnassus, and an immense number of less important works. Most of these editions are

---

(1) James of Bergamo, Trithemius, and Campi assert that Platina was kept in prison until the death of Paul II.; but in September, 1469, Cardinal Ammanati addressed a letter to our humanist, then at the baths of Petriola in the territory of Siena. (See *Epist. Card. Pap.*. no. 330.) Platina had contracted rheumatism in prison, and the Pope allowed him to visit these baths, Cardinal Bessarion going his security. Returning to Rome, he was never again disturbed by Paul; and the accession of Sixtus IV. greatly benefited him.

dedicated to Paul II. by John Andrew di Bussi, bishop of Alicia; and in his prefaces this editor declares that the typographic art owes its great progress in Rome to the liberality of that Pontiff (1). He could not have hated or despised letters who encouraged George of Trebizond, Theodore Gaza, Bartholomew Sicco, Filelfo, Flavius Blondus (2); who promoted many persons merely because they were learned (3); who sought among the poor for youths inclined to study, and himself defrayed the expenses of their education (4). Writing to Theodore Gaza, Filelfo says: "Immortal thanks are due to Paul for having recalled the Muses to the Roman court after a long exile;" and in a letter to Leonard Dathus, he says: "What do not I and all learned men owe to the great wisdom of Paul II.?" In another letter to Gaza, Filelfo declares that under Pope Paul "the Roman court was the sole refuge of learning and eloquence."

The artistic tastes of Paul II. utterly preclude the possibility of his having been a foe to letters; such refinement is incompatible with a hatred, or even a distaste, for learning. The immense sums which he lavished on architects, painters, and goldsmiths (5), and which form an argument for those who accuse him of ostentation, do not indicate the barbarian. He had collected, from far and wide, an immense number of manuscripts, and he gave much time to their study. He was a thorough connoisseur in sculpture and painting, and as a numismatist he was unrivalled. He is thought to have been the first to form a collection of medals. Both as cardinal and as Pope, his greatest pleasure seemed to be the exhibition of his archæological treasures to an amateur. Gaspar of Verona tells us that Paul had studied numismatics so profoundly, that by a cursory glance he could discover under what emperor an ancient medal had been produced. Does the reader deem it probable that such a man was illiterate, or a foe to learning in others?

It is safe to assert that much of the odium accruing to the Pontificate of Paul II. is to be traced to that event of his

---

(1) CHRISTOPHE; loc. cit.

(2) GASPAR OF VERONA.; b. III.; in Muratori, vol. III., pt. 2.—FILELFO; Epist., b. XXIII.

(3) CANENSIUS; passim.   (4) Gaspar; loc. cit.   (5) Idem, b. I.

early reign which cast a shadow over its whole course. **The**
reader has seen that, in accordance with a custom then for
some time in vogue, but afterward happily abolished, Cardinal Barbo, as well as all his brethren of the Sacred College,
signed a certain agreement at the commencement of the Conclave. The final clause, as we have remarked, was certainly
most humiliating to the head of the Church, but nevertheless
Barbo accepted it. Scarcely, however, had he been crowned,
when he manifested a design to cast aside the yoke imposed
upon him. Cardinal Ammanati, bishop of Pavia, then the
most renowned member of the Sacred College, who energetically resisted the abrogation of the compromise, narrates the
event in his *Commentaries* (1). Among the referendaries of
the court were two very learned and experienced prelates,
Stephen Nardi, archbishop of Milan, and Theodore Lelio, bishop of Treviso, whom even Ammanati praises as men of decided merit. These prelates reminded the Pontiff that the
right to govern the Church belonged to him, not to the cardinals, and urged him to cancel the obnoxious agreement. It
is for the canonist, not the historian, to decide whether the
promise of a cardinal can bind a Pope; but we may well ask
whether the abrogation in question was expedient. By this
revocation, Paul II. not only wounded the feelings of the cardinals, but subjected himself to the imputation of favoring
the abuses against which, generally speaking, the compromise
was directed. Nor did he boldly announce that he cancelled
the obnoxious agreement as injurious to the Church; he
simply declared the articles useless, and presented some
others to each cardinal, separately, demanding his signature
to them. Some yielded to promises, others to threats; a
few remained firm in refusal for a time, but at length they allowed the necessity for concord to influence them. Carvajal, a
Spanish cardinal, alone persisted, saying to the Pontiff that
he "had never, even in his youth, changed his mind without
reason, and he would not do so in his old age." From this
time there was a constant coolness between Paul II. and the
Sacred College. The cardinal of Avignon went so far as to
say to his Holiness: "For twenty-four years you have stud-

(1) These form a sequel to the *Commentaries* of Pius II.

ied how to finally deceive us " (1).   As to the tenor of the new laws, it is impossible to judge ; the Pontiff prohibited the cardinals to keep a copy of them (2).   Cardinal Quirini contends that Paul II. acted prudently in this matter (3).   Perhaps he simply wished to revenge upon the Sacred College the humiliations inflicted on the Papal authority.   The latter view is fortified by the fact that, having procured the retractations of the cardinals, the Pontiff never sought to avail himself of the abrogation of the compromise to exercise more latitude in governing.

<hr />

CHAPTER XI.

POPE SIXTUS IV. AND THE CONSPIRACY OF THE PAZZI.

Pope Paul II. having died on July 25, 1471, nineteen cardinals entered into Conclave on Aug. 6.   After some skirmishing among the partisans of Orsini, Ammanati, Bessarion, and d'Estouteville, the requisite two-thirds of the votes were ready for Bartholomew Roverella, archbishop of Ravenna; but before proceeding to the ballot, Orsini, Gonzaga, and Roderick Borgia demanded from the archbishop certain favors as the price of their adhesion.   Roverella returned the reply which has been erroneously attributed to Bessarion, that such trafficking would displease God, and that if elected, he would perform his full duty, untrammelled by any previous engagement (4).   Then Orsini, Gonzaga, and Borgia turned their attention to the cardinal Francis della Rovere, whose scruples did not forbid the required concessions, and on Aug. 9, Sixtus IV. ascended the throne of St. Peter (5).   Historians differ as to the rank of this Pontiff's family ; Panvini draws his descent from a very ancient and noble family of Piedmont which moved to Savona about the year 700.   Francis was born at Savona in 1414, and from his early childhood was remarkable for studious habits.   Having joined the Franciscans, he became distinguished as a theologian and philosopher.   For

(1) *Epistles* of Ammanati, no. 182.   (2) *Commentaries* of Ammanati, b. II.
(3) *Loc. cit.*, ch. ii.
(4) VESPASIANO ; *Life of Bart. Roverella*, in the *Spicilegium* of Card. Mai.
(5) *Epist. of James, card. Pav.*, no. 395 and 534.—BZOVIUS ; y. 1471, no. 2.

several years he taught in Padua, Bologna, Pavia, Florence, and Siena; and it was said that there was scarcely a man of note in Italy who had not profited by his lectures. Among his frequent auditors was Bessarion, who submitted all his writings to the revision of the judicious professor. After assisting four successive generals in the government of his Order, and having filled the office of general for some years, Friar Francis was enrolled in the Sacred College by Paul II. in 1467. As cardinal he conducted his household as though he was ruling a convent; all his leisure was devoted to study, and few historians do not praise the virtues which he manifested at that period of his life (1).

At the commencement of his reign Sixtus IV., like his predecessor, had two great objects at heart; namely, a Crusade against the Islamites, and the extinction of Hussitism. In order to actuate the first, he endeavored to cement the peace of Europe; sending preachers through Italy, and despatching legates to France, Spain, Poland, and Germany. Failing to unite the other powers, he collected from his own dominions, Naples, and Venice, a fleet of 112 galleys; and in 1472 he sent them to the East under command of the Neapolitan cardinal, Oliver Caraffa, and the Venetian admiral, Mocenigo. These commanders were instructed to co-operate with the Persian monarch, Uzum-Cassan, a mortal enemy of Mahomet II. But Mocenigo contented himself with ravaging the coasts of Asia-Minor, and with the pillage of Smyrna. The Persian became discouraged, owing to want of artillery, and abandoning his intention of besieging Mahomet II. in Constantinople, returned to his own land. In 1480 a formidable army of Turks captured Otranto, killing one half of its inhabitants; and again Pope Sixtus made superhuman efforts to stem the torrent which threatened to engulf Europe. Setting the example of self-abnegation, he forgot the injuries he had received from the Florentines, raised the interdict under which he had placed their capital, and soon completed the pacification of Italy. A league of all the Italian states was formed, the Turkish squadrons were dispersed, and Otranto retaken.

(1) PANVINI: *Life of Sixtus IV.*—FILELFO: *Letter to Sixtus IV.*, in b. XXXIII.— PIGNA; *Princes of Este*, b. VIII.—VESPASIANO; *Life of Bessarion.*

In order to eradicate Hussitism from Bohemia, Sixtus absolved its people from their allegiance to Vladislaus, and confirmed Matthias Corvinus of Hungary as their sovereign. Zealous for the purity of the faith, he condemned the doctrine of Peter de Osma, a theologian of Salamanca, who denied the divine institution of Sacramental Confession, and asserted that sorrow alone is necessary for forgiveness. Several errors tarnish the record of Sixtus IV., but no one will refuse him one glory—that of having restored modern Rome. He might have repeated the boast of Augustus, that he had found a Rome of bricks, but left one of marble. Rome owes to him, among innumerable other works, the beautiful bridge still called the *ponte Sisto ;* the acqueduct of the *vergine ;* the reconstruction and endowment of the finest hospital in the world, that of Santo Spirito; the elegant church and Augustinian convent of Sta. Maria del Popolo ; the restoration of the Lateran Basilica ; the Sistine Chapel in the Vatican.

The memory of few Pontiffs has been more bitterly attacked than that of Sixtus IV. Machiavelli says that he "was the first to show what (evil) a Pontiff could effect, and how many things, hitherto called errors, could be hidden under the cloak of Pontifical authority" (1). Infessura is virulent in regard to Sixtus. Even Muratori deems it proper to say that although this Pontiff "left beautiful traces of himself in Rome, which owes many of its ornaments to him, and although many of his qualities and virtues would have gained for him the name of a good Pontiff," nevertheless his excessive love for his relatives "led him to actions which have tarnished his memory not a little, and have caused the good to hope there will be no more Popes like him" (2). And the impartial Cantù thus summarizes the demerits of Sixtus : "He lavished benefices, bishoprics, principalities, dignities, and offices on his nephews, Riario and Della Rovere. Raphael Sansoni, made a cardinal when seventeen years old, had a train of sixteen bishops. The silly Peter Riario, legate for all Italy, had a court of five hundred persons. He founded the lordship of Imola for Jerome Riario, and designed for him a greater one in the Romagna ; but finding resistance in the Medici, he entered into

(1) *Florentine History,* b. VII.   (2) *Annals of Italy,* y. 1474.

the conspiracy of the Pazzi, and excommunicated Lorenzo for not allowing himself to be killed. He humored Venice so long as he hoped to find her an instrument for his nepotistic ambitions; then abandoning her, he allied himself with her enemies, the king of Naples and the duke of Ferrara, and placed her under an interdict. ... Machiavelli says that 'this ambitious mode of proceeding caused him to be more *esteemed* by the princes of Italy, and they all sought his friendship,' but the truth is that his shameless nepotism dishonored the Church, and his abuse of censures caused them to lose their terrors" (1). Panvini, who, probably more than any other author, is disposed to praise every action of every Pope, or at least to pass in silence over what he cannot approve, devotes considerable space to an enumeration of the shortcomings of Sixtus IV., and among other faults, he narrates that "as the many wars of this Pontiff entailed a great want of money, he was the first Pope to invent new offices for the purpose of selling them. He restored the Abbreviators, created by Pius II., and suppressed by Paul II., and he sold their positions at a very high price. He did the same with the offices of the solicitors. He also introduced the Janizaries, Stradiotes, and Mamelukes, but they were abolished by Innocent VIII. Sixtus was the first to sell the offices of procurator of the Chamber, of apostolic notary, of prothonotary of the Capitol, of notary of studies, of salt-weigher, and of chamberlain of the city. He invented new taxes, and increased the old ones. And not without stain of avarice, he exacted tithes from the prelates." And then Panvini quaintly tries to palliate these faults: "However, it seems to me that these things should be attributed to necessity, or rather to his relations and ministers, especially since there never was a Pontiff with a more generous soul, one more ready to benefit others" (2).

The nepotism of Sixtus IV. is indefensible; but when this Pontiff is charged with having instigated the attempted murder of Lorenzo dei Medici, and with unjustifiable severity

---

(1) *Univ. Hist.*, b. XXI.

(2) *Lives of the Pontiffs*, Venice, 1557.—The student will probably agree with Panvini when he says that "although Sixtus built churches and hospitals, improved streets and roads, repaired the walls, erected bridges, introduced the *acqua vergine* into the city, and had the intention of enlarging and fortifying the Vatican, nevertheless Rome owes him more for his generous and magnificent reorganization of the Vatican Library."

toward the Florentines in the matter of the interdict launched against them, we are not compelled to silence. Roscoe assumes the complicity of Sixtus in the conspiracy of the Pazzi to be certain; but it is well to note that this author betrays his animus against Sixtus at the very beginning of his notice of the Pontiff's reign, and by an unworthy misrepresentation. He says that "his knowledge of theology and the Canon law had not conciliated the favor of the populace; for during the spendid ceremony of his coronation, a tumult arose in the city, in which his life was endangered;" and he cites Muratori (*Annals*, y. 1471) as a support for this insinuation that the Romans hated the new Pope. Now Muratori simply states that "during the magnificent function there arose such a tumult among the populace, that he ran the risk of his life, being hit with several stones." The annalist does not tell us the cause of the tumult, nor does he at all imply that it was owing to any aversion to Sixtus. But we do learn from Ciac-conius, from Infessura, from Novaes, and from Panvini, that the tumult arose from the anger of the crowd on being too roughly pressed back by the Papal cavalry; that stones were thrown at the soldiers, and some struck the Pope's litter; that the influence of Cardinal Orsini soon restored order. When Roscoe so grossly misinterprets this incident, we are not surprised on finding Sixtus IV. represented by him as perfectly cognizant of, and approving the intention of the conspirators to murder Lorenzo. The English author agrees with Voltaire in regarding as "a proof of the political atheism of the times," this terrible event—"a transaction in which a Pope, a cardinal, an archbishop, and several other ecclesiastics, associated themselves with a band of ruffians to destroy two men who were an honor to their age and country; and purposed to perpetrate their crime at a season of hospitality in the sanctuary of a Christian church, and at the very moment of the elevation of the Host, when the audience bowed down before it, and the assassins were presumed to be in the immediate presence of their God." That the reader may the more fully understand this matter, we shall subjoin a brief narrative of the conspiracy, taking as our guide an author who is never deterred by sympathy from blaming the Roman Pontiffs when

he deems such action to be required by historical truth;
namely, Muratori (1).

The Pazzi were a powerful Florentine family, long envious
of the Medici. Francis dei Pazzi, treasurer of the Pope,
found that Jerome Riario, nephew of Pope Sixtus, hated Lorenzo intensely, because he had seen that this personage was
hostile to his aggrandizement when he became lord of Imola,
and because he anticipated trouble with the Medici after the
death of Sixtus. "From what can be gathered from subsequent events," says Muratori, "the old Pontiff allowed himself to be drawn by this wicked man into the dark design of
the Pazzi, and the more easily because not only he, but also
King Ferdinand (of Naples), was disgusted with Lorenzo dei
Medici, on account of his league with the Venetians and the
duke of Milan; and both hoped that if the Medici fell and the
Pazzi prevailed, Florence would unite with them." Francis
dei Pazzi was sure of the co-operation of Francis Salviati,

(1) Muratori has often been blamed for the freedom of his criticisms, and for the very
independent manner in which he sometimes judges the actions of the Holy See in temporal
matters. But a correspondence between Benedict XIV. and this author shows that the Holy
See itself did not regard his sentiments as condemnable, whatever the intrudingly officious and
self-appointed censors of Muratori may have thought. The grand-inquisitor of Spain having
placed the works of Cardinal Noris on the Index in 1747, Pope Benedict XIV. condemned this
action, and in a letter dated July 31, 1748, he told the inquisitor that the writings of great men
were not to be prohibited, when they contained some displeasing things, unless these things
affected faith or religion. Even Muratori, he said, had written some reprehensible things.
When Muratori heard this, he wrote to the Pontiff the following letter, which Catalani copied from a MS. in the Minerva Library at Rome, and inserted in his first *Preface* to Muratori's
Annals of Italy: "With all resignation and humility I learn from common report what your
Holiness, in a letter to the inquisitor-general of Spain, has said concerning me; and not
only from common report, but from the very words of your Holiness communicated to me,
I learn that while one of your hands wields thunderbolts, the other emits rays of great clemency. Nevertheless, I find myself in extreme confusion—nay, desolation—for this utterance,
so fatal to me, will last forever, and my contemporaries and posterity cannot forget that I
have been condemned, though with no formal condemnation; and they may believe my mistakes and demerits greater than they really are. In this too evident misfortune I have no
other comfort than the certainty that the paternal heart of your Holiness still warms toward your
unfortunate son. Animated, therefore, by this confidence, I take courage to prostrate myself
at your holy feet, and to implore the favor that your Holiness will deign to command that I be
informed of what is worthy of censure in my writings, so that I may retract it, and thus hope
to obtain pardon through my obedience. Thus then a cure will come from the same hand
that inflicted the wound, and I will not be exposed to the attacks of any one who might have
a heart less charitably disposed toward me than is that of your Holiness. May your great
charity—I almost say, your justice—be moved to grant this restorative to my poor name!
Kissing your holy feet with the most profound veneration, I resign myself, etc." Pope Benedict XIV. replied to this letter, assuring Muratori that in the letter to the Spanish inquisitor
he had complained, regarding our author, only of some passages concerning the temporal
doings of the Popes; that such passages, if written by some other person, might have been
censured; but that he was persuaded that an honorable man ought not to be troubled because

archbishop of Pisa (1); and by order of the Pope, Cardinal
Raphael Riario left Pisa for Florence with the title of legate,
and with orders to do whatever Salviati should suggest. A
Papal general, John Francis, was to lead two thousand men
to the aid of the conspirators, if necessary. The plot culmi-
nated on April 26th in the cathedral of Florence, and at the
moment of the elevation of the Sacred Host (2). Cardinal
Julian dei Medici, who had accompanied his brother and Cardinal Riario, was killed; but Lorenzo merely received a slight
wound in the throat, and fleeing to the sacristy, succeeded in
barring the door and detaining the assassins until help arrived. At once the entire population took to arms in favor
of the Medici. "Before the attempt, the archbishop of Pisa
had gone to the magisterial palace, to be ready to seize it on
the death of Lorenzo; but he was seized by the attendants of
the gonfaloniere at the first news of the attack, and, together
with a son of the historian Pozzo, was hung out of one of the
windows." Francis dei Pazzi was soon captured, and hung
by the side of Salviati; afterward other members of the family
of Pazzi met the same fate, and it was shared by about seventy of their followers (3). Cardinal Riario insisted that he

he thought differently from himself in matters not pertaining to dogma or discipline.—The
reader may be interested in the fact that a similar experience befell the great historian Cantù.
In his *Heretics of Italy* (disc. 31, note 7) he says: "That shameless thing which is called public opinion had rumored that the *Universal History* of Cantù was the work of a number of
Jesuits, he giving only the form and his name. On the other hand, the Jesuits blamed him
severely, in private and in public; therefore he begged that some of them would examine his
work, and indicate the errors, so that he might correct them in subsequent editions. The
charitable task was begun; then, perhaps because the size of the harvest frightened the pious
annotator, it was thought proper to send the notes to the Congregation of the Index rather
than to the author. Privately informed of this, Cantù declared that he submitted to any decision that the Holy See might pronounce, but that, in accordance with the Constitution of
Benedict XIV., he asked to be informed, and to be allowed to defend himself. After a long
time, which implies a minute investigation, he received notice that 'the Sacred Congregation, after mature examination, had been convinced that in the *Universal History* there are,
here and there, inexactnesses and also erroneous propositions; but in consideration of the
vast extent of the work, the many editions, the beautiful pages it contains, the rectitude of
the author, ... having regard to the Benedictine Constitution, the Congregation declares that
the said *History* be not condemned, although there are in it erroneous judgments which the
author himself, with his good sense and erudition, will perceive.' Accompanying this decision, on Sept. 7, 1860, the Cardinal-prefect of the Sacred Congregation congratulated the author
because he had not been attracted 'to that anti-papal and perhaps anti-Catholic party, which
furnishes the most noisy rewards. He has known how to keep himself at such a distance
from it, that he will never receive its applause.'"

(1) The magistrates of Florence had refused to allow Salviati to take possession of his see—
a plainly schismatical act. NARDI; *Hist. Flor.*, b. I.

(2) RAPHAEL VOLAT.; *Geog.*, b. V.—*Diary of Parma.*

(3) GIUSTINIANI; *History of Genoa*, b. V.

was unaware of the plot, "and probably he spoke the truth; he was afterward set at liberty, that the Pope might not be more angered. When the news of this horrible deed reached Rome, the Pontiff, finding it different from what he had desired, grew very angry at the Florentines, and under the pretext that Lorenzo and the magistrates of Florence had committed a too enormous crime in taking the life of an archbishop, in retaining a cardinal-legate in prison, and in having, before these events, given aid to the enemies of the Church, he launched against them all the excommunications and curses of heaven, and interdicted their city." Sixtus now declared war on Florence, and "sequestrated the property of the innocent Florentines who were in Rome;" but Louis XI. of France, the regency of Milan, the Venetians, Duke Hercules of Ferrara, Malatesta of Rimini, and other princes pronounced in favor of the republic. The emperor Frederick III. and Matthias of Hungary besought the Pope to make peace with the Christian state, and turn his arms to the defence of Christendom, every day more threatened by the Islamites. "They spoke to a deaf man; the heart of the Pope was influenced more by the ambitious policy of his nephew, Count Jerome, and of King Ferdinand, than by any reflection worthy of his office. ... Behold, then, to what extremes the Popes of that time allowed themselves to be brought by that nepotism from which we have seen certain wise Pontiffs of our time so exempt, and from which the glorious reign of the present Pope, Benedict XIV., is pre-eminently free." Such is the picture of the temporal side of the Pontificate of Sixtus IV. which we must accept as substantially correct. Were we disposed to avail ourselves of the *tu quoque* argument, we might palliate the action of Sixtus in fomenting rebellion in the states of his enemy and in aiding such rebellion by every means in his power; such statecraft has always been familiar to rulers, and never more so than at the present day. But granting the heinousness of such procedure on the part of a Pope-King, we turn our attention to the question of this Pontiff's cognizance and approbation of the design to assassinate the Medici.

Roscoe assumes this complicity as certain ; but if we may

credit the sworn deposition of John Baptist de Montesicco, the Pontiff was innocent of any murderous intent.   This
Montesicco was a *condottiere* in the Papal service, to whom the
conspirators had assigned the task of stabbing Lorenzo, but
who refused to commit such a deed in a church, and was replaced by one Anthony Maffei of Volterra, and by a wretched
priest, Stephen of Bagnone.   When the attempt had miscar-
ried, Montesicco was seized ; and before he was beheaded, he
was tortured to make him reveal all he knew concerning the
conspiracy (1).   According to his avowal, the intention of the
conspirators to subvert the power of the Medici was communicated to Sixtus by Jerome Riario, Montesicco, and James
Salviati, brother of the archbishop of Pisa ; and when they
remarked that such a project could not be actuated without
the death of Lorenzo and of Julian, the Pope exclaimed : "I
desire the death of no person, for any consideration ; one in
my office should compass the death of no one.   Although
Lorenzo is a villain, and treats us foully, I merely wish for a
change in the government; I do not want his death."   Then
Jerome replied that they would do what they could to content his Holiness, but that the Pope would pardon anything
reprehensible in the manner of the deed, when the object
was once attained.   Sixtus became indignant, and cried out :
"You are a beast.   I tell you that I want no death—only a
change of government."   The conversation continued, and Jerome often alluded to the possible death of Lorenzo ; but the
Pope constantly protested against it, and when the conspirators were departing, he said : "Go.   Do what you will, but
let there be no death !"   It is not improbable that Jerome, in
order to encourage his accomplices, so distorted the Pope's
approbation of the subversion of the Medici government, as
to make it appear that he consented to the assassination of
Lorenzo and his brother (2).

As for the severity of Sixtus IV. toward Florence, it was

(1) His testimony is given in the notes to the *Commentary on the Conspiracy of the
Pazzi,* by Angelo Poliziano, edit. Adimari, Naples, 1769.

(2) BRUTI ; *Hist. Flor.,* b. VI.—An old MS. entitled *The City of Florence,* in the Magliabecchi Library, states simply that Sixtus IV. and Count Jerome wished to change the
Florentine Government.   Nerli, in his *Commentaries on the Civil Events in Florence
from 1215 to 1537,* b. III., says that Sixtus wished to remove the Medici from the government, and to restore liberty to Florence.

in accordance with the letter and spirit of the Canons. If
the reader thinks that the Pontiff's connection with the attempt to revolutionize Florence, and the evident guilt of the
criminal, ought to be regarded as justifying the execution of
Archbishop Salviati, in spite of both the Canon and the civil
law; that the slaughter of many innocent followers of the
Pazzi and Salviati families, some of them ecclesiastics, ought
to be laid to the account of the unreasoning and irresponsible
mob: even then, Pope Sixtus IV. had good reason for launch-
ing an interdict against Florence and for waging war against
the Medici.   In the first place, there was the matter of Vitelli, lord of Città di Castello, a fief of the Holy See.   This baron, ambitious of becoming an independent prince (1), had
rebelled, and had been succored by Florentine troops.   Again,
the Medici had incited Charles of Montone to seize Perugia;
they had given hospitality and encouragement to the rebel
counts of Anguillara, who had warred on the Holy See during four successive Pontificates ; Florentine troops had attacked Cisterna, and Florentine vessels had ravaged the
Roman shores.   Such are some of the grievances which the
Pontiff narrates in the Bull in which he threatens an interdict against Florence (2), and any one of these would have
justified the punishment of the Medici.   But that which drove
Sixtus to the use of the interdict as a last resource was a
synod of the Tuscan clergy, which declared itself "a Council
met in the light of the Holy Ghost for the dissipation of the
Sixtine darkness," and which issued against the Pontiff a
diatribe of which even Roscoe says that "it is not in the
power of language to convey a more copious torrent of abuse,
than was poured out upon this occasion by the Florentine
clergy on the supreme director of the Roman Church."

A very prominent part in the contest between Sixtus IV.
and the Medici was played by the astute Louis XI. of France.
A brief sketch of this monarch's connection with the struggle
will serve to show the indomitable character and the diplo-

---

(1) Roscoe misrepresents the status of Vitelli, when he says that "the enmity of Sixtus to
Lorenzo had for some time been apparent, and if not occasioned by the assistance which
Lorenzo had afforded to Nicolo Vitelli and other *independent* nobles, whose dominions
Sixtus had either threatened or attacked, etc."

(2) Bull *Iniquitatis Filius*, in Raynald, y. 1478, no. 5.

matic ability of the Pontiff.   When Sixtus received the tiara, the legation of Avignon was in the hands of Charles de Bourbon, archbishop of Lyons, a prince of the blood-royal of France.   Very soon the cardinal Julian della Rovere was promoted to both the see and the legation, to the great displeasure of Louis, for, besides regarding the treatment of his relative as an insult to himself, the monarch was averse to Julian because that prelate had helped to influence René of Anjou to cede his county of Provence to the duke of Burgundy.   Julian added fuel to the flame by coming into collision with the seneschal de Beaucaire on the subject of certain rights which were not very precisely defined.   The king threatened to occupy Avignon, declaring that his predecessors had no right to countenance its purchase by the Holy See.   He went so far as to demand the execution of a decree of Constance, providing for a General Council every ten years; and he threatened, in case of the Pope's refusal, to convoke a national synod at Lyons by his own authority.   Although Louis was somewhat mollified by the elevation of Charles de Bourbon to the cardinalate, he manifested his aversion to Sixtus when the conspiracy of the Pazzi had failed.   Philip de Commines was sent to Lorenzo with three hundred men-at-arms, and assurances of the sympathy of Louis; and on Aug. 18, 1478, the king issued letters-patent to all the ecclesiastics in France, whether natives or foreigners, prohibiting all recourse to Rome for "expectatives," and all transportation of money from the kingdom.   He opened a national synod at Orleans in September of the same year, and all the royal complaints against Rome were there discussed; an embassy was also appointed which was to communicate the decisions of the prelates to his Holiness.   Sixtus IV. received the envoys on Jan. 27, 1479; and then he learned that Louis, moved by the prayers of Florence, Milan, Venice, and Ferrara, whom the Pontiff had attacked at the very moment when Mahomet II. was invading Italy, had determined to pacify the Peninsula.   Louis had held a national synod at Orleans, and this body had advised the Pope to lay down his arms, and to convoke a General Council to devise means of resisting the Turks.   To this speech Sixtus did not reply immediately; he requested the ambassadors to formulate their wishes in writing. This **was** done, and then it was found that Louis also demanded the punishment of all concerned in the conspiracy of the Pazzi, as well as the raising of the interdict in Florence, and the cessation of hostilities. If these conditions were not complied with, the king would appeal to a General Council, would compel all Frenchmen to abandon the Papal court, and would re-establish the *Pragmatic Sanction* in France. The reply of the Pontiff, also in writing, was singularly calm and firm. King Louis should presume that the Holy See did not act without reason, or without the advice of the wise personages who formed its council. His Royal Serenity gloried in his descent from Charlemagne; and he ought to imitate that prince, who never called his subjects from the Roman court, never spoke of a *Pragmatic Sanction*, never appealed to a General Council, but humbly submitted to the Apostolic decrees. The successors of St. Peter were obliged to render an account to no man; but out of deference to his Majesty, he would give certain explanations to the ambassadors. As to a General Council, it was not necessary to convoke one in order to decide whether the Florentines were justified in hanging an archbishop; both justice and ecclesiastical immunity had been violated by that action. Again, before calling a General Council, prudence would suggest that the emperor and other sovereigns should be consulted as to the opportuneness, the time, and the place; and above all, it should be remembered that it was the province of the Pope, not of this or that prince, to decide whether a Council should be convoked. Concerning the *Pragmatic Sanction*, the most serene king of France should reflect that here was a question involving his honor and his conscience. That *Sanction* was either just or unjust; if just, why had Louis abolished it? If unjust, why did he seek to restore it? So great a prince, thought Sixtus, should be more consistent. In fine, the Pontiff made no concessions to Louis XI.; in the very presence of the ambassadors, he reproached the bishop of Frejus, who had been his nuncio in France, for having referred the difficulty with Florence to the arbitration of the king; and then he indignantly dismissed the imprudent prelate.

But the capture of Otranto by the Turks caused Sixtus to show leniency to the Florentines ; and when, on Dec. 3, 1480, an embassy appeared before him, he received its members graciously and with great honor. They all knelt at the feet of the Pontiff, and in their name and that of their government, Louis Guicciardini confessed that Florence had sinned against the Church and its head, and begged for pardon. Then Sixtus replied: "We took measures against you with regret, and only because the honor of the Apostolic See demanded such measures. Now that you come to us in all humility, we accord you our favor, and absolve you from the sins you have confessed. Sin no more."

CHAPTER XII.

POPE INNOCENT VIII.

The mortal remains of Pope Sixtus IV. having been deposited in the basilica of the Apostles, twenty-five cardinals entered into Conclave on Aug. 26, 1484. The first care of the electors was to draw up a document which would serve as a rule of government for the coming Pontiff. One of the articles bound the new Pope to direct his energies to a reformation of the Roman court within three months after his coronation; by another he promised to call a General Council, in order to prepare a Crusade, and to correct many abuses in the Church (1). Only one cardinal, Peter Foscari, bishop of Padua, refused to sign this agreement. After some efforts in favor of Mark Barbo, a nephew of Paul II., the choice of the electors proved to be John Baptist Cibò, bishop of Melfi, and a native of Genoa, who assumed the name of Innocent VIII. The Cibò family was one of the most illustrious in Genoa, and for many hundred years had been prominent in the annals of the state; the father of our Pontiff, Aaron Cibò, had been viceroy of Naples for Alfonso of Aragon, and under Calixtus III. had been senator of Rome—then a very important office. John Baptist Cibò passed his youthful days at the Neapolitan court, but after the death of King Alfonso he en-

(1) BURCHARDT; *Diary.*

tered the University of Padua. After a few years we find him at Rome, enjoying the patronage of Cardinal Calendrini, a half-brother of Nicholas V. Paul II. made him bishop of Savona, and Sixtus IV. promoted him to the Sacred College and the see of Melfi.

Raphael of Volterra and Philip of Bergamo say that John Baptist Cibò had two natural children, Franceschetto and Teodorina Cibò, before his entrance into the ecclesiastical state. Ciaconius and Marino Sanuto state that he had been married. Panvini says that while in the Neapolitan court "a noble lady bore him two children called Francis and Teodorina, who were said to be legitimate, the mother dying at an early age." Ægidius of Viterbo mentions neither the marriage nor any illegitimate offspring. Muratori simply says that "before entering the ecclesiastical state Pope Innocent had some children, who were yet living." We are disposed to agree with Ciaconius and Sanuto, both because their authority is immeasurably superior to that of Raphael of Volterra and Philip of Bergamo, and because of intrinsic reasons, drawn from what is certainly known of Innocent VIII. In none of the circumstances of his life did the fact of his having children affect his good reputation; it did not prevent his becoming bishop of Savona under Paul II., who was most exact in probing the careers of all presented to him for preferment; it was not alleged as an argument against his elevation to the Papacy; finally, during his entire ecclesiastical life, his conduct was grave and almost severe in its moral tone (1).

Innocent VIII. was most affable in his manners, and of a most conciliatory disposition. In his funeral oration on our Pontiff, Leonello, bishop of Concordia, tells us that he was forgiving, simple, and modest. But all his contemporaries who have left memorials of his reign, agree in representing him as easily led by others. If Sixtus IV. was too determined, Innocent VIII. was deficient in the energy demanded by his

(1) Roscoe would allow his reader to suppose that there is no doubt concerning the illegitimacy of Cibò's children; and from his words one would not know whether these children were born while Cibò was a layman, or after he became an ecclesiastic. He simply says: " At the time of his elevation to the supremacy, he was about fifty-five years of age, and had several natural children." *Lorenzo dei Medici*, ch. vi.

evidently sincere desire to abolish abuses and to arouse the zeal of the clergy. Infessura says that Innocent was "personally good, ever intending justice, and had he not been thwarted by his rivals and enemies, he would undoubtedly have shown the real bent of his mind to the Church." One of Pope Innocent's first acts was to entreat the powers of Christendom to combine against Islamism ; reversing the policy of his predecessor, he expressed great admiration for Lorenzo dei Medici, and a sincere affection for his family. This change was due to a nephew of the late Pontiff, the cardinal Julian della Rovere, who had acquired the esteem of Innocent by his great talents and the ascendency of his character. Guid' Antonio Vespucci, writing to Lorenzo, advises him to write a good letter to this cardinal, for, he says, "he is Pope, and more than Pope" (1).

The most important event of this Pontificate was the struggle of Innocent with Ferdinand of Naples concerning the tribute due to the Holy See from that monarch as a vassal. Few historical facts are better established than that of the suzerainty of the Roman Pontiff over the Two Sicilies (2). Even though all other titles were wanting, the investitures repeated during a space of more than four hundred years before the time of Innocent VIII.—investitures asked for and received by the most powerful of the Neapolitan and Sicilian sovereigns—would have formed a just title for the Pontiffs. Even Muratori, who will never be accused of partiality toward the temporal claims of the Holy See, was so impressed by the evidence favoring Rome in this matter, that when speaking (at y. 1059) of the investitures granted by Pope Nicholas II. to Robert Guiscard, and supposing that the right in question originated in the once prevalent idea of the truth of Constantine's donation, he says : "We may believe that upon this foundation rests the origin of those rights which, from that day until our own, the Apostolic See has exercised over the Two Sicilies, where it enjoys so authentic a suzerainty by a prescription against which no argument whatever can be adduced." When Innocent VIII. received

(1) FABRONI ; *Life of the Magnificent Lorenzo dei Medici,* vol. I.
(2) See our dissertation on the *Deposing Power of the Pope,* in vol. II., p. 214.

the tiara, King Ferdinand trusted that since the youth of
John Baptist Cibò had been passed in the service of the house
of Aragon, and since he had received favors from King Alfonso, he would, now that he was Pontiff, reciprocate those
benefits and remit the customary tribute. The ambassadors
whom Ferdinand sent to congratulate Innocent on his elevation were instructed to dwell upon the fact that the royal
treasury had been depleted by the expenses contracted for
the recapture of Otranto, and that large sums were constantly
being spent in strengthening the kingdom against future ag-
gressions of the Turks. But the Pope insisted upon the
rights of the Holy See; and when, on Jan. 29, 1485, a second
embassy offered a white palfrey in sign of homage (1), he refused to accept it without the tribute. And Pope Innocent
VIII. had other causes of complaint against Ferdinand.
Philip de Commines tell us that this monarch " sold bishoprics, and to most unworthy persons; once he sold the bishopric of Tarento to a Jew for thirteen thousand ducats; on
another occasion he gave certain abbeys to a falconer on condition that he should keep a number of huntsmen and falcons
for the royal service " (2). Again, the harshness, vindictive-
ness, and treachery of Ferdinand to his subjects; the many
vices of his son Alfonso, duke of Calabria, of whom Commines
says no man was ever more cruel or wicked, had excited the
rage of the nobles, and they had already appealed to their lord-

---

(1) Sixtus IV. had consented to receive the palfrey and tender of homage, remitting the
tribute. Afterward, Julius II. decreed that on every eve or feast of SS. Peter and Paul the
king of the Two Sicilies should present to the Pope, " in recognition of the true, supreme,
and direct dominion of the Holy See over the kingdom of Sicily, and over all the territories
on this side the straits as far as the frontiers of the States of the Church, a tribute of 7,000
golden ducats and a gift of a splendidly caparrisoned palfrey." Though the amount of the
tribute varied, this custom was continued until 1788, when Ferdinand IV. ol Naples (of
Sicily, III.) offered the money, but not the homage. The formula of presentation of the
tribute was as follows: " NN, King of the Two Sicilies, of Jerusalem, etc., my sovereign lord,
presents to your Holiness, and I do so in his name this palfrey becomingly adorned, with
a tribute of 7,000 ducats for the kingdom of Naples. And I pray our Lord God that your Holiness may receive it again many years to the greater glory of our holy faith." The Pontiff
then replied: " We willingly receive and accept this tribute due to us and the Apostolic See
for the direct dominion of our kingdom of the Two Sicilies, on both sides of the straits; and
we beg the Lord (if the king was married, here followed a hope that he might have a numerous offspring). And to him, to his peoples and vassals, we impart the Apostolic benediction. In the name, etc." BORGIA; *History of the Temporal Dominion of the Apostolic See in the Two Sicilies*; Rome, 1789; no. 1509.

(2) *Memoires*; b. VII., c. ii.

paramount, the Pope (1). Finally, the barons held a Diet at Melfi, declared themselves free from their obligations to Ferdinand, and placed themselves at the disposal of the Holy See. Innocent then tendered the kingdom to René II., duke of Lorraine, whose Angevine ancestors had formerly ruled it. The revolted barons had already applied to Venice for aid, and that republic sent them a few thousand men under the famous general, Robert of San Severino. Lorenzo dei Medici now espoused the cause of Aragon; the duke of Milan followed his example; and the powerful family of Orsini joined the enemies of their sovereign. But the suspicious inactivity and, in all probability, the treachery of San Severino, prevented an energetic campaign. René, disappointed in his hopes of aid from Charles VIII. of France, who himself claimed a right to the Neapolitan crown, remained at home; and the Sacred College, supported by the complaints of the Romans, who suffered from the ravages of the duke of Calabria, besought Innocent to make peace. Accordingly, on Aug. 11, 1486, there was signed a treaty by which Ferdinand agreed to pay his homage and tribute of vassalage to the Holy See; to refrain from all nominations to benefices; and to not molest his barons for the course they had pursued (2). But Ferdinand soon violated this treaty; scarcely a month had elapsed, when his troops entered Aquila, and put the Papal representative to death. Many of the chief barons were imprisoned, and afterward ruthlessly slaughtered; the benefices of the kingdom were again put up for sale, and the tribute to Rome was refused. Even then, Innocent hoped for peace; he sent the bishop of Cesena to remonstrate with the king, but the prelate vainly sought an audience, and when he succeeded in intercepting Ferdinand on his way to the chase, the monarch answered that he would treat his barons as he saw fit, and ordering the huntsman's call to be sounded, he disappeared. Innocent bore this insult, and sought the mediation of the king of Castile, whose intercession, indeed, had been the main cause of the violated treaty. Nothing

---

(1) History of Aquila, in Muratori's Italian Antiquities, vol. VI.—MACHIAVELLI; Hist. Flor., b. VIII.—BRUTI; Hist. Flor., b. VIII.

(2) NANTIPORTO; Diary.—RAYNALD; y. 1486, no. 13.—GIANNONE; b. XXVIII., c. i.

came of this mediation, and finally, in Sept., 1489, Ferdinand
was deposed, and the Two Sicilies were pronounced to be in
the hands of the Roman Church, their suzerain. But the
Pontiff took no vigorous measures to enforce his rights;
though his decree produced the intended effect. Ferdinand
soon realized that though Innocent VIII. lacked the indomitable will of Sixtus IV., it would be very imprudent to leave
in the hand of an Angevine rival so powerful a weapon as a
Papal Bull declaring the vacancy of the Neapolitan throne.
In January, 1492, he made his submission to the Holy See;
he acknowledged the right of the Pontiff to tribute and homage; and promised to never again interfere in the collation of
benefices, and to indemnify the heirs of his slaughtered barons.   In return, the Pope revoked the decree of deposition,
and promised the future investiture of the kingdom to the
duke of Calabria.

   In 1487 Pope Innocent VIII. condemned certain propositions defended by the celebrated John Pico della Mirandola.
When only twenty-three years old, this philosopher and theologian had drawn from theology, physics, mathematics, magic,
and cabalistics, a series of nine hundred propositions, which
he offered to defend in Rome (y. 1486), "with all respect to
the authority of the Church." Some of these theses were
very unorthodox, but the young disputant protested that he
presented them only "for the sake of scholastic disputation,
and subject to the correction of the Apostolic See." About
four hundred of the propositions were taken from Latin, Egyp-
tian, Arabic, and Chaldaic philosophers; the others were
opinions of his own. No one appeared to attack the theses,
although Pico guaranteed all expenses of travel, etc. But the
learned were irritated by his daring, and they presented to the
Pope thirteen of the propositions as heretical, and after mature
examination they were condemned. Pico defended them in
several publications; and while, says Cantù, "we cannot derive a very clear notion of his meaning from his scholastic
jargon, his task may be regarded as an attempt to reconcile
Plato with Aristotle, and Pagan theology with the Mosaic and
Christian" (1). In his *Heptameron*, Pico says: "Moses and

(1) *Heretics of Italy*, disc. IX.

the Prophets, Christ and the Apostles, Pythagoras and Plutarch, and in general, all the priests and philosophers of the ancient world, veiled their knowledge under images, because the crowd could not appreciate the truth, and understood what the words by no means indicated. It is certain that Moses, in his enumeration of the six days, did not speak of the creation of the visible world (1). ... Christ confided, in secrecy, certain truths to His disciples, and the knowledge of these truths is the great foundation of our faith;" and this knowledge can be acquired, insisted Pico, only by means of the *Cabala*. "Who does not see," asks Cantù, "whither such eclecticism leads? If it was applauded by the Academies and by the Medicean court, where such things were fashionable, it could not please Rome; and although Pico repeatedly protested his submission to the Church, he really substituted himself for the Church when he defined and explained dogma by means of Hebrew or the *Cabala*." Innocent VIII. said of Pico : "Let him write poetry ; that is more consonant with his talent;" and although the Pontiff protected him from molestation, he would not withdraw his condemnation of the propositions. Pico very soon realized the vanity of merely human science, and devoted the latter years of his life to prayer and mortification. He recited the Office as though he were a priest, and as he himself tells us, he " day and night read those sacred pages which possess a celestial, vivid, and efficacious strength, which infuse divine love into the soul of the reader." He even thought of taking a crucifix in his hand, and

(1) " Man, according to this theory of Pico, is composed of a body and a reasoning soul, and of something intermediary which unites the two substances, and which physicists and philosophers call the spirit. Moses denominates the body slime; he calls the spirit, light; and he entitles the soul heaven, because it moves circularly, like the latter. The words of Moses, ' God created heaven and earth ... and there was evening and morning one day,' signify that God created the soul and body ; and as the spirit joined them, night and morning, or the darkening nature of the body and the luminous nature of the soul, gave origin to man. In the words of Moses, ' Let the waters that are under the heaven be gathered together into one place,' water represents the feeling faculty common to man and all animals. The gathering of the waters under heaven indicates the union of the corporeal senses in what Aristotle styles the *common sensorium*, whence they spread throughout the body. Moses places the sun, moon, and stars in heaven ; according to Pico, the sun signifies the soul soaring up to the spirit of God or the intellectual spirit ; the moon is the soul leveling itself to the plane of the senses ; the stars are the forms of the soul, the faculties of judging, etc. ... Supreme felicity consists in being re-united with God, after dropping all imperfections, which are the effect of plurality and complication."—BUHLE : cited by Cantù, *Univ. Hist.*, b. XIII., ch. xxx., note 9.

with bare feet preaching the love of Christ.   Finally, in 1493, Alexander VI. issued a Brief absolving Pico from any censures which he might have incurred.   The philosopher's last work was a defence, against the Jews, of St. Jerome's accuracy in translating the Psalms.   He had designed, says his equally celebrated nephew, John Francis Pico della Mirandola, who wrote an account of his uncle's life, to enter the Dominican Order ; and when he died in his thirty-second year, he was clad in the habit of that Order.

Some Protestant writers, seeking support for the theory that wine is not an essential matter for the Eucharist, have adduced, on the sole authority of Raphael of Volterra (1), the presumed fact that Innocent VIII. allowed the Norwegian clergy to consecrate the bread in the absence of wine.   The Catholic reader is probably aware that such a consecration would be grievously illicit, and perhaps invalid (2).   How, then, could Pope Innocent VIII. have granted such permission ?   It is evident that no such decree was issued.   In the first place, there exists no vestige of it, save in Raphael of Volterra.   Again, the reason assigned by this author for the admission of the exemption did not subsist.   He says that the reason was furnished by the Norwegian climate, which, he contends, causes wine either to freeze or to become vinegar.   This we know to be false ; and we also know that shortly after the time of the alleged decree the Norwegian reformers would allow no Communion unless the species of wine, as well as the species of bread, was employed.   If such a decree was really shown in the days of Raphael of Volterra (3), it must be classed among the many forgeries which our Pontiff detected and punished.   In 1489 it was discovered that there had been formed, among the officials of the various bureaus of the Apostolic Chancery, an association for the fabrication of false Bulls.   These documents were sold to the interested parties, who of course believed them to be genuine, and were willing to reward those to whose influence at court they supposed themselves indebted

(1) *Geography*, b. VII.

(2) Cardinal Lugo holds that if a priest *intends to consecrate only one species*, he acts invalidly, since he has received the power to consecrate the Holy Eucharist only *in sacrificiis*.—LIGUORI ;—*Opus Mor.*, b. VI

(3) He wrote the cited work about the year 1505.

for the favors presumably granted ; and the papers generally cost from one hundred to two thousand ducats. The chief forgers were one Dominick of Viterbo and one Francis Maldenti. Their property was confiscated, and although men high in power interceded for their lives, and their relatives offered to indemnify the losers, the culprits were hung, and their bodies given to the flames (1). If, therefore, there ever existed such a decree as that adduced by Raphael of Volterra, probably it owed its origin to these wretched men, and not to the Holy See.

CHAPTER XIII.

POPE ALEXANDER VI.

It is an almost general opinion that Pope Alexander VI. had neither the virtues which befit the Supreme Pontificate of Christendom, nor those of any ordinary man. His name is seldom mentioned without thoughts of simony, treachery, lust, avarice, and sacrilege. Other memories, long contemned and even accursed, have been rehabilitated ; but that of Alexander VI. remains, as yet, foul and detestable to a large number of Christians. Are we, therefore, to take for granted all that has been alleged against this Pontiff? Even Roscoe contends that " whatever have been his crimes, there can be no doubt but they have been highly overcharged. ... The vices of Alexander were accompanied, although not compensated, by many great qualities which, in the consideration of his character, ought not to be passed over in silence. Nor, if this were not the fact, would it be possible to account for the peculiar good fortune which attended him to the latest period of his life; or for the singular circumstance recorded of him : that during the whole term of his pontificate no popular tumult ever endangered his authority or disturbed his repose ?"

To Burkhard, master of ceremonies in the court of Alexander VI., we are indebted for most of the information which blackens the character of the Pontiff. But, granting that we possess the authentic work of Burkhard, which is very uncertain, of what weight is his authority? A master of cere-

(1) RAYNALD; y. 1490, no. 22.

monies in a royal court does not fill a position which would of itself imply a possession of accurate knowledge of the court's secrets. He may, at times, come into some kind of contact with great personages. His master, with that shadow of intimacy often affected with a superior servant, may condescend, now and then, to display good humor in his presence. A foreign ambassador, during the intervals of a tedious levee, may deign to gossip with him about unimportant matters. He may even be a great dignitary in the eyes of the lackeys on the staircase, or in the estimation of the dawdlers in the antechamber, and thus he may pick up a deal of tavern statecraft. His authority may be overwhelming when he decides on the proper color of a ribband, or even in a question of precedency. But his *Diary* can scarcely be regarded as testimony concerning the secrets of the court. Nor can we forget that until 1696 the *Diary* was known only by a fragment given by Godefroy in his *History of Charles VIII.*, published in 1684; and by some vague citations of Rinaldi in his continuation of Baronio. But in 1696 Leibnitz published at Hanover a quarto volume entitled *A Specimen of Secret History; or, Anecdotes of the Life of Alexander VI.; Extracts from the Diary of John Burkhard.* In his preface Leibnitz regrets that he could not find the text of Burkhard; but a few years afterward he thought that he had found the true text in a MS. given him by Lacroze, and would have published it had not death intervened. Eccard published the *Diary* at Leipsic in 1732, in his *Writers of the Middle Age*, following a Berlin MS., which may have been the one handed by Lacroze to Leibnitz. According to Eccard's own admission, this MS. was very defective (1), and the editor had frequent recourse to the extract of Leibnitz that order might be established. In Leibnitz there are articles which are wanting in Eccard, and toward the end the two become so dissimilar as to appear utterly different works. Eccard wished that some one would discover a good copy of the *Diary;* and finally Lacurne de

---

(1) Eccard adds that his edition contains the journal of the Pontificate of Alexander VI.; but this is an error, for even the extract of Leibnitz goes further back, commencing on Aug. 2, 1492, the day of Alexander's exaltation. The *Diary* given by Eccard begins four months later. The extract of Leibnitz goes as far as Aug. 3, 1503, while Eccard's finishes on Feb. 22d of the same year.

Sainte-Palaye found in the library of Prince Chigi at Rome a MS. in five quarto volumes, which seemed to contain the entire work,—beginning December 1, 1483 (the date of Burkhard's appointment as master of ceremonies), and ending May 31, 1506, a year after his death,—which fact demonstrates that the diarist had a continuator. In our day a third editor has appeared. Achille Gennarelli (Florence, 1855) has thought to produce the true text by uniting the dubious ones of Leibnitz and Eccard, and some other MSS. He admits, and most ingenuously, that he has filled up hiatuses with quotations from Summonte, Infessura, etc., etc (1).

Gregorovius (2), the latest Protestant historian to attack the memory of Alexander VI., has the assurance to say that the *Diary* of Burkhard " is, with the exception of the journal of Infessura, which ends at the commencement of 1494, the only work concerning the court of Alexander composed at Rome; and it has even an official (1) character. ... *He never repeats mere rumors.*" The *Diary* is before us, and there is scarcely a page where we do not read: " If I remember aright (*si recte memini*); " or " If the truth has been told me (*si vera sunt mihi relata*);" or "It is said (*fertur*)." Gregorovius opines that the apologists of the Holy See would feel less contempt for Burkhard, if they would consult the *Relations* of the Venetian ambassadors to their government. Well, Pasquale Villari, probably the most painstaking of all the editors of these *Relations*, is not such an apologist, and yet he says: " Doubts have been raised as to the authenticity of the *Diary* of Burkhard. New publications have lessened, but have not put an end to these doubts " (3). The German historian also presents the *Relation* of Polo Capello (ambassador at Rome from April, 1499, to September, 1500) as manifesting " the intrigues of the court of Alexander VI., the long series of crimes perpetrated therein, its exactions, the traffic in cardinals' hats, etc" (4). But, setting aside the numerous inexactnesses of

(1) It is the opinion of the abbé Clement (de Vebron) that all the weight of erudition displayed by Gennarelli does not add one particle more of authenticity to the *Diary*. See *The Borgias*; Paris, 1882.

(2) *Lucretia Borgia, according to Original Documents and Contemporary Correspondence,* 1876.

(3) See Villari's *Dispatches of Giustiniani,* vol. I., in preface. Florence, 1876.

(4) *Loc. cit.,* vol. I., p. 326.

this *Relation* of Capello, and not a few gross errors (1), we must regard it as of little value in the premises; since it was written not by Capello, but by the senator Marino Sanuto (2), who, while often furnishing us valuable historical documents, causes one to smile at his frequent credulity, and to hesitate to accept him as an authority (3).

After Burkhard, the great historian Guicciardini is the chief source of the accusations against Alexander VI.; Guicciardini, of whom even the arch-sceptic Bayle says that "he merits hatred" because of his partiality,—"a fault of gazetteers," but one "inexcusable in a historian;" whom even Voltaire regards as mendacious; and whose own conscience caused him, when asked on his death-bed what disposition should be made of his *History*, then still in manuscript, to reply: "Burn it." Cantù says of this author: "He regards the success, not the justice, of a cause. ... He not only examines and judges the Pontiffs as he does other rulers, but he always finds them in the wrong" (4). Capefigue (5) regards Guicciardini as "an impassioned colorist," who ever "breathes hatred of the Pope, the French, the Milanese, and Sforza. Florence, a city of pleasure, of libels, and of dissipation, loved the licentious tales of Boccaccio, the policy of Machiavelli, and

(1) For instance, it gives to Alexander a brother named Louis del Mila, while no such brother, but a cousin—John del Mila—existed. It narrates that Capello, before his departure from Rome on September 19, 1500, went to the Vatican to inform the Pontiff of the surrender of Rimini and Faenza; but Rimini did not fall until the end of October, while Faenza held out until the following April. It makes San Severino, instead of Ascanio Sforza, vice-chancellor of the Roman Church.

(2) An old law of Venice had obliged her ambassadors, after their term of office, to deposit a *Relation* of all they had learned in the Venetian chancery; but toward the end of the fifteenth century this law was almost entirely ignored, and was enforced again only in 1538. Marino Sanuto, in his *Diaries* embracing the period from 1496 to 1533, filled the hiatuses.

(3) The Venetian senator Malipiero, in his *Chronicle*, tells us that Sanuto informed the Venetian senate of the finding in the Tiber, in January, 1496, of a monstrosity having the head of an ass, a right arm like an elephant's trunk, a left arm like that of a man, one foot like that of an ox, the other like that of a griffin, a woman's bosom, and the lower part of the body like that of a dragon. The creature emitted fire from its mouth. The abbé Clement thinks that these details came direct from Germany, where, in 1524, Luther published his caricature of the "Pope-Ass." Rawdon Brown, in his *Information on the Life and Works of Marino Sanuto*, Venice, 1837, says that it would seem that such tales "were written for the Lutherans; but tor historians, they failed in their object." Nevertheless, says Clement, "certain candid minds believe the narrations of these pamphletary chroniclers: just as in Germany some persons, full of faith in Luther and his works, believe in the finding of the Pope-Ass in the Tiber. But one would suppose that Sanuto would not be so excessively credulous. Read the *Diaries*, now made public, and you will find the contrary."

(4) *Heretics of Italy*, Discourse IX.; Turin, 1865.

(5) *History of the Church during the Last Four Centuries*; Paris, 1855.

the stories of poison and treason unfolded in the books of Guicciardini." This historian was devoted to the Colonna and the Orsini families, and was also a partisan of Savonarola; quite naturally, therefore, he was a foe to the Borgias. Add to this that his hatred served his interest; for by exercising it he pleased the Florentines, the Venetians, and all who were then in opposition to the court of Rome.

The authority of Paul Jovius, bishop of Nocera, is of much less value than that of Guicciardini; for, being most venal, he is always either panegyrizing or calumniating. One day he was reproved for having narrated falsely, and he rejoined: "No matter; three hundred years hence it will be true " (1). Cantù styles Jovius the "lying gazetteer of that epoch " (2). Audin says that no historian ever "cared so little for his reputation as Paul Jovius. He represents himself as languishing with inertness because no one comes to purchase him " (3). Jerome Muzio asserted that Jovius showed diligence " only in obtaining the favors of the great, and he who gave the most was the principal hero of his works " (4). Vossius says that "for money Jovius would furnish posterity with a good character for any child of earth, but that he would calumniate all who did not pay for his services " (5).

Very little need be said of Tomaso Tomasi, another of the sources used by the defamers of Alexander VI. In his *Life* of Cæsar Borgia he had two objects in view: one was the favor of a princess of the Rovere family, which favor he thought to secure by decrying the Pontiff whom the cardinal of St. Peter's *ad Vincula*, her brother, had antagonized; the other was to exhibit in Cæsar a type of monstrosity which would exceed the efforts of the most rampant imagination. Even Gordon, to whom Roscoe attributes the reduction of history to below the level of romance, distrusts the authority of Tomasi.

As for the manuscript notices upon which many modern authors rely, they are of little or no value. Very few of them bear the names of their authors, and therefore they are unguaranteed. Most of them are diatribes, not narratives.

---

(1) The emperor Charles V. used to call Jovius and Sleidan "his two liars," one of whom spoke too well of him, and the other too badly.

(2) *Loc. cit.*, discourse XIII.   (3) *Leo X.*

(4) TIRABOSCHI; *Ital. Lit.*, vol. VII., p. 2.   (5) *Art of History*, c. ir.

They are positive where matters are at least doubtful, and carefully avoid everything creditable to our Pontiff. Many of them are needlessly prodigal with their venom. Casting aside, therefore, all such alleged authorities, and recurring only to facts and acts, we find that Alexander VI. had many virtues of a Pope and a sovereign; that, especially as king, he was more than ordinarily active and prudent, and nearly always successful in his enterprises; that his people loved him, and his reign was profoundly tranquil. One great fault he had, and perhaps this one was the source of all the others : he was passionately attached to the children—four sons and a daughter—who are generally supposed to have been born to him, but before he received Holy Orders; to aggrandize his family he made too much use of his presumed son Cæsar; and thus, in the eyes of posterity, he has shared the odium of that person's crimes.

Roderick Llançol was born on January 1, 1431, at Xativa, in the diocese of Valencia, in Spain. When his maternal uncle, Alfonso Borgia, was elevated to the Papacy under the name of Calixtus III., in 1455, the Llançol family assumed the name and arms of the Borgias, and only as such are they known in history. The young Roderick was noted for talent, and his first choice of profession was the bar, but he soon entered on the career of arms. Called to Rome by his uncle, and having evinced great aptitude for the business of a court, Roderick accepted offers of preferment, and was made successively commendatory archbishop of Valencia, cardinal-deacon, and vice-chancellor of the Roman Church. At this period, at least, his conduct must have been exemplary; for a contemporary writes that his fellow cardinals were "much pleased to have in their midst one who surpassed all in an abundance of gifts" (1). And Duboulai, who says that if the memory of Borgia had perished, we would not know how corrupt a man can be, admits that during his long cardinalate of thirty-five years Roderick never gave any public scandal (2). The rigid Sixtus IV. (1471–84) appointed him legate in Spain and

(1) *MS. Life of Roderick Borgia, under the name of Alexander VI.*, in the Casanatensian Library at Rome.
(2) *Life of Alexander VI.*

Portugal; and the cardinal of Pavia, a man of recognized sanctity, wrote to him during this legation: "I advise you to return; ... your influence here is sovereign; ... by your persuasion and wise opposition you can render great service to the Holy See." This same cardinal of Pavia slightly blamed Roderick for his ambition and love of pomp, but he predicted that he would become Pope (1). The manners of Borgia were grand and fascinating (2), and even Guicciardini credits him with rare powers of penetration, great tact, and diplomatic talent. Raphael and James of Volterra, Peter Martyr of Anghieri (3) waste no praise on Roderick, but they find in him vast genius and profoundity of thought. Ægidius of Viterbo admires his eloquence as natural and irresistible, his activity as indefatigable, and his sobriety as exemplary (4). Tomasi declares that whoever observed the young cardinal, could perceive that his genius marked him for empire. In 1476, having been appointed cardinal-bishop of Albano, Roderick received Holy Orders.

After the obsequies of Pope Innocent VIII., twenty-three cardinals entered into Conclave, and after five days of deliberation raised Roderick Borgia to the Chair of Peter, on August 11, 1492. As the foes of Borgia have tried to fasten the stigma of simony on this Conclave, it is well to note its members. The cardinal-bishops were: Roderick Borgia, then bishop of Porto; Oliver Caraffa, archbishop of Naples, whom even Roscoe styles a man of great integrity; Julian della Rovere, the future "Moses of Italy" as Julius II.; Baptist Zeno, bishop of Tusculum, whose piety and independence,

(1) *Epist.* 514, 670, 678, and in *Additions to Alduin.*—During Cardinal Roderick's legation in Spain there happened an event which gave occasion to one of Guicciardini's most barefaced lies. Sixtus IV. wished to give a cardinal's hat to Louis of Aragon, a natural son of King Ferdinand of Naples, but the stain of illegitimacy provoked the resistance of the Sacred College to the measure. Then there appeared several Spaniards, offering to swear to the candidate's legitimacy. The cardinals persisted, and the cardinal of Pavia wrote (*Epistles of James, Cardinal of Pavia*) to Roderick, urging him to use his influence with the Pontiff to prevent the promotion. The end was attained, but in after years, Alexander VI. conferred the hat which Roderick Borgia had kept from Louis. Now Guicciardini (*Hist.*, b. I.), in his hatred of the Borgias, travesties this event in a manner which precludes any supposition that he merely fell into an involuntary error. He changes the date to a period posterior by twenty years, 1493 (Roderick's legation in Spain terminated in 1473), and turns Louis of Aragon into Cæsar Borgia.

(2) Philip of Bergamo says that in Roderick "there was a celestial appearance very becoming to his name and office."

(3) Not to be confounded with Peter Martyr (Vermiglio) of Lucca, the Augustinian apostate who lectured at Oxford, 1547-53.

(4) This sobriety is admitted by Roscoe, *loc. cit.* See also Paris, *Diary,* at y. 1506.

according to Ciaconius, were remarkable; John Michiele, bishop of Palestrina and Verona, who, says the cardinal of Pavia, was learned, pious, and the friend of the poor; George d'Acosta, archbishop of Lisbon, and therefore, by national rivalry, a political enemy of Borgia. The cardinal-priests were : John dei Conti, venerated by all Rome ; Paul Fregoso, archbishop of Genoa, and thrice doge ; Lawrence Cibò and Anthony Pallavicini, Genoese ; Scalefetano, bishop of Parma; Ardicino della Porta, whose virtues even Infessura praises ; Gherardo, patriarch of Venice,—a holy Camaldolese monk, who died at Terni on his way home, but whom Infessura represents as having sold his vote to Borgia for 5,000 ducats, and as therefore deprived, on his return to Venice, of all his benefices. The cardinal-deacons were : Francis Piccolomini, afterward Pope Pius III., lauded by Roscoe ; Raphael Riario, leader of the Rovere party ; Ascanio Sforza, brother of the *Moro*, duke of Milan, and excessively praised by Paul Jovius ; Frederick da San Severino ; Colonna ; Orsini ; Savelli ; and John dei Medici, afterward Pope Leo X. The new Pontiff assumed the name of Alexander VI.,—a name famous, thought Roscoe, as " a scourge of Christendom, and the opprobrium of the human race." Probably no new Pontiff ever received so much flattery as that accorded to Alexander VI., at his coronation ; probably such wonderful deeds were never expected from any Pope as the princes and peoples awaited from him. The orators of the Italian States all vied in their congratulations with Tigrini of Lucca, who said that Christendom had a guarantee of its hopes in the Pontiff's many virtues and profound learning ; and Nardi, a famous Florentine historian, wrote shortly afterward that everywhere it was thought "that God had chosen this prince as His peculiar instrument to effect something wonderful in His Church, so great were the expectations universally conceived." And yet Roscoe asserts that " when the intelligence of this event was dispersed through Italy, where the character of Roderick Borgia was well known, a general dissatisfaction took place " (1).

(1) It is said that Cardinal dei Medici (afterward Pope Leo X.) remarked concerning this election : " We are in danger from the most ferocious wolf the world has ever seen ; he will devour us if we do not flee." Precocious though he was, the cardinal would scarcely have made this observation when sixteen years of age.

We must now touch briefly on the reputed simoniacal nature of Roderick's election. Raynald is chiefly responsible for the opinion prevalent, until very recent times, concerning the purity of the Conclave of 1492. If, instead of blindly relying on Infessura and his copyist Mariana, this annalist had consulted contemporary testimony less suspicious than that of Infessura, he would have been less severe toward this Conclave. Michael Fernus, whom Gregorovius calls "by no means a fanatical Papist," says that "in electing this Pontiff the cardinals showed that they had realized the appropriateness of the advice given them by Leonetti" in his funeral sermon on Innocent VIII (1). It would appear, therefore, according to Pernus, that merit, not simoniacal practices, procured the election of Borgia.

Sigismund dei Conti di Foligno tells us that "the qualities of Cardinal Roderick caused his brethren to esteem him as worthy of the Supreme Pontificate." Hartmann Schedel, author of the *Nuremberg Chronicle*, published in 1493, ascribes the election of Roderick to his "learning, excellent conduct, and great piety"(2). Porcius, a contemporary auditor of the *Ruota*, says: "He was unanimously elected, unanimously confirmed. Concerning this election I shall say only this: its principal authors were those same cardinals who had hitherto resisted all of Roderick's undertakings, both public and private "(3). Some of these were devoted to Julian della Rovere, Roderick's competitor in the Conclave; others were on the brink of the grave; but, with the exception of five—who, according to Burkhard, had declared that "votes should not be purchased,"—none denounced the alleged simony. And even these five voted for Borgia. But Infessura

(1) Leonetti, bishop of Concordia, had thus counselled the Sacred College: "As yet we know not whom God calls to succeed Innocent VIII.; what man is destined to avert the dangers menacing us. ... Elect a man whose past life is a guarantee; one who, according to the advice of St. Leo, has spent his days in the practice of virtue, and who merits the elevation because of his labors and the integrity of his morals; one without ambition, wise and holy; in a word, one worthy of being the Vicar of Jesus Christ." If the election of Borgia was a consequence of this advice, then the Borgia whom Fernus knew was not the acquaintance of Roscoe, Gregorovius, etc.

(2) "*Litteralis disciplinæ scientiarumque peritia, et optima vivendi ratio. Adest humanitas illa inclita cum auctoritatis ratione servata, optimum et salubre consilium; adest et pietatis cultus, et omnium rerum cognitio ... felix igitur tot virtutibus exornatus ... a Deo Optimo bene meritus.*"

(3) *Commentary of Jerome Porcius, Roman Patrician and Auditor of the Ruota;* Rome, 1493.

tells us that "it is said" that, in order to secure the votes of
Ascanio Sforza and his friends, Roderick sent, during the
Conclave, four mules laden with treasure to Sforza's palace.
It is strange, remarks Clement, that the indiscretion which
revealed this transaction did not betray it to the brigands who
were, just then, in possession of the streets of Rome. But
Manfredo Manfredi, ambassador of Ferrara to the court of
Florence, writes to the duchess Eleonora that it cannot be
supposed that Cardinals Colonna, Savelli, and Orsini would
have voted for Borgia unless seduced by money; and Manfredi
supports his charge by detailing the benefices given to these
cardinals by Alexander immediately after his enthronization (1). But where is the indication of simony in these appointments? The positions were necessarily to be filled.
The chancery, the abbey of Subiaco, given respectively to
Sforza and Colonna, had lost, the first its titular, the second
its commendatory; and we do not hear that the other benefices and fiefs were not vacant. Before dismissing this
charge of simony we must allude to a discovery made by
some Protestant polemics to the effect that since the death
of Innocent VIII. there have been no legitimate Popes, even
according to Roman principles. A papal decree nullifies any
election procured by simony; therefore, all appointments of
cardinals made by a simoniacal Pope are null; therefore,
there has been no legitimate Conclave since Alexander's delin-
quency. A mare's nest indeed; for the adduced decree was
issued by Julius II. on January 19, 1505, thirteen years
after Alexander's alleged simony.

One of Alexander's first acts was an instruction to the cardinals to lead an exemplary life. When his presumed son,
Cæsar Borgia, left his studies at the University of Pisa and
presented himself at court, the Pontiff rebuked him, saying:
"We certainly yearned most ardently for the tiara; but we
intended, if we obtained it, to use every possible means to promote the service of God and the exaltation of the Apostolic
See, in order to efface the memory of our past errors, and to
leave a worthy path to our successors." In many other ways

_____

(1) A. CAPELLI; *Acts and Memoirs of the Royal Deputations for the History of Modena*, vol. IV.; Modena, 1868.

Alexander VI. gave promise of a useful and glorious reign. The lives and property of his subjects, become more than precarious during the twenty months of serious illness endured by Innocent VIII., were assured of efficacious protection. A commission of four jurisconsults of known integrity was charged with the supervision of both civil and criminal causes. Another was instituted for the inspection and care of prisons. Every Tuesday any citizen could lay his grievances at the feet of an attentive sovereign, and if possible, they were redressed on the spot. So carefully did Alexander watch over the crops, the markets, the speculators in food, etc., that never, in the memory of man, had the poor been so abundantly and cheaply fed.

At this time the most powerful prince in Italy was Lodovico Sforza, called the *Moro*, of Milan. Sole guardian of his nephew, the son and heir of the assassinated Galeazzo Sforza, all his energies were directed to the acquisition of the sovereign authority for himself. Convinced that he would not succeed, so long as the Aragonese dynasty, faithful to his nephew, reigned in Naples, he laid a plan for the ruin of that house. He formed a league with the new Pope, who was then hostile to the house of Aragon, with Venice, the emperor Maximilian I., and Charles VIII. of France ; and finally tempted the last monarch to undertake the conquest of Naples, which had once belonged to a branch of his family. Florence was invited to aid Charles, but Piero dei Medici declared that no threat of war would induce him to break the alliance with the house of Aragon which his father and the Florentine senate had formed. Alexander VI. at once realized that neutrality in the coming struggle was impossible to the Holy See, for the Roman Pontiff was the suzerain of the menaced king of Naples ; he endeavored, however, to steer between Scylla and Charybdis by assuring the French envoy that the Holy See could not deprive King Alfonso of an investiture accorded by itself, unless Charles juridically established his own better right to it. But before Charles received this reply, the Pontiff promised Alfonso to invest him with the kingdom of Naples, to send a legate to crown him, and to confer the red hat on Louis of Aragon ; Alfonso promising in return to pay thirty thousand ducats to the Holy See, to marry his daughter Sancia to Geoffrey Borgia, and to confer on the bridegroom the principality of Squillace, as well as the protonotariate, one of the seven chief offices of the realm. While this alliance was being cemented, Sforza tried to secure the active aid of Venice for his enterprise; but the prudent oligarchs and merchants discerned a sure pecuniary profit in a wise neutrality. Although his preparations were made, Charles now hesitated to march; the old servants of the foxy Louis XI. had regained an ascendency, and for a time neither the clamors of Sforza nor the importunities of the French chivalry could overcome his fears. Finally he started, but paused at Vicenza. At this juncture the warlike cardinal Julian della Rovere waited upon him. This prelate, ever hostile to the Borgias, had retired to his fortress at Ostia immediately after the election of Roderick, and when he found that the new Pontiff bade fair to enter into the schemes of Sforza, he naturally espoused the cause of the house of Aragon; now that the Pope had allied with Alfonso, he fled to France. It is difficult to realize that this Julian della Rovere, encouraging the foreigner to invade his country, was the elevated and high-strung patriot who afterward, as Pope Julius II., effected more than even any other Pontiff for the independence of Italy. Nevertheless he now raised the drooping courage of the French monarch, insisting that his success in Italy was certain. In Aug., 1494, Charles VIII. began his Italian campaign. In Savoy and upper Italy the people, all hostile to the house of Aragon, welcomed another foreign invader to the peninsula; but the Florentines refused to ratify the arrangements made by Piero dei Medici with Charles, and since the Frenchman dared not leave a hostile Tuscany in his rear, they obtained very favorable terms of peace. When Alexander heard of the French occupation of Tuscany, he endeavored to come to an understanding with Charles. He chose for his ambassador the cardinal Francis Piccolomini, afterward Pope Pius III., one of the most conciliatory of men: but as the prelate was a nephew of Pius II., who had strenuously upheld the Neapolitan claims of Aragon, Charles would not even admit him into his camp.

Another source of anxiety to Alexander VI. at this time was the interception, by the prefect of Sinigaglia, who happened to be a Rovere, of certain letters purporting to come from the sultan Bajazet and addressed to the Pontiff; which letters, in the hands of an enemy, might seriously compromise the head of the Church. Alexander had sent a secret agent, one Buzardo, to inform Bajazet that the French king was about to march on Rome with the object of obtaining possession of Prince Zizim (1), whom he would place on the Turkish throne. Then Zizim, continued the Pope, would assist Charles VIII. in reducing the Mahometan empire to a vassalage to France. Alexander therefore suggested that Bajazet should send an ambassador to Venice to induce that state to join the league against France ; he also requested the sultan to advance the 40,000 ducats which he had promised to pay every year into the Roman treasury to defray Zizim's expenses. When captured at Sinigaglia by della Rovere, Buzardo had in his possession 50,000 ducats sent by Bajazet to the Pope, as also five letters. The prefect kept the money, but forwarded the letters to Charles VIII. In one of these the sultan asked Alexander to have Zizim put to death as quickly as possible, offering in return a sincere alliance and 300,000 ducats. Such a correspondence could effect, when known, much harm to Alexander ; for most persons would believe that the sultan knew his man when he proposed the murder of Zizim.

While Alexander was in this state of anxiety, the French monarch informed the world that he was about to make war against the Turks, but that he must first subdue the kingdom of Naples, both because the possession of its Adriatic coast

---

(1) On the death of Mahomet II. in 1482, his two sons, Bajazet and Zizim, inherited his dominions. The former dethroned his brother, who, to avoid death, fled to the protection of the Knights Hospitalers at Rhodes. Pierre d'Aubusson, the grand-master, received him most honorably, and protected him for some time ; but fearing that his presence would draw the entire infidel host upon the island, he sent the young prince to the care of the Holy See. Pope Innocent VIII., according to all writers of the day, Mahometan and Christian, loaded Zizim with honors, and even assigned him apartments in the Vatican. Bajazet was well content to pay an annual pension of 40,000 ducats for his brother's expenses, and he resided at Rome until Charles VIII. withdrew him from the care of Alexander VI. He died a few days after his removal, and, as Guicciardini and Sagredo record, the Pontiff was accused of having given him a slow poison. However, Corio (*Hist. Milan*) and Burkhard say that the prince's death was owing to the negligence of King Charles in regard to his diet. As to the letter of Bajazet mentioned above, Cautù insists that it was a forgery.

would facilitate his task, and because its crown belonged to him by right. Perhaps Alexander would now have made terms with Charles; for that monarch had promised, in his manifesto, to respect the authority of the Pope while passing through the Papal States, and to defray his own expenses. But the Pontiff suspected that the cardinals Ascanio Sforza, Colonna, Savelli, della Rovere, and San Severino, all partisans of Charles, and some of them in his camp, had plotted to assemble, with the help of that prince, a General Council which would elect a new Pope. And he felt that it was not unlikely that the young king, flushed with his good fortune, would acquire a taste for religious innovations, and would deem it a grand thing to pose as a reformer. He was encouraged to resist the French advance by the arrival in Rome of Ferdinand, son of Alfonso, with seventy squadrons; and when an embassy from Charles waited on him, he declared that he would not accord passage to a force destined to disturb the repose of Italy. But in a few days, when the French pickets were already at Monte Mario, the hopes of Alexander where shattered by news of a great calamity. Virginio Orsini, grand-constable of Naples, had allowed his sons to submit to Charles, and to offer him passage through their territories. The Pope would have abandoned Rome; but on Christmas eve Charles sent him assurances that he entertained no designs against his authority, and begged to be allowed to visit the capital of the Christian world. On Christmas morning the cardinal of Monreale gave the king of France permission to enter the Eternal City at his own convenience. Charles received the palace of St. Mark as a residence; but the Pontiff confined himself to the Vatican, to await the issue of negotiations. These were not easily concluded; among other things, Alexander resolutely refused to receive a French garrison in Castel San Angelo; when the discussion became bitter, he took refuge in the fortress, and although the French artillery was twice brought to bear upon it, he would not yield or come out. Fire was not opened, however, and the descendant of St. Louis steadily resisted those cardinals and barons who clamored for the deposition of Alexander. Finally the cardinals Pallavicini, Riario, and Carvajal prevailed upon him to abandon the matter of San Angelo, and to consent to the following treaty.   Firstly, the Pontiff would accord to the king of France the investiture of the kingdom of Naples; and the king would occupy Civita Vecchia, Terracina, and Spoleto until the said kingdom was subjugated. Secondly, Alexander would not punish the cardinals and barons who had sided with the king.   Thirdly, in return for the sum of 20,000 scudi, to be paid by the king, Prince Zizim was to be placed in the royal custody for six months; after which he was to be reconsigned to the Pontifical care.   Fourthly, Cæsar Borgia was to accompany the king for four months, in quality of Papal legate.   It is easily seen that by this last article Charles wished to secure a guarantee for Alexander's fidelity.

Eighteen months after his coronation as king of Naples, Charles VIII. was succeeded by Louis XII., who soon manifested a yearning for Italian territory.   Pope Alexander was thought to be not unwilling to aid him, provided, of course, that he himself was enabled to advance his family during the march of events.   Louis showed himself pliant; and Cæsar Borgia resigned his cardinalate and all his benefices, supplicating the Pontiff for secularization, as he "felt himself unequal to the burden of Holy Orders."   This request was proferred in full Consistory; and no voice was raised against its being granted.   Having secularized Cæsar, and seen him made duke of Valentinois by King Louis, Alexander now flattered himself that the House of Borgia would soon mount an Italian throne.   Of all sovereigns the French monarch appeared the most likely to second his projects; and he resolved to abandon the House of Aragon, and to uphold the cause of France in the peninsula, thus reversing the policy followed by the Holy See for sixty years.   Alexander's subserviency to France was rewarded by an admission of the Borgia stock into the proud blood of the Valois; Cæsar receiving the hand of Charlotte d'Albret, daughter of John, king of Navarre.   Certain of the support of the Pope, and having secured, by lavish promises, the favor of the duke of Savoy, of the marquis of Monferrato, and of the Venetians, who all hated Sforza, Louis XII. crossed the Alps to vindicate his claims to the duchy of Milan, derived from his grandmother, a Visconti. Sforza was immediately abandoned by nearly all his partisans; and without shedding a drop of blood, Louis became master of nearly all Lombardy. But the insatiable pretensions of Cæsar Borgia soon made enemies for the French. The Italian princes could not complacently look on while the arms of Louis were directed by Cæsar for his own benefit, now against Sforza, then against Malatesta and Riario; each one feared that he might be the next victim, and therefore they formed a league for common protection.

The second and definitive expulsion of the House of Aragon from Naples furnished Alexander VI. with the means of humiliating, of almost annihilating, the powerful and generally rebellious family of Colonna. Both Louis XII. and Ferdinand of Spain were hostile to these princes, and it soon became evident that absolute submission to their sovereign was the only means of safety open to them. Therefore they requested permission to surrender all their fiefs to the Sacred College; but Alexander quite properly announced that the sovereign authority in the Roman States pertained not to the cardinals, but to the Pope-King. The Colonna then placed the keys of their fortresses in the hands of the Papal envoy, the bishop of Cesena. In his determination to concentrate the government of the Papal States in the hands of their sovereign, Alexander directed his energies against all the great feudataries, the vicars of the Church, as they were styled. Through the skill of Cæsar Borgia, now nobly, then ignobly exercised, these lords were rendered nearly powerless. They were stained, as a rule, with every kind of crime; and it must be noted that for centuries the vicariates had been fruitful of misery to their inhabitants. If Cæsar Borgia had not seized for himself the fiefs of the subdued tyrants, his success would have completed the great work begun, a century and a half before, by Cardinal Albornoz.

After the destruction of the vicariates, and the weakening of the great families of Orsini, Colonna, and Savelli to the profit of the Borgias, Alexander VI. might have been satisfied; but the imperious ambition of the duke of Valentinois would be contented only with a royal crown. The Pontiff had already resolved to erect the Romagna, the Marches, and Umbria into a kingdom for Cæsar, and had even commenced to sound the minds of the cardinals in regard to such an iniquitous and unprecedented alienation of the patrimony of the Church (1), when death knocked at the doors of the Vatican. Several contemporary authors assert that Alexander and Cæsar were both poisoned; that either by error or by treachery they were made to partake of a poison which they had prepared for certain cardinals who were hostile to their projects. Ranke gives credence to this fable; Roscoe rejects it. Ranke says that " it is only too certain that Alexander formed the design of poisoning one of the wealthiest cardinals (Corneto); but this prelate so influenced the Pope's *maggiordomo* by presents, promises, and prayers, that the refreshment destined for the cardinal was served to the Pope." Now Ranke was well acquainted with the writings of Jovius; did he simply ignore the fact that this writer, in his *Life of Gonsalvo*, says that he learned from the very lips of Corneto that this cardinal had been really poisoned on the above occasion, and had suffered intensely, all his skin peeling off? It would seem, therefore, that the Corneto affair is not to be regarded as an undoubted historical fact; and that the murderous design of Alexander, said to have been frustrated by the *maggiordomo*, is not "only too certain." But the death of Alexander VI. was not the result of poison. In the Ducal Library of Ferrara there is a manuscript history by Sardi, a contemporary of Guicciardini and Paul Jovius, wherein the author speaks of ten letters written by their agents to Duke Hercules of Ferrara and Cardinal d'Este, in which it is shown that our Pontiff died of tertian fever, then rampant in Rome. " Attacked by this fever on August 10 [1503], he was relieved neither by bleeding nor by the use of manna, and he expired on the night we mentioned [August 18]. After death the body became swollen and blackened, owing to the putrefaction of the blood; and hence there originated, among such as knew not the cause of these appearances, a rumor that the Pope had been poisoned." In

(1) MURATORI; *Annals of Italy*, y. 1503.

a manuscript *Diary* of Burkhard, preserved in the Corsini Library, may be read the following : " On Saturday, August 12, 1503, the Pope felt ill; and in the evening, about the twenty-first or twenty-second hour, there came a fever which continually remained. On Tuesday, August 15, thirteen ounces of blood were drawn from him, and there supervened a tertian fever. On Thursday, August 17, at the twelfth hour, he took some medicine; and on Friday, August 18, he confessed to the lord Peter, bishop of Culm, who then cele-brated Mass in his presence, and after his own Communion gave the Holy Eucharist to the Pope, who sat up in bed. There were present five cardinals. ... At the vesper hour, having received Extreme Unction from the bishop of Culm, he expired."

And, strange to say, Voltaire is very firm in ascribing Al-exander's death to natural causes. Speaking of the report of poison (1), the cynic says : " All the enemies of the Holy See have believed this horrible tale ; I do not, and my chief reason is that it is not at all probable. The Pope and his son may have been wicked, but they were not fools. It is certain that the poisoning of a dozen cardinals would have rendered father and son so execrable that nothing could have saved them from the fury of the Romans and all Italy. The crime, too, was directly contrary to the views of Cæsar. The Pope was on the verge of the grave, and Borgia could cause the election of one of his own creatures; would he gain the Sacred College by murdering a dozen of its members?" Again, contends Voltaire—on whom, for rarity's sake, it is a pleasure to rely,—if after Alexander's death the cause of the catastrophe had transpired, surely it would have been learned by those whom he had tried to murder. Would they have allowed Cæsar to enter peaceably into possession of his fa-ther's wealth ? And how could Cæsar, almost dying, accord-ing to the story, go to the Vatican to secure the hundred thousand ducats ? They say that Cæsar, after the accident, shut himself in the stomach of a mule ; for what poison is that a remedy ? Finally, Pope Julius II., an unrelenting

(1) *Complete Works*, vol. XX. (*Hist. Miscel.*, vol. I.), p. 211 ; edit. Paris, 1818.—*Customs and Spirit of Nations*, i'., p. 115.— *Dissertation on the Death of Henry IV.*

foe of the Borgias, held Cæsar in his power for a long time, and he never charged him with the supposed crime. Well, therefore, did Voltaire exclaim: "I dare to say to Guicciardini: Europe has been deceived by you, as you were deceived by your passion. You were an enemy of the Pope, and you believed your hatred too readily."

And now a word on Alexander VI. as Pontiff. The assassination of the duke of Gandia (1497) produced a profoundly religious impression on his mind; he even thought of abdicating the Pontificate in order to conciliate the divine mercy. Deterred by Ferdinand the Catholic, he resolved to become a more worthy Pope, and as a first step he began to correct many abuses which had crept into the ecclesiastical administration. Among the abuses brought to light by an apposite commission was a systematic series of forgeries, or rather of supposititious issue of dispensations, in which rascality the chief offender was found to have been the archbishop of Cosenza, Bartholomew Florida, the secretary of Briefs. Florida confessed his guilt, was deposed, degraded, and imprisoned for life, on a diet of bread and water, in Castel San Angelo. Much good was effected by this commission, as Paul III. afterward indicated. Upon one point the zeal of Alexander was worthy of his position. As a defender of the faith he was never remiss. One of his first efforts was for the pacification of Bohemia, then ravaged by the Hussites; and it was owing to the kindness which he substituted for the harshness of his predecessors that the scourge vanished. In 1501 Alexander issued his Bull *Inter Multiplices* against the printing and reading of bad books. One of the most important Bulls issued by this Pontiff was the *Inter Cœtera* in 1493, whereby he drew a line of demarcation, which was to form, from pole to pole, the limit of the Spanish and Portuguese possessions in the lately-discovered New World. It required no small amount of daring to proclaim, as he thereby equivalently did, the rotundity of the earth,—a truth which then, and for centuries afterward, no scientific academy would have unhesitatingly patronized. And our astonishment is evoked by the fact that the line drawn by Alexander, at a time when the knowledge of cosmography

was as yet based on the most contradictory data, extends
from one pole to the other without encountering any land
whatever; had it happened otherwise, it might have furnished
a subject of discord to the rival nations (1). Naturally, the
enemies of the Holy See affect to regard this partition as a
crime; indeed, Marmontel termed it "the greatest of all the
crimes of Borgia." But Alexander simply exercised that
right of arbitration which all Christendom then admitted as
resident in the incumbent of the Papal throne.

We now enter upon a question, the very existence of which
may surprise some of our readers. It is generally supposed
that the cardinal Roderick Borgia was the father of several
illegitimate children, and that some of them were born while
he was in Holy Orders. But it is also asserted, and with
some show of reason, that these children were born to Roderick in legitimate wedlock. We shall submit the arguments
to the judgment of the reader, first premising that the contemporaries of Alexander VI. are utterly discordant as to the
identity of the mother of these children—a fact which shows
that during Roderick's career as cardinal and as Pope she
remained entirely in the background. Burkhard speaks of
her as Vanozza. Tomasi calls her Rose. In the MS. *Life* of
Roderick, preserved in the Casanatensian Library at Rome,
she is styled Virginia Vanozza. In the *Letters* attributed to
her, and preserved in the Modenese Archives, sometimes she
signs herself Vanozza Borgia, again Perpetua, and also Va-
notia Borgia de Cathaneis. Infessura says that she was the
wife of a certain Dominick d'Arignano, to whom at one time
Alexander wished to ascribe the paternity of Cæsar; but Tomasi says that Roderick "regarded her as a legitimate wife,
rather than as a sacrilegious concubine." When the young
Roderick Borgia was raised to the Sacred College (1466), he
was already the father of two children, Peter Louis and John
Francis. But if the reader were to imagine that the progeny

(1) M. Roselly de Lorgues, in his valuable work on the *Life and Voyages of Columbus,*
says: " Take the most perfect of all modern maps, ... and follow the mysterious line solemnly traced by the Sovereign Pontiff, and you will be astounded on perceiving that
underneath Europe this line courses over the entire surface of the planet, even to the south-
ern pole, without meeting any land. Try to draw a similar line to some point other than
that indicated by the Holy See, and you will strike some island or some part of a continent."

born to Roderick after this time was necessarily sacrilegious, he would be deceived by the title of cardinal which the Pope, in the actual discipline of the Church, confers only on bishops, or upon men at least in Holy Orders. At the time of which we are writing, the cardinalitial scarlet did not always presuppose Sacred Orders in its wearer; Mazarin and many other cardinals never received them. Nor did Roderick's archiepiscopate of Valencia, conferred on him in his youth, entail upon him the absolute necessity of taking Orders. His prelacy was merely " commendatory ; " that is, according to a detestable custom of the day, he enjoyed the emoluments of the benefice (1). He became, really and irrevocably, a member of the Catholic clergy, only during the last years of Sixtus IV. (1471-84), after that Pope had created him a cardinal-bishop, at first of Albano (1476), and then of Porto (1479). " Up to that time he enjoyed only the diaconal title of St. Nicholas, which he had received from his uncle Calixtus III., a title which by no means obliged him to take Orders " (2). Bearing these facts in mind, let us see whether there is good reason for believing that Cæsar, Lucretia, and their three brothers were born in wedlock. Ribadeneira (1527–1611) speaks of Julia Farnese as the mother of these children (3). This author had been intimate with St. Francis Borgia, and had, most probably, learned from him the origin of his immediate family. The illustrious Pompeo Litta, in his great work on the celebrated families of Italy, assigns Vanozza to the Farnese family, and says that her father was Ranuccio Farnese. Marino Sanuto preserves a pamphlet, written apparently during the last years of Alexander, in which a satirist gives a pretended dialogue between Death and the sick Pontiff. The latter invokes the aid of Julia, with whom he had lived in Spain. Although a mere diatribe, this

(1) The acting beneficiary was supposed, of course, to be above reproach. The commendatory was too often a scandal, especially in cases of royal patronage. The title of *abbé*, *abbate*, now given on the European Continent to all secular priests, was in those days adopted by a horde of perfumed gallants, who hung around the court in the enjoyment or expectancy of some abbey ' in commendam." One must therefore be careful not to credit the priesthood with every curled darling of an abbé of whom he reads in works of that time.

(2) CLEMENT (de Vebron) ; *The Borgias, a History of Pope Alexander VI., of Cæsar, and of Lucretia Borgia* ; ch. ii. Paris, 1882.

(3) *Life of St. Francis Borgia* ; Madrid, 1605.

document indicates the opinion of Alexander's contemporaries
that Julia Farnese was the mother of the children in question (1).   Now if Julia Farnese and Vanozza were one person,
it is more than probable that she was married to Roderick
Borgia.   The doubts raised by Guicciardini and other interested parties disappear, if we reflect that an illegitimate union,
so long prolonged, between a Borgia and a Farnese would
have been well-nigh impossible.   The nobility of the Roman
family of Farnese, dating from the thirteenth century, would
scarcely have brooked such an insult from the Borgias, who
were no more than its peers.   An implacable hatred, if not a
vendetta, would have ensued between the two houses; whereas history shows a contrary state of affairs.   Cardinal Alexander Farnese, afterward Pope Paul III., was greatly trusted
by Alexander VI., and was thoroughly devoted to him, even
at the time when the French ascendency enabled the enemies
of the Pontiff to plan his deposition.   Angelo Ferdinand
Farnese was killed in the service of Cæsar Borgia.   But
granting that Vanozza and Julia Farnese were different persons, there are other arguments for the legitimacy of Roderick's union with the mother of his children.   Only by the
supposition of a marriage—secret perhaps, but still legitimate—can we explain certain facts which are otherwise inexplicable.   How is it that Philip de Commines, so conversant
with all the affairs of his time, never applies the term "bastards" to Alexander's presumed children?   Whenever he has
occasion to speak of the natural children of a king, he uses
this epithet.   How is it that none of the writers who followed
Charles VIII. into Italy, none of Alexander's rebel cardinals,
all of whom accuse the Pontiff of other delinquencies, say
anything about his illegitimate family?   Unless we wish to
accept the theory that Lucretia and her brothers were not
Alexander's children, this silence alone would indicate their
legitimacy

But is it certain that Cæsar and Lucretia Borgia and their
brothers were children of Roderick?   Undoubtedly they were
Borgias; but after the election of Calixtus III. there were many

---

(1) *Diary*, vol. III.—"*Julia, me miserum cur non defendis?* ... *Ut peream, illius sus-
ceptus in ulnis quæ modo ab Hispania vecta puella mihi est.*"

Borgias in Rome. It is an incontestable fact that the children in question were frequently called "nephews" and "niece" of the Pontiff in documents of the time. Thus, Fioramondo Brugnolo, writing from Rome on March 19, 1493, to the marquis of Mantua, speaks of Cæsar as a "nephew of a brother of the Pope." The Venetian Senate, on Oct. 18, 1500, makes "Cæsar Borgia, duke of Valentinois, nephew of Pope Alexander VI.," a gentleman of the state. Peter Martyr of Anghiera, most hostile to the Borgias, calls Cæsar "the nephew of a son of a brother of Alexander." This hypothesis is not entirely new (1), but no one has so well presented and defended it as A. Leonetti, a religious of the Pious Schools (2). "If I may express my opinion," says Leonetti, "we may believe that all these children, born of the same mother Vanozza, were children either of a Borgia especially loved by the cardinal Roderick, or of a brother who remained in Spain, or of a son of his brother, the prefect of Rome." And if this hypothesis is rejected, continues Leonetti, in spite of the reasons confirming it, may not these children have been of some other Borgia? There were many in Rome. When their father died, and Vanozza had remarried, these children of his relative were cared for by the cardinal Roderick, and then some styled them his own children. Certainly there are good reasons for believing them to be children of that brother of Roderick who was the father of the cardinal John Borgia. Alexander is styled uncle (*patruus*) of this Borgia, and Cæsar is called his brother. "This morning," writes Cæsar from Forli on Jan. 16, 1500, "I heard of the death at Urbino of my brother, the cardinal Borgia." Duke Hercules of Ferrara, replying to Cæsar, calls the cardinal John the "carnal brother of Cæsar." The theory of Leonetti was attacked by M. de l'Epinois (3), who has merited well of the science of criticism, and whose views are to be respected. That the reader may judge of the soundness of Leonetti's theory, we notice his opponent's objections. Let us commence with Cæsar Borgia, whose "adulterous and sacrilegious" birth has been more harped upon than that of the

(1) It was advanced in the *Dublin Review* for Jan., 1859.

(2) *Pope Alexander VI., according to Documents of the Time,* Bologna, 1880. This work was highly commended by Pope Leo XIII.

(3) *Review of Historical Questions*; Paris, April, 1881

other presumed children of Alexander. M. de l'Epinois quotes: "He was always regarded as the son of Alexander." But who says this? Infessura, the enemy of the Popes, a personal foe of Alexander, the would-be destroyer of the Papal government. We refuse such testimony. Then, returns M. de l'Epinois, read the Brief of Sixtus IV., dispensing young Cæsar, then in his sixth year, from the impediment of infamy (1). This document, insists an erudite critic (2), must be regarded as a forger. In the fifteenth century the fabrication of false Papal documents was as much of a business as that of counterfeiting bank-notes in the nineteenth; M. de l'Epinois himself tells us how Alexander VI. imprisoned a bishop of Cosenza who had kept three secretaries at work in such forgeries. But let us examine this pretended Brief of Sixtus IV. What need was there to relieve the young Cæsar of the presumed irregularity, when the Brief itself declares that he was the issue of a married woman? He enjoyed a regular civil status, unless the husband of the woman disavowed him. Now in the immense quantity of diatribes which have rained upon the Borgia family, we read of no such disavowal. Why then should Sixtus speak of a defect in birth, especially when he has resolved to pass over it? Is it merely for the pleasure of publishing it? Why does not the Pope say: "You suffer from a defect in birth"? But no; remarks Morel; "Sixtus must explain to the world that this child is the son of a cardinal, even of a cardinal-bishop. This is scandalous in the extreme and scandalously futile; it is absurd enough to strike every mind not predisposed to credit anything unfavorable to a Borgia. ... We are asked to believe that Sixtus IV. informed

---

(1) "Sixtus, bishop, servant of the servants of God, to our dear son, Cæsar Borgia, a student, health and Apostolic benediction. The indications of very remarkable qualities which seem to abound in your tender age, as we have heard from trustworthy persons, furnish a probable hope that you will become a virtuous man, and lead us to encourage you with our Apostolic favor. Wishing to give you a proof of this our benevolence, because of the aforesaid indications, and considering that you, now in the sixth year of your age, are suffering from a stain of birth, being the issue of a cardinal-bishop and a married woman, in order that, when you have reached your seventh year, you may receive tonsure and the Minor Orders, and that, when arrived at the proper age, you may receive the Sacred Orders; we grant and cheerfully accord that you be not bound to mention the aforesaid defect of birth or this dispensation; and that all be valid and efficacious, just as though you were the fruit of a legitimate matrimony. Given at Rome, at St. Peter's, in the year of our Lord, 1480, Kal. Oct., and tenth year of our Pontificate."

(2) The Canon J. Morel, in *The Universe*; Paris, July 14, 1881.

the world that his vice-chancellor joined to his other dignities that of an adulterous and sacrilegious father. Would such an insulting proclamation, one so contemptuous of public morals, have been less culpable than the crime of the cardinal-bishop? ... It was just as easy to pass over the defect of birth when Cæsar was to be tonsured, as it was when he was to be made cardinal." M. de l'Epinois informs us that the cardinals Orsini and Pallavicini were appointed to inquire into the legitimacy of Cæsar, when there was a question of enrolling him in the Sacred College. Then, he says, Brancaccio wrote : "His being a natural child can be overlooked, for he will be regarded as legitimate, since he was born in the house of the living husband of his mother." So much for the pretended Brief of Sixtus IV. But Alexander calls Cæsar "his heart." Well, may not a nephew be "the heart" of his uncle? But once, it is objected, Cæsar signed a letter to Alexander, "the most devoted creature (*factura*) of his Holiness." It is absurd to suppose that here Cæsar implied anything more than his obligations to the Pontiff for his political preferment. As Morel well remarks, "Cæsar was too distinguished, too high-spirited, too princely, to sign himself like a hero of one of the romances of Paul de Kock."

And now for a few words as to the paternity of Lucretia. Gregorovius cites two notarial documents in which she is styled the daughter of a cardinal. One is a projected contract of marriage with John de Centelles—a contract made in Spain in the absence of the Borgias. Lucretia was then eleven years old. The lawyer's principal care seems to be to convince the world of the lady's cardinalitial origin. He describes her as "the carnal daughter of the said reverend cardinal ;" he informs us that the said cardinal gives such a dowry to "the said lady Lucretia, his carnal daughter ;" and lest we might not fully comprehend the situation, he assures us again that she is the cardinal's "bastard daughter." Certainly if Alexander confirmed this contract, he must have wished to boast of his crime before the world. The contract would have been just as valid if Lucretia had been styled his niece (1). Can it be that Roderick wished no one of his

(1) M. de l'Epinois would admit that, even though Lucretia were the daughter of the car-

diocesans of Valencia to ignore that his Eminence had an illegitimate daughter? If Roderick never confirmed this contract, it cannot claim our attention. The second notarial document quoted by Gregorovius annuls the marriage contract between Lucretia and the duke of Aversa, and calls her "a natural daughter" of Cardinal Roderick. But a few days afterward, the notary draws up another paper in which the lady is called the cardinal's "niece." However, these are not the only documents adduced to show the filial relation of Lucretia to Cardinal Roderick. The duke of Ferrara, writing to Pope Alexander, calls her "our common daughter." But would she not be such, even though she were the adopted daughter of Alexander? She was not the real daughter of the duke; why the real child of the Pontiff? The reader will judge of the value of Leonetti's theory. As for ourselves, we agree with the historian of the Pious Schools when he says that until more conclusive documents are produced, equity commands us to pronounce a judgment of acquittal in favor of the celebrated accused.

Gregorovius attributes to Roderick Borgia the paternity of a second daughter, named Girolama. He adduces as proof a contract of marriage between this Girolama and Andrew Cesarini, dated Jan. 24, 1482: "The most reverend Roderick Borgia, cardinal-bishop of Porto, moved and led by a sentiment of paternal love and affection for the noble, honest, and virtuous young maiden Girolama, sister of the excellent and virtuous youth, the lord Peter Louis Borgia, and of the minor, John Borgia, her full brothers, and wishing to treat and recognize as his daughter this young Girolama, who issues from his family and house, he gives to her for the honor of his house four thousand ducats, etc." But again we ask, cannot an uncle cherish a paternal affection for a niece? And if Girolama was Roderick's daughter, what need was there of adding that she "issued from his family and house?" Gregorovius also tries to prove that a child was born to Alexander VI. several years after his elevation to the Papacy. In

dinal Roderick, she might quite naturally be called his niece on this occasion. He himself alludes to the well-known adage, "*filii presbyterorum nepotes vocantur*," and says that decency demanded the use of the word "nephew" or "niece" in such cases, and that "these terms were current in the Chanceries."

1501 the Pontiff gave the duchy of Nepi to a child named John Borgia. Some critics have thought that this John was a son of the unfortunate second duke of Gandia; but documents recently published tend to show that John, the third duke of Gandia, and John, duke of Nepi, were different persons (1), and that the latter was a natural son of Cæsar. Gregorovius, in order to prove his thesis, adduces two Bulls of our Pontiff, both dated Sept. 1, 1501; the first being a legitimization of John as a son of Cæsar, while the second is a recognition of the boy as a son of Alexander. In the first Alexander declares that John, then three years old, is the son of Cæsar, an unmarried man, by an unmarried woman; and he legitimizes the boy, establishing him in all the rights of his parents. In the second, however, the Pontiff says: "But since you suffer from this defect, not by fault of the said duke, but by our own and by that of the said unmarried woman, which fault we could not avow for good reasons, in the preceding Bull; we now wish, in order that said Act may never be pronounced null, and in order that hereafter no difficulties may arise for you, to provide for your future welfare. Therefore by the present Act we freely and of our own generosity confirm the validity of all that is specified in the previous Act." Was Alexander VI. such a fool as to proclaim himself the father of the duke of Nepi? Did he wish to parade his own vices? And why did he not destroy the first Bull? Why allow it to go forth, if immediately afterward he deemed it necessary to declare that in it he had lied? When a man can easily retract a lie, and one not yet published, he does not utter the lie and its confession at the same time. But Gregorovius himself admits that "after Alexander's death the little John passed for a son of Cæsar," and he even cites documents which confirm this paternity of the Valentinois. Thus, in a Brief dated June 12, 1502, and addressed to the commune of Gallese, the Pontiff speaks of "the noble child, John Borgia, duke of Nepi, son of the noble Cæsar Borgia." And another argument for the falsity of the alleged Briefs is found in the fact that in the first Cæsar is styled "unmarried," while in the second he is pronounced "married."

(1) *Dispatches of Giustiniani*, 78, 97, 98, 109.—ALVISI; *Cæsar Borgia, Duke of Romagna*.

Many authors illustrate their theory of Pope Alexander's immorality by alleging the revolting orgy said to have been celebrated in honor of the prospective marriage of Lucretia with the duke of Ferrara—a banquet, etc., at which we are asked to fancy as participants the aged Pontiff, Cæsar, Lucretia, and fifty respectable (*honestæ*) prostitutes (1). Truly these females were *honestæ* beyond the wont of that ilk, and the favored servants were gems indeed, when all Rome did not ring, the next day, with the echoes of such Bacchanalia. Excepting Burkhard, if indeed he speaks in the cited quotation, not one contemporary, not one of those chroniclers who dilate so circumstantially on all the festivities given at the Vatican in honor of Lucretia's espousals, says a word of what would have been a mine of wealth to a gossiper. And why such silence on the part of the Ferrarese envoys who were then residing in the Vatican, awaiting the convenience of Lucretia, to conduct her to their royal master as a bride? They wrote every day to the duke, and we have their despatches. Why, again, silence on the part of the secret agent sent by the marchioness of Mantua, sister of the future bridegroom, who kept his mistress informed as to the most trivial incidents of the Papal court?

CHAPTER XIV.

SAVONAROLA.[*]

Jerome Savonarola was born at Ferrara in 1452. Naturally of a grave disposition, he soon manifested an enthusiastic piety, and at the age of twenty-three he donned the habit of a Friar-Preacher at Bologna. His strict observance of the

(1) Gordon quotes from the true or false Burkhard as follows: " *Dominica ultima mensis Octobris in sero fecerunt cœnam cum duce Valentinensi in camera sua in palatio Apostolico, quinquaginta meretrices honestæ, cortegianæ nuncupatæ, quæ post cœnam chorearunt cum servitoribus et aliis ibidem existentibus, primo in vestibus suis, deinde nudæ. Post cœnam posita fuerunt candelabra communia mensæ cum candelis ardentibus, et projectæ ante candelabra per terram castaneæ, quas meretrices ipsæ, super manibus et pedibus nudæ, candelabra pertranseuntes, colligebant; Papa, duce, et Lucretia sorore sua, præsentibus et aspicientibus. Tandem exposita dona ultima, diploides de serico, paria caligarum, bireta, et alia pro illis qui plures dictas mulieres carnaliter agnoscerunt, quæ fuerunt ibidem in aula carnaliter tractatæ, arbitrio præsentium, et dona distributa victoribus.*"

* This chapter appeared as an article in the *American Catholic Quarterly Review*, vol. XIV.

rule, his great talents, and, not least of all, his remarkably striking presence, drew upon him the admiration of the multitude to such a degree that his superior determined to utilize his influence in the pulpit. His first attempt at preaching, however, was not a success. It was made in 1482, in the church of St. Lawrence, in Florence; and when he had finished, says Burlamachi, one of his most zealous admirers, he found that only twenty persons had remained (1). Both he and his audience having decided that he was no orator, he occupied a chair of philosophy for a time, but soon abandoned the study of Aristotle and St. Thomas for that of Scripture. Now he was content, for his contemplative nature fully appreciated the lofty ideas and the mysterious and figurative style of the divine books. For several years he had devoted himself, night and day, to his Biblical studies, when he was again unexpectedly brought before the public. It was the celebrated Pico della Mirandola who was the means of pushing the retiring student into publicity, and of causing him to enter upon a career which was to prove his destruction. This great scholar, one of the brightest luminaries of his own or any other age, had heard Savonarola lecture at Reggio, and had been so impressed by his eloquence that he prevailed upon Lorenzo dei Medici to call the friar to Florence. In 1489 Savonarola was appointed professor of Scripture to the young religious of the convent of St. Mark, and as his oratorical powers had greatly developed since his failure at St. Lawrence's, he soon acquired a great reputation. Before long, impelled by the enthusiasm he excited, he reappeared in the pulpit; and voluptuous Florence was astonished at his denunciations of her vices and at the threats of chastisement which, according to him, God had commanded him to pronounce. The sermons of Savonarola, as we have them, are not from his own hand; they were taken down as delivered, by some of his auditors (2). But imperfect as they are, we can readily imagine the effect they must have produced. "His eloquence was not that which comes from the use of the orator's arts, or from a depth of reasoning, or from an emotion agitating the orator's self. It was an eloquence which seemed to

(1) *Life of F. Jerome Savonarola*, Lucca, 1761, p. 23.   (2) TIRABOSCHI; b. III., c. VI.

despise all human aids, and which, like the mystical figures
of Fra Angelico, looks toward heaven and does not touch the
earth. ... Savonarola is like no other orator. True or pretended, he is a prophet; he has the visions, the incoherence,
the seizures, the figurative language, the rashness of one.
For this reason, rather than by means of his talent, great
as it was, he captivated the multitude" (1). Several years
before the Italian expedition of Charles VIII., Savonarola had
predicted to his auditors that a foreign prince, led by the
Lord, would become master of Italy without drawing his
sword; and when, in 1494, he heard of the preparations being made in France, he quoted the passage of Genesis which
threatens the deluge, and cried out : " Oh! ye just, enter into
the ark. Behold, the cataracts of heaven are opened ; I see
the plains inundated, and the mountains disappearing in the
midst of the waters. Behold the day of the Lord's vengeance !"
His predictions were universally believed, and his authority
over the multitude became so great that a contemporary historian says that posterity will find it just as difficult to believe, as he finds it hard, having witnessed these events, to
describe them (2). A change came over gay and voluptuous
Florence. Vice of every kind disappeared, and piety became
so general that Burlamachi tells us that the days of the primitive Church seemed to have returned (3). Nor was the eloquence of the friar restricted to a combat with vice alone. The
Renaissance in letters and art had led men, for about a century, to give an almost idolatrous worship to the works of
Pagan antiquity, to the detriment of Scriptural and Patristic
lore. Paganism had so far corrupted many minds that even
the members of the Roman Academy of Pomponius Lætus
were accused of thinking that the Christian faith rested on
light foundations (4). Art, as well as literature and true
science, had suffered from this revival of Pagan sentiment (5).

(1) CHRISTOPHE; *History of the Papacy in the Fifteenth Century*; v. II., b. XVI.
Lyons, 1863.
(2) NARDI ; *History of the City of Florence*, b. II.   (3) *Loc. cit.*, p. 86.
(4) CANENSIUS; *Life of Paul* II., p. 78. TIRABOSCHI ; v. VI., p. 2., b. II.
(5) " Pagan ideas again flourish ; the books, statues, and buildings of Paganism are restored ; modern works are modelled after the ancient, to the sacrifice of originality and of nat-
uralness ; the authority of a philosopher or of a poet is weighed against that of the Scriptures:
or of a Father—professors even say, ' Christ teaches thus, Aristotle and Plato thus ;' the

The painter and the sculptor, influenced by the works exhibited in the Medici gardens, had adopted naturalism as a system, and, banishing the ideal, produced merely the expression of human beauty—decency and modesty were ignored, and Savonarola indignantly asked the artists why they put their mistresses upon the altars, and why they pictured the Blessed Virgin like a courtesan (1). All this was changed by the Dominican reformer. On two different occasions the Florentines made immense bonfires, and performed a real and meritorious *auto-da-fe,* by throwing into the flames their books on impure love, their lascivious pictures and statues, while joyous strains of music floated over the great square of the cathedral.

From the very commencement of his preaching, Savonarola had proclaimed the necessity of purifying the sanctuary; but at first he restrained his usual impetuosity, and confined himself to declamations against the laxity, then but too prevalent, of ecclesiastical discipline. But his growing popularity soon affected his judgment and banished his reserve. From the accession of Alexander VI. to the Papacy, he bitterly inveighed against the Pontiff, and consequently his auditors were divided into two factions. His partisans were known as *frateschi,* or "friarites," and sometimes as *piagnoni,* or "weepers," while those who, either in good or bad faith, trembled lest his denunciation would injure both Church and State, were called by his followers *tepidi,* or "lukewarm," and *arrabiati* or "madmen" (2). To neutralize the influence of the Dominican, the *arrabiati* made use of the Augustinian, Mariano da Gennazzano, a friend of the Medici, and a man esteemed as much for his austere morals as for his talents (3), and of whom Savonarola himself said that "if he had the eloquence of Mariano, he would be the first of orators" (4). But the impassioned genius of the agitator

Platonic sublimity disappears in theosophical delirium; only Pagan virtues are praised, and the names of Greeks and Romans are substituted for those received at baptism. ... Lorenzo dei Medici sings sacred hymns to please his mother, and makes obscene jokes to gratify his boon companions." CANTU; *Heretics of Italy, Discourse XI.*

(1) *Sermon for the Saturday before Second Sunday of Lent.* ·
(2) NERLI; *Commentaries on the Civil Affairs of Florence,* p. 68.
(3) Poliziano and Pontano greatly laud him as a preacher.
(4) TIRABOSCHI; v. VI., b. III.

still held the people entranced. A Franciscan named Dominic di Ponzo was then put forward to stem the torrent; but the Grand Council, a legislative body instituted after Savonarola had procured the expulsion of Piero dei Medici, prohibited his preaching. The Dominican had now become the real ruler of Florence, and the devotion of the citizens to their liberator took the form of insanity. Nerli tells us that they often interrupted their prayers to rush from the churches, and to the cry of " *Viva Cristo,*" they would dance in circles, formed of friars and laymen, placed alternately (1). But the *arrabiati* did not lose courage, and the war of factions became so general that the very children took part in it, and showed their zeal by pelting each other with stones (2). The opponents of Savonarola, most of them partisans of the exiled Piero dei Medici, now took the more efficacious means of discrediting their enemy by denouncing him to the Pope. Some of his most bitter sermons were sent to Rome ; and the Augustinian, Mariano, who had been exiled from Florentine territory, preached before the Pontiff and the Sacred College a most fiery sermon, in which he cried out : "Burn, Holy Father, burn this instrument of the devil; burn, I tell you, this scandal of the whole Church " (3). At first, Pope Alexander contented himself with charging Cardinal Caraffa, the protector of the Dominican order, to check the indiscretions of the friar ; but since the cardinal, himself a reformer, took no active measures, we must suppose that the Pontiff decided to let the matter rest.

At this time the worst accusation against Savonarola was that of being more of a tribune, yea, of a demagogue, than of an ecclesiastic and a friar. The charge of heresy, made by the *arrabiati*, was unfounded ; in the heat of improvisation he may have been, and doubtless was, inexact in his expressions, but he had deliberately attacked no Catholic teaching. As for his political notions, he was a thorough republican, and carried his principles to their utmost logical conclusions ; he was a firm advocate of universal suffrage. All, said he, are interested in the State ; all, therefore, should have a voice

---

(1) *Loc. cit.*, b. IV., p. 75.   (2) *Ibid.*, p. 74.
(3) BURLAMACHI; p. 34. NARDI ; b. II., p. 35.

in the government (1). Hence his institution of the *Consiglio Grande* of a thousand members, elected by the votes of all the citizens, and that of the *Consiglio degli Scelti* (Council of the Select) formed of eighty persons of over forty years of age, chosen by the former. Savonarola no longer inhabited the cell of a friar ; that modest apartment had been turned into a hall of audience and of political wrangling. Florence soon found that she had exchanged the despotism of the Medici for that of the friar ; for despite his liberal institutions, the reformer allowed no political measure to be taken without his permission. Marino Sanuto, a Venetian chronicler, tells us that "a stone could not be moved without his consent. ... He was lord and governor of Florence " (2). It is worthy of note that Machiavelli, though not a partisan of Savonarola, says, in his *Discourses*, that so great a man must be treated with respect ; and he tells Leo X. that the Florentine state can be firmly re-established only by the restoration of the friar's *Consiglio Grande.* Guicciardini, whose *History* was written with a different animus from that pervading his unedited works, allows, in these latter, his conscience to speak ; and in his book on the *Government of Florence* he admits : " We owe much to this friar, who, without shedding a drop of blood, knew how to accomplish what otherwise would have cost much blood and disorder. Before him Florence had been governed by a restricted circle of *ottimati*, and then she had fallen into all the excesses of popular rule, which would have produced anarchy. He alone, from the beginning, knew how to be liberal without loosening the reins." But the reader will be pleased to hear the reformer himself on this subject. In the *Abridgment of his Revelations*, published by Bzovius, he says to the Florentines : " After examining with care the state of your city, and the coming revolutions in its form of government which would seem inevitable, I have persuaded myself that the great change will not be effected without danger or without even the effusion of blood, unless Divine Providence comes to your aid out of consideration for the justice and piety of the citizens who are worthy. In this spirit, and relying on this hope, I ear-

(1) NARDI ; *b.* I., p. 18.   (2) *Chronicles of Venice.*—BURCHARD ; *Diary.*

nestly besought the people to be reconciled to the Lord, and
to merit His mercy by renewed fervor and sincere repentance.
I commenced my discourses on this point, on St. Matthew's
Day, Sept. 25, 1494. From that time the citizens appeared
so zealous in the good works I had prescribed, that it pleased
God to give tangible proof of His reconciliation with us ; in
fact, in the month of November, by a miracle of heaven's
protection, you witnessed the desired change, and without
bloodshed or other scandal. Now, since there was a question of proposing to you a new form of government, I assembled all the magistrates and notables of the city in the cathedral of Florence, excluding only those whose sex or condition prohibited their being called. ... Having discoursed for
some time on what had been written by philosophers, states-
men, and the most able theologians, touching the best way of
governing a state, I explained my opinion as to the form
most suitable to the genius and profit of the Florentines. In
the succeeding discourses I proposed four articles, the necessity of which was admitted : I. Religion should be the basis
and the first rampart of our government. II. All private interests should yield to the public good. III. By forgetting
all past injuries and quarrels, there would ensue a general
and sincere peace, and in no way should any trouble accrue
to those who hitherto administered the affairs of the state.
And I added that there should always remain liberty of appeal from the tribunal of the six judges, so that no private
person could ever usurp the sovereign authority. It was also
my idea to establish a Great Council, composed of the wisest
and most illustrious citizens, after the model of the Council
of Venice ; and that thereafter all offices, etc., should be conferred in the name of the people of Florence, and not in the
name of any single person, who might thus take occasion to
aspire to tyranny. I made no difficulty of assuring the assembly that all I had proposed was conformable to God's
law and to His will. ... It was not only because of my peculiar knowledge of the Divine Will, but because of many
conclusions of my reason, that I undertook to convince you
of the advantages of this new form of government, the best
fitted for your needs, the most favorable to liberty, and also

the most apt to give great glory to your republic, which will thereby become more flourishing, both in the spiritual and in the temporal order."

Great numbers, incited, of course, by the partisans of the exiled Medici, soon revolted against the dictatorship imposed upon the city, and allied themselves with those who opposed the friar on religious grounds. In 1494 the superiors of the Dominicans deemed it prudent to forbid Savonarola to preach the Lenten course, although a Brief of Pope Alexander permitted him to give it. His followers then appealed to the Pontiff; and then Alexander, who is wrongly said to have been Savonarola's foe from the beginning, quashed the prohibition. In fact, during the early troubles of the Dominican, Alexander VI. paid but little attention to him; when he thought of him at all, it was rather with admiration. He had even conceived the idea, says Burlamachi, of enrolling the friar in the Sacred College. But now Alexander, although not prohibiting Savonarola from preaching, summoned him to Rome to explain his conduct. The reply was an allegation of infirmity and the need that Florence had of his presence. Then the Pontiff threatened the friar with the censures of the Church, and menaced the city of Florence with an interdict. The Florentine merchants, fearing the results of this measure, and many of the cardinals, who were rather favorable to the agitator, prevailed upon Alexander to withdraw his citation. However, the Pontiff gave an eloquent rebuke to his stubborn son, by leaving it to his own conscience whether or not he would continue to preach. This moderation seems to have somewhat affected Savonarola, for he withdrew from the pulpit, substituting, however, the friar Dominic of Pescia, also a Dominican, and a man of reputed holiness, who was far less fiery than himself.

The enemies of the friar regarded this retreat from the pulpit as a triumph for themselves; but when, in October, 1495, he broke his silence, they suffered from one of his most virulent tirades. Heaven, he said, would take condign vengeance upon those who had presumed to interfere with its work, namely, the establishment of popular government. To this denunciation he added new declamations on the need of reform

in the Church.   Pope Alexander now ordered the vicar-general
of the Dominicans at Bologna to examine into the charges
against his subject, and to punish him, according to the rules
of the Order, if he were found guilty.   During the trial the
friar was not to preach; but, in spite of this prohibition, Savonarola continued in the pulpit.   The Pontiff now demanded
that the republic should place the agitator in his hands, and
as his request was not heeded, he launched an excommunication against him (1).   This sentence was read in six churches
of Florence on June 18, 1497.   At first Savonarola seemed
inclined to submit.   He withdrew to his cell, admitted no
visitors, and wrote a humble letter to the Pope.   Alexander's
answer was truly paternal.   Among other encouraging remarks, he says: "In spite of facts, we begin to believe that
you have not spoken in malice, but rather in simplicity,
and out of zeal for the vineyard of the Lord."   He concluded
wi*_ a promise that if the friar would abstain from preaching,
and come to Rome, he would annul the censures pronounced.
To this letter Savonarola replied, demanding to be judged at
Florence.   However, he, for some time, respected the censures,
and abstained from preaching.   But, after six months, being
asked by the magistrates, who were all _frateschi_, to reappear
in the pulpit, and reconvert the people, who, in the interval
of his silence, had resumed their gayeties, he yielded to the
temptation, and boldly defied his excommunication.   On
Christmas he celebrated the customary three Masses of that
festival, gave the Eucharist to his religious, and, after a solemn procession around his convent (2), announced that he
would at once resume his preaching in the cathedral.   When
this new departure was made public, the vicar-general, in the
absence of Rinaldo Orsini, archbishop of Florence, convoked
the Chapter of the cathedral, and a prohibition to assist at

---

(1) Alexander VI. said to Bonsi, envoy of Florence: "I have read the sermons of your
friar, and have talked with those who have heard them. He dares to say that the Pope is a
broken sword; that he who believes in excommunication is a heretic; that he himself,
sooner than ask for absolution, will go to hell. He has been excommunicated, not because
of false insinuations, nor at any one's instigation, but for his disobedience to our command
that he should enter the new Tusco-Roman congregation. We do not condemn him because of his good works; but we insist that he ask pardon for his petulant arrogance, and
we will gladly accord him absolution when he humbles himself at our feet."

(2) For some time Savonarola had been prior of the Convent of St. Mark.

the proposed sermons was issued to all the clergy ; the parish priests were ordered to inform the faithful that, owing to the censures hanging over Savonarola, any one who attended his discourses would incur the same penalties. In spite of this action of the Chapter, the friar announced that he would follow the inspiration of God (1).

From this moment, Savonarola was at a disadvantage. People felt, and he must have felt, that his rebellion destroyed the influence, by weakening the authority, of his words. To obviate this difficulty, he now attacked the validity of his excommunication, declaring, first, that the censures of a wicked Pope are of no weight; second, that Alexander had excommunicated him without reason ; third, that the censures were pronounced against the "sower of tares," and he was not such a one (2). The arguments with which he defended these propositions were of the weakest kind ; and to reassure his partisans, he, one day, had recourse to a device which was terribly impressive. With the Holy Eucharist in his hand, he called upon God to consume him with fire from heaven if he was deceiving the people, and if the Pope's censure, in his case, was valid. At this time, says Christophe, "his talent certainly appears great, but we can divine that he is not at ease, not sure of himself. Savonarola perceives, in the minds of his hearers, difficulties which disquiet them, and to which he is compelled to respond. He invents trivial similes that he may excite their laughter ; he encumbers himself with suppositions ; he advances hazardous and equivocal principles, the consequences of which he would certainly repudiate." In fact, from the day that Savonarola openly defied the Holy See, his waning eloquence and deficient logic proved that he recognized the anomaly of his position.

When the news of the friar's daring rebellion reached Rome, Pope Alexander threatened serious measures against Florence if the delinquent were not sent to the Eternal City. The republic yielded in part ; Savonarola was commanded to keep silent, but his disciple, Friar Dominic of Pescia, continued to preach in the strain of the master, and his rashness precip-

(1) NARDI; b. II., p. 42.
(2) *Sermon for last Sunday of Lent.*

itated the ruin of both. One day a Franciscan friar, named Francis of Puglia, while preaching in the church of Santa Croce, declared that Friar Jerome was an impostor; adding that he was ready to try the "ordeal by fire" with the said Jerome. At that moment Friar Dominic was holding forth in the church of St. Lawrence, and the news of the Franciscan's challenge was carried immediately to him. He at once informed his hearers, and accepted the defiance. When Friar Francis found himself called upon to make good his boasting offer, he lost courage, and tried to escape by pleading that he had challenged Savonarola, not Dominic. This incident was painful to Savonarola, but how could he disavow his companion when he himself had often declared that if his arguments did not produce conviction of the truth of his teaching, he was ready to invoke the supernatural in its defence? He accepted the challenge, and for himself, but insisted that a Papal legate and all the foreign ambassadors should be present at the ordeal; furthermore, he demanded that if he came unharmed out of the fire, the Church should at once be reformed. Friar Francis refused these conditions, but the factions had entered into the spirit of the thing, and the mob would not miss the show. The impetuous Dominic, unlike the timid Francis, was panting for the terrible trial, and there were many Franciscans more brave, or more confident, than their brother. Finally, the affair was laid before the magistrates, and they decided that the ordeal should be held. As champions the magistrates designated, on the part of Savonarola, Friar Dominic; and on the part of the Franciscan challenger, a lay-brother named Julian Rondinelli. Certain propositions, the truth or falsity of which was to be established, in the opinion of many, by this curious means, were drawn up by Dominic. They were: "The Church needs reformation. She will be chastised. She will be renovated. Florence will be punished, but she will afterwards prosper. The infidels will be converted. All these things will soon happen. The excommunication of Savonarola is null." The magistrates then appointed ten citizens, five for each party, as a commission to settle any differences that might arise; and all was ready for that trial, the worth of which we doubt, but which, in those days, commanded the confidence of the people (1). Previous to the experiment, however, the magistrates sent messengers to Rome to obtain the Pontiff's consent to the undertaking. A consistory was held, and the authorization was refused; Alexander simply wrote to the Franciscans, praising their devotion to the Holy See, and encouraging them to continue in their combat against error (2).

On April 7, 1498, in the centre of the Square of the Magistracy (in modern times, Square of the Grand Duke), was to be seen an immense scaffolding, paved with bricks, and covered with combustible material. Two tribunes arose before it, destined to be occupied by the magistrates and by the friars of the two Orders. The square was filled with anxious

(1) The Church never authorized or approved of ordeals; but, they being recognized in the laws of the barbarians, she was obliged to tolerate them. The prejudices of humanity are not easily eradicated; witness the number of superstitions in our own day, and among the most cultivated. As far back as the ninth century, Agobard, archbishop of Lyons, wrote against the *damnable* opinion that God interfered in the ordeals; in the eleventh, Ivo of Chartres supports his condemnation of them by a letter of Pope Stephen V. to the bishop of Mayence. Popes Celestine III., Innocent III., and Honorius III. condemned them, as did also the Fourth Council of Lateran. The scholastic theologians teach that they are injurious to God, and favorable to lies. As for the question, whether or not there was ever anything of the supernatural in the frequent success of these ordeals, see an excellent dissertation in the *Memoirs of the Academy of Inscriptions*, v. XXIV.—The following description of one of these "ordeals" may not be uninteresting to the reader. It is given by the Protestant Voigt, in his *Life of Gregory VII.* (b. III.), and the event occurred in Florence in 1063. In front of the convent of the Holy Saviour were "two platforms, each ten feet long, five in width, and four in height; they were separated by a path paved with dry and very inflammable wood. In the church hymns were sung, and fervent prayers were addressed to heaven, that it might be made known, who, in compliance with the order of the abbot, should enter the flames. The lot fell on Peter, a monk of Vallombrosa, a man of irreproachable conduct. Peter went to the altar to celebrate Mass; every heart was still. Four monks now approached the platforms; the first carried an image of Christ, the second the holy water, the third twelve blessed candles, and the fourth a vessel full of incense to nourish the fire. All raised their hearts to God, for the success of the perilous enterprise. When the priest had finished the sacrifice, he took the cross of the Saviour and solemnly made the round of the platforms, accompanied by the abbot and the monks. When he had approached the flames, the meaning of the ceremony was explained to the people. The fire was kindled, the flames waved in the air. The priest then kneeled to his God, and besought Jesus Christ to permit him to pass through the fire safe and sound, if the bishop were guilty; the multitude cried 'Amen.' Finally the monk made the sign of the cross over the fiery furnace, seized the crucifix, and with a serene countenance he passed through the flames without an injury. God and his faith had protected him."

(2) In reference to this request of the magistrates of Florence, the Abbé Christophe says that he is astonished to find that Carle, in his *History of Friar Jerome Savonarola* (Paris, 1848), cites the letter of Alexander VI. as an approbation of the proposed ordeal. "If we rightly understand the words of the Pontiff," adds Christophe, "they do not contradict the testimony of the historian (*Miscellanies* of Baluze, v. IV.; Burlamachi, p. 132), who affirms that the decision of the consistory was averse to the authorization. They simply contain a eulogy on the *fervor, zeal, devotion* displayed by the Franciscans in their struggle with Savonarola."

spectators, the house-tops were crowded. At the appointed hour Rondinelli, at the head of a long file of Franciscans, and Dominic of Pescia, flanked by Savonarola, and followed by a procession of Dominicans, entered the square, and took their places. It was observed that Savonarola carried a silver pyx, containing the Holy Eucharist. Rondinelli advanced to the magistrates, and cried out: "Behold me ready for the ordeal. Sinner that I am, I know the flames will consume me. But let not Friar Dominic therefore boast of victory; he must take his turn in the fire. If he comes out unharmed, let him be proclaimed the conqueror; otherwise, no" (1). The judges replied that his demand would be granted. Then ensued a curious scene. The referees feared that the champions might have concealed some charms under their robes, and ordered them to change them for others handed to them. Rondinelli was perfectly willing, but at first Dominic hesitated. "Never mind," cried the Franciscan, "his robe will burn with his body." Then the Dominican changed his garments, but retained a crucifix. When he was ordered to lay it down, Rondinelli said: "Let him keep it—it is of wood, and will burn with the rest." Then Savonarola handed the Holy Eucharist to Dominic. But the crowd, believing that the flames would, perforce, respect the Blessed Sacrament, declared that if the Dominican were allowed to carry it, the trial would not be fair (2). Savonarola persisted, and threatened to abandon the ordeal. An endless dispute ensued, and the promised spectacle vanished in ridicule.

This fiasco was the signal for the fall of Savonarola; for one cannot trifle with the mob. Had he not been protected by the Holy Eucharist, the agitator would not have regained his convent in safety. In vain he mounted the pulpit to pacify the crowd; his eloquence was not heeded, for all now felt that Savonarola was but an ordinary mortal. The day after was Palm Sunday, and, while one of the Dominicans was preaching in the cathedral, a crowd of young men burst upon

---

(1) NARDI, b. II., p. 48; BURLAMACHI, p. 140; Anonymous *Life of F. Jerome Savonarola* (Geneva, 1781), c. xxvi.

(2) NARDI, b. II., p. 45; NERLI, p. 78; Anonymous author, *supra*, pp. 101, 102.

the congregation, a voice cried : " To St. Mark's!", and in a
few moments the convent was attacked. The magistrates, tired
of him who had made them, more than winked at the outbreak, and ordered the few laymen who had rushed to defend the Dominicans, out of the building. The doors were
burnt away, and the mob rushed in search of its prey. Savonarola was found in prayer before the Blessed Sacrament,
in company with the imprudent Dominic of Pescia. He was
saved from the crowd by some municipal commissioners, and,
together with Dominic, lodged in prison ; a few hours afterwards Friar Sylvester Maruffii was also arrested.

Information of Savonarola's imprisonment was immediately sent to Pope Alexander, and he ordered the magistrates
to send the friar to Rome. Had the command been heeded,
the unfortunate man would, doubtless, have been confined,
perhaps even for life, but the catastrophe would have been
averted. The magistrates now appointed a commission of
six citizens and two canons (these latter as Papal commissaries) for the trial of the three Dominicans ; nearly all were
declared adversaries of the accused. The trial lasted from
the 9th to the 19th of April. During the first interrogatories
Savonarola was firm and collected ; but when, in accordance
with the detestable and foolish custom of the time, he was
put to " the question," as the torture was called, he quite
naturally weakened (1). Although the *Acts* of the trial are
printed with the title. *Authentic Copy of the Trial of Jerome
Savonarola*, and although the signature of the friar is found
at the end, there are strong presumptions against the value of
the admissions they contain. Firstly, the composition of the
tribunal, the preamble of the interrogatory, the testimony of
historians,—all prove that the proceedings were not conducted
with the calm impartiality of justice. Secondly, it is certain
that Savonarola more than once retracted, and showed much
vacillation, during the course of his interrogatory ; that he
frequently declared, in presence of the Papal commissioners,
that what he had said and predicted was the simple truth,

(1) The characteristic sneer of Roscoe that the torture is the "last reason of theologians "
is uncalled for, for in what civil tribunal, down to the last century, and in part of that, was
it not used ?

and that his own contradictions had been extorted by the fear of torture; that he acknowledged that torture would force him to admit whatever his enemies might wish, because he knew himself to be unable to support such pain. Hence the Pontifical representatives were much embarrassed. Finally, the commission has been accused of having falsified the depositions of Savonarola, they having realized the impossibility of obtaining real facts sufficiently serious, and it is said that a notary, called *Ser Ceccone,* aided in this odious stratagem. It is true that it is an apologist of Savonarola who asserts this (1), and that we should mistrust the testimony of those who trembled before the visions of the friar; but we find the same accusation, formulated, with no less directness, in several contemporary historians who had not the same interest as Burlamachi in attacking the equity of the commission. In fact, Nardi asserts (b. II., p. 47) that " at the time, and afterward, there was much doubt as to the truth and quality of the proceedings," and that he himself may not be accused of hiding the truth, he narrates the following anecdote : " A noble citizen, who had been one of the examiners of the said friars, and who had been chosen because of his enmity to them, was met by me in his villa; and being questioned by me with deliberate intention, concerning the truth of the said proceedings, he ingenuously replied, in the presence of his wife, that it was true that in the report of Friar Jerome's trial some things had been omitted and some things added " (2).

When the examination had come to an end, the magistrates deliberated as to the sentence to be passed upon the unfortunate religious. A few wished to refer the matter to the Pontiff, as the accused were ecclesiastics; and besides, they were leniently disposed, and thought that the friars' only chance of escaping the death penalty lay in their being placed in Alexander's hands. But the majority insisted that the culprits could not be accorded any ecclesiastical immunity, as they were excommunicated. The party of severity

(1) BURLAMACHI ; pp. 155-160.

(2) For other writers who bring the same charge against the commission, see MURATORI, *Annals of Italy,* y. 1498.

carried the day, and Pope Alexander was requested to appoint commissioners to preside at the sentence and its execution. The Pontiff commissioned Joachim Turriani, the general of the Dominicans, and Francis Ramolino, an auditor of the governor of Rome; and after some interrogatories they ratified the proceedings, and the friars were declared guilty of schism, heresy, persecution of the Church, and seduction of the people. They were sentenced to be burned at the stake. On May 23d Florence witnessed the last act of this terrible drama. In the square of the Grand Duke, where two months before Savonarola had seen his credit destroyed, another apparatus was now arranged for his death. Early in the morning the three friars went to confession, received Holy Communion with every manifestation of a sincere piety, and marched out to their last earthly suffering. Arrived in the square, they had to undergo the humiliating ceremony of degradation, being deprived, one at a time, of all their sacerdotal vestments. Burlamachi and Nardi assert that the prelate, whose duty it was to perform this act, said to Savonarola: " I separate thee from the Church militant and triumphant;" and that the unfortunate firmly and loudly replied: " From the Church militant, yes—from the Church triumphant, no!" The three friars were then asked whether they accepted the plenary indulgence which the Pontiff accorded them, and they all three bowed their heads and answered in the affirmative. They were then strangled, and their bodies reduced to ashes, which, to prevent any superstitious veneration, were thrown into the Arno (1).

The following reflections of Christophe on the character of Savonarola are worthy of the reader's attention: "Some make a fanatic, a sectarian, an impostor, of Savonarola; others, an apostle, a saint. The fact is, there is something of all these in the Dominican. If we open the door of his cell in St. Mark's and there contemplate him at the foot of the crucifix, attenuated by fasting and drowned in an ecstasy of prayer; if we follow him to Santa Maria del Fiore and hear him reproaching voluptuous Florence with her vices, Savonarola is a saint, an apostle. But if we turn to the other side,

(1) RAZZI; *MS. Life of Savonarola.* SANUTO; *loc. cit., b.* VI.

and behold the tribune who mixes politics with religion, the
declaimer who inveighs against the existing powers, the seer
who opposes a divine mission to the authority of the head of
the Church, Savonarola is very like a fanatic, a sectarian, an
impostor. Unfortunately he finished his life with the latter
character; such was the impression he left with the spectators when he left the scene, and we may well ask ourselves
whether, if he had preserved the popular favor, he would
have anticipated the role of the monk of Wittenburg. Protestants appear not to doubt it, for they claim Savonarola
as one of their forerunners. But they forget that this monk
broke the link which might have connected him with their
rebellion, on the day when, at the foot of the stake, he accepted the absolution of the Pope, and handed down to posterity that tardy but solemn proof of his repentance. . . .
Savonarola knew not how to be either saint or apostle. We
would hesitate to call him a sectary, and we would dislike
still more to style him an impostor. We regard him as a
sincere, but a prodigiously imaginative preacher. If we have
studied him rightly, he appears to have been carried away
in the current of an unregulated imagination from the day
when he began his prophetic exposition of the Apocalypse,
to that when he openly substituted for the authority of the
Church that of his own pretended celestial mission. Undoubtedly his eloquence is wonderful, but it is that of a vehement declaimer rather than that of a solid and enlightened
teacher. We see in it the violent and convulsive agitation of
a fever, rather than an effort of powerful and healthy thought.
His strength does not warm; it burns, it boils over like the
lava from a volcano. It does not illumine, it dazzles; it does
not guide, it pulls; it does not march, it tumbles. His spirit
cannot understand the positive side of things. Savonarola
is seldom true; exaggeration seems to be his domain, his
figures are colossal, his situations forced, his end greater
than his means. We need not be surprised if a man so organized, with such power of imagination and such weakness
of sense, influenced by the enthusiasm which drinks his
words, and by an idolatrous worship accorded him,—if such
a man becomes intoxicated with himself, . . . and if he be-

lieves himself to be the envoy of the Lord. Savonarola succumbed to the hatred of factions which he himself had excited. In our days he would have succumbed to ridicule."

Protestants have frequently spoken of Savonarola as a precursor of the "Reformation." Luther insisted that the unfortunate Dominican taught the doctrine of justification by faith alone; and in 1523 he caused Savonarola's meditation on the 70th psalm to be circulated throughout Germany, together with a preface by himself, in which he declared that Friar Jerome was his forerunner, "although some of the theological mud yet stuck to the feet of the holy man." He asserts that Savonarola taught his own cardinal doctrine, and that "*for this reason* he was burnt by the Pope," and he adds: "Christ canonized him because he did not rely upon vows or a cowl, upon Masses or a rule, but upon meditation on the gospel of peace; and covered with the breastplate of justice, armed with the shield of faith and the helmet of salvation, he enlisted, not in the Order of Preachers, but in the army of the Christian Church." Savonarola was not put to death by the Pope, nor was his fate owing to the cause alleged by the ex-Augustinian; and the very work upon which the latter relies to prove his point shows the former's orthodoxy in the doctrine of grace. Luther draws comfort from the following passage: "I will hope in the Lord, and soon I shall be freed from all tribulation. And by what merit? Not by mine, but by Thine, Lord. I offer not my own justice, but I seek Thy mercy. The Pharisees gloried in their justice; hence they had not that of God, which is obtained by grace alone, and no one will ever be just before God, merely because of having performed the works of the law. Soldier of Christ, what is your mind in these combats? Have you faith, or not? Yes, I have (you answer). Know, then, that this is a great grace of God, for faith is His gift, and not for our works." But this passage is explained by its continuation, for, meditating upon the next verse, "Incline Thy ear unto me, and save me," Savonarola says: "Let thy sorrow show, if it can, one sinner, even the greatest one, who has turned to the Lord, and has not been received and justified. ... Hast thou not heard the Lord saying that whenever a sinner weeps, and grieves for his sins, He will not remember his iniquities? ... Hast thou fallen? Arise, and mercy will find thee. Art thou being ruined? Cry out, and mercy will come." That Savonarola's belief concerning grace was far from the Lutheran is shown by the *Rule for a Good Life*, which, when requested by his jailor to leave him some souvenir, he wrote on the cover of a book. In it he says: "A good life depends altogether upon grace; hence we must *strive to acquire it*, and when we have received it, we must try to increase it. ... It is certainly a free gift of God; but examination into our sins, and meditation on the vanity of worldly things, prepare us for grace; confession and Communion dispose us to receive it. ... *Perseverance in good works*, in confession, and in all that disposes us to grace, is the true and sure means to increase it." Protestants who would like to claim Savonarola as a precursor of the Lutheran movement, should attend to the following passage, taken from the fourth book of his *Triumph of the Cross*. "Since Peter was made His vicar by Christ, and was constituted by Him pastor of the whole Church, it follows that all the successors of Peter have the same power. And since the bishops of the Roman See hold the place of Peter, it is evident that the Roman Church is the leader and mistress of all the churches, and that the entire congregation of the faithful should be united with the Roman Pontiff. He, therefore, who differs in doctrine from the unity of the Roman Church, certainly recedes from Christ. But all heretics differ from that Church; therefore, they are out of the right path, and cannot be called Christians. He is to be styled a heretic who perverts the sacred pages and the doctrine of the Holy Roman Church, and, following the sect of his own choice, obstinately perseveres in it. As has often been said, truth agrees with truth; all truths confirm each other. But heretics so differ among themselves that they agree in almost nothing; it is very plain, therefore, that they are strangers to truth. However, the doctrine of the Roman Church, in all that pertains to faith and morals, is one; and although Catholic teachers are almost innumerable, they neither depart from that doctrine nor wish to differ from it. The kingdom of Christ and of the Church militant is established not only to endure until the end of the world; after the renovation of the universe, it will exist forever, as the Gospel and all the Scriptures and the monuments of the saints testify. Heretics, who have bitterly persecuted Catholics, have not been able to preserve their lines against the Roman Church; but have been utterly routed, together with their depraved dogmas and the obstinacy of their followers. It is certain, then, that their false volumes come not from God; that their doctrine is not Christian."

In 1548 the celebrated Dominican, Ambrose Catarino (Lancellotto Politi), published at Venice a *Discourse against the Doctrine and Prophecies of Friar Jerome Savonarola*, in which he drew attention to many propositions which he deemed contrary to Catholic teaching; but he declared that he did "not combat Savonarola, who was worthy of compassion rather than of blame, but only his errors, which yet survived in the minds of those who, not without scandal and danger to their souls, believed in him" (1). Probably in consequence of this work, Pope Paul IV. ordered an inquiry into Friar Jerome's works, and when the commissioners read to him some extracts, he exclaimed: "Why, this is Martin Luther!" But after the examination was finished, the sole decision pronounced was a "suspension" of fifteen of the sermons and of the dialogue on *Prophetic Truth*. And in the *Index* of the Council of Trent these works are prohibited only "until corrected," which certainly implies that they contain only accidental, not essential, errors.

The sermons of Savonarola were placed upon the Roman Index "until corrected;" but his other works are animated by a spirit of the most tender piety, and are thoroughly orthodox. His *Triumph of the Cross* consists of four books on the evidences of Christianity, and is written in a vein of calmness very surprising to one who has just been subject-

---

(1) Catarino had a perfect mania for scenting heresy nearly everywhere and in nearly every author. He even denounced to the Faculty of Paris many propositions of the great Thomas de Vio (called Cajetan, from his birthplace and See of Gaeta). But he was well rebuked by Bartholomew Spina, master of the apostolic palace, who, when Catarino was named to a bishopric, brought forth fifty propositions, taken from the zealot's writings, which, the critic insisted (though without reason), were heretical.

ed to the fire of the author's sermons.   His five books on
the *Simplicity of the Christian Life* are preceded by an epistle
to the citizens of Florence, in which he thus describes his
work : "I shall try to adopt natural reason, rather than the
authority of the divine writings.   And I shall do so, because
of the incredulous, the wise ones of this age, that is to say,
the philosphers and orators, the poets and others of inflated
intellect, who think that the Christian life is superstition,
and that its simplicity is foolishness ; also, because of the
condition of our unhappy age, in which faith has grown so
weak, and the supernatural light has been so nearly extin-
guished, that I am unable to decide whether those who acknowledge their belief merely regard it as an affair of opinion, and hold it because it was taught them in childhood,
or whether they really cling to it as something taught by supernatural authority.   I hesitate in pronouncing upon the
faith of Christians of to-day ; for charity has grown cold, and
the 'fruit of good works does not appear.   But since the natural light does not fail in man, so long as he acts according
to natural reason, let the intellect, at least, of these people
be convinced, and let them understand that the Christian
life is truth and simplicity ; that it is not foolishness, but
the wisdom of God ; then perhaps they will cease to calumniate it.   I trust, however, in the Lord Jesus, that you will
find in this book nothing contrary to Holy Writ, or to the
sayings of the holy Doctors, or to the teaching of the Holy
Roman Church, to whose correction I have always submitted, and do submit ; but that you will discover in it the full
truth, which came down from heaven to our fathers who
everywhere preached it, and left it to us in writing, confirmed by signs and miracles " (1).

In this work Savonarola leads his reader to come, in each
book, to a certain number of *Conclusions.*   Thus, in the first
book, the conclusions are as follows :   The Christian life is
that in which the doctrine of Christ is followed, and His
conduct imitated.   It is better than any other which can be
found or excogitated.   It is not founded in any natural love.
Nor is it based on the sensitiveness of man.   Neither is it

(1) *Works of Friar Jerome Savonarola* ; Grenoble, 1606, vol. II.

founded on the sole natural light of reason. It proceeds from no natural cause. It proceeds from no spiritual creature. Its root and foundation is the grace of God. It tends, with all its powers, to augment and preserve the gift of grace. For these ends, prayer is a better means than any other good work. The devout and frequent use of the sacraments of Penance and the Holy Eucharist furnish the best means to preserve and to augment the gift of grace. The second book treats of simplicity of heart; the third, of exterior simplicity; the fourth, of rejection of superfluities, and of almsgiving; the fifth, of the happiness of the Christian life. The *Meditations* on the Psalms *Miserere, In Te Domine speravi*, and *Qui regis Israel*, form, to use the words of the Dominican censor of the edition before us, "a honeyed book, full of the sweetness of piety, and it cannot be read without fruit if it is read attentively." This book is peculiarly interesting from the fact that Savonarola composed it while in prison. The following touching prayer is prefixed to the meditation on the *Miserere*. "Unhappy me! I have offended heaven and earth, and am destitute of help. Where shall I go? To whom shall I turn? Who will have mercy on me? I dare not lift my eyes to heaven, for I have grievously offended heaven. I find no refuge on earth, for I have been a scandal to earth. What then shall I do? Shall I despair? God forbid! God is merciful, God is piteous, my Saviour is kind. God alone, then, is my refuge; He will not despise His work; He will not spurn His image. To Thee, therefore, most kind God, I come, sad and dejected; Thou alone art my hope, my encouragement. But what shall I say to Thee, since I dare not raise my eyes? I must pour forth the words of contrition, and implore Thy pity, crying: *Miserere!*" Another interesting work of Savonarola's is a dialogue between the soul and the spirit, entitled *The Solace of My Journey*, the tone and object of which may be gathered from the first sentences: "*Spir.* I am now thinking of returning to my home, to see the God from whom 1 was banished; but thou shalt go with me, my spouse. *Soul.* But I know not the way to so great a joy. *Spir.* Our way is Christ. *Soul.* But faith wavers. *Spir.* He who approaches

God should believe that He is. *Soul.* And yet, he that is. hasty to give credit, is light of heart (*Eccles.* xix. 4). *Spir.* But to believe in God is the part of gravity and of wisdom. *Soul.* Has God ever spoken to thee? *Spir.* I believe those to whom He has deigned to speak. *Soul.* But how do you know that they heard God speaking? *Spir.* Miracles have proven it. *Soul.* Miracles have ceased; what then shall persuade me? *Spir.* Doubtest thou that God is? *Soul.* Many doubt, for no one has ever seen God (*John* i. 18). *Spir.* But such have no intellect, according to the Psalmist (xiii. 1): 'The fool hath said in his heart, there is no God.' *Soul.* How canst thou prove that God is? ... I admit the force of thy argument, but I ask, ... what is God? *Spir.* If carnal men could know what God is, He could not be God. For we can know only tangible and sensible things; God is not one of these, nor can He be presented to our intellects as He really is; it is sufficient that we know what He is not. ... *Soul.* Thy words have convinced me, and I already yearn for the sight of God; but I ask myself, what if God does not grant it? Has He promised to thus bless those who love Him? *Spir.* Let what thou hast now learnt suffice for to-day. The night approaches; let us seek our abode in silence, and pray God that to-morrow thou mayest acquire more of the science of salvation." The first book of this *Dialogue*, as we have seen, treats of God; the second, of the truth of the faith; the third, of the Messiah, against the Jews; the fourth, of the articles of faith, against philosophasters; the fifth, of the reasons of probability which favor the articles of faith; the sixth, of the future life; the seventh, of heaven.

We now ask the reader's attention to the following remarks of Cantù: "A man of faith, of superstition, of genius, Savonarola abounded in charity. Contrary to Luther, who confided entirely in reason, he believed in personal inspiration. From his works may be taken arguments both for and against him; and by comparing them, we may perceive how he sought to harmonize reason with faith, the Catholic religion with political liberty. He never denied the authority of the Holy See; although he resisted him whom he regarded as an illegitimate Pope, and against whom he invoked a Council which should reform the Church. ... He thought to guide the crowd by means of its passions; and, as always happens, he became the victim of these passions. He alone is a heretic who obstinately defends something contrary to what is defined to be of faith. The fame of Savonarola remained suspended between heaven and hell; but his end was deplored by all, and perhaps first by those who had caused it. In the churches of Santa Maria Novella and San Marco he is depicted as a saint, and Raphael placed him, in the *Loggie* of the Vatican, among the Doctors of the Church; portraits of him were kept and venerated, not only by the pious of Florence who continued to oppose corruption and its consequent slavery, but even by great saints. ... It is said that Clement VIII. swore, in 1598, that if he succeeded in acquiring possession of Ferrara, he would canonize Savonarola. If the philosophical Naudet called him a modern Arius or Mahomet, the devout Father Touron thought him a messenger of God; Sts. Philip Neri and Catharine de Ricci venerated him as blessed, and Benedict XIV. deemed him worthy of canonization. *Not one of the followers of Friar Jerome became a disciple of Luther or a betrayer of his country's liberty.* Michelangelo, who raised bastions for his native city and the greatest temple in Christendom, always venerated Savonarola. Machiavelli, who never embraced any opinions not in vogue, admired him at first; he commenced to ridicule him only when he himself had fully developed a policy that was diametrically opposite to that of the friar, namely, a policy without God, without Providence, without morality—an innate depravity, though without original sin and without a Redeemer—and which expected to regenerate Italy, not only without the Church, but in spite of the Church" (1).

Much has been written for and against Savonarola's claims to the gift of prophecy. It is certain that very many wise and cool-headed men among his contemporaries credited his predictions; for instance, Pico della Mirandola, Marcilio Ficino, and St. Philip Neri. The reader may be interested

(1) *Heretics of Italy*, Discourse xi.

in the following remarks of the prudent and observing Philip de Commines. "I have already told how a Friar-Preacher, or Jacobin, a resident of Florence for fifteen years and enjoying a reputation for great sanctity—whom I conversed with in 1495—Jerome by name, foretold many things which afterward happened. He had always insisted that the king would cross the mountains, and he publicly declared that this and other things had been revealed to him by God. He said that the king had been chosen by God to reform the Church by force, and to chastise the tyrants (of Italy); and because he declared that he knew these future things by revelation, many murmured against him, and he acquired the hatred of the Pope and of many of the Florentines. His life was the most beautiful in the world, as every one could see, and his sermons against vice converted many in that city to a good life, as I have said. At this date of 1498, when King Charles died, Friar Jerome also passed away—four or five days intervening between the two deaths, and I will tell you why I note the date. He had always publicly preached that if the king did not return into Italy to accomplish the task God had assigned him, God would cruelly punish him; and all these sermons were printed and sold. And this same threat of cruel punishment had been often written to the king before his death, by the said Jerome, as the friar himself told me in Italy, saying that the sentence of heaven was pronounced against the king, if he did not accomplish God's will and did not restrain his soldiers from pillage. He predicted many true things concerning the king, and the evils to befall him; the death of his son, and his own, and I have seen the letters to the king" (1). On May 13th, 1495, the duke of Ferrara wrote to Manfredi, his agent at Florence, that he had understood that Friar Jerome "had said, and says, many things about the present affairs of Italy, and it appears that he threatens the Italian princes. And since he is a virtuous person and a good religious, we greatly wish to know what he has said and says, with all particulars; we desire you to see him, and to request him, in our name, to tell what he thinks is to happen, especially in matters con-

(1) *Memoirs*, b. VIII., ch. III.

cerning us." And Savonarola replied that he would pray to
God, and then answer the duke. On August 8th, 1497, this
same prince wrote to the friar: "We declare to you that we
have never doubted the future occurrence of all the things
you have predicted."

The figure of Savonarola is intensely poetical, and therefore it appeals to the imagination. This alone would account
for much of the sympathetic interest which his memory has
ever evoked; but it is indubitable that where the incense of
praise has been offered to him by Catholics, such persons
have been influenced by the un-historical and un-theological
theory of a distinction between the Church and the Papacy.
As to the acclamations of the heterodox, it is natural that they
should gloat over the spectacle of a son of the Church flinging
mud on his mother. Truly Savonarola was a wonderful genius, and it is difficult to deny the purity of his inmost heart.
His power over the souls of men was such as it has been giv-
en to few to exercise; he dominated the sage Commines
and the simplest *piagnone* in the Duomo with equal facility.
Above all his qualifications, however, should be ranked that
political capacity which made him, for eight years, the absolute master of the Florentine state. And it is upon this capacity that his latest apologist, Pasquale Villari, lays particular stress. But what was the first duty of this man whom
Villari, with apparent sincerity, strives to vindicate? It was
that of a sworn servant of God's altar. Had this priest the
right to become derelict to his priestly vocation by descending into an arena of legislative squabbles? Had this friar
the right to trample upon the Constitutions of his Order?
So long as Savonarola directed his pulpit eloquence toward
the expulsion of the Medici from Florence, possibly his intervention was a ministry of charity; but he should not, thenceforward, have sunk the preacher in the tribune, and have
ceased to be the obedient religious. But he disobeyed, urges Villari, because he suspected the trap which Alexander
VI. had set for him. The existence of this trap is a gratui-
tous assertion; but even had the Pontiff laid such a snare, it
was the duty of the friar to obey. Villari seems to have
anticipated this observation; for he says: " Savonarola would

have sacrificed himself willingly for the peace of the Church, had there been a question of his own person alone; but the attacks directed against him were aimed chiefly against the Florentine Republic, of which he was the living and speaking representative." Such a reply merely emphasizes the fact that in the later career of Savonarola, the priest had vanished in the politician (1).

CHAPTER XV.

POPE JULIUS II.

At the commencement of the sixteenth century, the Italian factions of the Guelphs and Ghibellines had almost entirely disappeared; and the numerous small Italian republics having been absorbed into other states, or combined, in some instances, to form others, Italy was divided politically as follows. The illustrious House of Savoy, then enjoying a ducal title, reigned over Piedmont. The marquisate of Monferrato was ruled by Boniface, of the stock of the Paleologi. Genoa was an aristocratic so-called republic, but under the protection of the king of France. The duchy of Milan, a recent conquest of Louis XII., was occupied, for the nonce, by French troops. Modena, Reggio, Ferrara, and certain surrounding districts, acknowledged the ducal sway of the House of Este. Venice possessed, besides her Adriatic shores and the mouths of the Po, the provinces of Bergamo, Brescia, Verona, Crema, Vicenza, and Padua; she also ruled over Treviso, Feltre, Belluno, the Polesine di Rovigo, and Ravenna; she exercised supremacy over Gorizia excepting Aquileja, and over Istria, excepting Trieste; along the Adriatic, she owned Zara, the islands opposite Dalmatia and Albania, and Spalatro; in the Mediterranean, she held Zante, Veglia, Crete, and Cyprus; and of the late Lower Empire she owned

---

(1) " The question is simply one of a Pope commanding a religious, and of a religious refusing obedience to a Pope. Friar Jerome was a rebel, and all the virtues which he had so laboriously cultivated, the grand edifice of talents and merits which men properly admired, cannot hide that damning fact from the eyes of a true Catholic. Let us pity his fate if we will; and if it appears to have been undeservedly severe, let us ascribe the blame to those to whom it properly belongs. The criminal legislation of those days was terrible; for then, in spite of a wickedness apparently grosser than our own, men at least believed in such things as truth and error with the utmost simplicity."—BARBEY D'AUREVILLY; *Men and Works*, vol. VIII., p. 143. Paris, 1887.

some of the richest territories, such as Modone, Corone, Nea-
polis, Argos, and Corinth.   Mantua and its duchy were ruled
by the House of Gonzaga.   Florence was waiting for the return of the Medici, momentarily expelled.   The States of the
Church were still subject to the sceptre of the Pope-King,
saving those which Cæsar Borgia had managed by force or
fraud to appropriate.   The two kingdoms of Naples and Sicily, which had been taken from the House of Aragon by the
united forces of France and Spain, and from which a Franco-
Spanish war had afterward expelled the French, were now
provinces under the sway of the Spanish monarch, Ferdinand
the Catholic.

After the funeral of Pope Alexander VI. the cardinals, to
the number of thirty-seven, entered into Conclave, and on
Sept. 22d, 1503, Francis Piccolomini (1), a cardinal-deacon
and archbishop-elect of Siena, was chosen Pontiff.   He assumed the name of Pius III.; and so eminent was his virtue,
that great advantages were anticipated from his reign.   But
after only twenty-six days of Pontificate he died, and was
succeeded on Oct. 21st by the cardinal Julian della Rovere,
who took the name of Julius II., "more mindful " thinks
Alexandre, "of Julius Cæsar than of St. Julius I."   Muratori, who is not too favorable to Julius II., says that he possessed all the gifts of a magnificent man.   "He had a grand
mind, much shrewdness, and no less courage.   He had enjoyed a long experience in things of the world, and was
loyal and truthful."   Blanc thinks that if this Pontiff had
been less warlike, less politic, less intrepid, he would have
been regarded as a great Pope.   Cantù recalls the saying of
the contemporaries of Julius, that he threw the keys of
Peter into the Tiber, and preserved only the sword of Paul;
but this author also sees in Julius, "A Pontiff superior to
either personal or family interests, and one who knew not
how to yield when he thought the advantage of the Holy
See was concerned.   Disgusted with the brutal soldiery who
disposed of Italy as they willed, and before whom Alexander VI. had trembled, he formed the noble design of 'free-

(1) His father was one of the Todeschi ; but his mother being a sister of Pope Pius II.,
that Pontiff had induced him to assume the name and arms of the Piccolomini.

ing Italy from the barbarians.' ... Even in the agony of death he exclaimed : ' Chase the French out of Italy'(1), and if all his actions had tended toward this end, he would have merited well of his country. He proved himself fit to govern a much larger state ; he was generous in his designs, a stranger to his personal interests, and was respectful of the liberties of his people." Audin finds in Julius II. only one object, one plan, one idea ; namely, the freedom of his country from foreign servitude. "Without him Italian nationality was lost ; Italy would have become a French province." Ranke discerns in this Pontiff "a noble soul, cherishing grand designs in favor of all Italy." Leo, also a Protestant, says that "surrounded by the passions and weaknesses of his time, Julius II. was one of the most worthy characters produced by Italy." But the early Reformers, ever venomous toward all the Pontiffs, were especially malignant toward Julius II. Ulrich Hutten, who has been styled the German Demosthenes, and whose *Epistles of Obscure Men*, despite their obscene inanities, have been compared by Germans to the *Letters* of Pascal, would have his credulous compatriots believe that : "The robber Julius was polluted with every species of crime. He pretended to open Heaven to whom he would, and he doomed to Stygian darkness men of pure life. He filled the world with crime, and ever confused right and wrong." The same rampant declaimer saw in our Pontiff an anomaly, a ruffian with unkempt beard, a savage eye, and colorless lips ; and he invoked a Brutus to rid Rome of such a hateful presence (2). According to Hutten, the Pope should possess no property ;

(1) Muratori (*Annals of Italy*, y. 1513) thus alludes to this event : "After a few days of illness, during which he constantly preserved his wonted prudence and that severity which dominated every member of the Sacred College, he devoutly received the Sacraments of the Church during the night of Feb. 20th, and at the dawn of the next morning he yielded up his soul. I read in some authors that toward the end he fell into delirium, and cried : ' Out of Italy with the French ! Out with Alfonso d'Este !' But more reliable writers state that his mind was clear. Venetian historians tell us that the death of Julius was hastened by his anger on hearing of the alliance which was being promoted between their republic and the king of France, and by his consciousness of the hatred borne him by all the cardinals because of his martial designs. But probably this is mere imagination.... One of his merits was his freedom from any excessive attachment to his family. Only at the end of his life he asked from the cardinals the concession of the vicariate of Pesaro for his nephew, the duke of Urbino."

(2) "*Julius est Romæ ; quis abest ? Date, numina, Brutum : Nam quoties Romæ est Julius, illa perit*"

the emperor should be lord of the earth. It was natural that this literary light of the Reformation should utter such sentiments; for though he owed his own education to the University of Pavia, he could see no good in Italy, and least of all in Rome. He informs us that the visitor to the Eternal City invariably brought away three things: an evil conscience, a disordered stomach, and an empty purse. There are three things which, according to this pious censor, are not taught in Rome: the immortality of the soul, the resurrection of the dead, and the existence of Hell. And he says that in Rome there are three principal articles of commerce: the Grace of God, ecclesiastical dignities, and the virtue of women. It is not strange that Hutten acquired the praise of Luther as a model of epistolary excellence; but the cleaner taste of Cantù finds in the writings of the Hessian Demosthenes, "the slang of taverns and brothels, and the discharges of a sewer; an orgy of sentiments and words which disgusts even one who has perused the writings which the leaders of the Reformation produced in the same style."

It is certain that the prudence, foresight, and indomitable energy of Julius II. alone thwarted the designs of Louis XII. in Italy. As the enthusiastic but generally perspicacious Audin expresses the idea, "The French were chased out of the Romagna and Lombardy, not by the knives of the Milanese, or by the guns of the peasants, or by the cannons of Peter of Navarre, or by the pikes of the Swiss mountaineers, but by that cry of the Pontiff: 'Deliver us from the barbarians, O Lord!'" During this war, not one of the adversaries of the French monarch, saving Julius II., was more honest than his allies; and certainly Julius II. alone cared for the interests of the Holy See, for the freedom of Italy, and for art and science. "Prate not about his ambition; for it was justified by his object, which he attained in spite of the fever which confined him to his bed, as it did after the proclamation of the pseudo-council of Pisa; in spite of the seditions of the Roman people, as on the day when Pompeo Colonna and Antonio Savelli spoke of proclaiming the republic on the Capitol; in spite of the oath 'I shall destroy the very name of Babylon,' which Louis XII. inscribed on his coins at Milan;

in spite of the tears of his cardinals, as they showed him at Ostia, after the battle of Ravenna, the ships that were already prepared to carry off the conquered Pope. It is possible that Julius II. was too fond of the helmet and the cuirass, that he knew too well how to handle the sword, and that he was too often on horseback; all this is possible, for it is written not only in history, but in bronze, on stone, and on canvas. But it must be admitted that the most beautiful work which a monarch can undertake in the interest of his people, the preservation of their nationality, is never accomplished by one of those tepid temperaments which are wanting in both faults and virtues" (1). To us who have experienced the sweetness of Pius IX. and Leo XIII., and who have talked with many who had known the gentleness of Pius VII. and Leo XII., it appears strange that a Roman Pontiff of comparatively modern days should have inspired fear rather than love. But historians are prone to dilate on such salient characteristics as most readily captivate the imagination of the many; and we do not know that the only amiable traits of Julius II. were those which he persistently displayed toward the votaries of the Muses.

That the transcendent conceptions of the Papacy which are so natural to Catholics, must necessarily be strangers to the average heterodox brain, is evinced by the judgments passed on Julius II. by such historians as Sismondi and Daru. Pope Julius II. was too prominent a figure in the history of the sixteenth century to be ignored; and since his portrait could not well be represented, like that of Alexander VI., as a kind of Medusa's head,—since, in fact, there was too pronounced a halo of real glory hovering over his reign,—he shall receive credit where credit is indeed due him, but for matters comparatively extraneous to his sublime office, and in such a guise that his greater merits shall be relegated to oblivion. Men must be led to regard him and his enemy, Louis XII.; him and the emperor Maximilian, Ferdinand of Aragon, the Bentivoglio of Bologna, and the Baglioni of Perugia,—all as so many politicians of the same ignoble stamp, all with equal rights or absence thereof, and all equally bent

(1) AUDIN; *History of Leo X.*, ch. xiii.

on stealing as much territory as possible. But Julius II. was a connoisseur in matters of art and of artists; and he was the generous protector of Bramante and of Michelangelo. For this striking evidence of his appreciation of worldly merits, our critics will laud him to the skies; for such praise can work no harm to their pet theory of an ideal Pontiff, despoiled of one of the three crowns of his tiara,—a theory which Julius so successfully combated against the robber princes and princely robbers of his day; and which was no new theory even then, although it was reserved to our nineteenth century to reduce to a philosophico-political formula a conception which hitherto had been merely a matter of exceptional practice.

It is often observed by the adversaries of the Holy See that the policy of Pope Julius II. and his military enterprises left no enduring traces. What remains of that policy to-day? asks a recent writer. "Merely the narratives of some annalists, who frequently contradict one another,—some praising his course, others belittling his qualities and drawing attention to his vices. But no matter what opinion history may cause us to form of his character, so long as a love of the beautiful survives among men, St. Peter's Basilica, the Vatican Palace and its chapels, *stanze*, and frescoes, the statue of Moses at the tomb in St. Peter's ad Vincula, will inspire a veneration for his memory in the minds of each new generation which comes to admire them" (1). This latter sentence shows that had the artistic sympathies of the author not been excited by contemplation of the fascinating side of our Pontiff's character, he would have abstained from penning his work. And yet the glory of Julius II. is more far-reaching than it would have been, had artistic proclivities alone been his salient characteristic. We must remember that the Papacy was not instituted for the encouragement of architects, painters, sculptors, or musicians; the Divine Founder of the Church did not even intend that the primary duties of the successors of St. Peter should tend to a fostering of literature, of sound historical criticism, etc. However intimately the arts and sciences may be connected

(1) *History of Julius II.*, by M. A. J. Dumesnil. Paris. 1886.

with the development of civilization and the delectation of men, they enter very indirectly, if at all, into the scheme of salvation. The real grandeur of a Supreme Pontiff, in the eyes of history as well as in those of God, will ever depend upon the manner in which he advances the interests of the Church which he is appointed to govern, and to maintain in all the force of its integrity. The duties of the Pontiffs vary with the circumstances of their respective times; thus the dangers and prospects of the Papacy were very different in the days of Julius II. from what they were in the time of Hildebrand. But Julius was as zealous a Pope as St. Gregory VII.; and it was because of his heroic accomplishment of the tasks devolving upon him as guardian of the flock of Christ, and not because of his protection of artists, that we designate him as a grand Pontiff.

All the Popes have defended the independence of their See as an indispensible requisite for the proper performance of their pontifical duties; and all, from the first foundation of their temporal dominion, have guarded the integrity of their States as an essential of their independence (1); but Julius II. may be styled as pre-eminently the Pope of the temporal power. His predecessor, Alexander VI., utilizing the services of Cæsar Borgia, had defended his temporal rights with all the ardor of the most irreproachable Pontiffs; and Julius continued that policy even against Borgia, compelling him to surrender the fiefs which he had usurped. Though he was far advanced in years when he donned the tiara, his entire pontificate was a defence of the Papal territory from the "barbarians" who had appropriated much of it, and were yearning for the remainder. We may smile when we here this fiery Pope-King shouting his battle-cry: "Out of Italy with the barbarians!" But we must remember that at that time the refinement of the Cisalpine nations, if compared with the culture of the Italians, was not worthy of the name; and certainly the uncomplimentary designation was a natural one in the mouth of the sovereign of that people whose ancestors had been accustomed to flatter themselves, by the same use of the term, on the exclusive posses-

(1) See our chapter on " St. Leo IX. and Pius IX.," in vol. I.　. .

sion of the traits which mollify the human animal. And besides the Gaul and the German, whom Julius naturally apostrophized as "barbarians," there were other enemies of the Papal royalty who were intestine, and whose conduct in face of their priestly sovereign but too frequently proved that they also were not unworthy of the same characterization. It is remarkable that in his desperate struggle with these imperialists, Julius II. invoked no aid from a foreigner. He wanted no other swords than Italian ones to preserve the independence of the peninsula and of the ecclesiastical domain.

Julius II., with his sword, settled for his day that question of the Papal temporal royalty which our day thinks it has solved in a very different sense. That is "what is left of his policy and of his military enterprises." But does this soldier-priest correspond to the ideal of that sanctity which befits a Pontiff? Well, if holiness consists solely in austerity and peaceful contemplation, then there have been many Popes more holy than Julius II.; but if there is, for a Pontiff, a sanctity founded on the fulfilment of his tremendous responsibilities, in spite of every danger, then Julius also had much of that sanctity. But he drew the material sword, and the Church is supposed *abhorrere a sanguine*—to abstain from blood. True, yet Popes who are canonized saints have not hesitated to wield the sword in defence of the Patrimony of the Church; and the blood which they would have abstained from shedding was that which would have been unjustly or uselessly spilt, not that the loss of which would have redounded to the glory of God and the good of His Church. There are some Catholics nowadays in Italy and France who are called "Catholics of resignation"— those who are fain to believe that since Our Lord was crucified for the foundation of the Church, that Church should willingly offer herself to be crucified in turn. But such is not the mind of the Church herself. She shuddered not because of the blood shed in the Crusades; nor because of that, for instance, poured forth by Peter d'Aubusson, a religious at Malta; or by that shed by more than a hundred cardinals (Vitelleschi, for example), who have successfully command-

ed her armies. Michelangelo was a devout Catholic, yet
he scrupled not to portray Julius II. sword in hand; and
while Catholics like Ciaconius have misunderstood this Pontiff, and Protestants like Sismondi have calumniated him,
the great artist is his real historian. Unfortunately, the
history recorded in bronze by Michelangelo no longer exists; the French enemies of Julius destroyed this masterpiece when they sacked Bologna; and the duke of Ferrara,
who discerned the hero in the Pontiff, used some of the frag-
ments in the construction of a cannon, which he nobly
named *Julius II.* "But the head of the statue escaped; and
it was of such majestic beauty, and showed such an ascendency of expression, that it impressed even the Bolognese
insurgents; and they did not dare to touch it, any more than
those historians—blindly religious or philosophistic—who
wrote before Rohrbacher and Audin, have touched the figure
of the heroic Pontiff" (1). Audin and Rohrbacher were
both Frenchmen; but they did not imitate King Louis XII.,
the foe of Julius, complaining that a Pope had no business
to fight a French monarch. They realized that the Julius
II. who scaled the ramparts of Bologna was the same Pontiff who thundered against the second schismatic Council of
Pisa, and that in both instances he but fulfilled his duty.
This Pope, in fine, may well be styled the Julius Cæsar
of the Papacy, but conquering the Gauls, not in their own
country, but in his dominions, which they had invaded; and
amid all his bloody contests he ever shone forth as a true
priest. He was a thorough Pope, whether in the field or in
the Vatican; always surrounded by his cardinals, even in
battle, where these latter, like Cardinal dei Medici at Ravenna, assisted the dying.

The only "vice" with the possession of which Julius II.
has been reproached is anger. But a careful study of his
life will evince that the choler in which he sometimes indulged was of that kind which besieges Heaven. His anger
was generous; for it was externated only when there was a
question of the honor of God or of the welfare of his country.
In vain do certain writers charge him with an implacable

---

(1) BARBEY D'AUREVILLY; *Men and Works*, vol. VIII., p. 171. Paris, 1887.

hatred for the French. Was it to be expected that he would remain passive while Louis XII. pitched his tents on Italian soil, in the very territories of the Holy See ? Julius II. left the world, says M. Dumesnil, "tired of his ambitious projects.' Twice he conquered Bologna; he restored Perugia to the Papal obedience ; he added Parma, Piacenza, etc., to the States of the Church ; and was about to seize Ferrara when death overtook him. All this simply signifies that our Pontiff retook what belonged to the Holy See. However, as we have observed, Julius II. is not entirely reprobate in the eyes of our philosophistic friends ; his artistic tastes almost merit for him a place among the elect. "The conduct of Julius II. in reference to art and artists is as worthy of all praise as his policy is worthy of reprobation." So thinks M. Dumesnil, incapable as he is of realizing that to the world-scanning eye of a Roman Pontiff art and artists must be, comparatively speaking, things of minor consequence.

CHAPTER XVI.

THE SEVENTEENTH GENERAL COUNCIL ; FIFTH LATERAN.

When Pope Julius II. had resolved upon the actuation of his policy regarding Italy, he began by forming the " League of Cambray," concluded in 1508 between the Holy See, the king of France, the emperor Maximilian, and the king of England, against the Venetians whose usurpations of the Pontifical rights and territories had become intolerable. Reduced to extremity, the Venetians yielded ; and as Venice alone could then restrain the Turkish advance into Europe, Julius granted her pardon and dissolved the League. But the French remained in Italy ; and they aided Alfonso d'Este, duke of Ferrara, in a revolt against the Pope, his suzerain. In 1510 Julius excommunicated the king of France, and entered into an alliance with the Swiss and the kings of Spain and England. In the war which followed, Louis XII. was not content with the use of merely material weapons. He immediately convoked an assembly of the French clergy at Tours, and caused the adoption of a number of "Conclusions," all hostile to the claims of the Pontiff. The first question proposed was: "Is it allowable to the Pope to war on secular princes concerning territories not belonging to the Church?" The unanimous reply was in the negative. The other Conclusions were logical consequences of this one (1). Louis XII. then proceeded to further and most unjustifiable extremes. In conjunction with the emperor Maximilian I. he assembled a "General Council" for the purpose of deposing Julius. Nine cardinals, feigning indignation because, as they asserted, the Pontiff would not convoke a Council, as he had sworn to do, were found willing to promote this imitation of the Pseudo-Council of Basel; but only four of them attended the sessions. At the opening of the conventicle, two archbishops and fourteen bishops, with the abbots of St. Denis and St. Menard (all Frenchmen) were present; before the close sixteen other French bishops attended. The first three Sessions of this would-be Second General Council of Pisa were held in that city in November, 1511; five were held in Milan, January to April, 1512; and finally the members adjourned to meet at Asti, and then in Lyons, but as a Synod they transacted no more business. The principal act of this factious assembly was a pretended suspension of Julius II. in its Eighth Session.

Scarcely had Pope Julius been informed of the schismatical action of the emperor and the French king, than, under date of July 18, 1511, he issued the Constitution *Non sine gravi*, convoking a General Council to meet in the Lateran Basilica on April 19, of the following year. He denied that he had been reluctant to call a General Council, appealing to the well-known fact that his vivid desire to behold such an assembly had procured for him the hostility of Alexander VI. He gave good reasons for having deferred the convocation; and insisted that Rome alone was, in the circumstances, a proper place for the meeting. Finally, in the fulfilment of his duty, he invalidated whatever would be transacted in the Pisan conventicle.

In accordance with the above convocation the Seventeenth General Council was solemnly opened by Julius II. in per-

(1) They are all given by Alexandre, *Cent. XVI., dissert. XI., art. 3.*

son on May 3, 1512; the battle of Ravenna having interfered with the prescribed date. The sermon was preached by the famous Ægidius of Viterbo, general of the Augustinians, and afterward a cardinal. Ægidius began by stating that he had predicted, some years before, while explaining the *Apocalypse*, that the Church was threatened with evils, but that a reformation of morals would remedy them. "I rejoice," he then said, "on perceiving to-day that my prediction was not entirely false. Things are reduced to the last extremes; we are engulfed in a sea of evils; furious tempests assail us from every quarter; but we find consolation in one ray of hope." He then spoke of the good and the need of Councils, and described the miseries which the synodals were expected to alleviate. "Can we see without moaning, and without shedding tears of blood, the corruption of this perverse age; the monstrous disorder reigning in the morals of men; the ignorance, ambition, uncleanness, libertinage, and impiety, which triumph even in the sanctuary, whence such shames ought to be eternally banished? Who can behold with dry eyes the plains of Italy more drenched with blood than with the waters of heaven? Innocence is oppressed; cities are stained with the blood of their pitilessly slaughtered citizens; the public squares are filled with the unburied dead. The whole Christian world has recourse to you, and implores your protection." Addressing the Pontiff, the orator praised him for having rendered travel secure in his dominions, and for having reclaimed and restored many cities to the patrimony of the Church. "But Christian Europe expects something greater than all this from your prudence, courage, and zeal; if I may dare to so express my thoughts, she awaits something more worthy of your Holiness. The establishment of concord among Christian princes; their union in arms against the common enemy(the Turk); their use of all their strength in repelling this cruel and redoubtable foe of our holy religion—behold a more glorious design, and the only one which will immortalize the name of your Holiness."

At the first assembling of the prelates, there were counted sixteen cardinals, eighty-three archbishops and bishops, and a few abbots; but when the eighth session was held, there were in attendance twenty-five cardinals, one hundred and twelve archbishops and bishops, and four generals of orders. The First Session, held on May 10, was devoted to the ceremonies usual at the commencement of a Council. In the Second, celebrated on May 17, the Papal Bull invalidating the acts at Pisa was read. The Third Session was not held until Dec. 3, owing to the presence of contagious diseases in the Eternal City. When the fathers reassembled, the secretary read an act of procuration whereby the emperor Maximilian empowered the bishop of Gurk to condemn, in his name, the proceedings of the conventicles of Tours and Pisa. The Fourth Session took place on Dec. 10. The Pontiff ordered the secretary to read the *Letters Patent*, whereby Louis XI., addressing Pope Pius II., had abrogated the *Pragmatic Sanction*. Then the conciliar advocate pronounced a discourse against this famous procedure, demanding its revocation, and advising the citation of all the prelates, chapters, and parliaments of France, that they might furnish the Council with their reasons for impeding its abrogation. Such a citation was drawn up, the summoned parties being allowed sixty days within which to appear before the Council. The Fifth Session, celebrated on Feb. 16, 1513, found Pope Julius seriously ill, and the cardinal Raphael Riario presided. The Council received and approved a Constitution whereby the Pontiff not only prohibited all simony in a Papal election but invalidated any simoniacal election, and deprived all the concurrents therein of the cardinalate and all benefices, also excommunicating these participants, and reserving their cases, unless at the point of death, to a Pontiff legitimately elected. On Feb. 21 Pope Julius II. died, and was succeeded on March 11 by the cardinal John dei Medici, who assumed the name of Leo X.

In the Sixth Session, held on April 27, Pope Leo X. presided. The new Pontiff addressed the synodals, declaring his resolve to continue the Council until a solid peace was secured to Christendom. He signified his wish that the Council would choose fourteen of its members who, joined with certain cardinals whom he would select, would form three congregations for the purpose of procuring, firstly, peace among Christian princes; secondly, a general reformation, embracing also the Roman court; thirdly, the abrogation of the *Pragmatic Sanction*. In the Seventh Session, held on June 17, the cardinals Carvajal and Sanseverino abjured the schism of Pisa, but were not at once restored to their dignity; not until the 27th were they reinvested with the cardinalitial scarlet, and admitted to the kiss of peace, receiving as penance the obligation of fasting once a week for the rest of their lives. In the Eighth Session, on Dec. 17, the ambassadors of Louis XII. presented that king's renunciation of the coventicle of Pisa, then sitting at Lyons, and his recognition of the Lateran Council. The Pontiff condemned the doctrine that the intellective soul of man is mortal; also the teaching that the soul is one and the same, *unica*, in all men. It was resolved to send legates to all Christian sovereigns, imploring them to turn their arms against the Turks. In the Ninth Session, held on May 5, 1514, the procurator charged the absent French bishops with contumacy; but it having been shown that these prelates had started on their journey, but had been detained by the duke of Milan, Pope Leo extended the time allowed for their appearance. Then a reformatory Bull was read, and among the passages relating to the cardinals we note the following. "Out of reverence for the Apostolic See, ... we decree that no cardinal shall reveal, by word, writing, or in any other manner, anything heard, said, or performed, in the Consistory, which might turn to the scandal or prejudice of any person; and this we decree under pain of perjury and disobedience." In the Tenth Session, on May 5, 1515, was issued a Constitution declaring the lawfulness of the *Monti di Pietà*, institutions for the relief of the poor, common in Italy from the days of Paul II., and which, unlike the pawnbrokers, charged an interest merely sufficient to meet the necessary expenses of the establishments. Another decree concerned the printing of books. Pope Leo X. says that the Holy See has heard that many persons are publishing translations from the Hebrew, Arabic, Chaldean, and Greek, of works containing pernicious dogmas. He orders that hereafter there shall be printed no book which has not been examined and approved by the ecclesiastical authorities.

The Eleventh Session was delayed until Dec. 19, 1516. The deputies of Peter, patriarch of the Maronites of the Lebanon, were admitted to tender their obedience to the Pontiff. In the patriarch's letter was a *Profession of Faith*, wherein the Maronites avowed their belief in the Procession of the Holy Ghost from the Father and the Son; in the doctrine of Purgatory; and in the necessity of communicating at the Paschal time. The patriarch thanked his Holiness for having sent a Franciscan friar to the Lebanon to instruct the Maronites on certain points of Catholic doctrine, and in regard to certain ceremonies which they failed to observe. Then was read a Concordat (1) made at Boulogne with the king of France. Then followed the reading of a Bull abrogating the *Pragmatic Sanction.* We quote the following passages : "Following the instructions of St. Peter, we ought to use every care in upholding the regulations of our predecessors in everything concerning obedience, ecclesiastical liberty and authority, and the deliverance of simple souls from the snares set for them by the prince of darkness. Pope Julius II., our predecessor of happy memory, having assembled the Holy Council of the Lateran; and having considered that the *Pragamtic Sanction* was still in force, to the injury of souls and the detriment of this Holy See; he appointed certain cardinals to examine it. And although said *Sanction* was notoriously null for many reasons; although it entailed a manifest schism in the Church; and although it might properly have been pronounced abusive, and have been abrogated; nevertheless our predecessor

(1) By this agreement the king of France received the right of nominating to bishoprics, and other prelatures during the six months following the vacancy ; the nomination was to be referred to the Pope, who could refuse to confirm it; if this confirmation was refused, the king could make another nomination in three months ; if he did not do so, the right pertained to the Pontiff. Many of the Gallican prelates opposed this Concordat ; the famous Genebrard, archbishop of Aix, styled it "a mystery of iniquity whereby the French church was ruined" (*Chron.*, b. IV., y. 1517). This convention remained in force in France down to 1789. It was partly reproduced and partly replaced by the Napoleonic Concordat of 1801. After the restoration of the Bourbons, it was renewed in a Concordat concluded on June 17, 1817, between Pius VII. and Louis XVIII., which annulled the Bonaparte instrument of 1801 ; however, the Chamber of Deputies rejected the new convention, and hence it was not enforced. The revolution of July, 1830, restored the Concordat of 1801, together with its " organic articles ; " but in practice it was often ignored.

wished, by way of precaution, to examine into its abuses, and to cite the bishops ... who enforced it. As this citation was of no avail because of various impediments, and as death visited Pope Julius before the affair could be decided, we ourselves deemed it proper to resume it. ... Therefore having consulted the cardinals of Holy Roman Church and many very learned persons, we deem it proper to entirely abolish that *Pragmatic Sanction*—already, indeed, revoked by King Louis XI.—just as did our predecessor, Leo I., whose footsteps we follow, when in the Council of Chalcedon he revoked all that had been rashly ordained against Catholic faith and justice in the (Pseudo) Council of Ephesus. It is in imitation of him that we believe we can and ought to abolish this *Pragmatic* and all its contents, without any consideration for its pretended authority from the Council of Basel and the assembly of Bourges ; for its acceptation occurred after Pope Eugenius IV. had condemned that Council. ... In the fulness of our Apostolic power and authority, and with the approbation of the Holy Council, we ordain and declare that the *Pragmatic Sanction* possesses no authority. We annul all the decrees, statutes, regulations, and ordinances therein contained ; and all which have been inserted therein, no matter whence they may have emanated " (1). In the Twelfth Session, March 16, 1517, the usual Mass of opening was sung by the cardinal Carvajal, who had been the chief promoter of the conventicle of Pisa. A Bull was then published to the effect that there was no need of prolonging the Lateran Council, since peace was now established between Christian princes ; a reformation of morals had been regulated ; the conventicle of Pisa had been abolished. An imposition of tithes on all benefices was ordered, said tithes to be devoted to a war on the Turks.

More than mere mention should be accorded to the decrees issued by this Council in reference to the *Monti di Pietà* and the publication of books. The reader of Dante will remember that the divine poet assigns the unnaturally

---

(1) Concerning the history and meaning of the *Pragmatic Sanction*, see chap. viii. on Pope Pius II.

impure and usurers to the same place in hell. From this fact we may form some idea of the extent of what was really the queen social evil of the Middle Age; for the theologically accurate mind of the sublime Florentine would not have likened the heinousness of usury to that of the Gomorrhaites, had his heart not bled at the sight of the woes entailed by the rapacity of the money-lending Jews of his day. The first person to excogitate a remedy for an evil which sapped the source of public prosperity was a Franciscan friar, Barnabo of Perugia, who flourished in the middle of the fifteenth century. In one of his sermons this real reformer besought the wealthy and the well-to-do to enable him to establish a new kind of pawn-broker's shop under municipal control, which would lend money on portable securities, but at a rate of interest as low as the mere expenses of the institution would permit. The eloquence of the friar produced the desired effect; from all sides money, jewels, and precious objects of art were laid at his feet, and funds were immediately obtained for the first Mountain of Charity—so-called because of the immense space which was occupied by the securities, grain and other bulky articles being commonly pledged. The new institution was immediately approved by the Holy See, and throughout Italy similar ones were established by the charity of the wealthy, who thus, under ecclesiastical guidance, became the bankers of the poor. In vain did the Jews exercise every art to prevent the spread of an institution which deprived them of their chief source of wealth; men like the friars, Barnabo of Perugia and Bernardino of Feltre, were superior to bribes, and even courted death in the cause of God's poor. However, the usurers gathered some grains of comfort when the great Dominican theologian, Cajetan, attacked what he styled the Mountains of Impiety. This erudite casuist and exemplary churchman, a rigid Thomist, contended that if the twenty per cent. of the Jews was condemnable, the two per cent. of the new institutions was just as bad in the eyes of the true moralist. He who charges one cent of interest, contended Cajetan, let the form or the person be of any nature whatsoever, violates the commandments of God. The Dominicans ranged themselves on the side of him who was one of the great ornaments of their Order; while the Franciscans planted themselves on the firm ground of the needs of society. In 1484 Sixtus IV., and in 1506 Julius II., pronounced in favor of the *Monti*. Finally, in the Fifth Lateran Council, after a brief but lucid explanation of the controversy, Pope Leo X. declared that the founders of the *Monti di Pietà* had been animated by an enlightened zeal for truth, as well as by an ardent charity for men; and in the exercise of his Apostolic authority, the Pontiff prohibited the application of the term "usurious" to institutions approved by the Holy See, establishments which demanded, by way of interest, a comparatively trifling sum in liquidation of their necessary expenses.

That the invention of printing was one of the most beneficent ever welcomed by man, no sane mind will deny; but that its abuse has been fraught with consequences more deleterious to civilized man than those produced by any other human agency, is so evident that the presentation of any proof of the fact would excite derision. When this subject was laid before the Seventeenth General Council, the synodals were as firmly convinced as is any impartial thinker of our day, that the passions of men too often turn one of the most beautiful gifts of God into an engine of intellectual and spiritual death. Pope Leo X. could tell of the dangerous power of printed words, as experienced by him in the city of Lorenzo the Magnificent; fresh in his memory were the thuds of the press which struck off the improvisations of Savonarola, destined to subvert his family as well as to excite contempt for Pope Alexander VI. And he may have thought as Audin did in our day, that the unfortunate friar of St. Mark's would not have ascended the pyre, if at that time every lucubration of an ecclesiastic was submitted, before publication, to the censorship of his natural judge, his episcopal ordinary. Many years before this Council, the Christian pulpit and professorial chairs had denounced the license of the press. In 1500, Vitalis of Thebes, professor of law, complained of those many printers who, for shameful profit, published works written "in language which would not have been heard in the ancient *Lupercalia*." Gerson publicly proclaimed that he would no more pray for the author of the *Romance of the Rose*, than he would for Judas; did he not know that the wretched man had repented before he died.   In 1486 we hear Berthold, archbishop of Mayence, warning his flock against the many licentious books then circulating on all sides.   It is not surprising, therefore, that the Seventeenth General Council published the following decree : " In order that what has been invented for the glory of God, for the propagation of the faith, and for the better cultivation of literature, be not distorted to contrary purposes, and thus become a danger for the faithful of Christ ; we have deemed it our duty to direct our attention to the printers of books, so that henceforth thorns may not grow with the good grain, and poisons may not be mixed with remedies.   Wishing to arrange this matter in a proper way, in order that the printing-press may be the more successful through proper supervision ; we decree and ordain that now and ever hereafter no person dare, either in our city or in any other city or diocese, to print any book or writing whatsoever, unless said books or writings have been carefully examined, in Rome by our vicar and by the master of our apostolic palace, and in other cities or dioceses by the bishop or by some one deputed by him ; etc."

CHAPTER XVII.

THE PONTIFICATE OF LEO X.

We now approach the reign of a Pontiff whom historians have glorified by giving his name to the age in which he flourished.   Just as we read of the Age of Pericles, of Augustus, and of Louis XIV., so we read of the Age of Leo X. Only one Pope, St. Gregory VII., has been similarly distinguished ; and in his case, the presumed honor has not been so universally accorded.   It may be doubted, however, whether this species of apotheosis befits the favored son of Lorenzo the Magnificent more specially than it would several other successors of St. Peter.   Certainly the seventh Gregory and Innocent III. dominated their epoch as Leo X. never dreamed

of influencing his times. A historian should not very readily bestow the qualification of "grand" upon a particular
Roman Pontiff; upon one of that long series, the immense majority of whose members were men of uncommon
intellectual calibre, of heroic force of character, and of consummate sanctity—men who influenced the society of their
day as no secular leader did, and for whose lives nearly all
thinking men of succeeding years have thanked the Giver of
Mercies. The calm investigator will hesitate, ere he styles
the tenth Leo a great Pontiff; but the reign of this Pope
will ever claim especial attention until its course has been
run by the heresy which was born at that time. When Protestantism shall have met the fate which must inevitably over-
take all systems which oppose the teaching authority of the
Spouse of Christ, then men may show less interest in Leo
X. When treating of Pope Julius II., we deprecated the
tendency of certain writers to discern in that Pontiff merely
a Mæcenas for artists; but historical justice demands that
the chief claims of Leo X. to our admiration be recognized
as founded in the literary and artistic features of his character.

Giovanni dei Medici, born in Florence in 1475, was the
second son of Lorenzo the Magnificent, who was a grandson
of that Cosmo dei Medici who had quietly founded a tyranny
of wealth in Florence, without any apparent change in the
constitution or laws of the republic, and had thus laid the
first foundations of a dynasty which was to rule over Tuscany
during two centuries (1531–1737), and to fill the annals of Europe with its renown for both good and evil (1). An atmosphere of art and learning environed Giovanni in his infancy;
as a child he played at the knees of that Gentile of Urbino
who had been the first tutor of his accomplished father;

(1) As in the case of all families which have become pre-eminently celebrated in the annals of history, some genealogists have been found able to discover for the Medici a very
ancient and honorable pedigree. But with the exception of Cantù, no modern historian
has drawn attention to the genealogy furnished to the Medici by a Grecian tradition.
According to this legend, the Medici descended from the Mikali, a family which has been
famous for many centuries, even to our day, in the Peloponnesus. Be this as it may, the
first of the Medici to become prominent in the Florentine annals was Giovanni di Bicci
(1421-29), from whose two sons, Cosmo and Lorenzo, descended the two great lines of the
family. The line of Cosmo is as follows:

and his early youth blossomed unto glorious promise under the inspiration of such preceptors as Poliziano, Chalcondyla, and Verino. Quite naturally his special masters were

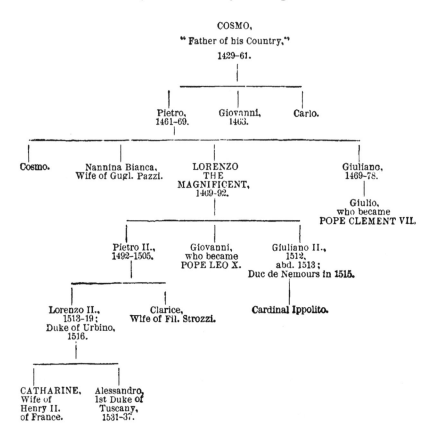

THE LINE OF LORENZO:

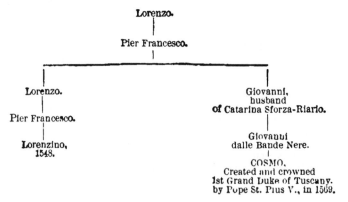

the best that Italy, and therefore Europe, could furnish; and a much weaker intellect than his would have thrived unto magnificent fruition when cultivated by professors like Marsilio Ficino and the truly wonderful Pico della Mirandola. Destined to the priesthood from his birth, Giovanni was only seven years old when he received the clerical tonsure; and only eight when the abbey of Passignano was conferred upon him by Pope Sixtus IV. It is sad, rather than amusing, to note that Audin, the ultra panegyrist of Leo X., describes this and other premature collation of benefices on the child of the Magnificent as "the first of the innumerable favors which Heaven had reserved for the ducal boy;" and that the same author sympathizes with "the new joys which nearly every day filled the heart of Lorenzo" as he saw the ecclesiastical emoluments rapidly accumulating for one who was almost a mere babe in arms. When the boy was scarcely able to dispense with the cares of a nurse, "nothing was wanting but a cardinal's hat, and that was ardently desired by Lorenzo and his court." However, it is certain that Giovanni was a lad of marked virtue, as well as of great precocity; and when, in his thirteenth year, he was nominated to the Sacred College by Innocent VIII., on condition that he should pass three years in the study of Canon Law before being invested with the insignia of his dignity, his piety was acclaimed as sufficient to preclude scandal. He spent the probationary period at the University of Pisa, the institution whose very walls spoke of Dante, and where the students always lifted their caps when they passed the statue of the divine poet which stood in the great hall. In 1491, having taken his degree in Canon Law, Giovanni received his cardinalitial robes, and proceeded to Rome. Warmly welcomed by Pope Innocent VIII., he entered the august Senate of the Church, and there made his first acquaintance with those cardinals who were to be the Pontiffs, Alexander VI., Pius III., and Julius II. In the Eternal City the young cardinal easily satisfied his tastes as philosopher, archæologist, poet, and musician; and his most exquisite enjoyment was the society of the Academicians who assembled around Pomponio Leto. If we may

judge by the almost unanimous voice of authors who knew
him well, Cardinal dei Medici always conducted himself as
his father had advised, when, shortly after the young prelate
had entered the Sacred College, the doting though prudent
parent wrote : " Never forget that you do not owe the cardinalate to your own merits. ... Continue the studies which
are so necessary to success in your state of life.   You edified
me greatly last year, when you approached the Sacraments
of Penance and the Holy Eucharist so frequently ; persevere in this course, for through it alone will you remain in
the grace of God. ... You will find many men of piety and
learning in the Sacred College, and they should be your
models.   In the arrangement of your household, think more
of an appropriate respectability than of a show of wealth.
Jewels and silks are not things for a man of your profession ;
but surround yourself with books and antiques.   Employ
very few, but worthy domestics.   Give more hospitality than
you accept, but have the simplest dishes at your table. ...
I would especially recommend you to form the habit of rising early from your bed ; for you will thus not only preserve
your health, but you will assist with greater promptitude at
the divine offices, and you will have more time for study, audiences, etc.   I would give you another bit of advice.   When
you retire at night, think of what you will have to do on the
following day, so that you may be somewhat prepared for
emergencies."

On the seventh day of the Conclave which had met to select a successor to Julius II., the cardinal Giovanni dei Medici was raised to the Chair of Peter as Leo X.   Among the
letters of congratulation which the new Pontiff received from
all parts of Christendom, two are remarkable, one from a
poor monk who had been his first teacher of Latin, and the
other from a philosopher who probably expected a rich reward for his flatteries.   Peter Delfini, superior of the Camal-
doli Benedictines at Venice, spared a few moments from the
study of the precious manuscripts which ever surrounded him,
in order to give another lesson, though indirectly, to his quondam pupil.   " You have assumed the name of Leo as a sign
of wisdom and of terror; of wisdom in regard to the obedient,

and of the fear which the rebellious must entertain. That name will be the object of veneration, on the part of all who bear the Christian name. May you be blessed; for you have followed the examples of the old race of the Medici, keeping your ears ever open to the cries of the poor. Undoubtedly you still attend to the duty of hospitality enjoined by the Apostle, and you remember that many have found grace in the Lord, because of the hospitality which they accorded to angels." Now hearken to the adulation proferred by Erasmus: " Leo X. will give us the successful administration of Leo I.; the pious erudition and the musical tastes of Leo II.; the fruitful eloquence and the soul of Leo III., which never failed in either good or evil fortune; the simplicity and prudence of Leo IV.; the holy tolerance of Leo V.; the love of peace of Leo VI.; the truly celestial life of Leo VII.; the integrity of Leo VIII.; the beneficence of Leo IX. All these you will give us ; we have a guarantee of them in those holy names which are so many oracles of the past and of the future." The elevation of Giovanni dei Medici to the supreme magistracy of Christendom was hailed with joy by the learned and the artistic; and the reader will find graphic details of all that he effected to justify their acclamations, in the pages of Cantù, Audin, and Roscoe. We shall merely allude to a few of the acts which illustrate this side of his character.

Pope Alexander VI. had greatly developed and magnificently endowed the University of the Sapienza; and Pope Julius II., far from diverting its revenues, as Roscoe falsely asserts, had granted to its purposes certain revenues of the Capitol. With its means for usefulness thus augmented, the Sapienza expected to fulfil the destiny augured for it by Pope Nicholas V., when, in the words of the Protestant Casaubon, "He raised the banner of science, apparently buried forever in the ruins of Byzantium; and thus he dissipated the darkness which was lowering over the world, and caused Rome to emit the light of literature and art." But it was not enough for Leo X. that the Sapienza should merely rival the Universities of Bologna, Milan, and Pavia, in the intellectual primacy of Europe. By a Bull dated **Dec. 19, 1513,** he urged the students to abandon the false philosophy of Plato, and to disregard the allurements of a poetry which corrupted the soul; reminding the professors that they were to teach virtue, even more than science—a strange proceeding, if, as we are asked to believe, the tastes of this Pontiff were more pagan than Christian. He took care that the corps of instructors should be sufficiently numerous to ensure a thorough care for the progress of each student. Thus, for instance, Rhetoric was taught by six professors; Greek by three and many assistants; Canon Law by eleven; Civil Law by twenty; Moral Philosophy by five; Medicine by fifteen. He provided for the payment of professorial salaries which must have caused the managing boards of the universities in other lands to stand aghast; for example, the professors of Greek—Valdo, Chalcondyla, and Varino Favorino—received 300 golden florins a year, and many other emoluments, while similar posts were elsewhere generally filled for 60 florins (1). Many writers follow Pallavicino in asserting that Leo X. was so entranced by the beauties of secular literature, that he neglected theologians; but it is certain that the most prominent theological luminaries of the Council of Trent came from the Sapienza. Certainly, Leo X. did not neglect Thomas de Vio (Cajetan), when he made him a cardinal; nor did he forget Prierio, when he appointed him to the mastership of the Apostolic Palace; nor did he frown on the great canonist, Jacovacci, or on the exegetist, Sadoleto, when he gave the red hat to the former, and made the latter his private secretary. We read that in the early days of Christianity, the bishops used to turn their sacristies into libraries; and much of that spirit was evinced by Leo X., in his zealous search for valuable books and manuscripts. Nicholas V., Calixtus III.,

(1) Among the many celebrated men of genius whom the wise liberality of Leo X. drew to the Sapienza or to the papal court, we may mention Machiavelli; Bembo, who, when yet a boy, was one of the best Hellenists in Europe, but whose ultra-classicism has led many to regard him as a personification of paganism; Sadoleto, the private secretary of the Pope; Musuro; Calergi, the editor of Pindar and of Theocritus; Aldo Manuzio, the printer; Favorino, the papal librarian; Forteguerri, the philologist; Beroaldo, the editor of Tacitus; Ambrogio, the orientalist; Guidacerio, the hebraicist; Pagni, the biblicist; Alemanni, the philologist; Fracastoro, the physician-poet; Tristino, the diplomat-poet; Calcagnini, the astronomer; Inghirami, the orator, and conservator of the Vatican Library; Merino and Paoloso, the musicians; the poets Ariosto, Accolti, Berni, Folengi, Racellai, Sannazzaro, Vida; and the humanist, Flaminio.

Pius II., and Paul II. had greatly augmented the Vatican Library; and Sixtus IV. had conceived the idea of opening it to the literary public. Leo X. sent the humanist Beroaldo and other bibliophiles into all parts of the civilized world, with instructions to spare neither money nor fatigue in the effort to acquire precious manuscripts; and Beroaldo is quaintly pathetic in narrating how, in obedience to his enthusiastic master, he suffered from hunger, thirst, heat, and dirt, in his efforts to give liberty to long-immured ancient writers. Among the innumerable manuscripts which our Pontiff thus procured for the literary treasury of the Vatican, we may mention one of Tacitus, found in the abbey of New Corbie in Saxony, and for which the then enormous sum of 500 sequins was paid. In the decree whereby the Pope forbade any infringement of the authorized printer's rights in the matter of this work, he termed literature, "the most beautiful gift, after religion, which the goodness of God has proferred to man; our glory in misfortune, and our consolation." When the printed work appeared, its title-page bore the announcement, beneath the escutcheon of the Pontiff, that this fosterer of classical studies would reward munificently all who would bring to him any ancient book which had not yet been edited. It was with money donated by Leo X. that Ariosto published his *Orlando Furioso;* but if the reader is disposed to blame the papal Mæcenas for encouraging this lucubration, he should remember that the *Furioso* which we read is not the one which the poet submitted to his protector in 1515. The latter effusion was in forty cantos; and when the author issued another edition in 1532, from which the modern ones are copied, he had added six cantos, and had effected many notable changes in the poem. Leo X. was an enthusiast in chess; and when he learned that the Eternal City was harboring Vida of Cremona, a canon-regular who had written a curious poem on the far from poetical game, he caused the scribe to be led into his presence. The result of the interview was the poem *Cristiade;* for Leo had told Vida that the time had come when poets should abandon the mountain of Helicon for that of Calvary. "In the crib of Bethlehem," said he, "is enshrined a magnificent epic, the *Cris-*

tiade ; that is, an account of how the world escaped from the clutches of the demon, culpable humanity being redeemed by the blood of Jesus. Away with pagan books! A Christian should open but one book, when he desires a subject well worthy of his contemplation." It was through the encouragement of Leo that Sannazaro, the author of the *Arcadia,* probably one of the most beautiful of the inspirations of the Italian Muse, forsook worldly for religious poetry. The great professor, Zerrabini, whose academical name of Flaminio may be more familiar to the reader, entrusted his son, Marc' Antonio, to the protection of Leo; and it was the fostering care of the Pontiff that developed one of the most illustrious minds of the Renaissance.

When Leo X. assumed the direction of the Universal Church, the fanciedly keen observers who then, as ever, abounded in the world, proclaimed that the great intellectual movement of the Renaissance, begun (so far as Italy was concerned) toward the end of the thirteenth century, had reached its zenith; and that therefore the reign of peace and justice was now at hand. On April 6, 1513, our Pontiff opened the sixth session of the Council of the Lateran; the schismatic cardinals nearly all returned to their duty, and the pseudo-synod of Pisa was as though it had not been. Louis XII. of France was reconciled with the Holy See, but when that monarch had been succeeded by Francis I. (Jan. 1, 1515), the Pontiff saw with chagrin that the French aspirations for the domination of the Milanais were again encouraged. He immediately made an offensive and defensive alliance with Spain and the empire; for, ever faithful to the traditional policy of the Popes—the deliverance of Italy from a foreign yoke, and the perpetuation of the papal temporal dominion—such a course appeared to be the sole means of checking the enterprising spirit of Francis I. The late king of France, Louis XII., called by his subjects, "the father of his people," and forced by popular delirium to cross the Alps with drawn sword, had derived no serious advantage from his thirteen years of campaigning; having vindicated his rights as grandson of Valentina Visconti, and posed as "King of Jerusalem and of Sicily, and Duke of Milan," he allowed himself to be drawn into an attempt on the kingdom of Naples. Oppressed by sickness, he had not sufficient energy to combat the energy of Julius II.; nor had he enough of cunning to oppose successfully that Ferdinand of Aragon who, when he heard of the French king's complaint that his Aragonese majesty had deceived him twice, cynically replied that he had duped Louis at least ten times. By the defeat on the Garigliano, the French lost the kingdom of Naples for the second time. The victory of Agnadel, as unfortunate as a defeat, and the victory of Ravenna, in which the death of Gaston de Foix deprived France of hope in the near future; finally, the defeat of Novara, which entailed the loss of the Milanais; formed the culmination of the deplorable enterprise. But Francis I., the veritable hero of that epoch, was of calibre very different from Louis XII.; and after his great victory of Marignan over the Swiss Confederates, a victory which deprived the Swiss of all future influence in Italian matters, the combined power of Spain, Germany, and their Italian allies could not have prevented his reduction of the Two Sicilies, and, if he had been so disposed, his dismemberment of the States of the Church. In this emergency, our Pontiff entered into negotiations with the conqueror; but the conditions offered by Francis were very severe. Certainly, the Pontiff's family pride was gratified by the guarantee of the authority possessed by the Medici, in the Florentine state; but the king insisted on the cession of the pontifical territories of Parma and Piacenza, a step which would have established definitively the French domination in Italy. Leo determined, contrary to the advice of many of the cardinals, to hold an interview with the French king. Three places were proposed for the conference; Rome, Florence, and Bologna. The monarch would not choose Rome, and the Pope feared to name Florence, because the *frateschi* (now termed " patriots ") might have made trouble ; hence on Dec. 11, 1515, Bologna saw the meeting of the two most influential personages of Europe (1). The negotiations lasted for

(1) Contemporary writers tell us that when the two great personages met, the king knelt, kissed the papal slipper, and having been raised by the Pontiff, kissed his cheek. When the Pope invited Francis to be seated, and the king had done so, the royal chancellor advanced, and read, on the part of his Majesty, a protestation of profound homage; and

three days, and the chief points considered were the French
demand for the Papal renunciation of sovereignty over Parma and Piacenza; the French desire for the papal sanction
to a French conquest of the Two Sicilies; the fate of the
rebel duke of Urbino (a nephew of Julius II.); the papal
restitution of Modena and Reggio to the duke of Ferrara;
and most important of all, the definitive abrogation of that
Pragmatic Sanction of which we have already treated when
scanning the events of the Pontificate of Pius II. Leo X. was
forced to the conclusion that prudence bade him yield in the
matter of the Parmesan and Piacentine duchies; time might restore them to the Holy See. As to the desire of Francis I. to
reign over the Two Sicilies, vassal territories of the Roman
Pontiff, here also Leo relied upon time to either moderate
the aspirations of France, or to furnish some other attrac-
tion for them. Meanwhile he impressed successfully in the
mind of the monarch the idea that the king of Aragon was
an infirm old man, could not live very long; and that future
circumstances might enable the Holy See to find a way of
disengaging itself from its engagements with the House of
Aragon. Concerning the duke of Urbino, the Pope convinced
Francis that his sympathy for that prince was, despite the
duke's services to France in the late troubles, very much out

whenever there occurred a passage implying especial submission and devotion to the Holy
See, Francis always lifted his cap, although requested by Leo to remain covered. The dis-
course concluded with the asseveration that the king was the Pontiff's submissive son:
"*Tuus c religione, tuus jure, tuus more majorum, tuus consuetudine, tuus fide, tuus
voluntate.*" On the next day, the Pope proceeded processionally, preceded by the king surrounded by his highest officers, to the church of S. Petronia, for the celebration of Mass.
When his Holiness advanced toward his throne, King Francis insisted on carrying the
Papal train, despite the demurrer of Leo; and when the initiatory psalm began, his Majesty knelt, *more acolythi*, and made the responses. He remained on his knees at the foot
of the altar until the elevation; and thenceforth, until after the Pope's communion, he
was stretched prone on the pavement. When the Pontiff, the deacon, and the sub-deacon
had communicated, his Holiness asked the king whether he wished to receive his Lord and
God. Francis replied that he was not in the state of grace; but that many of his officers
would like to receive the Body and Blood of Jesus Christ from the hands of His Vicar.
As the veterans were approaching, one old soldier cried out from the rear: "Holy father,
I would be too happy to communicate at your sacred hands; but since I cannot whisper in
your ear, I confess aloud that I fought, and vigorously too, against Pope Julius II." Others
then repeated the avowal, and from all sides came the cry: "Pardon, pardon!" King
Francis also cried: "Most holy father, be not surprised that these gentlemen were foes
to Pope Julius. He was by far the greatest of our adversaries, and I never knew a fiercer
warrior in a battle. To tell the truth, your Holiness, he would have been better as a general
than as Pope." Leo pronounced absolution, and the ceremony proceeded. King Francis
communicated in the Dominican church on the following day.

of place ; since the nephew of Pope Julius had become a rebel to the Pope-King. The question of Modena and Reggio was reserved for consideration until the time when Francis should be in condition to reimburse the Holy See the money which Julius II. had paid to the emperor for the investiture of the duchies. No difficulty was experienced in the matter of the *Pragmatic Sanction ;* but there were many serious details to be arranged. For that purpose the Pontiff deputed two cardinals, and the king his chancellor, to draw up the terms of a new *Concordat ;* and finally, on Aug. 18, 1517, was published at Rome that instrument which regulated French ecclesiastical affairs until the Revolution of 1789.

Leo X. did not hesitate to use his power to consolidate that of the House of Medici. He appointed his brother Giulio to the archiepiscopal see of Florence ; he invested his nephew Lorenzo with the ducal crown of Urbino which had been worn by La Rovere ; and he strengthened the Medicean influence in Florence by many powerful alliances. Nevertheless, you will seek in vain for any unworthy or even improper means in the actuation of these projects. But the Pontiff's pride of family made many enemies for him ; and one of the consequent conspiracies resulted in the degradation of three cardinals, and the execution of one. Alfonso Petrucci had been one of the most zealous advocates of the elevation of Cardinal dei Medici to the Popedom ; and after the enthronization of Leo X., he had counted on the gratification of his desire to become governor of Siena—a desire which was quite natural to a scion of that family (Altomonte) which had, for many centuries, almost constantly dominated in that province. When Petrucci saw the coveted magistracy bestowed on the bishop of Grosseto, he began to ruminate on other causes of complaint which his family had against the Medici, and concerted measures for revenge. During many years a painful abscess had afflicted the Pope ; and even in the Conclave which elected him, his trusted surgeon had been obliged to operate for his relief. In the spring of 1517, this practitioner was absent from Rome, and his place was filled by Baptist Vercelli, who was a consummate toxicologist as well as an

able surgeon. Petrucci succeeded in buying the services of
Vercelli; and it was arranged that the physician should
place a poisoned bandage upon the sore of his august patient. But the modesty of Leo saved his life; he could not
bring himself to submit to the ministrations of the stranger.
Those who were involved in the plot persistently urged the
sufferer to admit Vercelli to the confidence which the regular
body physician had enjoyed; but while they were endeavoring to overcome the obstinacy of Leo, the plot was discovered.
When arrested, Cardinal Petrucci was confronted with the
confession of his secretary, and he finally avowed that he had
designed "to rid the world of a tyrant," and to procure the
tiara for Cardinal Raphael Riario, the same whom we have
seen engaged in the Conspiracy of the Pazzi. He added that
besides Riario, he had for accomplices the cardinals Soderini,
brother of the famous *gonfaloniere* of Florence; Adrian of
Corneto, and Bandinello de Sauli. In the Consistory of June
3, 1517, Soderini and Adrian confessed their crime, after the
Pontiff had informed the assembly that he knew that there
were two felons in the hall, and that, "in the name of the
Crucified Saviour, he would spare their lives, if they avowed
their crime." Riario and Sauli had already been arrested.
On June 22, Bembo read to his fellow cardinals the sentence
of degradation pronounced against Petrucci, Riario, and Sauli.
Petrucci was executed in his prison on the following day.
There seemed to be much doubt as to the extent of Riario's
culpability; that both he and Sauli were cognizant of the
plot would appear from their mutual recriminations in the
Consistory. It was because of this doubt that though both
were condemned to death, the Pontiff commuted the punishment of Riario to a fine of 50,000 ducats (which was paid by
that rich Sienese merchant, Chigi, whose palace in the Via
Longara was adorned by Raphael); while Sauli was consigned to perpetual imprisonment, but was soon liberated.
A few days after the commutation of his sentence, Riario was
among the assistants at the Pope's celebration of the Holy
Sacrifice; and to his utter astonishment, the Pontiff suddenly turned from the altar, and walking over to him, said:
" Most reverend lord, in order that your heart may be at rest,

I offer you my pardon here, in the presence of the Body and Blood of Jesus. In the name of God I forgive you for all that you may have done against me; and as a return I ask you, in the name of Our Lord here present, to banish from your breast all resentment which you may now feel in my regard." And then he tenderly embraced the culprit.

The conspiracy of Petrucci warned Leo X. to reinforce the Sacred College with members whose religious zeal, learning, and tried prudence would contribute to the glory of God, as well as add to the *eclat* of his pontificate. It is well to note the merits of a few of the thirty-one cardinals created in the Consistory of June 26, four days after the degradation of Petrucci and his associates. 1. Ægidius of Viterbo, an Augustinian friar, was of such humble stock that he is known only by his monastic name. A pupil of that Mariano of Genazzano, whom Savonarola regarded as a master of eloquence, Ægidius acquired so great a reputation for every virtue that a religious should possess, that in 1507, in the General Chapter held at Naples, he was elected general of his Order. In 1512, he was deputed by Julius II. to deliver the opening oration in the Council of the Lateran, and his eloquent and practical discourse justified the Pontiff's selection. Ægidius was an able humanist; he was at home with Hebrew, Chaldaic, and Greek, and he was at once theologian, philosopher, historian, and poet. Sadoleto compared him to the aurora, and he was one of the luminaries of the Renaissance. The reader will find many of the *Letters* of Ægidius in the *Collection* of Martene and Durand; and they merit attention from him who seeks for details as to this period of history (1). II. Adrian of Utrecht, the son of a poor artisan, owed his education to the charity of a priest and to the admiring commiseration of the widow of Charles the Bold, Margaret of Austria, who then governed the Low Countries. He acquired such learning that he became a professor in the Uni-

(1) The chief works of Ægidius of Viterbo are, *Observations on the Three First Chapters of Genesis*; some *Commentaries on the Psalms*; many *Dialogues* and *Epistles*; some *Odes* in praise of the statesman and writer, Jovianus Pontanus; and a fine treatise on *The Growth of the Church*. See SADOLETO; *Epist.*, b. III.—BEMBO; *Epist.*, b. II., nos. 13 and 14.—GUICCIARDINI; bk. XII.—PAOLO GIOVIO; *Eulogies on The Learned*, ch. lxxxv.;— UGHELLI; *Sacred History.*—AUBREY; *History of the Cardinals.*

versity of Louvain; and in 1507 he was chosen by the emperor Maximilian I. to be the preceptor of his grandson, the future Charles V. He so won the confidence of his pupil that in 1515, when the death of Ferdinand the Catholic (the maternal grandfather of Charles) appeared imminent, the prince sent him to Spain to take possession of the kingdom as soon as the throne was vacant. Ferdinand having died on Jan. 23, 1516, Cardinal Ximenes exhibited a document whereby the late monarch had appointed him regent until the arrival of the hereditary prince; and Charles solved the difficulty by naming Adrian ambassador to the regent, Ximenes. Shortly afterward, Ximenes named Adrian bishop of Tortosa and grand-inquisitor of Aragon. When the revolt of Luther began, Adrian, then cardinal, thought that it could be repressed by an abolition of the abuses of the Curia Romana. "The old professor of theology," says Hefele, "thought that the teachings of Luther were worthy of no person's serious attention; that their sole weight lay in their being an attack on certain real abuses in the Church; and that when those abuses were removed, the Lutherans would abandon their doctrine on grace. But he was mistaken." III. Thomas de Vio, generally mentioned as Cajetan, from the fact that his family were illustrious in Cajeta (Gaeta), was termed emphatically "the great mind, and the miracle of the minds of his time." In spite of the opposition of his parents, he became a Dominican at the age of fifteen (1484); made his first ecclesiastical studies at Naples; and finally received the doctorate at Ferrara. After several years of successful teaching in Padua, his reputation led Cardinal Oliver Caraffa, the cardinal-protector of the Friars-Preachers, to procure his transfer to Rome. In 1500 he became procurator-general of his Order, and in 1508 general. On the occasion of the Pseudo-Council of Pisa, sustained by the faction of the emperor Maximilian and Louis XII., Cajetan greatly encouraged timid spirits, and confounded the rebellious, by his work *On the Power of the Pope.* We shall see him acting as legate of Leo X. in Germany, endeavoring to combat religious revolt by an admirable combination of adroitness and authority; and the student of his entire career will find that his teaching was ever regarded as a guide for others, and his silence as an implicit censure. He had, like all great men, zealous partisans and rabid censors. Melancthon portrays him in no flattering terms. Catarino, his fellow-religious, combatted some of his writings, especially his *Commentaries on the Scriptures*, most furiously. Chamier praises his rectitude, candor, and moderation. Sixtus of Siena cannot find enough eloquent words to express his admiration of the man and the theologian (1). IV. Scaramuccio Trivulzio, a nephew of the great Italian commander in the service of France, the marshal Gian-Giacomo Trivulzio, merits mention for his ascetic piety and his profound juridical attainments. V. Campeggi, so famous for his legation to England in the matter of the divorce of Henry VIII. and Queen Catharine, was as noted for his virtue as for his learning. The praise of Erasmus may be of suspicious sincerity; but it is interesting to observe that the humanist acknowledged a present from his Eminence in these words : " The brilliancy of the gold shall be a lasting symbol of your cardinalitial wisdom ; but the flash of the diamond can be only a faint image of the glory of your name "(2).

Probably the most meritorious work of the reign of Leo X. was his endeavor to hurl back into Asia the ever-threatening hordes of Islam ; like all his predecessors, since the day of the first Mahometan advance into Europe, this Pontiff moved heaven and earth to protect Christendom and civilization. Julius II. had continued the task of Pius III., entreating all the European peoples to don the Cross ; and at least Venice, Genoa, and Naples had undertaken expeditions blessed by the successor of St. Peter. But the power of the Crescent was not diminished ; and if Europe was not already overrun by the cavalry of Bajazet, it was simply because that son of Mahomet II. was, to use the words of Commines, a man of little valor, preferring the pleasures of the seraglio

<hr>

(1) The chief points of the career of Cajetan are treated by Ughelli and by Capiccio, and oy his secretary, Flavio. See also PIAZZA; *Cardinalitial Hierarchy.—*PEYRAT ; *Origin of the Cardinals of the Holy See.—*VICTORELLI; *Lives of the Pontiffs and Cardinals.—*ALBY ; *Illustrious Cardinals* . Paris, 1644.'

(2) SIGONIUS; *Bishops of Bologna.—*PANVINI ; *Chronicle.—*SANDER; *English Schism.* -SLEIDAN : *Annals.—*BUMALDI; *Library of Bologna.—*AUBREY ; *loc. cit.*

to the din of battle. But when Selim mounted the Ottoman throne, promising his Janizaries the spoils of the western world; when Europe heard that Selim had subverted the power of the Mamelukes, conquered Palestine, and profaned the Sepulchre of Christ; a shudder ran through every Christian community, as though Jerusalem had bowed before the Crescent for the first time. Therefore it appeared not impossible to resurrect the spirit of the Middle Age, when Leo X. preached another Crusade in the Lateran Council. Soon after the dissolution of this assembly, the Pontiff sent legates into France, Spain, England, Germany, Hungary, and the northern countries; exhorting the nations to form a Christian league against the common enemy, declaring himself the head of that league, proclaiming a truce of five years between all hostile Christian States, and excommunicating all violators of the Peace of God. In order to draw down the blessing of Heaven upon his project, he ordered solemn fasts and deprecatory processions in the Eternal City; and himself attended tearfully at the public services in St. Peter's, having walked thither barefooted, distributing enormous alms on the way. Writing to Henry VIII. of England, he said: "My heart is inflamed with joy, since I have learned that the emperor Maximilian, the king of France, and the king of Spain have resolved to make common cause against the Turk. Our dissensions have always benefited the Turk, and he has continually grown more formidable; but now, thanks to God, his advance will be checked. I have sent legates to all the sovereigns, urging the immediate departure of the promised succors. ... Certainly you will not be the last to join the Crusade, for your glory is at stake. Listen to the call of God, the Master of us all!" And writing to Francis I., the Pontiff warns him: "Let us beware lest, on the Judgment Day, the Lord condemn us as faithless servants who have abused His gifts; lest the accusation of indifference and cowardice be brought against us, to whom He has entrusted the care of His flock!" Such language on the part of the Father of the Faithful was not entirely without effect. The emperor promised to send an army to aid the Polish and Hungarian cavalry in an attack on both sides of the Balkans; the French, together with large Venetian and other Italian bodies of veteran troops, and 16,000 Swiss, were to embark at Brindisi, destined for the shores of Greece; while Spanish, Portuguese, and English fleets were to gather at Carthagena, there to receive the formidable Spanish infantry which was apparently destined to win new laurels on the shores of the Hellespont. But the brilliant prospect was soon dissipated; the spirit of the vaunted Reformation had begun to exhale its venom, and the projected Crusade of Leo X. served only to rekindle the fanaticism of the Osmanli. While the Pontiff was perorating the cause of Christendom, an apostate friar was calling upon the Germans to realize that the rule of the Turk was a thousand times preferable to that of the Pope, the faith of Islam much purer than the idolatry of the Mass. "The Turk peoples Heaven with saints; but the Pope peoples hell with Christians. However, if you wish to fight the Turk, begin with the Papacy! By my faith, if the Turk marches on Rome, I shall not weep. ... To war on the Turk is to war on God. ... I have never regarded Mahomet as Antichrist; but the Pope is the real Antichrist. ... Hear, all ye who have ears! Do not enlist against the Turk, so long as there is a Pope under the vault of Heaven!" And the polite German Demosthenes, Ulrich Hutten, mouthed the same ravings: "No money for a war against the Turk! You must make a crusade; but it must be against Rome—that Rome where there are only lawyers, notaries, procurators, Bullists, jurists, who fatten on our sweat and blood. Throw off this insulting yoke! Germans, break your chains!" Perhaps a St. Pius V. would have cured the fever which had begun to make sad havoc in the German body; but the disease ran its course, and so distracted the rest of Christendom that not until St. Pius V. did come, was a temporary check experienced by Islam.

In 1519 the throne of the Holy Roman Empire, then practically that of Germany alone, and such other countries as the incumbent of the moment might happen to rule, became vacant by the death of Maximilian I. of Austria. Immediately the enterprising and externally chivalrous Francis I., king of France, announced himself as a candidate (1). Of course, the electors were Germans, and the Holy Roman Emperor would be king of the Germans; but Francis relied upon what he not foolishly regarded as just titles for their preference. He was a man of spirit, presumedly elevated character; he had recently been victorious in "the combat of giants" against those Swiss who had been styled "the tamers of princes;" and he was master of solidified France— a country which, unlike Germany, was thoroughly *one*, with no independent subordinate sovereigns or privileged communes, and with an almost perfect political constitution. And then the German electors were all, at that time, basely venal. "Glut them with everything!" said Francis to his agents; and up to the very moment of the election they swallowed his gold, as well as that of his competitor, finishing the comedy with the sacrilegious declaration, before the Holy Communion, that they were acting in perfect freedom from any illegitimate influences. But the very talents of Francis militated against his success; the German princes preferred to be ruled by one who had, as yet, given no sign of ability. King Charles I. of Spain (Fourth of Naples, Second of Sicily), was the grandson of Ferdinand and Isa-

(1) " Francis of Angouleme, who became king at twenty years of age, merits description. He was a spoiled child of fortune, a man of persuasive tongue, and a facial expression which won all hearts. He was well trained in chivalrous habits, a brilliant inheritor of the traditions of the feudal nobility, and totally unlike the sombre Louis XI.; in a word, he was a royal chevalier. From his tutor, Arthur Goufier, lord of Boisy, a noble veteran of the Italian wars, he had received an artistic and literary education which grafted itself upon a character as variable as it was passionate. From his earliest years, an extravagant temerity, often justified by success, led him to mad acts of audacity and intrepidity. ... His height was above the ordinary; his physiognomy was open and very seductive; his speech was rich, flowing, and persuasive. But beneath all these imposing externals, there was not a great soul; rather was there a weak and capricious character, governed entirely by the moment. Military life is a school of discipline for ordinary men; one of despotism for rulers. Strong and ardent, the pupil of Marshal de Gié had learned from that veteran how to so enforce obedience as to experience no resistance or hesitation; and therefore he was for others an imperious master, even though he was a blind slave to his own passions. Thus it was that to Louis XII., a king who had exhibited one side of the character of St. Louis, namely, submission to rule and attachment to duty, there succeeded a prince who knew no law other than that of his own instincts and his own will, no other authority than the omnipotence of his own caprice. When perchance Francis sometimes yielded to outside pressure, it was because he was under influences, for which he should have blushed. His defects, perhaps, more than his good qualities, seduced the French nobility. When Bayard knighted Francis on the battle-field of Marignan, he could not then confer upon his sovereign the truly chivalric grandeur of his own soul, without fear and without reproach. In truth, Francis I. was only externally a chevalier." PELLISSIER; *The Sixteenth Century; Ten Anecdotical Essays on the Renaissance and the Reformation.* Paris, 1888.

bella ; those sovereigns having united their daughter Jane to Philip of Austria (d. 1506), son of the emperor Maximilian I. With the crown of Spain, he inherited the mastership of nearly all the New World; and from his grandmother, Mary of Burgundy, he derived the sovereignty of a large portion of the Low Countries, as well as of that ancient province of France, then called Franche-Comté. From his grandfather Maximilian he inherited a sceptre which dominated over Austria proper, Styria, Carinthia, the Tyrol, Carniola, and Austrian Suabia. The student who wishes to form a correct idea of the character and career of this extraordinary man will do well not to rely upon the olden historians who are the most quoted, Paul Jovius the Adulator (of Charles) and Sleidan the Malevolent. Still less ought the reader turn for knowledge to the pages of Robertson, whose reflections are Voltairian, though his spirit is not as diabolic as that of the followers of the Sage of Ferney ; who, royal historiographer in England, could be scarcely independent and impartial, even though he did not cater for the cravers of tales of papistical absurdities ; and of whose work our judicious Protestant countryman, Henry Wheaton, said that it was full of errors (1). Cantù institutes a comparison between Francis I. and Charles V. which will interest the reader. " One of these two young arbiters of Europe had already shown his warlike nature ; the other his preference for intrigue. Francis, educated as a private gentleman, had preferred to the glorious title of his predecessor that of ' king of the nobles,' and that of the ' first gentleman of France.' Indeed, Francis had all the defects and virtues of a ' gentleman.' He was like a hero of the Middle Age ; Charles was a modern king. Francis was addicted to inordinate parade and splendor ; Charles sought only for substance and success. Francis affected to be scru-

(1) See his letter to the Secretary of the National Institute at Washington (1843).—Among the general Histories, the searcher for information concerning the two royal rivals will find none so satisfactory and impartial as that of Cantù. The seeker for details will profit by GACHARD ; Correspondence of Charles V. and Pope Adrian VI. Brussels, 1841.—LANZ ; Correspondence of Charles V., Taken from the Imperial Archives and the Burgundian Library in Brussels. Leipsic, 1844.—Relation of Giovanni Correr to the Venetian Senate in the Relations of Ambassadors. Paris, 1838.—LEGLAT ; Essay on the Negotiations between France and Austria, During the Thirty First Years of the Sixteenth Century. Paris, 1850.—Vatican Documents Illustrating the Ecclesiastical History of the Sixteenth Century. Freiburg, 1861.

pulously honorable, while Charles feigned to persevere in the simple loyalty of his family ; but both could deceive, when they deemed such conduct opportune. Charles never rested ; Francis often sought quiet. Charles travelled continually, and thus seemed to bring nearer together his widely separated dominions ; he retained the fidelity of his generals, but never allowed them to guide him ; he permitted no influence to his feminine friends, and no man ever knew who was the veritable mother of his bastards. Francis squandered his wealth in display and libertinage, confided office to the least worthy, and because of the female intrigues and court punctilios he disgusted the constable de Bourbon, Doria, the prince of Orange, who all passed over to the service of his more prudent foe. The most fortunate wars of Charles were conducted by his generals ; but he always directed his policy. In the art of conducting an intrigue, promising, eluding, and corrupting, he far excelled the soldier-king. Reflective even when a child, and quick to foresee, Charles surrounded himself with advisers ; but he never abandoned himself to them. Inexorable and circumspect, he sought continually to satisfy his personal interests ; and he knew well how to wait, as his motto 'Not yet' testified. The easy conquest of America so exalted the ambition of Charles, that he imagined the entire world to be waiting for his grasp— an idea which was encouraged by victories which were rather lucky than merited, which dazzled his contemporaries, and afflicted his subjects with the bewilderment in which the blind obedience of the soldier is taken for heroism, and in which men regard as honorable any course which entails advantage for their master " (1).

Pope Leo X. could not regard the imperial aspirations of either the French or Spanish monarch without apprehension ; for the success of either would be fraught with danger for the equilibrium of Europe, the repose of Italy, and the security of the Holy See. Therefore he tried to induce Francis to advocate the election of a prince whose moderate political influence would promise quiet both for Rome and France ; and the elector of Saxony was suggested as the

(1) *Universal History*, bk. XVIII., ch. vi.

person. But the heart of Francis was filled with the desire to don the crown of Charlemagne ; and the Pontiff was compelled to trust in the energy and skill of Cajetan, whom he had sent as legate to the Diet of Nuremburg, in which the emperor was to be chosen. The cardinal reminded the princes that Charles of Spain and Austria was also king of the Two Sicilies, and that the Constitution of the Holy Roman Empire forbade a king of Naples to mount the imperial throne ; then he showed the danger to both Italy and Germany, if Francis, who already was duke of Milan and lord of Genoa, were hailed as King of the Romans. An impression was produced ; and the elector of Treves proposed Frederick of Saxony as future emperor. The other electors assented ; but Frederick declined the burden. Then the electors agreed to reward the modesty of the Saxon prince by allowing him to name his substitute ; and he pronounced in favor of the Austro-Spaniard. On June 28, 1519, Charles was proclaimed King of the Germans and Emperor-Elect, and was crowned as the first at Aix-la-Chapelle a few days afterward ; but he did not receive the imperial crown until 1529, and then at the hands of Pope Clement VII (1). The power of Charles V., at this time, was greater in appearance than in reality, not only because it was derived from heterogeneous elements, but because his most important states were afflicted by disorders which threatened their national existence. Spain was lacerated by civil discords, because the young monarch, contrary to the advice of the wise Cardinal Ximenes, had interfered with her time-honored *fueros* or local privileges. Germany was not only trembling in anticipation of Islamite invasion, but was the prey of the disintegrating forces of the new religionists. The populations of Naples and Sicily, ever hostile to the Spanish yoke, were

---

(1) As Pope Adrian IV. expressed the proper conception of the imperial tenure, in a letter to the bishops of Germany: "The king of the Germans cannot be styled Emperor and Augustus, until he is consecrated by the Roman Pontiff, who promoted Charles (Charlemagne), and gave to him the great name of emperor." The modern German emperors, though hailed by their subjects as such, were never styled by the Popes, the real and historical source of their imperial dignity, in other fashion than as "emperors-elect;" simply because those modern emperors had not been confirmed as such and crowned by the Roman Pontiff. For the distinction between a King of the Germans and a Holy Roman Emperor, see our dissertation on the *Revival of the Empire*, in vol. II., ch. ii.

kept in subjection only by large bodies of troops which Charles would gladly have employed for other purposes. The Low Countries, jealous of their venerable franchises, obeyed or scorned their foreign ruler pretty much as they willed. Therefore Francis I. deemed the time propitious for a war against his rival ; and in 1521 Spain, Italy, and Flanders became theatres of carnage. Pope Leo X. was involved in the struggle. 'The French governor of the Milanais having violated the territories of the Church, the Pontiff decided to accept the offers which Charles V. made in return for an alliance. If the Pope would aid the emperor in expelling the French from Italy, Charles would see that Parma and Piacenza were restored to the papal dominion ; he would also aid the Pope against certain rebel feudataries, and would augment the tribute which, as king of Naples, he was bound to pay to the Holy See, suzerain of that kingdom. Probably the Pontiff was impelled the more easily to enter into this alliance, because of his belief that Charles could and would put an end to the religious revolt which Luther had excited in Germany. In reference to the military operations which now ensued, we need say but little. The historian, Guicciardini, held the title of commissary-general of the pontifical army ; and the veteran, Prospero Colonna, was commander of the allied forces. The Milanese, tired of the exactions of Marshal Lautrec, the lieutenant of Francis, rose in arms, expelled the French from nearly all the duchy, and recalled the Sforzas to the ducal throne. Then, supported by the Spanish, Papal, and German forces, they forced Lautrec to retreat into France. Our Pontiff was at his villa of La Magliana, when he received the news that Parma and Piacenza had been restored to his temporal dominions, and that Italy was freed from the sway of the French. If he then began to cogitate as to the possibility of actuating the dream of Julius II. by driving out of the peninsula the other "barbarian," time for the purpose was denied him.

On Nov. 24, 1521, Leo X. returned to Rome amid the plaudits of his subjects, nearly all of whom, that day, carried crowns of olive leaves in their hands. During three days court and people abandoned themselves to transports of joy ;

and when, on the 27th, the news circulated that the Pontiff was indisposed, men thought that the most serious consequence would be a postponement of the Consistory which had been ordered for that day. But in the early morn of Dec. 1, the attendants of his Holiness saw him join his hands, move his lips in prayer, and fall back dead upon his pillow (1). When we contemplate the reign of Leo X., we can scarcely avoid the question as to whether he was the Pope for his time; whether his attitude toward nascent Protestantism, which we shall notice in its proper place, was that which befitted the Head of the Universal Church. Certain writers have amused themselves, and perhaps their readers, by speculating as to whether Luther, if he could have changed places with the son of Lorenzo the Magnificent, would not have subdued the religious revolt, while it was, as yet, confined to an obscure corner of what was then comparatively uninfluential Germany. The imagination will not be directed toward such a supposition by one who has studied the character of the ex-Augustinian ; for he realizes that this consummately successful agitator possessed none of even the most rudimentary qualities of a true statesman. But Luther struck the key-note of popular discontent, and drew the salient outlines of a successful campaign, when he made his onslaught on the abuses which were too frequently practised by the preachers of Indulgences. At that moment, if Leo X. had disciplined the culprits severely, and had he then repressed energetically other abuses which had been denounced again and again by devoted children of the Church, the heavy shower might not have become a storm. But the elegant and fastidious scion of the Medici, the lover of literary repose, the man who manifested such zeal when there was a question of scientific or artistic import, discerned in the gathering clouds merely a sign of a "monkish squabble," and in the turbulence of Luther he recognized simply the vaporings of a " drunken German, who would sing another tune, when he

(1) There is no need of dilating upon proofs that refute the assertion made by some au_ thors that Leo X. was "probably " the victim of poison. Mere rumors to that effect were current among the people : and although Malespina, the Pope's cup-bearer, was suspected, and dragged by the mob to the Castel San Angelo, nothing was proved against him. The most reliable records of the time ascribe the castastrophe to suffocation by catarrh.

had digested his liquor." The apathy of the Pontiff in the premises contrasts vividly with the impetuosity of the aggressor ; and the former was so preoccupied with his arts and sciences, with the cares of his worldly state, or at best with an apparent consolidation of his authority, that he preferred to disdain the rebel whom, possibly, he might have disarmed. This apathy is eloquently illustrated by a comparison of the dates of the three events which were the main signal lights during the first phase of the Reformation. It was on Nov. 11, 1517, that Luther affixed his propositions on the church doors of Wittemberg; not until nearly three years afterward, on Sept. 15, 1520, did the Pontiff promulgate the Bull which condemned forty of these theses ; and on the following Dec. 10 the apostate publicly burned the papal document. We perforce agree with the Benedictines who afterward, though with a truly filial sorrow, reproached Leo X. for allowing his temporal preoccupations to jeopardize the spiritual authority of the Holy See. Certainly he showed much care in perfecting the administration of Church affairs, inasmuch as he strove to consolidate the hierarchy of the Church ; but he gave little attention to the banishment of cupidity and ambition from the sanctuary. Therefore we cannot term Leo X. a grand Pontiff. On any other throne than that of the successor of St. Peter, he would have surpassed any one of his line in commendable qualities ; but he should not receive a title which the judicious confer on a Gregory the Great, a Gregory VII., an Innocent III., a Nicholas V., or a Pius V. Undoubtedly Bembo, Ariosto, Raphael, and Michelangelo were apostles of the beautiful in literature and art, and upon his encouragement of such luminaries Leo X. relied for the future glorification of his pontificate ; but the beauty of which they were the apostles could not give to him either true strength or true grandeur (1).

(1) In illustration of the immense latitude of speech which was then allowed in the land of the Inquisition to criticizers of the Popes, and to show that the eulogies of Leo by his courtiers were not entirely endorsed by the clergy of Italy, we cite a passage from a sermon delivered in Mantua, in 1537, by Fra Callisto da Piacenza, one of the most popular preachers of his time : " Poor Pope Leo ! He had attained to so many dignities, had amassed such immense treasures, and had at his beck so many friends and servants ! But in that last journey with the bottomless sack, out of the bag fell everything, excepting only Fra Mariano (the Pope's confessor), who, being a buffoon, was as light as a straw, and therefore

But we must not suppose that Leo X. ignored entirely the duties of his sublime position. He exhibited much zeal in furthering many of the reformatory projects of the Lateran Council. He was active in suppressing the remnants of Hussitism in Bohemia. He did much toward propagating the faith among the still barbarous Muscovites. He endeavored to bring the Abyssinians out of their schism. He founded many dioceses in America. He terminated the long and vexatious dispute concerning the legitimacy of the Monti di Pietà (1). He introduced the sublime ceremonies of the Holy Week which are still practised in the Vatican Basilica, and the writers of the day are concordant in their praise of his edifying demeanor on all such occasions. When urged to confer benefices on the unworthy, he generally preferred to supply the wants of such persons with his private funds. His sobriety was that of an anchorite; he never drank anything but water. He never ate meat on Wednesday; on Friday he ate greens alone; and on Saturday he never dined. That his chastity was truly priestly, we may suppose, since Luther never dared to question it; Ranke is discreetly silent as to the matter, and Roscoe says that his morals were irreprehensible. Ranke tells us that he does indeed find in a passage of Navigero that Leo X. thought of a war against the Turks; but the German historian stoops to an unworthy insinuation when he says that "Leo did not think of the interests of Christendom when he tried to regain the Sepulchre of Christ, but rather of the lost Greek and Roman manuscripts which he might recover." Now Ranke makes much parade, in his preface, of the numerous olden authors whom he consulted in the preparation of his frequently valuable work; and he must have known that it is not only in an incidental passage of a comparatively obscure writer that indications of Pope Leo's crusading intentions are to be found. This feature of his papal career is as salient as any other of

clung to the side. When the poor Pope came to the point of death, of all that he had gathered in this world, nothing remained to him but this friar, and he recommended Leo to think only of his soul, saying: ' Remember God. Holy Father!' And the poor Pope could only cry out in his agony, ' Good God, good God!'; and thus he gave his soul to his Lord. See how true it is that he who amasses riches puts them into a bottomless sack."

(1) See page 271.

which Ranke treats. As for the assertion of the Pontiff's indifference to what had been dearest to the hearts of all his
predecessors, since the day when the Crescent first floated over
the towers of Jerusalem, the German author does not attempt
to furnish a morsel of evidence. The same writer says that
Leo X. did not always observe the usual Papal decorum;
for instance, he would often go forth from his palace, "not
only without his surplice, but even with boots on his feet."
And alas! He was wont to "pass the autumn in the pleasures of the Campagna, in hunting near Viterbo and Corneto,
in fishing in Lake Bolsena;" and the pleasures of his court,
"while not like the outrageous ones of Alexander VI., were
unworthy of his high position." Well, Leo X. did hunt very
frequently; but his physicians had ordered him to take that
exercise, insisting that it was the sole means whereby he
could avoid an early and sudden death. But the last complaint of Ranke cannot be dismissed with a smile. We cannot
admire our Pontiff as, surrounded by his courtiers and noble
visitors, he listens complacently to certain effusions which
were meritorious from a literary point of view, but certainly
not calculated to promote that purity of heart which ought
to dominate in the ecclesiastic (1). But may we not suppose
that the literary preoccupations of Leo X. and his court,
while listening to the dulcet measures of Ariosto, or even to
the lubricious ridiculosities of Della Casa, deprived those
productions of much of their immoral consequences? And
it is well to remember with Saint-Cheron, that plain language is not always an indication of a depraved mind; that
"experience proves that the more corrupt a society is, the
more delicate and susceptible it is as to its language."
Ranke is of opinion that "the sentiments of Christian faith
were necessarily enfeebled" in the minds of Leo X. and his
court; and as proof he adduces Pomponazio, "the most cele-

---

(1) It is not edifying to note that although Leo X. was himself an exceedingly sober man,
he delighted in entertaining that Friar Mariano who could swallow a pigeon at a mouthful,
and eat forty eggs at a meal; that among his habitual boon companions of the leisure hour
he numbered that Nobili il Moro, who was one of the most disgusting gluttons of the day;
and that one of his favorite pastimes was to play cards with his intimates, on which occasions, whether he won or lost, he scattered handfuls of florins among the spectators. What
is still more sad, Paul Jovius when narrating these things. regards them as "worthy of a
noble and gentlemanly prince."

·brated of the philosophers of the time," contending that the soul of man is not immaterial and immortal. But Ranke himself has narrated how Pomponazio, because of this assertion, was ordered, on June 13, 1518, to retract; "otherwise proceedings would be instituted against him." Like the philosophasters of our day, Pomponazio affected to discern an opposition between reason and faith; and in his treatise on the *Immortality of the Soul* he pretended that the immortality could not be proved by reason, and that the Church would not permit the exercise of reason in the premises. His position was attacked at once; and although Cardinal Bembo ·defended it, Pomponazio issued a new edition with the necessary corrections. Ranke studiously ignores the fact that the philosopher died a submissive son of the Church, and with all the signs of an edifying piety. Ranke unhesitatingly avers that so paganized had the Roman priesthood become, under the influence of Leo X., that "at the very moment of the consummation of the Sacrifice of the Mass, the priests were wont to utter blasphemous words, wherewith they denied (the truth of) the Sacrifice." One has a right to demand proof in corroboration of this tremendous accusation; but whom does this praised-as-impartial historian adduce? Martin Luther!

CHAPTER XVIII.

THE COMMENCEMENTS OF PROTESTANTISM : LUTHER.

It is futile to deny that a reformation in the Church was necessary at the beginning of the sixteenth century; the student of the history of that period is familiar with the lamentations of the most submissive children of the Church, because of corruption in the sanctuary. Fallen humanity is ever prone to an abuse of even the holiest things, and this tendency had been favored, during several centuries, by the disorders of several Pontiffs and of many of the clergy, as well as ·by the criminal ambition of nearly all the Holy Roman emperors and of many other sovereigns. And above all, the ·Great Western Schism, that natural outcome of the removal

of the Papal residence from its legitimate seat, had greatly
weakened the strength, and marred the beauty, of the human
element of the Spouse of Christ.   In the universal uneasiness
consequent upon this state of ecclesiastical affairs, proud
spirits found their opportunity, and, observes Bossuet, "The
weak-minded lost their good sense, and instead of remembering that the Son of God inculcated respect for the Chair of
Moses in spite of the iniquity of the doctors who filled it,
very many yielded to the temptation to hate the chair itself.
All was ready for a great rupture ; the materials for schism
were collected, and the architect alone was wanting" (1).   Circumstances elicited the architect.   Two great tasks, undertaken by Roman Pontiffs, furnished the occasion for revolt.
Julius II. had begun the erection of the grandest architectural glory of either olden or modern Christendom, St. Peter's Basilica at Rome ; and Leo X. was straining every nerve
to prevent a threatened invasion of Europe by the sultan
Selim I.   These works required money, and Pope Leo offered
indulgences to those who would contribute.   The Dominican
Friars were charged with the task of preaching the Indulgences, and the work in Germany was entrusted to one Tetzel,
whom John Lindner termed a light of his Order (2), and
whom Buddæus praises (3).   These Indulgences found much
opposition in Germany, for it would seem that many of the
ignorant regarded the money as the price of a sacred thing,
and that the more educated frequently acted, in regard to
the concessions, in such a manner as to divest them of much
claim to respect (4).

Protestant authors have dilated greatly upon the alleged
infamy of Tetzel's proceedings ; but they have no other proof
than Luther's assertions.   As an indication of Luther's bad
faith in this matter, we need only to adduce that passage in

(1) As Erasmus expressed the idea, " the egg was laid ; Luther had only to hatch it."

(2) *Life of the Papistical Indulgence Preacher*, by James Vogel. Leipsic, 1727.

(3) *Ibid.*

(4) The sovereigns often demanded a lion's share in the collections. Thus six years before the publication of Luther's theses, an indulgence was preached in Saxony for a crusade
against the Turks, and all the funds were appropriated by the emperor and that elector
who afterward patronized Luther. As a rule the German princes took two-thirds of the
amount accruing from the collections, and the reader should bear this fact in mind when
he reads the declamations of those princes, justifying their patronage of the Lutheran idea
with the plea that the Popes were ruining Germany by the sale of indulgences.

his *Table Talk* where he avers that " Tetzel was an arrant
rascal who dared to preach that if one were to violate the
Mother of God, an Indulgence would wash away the sin."
Now, Seckendorf, the chief apologist of Luther, tells us in his
Commentary on Lutheranism, that the words of Tetzel were :
" However enormous a sin against the Mother of God must
be, it is less than that which is committed against her Son,
and even this latter sin may be forgiven, as Christ tells us."
Some writers attack the morals of Tetzel ; but since Luther
himself, in the torrent of his vituperations, made no such reproach, we may be sure that he had no reason to utter any.
But there were real reasons for discontent ; and if we consider
the chagrin of the Augustinian Friars, who had hitherto, as
a rule, preached all Papal Indulgences in Germany, we will
have a conception of the spark which, falling upon inflammable materials, produced one of the direst conflagrations
that God has permitted to devastate His Church.

Martin Luther was born in 1483, at Eisleben in Upper
Saxony.   His first studies were made by the aid of alms obtained by singing in the streets, and by the help of a small
salary earned as chorister in the churches.   Having excited
the interest of a widow named Cotta, he was enabled to devote himself more freely to study, and in time he received
his degree in philosophy at Erfurt.   Profoundly affected by
the sudden death of a companion, he resolved to join the
Augustinian Order ; and two years afterward, in 1507, he
made his profession and received the priesthood.   During
many years, according to his own testimony, in the *Preface*
to his *Works*, he " was so besotted with the Papacy, that he
would have killed or helped to kill any one who rejected one
iota of the Pope's teaching."   And nevertheless, in 1516, long
before his collision with Tetzel, he had written a work on the
will of man, directed " against the doctrine of the Pope and
of the sophists."   We may suppose, also, that rebellious
thoughts were already agitating his mind at that time, for he
wrote to the priest Leitzken : " Pray for me, for I grow more
miserable every day.   I am constantly drawing nearer to
hell."   Toward the end of 1517, while Luther was stationed
at Wittemberg, Tetzel proceeded to Juterbock.   Protestant

writers tell us that so great was the desire to procure " par.
dons," crowds surrounded the Dominican, but all returned
without any exterior signs of compunction. The confession-
als of the Augustinians were deserted ; and these friars became jealous. Luther, who had already declared that "with
God's help, he would put a hole in Tetzel's purse " (1), announced that he would preach on indulgences. On the appointed day, an immense throng listened to a number of innovations which appeared so revolutionary to Luther's brethren, that one of them mounted the pulpit, and pulling the
orator's tunic, he whispered : " You are rash, doctor. The
Dominicans are laughing in their sleeves. Our order will
suffer for your words." Then Luther retorted in language
which is much admired by Protestants, but which would
come with more grace from Moslem than from Christian lips :
" If my teaching is not from God, it will fall to the ground ;
if it comes from His holy name, leave it alone." On the
following day, Tetzel publicly analyzed Luther's proposition.
"The polemical style of Tetzel," observes Audin, " has nothing striking ; and we cannot understand the effect which he
produced in the pulpit ; for the reader is not treated to those
instances of bad taste, those indecorous comparisons, with
which his sermons are said to have been tainted. It is the
style of a theological professor who, feeling sure of victory,
has no need of harsh expressions " (2).

On the Feast of All Saints, although he had promised the
bishop of Brandenburg that he would not publish his ideas on
Indulgences, Luther prevailed on the porter of his convent
to affix on one of the outer pillars of the church of All Saints,
his famous 95 theses. The revolutionary manifesto began:
" For the sake of love and truth, the following theses will be
upheld at Wittemberg, under the auspices of the Reverend
Father Luther, of the Order of St. Augustine, Master of Arts
and of Theology, and Lector-in-Ordinary. Wherefore it is
requested that those who are unable to discuss them with us
in person will do so in writing. In the name of Our Lord
Jesus Christ. Amen." We quote the principal theses. I.

(1) *MS. Chronicle of Grimma*, at year 1516.
(2) *Life, Writings, and Doctrines of Luther.* Paris, 1841.

When our Lord and Master says, "Do penance," He desires that the lives of the faithful shall be lives of constant penance. II. Unquestionably He never spoke of the Sacrament of Penance ; that is, of confession to a priest. XIII. The dead cannot be affected by canonical judgments. XXVI. If the Pope can relieve souls in Purgatory, he does so by prayer, and not by the power of the Keys. XXIX. Who knows whether all the souls in Purgatory desire relief? Read what is narrated of Sts. Severin and Paschal. LXXXII. Why does not the Pope empty Purgatory at once ?

Alphonsus de Castro thinks that when Luther published these theses, he was, as yet, merely afflicted by a false zeal (1). Surius thinks that he was, at that time, merely an opponent of abuses which were lamented on all sides (2). The impartial Protestant historian, Schrock, regards him as being still submissive to the authority of the Church (3). But although Luther did protest to the public, at that time, that he deferred to the judgment of the Church, he used different language to his friends. Ten days after the Wittemberg episode, writing to Langus, he styled the archbishop of Mayence and the bishops of Saxony, who had condemned his theses: "Buffoons and earthworms." Three months afterward, he wrote to Spalatinus : "I declare to you and our friends, that Indulgences are mere mummeries. I know well that I am raising up against myself six hundred Minotaurs, Rhadamanthotaurs, and Cacotaurs ; but what is that to me?" At first, Rome was disposed to regard this matter as one of the petty monastic squabbles which Germany frequently produced. The learned of Italy could not realize that a "barbarian" could effect anything extraordinary. Leo X. was rather pleased by Luther's subtleties; and regarding him as a German drunkard, he advised that "the friar should be allowed to digest his wine." And perhaps the Pontiff was right in favoring leniency, for, under date of Trinity Sunday, 1518, Luther had written to him, saying: "The propositions which I put forth, Most Holy Father, are in the form of theses. and not of doctrines ; of enigmas pro-

(1) *Against Heresies*, art. *Absolution*, b. XI.
(2) In Appendix to the *Chronicle* of Nauchler.
(3) *History of the Church*. vol. I., p. 129.

pounded in an enigmatic style. ... Prostrate at your feet, I resign to your Holiness all that I am and all that I possess. *Vivify, kill, recall, approve, reprove; as it may please you to do. I acknowledge your voice as that of Christ who presides and speaks in you.*" The rank hypocrisy of this effusion is shown by the friar's declaration to Spalatinus at that very time: "I am not quite certain whether the Pope is really Antichrist or merely his apostle."

The emperor Maximilian had conceived the idea of using Luther as a weapon against the Pope; he had even written to the elector of Saxony : "Keep an eye on Friar Martin, for he may be of great service to us." But the wily prince soon discerned the troubles menacing Germany, and formally denounced the agitator to the Holy See. Therefore on August 7, 1518, Leo X. commissioned the bishop of Ascoli to summon Luther to Rome; but the elector Frederick requesting an examination in Germany, the cardinal Cajetan, a man of great reputation for learning and piety, was delegated for that purpose (1). The meeting occurred at Augsburg on October 12; and when the friar tried to dispute, the cardinal said : "I have not come here to argue with you as boys do in college ; nor am I your judge. I have been sent by our common father, to whom you wrote only the other day : 'Approve, condemn, etc.' Retract, therefore, for such is the will of the Pontiff." After several hours of conversation, Luther asked for a delay of three days, and it was granted; but on the following morning he gave a protest to his Eminence, declaring that "he had never intended to teach anything offensive to Catholic doctrine, to the Holy Scriptures, to the authority of the Fathers, *or to the decrees of the Pope.*" Then Luther departed from Augsburg, and a fews days afterward, he gave the world a proof of his duplicity by having

---

(1) Thomas de Vio, surnamed Gaetano (*anglice*, Cajetan) because he was from Gaeta, became a Dominican, and first attracted public notice by a disputation with the celebrated Count Pico della Mirandola, held at Ferrara in 1492, in a General Chapter of his Order. Though only twenty-two years old, he so distinguished himself in this contest of intellect with the great man who could argue well on everything, "and on some other things" (so it was said of Pico), that at his opponent's request, he received the doctorate on the spot. In his thirty-ninth year, he became General of his Order, and in 1517 Leo X. gave him the red hat. Cajetan was remarkably gentle in manner ; and was greatly beloved by the workingmen of Rome, because he had espoused their cause against the usurers.

affixed to the gate of the Carmelite monastery where he had lodged, an appeal to the effect that if he had attacked Indulgences, it was because they were not enjoined by God. His judges, he averred, were not to be trusted; he had not gone to Rome, because there where justice once abided, homicide now dwelled. Finally, he "appealed from the Pope badly informed, to the Pope better informed" (1).

We omit any account of the mission of Miltitz, and of the dispute between Luther and Eckius on July 4, 1519, because they were without results. On April 6, 1520, the friar wrote another letter to Pope Leo, some passages of which are models of sublime effrontery. "I protest, and my memory is not at all treacherous, that I have never spoken of you otherwise than with honor and respect. ... You cannot deny, my dear Leo (*optime Leo*), that your See is more corrupt than Babylon or Sodom. It is against that impious Rome that I rebel. ... Rome is a stinking cave of robbers, the most brazen of brothels, and the throne of sin and hell. ... Filled with love for your person, I regret your elevation to the Pontifical chair in such an age as this; for you merit to have been born at another time." Seckendorf tries to palliate this impudence by alleging that it was provoked by the Bull of Excommunication; that it was written in the October following that Bull. If such was the case, why did not the fiery object of the Bull allude to it? But the question of date has been settled by Roscoe (2), in favor of April 6, as it is given in the Jena and Aurifaber editions of Luther's works.

There was a limit to the patience of Leo X. On Sept. 15, 1520, the long-delayed Bull of Excommunication was launched (3). Then the unfortunate issued his famous diatribe *Against the Execrable Bull of Antichrist.* "At length, thanks to the zeal of my friends, I have seen this bat in all its beauty. In

(1) SECKENDORF, *loc. cit.*

(2) In the second edition of his *Life of Leo X.*, Henri's French translation of Roscoe omits this dissertation. The Italian version by Bossi gives it.

(3) Audin thus comments upon this Bull: "It is not for us to appreciate the pontifical Bull as a dogmatic work, for the words of the successor of the Apostle are above our examination. But if, descending from the regions of faith, we consider it as a work of art, it is impossible not to discern in it a complete revelation of the classical regeneration of Rome at that period. ... We see that Italy had made a serious study of the Ciceronian style. ... Yet Luther said that Rome did not then harbor more than two or three cardinals of intelligence." *Loc. cit.*

truth, I know not whether the Papists are joking. This must be the work of John Eckius, the man of lies and iniquities, the accursed heretic. ... I maintain that the author of this Bull is Antichrist; I curse it as a blasphemy against the Son of God. ... I trust that every Christian who accepts this Bull will suffer the torments of hell. ... See how I retract, daughter of a soap Bull. ... It is said that the donkey sings badly, simply because he pitches his voice on too high a key. Certainly, this Bull would sound more agreeably, were its blasphemies not directed against heaven. ... Where are you, emperors, kings, and princes of the earth, that you tolerate the hellish voice of Antichrist? Leo X., and you the Roman cardinals, I tell you to your faces. ... Renounce your satanic blasphemies against Jesus Christ." Luther now remembered that Jerome of Prague had burnt the sentence of the Council of Constance against Huss ; and on December 10, he was able to write to Spalatinus : " There have just been burned, at the eastern gate of Wittemberg, opposite the church of the Holy Cross, all the writings of the Pope, the *Rescripts*, the *Decretals* of Clement VI., the *Extravagantes*, and the last Bull of Leo X., together with the *Summa* of the Angel of the Schools." On the day after this exhibition, Luther preached to the people, and said : " Yesterday I burned in the public Square, the devilish works of the Pope ; and I wish that it was the Pope, that is, the Papal See, that was consumed. If you do not separate from Rome, there is no salvation for your souls."

Previous to the Diet of Worms, opened on Jan. 28, 1521, Luther sent to each elector of the empire a copy of his *Address to Cæsar and to the German Nation*, a political and religious manifesto dilating on what he termed the encroachments of Rome—encroachments which, by means of "three walls," he insisted, had made captives of princes and peoples. *First Wall.* Rome pretends that the spiritual authority is above the civil ; but this is false, for all Christians "are spiritually alike." He did not assume to evince the logicality of this connection. The secular power is from God ; therefore, contended the friar, it should be exercised over the Pontiff. *Second Wall.* St. Paul declares that all men are priests ;

and nevertheless, the priest now judges, and is not judged. But "*we* know more about heaven than a wicked Pope knows." *Third Wall.* It was the emperor Constantine who convoked the Council of Nice (1). If a city is about to be surprised, and some one cries, "To arms!" do men inquire whether the warning was given by a magistrate or a citizen? "Miserable Germans," cries the blatant demagogue, "we have been deceived. We were born to be masters, but we must bend our necks. ... The Popes have the grain; we the straw. ... It is time that the glorious German nation should cease to be the puppet of the Roman Pontiff." It was from a nobility inflamed by this document that Aleandro, the Papal nuncio, vainly demanded, in the Diet of Worms, the condemnation of Luther. He produced some impression; but the elector of Saxony insisted that the friar should be heard. Accordingly, the emperor Charles V. cited Luther to appear before the Diet; and when, on April 17, he obeyed, but refused to retract, an edict was issued, forbidding any one to harbor the rebel after May 15, the last day included in the safe-conduct which Charles had sent to him. Luther now departed from Worms; and by pre-arrangement with Frederick of Saxony, he was apparently kidnapped, and carried to his friend's castle of Wartburg. This master-stroke of policy was designed less for the purpose of foiling the friar's enemies, than in order to keep him from imprudences. Luther remained in his Patmos, as he styled it, until the death of Leo X.

While at Wartburg, the heresiarch began to formulate a Creed; and here also he first told the world that he had learned the wickedness of clerical celibacy. Not long before his conversion to the idea of the necessity of marriage for the clergy, he had laughed at the theory of his co-reformer, Carlstadt, that a wifeless priest was apt to *semen immolare Moloch;* and he had declared that the ex-archdeacon made the reformers "the laughing-stock of the Papists," it being strange that the learning of Carlstadt had not informed him that the quoted Biblical phrase "merely signified the sacrifice of one's children to Moloch" (2). Again, Luther had

(1) For the falsity of this assertion, see our vol. I., p. 201.
(2) Epist. to Spalatinus, Aug. 15, 1521.

already exclaimed : " Good God! Our Wittembergers will end by giving a wife to every monk ; but they shall not force one on me " (1). But his letters of this period indicate a change of mind.

During this retreat, Luther completed his translation of the Bible into German. It is frequently asserted that he was the first to translate the Scriptures into a vernacular. But as far back as the eleventh century there was a German version by William of Ebersberg ; and the curious reader may inspect it, for it was printed at Vienna in 1864. And as early as the eighth century, the Anglo-Saxons had their version by Ven. Bede. Leroux de Lincy edited, in 1841, a French translation of the *Book of Kings*, which internal evidence shows to be of the twelfth century. There were several other French versions in the twelfth century ; for Pope Innocent III. speaks of them in a letter to the bishop of Metz. In 1294 appeared the French translation by Guyard des Moulins, which was corrected as to style by John de Rely in 1487. While Luther was working at his German version, James Favre d'Etaples (Lefevre) published his French version at Antwerp with the approbation of the Inquisition. Mariana speaks of a Spanish translation made by order of Alphonsus of Castile in 1280 (2) ; and Richard Simon (3) praises another Spanish one made in the time of St. Vincent Ferrer (b. 1357). The Italians needed no translation in those days ; for their present beautiful language was then a mere infant, and Latin was spoken at least moderately well by whoever could read. Nevertheless, the Dominican, James de Voragine, archbishop of Genoa (b. 1230), made an Italian translation of the Bible.

It was probably at Wartburg that Luther, according to his own account, had a conference with the devil on the subject of the Mass, at which interview Satan appeared in the guise of a saver of souls, earnestly impressing on the friar's mind the idolatrous nature of the Divine Sacrifice (4). Here

---

(1) To same, Aug. 6.　　　　(2) *History*, b. XIII., ch. xiii.
(3) *Crit. Old Test.*, vol. I., p. 336.
(4) *Works*, vol. III.—See Claude's *Defence of the Reformation*, pt. 2.—Nicole's *Legitimate Prejudices*, ch. 11.—Basnage's *Hist. Ref. Churches*, vol. III., ch. v.—Bayle's *Dict.*, art. *Luther*.

also Luther heard of the revolt of Carlstadt, Munzer, Stubner, and innumerable other Reformers against his leadership ; and naturally, therefore, he wished to re-enter the world. His princely protector forbidding the design, he donned the dress of a soldier, and made his way to Wittemberg, where, three days after his arrival, he thus upbraided his rivals in the manufacture of religions : "Do you wish to found a new Church? Then tell us who sent you. Whence do you derive your ministry? Since you alone testify about it, we refuse to believe you, as St. John advises. ... Where are your miracles? When the law is to be altered, miracles are necessary." Logical or not, the ex-friar procured the expulsion of Carlstadt from Wittemberg. At this time Luther preached that famous discourse on marriage, the language of which, as his apologist Seckendorf gives it, is too utterly foul for record in this work (1). There was, however, one consoling consequence to this sermon; it opened the eyes of Staupitz, the friar's olden superior, who had hitherto followed him in his aberrations. He now said to Luther: "I leave you, brother, because I perceive, at last, that you have the sympathies of all who frequent brothels " (2). Thereupon, the old man returned to the faith, and died, some years afterward, abbot of St. Bridget's in Salzbourg. Many monks and friars adopted the creature-comforting practice of the New Gospel; but since very few of the nuns showed an inclination to break their vows, Luther encouraged them in his treatise, *Reasons Why Nuns Should Abandon Their Cells;* which he dedicated to Kœppe, a handsome young lord of Torgau, whose chief occupation was the "scaling of nunneries" in aid of such religious as might be induced to doff their veils. It was this gallant who afterward carried off Catharine Bora, destined to the worldly solace of the ex-Augustinian. About this time, the heresiarch completed his treatise against the hierarchy, the general trend of which work may be perceived in this passage : "Colleges, bishoprics, monasteries, and universities are so many jakes and

(1) In *Works*, edit. Wittemberg, 1544. Few of the later editions of the *Works* contain this sermon.
(2) SECKENDORF, *loc. cit.*, vol. I.

sinks in which the gold of princes and of the whole world is
buried. Pope? You are not Pope, but Priapus. ... Whoever shall help, with person, means, or influence, to destroy
the rule of bishops, is a beloved child of God."

The Edict of Worms had been forgotten; the scheming
brain of Charles V. was revolving other ideas than those of
religion. However, one crowned head occupied itself with
the defense of Holy Church—with the pen. Henry VIII. of
England, with the approval of Erasmus, and after a course
of study under Fisher, bishop of Rochester, and other prelates, issued his *Defence of the Seven Sacraments against
Doctor Martin Luther* (1). We have no space for a synopsis
of this work; suffice it to say that its theology was so excellent
that many thought it a dictation by Erasmus or by one of
the bishops, and that its Latinity was almost worthy of the
court of Pope Leo X (2). This treatise merited for Henry
and his successors, by a pontifical decree, the title of "Defender of the Faith." The heresiarch took up his pen against
Henry, spattering his usual amount of filth, which, of course,
we omit. "It matters not whether this treatise was written
by Henry or by the devil; whoever lies, is a liar, and I do not
fear him. I do think, however, that Henry gave one or two
ells of coarse cloth, and that snivelling sophist (Lee), such as
the fat Thomist hogs cherish, the same who wrote against
Erasmus, then took up needle and scissors, and made the
garment." After great pretence of refutation of the royal
arguments, Luther proceeds: "When the king of England
spits his impudent lies into my face, I must be allowed to
cram them down his throat. ... I think that he wrote his
book as a penance, for his conscience tells him that he stole
the crown of England by putting to a violent death the last
offspring of the royal line. ... Henry and the Pope are
equally legitimate; the Pope has stolen his tiara, and Henry
his crown; this fact accounts for their rubbing each other,
like two mules. ... Henry spits out poison like an angry
prostitute—a good proof that he has no royal blood in his

(1) The royal MS. is preserved in the Vatican Library.

(2) Once, unfortunately for his sense of decency, Henry falls into Luther's own style, and
dismisses the friar, "*cum suis furiis et furoribus, cum suis merdis et stercoribus, cacan-
tem, cacatumque.*"

reins. ... Courage, ye swine (1). Burn me, if you dare! Luther will be the bear in your road, the lion in your path; ever following you and giving you no rest, until he shall have broken your iron skulls and brazen faces." If the reader should be almost tempted to admire what he may deem the boldness of Luther in thus bearding the ally of Charles V., let him reflect that just then the stars of Charles and Henry seemed to be in the descendent; for the French had expelled the English from their territory, and Charles had failed in his attempts upon Burgundy and Guienne. But two years later, when the pretty face of Anne Boleyn was luring Henry toward a rupture with Rome, and when therefore the heresiarch discerned a companion incendiary in that monarch, he changed his style, and thus addressed him: "Most Serene and Illustrious Prince, I ought to fear to write to your Majesty, remembering how I insulted you in that pamphlet which I, a vain and haughty man, yielding to evil advisers, and not of my own inclination, published against you. But your royal goodness encourages me to address you, that goodness being made known to me in my daily correspondence. Since you are mortal, you will not harbor immortal anger. Besides, I have good reason to know that the document which was published in the name of your Majesty, was not composed by the king of England, as certain shameless sophists would have us believe. ... I blush for myself, and scarcely dare to raise my eyes to you, I being a worm of rottenness and dust, meriting only contempt and disdain. ... If your Majesty thinks that I ought to deny my words, and to laud you in another work, deign to so command. I am ready and willing to comply." In his reply to this apology, Henry plainly insists that he was the author of the *Defence*. Burnet, in his *History of the Reformation of the Church of England*, lauds the theological learning of Henry, and does not even allude to Luther's allegation of fraud on the part of Lee. Seckendorf thinks that this silence would not have been maintained by Burnet, if he had suspected the origin of the work to have been of another hand than that of Henry. However, Lingard

---

(1) This apostrophe is addressed to the disciples of the school of the Angelic Doctor, St. Thomas of Aquin.

perceives a corroboration of the public opinion that the king was not the author, in a remark of Sir Thomas More that "by his Grace's appointment, and *the consent of the makers of the same*, he (More) was only a sorter out and placer of the principal matters therein contained."

In 1524 a Diet met at Nuremberg; the Pope being represented by Cardinal Campeggi, a man of high character and fine ability. Charles V. had sent to the Diet a mandate ordering the execution of the Edict of Worms, while the Lutheran princes wished to resist that decree. A compromise was tried, the Diet resolving that the Pontiff should convoke a General Council in Germany, while the Estates should assemble at Spires, and decide whether to accept or reject the New Gospel. Naturally this compromise pleased neither party ; Campeggi protested, and in a rescript to the German princes Charles threatened death to all contemners of the Edict of Worms. Very soon, in all Northern Germany, the innovators began to oppress the Catholics, churches were seized, images destroyed, and superstition, said the despoilers, was about to vanish. In July, 1524, the Catholic princes met at Ratisbon for consultation. Naturally, they resolved that the Edict of Worms should be observed, and that they would aid each other if attacked by the Lutherans. Meanwhile there had begun a movement among the peasants, which caused all the nobles, irrespective of religion, to tremble. It is not for us to describe the horrors of the Peasants' War (1524-25) ; we allude to it, merely to show Luther's connection with it. If victory rested with Munzer, the man of the mob, Melancthon's "devil incarnate," the ex-Augustinian would cease to be the Pope of Wittemberg. Luther realized this danger, and he met it with a manifesto counselling the peasants to moderation ; but the logical Munzer sent to him a page torn from Luther's own work on the hierarchy, in which the innovator had said "Whosoever, with his arm, his fortune, and his estate, shall assist in destroying the bishops and the episcopal hierarchy, is a true son of God." And Osiander regretted that the Anabaptist was unacquainted with the following passage in the tirade of Luther against Prierias : "If we hang robbers, behead murderers, and burn heretics, ought we not wash our hands in the blood of these masters of perdition, these cardinals, Popes, serpents of Rome and Sodom, who defile the Church of God?" Then Osiander thus rebukes his co-reformer: "Alas! Poor peasants, whom Luther flatters and caresses when they attack only the bishops and priests; but when the insurgents, laughing at his Bull, threaten him and his princes, then he sends forth another Bull, decreeing their slaughter as so many wild beasts." Erasmus adds his rebuke to Osiander's: "You indeed disclaim all complicity (with the insurgents) in your most cruel tirade against the peasants, but you cannot make men believe that these troubles were not occasioned by your writings, especially those in German, directed against bishops and monks." When the peasants had made great progress, Luther resolved to prevent the triumph of his rival. Thus he addressed his noble followers: "To arms, my princes, to arms! The time has come, the wondrous time, when princes can win heaven with blood more easily than others can with prayers. Slay, front and rear! Nothing is more devilish than sedition: it is a mad dog that bites you if you do not kill it. There must be no more sleep, patience, or mercy; the times of the sword and of wrath are not those of grace." The "gentle" Melancthon coincided with these sentiments. Well might the Sacramentarian Hospinian say to Luther that he it was who excited the Peasants' War, and the heresiarch admits that he "shed all that blood by God's commands." In fact, Luther had little love for the inferior orders. He would say: "Give the ass thistles, a pack-saddle, and the whip; give the peasants oat-straw. If they are not content, give them the cudgel and the carbine; these are their due." Munzer, just before his execution, accused Luther as the author of his misfortunes.

It was amid the horrors of the Peasants' War that the ex-friar took to himself a "wife" in the person of an ex-nun, Catharine Bora (1). Dollinger thus speaks of this event: "So

(1) Regard for decency must ever prevent any but a lubricious author, be he Catholic, Protestant, Jew, or pagan, from quoting at random the arguments with which Luther insists on marriage for all, without exception. It is necessary, however, for our purpose that we give some notion of the apostate's ideas. The first requisite for one of his preachers was

sudden was this marriage, and so precipitately was it performed, that it astonished even his most intimate friends.
On June 3, 1525, he had told the cardinal prince-elector of
Mayence that although he had urged that prelate to marry,
nevertheless he himself had not married, because he did not
feel that he was made for a conjugal life. And a few days
after writing this letter, he very secretly espoused Catharine
Bora, an escaped nun; and on June 27, he gave the nuptial
feast. One cannot perceive clearly what motive actuated him
in this manner of procedure. The letters written by him at
that time give no satisfactory explanation of it. Munzer and
his peasants, he writes, so oppress the Gospel—that is, the
revolt of the peasants had caused many to distrust Luther's
doctrine—that he has married a religious in order to show
his contempt for his foes, and in order to give testimony to
the Gospel by deeds. Then again he falls back upon a desire which he says that his father had expressed concerning
the necessity of silencing evil reports about his relations
with Bora. On another occasion he tells how, all of a sudden, and when he was thinking of anything but her, the Lord
miraculously urged him to marry the nun; and how his obedience to the command entailed upon him nothing but confusion and abuse. He seems to glorify both himself and

the possession of a wife; and when the preacher had taken unto himself an ex-nun, whether
she was a voluntary fugitive or a stolen prey, Luther decreed that no ceremony of ordination was necessary. (*Table Talk*, fol. 389, Dresd.) When Luther speaks of marriage, he is
the mere animal; he thinks of none of the relations of matrimony toward God or society. It
is merely an opportunity for the gratification of a carnal appetite, and a means to propagate
the race. He says that "the fire of voluptuousness which is in human nature can be ex-
tinguished neither by vows nor by laws" (Letter to Wolfgang Reissenbusch, March 27,
1525, no. 686 in edit. Wette, Berlin, 1826, vol. II.). In a letter to the archbishop of Mayence
and Magdeburg, he tells the prelate that he will be damned, if he does not marry, and asks
him what he will reply to God, when he is told: "I made thee a man not to be alone, but to
have a woman" (Letter of June 3, 1525, no. 710). To some nuns who hesitated to break their
vows, he wrote: "A woman does not belong to herself God made her body to be in the
society of a man. Just as God made the need of eating, drinking, sleeping; so he made man
and woman to be united in marriage. That is enough, and no one should blush because of
a thing for which God made him. This you will understand when you are outside, and hear
preaching such as you ought to hear" (Letter of Aug. 6, 1524, no. 615, vol. II.). Writing to
the soldier-monks of the Teutonic Order, he says: "Priests, monks, and nuns ought to
break their vows so soon as they feel that they have the strength and power to propagate; and
they have no right, because of any law or authority, to impede the effect of the power which
God has placed in them. You cannot promise not to be men or women; and therefore you
cannot renounce marriage. The command to multiply is a thunder-clap for the Pope's law.
If you want to make a vow which perhaps you can keep, vow to never bite your own noses."
Some of Luther's letters to his married priestly friends will not bear reproduction. Here
are some of the cleaner specimens. Writing to Amsdorf on Feb. 10, 1525 (no. 673, vol. II.),

the woman on account of their violation of their vows, by a union which was declared invalid by both the religious and civil law, more than a thousand years before his time. But his friends and very many of his followers thought different-ly; and he could write: 'I have been so humiliated and despised on account of my marriage, that I trust that the angels smile on it, and all the devils of hell shed tears be-cause of it.' In the letters which he wrote at this time, we read expressions regarding the conjugal relation which are cynically gross and scandalously smutty ; but behind all his effrontery and his apparent ease of mind, we discern a hu-miliating recognition of the fact that his personal considera-tion has been gravely diminished, and of the fact that his most fervent admirers cannot understand why he selected for his marriage a time when the Peasants' War was filling the land with bloody atrocities."

We omit any account of Luther's disputes with Zwingle and Carlstadt ; of the sacking of Rome by the imperial army, mostly Lutheran; and come to the Diets of Spire and of Augsburg. Of the first, held in 1529, it is sufficient to say that it was decided to preserve the *status quo* temporarily, thus discouraging the spread of the Reformation. Against this decision, the innovators, headed by the elector John of Saxony, the elector George of Brandenburg, the dukes Er-

he says: " *Vale, et pinguem maritum, Melchiorem saluta, cui opto conjugem obsequen-tem, quæ per diem septies cum capillo circum forum ducat, et per noctem ter bene ob-tundat verbis connubialibus, ut meretur.*" Writing to Spalatinus on Dec. 6, 1525, he says: " *Saluta tuam conjugem suavissime, verum ut id tum facias, cum in thoro sua-vissimis amplexibus et osculis Catharinam tenueris, et sic cogitaveris : En hunc homi-nem optimam creaturalam Dei mei, donavit mihi Christus meus ; sit illi laus et gloria. Salutat te et costam tuam costa mea. Gratia vobiscum. Amen.*" Luther composed the following epithalamium for his nuptials : "O God, in Thy goodness, give us gowns and hats, mantles and petticoats, fat calves and goats, oxen, sheep, and cows, plenty of women, but few children " (*Table Talk*, Eisl., pp. 307, 309, 442). It was on Good Friday of 1523 that Luther commissioned Koppe to abduct Catharine Bora and nine of her companions from the Bernardine Convent of Stimptsch, near Grimma ; and because of the date, Luther com-pared Koppe to our Lord, both having accomplished, he said, the Redemption on the same day. Luther seems to have taken pains to select great feast-days for this kind of work. Thus we find him carrying off thirteen nuns in Saxony on the feast of St. Michael, 1525. At this period these verses began to circulate among the Catholics of Germany :

> I Cuculla! Vale Cappa !
> Vale Prior, Custos, Papa!
> Cum Obedientia!
> Ite Vota, Preces, Horæ !
> Vale Timor, cum Pudore !
> Vale Conscientia!

nest and Francis of Lunberg, the landgrave Philip of Hesse,. the prince of Anhalt, and thirteen imperial cities, protested; thus originating the term " Protestants "—a term which, though purely negative, has been accepted by all the offspring of Luther's revolt, as the only collective designation befitting the innumerable sects which have no bond of union save opposition to the Catholic Church. The Diet of Augsburg was opened by Charles V. in person, on June 20, 1530. The Protestant princes presented their *Confession of Faith,* which had been drafted by Melancthon. It was in two parts; the first containing twenty-one articles on religious doctrine; the second, in seven articles, treated of the ceremonies and usages of the Church. We give a summary of the articles. I. The teachings of the first four General Councils on the unity of God and the Trinity of Persons were accepted. II. Original sin was admitted, but was made to consist entirely in concupiscence, in a lack of fear of God, and in a want of confidence in His goodness. III. All that is taught in the Apostles' Creed concerning the birth, life, passion, death, resurrection, and ascension of Christ was received. IV. It was held, against the Pelagians, that man cannot justify himself of his own strength; but it was held, against the Catholics,. that justification is obtained by faith alone, good works excluded. V. The Holy Ghost is conferred by the Sacraments; but He works only by faith. VI. While faith ought to produce good works, these lead not to justification, being performed only in obedience to God. VII. The Church is composed of the elect alone. VIII. The word of God and the Sacraments are efficacious, even when the minister is wicked and a hypocrite. IX. Infants are to be baptized. X. The Body and Blood of Christ are really present in the Holy Eucharist. XI. Absolution is necessary for the remission of sins, but confession is not necessary. XII. The amissableness of justice is asserted against the Anabaptists; against the Novatians, penance is declared to be useful; against the Catholics, it is denied that a sinner can merit forgiveness by penitential works. XIII. Actual faith is necessary for all who receive the Sacraments, even for infants. XIV. Without a legitimate vocation, no one can teach religion publicly, or administer the Sacraments. XV. Holy days and prescribed ceremonies are to be observed. XVI. Civil laws, magistracies, property, and marriage, are legitimate. XVII. A last judgment, heaven, and hell are acknowledged; and against the Anabaptists it is taught that hell is eternal. XVIII. Man possesses free will, but he needs grace to be saved. XIX. God is not, and cannot be the cause of sin. XX. Good works are not altogether useless. XXI. The saints in heaven pray for us, and on stated occasions we should celebrate their memory ; but the *Confession* neither condemns nor approves our invoking them. In the second part, I. Holy Communion should be administered under both species, and processions with the Blessed Sacrament are prohibited. II. Clerical and monastic celibacy should be abolished. III. Private Mass should not be celebrated, and in all Masses the vernacular should be used. IV. The faithful ought not to be obliged to confess their sins, or at least they should not be compelled to an exact and circumstantial enumeration of them. V. Fasting and the monastic life are condemned. VI. Monastic vows are plainly reprobated. VII. Such a distinction is established between the ecclesiastical and civil powers, as to deprive the former of all temporal power. At the same time that the chiefs of the Lutheran party presented this *Confession* at the Diet of Augsburg, four imperial cities, Strasbourg, Constance, Memingen, and Landaw, which had become Zwinglian, offered one of their own, composed by Martin Bucer, and this was regarded as a prodigy of doctrine by the Calvinists. This separate *Confession*, however, did not prevent Bucer from signing that of Augsburg and the prohibition of his own. Melancthon himself, who, in the second part of the *Confession of Augsburg*, so strongly condemned the Roman ceremonies, did so in contradiction to his own sentiments, and merely to please Luther.

One cannot avoid noticing the inconsistency of Luther, who having proclaimed the right of private interpretation, imposes at Augsburg a Creed upon men, and anathematizes those who reject it. And yet this same Creed was again and again altered. While at first Luther denied the free will of man, because of divine predestination, he subscribed to Melancthon's article 18, asserting that "free will is to be acknowledged in all men who have the use of reason." He had insisted that "God works sin in us," but article 19 says that "the will of man is the cause of sin." He had rejected good works, but article 20 says that they are useful. However, taking the *Confession of Augsburg* in its entirety, we may agree with those who believe that if Luther had made it some years before, or if there had been a Melancthon in 1519, the revolt would not have occurred; that if, even in 1530, Luther had been no more, the revolt would have ended. Melancthon was certainly tired of controversy; several times at this period he wrote to his master, "We are in grief and despair; Brentz, who accompanies and tries to console me, unites his tears with mine" (1). And Obsopæus wrote to Camerarius: "They say that Melancthon behaves like a man in the pay of the Pope; and that he lauds the Popedom with the best of them. It is often said that he is like Architophiles; some compare him to Erasmus" (2). Writing to Camerarius at this time, Melancthon says: "Shall I give my real opinion? I would restore to the bishops both their power and their spiritual administration. Unless the Church really governs, the new tyranny will be worse than the old one." But it was not the interest of the Protestant princes to restore religious unity, and Melancthon was fain to remark to Luther: "They care little for religion; they desire only despotism and licentiousness." And his master replied: "Whoever dies from fear, should have asses bray at his funeral. As to you, what kind of requiem ought you to have when you are dying from sheer cowardice?"

We must now notice an episode in the early history of this "emancipation of humanity," which illustrates both Luther's subserviency to princes, and his disregard for morality. Philip, landgrave of Hesse, had been married sixteen years to Christina of Saxony, and she had borne eight children to him, when he became enamored of Margaret von Saal, a maid of honor to his sister Elizabeth. He had been of much service to Lutheranism, and he felt justified in ap-

---

(1) CHYTRÆUS; *Hist. Conf. Augsburg.*
(2) CAMERARIUS; *Life of Luther.*—CHYTRÆUS; *loc. cit.*

plying to his spiritual leader for permission to take another wife. Our account of this matter is taken from a book printed by order of the elector-palatine, Charles Louis, in 1679, under the name of Daphuæus Arcuarius (Lawrence Baeger), one of the elector's councillors (1). Martin Bucer was employed by Philip to draw up his petition to Luther, and from it we take the following passages: "I have a wife, and cannot abstain from women. When I married Christina, it was from neither passion nor inclination. The officers of my court may be examined as to her temper, charms, and love of wine. I am of a warm temperament; used to the irregularities of camp life, I cannot exist without women; I have not kept conjugal fidelity for more than three weeks. My clergy wish me to approach the holy table, but I shall exercise my judgment in that matter, for I wish not to change my life. If I must fight for the confederation, a stroke or a shot may kill me, and then I say to myself that I shall go straight to the devil. Now I have read in the Old Testament that holy persons such as Abraham, Jacob, David, and Solomon, had many wives; and yet all believed in the coming of Christ. Neither has God, in the Old Testament, nor Christ in the New, nor the Prophets, nor the Apostles, forbidden a man to have two wives; never have the Prophets or Apostles blamed or punished bigamy, and St. Paul never excluded from heaven the man who has two wives. Again, when St. Paul says that a bishop should be the husband of one wife, he would have laid the same injunction on laymen, had he wished each of them to have only one wife (2). Besides, I know

---

(1) *Conscientious Considerations on Marriage, with an Explanation of the Questions Agitated to Our Day Concerning Adultery, Separation, and Polygamy.*—De Wette gives Luther's license in his collection of the friar's letters, vol. V. It is also found in the editions of Altenburg, vol. VIII.; of Leipsic, vol. XXII.; and of Halle, vol. X.

(2) Probably the landgrave, or rather Bucer, adopted this misinterpretation of St. Paul's saying from the wretched Anabaptist, John of Leyden. After the capture of this fanatic, Corvinus, one of the Lutheran ministers of Hesse, challenged him to a disputation, and the "prophet" accepted the cartel. The debate having turned on polygamy, the ex-king of Leyden said: "Does not St. Paul teach that a bishop should be the husband of one wife? If therefore, in the Apostle's time, a man was not a bishop, he could have two or three wives." When Corvinus quoted St. Paul as saying that every man should live with his "wife," not "wives," John encouraged him in the Lutheran system of private interpretation of Scripture by this explanation of the Pauline text: "St. Paul did not speak of all wives, but of each in particular; the first is my wife, and I live with her; the second is my wife, and I live with her; the third is my wife, and I live with her. All that is very simple. Besides, is it not better to have several wives than several concubines?"

that Luther and Melancthon have advised the king of England not to divorce his first wife, but to take a second. But
let them not suppose that, because I had another wife, I
would maltreat the first one, or even cease to cohabit with
her. No! I would be resigned to my cross and would render her every duty, even the conjugal debt. Let them, then,
grant my demand, so that I may live and die like a good
Christian, for the honor of the Gospel; and all that is just
and reasonable, *even the property of the monasteries and such
like, I will grant to them.*" The chief clergy of Wittemberg
and Hesse, that is, Luther, Melancthon, Bucer, Corvinus,
Leningen, Winther, and Melander, soon emitted an opinion,
couched in twenty-four articles, of which the twenty-first
says: "If your Highness is determined to marry a second
wife, we judge that it ought to be done privately, as we have
said when speaking of the dispensation which you request;
that is to say, that no one should be present save the cele-
brant and a few witnesses, who must be bound to secrecy, as
though under the seal of confession. Then there will be no
fear of opposition or great scandal, for it is not uncommon
for princes to keep concubines; and although the common
people may be scandalized at it, the more enlightened will
suspect the truth. We need not be very anxious about the
world's remarks, when the conscience is at rest. Therefore,
your Highness has in this writing not only our approbation
of your wish, but also the reflections which we have made on
it." The marriage took place on March 4, 1540, and Christina, very different from Catharine of Aragon, consented to it.

It is very improbable that any religious innovator started
out with a complete programme; and certainly Luther developed his doctrines by degrees, now modifying, then withdrawing some of them. He could not have foreseen, when fostering his bitterness during his visit to Rome in 1510, that his
German hatred of Italy was slowly disposing him to refuse
obedience to Roman authority. When Luther visited Italy,
he felt nothing but contempt for everything he saw. And
yet he tells us that he found "everywhere well-built and well-
provided hospitals, with excellent food, attentive nurses, ex-
pert physicians, clean beds and linen, and everywhere pict-

ures." He is astonished on finding that when a patient enters an Italian hospital, " he receives a white night-shirt, and
is put into a good bed ; the nurses give him food and drink
in vessels which they scarcely touch with their fingers ; then
two physicians visit him, and ladies, veiled so as to be unknown, wait upon him." The northern European of that
day could not comprehend such refinement as Italy everywhere exhibited. And then, observes Cantù, "His soul,
wanting in love as in humility, does not comprehend the poetry of our sky, our arts, or our history. Sculpture along the
roads, the marbles and gold in the churches, stupefy him. ...
For Luther, Rome is not the city from which the Apostles
repelled Attila, the Scourge of God, the city where emperors
and kings pause to venerate or to tremble; the city which
personifies the domination of intelligence over brute force.
When he sees so many masterpieces of the ancients rivalled
by the moderns with pen, chisel, and color; when he beholds the Papal robes sheltering so many geniuses, any one
of whom would immortalize a country or an age ; the ice of
his soul is not melted by one of the rays from the aureolas
of Raphael or Michelangelo. ... But he swallows greedily
all the scurrilities of the taverns; he declares that in the
garden of a certain convent—which one, he does not state—
the skulls of 6,000 babes have lately been disinterred ; he insists that Rome has poisons so delicately powerful, that one
would be killed, if he but looked into a mirror sprinkled
with them. He despises the universities and the course of
studies in Italy, because reason is there interposed between
science and faith ; because the Italian schools teach that the
divine increases the natural light, as the sun illumines a
beautiful picture. ... Returning with these sentiments to his
own land, even in his first letters, especially in those of 1518
to Spalatinus, he manifests his malignity in regard to the Romanists, his contempt for scholastic theology, a passion for
every novelty—no matter where found; and he yearns to
emerge from obscurity, and to give a shock to the world" (1).

It is also improbable that in the beginning of his demolition of the sacerdotal edifice, Luther foresaw that he would

(1) *Heretics of Italy*, Discourse 15.

be led to deny that man can do anything toward his own salvation; that then, from this idea of the inutility of good
works, he would infer that there should be no penances, no
prayers for the dead; that since evil is the normal condition
of finite man, faith in Christ is alone requisite for salvation;
that, in fine, man's motto should be: "Sin, and sin strongly, but believe more strongly!" Yes; such is the moving
principle of all the teaching of the father of the so-called
Reformation: "Be a sinner, and sin boldly; but more boldly still believe and rejoice in Christ who is the Conqueror of
sin, of death, and of the world; we must sin, so long as we
are here. ... Sin cannot separate us from God, even though
we were to fornicate or murder a thousand times in one
day" (1). With the picture of strange prospects looming
up before it, if such teaching were generally received, the
Christian world was asked to accept the following heads of
doctrine. I. By the sin of Adam the free will of man was
entirely destroyed. II. In no way can man merit salvation.
III. Man can be justified by faith alone. IV. The sacraments do not confer grace, nor do any of them impress a
character in the soul. V. Auricular confession is a human
invention. VI. In the Holy Eucharist, after the consecration, there remains, together with the Body and Blood of
Jesus Christ, the substance of bread and wine. VII. The
Body and Blood of Christ are not permanently present in
the Eucharist, but only *in usu*. VIII. Holy Communion
should be administered to the laity under both species. IX.
The Mass was not instituted by Christ, and it is not a Sacrifice. X. Priests are not bound to celibacy. XI. Monastic
vows are reprehensible. XII. Indulgences are pious frauds.
XIII. That contrition which proceeds from a fear of hell is
a sin. XIV. The saints in heaven are not to be revered or
invoked. XV. The Church consists of only the just. XVI.
The existence of Purgatory cannot be proved from the Scriptures. XVII. God commands man to do impossible things,
and is the Author of sin. XVIII. The primacy of the Roman Pontiff is not by divine right. XIX. To fight against
the Turks is to resist the will of God who, by means of them,

(1) Letter to Melancthon, Aug. 21, 1521.

punishes us for our iniquities. XX. Bishops and princes would not do wrong if they were to abolish the Mendicant Orders. XXI. There are only two Sacraments, Baptism and the Eucharist. XXII. All Christians are equally priests. Luther propounded many other errors, but they are all included in the above.

Concerning the death of Luther, we need merely state that his last words were an affirmative reply to the dread question put by Justus Jonas, a minister of Wittemberg, as to whether "he wished to die in the faith and doctrine he had preached." The character of Luther was very peculiar. Exceedingly jolly at times, he was generally haughty, and as rash as cunning. His utter want of urbanity, and his absolute ignorance of any moderation of language, may be excused in an inhabitant of a country which knew, at that time, very little of either of these tokens of refinement. But his scurrility, even when treating of the most sacred things, was his own. In a tavern at night, he would laugh at the matter of his discourse in the morning; and no gutter-tramp could have desired a more brilliant school for foul-mouthings than that furnished by the ex-friar on such occasions. He was fond of ridiculing superstition, and even prejudice; but he gravely tells us that he often hears the noise of three thousand barrels being rolled down the stairs by the devil; that he often sees the *Killkropft*, a child born of Satanic parents, sitting among his own offspring; that whenever the demon disturbs him at night, he exorcises him with three words which the reader will excuse us from repeating. When young, he had studied carefully and thoroughly; therefore, when nature had given to him much fecundity of imagination, a fine presence, and a sonorous voice, he was an impressive orator. Spirit he undoubtedly possessed, even to superbundance; his genius may be questioned. Cunning though he certainly was, some of his most important actions were the results of impulse, even of momentary anger. As to his teachings, he advanced not one new doctrine; he merely selected among the speculations of previous heretics, and presented them at a time when men were more disposed to welcome them, than they had been, when the same notions were originally emitted. His attacks on the Keys were mere developments of the olden struggle between Church and Empire. And, remarks Cantù, "the world had already proclaimed the superiority of force over thought. The Waldenses and such had already set up the Bible as the sole rule of faith. Every heresiarch of the Middle Age had marched under the banner of private judgment; and in that period, every possible error on grace, justification, and Purgatory, had been discussed. ... History shows that abnormal force is always admired, and draws every one who cares not to do his own thinking. The Germans had become hostile to the Popes from the time these opposed the emperors, who tried to confuse the temporal and the spiritual. A feeling of malevolence was cherished against everything from across the Alps, and especially against those Pontiffs who had preserved civilization. The Germans, growing fond of the new Arminius, declaimed against a delicacy they did not know, and against a culture of which they were not capable" (1).

Most of the questions in the mind of the student, after he has become acquainted with the origin and early career of the Reformation, and which are vigorously debated by theologians and polemics, pertain to other provinces than that of the historian. But two claim our attention. We took occasion, when treating of the rapid propagation of Christianity during its first three centuries (2), to show that this progress furnished our ancestors in the faith with an encouraging proof of its divine origin. Now, heterodox writers are fond of dilating on the readiness with which numbers, especially in Germany, abandoned the Church of Rome at the call of the new apostles. But the reader will remember that in the case of early Christianity, our argument was that since Pagan resistance was at the maximum, and the force of the Church was, humanly speaking, at the minimum, therefore the effect, namely, the propagation of Christianity, should have been, according to all human forethought, zero, that is, a failure. In the case of the Reformation, however, the resistance of the world was not at the maximum, and the force at the command of the innovators was not at the minimum; therefore, humanly speaking, it was quite natural that the movement should succeed. Very little reflection is necessary to establish the conviction that the spirit of the world was with the early Reformers, and that, which is the same thing, their strength was immense. Paganism, Gnosticism, Manicheism, Islamism, and scores of other religious systems, have been propagated by the passions of men. And these immense levers, apt to move the mental and moral world, were in the hands of Luther and his brethren. And how could it be otherwise, when free will was denied, good works declared useless, and hence every one was at the beck of his own inclinations? Many Protestants have observed this work of the passions in furthering the Reformation. Frederick " the Great " remarked : " If you wish to reduce the causes of the progress of the Reformation to simple principles, you will find that it was the work, in Germany of interest, in England of lust, and in France of a liking for novelty " (1). Even Calvin said : " Among a hundred Evangelicals, scarcely one can be found who became an Evangelical for any other motive than to be able to abandon himself with greater freedom to all kinds of pleasures and lusts " (2). Melancthon lamented to Luther that " Our companions dispute, not for the Gospel, but for their interests " (3). Bucer declared that " In the Reformed Church nothing is so much desired as the pleasure of living as one wishes " (4). But not only by the passions of men were the early Reformers aided ; in the majority of the German principalities the strong arm of the secular power was in their favor. Frederick III., elector of Saxony, styled Luther his friend, his father, the chosen one of the Lord, the man of God, etc. Louis, count-palatine and vicar of the empire, was also a staunch ally of the innovators. Albert of Brandenburg, grand-master of the Teutonic knights, entered into the new dispensation, took a wife, stole nearly all the domains of his order, and thus laid the foundation of the Protestant kingdom of Prussia. Philip, landgrave of Hesse, was ever ready to aid the New Gospel with his sword, and

(1) *Memoirs of Brandenburg.*   (2) *Commentary on Second Epist. of Peter.*
(3) *Epist.*, b. I., no. 10.
(4) *Epistles of Calvin*, cited by Bossuet, *Variations*, b. V., no. 14.

received his reward in a permission to have two wives at the same time. Even the emperor Charles V., during several years, sacrificed the interests of religion to his conception of policy. Frederick I., duke of Holstein, having ascended the throne of Denmark, forced his subjects into Lutheranism. Gustavus Vasa did the same that he might appropriate the property of the Church. The apostasy of the two powerful archbishops of Cologne, Hermann and Gebhard, had much to do with the success of Lutheranism. Nor can it be forgotten that the German nobility hated the clergy. They had more to fear from the Pope than from the emperor; although little better than freebooters, they were sometimes sufficiently powerful to frighten the latter, but the former was superior to their threats. Again, the heavy tribute paid to Rome was a powerful incentive to their rebellion. Jurieu, one of the most venerated of Protestant apologists, admits that it was only by the aid of the civil power that the Reformation triumphed in Geneva, and in the free cities and most of the principalities of Germany (1). This is especially true of Saxony, immediately after the death of Duke George (2).

Most Protestants fondly believe that the intellectual movement of the sixteenth century, the Renaissance, was the work of the Reformation. But the "rebirth" of literature had occurred long before the birth of Luther; and the movement was well under way two centuries before that event, so that it is incorrect even to assign its initiation, as some have done, to the influx of Greek science which was consequent on the fall of Constantinople. To say nothing of the universal appreciation of Dante by his Italian contemporaries—an appreciation in comparison with which that of Erasmus by the learned of his time was calm indifference, and which showed that those Italian intellects were by no means beclouded— the careers of Petrarch, Boccaccio, Colluccio Salutato, John of Ravenna (Malpaghino), Poggio Bracciolini, Traversari, Leonardo Bruni, Ognibene, Carlo Aretino, Guarini, Francesco Filelfo, Barbaro, and innumerable other luminaries, repel the claim of Protestantism to be regarded as the enlightener of

(1) MARX ; *Causes of the Rapid Spread of the Reformation.*
(2) HAGEN ; *Spirit of the Reformation,* vol. I., p. 116.

a besottedly ignorant society (1).   Undoubtedly, the Renaissance, the Reformation, *and the Revolution* are affiliated.   All
three had a more or less real point of departure in legitimate
and healthy aspirations, and all three deceived many generous souls, the first superficially and for a few years, the second and third radically and for centuries.   The excesses of
the first told principally upon Italy ; those of the second upon
Germany ; and those of the third upon France.   But what
was evil in all three eventually infected nearly all Europe ;
and to-day we find a large portion of what was once, not a
mere aggregation of Christian peoples, but the *Populus
Christianus,* suffering from the poison which, in the fifteenth
century, was injected into the social body by the pagan excesses of the once Christian Renaissance.   The connection between the paganized Renaissance and the Reformation has
not escaped the notice of Pastor, the latest Catholic historian
whom Germany has produced ; and scrutinizing the hybrid
influence of the humanist movement, he feels " the difficulty
of fixing the exact balance of good and evil with which it af-

---

(1) Even Cola di Riènzi was distinguished as a humanist long before he became a revolutionist ; and nearly all the Italian princes of his day were patrons of literature.   PETRARCH
(b. 1304).   The literary faculties of Petrarch were prodigious ; when a mere child, and unable to understand the meaning of Cicero and Virgil, the harmony of their language
charmed his ear.   He excited the energies of the erudite among his contemporaries by his
eulogies of the great writers of antiquity, and by his own excellent imitations of the same.
It was he who introduced among the Italians that worship of the antique which was to be
their fanaticism in the sixteenth century.   Would the works of Petrarch have excited an
enthusiasm of admiration which was almost comparable to that felt for Dante, if there had
not been, at least among the Italians, a notable advance in classical attainments and in
good taste ?   BOCCACCIO (b. 1313).   This celebrated author of the *Decameron* is known by
most persons solely because of that licentious work ; which, by the way, is purity incarnate
when compared with the *Heptameron* of Margaret of Valois, the idol of French Protestants, who wrote under the inspiration of the New Gospel.   During his entire life Boccaccio
exhorted his contemporaries to study the ancient authors ; and aided by the Florentine government, he travelled extensively in search of old manuscripts, which, when money for their
purchase failed him, he copied with his own hand.   COLLUCCIO SALUTATO (b. 1320), at first
secretary to Pope Urban V., and then chancellor of Florence, was allied with Petrarch and
Boccaccio in friendship and literary pursuits.   His chief efforts were devoted to the detec-
tion and correction of copistical errors in ancient MSS.   His contemporaries laud him as unequalled in eloquence, poetry, and historical knowledge, by any one of their day ; Philip
Villani places him on the same plane as Cicero and Virgil.   JOHN OF RAVENNA (b. 1350),
a famous grammarian, was the instructor of many celebrated men, whom Philip of Bergamo enumerates, and of whom the best known by us are Leonardo Aretino, Paolo Sforza,
Poggio, Traversari, and Filelfo.   Raphael of Volterra compares him to the horse of Troy
which held in its bosom the flower of the Greek army.   POGGIO (b. 1380), whose real name
was Bracciolini, was an employee of the Roman court, and devoted all his leisure to literature.   While at Constance, in the suite of Pope John XXIII., he heard that in the neighborhood there were many rare manuscripts which ran great risk, during the troubles incident-

fected the Church and religion" (1).   When Friar Martin
began his work of destruction, the Rome of Pope Leo X. was
paying so much attention to intellectual and artistic culture,
that many, not without some reason, charged it with fostering a Pagan, rather than a Christian spirit.   The science of
criticism alone owes a little to the Reformation ; but, as
Balmes remarks, this debt was like that of the science of medicine to a pest which decimates the nations.   As to philosophy, it was not Germany (which produced no great philosopher before the very un-Protestant Leibnitz), but France,
which, by means of the Catholic Descartes, inaugurated the
new era.   England has no claims in the premises, for all her
schools of philosophy are posterior to Descartes.   Speaking
of the period preceding the Reformation, Balmes says :
" Whoever examines dispassionately this epoch of history,
will acknowlege that then society received its most fortunate
impulse, and that then were discovered and rapidly developed most of the great means of action.   In the face of such
positive facts, one cannot understand how history has been
studied by those who flatter Protestantism with the notion
that it awakened the human mind from a lethargy, and that

al to the Great Schism, of being lost or destroyed.   He set himself the task of saving the
treasures; and he discovered a complete Quintilian, part of the *Argonotic* of Valerius
Flaccus, the *Commentary* of Asconius Pedianus on the *Orations* of Cicero, the work of Lac-
tantius *De Opificio Hominis*, the architectural treatise of Vitruvius, and the treatise of
the grammarian, Priscianus.   In posterior investigations in the monasteries of France and
Germany, Poggio found many orations of Cicero, Lucretius, the *Bucolics* of Calphurnius,
a book of Petronius, what we have of Ammianus Marcellinus, Vegetius, the work of Fron-
tinus on acqueducts, the mathematical writings of Firmicus, Nonius Marcellus, and Colu-
mella.   Literature owes much to Poggio's own writings, in the line of elegant style.
LEONARDO ARETINO (b. 1382).   This humanist rediscovered the principles of correct and
attractive literary style ; he introduced harmony where hitherto it had been lacking, and
if he himself is not as elegant as the *Seicentisti* came to be, these polished gentry merely
followed his direction.   CYRIAC OF ANCONA.   This writer was the literary Marco Polo of
his time.   After having investigated the literary treasures of every city of Italy, he pursued his literary and archæological studies in Egypt, Syria, and the Archipelago.   At Adri-
anople he learned Greek, and on his other travels became acquainted with Persian.   He
formed the design of exploring Abyssinia, finding the sources of the Nile, travelling
through ancient Getulia, and returning between the Pillars of Hercules ; but he was prevented by obstacles unknown to us.   Join to the names of Petrarch, Boccaccio, Colluccio,
John of Ravenna, Poggio, Aretino, and Cyriac, those of Pope Nicholas V., Filelfo, Giannozzo Mannetti, Barziza, Victorino de Feltro, Blondus Flavius, and Carlo Marsuppini ; and
you know the true fathers of the Renaissance.   TIRABOSCHI ; *History of Italian Literature.*—MANNETTI ; *Life of Boccaccio.*—GINGUENE ; *Literary History of Italy.*—HALLAM ;
Literature in the Middle Age.—*Life of Poggio*, in MURATORI, vol. XX.—RAPHAEL OF
VOLTERRA ; *Anthropology*, b. XXI.—TRAVERSARI ; *Letters*, b. XXIV.—CORTESE ; *Dialogues.*

(1) *History of the Popes since the Middle Age.*

it gave a new life to the peoples of Europe. Undoubtedly, the organization of European society, as Protestantism found it, was not what it was, one day, to be; but, considering the natural course of events, it was all that then it could be. Had human intelligence, in its development, continued in the path traced by the Church, civilization would have advanced regularly, and would have been fully secure. Unfortunately, the Reformation precipitated it into a road choked with obstacles, amid which it is now, perhaps, on the point of destruction."

Undoubtedly the orgies of pagan philosophy, encouraged by the Renaissance, had already weakened the Christian faith of many of the cultivated spirits of Europe, when Luther appeared upon the scene. But the Catholic spirit still permeated the masses, and even the great majority of the learned; so that the self-styled Reformers, far from addressing men who were ready to throw off the yoke of the priesthood, were obliged, in order to obtain recruits for the army which was to level the gates of Babylon, to recur to deceits of many kinds, and finally to avail themselves of royal authority. Of course there was an attractive sound, for many good Catholics, in the word "Reformation;" but they acclaimed it merely as a próbable prelude to a cessation of scandals. Modern Protestants would be astonished, if they were to read the annals of that time describing the full liberty of thought and expression then exercised in the supposedly slavish Catholic pulpit, as it hurled anathemas against many mitred defilers of the sanctuary. To cite one of innumerable such instances, Florimond de Remoud (b. 1540) narrates how Friar Thomas, a Franciscan, travelling through Europe, a few years before the Lutheran outburst, used the most audacious language in the sermons which he delivered everywhere, denouncing prelatical libertinage, and predicting the punishment soon to be inflicted by God on His Church (1). But the desire for a reformation of both clergy and people did not interfere with the faith of those days. The people were too well acquainted with the history of the Church; they knew too well that the vices of humanity are pretty

(1) *History of the Birth, Progress, and Decay of Heresy*; vol. I.

much the same in all ages; and hence they never invoked that phantom of a primitive Christianity which was depicted by Luther and his imitators as absolutely pure and perfect. The Catholics of the sixteenth century believed no more in the Golden Age of Christianity, than they did in that of the poets ; and Cardinal Pallavicino knew whom he was addressing when he wrote, concerning Sarpi, the mendacious "historian" of the Council of Trent: "He may perhaps persuade the simple of the truth of his dream that the early Christians lived in unalterable concord and exquisite sanctity ; but he cannot convince those who know enough of Latin to understand the Mass. The *Epistles of St. Paul* complain loudly of many enormities ; among others, of schisms and revolts which were unmasked by that aurora of Christianity. God wished to leave a certain testimony of this fact in the Scriptures which He dictated ; so that the censors of their own time, and they who burn incense in honor of the past, might have no right to believe that the Church, being composed of members so faulty as those we now see, cannot be the True Spouse of Christ. And if this be true of the primitive Church, what shall we say of that of the following centuries, down to the time of that St. Cyprian who, according to Sarpi, represents the undivided jurisdiction of the bishops ? (1) Does not St. Cyprian himself lament the deplorable divisions among those who governed the Church in his day ? Do not ecclesiastical annals tell us of scandalous quarrels, even among the courageous confessors of Christ who were waiting in prison for martyrdom ?" (2) Bearing these facts in mind, we may realize that the scandals imputed to the generality of the clergy by the Reformers, and for which comparatively few were responsible, aided the progress of heresy in merely an indirect manner. The peoples of that day were really affected, however, by the declamations of the truly orthodox in favor of a reformation; for men became accustomed to the cry, and desired it as a good. Then the heresiarchs came with that cry ever on their tongues; and the simple never dreamed that the motto hid a scheme for

(1) A thesis sustained by Sarpi and the contemporary heretics.
(2) *History of the Council of Trent*; vol. II., b. VI., ch. iii.

their deprival of the faith of their fathers. Luther proposed, at first, no change of doctrine ; he spoke in the name of the faith which was dear to his auditors, and urged only a removal of excrescences which were soiling it. The very name of Catholic was preserved by the new doctrinaires for several years ; and they spoke, at first, as men having authority, giving an idea of liberty different from that which they afterward espoused, and which all succeeding revolutionists have so curiously developed. And when the time came that witnessed the repudiation of ecclesiastical tradition, the majority of those who had followed the Will-o'-the-Wisp were kept only by violence in a position which they had not dreamed of occupying. Wherever the Reformation succeeded definitively, as in a large part of Germany, in England, in Sweden, and in Bearn, it owed its success to the civil power ; and wherever the sovereigns abandoned it, as in England under Queen Mary, and in Bearn under the converted Henry IV., the peoples returned to the ancient faith. Wherever the monarchs remained undecided, sometimes favorable and again hostile to heresy, as in France, the new religion tried the power of the sword to secure its domination, but failed. Wherever the ruler manifested determination to repel the monster, as in Spain, the Catholic faith remained victorious, *semper et pro semper*. We have said that Luther spoke very little of liberty ; certainly he did not favor that freedom of thought and private interpretation which became the vogue among his progeny. " It was in the inspiration by the Holy Ghost that Luther found the sovereignty, as well as the equality of men. But when the anathemas of the Papacy, and his own success, had effected his exclusion from the Church, he marched immediately toward an autocracy which allowed no discussion (1). He always affirms what our contemporary theosophists term the rehabilitation of the flesh. Then we hear him exclaiming, with his habitual bestiality of language, that a man can no more easily get along without a woman than without wine (2). But once that he has sati-

<hr/>

(1) See the proofs of this autocracy in Bossuet's *History of the Variations of Protestantism*, especially the letter of Luther to the bishops, in which he affirms the divinity of his mission, and assumes the title of Ecclesiast of Wittemberg.

(2) FLORIMOND DE REMOND ; vol. I., p. 33.

ated men's appetite with this morsel, he thinks only of founding a church on his doctrine. We know his disputes with
the other sectarians, and the anathema which he launched
against Zwingle's version of the Bible. Discouraged when
he saw that discord flourished among the Reformers, he
cried: 'When I close one mouth of the devil, he opens ten' (1).
From this moment he had followers; anarchy having only hired
assassins. But it must be remembered that these followers,
saving only the plotters and some demoniacs, were led astray
in the name of Catholicity—by the fact that, at first, the
Mass had been preserved, also the episcopate and most of
the sacraments, and even, in the hearts of the more pious, a
hope of reunion with the Pope. And in spite of all these
semblances of essential unity, all these assuagements of a too
deep and too real separation, fire and sword alone tore the
Roman Faith out of the hearts of the populations. The rest
was accomplished by the legislation of princes who had been
bought with Church property; these rulers fashioned the
succeeding generations, born in an ignorance and a blind
hatred of Catholicism, to a spiritual servitude which results
from the identification of Church and State" (2).

CHAPTER XIX.

ERASMUS.

This celebrated scholar was a natural son of Gerard Helie
by a daughter of a physician of Zevenberg, in Holland. He
was born at Rotterdam in 1467, and his early education was
obtained in the then celebrated school of Deventer, under the
direction of the Brothers of the Community Life. While yet
a mere child, he became an orphan; and from the day of his
bereavement his guardians tried to impress upon his mind
the idea that God called him to a monastic life. Erasmus,
however, thought otherwise; and he seems to have imbibed,
even at that early day, very strong prejudices against the religious orders, prejudices which were to manifest themselves
in nearly all of his writings. His tutors withdrew their pro-

(1) In his *Treatise Against the Anabaptists.*
(2) SEGRETAIN; *Sixtus V. and Henry IV.,* ch. ii.   Paris, 1861.

tection, and in his fourteenth year the boy found himself poor, sick, and abandoned. At this juncture, he met one of his old schoolmates who had just returned from a visit to Italy, and had entered a community of Regular Canons at Emmaus, near Gouda. This friend persuaded Erasmus to reconsider his resolution to follow a secular career; dwelling especially upon the advantages offered by the monastic life to one who is fond of study, and whose talents are as great as those of Erasmus undoubtedly were. The youth yielded, entered the community at Emmaus, and in time made his solemn vows. In after days he often regretted this step; but tried to find consolation, as he wrote, in the thought that " an honest man may find contentment, in any vocation which Providence may assign to him." During his residence at Emmaus, he devoted the greater part of his time to a study of the works of the celebrated Italian scholar, Lorenzo Valla (1), but he by no means neglected theology, as he very soon proved. It was during this period that he composed his *Canticles* in honor of the Blessed Virgin, his Discourse on the *Evils of Disunion,* and his treatise on *The Contempt of the World.* Erasmus did not receive the priesthood until 1492, and then he was no longer a resident of Emmaus. The bishop of Cambrai, Henry de Bergis, having admired his classical attainments, had obtained permission from his abbot and from the bishop of Utrecht, for his residence outside the community, and had made him episcopal secretary. In 1496, this prelate yielded to the desire of Erasmus to perfect his theological studies at the University of Paris, and procured for him a position in the College of Montaigu, whereby his maintenance was assured.

Although Erasmus afterward admitted that the declaration " Thus decides the Theological Faculty of Paris " was an authoritative stamp for the value of an opinion (2), he now became dissatisfied with the scholastic system as taught by that Faculty; and when certain of his wealthy English fellow-students invited him to visit their country, he accepted,

(1) This scholar, born at Rome in 1406, was a canon in the Lateran. He was one of the foremost contributors to the revival of classical studies, especially by his work on *The Elegancies of the Latin Language.*

(2) In his Epistle to the Sorbonne, no. 12, b. XXII.

and aided by a pension of 100 florins from Prince Adolph of Burgundy, he resided some time among the islanders. He became the vogue among learned·men, and won the hearty friendship of the future chancellor (now Blessed) Sir Thomas More, as well as that of the Hellenists, Latimer and Linacer. The prince of Wales, afterward Henry VIII., felt much affection for Erasmus, and he never quite ceased to love him. While in England, our scholar imbued many persons with what was then there an almost unknown taste for letters, and he amassed great wealth. But be it said to his credit, he devoted to literary purposes all the money not needed for his modest support, and for the care due to his always miserable health. In 1499, he departed, for a time, from England, and devoted several years, spent in various places, to a severe study of the Fathers and the Scriptures. The year 1505 found him again in England, but in 1506 he repaired to Italy. At Turin he received his laureate in theology, and then visited the principal cities, everywhere seeking the society of the learned, and burying himself among the tomes of learning with which he found nearly every Italian library filled. His reputation had preceded him to the Eternal City, and he was warmly welcomed by that prince among patrons of learning, Cardinal John dei Medici, afterward Pope Leo X., while Pope Julius II. tempted him to remain in Rome by the offer of a cardinal's hat in the near future. But the death of Henry VII. of England in 1509, and the consequent accession of his friend Henry VIII. to the throne, caused Erasmus to hearken to the solicitations of his English admirers, and to return to their island. The new monarch would fain have retained the scholar near his own person ; but the professorship of Greek and of theology in the University of Cambridge, tendered him by its chancellor, the Blessed John Fisher, was more to his taste than the atmosphere of a court. His lectures at Cambridge continued until 1521, interrupted only by a few trips to Brussels, Louvain, and Basel, all undertaken in the interest of science, as furthered by his numerous publications. When he had definitively settled at Basel, and had entered upon the most brilliant period of his marvellous literary activity, Francis I.

vainly endeavored to attract him to the newly founded College de France; and Ferdinand, archduke of Austria, just as vainly tried to induce him, by an offer of a large pension, to simply reside in Vienna, that his capital might be the envy of all others, because of its possession of "Erasmus, whose incomparable erudition was praised by the entire world."

No man of letters was more celebrated than Erasmus at this period. Popes and princes, ecclesiastics and laymen, all vied with each other in doing him homage. Fierce adversaries he naturally had, being a man of genius; but if he was not the centre of the literary movement then so active in Europe—that centre being the court of Leo X., no single man of letters then enjoyed more consideration. When Basel was invaded by the so-called Evangelicals in 1529, Erasmus, like all Catholics who could do so, left the city. He took refuge in Fribourg, but in 1535 he returned to Basel. During the autumn of that year he was confined to his bed by a slow fever, but he did not allow his malady to interfere with the completion of the works he had in hand, and with the classification of his immense correspondence. Once, while engaged in this latter task, he happened to take up a letter from his dear and faithful friend, the Blessed Fisher, the martyred bishop of Rochester, and he cried: "I also want to die, if it be the will of God." It is gratifying to know that the last years of Erasmus were rendered as comfortable as money could make them. In 1533, Pope Paul III. secured to him an annual revenue of 5,000 ducats. The entire Roman court desired to see the great scholar enrolled in the Sacred College, and he would have received the hat had he not begged to be left in a humility which, he thought, better befitted his dying condition. The only detail of the circumstances of his death which has come down to us, is that his last words were: "Have mercy, Jesus! Lord, deliver me! Lord, put an end to my life! Lord, have mercy." He died in July, 1536 (1).

In their intense desire to impress in the minds of men the conviction that all that was grand and noble, and especially all that was intellectual, in the sixteenth century, entered in-

(1) The following was the epitaph inscribed on the grave of Erasmus:

" *Fatalis series nobis invidit Erasmum*
Sed Desiderium tollere non potuit."

to the ranks of the Reformers; while all that was degraded
or besotted remained subservient to priestcraft and monkery;
Protestant polemics have claimed Erasmus as their own.
Certainly, it cannot be denied that very frequently the tone
and even the tenor of this scholar's writings contributed,
without any such intention on his part, to make the way of
the Reformation comparatively easy. His lashing of the
ecclesiastical abuses of the time was merciless; but just as
severe have been the castigations given in every age by men
of God to the wicked ones in the sanctuary, and yet they
gloried in their Catholic faith. Again, it is true that Erasmus often treated theological matters in so caustic and flippant a manner, that in the minds of the weaker sort of men
doubt might take the place of faith, when they read these
passages in a superficial manner, and when they were already
pre-occupied in complaints against certain real evils. Erasmus felt the force of the accusations based upon this fact,
especially in the case of certain passages concerning indulgences, infant-baptism, and devotion to the saints. But in
his later writings he endeavored to do away with the impression he had unwittingly made; and he repeatedly insisted
that he was a submissive son of the Church. Listen to some
passages from his letter to Card. Campeggi, in which he
repels the charge that he was a Lutheranizer. " I was the
first to condemn the writings of Luther, because they caused
disorder, which I always abhorred; I was the first to oppose
the publication of those writings; I was almost the only one
who never read them; I was the only one who never found
anything in them to defend. I constantly urged those who
could do so, to speak and write against Luther. ... The
Bull against Luther seemed to all to be unworthy of the lenity of our Leo; but no one ever heard that Erasmus was discontented because of it. ... I am not so impious as to dissent
from the teachings of the Catholic Church. ... I have written,
thus prolixly to you, that you may know that Erasmus is a
devoted subject of the Roman See." It is true that in the
beginning of the Lutheran agitation, Erasmus favored a policy of conciliation; and that he hoped much from the Diet of
Cologne (Dec., 1520); and that he excused himself, on the

plea of ill health, from appearing at the Diet of Worms (April, 1521). But in vain did Luther, Ulrich von Hutten, Melancthon, and Zwingle, try to make of him a rebel to Rome. As soon as he realized that his conciliatory views were misinterpreted by many Catholics as well as by many Protestants, he proceeded to set himself right by the publication of his treatise on *Free Will*, to which Luther replied with his *Free Will a Slave.* Then followed the *Hiperaspistes* of Erasmus in which he bitterly reproved the bitterness of Luther, and repelled the charge of scepticism, insisting that now the Church had pronounced on the matters in dispute, he saw no room for further doubt. From that time the ex-Augustinian declared that Erasmus was a free-thinker and a pest to be shunned.

But it is said that Erasmus discarded his monastic tunic. He did, *secundum quid*, as the scholastics say. In 1506, after he had taken his doctor's degree in Turin, he proceeded to Bologna. He was dressed in the costume of his Order, which was the same as that of a secular priest, but with a white band around the waist. Just at that time, a pest was ravaging Bologna, and the magistrates had ordered that all the ministering-clergy, physicians, nurses, etc., should wear a white band as a warning to others to keep at a distance. Hence it happened that our Regular Canon was taken for a priest fresh from the beds of the stricken; and as he persisted in mixing with the crowd, evil would have befallen him, had not a sympathetic citizen pulled him into his own house. Then he removed the band; and afterward received from Rome a dispensation to dress like a secular priest. Hence the story that he had unfrocked himself. That Erasmus did not, at his death, belie the known sentiments of his entire life, is almost evident from a letter which he wrote to a friend on June 28, 1536, that is, scarcely two weeks before his demise: "Although I am residing here at Basel among kind friends, I would rather die in some other place, owing to the difference in our religious belief" (1). And during the previous year, writing to the treasurer Bouvalot, he said : " I allow no person who is infected with the new doctrines, to come into.

(1) Epistle no. 1299, to John Gocien.

my house." We refuse to believe, therefore, with the Protestant Henke, that " The Roman Church cannot claim the honor, if it be an honor, of having seen Erasmus die in her bosom ; for he departed, according to the monkish jargon, ' without cross, without candles, and without God. ' " Neither, by the way, can we accept the assertion of Henke, presumedly conversant with the olden monastic phraseology, that the saying " *Sine crux, sine lux, sine Deus* " is a fair specimen of the Latin current in the religious establishments of the sixteenth century. Like the colleges of every day, monasteries have their jokes and their plays on words ; but that the adduced jargon was ever seriously spoken by monks, least of all in the Age of Leo X., unless by lay-brothers in the monastery kitchen, "*Credat Judæus Apella !* " But is it probable that a hypocrite and an obstinate heretic would have been a bosom friend of those glorious martyrs to Catholic truth, Blessed Fisher and Blessed Thomas More ; and that such a person would have won and preserved the enthusiastic admiration of four Roman Pontiffs ?

CHAPTER XX.

POPE CLEMENT VII. THE SACKING OF ROME BY THE TROOPS OF THE EMPEROR CHARLES V. THE DIVORCE OF HENRY VIII.

Adrian VI., the successor of Leo X., was a pious and learned man, but utterly strange to political craft ; and as a Fleming he cared nothing for the interests of Italy. A lover of peace, he thought he could secure it by heading a league composed of the emperor Charles V., the archduke Ferdinand of Austria, Henry VIII. of England, and Florence, Genoa, Siena, and Lucca, to the detriment of France. As a rule, the Italians disliked Charles V.; each side of the quadruple aspect which he presented being hostile either to their interests or to their dearest sentiments. He was king of Spain, and therefore master of the New World, the discovery of which had entailed upon Italy the loss of maritime supremacy ; he was Holy Roman emperor, and therefore, an heir to exorbitant pretensions in regard to Italy ; he was chief sovereign of Germany, the land which had furnished the new heresy which was trying to subvert the Popedom, the chief glory of Italy; and he was a Fleming, one of a race which was just then rivalling the Italian in commerce. Then the French, despite the many contrary lessons of recent history, had been regarded as liberators. It was natural, therefore, that his temporal subjects should feel little regret, when the Flemish Pontiff died, after a reign of twenty months. His successor, Clement VII., elected on Nov. 18, 1523, was an illegitimate child of Giuliano dei Medici, and therefore a cousin of Leo X., who had legitimated him. The accession of Giulio dei Medici was gratifying to the Romans; for they had quickly tired of the simple manners of Adrian VI., and yearned for the magnificence which a Medici would naturally display. Vettore describes Giulio at Florence as "not haughty, not a simoniac, not miserly, not libidinous; sober, modest in dress, religious, and devout;" and he was learned, fond of art, a dexterous politician, and a pleasing talker. Hitherto he had favored Spain; and he gloried in having prevented Francis I. from reducing Naples, at the time of that prince's first Italian campaign. In fact, it was Giulio dei Medici who had reconciled Leo X. to the election of Charles to the Holy Roman Empire; and he had advised that Pontiff to abrogate the papal decree which forbade a Holy Roman Emperor to wear the crown of Naples. Afterward, however, the spectacle of the Spaniards camped in Lombardy wrought a change in his policy.

After the victory of the imperialists at the passage of the Sesia, the marquis of Pescara and the arch-traitor, the constable de Bourbon, invaded Provence, with the declared intention of dismembering France (1). But Francis I. rebuked

(1) Charles de Bourbon, a lineal descendant of St. Louis, was the second prince of the blood-royal of France, being the son of Gilbert de Bourbon, count de Montpensier, by Clara di Gonzaga. In 1515, recognizing his incontestable valor and talent, Francis I. made him high constable, or commander-in-chief of all the armies of France. Left a widower in 1521, the queen-dowager, Louisa of Savoy, asked him to marry her; but he refused the honor. This slight embittered the royal lady, and she led her son to distrust his constable. During the campaign of 1521, in which Francis commanded in person, the command of the advance, which was a prerogative of the constable in such circumstances, was given to the duke d'Alencon: and shortly afterward, the unlucky man was deprived of the governorship of Milan. But not content with these revenges, Louisa thought to deprive her contemner of the heritage of the House of Bourbon, claiming it herself, as the daughter of Margaret de Bourbon, the wife of Duke Philip of Savoy. The fiery constable would not wait for the decision of the Parliament of Paris, but hastened to take revenge

the "Spanish rodomontade" of the emperor by driving his troops over the Alps, and then marching on Milan, which he entered in triumph. Many of the imperialists now deserted, and the leaders could not agree. If Francis had not listened to the counsels of his favorite general, Bonivet, losing valuable time in taking unimportant fortresses, he could have ruined his adversary. As it was, the famous Spanish general, Anthony de Leyva, who had fought thirty-three battles and conducted forty sieges, succeeded in fortifying Pavia; and while Francis was besieging that important place, Gian Giacomo Medeghino captured Chiavenna, thus preventing the Grisons from succoring the French. The imperialists now gathered from all sides, and Francis, having foolishly detached nearly half of his army for an attempt on Naples, was defeated and captured in the battle of Pavia, on Feb. 24, 1525. This victory of Leyva gave to Charles V. a power which he preserved to the end of his career. The immediate effect of the triumph was to place Italy at the feet of the emperor, almost as in the days of Barbarossa : and unfortunately for Italy, a Lombard League was impossible, and an Alexander III. was not on the papal throne. Clement VII. and the Florentines, who had sided with the French, hastened to make peace with the conqueror ; and Venice, Lucca, and Siena were obliged to exhaust their treasuries in return for pardon. But when King Francis returned from his year's captivity in Madrid, Pope Clement, Florence, and Venice hastened to renew an alliance which promised to relieve Italy from the presence of an undisciplined and licentious soldiery. A secret league was formed at Cognac, with the understanding that the Austro-Spaniards were to be expelled definitively from Italy ; Ferrara was to be restored to the Holy See ;

by traitorous overtures to the emperor. Of course his proposals were received with joy, and Charles tendered the following terms. The traitor was to marry Leonora, the sister of Charles and widow of the king of Portugal, receiving as dowry 200,000 ducats, and the succession to all the states of the House of Austria-Spain, in default of heirs to Charles V. and his brother, Ferdinand. Henry VIII. of England also had his part in this precious agreement ; he promising the other contracting parties to aid in the dethronement of Francis I., and in the elevation of the constable to an impoverished French throne, England to receive Normandy and Guienne, and the empire to receive Burgundy and the Artois. Of course, the intending usurper was to leave a clear field in Italy to Charles V. BELCARIUS ; b. XVII.—DANIEL; *History of France*, edit. 1729, vol. V., p. 498, and vol. VII., p. 501.—DE THOU; b. I, y. 1523. *Memoirs of Bellai*; b. II.

Francesco Maria Sforza was to be once more duke of Milan;
and the crown of the Two Sicilies was to be given to the
count de Vaudemont, a descendant of the House of Anjou.
Our purpose precludes the necessity of entering into any details of the war which now ensued, saving those which affected the Holy See; the pages of Guicciardini and Cantù will
satisfy the scholar who wishes fairly accurate information,
while the ordinary reader, if provided with abundance of
salt, may learn much from Robertson. Coming, therefore,
to the campaign which immediately concerned Pope Clement VII., we observe that the imperial forces greatly out-
numbered those of the allies; and that while the latter were
animated by various and divergent interests, the imperial
generals—the Frenchman, Charles de Bourbon, and the Spaniards, Pescara and Del Vasto—had but one thought, the humiliation of the Pope-King. Add to this source of imperial
strength the fact that the constable was fighting for the safety of his own head, and you will understand how comparatively easy was the reduction of the Eternal City. Nor should
it be forgotten that when Francis I. found himself "still a
king," when he sprang to the French bank of the Bidassoa,
his first use of freedom did him little honor. Instead of
sustaining his troops in Italy, he allowed the ferocious
hordes of the constable to glut their insensate fury against
the capital of Christendom, while he plunged into dissoluteness, as a consolation for the ennui of his captivity; and although, when too late, he sent Lautrec to repair the evil,
he forgot his brave soldiers in Naples, where, without money
or reinforcements, they became disorganized, and the gallant
commander died of the plague.

The allied army was unable to check the onward march of
the constable, who had told his followers, when he led them
out of Piacenza, that they should not disband because of
their not having been paid, since he was about to lead them
to the pillage of a city which would yield them wealth, wine,
and women. The army of Charles de Bourbon numbered
30,000 men, about 18,000 of whom were German Lutherans
who had been recruited by that general of the archduke
Ferdinand of Austria, George von Freundsberg, who was

wont to direct the attention of his applauding Gospellers to two halters which dangled from his saddle; one of gold thread which was destined to strangle Pope Clement, and one of silk with which he would hang such cardinals as fell into his hands. These Germans panted for an opportunity to wash their hands in the gore of those Roman vampires who, as they had been taught by Hutten, Luther, etc., had been fattening on the blood sucked from the veins of the honest fatherland. The remainder of the army—if that could be called an army which was without discipline, commissariat, or baggage, and which always answered the appeals of its officers with the cry, "Pay us!"—was composed of 2,000 Italians, and of 10,000 Spanish subjects of the Hispano-Austro-German Cæsar, who, although Catholics as Spaniards must ever be, were nevertheless anxious to share in the spoils of a city which had been represented to them as overflowing with riches which had been wrung from every land in Christendom. When Pope Clement heard on May 5, 1527, that the constable was at the gates of Rome, he confided the defence to his general, Renzo da Ceri, and retired to Castel San Angelo, accompanied by nearly all the cardinals then resident in the city. The papal commander arranged his four or five thousand improvised warriors as best he could; and when the assault was made, it seemed as though the capital might yet be saved, even though the expected Venetians and French did not arrive. Then the Bourbon, brave though traitorous, headed a second attack. With his own hands he placed a scaling ladder, and had mounted nearly to the ramparts, when he fell to the ground mortally wounded, and almost immediately expired. The prince of Orange prudently covered the body with his cloak, lest the sight of their dead leader might discourage the on-rushing soldiers, and the struggle progressed, terminating finally in the capture of the city. By the death of the constable, the prince of Orange became commander of the imperial forces, who now engaged in one of the most horrid, and certainly the most sacrilegious, of all the war dramas of modern times; but we do not read that the noble Netherlander made any effort to prevent it. In the name of his Catholic Majesty of Spain, of

.ı Holy Roman Emperor, of a German Cæsar, all united in the person of Charles V., was performed a crime which an Alaric would probably have scorned to imitate. Thousands of men, women, and children were murdered outright. Not one palace or church, not one house of any promising appearance, escaped pillage and destruction. Atrocious tortures were applied to make the presumedly wealthy avow the recesses where their riches were supposed to be concealed; and often, when the victim had purchased life from one band, he underwent the same experience at the hands of another. Husbands, fathers, and brothers, bound and helpless, beheld their wives, daughters, and sisters violated by human monsters. Crimes like these were committed by Spaniards as well as by Germans. But great was the joy with which the German Lutherans manifested their hatred of the idolatries of "the whore of Babylon." The drunken Teutons, crazy less with wine than with the teachings of Luther, rushed to the sanctuaries; defiled the altars in an unmentionable manner; used the sacred vessels for the vilest purposes, after having trampled on the Body of Our Lord; destroyed every painting and statue; and in the very House of God outraged the sacred virgins whom they had dragged from their cloisters. When such deeds of hell were the order of the day for the reformed gentry of Germany, we need say but little about such exhibitions as the placing of a cardinal in a coffin, and after a mock Mass for his soul, the performing of an obscene dance around him; the sending of another cardinal, accompanied by a guard, to beg for money for his ransom, from door to door; the using of Papal Bulls and works of the Fathers instead of litter for the German horses; the attempted compulsion of a priest to give Communion to an ass; the donning of sacred vestments amid scenes of disgusting lubricity; the holding of a mock Conclave in the Vatican, in which Luther was elected to the Chair of Peter; etc (1). For two months this diabolic Carnival went on; and in the meantime, the Pontiff and his attendants, surrounded by a small

(1) CIACONIUS; *Life of Clement V.*—DUCHESNE; *Hist. of Clem. V.*—BELLAI; b. III.—GUICCIARDINI; b. XVIII.—GLORIERI; *Capture of the City.*—RINALDI; y. 1527, nos. 18, 19.—JOVIUS; b. XXVI.—MEZERAY; *Life of Francis I.*, vol. IV.—CANTU; *Univ. Hist.*, b. XV., ch. vi.

garrison of Roman noblemen and gentlemen who were faithful to the last, were suffering the extremes of starvation in
the besieged fortress. Many attempts were made by the
Roman people to smuggle provisions into the Castle, but all
failed. One old woman was detected in the act of tying a
basket of lettuce to a cord which had been lowered from the
ramparts; and the imperial commander had her hung on the
spot. Cardinal Pucci succeeded in leaving the Castle; but as
he mounted a horse at the gate, the animal was wounded by
a pikeman, the cardinal lost his seat, and his foot catching in
the stirrup, he was dragged to death on the pavement of the
bridge. These and similar catastrophes were witnessed by
Pope Clement, and combined with the entrance of the plague
into the castle (it had appeared in Rome almost simultaneously with the imperialists), they induced him to capitulate.
He was forced to pay to his Cæsarean Majesty 400,000 ducats
as a ransom, and to remain a prisoner until one-half of the
amount was delivered; to cede Parma, Piacenza, and Modena to the Germans; to receive imperial garrisons in all cities
of the Papal States, wherever the emperor might choose to
plant them; and he was to await, at Nola or at Naples, the
further orders of Charles. The prince of Orange assigned
as chief jailer of the august prisoner the same officer who
had held that position in Madrid toward Francis I.; and six
companies, half Lutherans, and half Spaniards, entered the
castle to assist him. For several months the Pontiff besought his enemies to remove him, if not to the Vatican, at
least to some city in his States where he could attend properly to the affairs of the Church; and when they refused his
demand, occurrences in his desolate capital added to his
chagrin, and gave him good reason to fear that his life was
in danger. The imperialist soldiers had not yet received
their pay, and their robberies in Rome had not satisfied them,
although the most moderate estimate of their booty sets its
value at twenty millions of our money. When the Germans
saw that the Pope found it difficult to raise the amount necessary to pay the second instalment of his ransom, they
cried aloud in the streets for his head. On three occasions
they dragged around the Campo dei Fiori a number of bish-

ops and Roman patricians, chained together, the hostages whom the Pope had given to the prince of Orange; and they would have hung them all, then and there, had not the Romans succeeded in making them so drunk, that they became incapable of action. These facts impelled Pope Clement to risk much in an attempt to regain his liberty; and having succeeded in opening a correspondence with Prince Louis di Gonzaga and other faithful and determined personages in Rome, he escaped from his prison on the night of December 9. At the gate of the fortress, where he appeared in the disguise of a merchant, he was met by Gonzaga and certain imperial soldiers whom that prince had bribed; and in a few days he was safe in Orvieto, then in the possession of the troops of Lautrec. It was here that he received Knight, secretary of state to Henry VIII. of England, who had been sent by that monarch to sound the Pontiff in reference to his projected divorce from Catharine of Aragon.

It is not probable that Charles V. was guilty of that stupendous crime which we have recorded, unless in the sense that one is culpable when he wantonly launches an engine of destruction, all the capabilities of which he has not estimated. He tried to deceive others, and to lull the reproaches of his own mysterious conscience, by ordering prayers to Heaven for the liberation of him whom he had enchained; by making a parade of himself and friends, dressed in penitential guise; and by lame excuses to the sovereigns of Christendom. But he refused to subtract one pennyweight from his promised pound of flesh; and he, then residing in Valladolid, would have ordered the transfer of his august prisoner to Madrid as a testimony to his grandeur, had not all Spain, ecclesiastical and lay, manifested its horror at the design. However, circumstances, or rather Providence, impeded the design of Charles V. to the detriment of the Pope-King; and when, at length, there occurred a reconciliation which was necessary to both Church and Empire, it was found that the Holy See occupied a position which could be justified, to human understanding, much more easily if the pontifical forces had repelled the imperialists from the walls of Rome. In June, 1529, the emperor agreed to the following conditions of peace with Pope

Clement VII. The Venetians were to restore Ravenna and
Cervia, and the duke of Ferrara would yield Modena, Reggio,
and Rubiera, to the States of the Church. The Medici were
to recover their pre-eminence in Florence. Sforza was to
again don the ducal crown of Milan. Charles was to use all
his energies to repress heresy in Germany. In return for all
these favors, Clement VII. agreed to confirm the election of
Charles to the Holy Roman Empire, and to give to him the
imperial crown. Charles was also to receive from the Pontiff
the investiture of the kingdom of the Two Sicilies; Clement
agreeing, for the nonce, to be satisfied with receiving, as tok-
en of the pontifical suzerainty over that kingdom, merely the
white palfrey. When the time came for the coronation of
Charles, he had sufficient good taste, or perhaps remorse, to
refrain from insisting upon Milan as the place for his reception of the iron crown of Italy, and upon Rome for the reception of the imperial diadem; and Bologna was gay with the
festivities which announced another accord between the Church
and the Empire. Charles V. was the last German emperor
to be confirmed and crowned by the Roman Pontiff; and
hence, from that day down to the abolition of the empire by
Napoleon, every emperor was always styled in the official
language of Rome, and in the Liturgy where his name occurred, as "emperor-elect." So true was it, in the words of
Pope Adrian IV., writing to the bishops of Germany in 1156,
that " the king of the Germans cannot be called emperor and
Augustus, until he is consecrated by that Roman Pontiff who
promoted Charlemagne, and gave to him the great name of emperor " (1). Bologna was gay on Feb. 22, 1530. " Painting,
poetry, and the theatre rivalled each other in that solemnity,
the most splendid that occurred in that age of splendor (2).
Tired and dismayed, our people congratulated Charles, and
they said to each other that they would never have expected
to discover such amiability and courtesy in the author of so
many horrible disasters. Amid those rejoicings was consummated the humiliation of Italy; a humiliation begun in the

(1) AIMOIN; b. V., ch. xxv.—See our vol. II., p. 26, et seqq.
(2) The duke of Savoy wore a dress which cost 300,000 dollars. What would it cost in our
day? GIORDANI; On the Arrival and Stay of Clement VII. in Bologna, for the Coronation of Charles V. Bologna, 1842.

discords, and finished in the harmony of the powerful. Every equilibrium between the small states, whether loyal to the empire or not, was broken. The Pope, frightened at the progress of the Reformation, embraced the knees of that Majesty which his predecessors had so often caused to tremble ; and if a regulated opposition had heretofore formed the glory and grandeur of the Popedom, that power now changed its motto, and camped with the Ghibellines. If our land had hitherto suffered from wars and plagues, transient evils which do not attack the roots of prosperity, it now saw the introduction of an absurd administration, of homicidal principles, and of a systematic oppression of thought, of genius, and of industry " (1).

At this time the principal members of the Medici family, besides Pope Clement VII., were Ippolito, created cardinal by Clement ; Catharine, afterward queen of France ; and Alexander, who was to marry Margaret, a natural daughter of Charles V. Catharine and Alexander were children of Lorenzo, duke of Urbino, son of that Peter who had succeeded to his father, Lorenzo the Magnificent, had been expelled in the time of the French Charles VIII., and had perished in the defeat of the French on the Garigliano. The promise of Charles V. to see that the mastership of Florence should accrue to Alexander opened the eyes of the Florentines to the fact that they were called to make an extreme and desperate struggle for freedom. But unfortunately, the two great parties of the *Piagnoni* (the olden "weepers" of Savonarola's day) and the *Palleschi* (partisans of the Medici, so called from their war-cry of "Palle," taken from the balls which formed the Medicean device), were irreconcilable, because of ancient animosities and recent broils. Then there was a third party, termed Neutrals, who desired popular government, but were favorable to a return of the Medici, provided that those enterprising persons would be content with the rank of private citizens. This party, called also Optimates, because it was composed of most of the nobles and the wealthy, followed the leadership of that Nicholas Capponi who, in 1527, had so vividly represented the woes of the re-

(1) CANTU ; *loc. cit.*

public as punishments of Heaven, that his many thousands
of hearers fell upon their knees, begging aloud for divine
mercy.   Then these men of faith induced the government to
solemnly proclaim Christ King of the Florentine State, re-
cording the decree on the door of the government palace,
where it may be read to-day, if the modern regenerators of
Italy have not obliterated the inscription which recognizes
the sovereignty of the Crucified One of Calvary.   When the
Florentines realized that war alone could preserve their self-
respect, they resolved to defend themselves with an ardor
rarely equalled in the annals of any people.   They deposed
the gonfaloniere Capponi, whom they suspected of holding
correspondence with Pope Clement, the real head and main
strength of the Medici.   Then they brought into Florence,
with great pomp and devotion, the holy image of the Virgin
dell' Impruneta, and the table of Santa Maria Primierana of
Fiesole ; which they placed, as a Palladium for their capital,
in the church of Santa Maria del Fiore.   Then they hired a
number of mercenary officers, among whom were several who
had commanded in the famous Black Bands ; and with 16,000
devoted citizen soldiers, under the command of Malatesta
Baglioni, they hoped to withstand the attacks of the prince
of Orange, who was advancing from Fuligno with 40,000
Hispano - German imperialists.   Michelangelo Buonarroti,
military and civil engineer as well as painter, sculptor, architect, and poet, did as Archimedes of Syracuse did in similar
circumstances ; he devised and actuated an improved system
of fortifications, which the event proved to be valuable.
However, Perugia, Cortona, and Arezzo were taken by the
Cæsarians ; and when the news reached Florence, many of
the Medicean party, moved either by hope or by fear, and
among whom was the historian Guicciardini, abandoned the
city.   A delay of fifteen days in the Val d'Arno, on the part
of the Netherlander, allowed the Florentines to augment their
advanced fortifications, levelling every one of their suburbs,
and also a great many magnificent buildings in the contigu-
ous parts of the city, which might be occupied by the enemy.
In this work of patriotic destruction the owners of the doomed
edifices assisted, calmly helping to raise bastions out of

the ruins of their luxurious villas, and turning their prized fruit-trees into *chevaux de frise*. If the reader has seen the beautiful picture of the Last Supper by Andrea del Sarto, he will be interested in the following episode of this struggle, narrated by the historian Varchi, a contemporary of the event. A mixed multitude of soldiers and artisans were engaged in the destruction of the church and convent of San Salvi, which the engineers had thought proper to demolish ; and having dismantled the upper part of the buildings, they came to the refectory, on one of the walls of which the great artist had painted his most celebrated tableau. Immediately, says Varchi, the entire body refused to prosecute the demolition any further ; so deeply were they penetrated by a sense of the beautiful in art. To the good taste of those probably uneducated men the art student of to-day owes the survival of a grand source of inspiration. On Nov. 10, 1529, the prince of Orange led in person his first assault on the resolute Florentines, and was repulsed with great loss. During the night of Dec. 11, Stephen Colonna led a successful sortie into the imperial camp, inflicting great damage on the enemy. Many other sorties were made, and with considerable success ; but the Florentine commander, who had begun to think favorably of the overtures secretly made to him by Pope Clement (1), always recalled his troops at the decisive moment. The siege progressed, the Florentines meanwhile suffering greatly from the plague and starvation. When things were at their worst, Francesco Ferruccio, one of the best guerillas of that day, who had administered many severe checks to the imperialists in Central Italy, marched to the aid of Florence ; but on Aug. 2, 1530, the prince of Orange attacked him at Gavinana, and although the prince was killed, and his army routed, the arrival of the imperialist *condottiere* Vitelli, with a reinforcement of Pistojesi, turned the victory into a defeat, in which Ferruccio was made prisoner and massacred. When the news of this event reached Baglioni, he introduced the imperialists into the bastions, and the cannons which had been pointed away from the city were immed-

(1) The Pontiff had promised him Perugia in fief. When Andrea Gritti, doge of Venice, read the terms of the pacification of Florence, he said of Baglioni : " He sold the blood of those citizens, ounce by ounce ; and he has made of himself the blackest traitor on earth."

iately turned against it. No other resource was now left to the *Signoria* but an honorable capitulation; and deputies were sent to Don Ferrante Gonzaga, upon whom the command of the imperialists had devolved. Gonzaga referred the matter to Baccio Valori, the papal commissary in Tuscany; and on Aug. 12 it was agreed that the emperor should provide for the security of the Florentine State, "respecting always the popular liberties." The destinies of Florence now depended on Valori, Guicciardini, Vettore, and Acciaiuoli; and on July 5, 1531, accompanied by Muscettola as imperial ambassador, Alexander dei Medici arrived, bearing for the *Signoria* an imperial letter declaring that Charles confirmed the ancient liberties of Florence, but on condition that Alexander was accepted as duke, the succession to reside in the Medici family (1).

While the chief anxieties of Clement VII., the expulsion of the imperialists from Italy, and the restoration of his family to the domination of Florence, were consuming time which might better have been devoted to the weal of the Church whose Pontiff he was, the incendiary tenets of Luther and Zwingle were being rapidly propagated in Germany, the Scandinavian countries, and Switzerland; and Germany was reeking with the blood which had been shed in the Peasants' War. In 1529 the word "Protestant" was given to the world in the Diet of Spire; and in 1530 the reformers presented their Confession of Augsburg. In 1531 the Catholics of Switzerland had to sustain a terrible war against the partisans of Zwingle, in order to preserve the right to practise their religion. The sultan Soliman was menacing Christendom with an utter overthrow. The Pontiff vainly besought the princes of Germany to rally around the standard of the ancient faith, and to join the emperor in an endeavor to subdue a heresy which was dividing forces which were all needed to check the advance of nearly triumphant Islam. But the Protestant princes were deaf to the voice of Rome; and the very danger of his hereditary states induced Charles V. to show a condescension to the German heretics, without whose aid he could

(1) SEGNI; *Hist. Flor.*, b. IV.—VARCHI: *Hist. Flor.*, b. II.—VETTORE; *Summary of the History of Italy from 1514 to 1527.—Venetian Relations*, series II., vol. I.—JOVIUS; *loc. cit.*

scarcely hope to withstand the Turk. At the Diet of Augsburg, and more strongly during his conversations with Charles at Bologna, Pope Clement had announced his intention to convoke a General Council, to be held either at Bologna, or at Mantua, or at Piacenza; but the Protestant princes of Germany were fertile in pretexts to prevent the actuation of an idea which boded ill for the success of their schemes. Again and again did Clement endeavor to bring about an assemblage of the bishops of Christendom, that means might be devised to preserve the integrity of the seamless garment of Christ; but he had the grief of seeing not only that predominance of Charles V. in Europe which he so much dreaded, but also the definitive separation of a large portion of Germany from the Church, and tl e beginning of a revolt which was to involve in heresy what had been the Island of Saints.

Probably the most anxious moments of Pope Clement VII. were those in which he tried to divert the English monarch, Henry VIII., from his project of divorce from his wife, Catharine of Aragon. For the details of the lubricious origin of the Anglican Church Establishment, we refer the reader to the pages of Lingard; we shall notice merely the position occupied by Clement VII. in regard to the first stage of a movement which, at first schismatic, in time became heretical. It was probably in the early part of 1526 that Henry VIII. became enamored of Anne Boleyn, a sister of that Mary Boleyn who had succeeded Elizabeth Tailbois in his transient affections, and whom he had foisted as a wife on William Carey, a gentleman of his privy chamber. During the ensuing year he sounded many divines and lawyers as to the validity of the dispensation whereby Pope Julius II. had allowed him to marry the virgin-widow of his brother, Arthur; but on Aug. 30, 1527, we find him writing to the bishop of Bath : "The Bull is good, or it is naught. If it is naught, let it be so declared; and if it be good, it shall never be broken by no byways by me " (1). However, about this time, the king despatched his secretary, Knight, to Pope Clement, then a prisoner in Castel San Angelo, to prepare the way for the desired divorce. Knight arrived in Italy after the Pontiff's

(1) In Herbert, 99.

escape to Orvieto; and on Dec. 16, he presented his master's letter to his Holiness. Many authors are prone to descant upon the supposed quandary in which our Pontiff was placed by this application of Henry. Unwilling to disoblige the king of England, who had shown considerable friendship for him; yet dreading to displease Charles V., the nephew of the persecuted queen; Clement is often represented as hesitating as to his course. There is not the slightest evidence that in this matter Clement VII. ever, for one instant, closed his eyes, wilfully or by chance, to his duty as the Vicar of Christ, the supreme interpreter of Christian doctrine, the custodian of Christian morality, and the natural protector of outraged innocence. But Rome never hurries in important decisions; and if Clement availed himself of this proverbial prudence of the Holy See, trusting that time—so often the best solver of difficulties—would come to his aid, he should not be blamed. He had good reason to hope that Henry would, after a season of dalliance with the Boleyn, abandon her as he had her mother, her sister, and many other Circes of the hour. As priest and as man of the world, he knew full well that the alleged scruples of Henry in regard to his union with Catharine were simply tricks devised to deceive the ignorant or the unwary; and therefore he felt that, were the royal lecher loosened from Anne's embraces, there would be no more talk about divorce from his lawful spouse. In the meantime, he would do all that he could conscientiously do to humor Henry, and to please Francis I., who, for political reasons, and chiefly because of his hatred of the House of Aragon, had ranged himself among the favorers of the divorce. Therefore the Pontiff consented to sign two documents which Knight presented to him, on the part of his master. By the first, he allowed Cardinal Wolsey to hear and decide the cause of the divorce, subject to the papal approbation; and by the second, he agreed, in case the divorce were granted, to grant a dispensation for Henry's marriage with any woman who was already promised to another, or who was related to himself in the first degree of affinity. We are not bound to explain the inconsistency of Henry—an act which really cut the ground from under his feet—in asking from Clement a dispensation which, according to the royal contention, Julius II. had no right to grant (1).

The ambitious Wolsey was not content with the agreement handed to Knight by the Pontiff; for it left Clement at liberty to revise any sentence which the cardinal might pronounce. Therefore he employed his secretary, Stephen Gardiner, an eminent canonist and a fine lawyer, to procure from Clement a commission authorizing the cardinal, with the aid of any other English bishop, to decide definitively in the case. This commission was granted on April 13, 1528; but the conscience of Wolsey was fully awakened by the now manifest sense of his tremendous responsibility. Accordingly, Gardiner was told to request that Cardinal Campeggi be joined with the English members of the court; and Wolsey himself avowed to the now exultant monarch that while he was ready " to spend his goods, blood, and life " in the service of his royal master and friend, nevertheless, if he found that the dispensation granted by Pope Julius II. had been valid "he would so pronounce it, let the consequences be what they would "(2). Henry received this announcement with dismay and every token of rage; and the cardinal, foreseeing that the worst might happen to himself, hastened to complete the endowment of the colleges and other institutions which he had founded, and to put his other affairs in order. The request to appoint Campeggi as a co-judge with Wolsey was pleasing to the Pontiff; for the cardinal was an adroit statesman,

(1) " This dispensation was thought necessary to secure the intended marriage with Anne Boleyn from two objections, which might afterward be brought against it. I. A suspicion was entertained that she had been actually contracted to Percy, and was therefore his lawful wife. On this account the dispensation was made to authorize the king's marriage with any woman, *etiamsi talis sit quœ prius cum alio contraxerit, dummodo illud carnali copula non fuerit consummatum.* II. Mary Boleyn had been Henry's mistress. Now the relationship between sister and sister is as near as the relationship between brother and brother; whence it was argued that if Henry, as he contended, could not validly marry Catharine, on the supposition that she had been carnally known by *his* brother Arthur, so neither could Anne validly marry Henry, because he had carnally known *her* sister Mary. On this account the following clause was introduced. *Etiamsi illa tibi alias secundo aut remotiore consanguinitatis aut primo affinitatis gradu, etiam ex quocumque licito seu illicito coitu proveniente, invicem conjuncta sit, dummodo relicta fratris tui non fuerit.* Thus the king was placed in a most singular situation, compelled to acknowledge in the Pontiff a power which he at the same time denied, and to solicit a dispensation of the very same nature with that which he maintained to be invalid." LINGARD; edit. 1883, vol. IV., p. 498.

(2) LE GRAND; III., 164.—STRYPE; I., App., 84.

upright, and experienced (1). Then he was also troubled
with the gout, and tried to avoid the appointment—a fact
which militated in his favor in the mind of the Pope, who
saw that a comparatively slow and inactive colleague of Wolsey would be more apt to further his wish to gain time.
Clement even instructed his legate to journey slowly to England ; and when there, to conduct the trial with all due deliberation and every formal observance. Above all, he should
not pronounce judgment, until he had consulted the Holy
See (2). We pass over the proceedings which now occurred,
for they are at the ready command of the reader. The hopes
of Henry and his paramour were nearly blasted, when, on
Feb. 6, 1529, they were revived by the news that Clement VII.
was dying. Forgetful of the historical fact that an easy-
going and much promising cardinal has often made an un-
compromising Pope, and apparently inconsiderate of the
fact that Christ lives in His Vicar, both Henry VIII. and
Francis I. started the machinery which they deemed calculated to land Wolsey on the Chair of Peter (3). But Clement recovered, and the English and French agents devised
new means to further the scheme of their sovereigns. During
the Pope's tedious convalescence they not only cajoled him,
but they presumed to warn him of the dangers which his soul
would run, if he persisted in refusing so small a thing as
allowing a powerful king to put away a distasteful woman,
seeing that the refusal would probably entail the loss of England to the Catholic Church. Clement showed himself the
true Pontiff ; to all flatteries and menaces he replied that the
law of God was his guide, and that he was insensible to all
considerations of temporal interest or danger, when the duties
of the Supreme Pontificate were involved.

In the spring of 1530, King Francis obliged his friend of
England by procuring a forged decision of the theological
Faculty of Paris in favor of the divorce ; and Henry hastened

(1) Burnet represents Campeggi as an immoral man ; proving his assertion by the fact
that the cardinal brought with him to England a young man whom he introduced everywhere as his "second son, Ridolfo." Now the entire life of Campeggi was well known
throughout Europe ; and every well-informed person knew that his wife had died in 1509,
and that he entered into Orders only after that event, receiving the red hat in 1517.

(2) PALLAVICINO ; I., 258.—SANDERS ; 32.

(3) LE GRAND ; III., 206.—BURNET ; Records, II., 20.

to publish it as the real opinion of a truly celebrated body of theologians and canonists. The document, together with similar ones which really came from the Universities of Orleans and Toulouse, was forwarded to Pope Clement; but the Pontiff most properly contemned them, since they all were founded on the supposition that the marriage of Catharine with Arthur had been consummated—a point which the queen solemnly denied, and which Henry tried vainly to prove (1). Then, on July 30, the king succeeded in inducing all the spiritual and temporal lords, and a few of the commoners, to sign, in the name of the nation, a remonstrance to his Holiness, asking what crime Henry had committed, that he should be refused what so many learned men had deemed legitimate. England, insisted this precious instrument, was threatened with the calamities of a disputed succession; and Clement declined to permit a marriage which was the sole means of preventing those miseries. On Sept. 27, the Pontiff replied to this impudent address with spirit, drawing the attention of England to the truth, that if she was menaced with a disputed succession, the danger would be simply increased by any procedures which were unjust; and that the originators of lawless measures would alone be responsible for the results. On Jan. 25, 1533, Rowland Lee, one of the royal chaplains, went through the farce of a marriage ceremony for Henry and his mistress; but owing to the prayers of King Francis, the Pontiff did not excommunicate the paramours until July 2, and then only in case they would not have separated, before the end of September. When that term had arrived, Clement prolonged it, trusting in the confident assurances of Francis that when the Pope arrived in Marseilles, whither he was about to proceed for the negotiation of a marriage between his niece and the duke d'Orleans, the son of Francis, the English monarch would announce his submission. The

(1) Cardinal Pole, a relative of Henry, being a grandson of that duke of Clarence who was put to death by his brother, Edward IV., says that Henry himself admitted the truth of Catharine's claim. Writing to Henry a letter entitled *A Defence of Ecclesiastical Unity*, he says: " *Tu ipse hoc fassus es, virginem te accepisse, et Cæsari fassus es, cui minime expediebat, si tum de divortio cogitares, hoc fateri.*" Even that virulent apostate, Peter Martyr (Vermiglio) says that the Spaniards all insisted that Catharine was a virgin when she married Henry. That the same was the common opinion in England, is shown by the fact that when she was married to Henry, Catharine was dressed in white, and wore her hair loose—observances then peculiar to the wedding of a maid. SANFORD ; 480.

French king probably believed that Henry would yield ; but the Pontiff returned to Rome unsatisfied. The climax was now at hand. On March 24, 1534, in full Consistory, all the proceedings in the momentous cause were explained by Simonetta, a deputy auditor of the *Ruota ;* and then, out of twenty-two cardinals, nineteen voted for the validity of the marriage of Henry with Catharine of Aragon, three voting for a further delay. Pope Clement now pronounced his definitive sentence in favor of Catharine ; but before the news reached England, the wretched Henry had taken his resolution to erect a Church Establishment which would recognize no other Pope than his own royal self. In the following September, Pope Clement VII. died, and Alexander Farnese ascended the papal throne as Paul III.

CHAPTER XXI.

CALVINISM.

John Cauvin, better known as Calvin, from the Latin form of his name, was born at Noyon in France in 1508. He was the son of a cooper, and like the first chief of the Reformers, his early education, remarked Florimond, was "at the expense of the Crucifix," for it was due to the charity of a pious Catholic family. His father destined him for the service of the altar, and when twelve years of age he was sent to Paris for study. In his fifteenth year he made the acquaintance of Farel, and this "lying, virulent, and ambitious soul," as Erasmus termed him, sowed the first seed of religious doubt in the young student's mind. When nineteen years old, and although not in Holy Orders, Calvin obtained a curacy, but he continued to attend lectures in ecclesiastical science. After a short stay at the University of Orleans, he studied at Bourges under the famous Italian jurist Alciato and the Lutheran Wolmar, and here he became intimate with his future biographer, Theodore Beza, styled by his admirers, "the Phœnix of his age." In 1532 Calvin returned to Paris and founded a conventicle of heresy which soon attracted the notice of the civil authorities ; and to avoid imprisonment he fled to the court of Queen Margaret of Navarre (1), already an avowed patroness of such innovators as sought her protection. The year 1535 found him at Basel, publishing his *Christian Institutions*, wherein he prescribes the Bible as the sole rule of faith. God, he says, will inspire each seeker with a knowledge of the true meaning of the text. This work made him famous, and his presence was desired by the Genevans, who had overthrown the dominion of their prince-bishop (2) and the suzerainty of the duke of Savoy in 1526, and had received the new Gospel from Bearn in 1533. Farel, the first Reformed pastor of Geneva, felt himself unequal to the task of legislating for the new church, successful though he had been in disorganization. Calvin seemed to be the man for their purpose, and the magistrates and consistory of Geneva tendered him the office of preacher and of professor of theology. He accepted in 1536, but after two years of tyranny he had so disgusted all but his immediate partisans, that his position became insecure ; and finally, when he refused to obey a decree of the synod of Bearn, ordering the use of unleavened bread at the Lord's Supper and the observance of holy days as well as Sunday, he, Farel, and Couraud were ordered to leave Geneva in three days. Calvin went to Strasbourg, where he was received by Bucer with open arms ; and here, in 1539, he married the widow of an Anabaptist. Meanwhile indescribable disorder was rampant in Geneva ; and the French partisans of Calvin—immigrating thither in greater numbers day by day—having convinced the magistrates that their idol alone could remedy the evil, he was recalled in 1541, and received absolute power to regulate ecclesiastical matters as he might deem best. From that moment, woe to all who resisted the will of Calvin, the man who, above all the other Reformers, had insisted on the right of private judg-

(1) Margaret de Valois, sister of Francis I. and widow of Charles d'Alençon, first prince of the blood and constable of France, married Henry d'Albret, king of Navarre, in 1527, and became the mother of Jane d'Albret, who married Anthony de Bourbon (lineally descended from the Count of Clermont, youngest son of St. Louis), and gave birth to Henry IV. She was addicted to religious speculation, but gave time also to labors of a lighter character, such as the *Heptameron*, written in the vein of the *Decameron* of Boccaccio, but redolent of far grosser obscenity and with none of the latter work's redeeming features.

(2) Geneva ceased to depend from the emperor when Henry V. was excommunicated by the Lateran Council in 1112, and its bishop, who swore not to violate the rights of the citizens, was also its temporal lord.

ment.   At the head of his *Institutions* he had declared that
he came to bring war, not peace; and the history of his
entire reign at Geneva justifies the assertion.   A Protestant
author of our day, whose work was published at Geneva (1),
says that " In his reformation of the Genevans, Calvin ignored
all that is good and honorable in humanity, and established
a regime of the most ferocious intolerance, of the most besotted superstitions, and of the most impious doctrines.   At
first he effected this by cunning; but he soon used force,
threatening the council with a revolt and with the vengeance
of his followers, when it tried to uphold the laws against his
usurpations.   He was adroit and profound, but after the fashion of the many little tyrants who have undermined republican government in many different countries."   This heresiarch's rule was very different from that of the prince-bish-
ops of Geneva, under whom, says the Protestant Pazy, " the
laws were mild, torture was very seldom applied, confiscation was unknown, and there was nothing like that monstrous
persecution of opinion made common by Calvin " (2).   The
amenities of polite polemics were unknown to Calvin; he
fairly exhausted the language of vituperation when addressing
his adversaries, even though they were Luther, Melancthon,
Osiander, Capmulus, Memnon, or Westphalius.   To this last
opponent, who was a zealous Lutheran, and most hostile to
any figurative view of the Eucharistic Presence, Calvin cried:
" Your school is a rotten pig-sty.   Do you hear me, you dog?
Do you understand me, you lunatic, you beast? " (3).   He
styled the members of the Council of Trent ignoramuses,
asses, hogs, fat bulls, legates of Antichrist, blatherskites,
sons of the great whore, etc."   Nor was his virulence satisfied with vituperation.   Bolsec, an apostate Carmelite, was
banished for showing that Calvin made God the Author of
sin; and the heresiarch tried to have him capitally punished
as a Pelagian and a rebel.   Gentile was condemned to death,
at his instigation.   He procured the banishment of Ochino.

(1) GALIFFE: *Genealogical Notices*, vol. III., p. 21.
(2) *Essay on the History of the Republic of Geneva*, vol. I., p. 276.
(3) The title of Calvin's last work against Westphalius, written in 1557, is interesting:
" The last warning of John Calvin to Joachim Westphalius, and if it is not heeded, Westphalius will be put where St. Paul orders us to place all heretics."

When consulted by the Genevan magistrates concerning the writings of Gruet, he urged an immediate infliction of the highest penalty; and it is to be noted that the decree ordering the search of Gruet's private papers was issued "in the name of the Father, Son, and Holy Ghost, with the gospels before our eyes." But the case of Servetus would alone suffice to illustrate this phase of the character of Calvin.

Michael of Villanova, a native of Aragon, and generally known as Michael Servetus, was born in 1509. Studying at Paris, he acquired some reputation in medicine, but soon manifested an inclination for theological speculation. In 1531 he published at Haguenau a pamphlet on the *Errors on the Trinity*, in which his brutal attacks on the dogma as a popish hallucination and a mythological chimera astounded Christendom. Having settled at Vienne in Dauphiny as a physician, he secretly issued, in 1553, his *Restoration of Christianity*, the fourth book of which contained thirty letters addressed especially to Calvin, in all of which the autocrat was severely handled. Years before, Calvin had disputed with Servetus at Lyons, and had conceived such hatred for him that in 1546 he wrote to Viret, a colleague of Farel, " If Servetus ever comes to Geneva, he will not leave it alive." Now his spies forwarded him advance sheets of the *Restoration*, and at once the ecclesiastical authorities of Vienne received a denunciation of the author, accompanied by the index and some pages of the new work. Servetus was arrested, but escaping from prison, he fled to Geneva where he naturally expected to find safety; but by order of Calvin he was seized on Aug. 13, 1553, and held for trial as a heretic. After five weeks of suspense, Servetus wrote to the council of Geneva: " Vermin are eating me alive; my underclothing is in tatters, and I have not even a shirt for a change." The magistrates would have sent him some sheets and a shirt, but Calvin objected. After three more weeks, during which Servetus vainly applied for relief for the *pauvretés* of his body (1), the judges met for deliberation. On Oct. 26, the unfortunate was notified that he had been condemned to death by slow fire. Calvin afterward thus commented on the horror with which

(1) GALIFFE; *loc. cit.*

Servetus heard his sentence : " Let not the blackguards take pride in the obstinacy of their hero, as though it were the constancy of a martyr. When he heard his fate, he manifested the stupidity of a brute. Now his eyes were fixed like those of a fool, and he drew deep sighs; then he would howl like a madman; he never ceased to bellow, after the fashion of the Spaniards, ' Mercy, mercy!'" (1). On Oct. 27, Servetus was led to the stake, and the green faggots showed him that his death was to be a lingering one. "The axe!" he cried, "the axe! Not fire, lest I lose my soul in despair! If I have sinned, it was through ignorance." But he made no retractation. From a neighboring window Calvin coolly gazed on the spectacle (2). When the "gentle" Melancthon, the "Fénelon of Lutheranism," heard of this event, he wrote to Calvin: "By putting Servetus to death the magistracy of the republic of Geneva gave a pious and memorable example to all posterity. ... I am entirely of your opinion, and I hold for certain that the matter having been conducted according to law, your magistrates acted justly in putting the blasphemer to death" (3). Calvin himself justified his course in the matter by publishing an exposition of the errors of Servetus, "together with a defense of the proposition that heretics are to be put to death." And he wrote to the marquis du Poet, grand-chamberlain of the court of Navarre, "Take good care to rid the land of these despicable rascals who excite the people against us. Such monsters should be executed like Michael Servetus the Spaniard. You may well believe that he will have no imitators in these regions." Nevertheless, Calvin could write that "lamentable indeed is the state of the Papal Church when it can be upheld only by violence;" and this he presumed to say, remarks the Protestant Castalion (4), precisely at the time " when his hands were yet dripping with

(1) *Epist. to Farel*, Oct. 29, 1553.

(2) For the whole affair of Servetus, see DE THOU, b. XII.; SPONDANUS, y. 1553, no. 14; VARILLAS, *Heresies*, vol. IV., b. XX.; LUBENIESKI, *Reform Pol.*; SLEIDAN, *Comment.*, b. XXV.; BEZA, *Life of Calvin*, y. 1553.

(3) *On Servetus—Corpus Reform.*, VIII., 523; IX., 133.—See the *Defense of Calvin*, by the Protestant Grellincourt.

4) Sebastian Castalion, a Savoyard, became involved in a dispute with Calvin concerning the merits of the former's translation of the Bible (1555). The case was tried by the Senate of Geneva. Castalion was convicted of calumny, and he was deprived of his professorial chair.

the blood of Servetus." And it is worthy of note that Calvin reserved for himself the utmost latitude of opinion regarding the Trinity, so that another reformer, Stancarus (1), ventured to thus reprove him : "What demon has prompted you, Calvin, to join Arius in declaiming against the Son of God?... You presume to worship that Antichrist of the North, the grammarian Melancthon. ... Beware, my readers, and especially you, ministers of the word, beware of the writings of Calvin! They contain impious doctrine, the blasphemies of Arianism, as though the spirit of Michael Servetus had transmigrated into the author."

The death of Calvin, if we may credit his Lutheran contemporaries, was one of despair. Schlussenberg says: "God so struck this heretic with His omnipotent hand that, despairing of salvation, and calling upon the demons, cursing and blaspheming, he miserably yielded his soul" (2). John Haren, one of Calvin's disciples, tells us that he witnessed, "with his own eyes, that miserable and horrible death" (3). Schlussenberg says that God punished the crimes of Calvin, even in this life; that He "*in virga furoris visitavit, atque horribiliter punivit ante mortis infelicis horam ... vermibus circa pudenda in aposthemate seu ulcere fœtentissimo crescentibus, ita ut nullus assistentium fœtorem amplius ferre posset*" (4). His Lutheran enemies insisted that during his life Calvin bore on his back the defaming brand which attested the unnatural immoralities of his youth. They declared that he had been convicted of sodomy by the tribunal of Noyon, and condemned to the stake; but that owing to the intercession of his bishop, the punishment was commuted to the infamous brand of the galleys. The chief authority for this accusation was Bolsec, who insisted that he had read a copy of the sentence, drawn from the records at Noyon by Berthelier, who had been sent from Geneva to investigate the charge. The Lutherans

(1) *In Calv. Inst.*—Stancarus, a native of Mantua, fleeing from Italy to avoid prosecution for heresy, became professor of Hebrew in Cracow, and afterward founded a Lutheran school at Pinczovia in 1550. Konigsberg calling him to its chair of Hebrew, he there disputed with Osiander on the mediatorship of Christ, he contending that our Lord mediated between God and man only according to His human nature, whereas Osiander taught a divine mediatorship The Polish Synods declared against the opinion of Stancarus, and after his death, his partisans became avowed Arians.

(2) *In Theol. Calv.* b. II., fol. 72·   (3) *Apud Pet. Cutzemium.*   (4) *Loc. cit.*

of that day regarded the alleged crime as indubitable (1);
and Campian says that his adversary, Whittaker, admitted
the fact, simply remarking that "Calvin had been stigmatized,
and so had St. Paul" (2). Stapleton says that the relatives
of Calvin vainly endeavored to procure the erasure of the
record which entailed such disgrace on their family (3).

The spirit of Calvin was far more bitter than that of Luther toward Catholicism, even if the ex-Augustinian's heart be
studied in his most fiery ebullitions, or in the mouthings of
his *Table Talk;* but, like all the early Reformers, he at first
affected to be a regenerator, not a destroyer. We find him
writing, in November, 1557, to the king of France: "Herein
we have arranged in simplicity a short *Confession of Faith,*
the one that we profess; and we trust that you will find it
concordant with that of the Catholic Church " (4). Afterward, however, wherever he held the upper hand, he washed
away the "abominations of the Mass and other papistical
idolatries " with the blood of the faithful ; and always in virtue of the right which, as a civil ruler, he professed to hold from
God. "The rulers, to whom God has given the sword of
authority, must not permit in their jurisdictions any blasphemy against the faith which they have received" (5). Like
the Terrorists of the first French Revolution, he often mixed
the grotesque with the frightful in his application of the extreme consequences of his self-arrogated authority ; but unlike those brutally frank homicides, he showed the grotesque
in a hypocritical zeal for at least outward virtue. He imprisoned women who allowed a tress to escape from under
their coifs ; and he prohibited the wearing of slashed stockings, "because by the windows of those stockings all sorts
of dissoluteness are encouraged " (6). But he could tolerate,
nay, absolutely approve bigamy, as in the case of the Italian
apostate Caracciolo, of whom we shall speak, when treating

---

(1) *De Calvini rarus flagitiis et Sodomiticis libidinibus, ob quas stigma Joannis Calvini dorso impressum fuit a magistratu sub quo vixit.*" *Ibi.* The Lutherans of that day
were prone to credit any report which might entail obloquy on Calvin. Thus Beza quotes
Westphale (b. 1510), superintendent of the Lutheran churches in Hamburg, as saying that
Calvin's mother was a priest's concubine.

(2) *Third Reason.*   (3) *Promptuarium.*
(4) *French Letters of Calvin* ; edit. Bonnet, vol. I., p. 152.   (5) *Ibid.,* vol. II., p. 20.
(6) *Ibid,* vol. I., p. 215.

of the attempted Protestantization of Italy. Only the iron rod was sufficient to keep in subjection those who were deceived by Calvin; so true was it, as we have observed in our chapter on the beginnings of Protestantism, that even among the most ardent of the new religionists there long subsisted an affection for the ancient faith (1). As Calvin observed, "The superstitions of Antichrist have struck such deep roots, and have been fastened so long, that they cannot be easily torn out of the hearts of men" (2). An excellent illustration of this fact is seen in the career of Renée of France, duchess of Ferrara, deeply penetrated by the Calvinistic poison, and through whom the heresiarch calculated to introduce that poison into Italy. This misguided princess had appointed an apostate friar as her private chaplain, and Protestant though she termed herself, she could not crush her belief in the Real Presence, and therefore compelled the unfortunate renegade to celebrate the Divine Sacrifice every morning in her apartments. Then there was Margaret of Valois, that mixture of mysticism and lubricity of thought, whose court was the favorite refuge of unfrocked priests, and who was apparently a fanatical Calvinist. Her faith was never completely crushed; and in 1550 she proclaimed it openly, and died with its consolations. The same happiness befell her equally fanatical husband, Henry II. d'Albret, in 1554. In fine, "there was really then a common patrimony shared by the faithful children of the Church and her wayward ones; whereas in our days the diminution of Christian dogmas in the bosom of Protestantism, now become almost an annihilation, leaves nothing positive in the struggle, Protestants cherishing only that antipathy to the Papacy which is common to all revolutionary sects" (3). The permanence of a residue of Catholic sentiment in the early Calvinists explains the facility with which many passed from the Church to the Conventicle, and then from the latter to the former. The ordinary reader is familiar with those many official changes of religion in the France of the early sixteenth century, changes made by royal decree, when entire provinces substituted one

---

(1) See p. 333. (2) *Letters*, vol. I., p. 162.
(3) SEGRETAIN ; *Sixtus V. and Henry IV.*, p. 40. Paris, 1861.

cult for the other, according to the momentary policy of the court. But if the student delves deeply into the records of those days, he will find that there were an immense number of individual apostasies and repentances in that period when questions of faith were the chief concern of men. All these reflections bring us to the conclusion that the prime seducers of the populations found an almost invincible attachment to the ancient faith in the masses; and that even those who plunged into the abyss of heresy seldom followed those dictates of conscientious conviction which guarantee a firm perseverance in the new condition. No wonder, therefore, that Calvin relied so much upon the power of force.

The system founded by Calvin was a repetition of almost all hitherto known errors; he drew upon the early Predestinationists, Donatists, Iconoclasts; upon Berengarius, the Albigenses, and the Waldenses; and upon Wycliffe, Huss, Luther, and the Anabaptists. His essential teachings may be reduced to six heads: I. Jesus Christ is not really present in the Holy Eucharist; He is received by the communicant only by faith. While Zwingle taught that the Eucharist is a mere sign of the Body and Blood of Christ, Calvin held that the Sacred Body and Blood are truly received, although only by faith. As to the Lutheran system of a Real Presence by impanation, Calvin pronounced it due to "a fascination of the devil;" and he styled its followers "eaters of human flesh," and their communion "a repast for Cyclops." According to Schaffmacher, the minister Claude, the famous adversary of Bossuet, regarded Calvin's theory as "inadmissible" (1). II. Predestination is absolute, independent of God's foreknowledge of the good or evil deeds of each person. The decree of one's salvation or of his damnation depends from the pure will of God, without any regard to one's merits or demerits. III. God gives an inamissible justice and an inamissible faith to His elect, and does not impute their sins to them. IV. Original sin so weakened the will of man, that he cannot perform any good work meritorious of salvation, nor even any act which is not in itself sinful. V. Man cannot resist concupiscence; the

(1) BOSSUET; *Var.*, b. IX., c. xxiv., xxxvii., lix., lxxxii. – FELLER; *Catech.*, vol. II., p. 268.

freedom of his will consists merely in its being exempt from coercion, but not from necessity. VI. Man is justified by faith alone, and hence good works are of no avail for salvation. The Sacraments are of value only inasmuch as they excite faith.

The followers of Calvin did not long leave his dogmas unchanged. Concerning the Eucharist, the ideas of Zwingle soon became general. But the greatest discontent arose from the horrible nature of the Calvinian idea of predestination. The theory that Christ died only for the predestined, also formed matter for discussion. Nor did the notion of the irresistibility of grace meet with universal acclamation. Finally, the doctrine of the inamissibility of grace found many enemies. Arminius, a minister of Amsterdam, attacked the Calvinian teachings on all these points; while Gomar, a professor at Groningen, assumed the championship of the rigidists. After many years of violent disputation, the Calvinists of the Low Countries were on the verge of civil war, when the Synod of Dordrecht, in 1619, decided against the Arminians or Remonstrants. At this convention, which was composed of deputies from all the Calvinist consistories except the French, the more rigid of the Gomarists tried in vain to obtain a sanction of their opinions. Like Calvin, these held that God, from all eternity, had predestined some men to heaven, and some to hell; that God, therefore, had so determined the fall of Adam, and had so predisposed events, that Adam was obliged to sin. They were called *supralapsarii*, because they supposed a predestination before the fall, *ante* or *supra lapsum*. Others, who were styled *infralapsarii*, held that predestination was accorded *infra lapsum*; that is, that God did not positively predetermine the fall of Adam, but merely permitted it; that then the human race having become a mass of perdition, God resolved to save a certain number of men, while allowing the rest to remain in their miserable condition, and refusing them the graces necessary for salvation. The *infralapsarii* triumphed at Dordrecht, thanks principally to the English deputies; nevertheless four provinces of Holland refused to subscribe to the decrees, and in the churches of Geneva, Brandenburg, and Bremen,

Arminianism prevailed. The Calvinists of France received the decrees in a national synod of their religionists held at Charenton in 1623. Mosheim shows that the Synod of Dordrecht adopted the doctrine of Calvin which makes God the Author of sin; that the articles it condemned were held by the Lutherans and most Anglicans; and that even the condemnation was couched in such ambiguous terms, that it could be variously interpreted.

CHAPTER XXII.

THE ATTEMPTED PROTESTANTIZATION OF FRANCE.

Just as in Germany the Reformation furnished a pretext for a revolt of certain princes against the emperor, so in France the introduction of the new religion was an occasion for aggressive movements of the feudal nobility against the king. But to the honor of French Protestants be it remembered that in the Land of the Lilies the stealing of Church property played but a minor part in the struggle between the ancient and the new religion; whereas for Frederick and Maurice of Saxony, for Henry VIII. and the English nobles, and for Gustavus Vasa and his poverty-stricken companions in their kingdom of snow, the pillage of ecclesiastical possessions was the chief medium through which the beauties of the New Gospel were discerned. This exemption of the French nobles from the stain of rapacious cupidity, even while they committed acts of crime and of stupendous folly during their temporary religious aberration, was very unfavorable to a permanent substitution of the bands of Geneva for the Catholic mitre. Nor was the general situation of France such as to promise a profitable field for the labors of a heresiarch. Since the baptism of Clovis by St. Remy, nearly eleven centuries before the Calvinistic irruption, Catholicism had been associated with all of the grandest and worthiest emotions of the French nature; the union of Rome and France had been cemented by every possible exertion of intellect, heart, and imagination; in the eyes of all Europe the people of France had come to be regarded as, if it be permitted to use such a term, the special pet of Heaven—so much so, that in 1556, just at the time when the Calvinists were essaying their favorite scheme of slaughter in the name of a sweeter and purer faith than that of Rome, the keen observer of men and things, Charles V., who knew no such thing as enthusiasm, pronounced his deliberate opinion: "No people have so often done what ought to destroy them as the French; but they always recover, because they are specially protected by God." Neither the king nor the people of France had any great temptation to turn their backs to that Church by whose means had been produced the *Gesta Dei per Francos*—the action of God through the visible arm of the Franks. For the monarch, whose proudest title was that of Most Christian King (1), there was no yearning for a secularization of the goods of the Church; that transformation had been pretty well effected by the Concordat of 1516. As to the people, they needed not

(1) The antiquity of the title " Most Christian King," borne by the French kings, has been the subject of much discussion ; many contending that the first monarch to bear the title as a special prerogative was Louis XI., to whom it was accorded by Pope Paul II. in 1459. This opinion was held by the great Benedictine writer, Mabillon in his *Diplomatics* (y. 1704) ; by the Jesuit historian, Daniel, in his *History of France* (y. 1713) ; and by Henault in his *Chronology* (y. 1744). Daniel seemed to have proved his side of the question quite conclusively ; but in 1720 the Abbé de Camps showed that the famous title had been borne by all the French monarchs since the days of Clovis. Griffet gave a new edition of Daniel's work in 1755, and profiting by the researches of De Camps, assigned the origin of the title to the reign of Charles V. (1337–80). In 1760, the learned Bonamy demonstrated to the satisfaction of the Academy of Inscriptions that the title was accorded to King Pepin, the father of Charlemagne. After a careful consideration of all these arguments, it appears to us that the title of Most Christian King was not only recognized by the Popes as a special prerogative of the French kings, long before the days of Louis XI., but was transmitted by the first Christian king of the Franks as part of that inheritance of faith and devotion to the Church which was guarded by his successors, almost without exception, as their most precious possession. In the first place, Pope Paul II., who is represented as according, for the first time, the title of Most Christian King to Louis XI., acknowledged in a letter to Charles VII., the father of Louis XI. (*Epist*. 385), that the French sovereigns held the famous title by heredity, and because of their constant defence of the Holy See. And Louis XI. himself, in his *Institution* drawn up at Amboise in 1482 for the guidance of his successor, declares the same fact : "Considering that God our Creator has given to us such great graces ; that He has been pleased to constitute us the king of the most notable nation on earth, this kingdom of France, many of whose sovereigns, our predecessors, have been so great, virtuous, and valiant, that they have acquired the name of Most Christian Kings, etc." Secondly, St. Avitus, a contemporary of Clovis, tells us (See Ruinart's *Preface to St. Greg. Tur.*, No. 18) that there was no province in the West that did not owe its safety to the Franks ; alluding, of course, to the combats of the first successors of Clovis against the Arians and the pagans. When Clovis was baptized, he was the sole veritable Catholic king in Europe, and hence would properly be addressed as Most Christian. Therefore it is that we find Romanus, general of the Roman armies in Italy, addressing King Childebert as " your Christianity—*Christianitas vestra*," in the same sense as that of our phrase, " your Majesty." Therefore also we find the

to blush for their clergy; abuses there sometimes were in
the French ecclesiastical body, but the finger of scorn was
not necessarily pointed at the bishops, as in the cases of the
German prelates whom Luther with but too much reason denounced. At that time a De Retz or a Rohan was impossible
in the French episcopacy; such scandals were to be seen only
when many years of experience of the Concordat of 1516 had
demonstrated that it was unwise to entrust a king with nominations to the crozier. Nor were the populations of France
attracted by the moral system proposed by Calvin; real austerity was sufficiently repugnant to them, but a fantastic
prudery which verged upon hypocrisy was unendurable.
But if neither monarch nor people were naturally well-dis-
posed toward the religious innovators of the time, the minor
nobles of the provinces, ever envious of the nobles of the
court, often felt an inclination for novelties, and many thought
that a change in religion might work a change in political
forms—a recovery, in fine, of what feudalism had lost under
Louis XI. and Francis I. Reflection on this disposition of
the nobles, especially those of the South, who rushed to the

same language in the letters of the emperor Mauritius, to Childebert, and in those of Pope St.
Gregory I. to the kings, Thierry and Theodebert, sons of Childebert II. Thirdly, even in the
time of Charles V. of France, to whose reign rather than that of Louis XI. Griffet would ascribe the origin of the glorious title, we find Raoul de Presles (in his *Prologue to St. Augustine's City of God*) saying to Charles V : "You are and ought to be the sole chief protector of the Church, just as your predecessors were ; and this is held by the Holy See of Rome,
which has been accustomed to address you *and your predecessors* as Most Christian Princes." Fourthly, when the emperor Frederick III. wrote to Charles VII. about a projected
Crusade, he admitted that the title had belonged to the French monarchs as an inheritance,
at least from the time of the first Holy Wars. Fifthly, Pius II., predecessor of Paul II.,
writes to Charles VII. that the monarch "has inherited the name of Most Christian from his
ancestors" (See the *Glossary* of Ducange, at word *Christianitas*). And the same Pontiff
says that this title has been an ornament of the French monarchs *per longissimam tempo-
rum seriem* ; and that it has been accorded, *consensu populorum, gentium, nationumque.*
It is true, and also very strange, that in spite of these declarations of his immediate predecessor, Paul II. at first told Cousinot, the ambassador of Louis XI., that the Popes were not
accustomed to term the French monarchs Most Christian Kings ; but we must remember
that the Pontiff was just then very angry with Louis on account of that prince's severity
toward the traitor, Cardinal de la Balue. However, Paul II. did agree to style the monarch
in the usual fashion ; though he gave no Bull confirmatory of the long possessed title. Griffet seems to imply that this Bull was expedited, when he says that "we must regard this decision of Pope Paul II. as marking the remarkable epoch when the title of Most Christian was
assured to our kings by a juridical act which undoubtedly gave to the already established
usage a degree of authenticity which it had not yet possessed." If there had been any formal Bull issued in the premises by Paul II., Alexander VI. would scarcely have tried to deprive Charles VIII. of the title, in order to confer it upon Ferdinand of Spain, giving instead
of it the style of Catholic to the Spanish sovereign, only because the Sacred College protested against the innovation. See the *Memoires* of Commines, b. VIII., ch. xvii.

standard of Condé with the cry that they all were kings, made Montaigne say of them: "All the leaders made a parade of religion; but they were influenced more by ambition." Thus was formed a clandestine religious faction, which remained clandestine until the minority of Charles IX. and the Machiavellian policy of Catharine dei Medici allowed it to manifest itself in its true colors.

Luther, Melancthon, and Zwingle discerned an excellent opportunity for the introduction of their errors into France, when it became known that Francis I. accorded a hearty welcome to all foreigners who could contribute, by their learning, to the intellectual improvement of his subjects. All three sent most specious letters to the monarch, and recommended to his protection many of the humanists whom they had imbued with their doctrinal notions. By sheer force of impudence these spouters of Greek and of a little Hebrew impressed many with the idea that they were prodigies of learning; in Italy they would have been appreciated at their true value They soon assumed oracular airs, giving new interpretations to both the New and the Old Testament, accommodating numberless passages to the theories of the Reformers; always insisting that their point of view was strictly concordant with the Greek and Hebrew texts, though perhaps opposed by the Latin Vulgate, which they affected to despise. From the year 1535 the works of Calvin spread throughout France, and he soon came to be known as the French Luther. In regard to the new doctrines Francis I. was severe or tolerant, according as he was, for the moment, under the influence of his mother, Louisa of Savoy, or under that of his sister, Margaret of Valois. This latter princess, whom Francis loved most tenderly, who had been married to the duke d'Alençon, and afterward to the king of Navarre, Henry d'Albret, was addicted, as we have already observed, not only to poetry of a worse than light vein, but to a superficial investigation of religious mysteries which she mistook for profound theological study. Such a woman was an easy victim to the wiles of the Calvinists. By dint of flattery of her success in penetrating mysteries which had defied a Thomas of Aquino, and by dedicating to her some of their works which they presented to her in superb bindings (1), they filled her with a temporary aversion for many of the practices of the Catholic religion. Margaret did penance, eventually, for these aberrations; but her daughter, Jeanne d'Albret, who married Anthony de Bourbon, and became mother of the future Henry IV., plunged into the depths of heresy, and never emerged. A brief sketch of the work of this princess in the establishment of the Reformation in Bearn will serve to illustrate the methods of all the Calvinist leaders in France. Jules Bonnet, in his edition of the *French Letters* of Calvin (2), naively writes : " Docile to the counsels of Calvin, and not at all alarmed by the anathemas of Rome or by the menaces of Spain, Jeanne d'Albret had *courageously* undertaken the work of the Reformation in her states. She abolished the worship of images, interdicted public processions, and changed the churches into Protestant temples. So thorough a revolution could not be accomplished without great difficulty ; but the genius of the queen triumphed." Each word of this eulogy shows the animus of the writer no less than it recalls, to a mind which is acquainted with the history of Bearn, a number of atrocious massacres in the prostituted name of religion, and one of the most tyrannical codes of laws ever invented by a despot. " It would seem that toleration execrates princes who, like Philip II., appeal to force for the preservation of a nation's religion from the attacks of foreigners and the preachers of heresy ; but that it can discern only courage and genius in sovereigns who, like Jeanne d'Albret and her odious model, Elizabeth of England, violently change the religion of their subjects in accord with their own caprices "(3). During the lifetime of her husband, Anthony de Bourbon, although he favored the Reformation, Jeanne merely prepared the way for future triumph over Rome ; contenting herself with exhortations to the priests to marry, and with an imposition of a tax on the clergy for the support of the Protestant preachers. But when Anthony died,

(1) Such as *The Pure Gospel*, *On Adoration in Spirit and in Truth*, *The Faith Detached from Superstition*.

(2) Paris, 1854. This author, one of the most fervid of modern professors of toleration, was Secretary to the Society of the History of Protestantism.

(3) SEGRETAIN ; *loc. cit.*

in 1562, she openly participated in the Calvinistic Lord's Supper, and instantly entered on her never-interrupted course of persecution. All the cathedrals were pillaged; and although their walls were allowed to remain, and a semblance of divine service continued to be performed, their Chapters were forced to admit Calvinist ministers to beneficed stalls in their desecrated choirs. The sons of St. Dominic were chased from their convent in Orthez, and the building was turned into a nursery for future preachers of the Gospel of Liberty. The estates of Bearn vainly protested against these and many similar measures; the queen did indeed defer sufficiently to the energetic clamors of her subjects to issue, in 1563, an Edict of Toleration, but by it the Catholics were prohibited to restore their dilapidated temples or to erect new ones. During the journey of Charles IX. through her Bearnese Majesty's dominions in 1564, the French court was so horrified by the desolation on every side, that Jeanne agreed to allow full liberty to the Catholics in the district of Nérac; but in 1569 she promulgated an edict by which she decreed the total and immediate abolition of the Catholic religion throughout the kingdom of Navarre. A few months before the publication of this drastic document, Jeanne having perceived that her people manifested an inclination to throw off her yoke, she had requested and received from Elizabeth of England a subsidy of 100,000 golden scudi, ten cannons, and a large quantity of munitions of war. Of course this appeal to a foreign power was regarded by Charles IX. as a violation of his rights as suzerain of Navarre; and he ordered the viscount de la Terride to seize the dominions of the rebel queen. Therefore it was that the Navarrese, having accepted the protectorate of France with enthusiasm, heard, in Nov., 1569, that thereafter the public preaching of heresy was prohibited. But Montgommery invaded the land, captured the viscount at Orthez, and after committing enormous excesses, proclaimed the supremacy of the Reformation. By order of Montgommery, the most illustrious of the Catholic nobles of Bearn, in violation of a capitulation which had guaranteed their lives, were massacred.

It is well to note the provisions of the Edict whereby

Jeanne d'Albret merited the homage of Protestant publicists—a homage which is extended to her memory to-day by nearly all heterodox historians, and precisely because of an Edict which served as type for Protestant legislation wherever Protestantism triumphed. Having been informed of the success of Montgommery in Bearn, the royal zealot ordered Arros and Montamat to publish the following articles. I. "The queen orders that the word be announced by those who, having been called by God, are alone in possession of a legitimate vocation; and to this effect she annuls, quashes, banishes, and proscribes all the practices of the Roman Church, and without exception: The Mass, vespers, processions, litanies, vigils, feasts, painted or sculptured images, luminaries, etc." II. "She wishes that the rural oratories, sites of superstitious follies, and also all the altars and every reredos in each and every city and village, be razed and demolished, the stone and wood to be converted to useful purposes." III. "She commands all the inhabitants, be they who they may, to attend at all the preachings and instructions delivered by the ministers of the word of God. Those who reside where these services are held, must assist at them whenever they are performed; and they who live at a distance, must come to them at least every Sunday." IV. "She commands that all the inhabitants, both they who have made public profession of the Reformed Faith, and they who have not, hold themselves subject to the authority of the Cousistories; and all are obliged to present themselves before those Consistories, at the first requisition, there to receive the proper instructions, corrections, or reprimands." Perhaps the reader may think that the unfortunate Catholics were still at liberty to practise, in the quiet of their own homes, such rites of their faith as laymen could perform, when their priests had all been massacred or banished. But this female Protestant Pope would not allow to her Catholic subjects even the consolation of pouring the waters of regeneration on their own offspring; they were forced to submit to the abhorred ministrations of apostates. V. "Since the Reformed Church recognizes Baptism as that Sacrament which was established for the reception of the marks of a remission of sin (*sic*), and since it is a duty for parents to present their children to Holy Church for baptism, and since, nevertheless, a very large number refuse to do so, pretending themselves to administer this Sacrament ; therefore the queen prohibits all parents, matrons, and others, to baptize, under the pain of punishments which she will soon provide." Another article pronounces all marriages invalid which were not "blessed" by a Protestant preacher. "If any persons make reciprocal promises of marriage, they are prohibited to live conjugally, until they have announced such promises, and receive the blessing of the Reformed Church ; under pain of punishment as concubinaries." In another article we read a law like that which was enforced at that time, and for centuries afterward, in the dominions of his Britannic Majesty, with such success that certain youthful ears, still in service, used to tingle with Protestant declamations about Papistical ignorance. It was ordered that in all her Navarrese Majesty's dominions, no one should be allowed to teach, either the young or the old, unless he was a professed member of the new Church. Finally, for our limits warn us not to say too much about this pioneer of "the religion" in France, we find a confirmation of a remark which we have already made concerning the facility with which certain parties fluctuated between the old and the new "systems." In one of the last clauses of this memorable Edict of the precious Jeanne d'Albret, we read : "And since, through the suggestion of the Evil Spirit, many persons have withdrawn from the Church, after having received her teachings, it is ordered that they shall be chastised by the magistrates, forasmuch as they are scandalous persons, rebels, and disturbers of the Church." And this authentic testimony to the sweetness of the Protestant sway ends with a prohibition to all priests and religious, "without the permission of her Majesty," to enter the country ; but it is declared that this consent will be accorded, "if said priests and religious will agree to conduct themselves like decent persons, and like fearers of God, ranging themselves on the side of the Church and its discipline." Such were the means by which Protestantism tried to obtain a foothold in France. It is absurd to attempt to justify them by adducing the presumedly similar conduct of the Spanish kings, especially Philip II., in their repulsion of heresy from the Catholic soil of their country. We admit that the Spaniards defended the integrity of the Christian faith with a severity which was sometimes excessive; but they exercised their power in accordance with the will of the entire nation, protecting it from the assaults of a few fanatical and unpatriotic theorists. In France, an audacious minority used violence to transform the faith of an entire nation, and after a partial success, it legalized its crime. We read much about Catholic retaliations, and it cannot be denied that when a civil war is accentuated by religious animosity, the ferocity of the human animal assumes terrible proportions. But the cold fact remains, that the Catholics of France resisted an invasion of their rights, and that it was only by oppression and by the vacillation of their monarchs that their adversaries succeeded in imposing, for a time, religious novelties upon them.

It is certain, however, that France was less unanimous than Spain in her devotion to the faith, and that the French clergy of the sixteenth century were more apt than the Spanish to seek inspiration in the royal court, rather than in the counsels of Rome. While all the more intimate elements of the national life—the people, the bourgeoisie, and the religious orders, organized to defend the integrity of the deposit of faith; a portion of the French nobility and of the episcopacy yielded to the attractions of the worst characteristic of the Renaissance, and became, for a time, victims of the Calvinist wiles. And indeed, for a considerable space of time, few Frenchmen perceived that the very existence of the Church was imperilled by the Reformers. Hence it was that Francis I. and Henry II., although passionately attached to the faith, aided Protestantism in Germany, realizing its disintegrating properties, while they at least frowned on it at home; and it is painful to a French Catholic to be obliged to admit that French monarchs were so determined to reduce the power of the House of Austria–Spain, that they threw themselves into the arms of the foes of Charles V. By the victory of Muhlberg, April 15, 1547, the emperor had reduced to a minimum the influence of the innovators in Germany, and Calvin himself had regarded his cause as lost. The French king did not realize that all means are not licit, even though they may tend to ruin an enemy. "He did not perceive that in order to crush a rival, he was precipitating the entire Christian body into the revolutionary unknown; and we know by what diversion, favorable to the heretical princes, our arms restored their fallen fortunes, and forced Charles V. to enter on that path of negotiations and compromises which was to undermine the civilization of Europe" (1). But if the foreign policy of the French court, in the matter of rising Protestantism, was unfortunate, its policy at home was unconnected and inconsequent for good. Even while it sent heretics to the scaffold, it allowed Marot, one of the most ribald of poets, to popularize Calvinistic ideas in his translation of the Psalms; and it became quite the fashion, among the young nobles, to sing the sermon-chants of the poet-valet. There is much talk about the repressive legislation which Francis I. and Henry II. enacted to combat the audacity of the Protestants; but while the language of the edicts was severe, they were often neutralized by suspensory decrees. In fact, during the first period of French Protestantism, the parliaments, especially that of Paris, more or less connived at the efforts of the innovators; for the French magistrates, though Catholic at heart, were still much influenced by the prejudices which the Council of Basel had entailed upon their predecessors, and the warmth of their affection for the Holy See had been greatly diminished. Only when, thanks to this very complicity and to the capriciousness of the court, the sectarians had become powerful; and when it became evident that there was not a mere question of some half-schism such as gratified parliamentary Gallicanism; did the great French courts of justice experience a Catholic reaction. The pressure of the national sentiment induced the parliaments to take a firm stand against heresy; and when the famous chancellor, L'Hopital, endeavored to force upon them the ordonnance of Orleans, which proposed the revival of the *Pragmatic Sanction* (2) as a remedy for religious dissension, he en-

(1) SEGRETAIN; *loc. cit.*, p. 58.

(2) See page 170 of this volume.

countered an almost invincible opposition. And now for a
brief notice of this celebrated man, both because he is an excellent illustration of the uncertain conscience of the magistracy during the debut of the Reformation in France, and
because all Protestant and many Catholic (1) publicists regard him as a type of integrity, and a marvellous instance of
moderation, ignoring the fact that he represents that system
of double dealing which precipitated his country into anarchy, and which necessarily led to the Massacre of St. Bartholomew's Day, and nearly ruined Catholicism in France (2).

Among the railleries to which Beza, the Calvinist theologian, was addicted, and sometimes happily, was his representation of L'Hopital holding a torch behind his back, the
chancellor having been afflicted with a constant dread of
looking straight at a truth. Michel de L'Hopital, born in 1507,
became an auditor of the Roman *Ruota* in 1524, counsellor
to the parliament of Paris in 1537, envoy to the Council of
Trent in 1547, master of requests in 1553, president of the
chamber of accounts in 1554, and chancellor of France in
1560. At best an equivocal Catholic, he obtained the favor
of the court for the Protestants, procured authorizations for
Protestant assemblies outside the cities, and applied the famous Edicts of Pacification. When he found that the influence of the Guises predominated, he withdrew from the court
in 1568 ; but he retained his chancellorship until six weeks
before his death, which occurred in 1573. If his attempt to
prove, at the Colloquy of Poissy, that the Calvinistic tenets
were not heretical ; if his constant cession to the Huguenot
demands, when he could yield without compromising himself ; if his long course of defending contrary doctrines at the
same time ; if these constitute honesty, impartiality, and
moderation ; then L'Hopital deserves the praise which the
modern French bourgeoisie accord to him, but which his

(1) For instance, Pellissier, in his excellent work, *The Sixteenth Century*, p. 230. Paris,
1887.

(2) Dufey, in his edition of the *Complete Works of L'Hopital* (Paris, 1824), tries indus-
triously to show the disinterestedness of his hero, and also to prove that he held the Barthe-
lemy in such horror that he could not restrain himself from assuming a severe attitude
toward Charles IX. But in all the letters which this disinterested man wrote to the king and
queen, after the massacre, there is scarcely else than a continued reiteration of requests for
offices and other favors.

contemporaries of that class refused him. He acquired the ill will of the Catholics by trying to abolish religious confraternities; but he countersigned the Edict of Romorantin, which, by its reservation of all cases of heresy to the ecclesiastical tribunals, was tantamount to an establishment of the Inquisition in France. Notwithstanding this piece of diplomacy, so repugnant to all the theories of modern toleration-ists, these gentry style L'Hopital an apostle of religious liberty. It is interesting to note that the chancellor denounced as a "seditious rabble, without God, and bent on confusion and pillage" those very Huguenots whom he so often favored, and whom our modern liberals applaud as so many lamb-like innocents, seeking only for permission to adore the Lord in spirit and in truth (1). Certainly our Protestant friends are very generous to L'Hopital. "His memory is more cherished in our day, because he is an exact personification of that absence of principles which hides itself under the name of moderation, of that undulating conduct which is termed prudence, of that yearning for novelty and that blind hatred of tradition which our day calls a love of progress; all of which have become characteristics of a statesman in a society which has neither compass nor helm. In fine, L'Hopital, distinguished as a jurisconsult, a magistrate ever attentive to his functions, preserving the dignity of the judges of that period, moderate in his desires without neglecting to secure his fortune, was a minister without elevated ideas, deplorably feeble and indecisive, hostile to the Church in intention rather than in fact, and capable only of exasperating the national Catholic sentiment, while affecting an indifference which his contemporaries did not profess. L'Hopital is a man of straw for those enemies of Catholicism who wish to hide their hatred under the cloak of a pretended impartiality, and under the appearance of a false wisdom which is simply a paralysis of reason" (2).

The French prelates held numerous Councils to oppose the

---

(1) "Y a esdictes compagnies séditieuses force bannis et canailles, qui tous se couvrent du manteau de la religion. Si est-ce qu'ils ne sont luthériens, mais plustot sans Dieu; ne veulent vivre dans leurs maisons ne hors, *sub legibus*, mais à la force. Quelle esperance peult-on avoir de telles gens, aultre que de confusion et de pillerie?"

(2) SEGRETAIN; *loc. cit.*, p. 69.

Calvinistic invasion, and the Universities proscribed heretical books. The parliaments passed many sentences of death, the kings issued many decrees ; but the contagion established itself firmly in nearly every province of the kingdom, and in 1559 Paris beheld a " National Synod of the Reformed Churches of France." Here a small number of preachers, without authority and mission, and in violation of the lauded principle of " freedom of examination," presumed to decree, for all their fellow-rebels against the Church, a uniformity of doctrine which their followers would not and, if consistent, could not, allow them to enforce. But this parody of Catholic Councils failed, as its members, unless blind, must have foreseen that it would fail, to end the divisions of the Protestant Babel. "The *œuvre constitutionelle* of the Synod of 1559 could not unite churches which were essentially free and independent, nor determine a belief which was necessarily variable, being founded on the individual interpretation of Scripture by each person. Therefore it was soon ignored by the Protestants ; one of the ministers termed it ' a paper Pope, the worst of all Popes ' " (1). In this same year, 1559, at Ferté-sous-Jouarre, after a " doctoral decision" by all the ministers of Germany, France, and Geneva, the Calvinists entered into a conspiracy for the violent abolition of Catholicism throughout France, to be begun with the murder of all the family of Guise, and according to some authors, with that of the entire royal family. However, the plot was discovered by the duke of Guise, and frustrated at Amboise. At this time, the two powerful families of Guise and Montmorency shared all the honors and authority which the court could bestow. Several of the Montmorencies embraced " the religion," as the Calvinists designated their sect, at an early period of its existence—Louise, sister of the famous constable, and married to Gaspard de Coligny, lord of Chatillon ; her three sons, the admiral Coligny, the colonel-general d'Andelot, and the cardinal Odet de Chatillon, bishop of Beauvais. The Calvinists could also boast of the accession

(1) *Pastoral Letter of the Bishop of Nimes to the Protestants of Gard.* 1859.—The egregious failure of this Protestant Council did not prevent the Protestants of France from celebrating, with high-flown declamation and other noise, its third centennial

to their party of the prince de Condé, who became the commander of the Huguenot forces (1). Francis, duke of Guise, opposed this triumvirate with a Catholic one, of which the other members were Anne de Montmorency, uncle of Coligny, and the marshal de Saint-André. This triumvirate took for its device : " One faith, one law, one king." The queen, Catharine dei Medici, indoctrinated in the principles of Machiavelli, now favored one of these parties, then another, according as either became too powerful. Her policy served merely to foment their discord ; personal hate, political ambition, and fanaticism, were all confusedly mingled by both factions ; and this reflection leads us to note the absurdity of which so many writers are guilty when they apply the term " war of religion," to every hostility of those days between the orthodox and heretics, and thus make religion responsible for the consequent effusion of blood. The holy name of religion, well observes M. de Falloux (2), whether used in attack or defence, was frequently only a war-cry, well adapted to rally the masses and to captivate their confidence.

On the Ash Wednesday of 1562 the duke de Guise was at Vassy, in Champagne, and with a number of retainers assisted at Mass in the parish church. During the sacrifice a great noise of psalm-singing in a neighboring farm-house disturbed the worshippers, and the duke sent to the Huguenots a request for them to be quiet for a quarter of an hour. The messengers were received with insults, and the psalms were vociferated with more energy. Then the indignant Guisards attempted force, and the duke rushed to the spot to preserve peace. Scarcely had he arrived at the door of the farm-house when a heavy stone struck his face, and then, despite his commands, his followers attacked the Huguenots, killing, says the Protestant La Popelinière, forty-two. To his last day Guise insisted that this affair was fortuitous ; and that the slaughter was against his will is admitted by the Huguenot sympathizer De Thou, by the Protestant La Popelinière,

(1) According to Berault-Bercastel, this word is derived from the German *eidgenossen*, signifying "confederated." Some contend that the French innovators assumed this name as the pretended champions of the royal race of Hugues Capet, against the " Lorrains-Guisards," or " Charlins," descendants of Charles of Lorraine.

(2) *Life of St. Pius V.*, Paris, 1841.

and by Marcantonio Barbaro, Venetian ambassador at Paris, in his *Relation* to his government for 1565 (1). Throughout the kingdom the Calvinists now demanded vengeance for this massacre; and to this day Protestant polemics urge, in palliation of the atrocities committed by the Huguenots, that those horrors were mere retaliations for the Catholic persecutions initiated at Vassy. But the excesses of the Calvinists had begun before this event. On December 21, 1561, they had driven the bishop, clergy, and nuns from Nimes, had burnt the holy images in the cathedral, and had turned the edifice into a meeting-house. On December 27th they had destroyed the furniture of the church of St. Medard at Paris, and had tried to burn to death such Catholics as had fled to the belfry. They had dragged thirty-four citizens from the sanctuary, and had exposed them to the outrages of the mob, as we learn from the *Journal* of the minister Deyron, given by Menard in his *History of Nimes*, and also from Mezeray's *Chronological Abridgment*. On the return of Guise to Paris, the citizens received him with enthusiasm; therefore the jealous Catharine regarded the Huguenot complaints with favor, even resolving to entrust the care of the young king, Charles IX., to those sectarians. She wrote from Fontainebleau to Condé: "Come, and save mother and child!" Condé and Coligny wished to profit by the invitation; but, the design transpiring, the Parisians rushed to arms, and by their aid Guise seized the person of the royal child, bidding the mother go whither she pleased. One day too late the Condean troops arrived at Fontainebleau, and then, realizing that he had gone too far to recede, the prince prepared for civil war, openly enlisted men against his sovereign, made alliances with England and other powers, seized Orleans, Rouen, Bourges, Tours, Grenoble, and many minor towns. The first civil war (1562–63) produced monsters of cruelty on both sides. The Huguenot baron des Andrets put Auvergne, the Forez, the Lyonnais, Dauphiny, and Provence to fire and sword, and in order to deaden their sensibilities literally bathed his own children in Catholic blood.

(1) In the *Relations of the Venetian Ambassadors Concerning the Affairs of* France Paris, 1838.

One of these boys, Blaise de Montluc, lived to make the Huguenots curse the lessons they had given to him; for he became a Catholic, and was as savage toward them as his parent had been in regard to the Papists. This war terminated with the assassination of Duke Francis by a Huguenot named Poltrot, who died accusing Coligny as his instigator; and Coligny could never repel this accusation. Bossuet holds that when the admiral was informed of Poltrot's design, he gave him 120 scudi to enable him to prosecute it and escape. Certainly, in a letter to Catharine, Coligny admitted that "for the last five or six months he did not strongly" oppose the killing of Guise, and he gave as a reason for said implicit compliance that certain persons had tried to kill himself; and in another letter to Catharine he spoke of the death of the duke as "the greatest benefit that could accrue to the kingdom and to the Church of God, and a personal advantage to the sovereign and to the whole family of Coligny." After the murder of Francis de Guise, Catharine made every effort to secure peace, and in 1563 the Edict of Amboise conferred many privileges on the Huguenots, but did not satisfy them. The free exercise of Calvinistic worship was allowed to the lords high justiciary in their jurisdictions; the same was permitted to the nobles in their houses; the bourgeois could practice Calvinism in one city in each *bailliage;* and wherever the Huguenots were in the majority their worship was permitted. Several years previously Catharine had asked Pope Pius IV. for concessions to the Protestants, then increasing in number. For instance, she requested the abolition of images, the suppression of the exorcism and of the use of the priest's saliva in baptism; she asked for the Communion under both species for the laity, for a simplification of the ceremonies of the Mass, for the use of the vernacular in the Liturgy: "hoping thereby," she said, "to unite the two Churches." Then the Colloquy of Poissy was held, and here Peter Martyr (Vermiglio) and Theodore Beza were summoned by the Navarrese monarch to combat the cardinal of Lorraine and Claude Despense; but this dispute, like so many others, availed nothing. The Guisards now excited the ambition of the Navarrese by a promise of the restoration of his lost kingdom; therefore he joined the triumvirate of his former enemies, who permeated the court and neutralized the influence of the queen. Resolved to rule at all hazards, the Medicean diplomat made overtures to Condé, and by the advice of L'Hopital allowed the Protestants to freely exercise their form of worship if they did not disturb Catholic devotions.

In 1567, encouraged, admits Sismondi, by the rebellion of the Scotch Calvinists against Queen Mary, the French Huguenots again tried to seize the person of their young king while he was sojourning at Meaux. Foiled in this attempt, they besieged their sovereign in his capital, but were defeated in a bloody contest under the walls, and compelled to a truce of six months. In 1568 the second civil war began. The historian, De Thou, most partial to the Huguenots, admits that their atrocities surpassed everything hitherto experienced during these terrible times (1). Their bloody onslaughts were directed especially against priests and nuns; the savage De Briquemaut wore a necklace made of the ears of priests whom he had murdered. The exasperated Catholics retaliated, and France became a scene of carnage. Finally, when Condé had perished, and the Huguenots had been nearly crushed, the Machiavellian daughter of the Medici signed, in 1570, a treaty favorable to the Protestants. A general amnesty was proclaimed: the rebels were allowed freedom of worship; their confiscated property was restored; they received the privilege of appointing six judges in the parliaments: and La Rochelle, Montauban, Cognac, and La Charitè sur Loire were accorded them as "cities of safety," with the right of naming the governors and controlling the garrisons. But Charles IX., ever remembering the attempt at Meaux, did not heartily approve of these concessions; hence Coligny sought to conciliate the young monarch, obtaining very soon such an influence that the queen-mother feared for her own. She hearkened to Henry de Guise, who yearned to revenge his father's murder on the reputed assassin. Coligny

(1) The contemporary poet, Ronsard, asks:

> " Et quoy ! bruler maisons, piller et brigander,
> Tuer, assassiner, par force commander,
> N'obéir plus aux rois, amasser des armées,
> Appelez-vous cela Eglises réformées ? "

was only slightly wounded, and Catharine rushed to her son, declaring that the Huguenots were on the eve of open revolt, and that they had sworn the death of his Majesty. These charges were rendered probable by the past conduct of the sectarians and by the open threats of their leaders; therefore Charles determined to forestall his enemies, and on August 24, 1572, the massacre of St. Bartholomew's Day, of which we shall treat in an apposite chapter, blighted the fair fame of France.

Henry III., the last of the Valois, was the worst of a bad race; an object of disgust and almost universal contempt, religion was dishonored by his routine of processions and balls, masquerades and penances. Naturally the court reflected, to a great extent, the habits of the sovereign; and it was extremely delicate and extremely corrupt, sickening the good by its mixture of libertinage with an appearance of religious mysticism. In an endeavor to procure rest for his sorely-tried kingdom, Henry, always partial to heresy, accorded to the Calvinists, in 1576, an edict more favorable than any preceding one; allowing the public exercise of their worship, granting them full representation in each parliament, and decreeing that such priests and nuns, etc., as had married, were not to be disturbed, while their children were to be held as legitimate. Nevertheless, the Calvinists now constituted themselves into a regular federation, bound by oath to "a more intimate union, association, and fraternity." To counterbalance this, the famous League was devised—a vast association of citizens of every class, under the direction of Henry de Guise. Picardy was the first province to inaugurate this great association in the interest of religion and of the kingdom; James d'Humières, then commanding the troops in those parts, having begun it with some of his friends. His example was soon followed at Paris and in other cities. "The heretics combine together," said Louis d'Orleans; "let us form a League. They sustain each other; let us do the same. They hold meetings; let us meet. You are of no worse blood than these traitors to their God, their king, and their country. Shall they, then, be allowed to league, while we remain quiet?" In a few months, every town had its league, and in 1577 the States-General and the king himself sanctioned the confederation. Modern impiety, embittered by the spirit of the Revolution, cannot do justice to the League. It was a glorious manifestation of the Catholic and national spirit of the better part of the French of their day; a manifestation which was almost general and entirely spontaneous, developed by the force of circumstances and the crying needs of the country. The Guises certainly directed it, but before they did so, they had followed it; they were not its authors. Some writers hold that the League never obtained the approbation of the Holy See; others again hold that it received a verbal sanction, at least, from Gregory XIII. Certainly Sixtus V. condemned it as pernicious to the royal authority, to the good of the state, and to the true interests of religion. But the principles and beginnings of the League must not be confounded with its posterior deeds and its excesses. The judgments of Gregory XIII. and Sixtus V. are not contradictory of each other; for they are founded in the same principle, and, as Saint-Victor observed, they are one and the same judgment, and both are useful to a person who wishes to properly appreciate the great association. Certainly Rome, whose prudence and foresight is proverbial, always regarded the League as though she was preoccupied with its final result, as though she suspected that its consequences might reach beyond the object that had inspired it (1). In 1588, Henry III. procured the assassination of Guise and his brother, the cardinal of Lorraine. Then seventy doctors of the Sorbonne decided that Henry had forfeited his crown, and Pope Sixtus V. having excommunicated him, the wretched prince openly threw himself into the arms of his Huguenot friends and of Henry of Navarre, who began a siege of Paris. In 1589 Henry III. was assassinated by Clement, a fanatical friar, instigated by Mme. de Montpensier, a sister of the murdered Guise (2). Six months before this event, Cath-

(1) BÉRAULT-BERCASTEL; vol. X., p. 234.—MAZAS; vol. II., p.459.—FELLER; art. *Henry III.*

(2) " Chateaubriand, with more imagination than proper spirit of criticism, and allowing himself to be attracted by a fortuitous similarity of numbers, instituted a parallel between the three Valois, the three Stuarts, and three of the Bourbons. Chateaubriand paid too much honor to the Valois, and did a grave injury to the Bourbons. In reality, the Stuarts paid with their heads or their crowns for their blindness, and for their non-recognition of the legitimate needs of their subjects; the Bourbons strove seriously to reconcile historical tra-

arine dei Medici had preceded her son to the grave; and as Pierre de l'Estoile brutally but truthfully said, "She who had been styled the Juno of the court had no sooner taken her last breath, than men cared no more for her than for a dead goat." Civil war and all its accompaniments again desolated France until the conversion of Henry IV. in 1593. The celebrated Edict of Nantes, of which we shall treat when we approach the matter of its revocation, was issued by Henry IV. in 1598, the parliaments registering it with a clause added by themselves, to the effect that future monarchs would be free to revoke the instrument, if they should deem such action conducive to the good of Church and State. This Edict placed the Protestants on nearly the same footing as the Catholics; the only preference accorded the latter being that their worship could be publicly exercised everywhere, whereas the former could worship publicly only in certain districts. The Catholic worship was to be restored wherever it had been abolished; restitution of all ecclesiastical property stolen by the Huguenots was to be made; freedom of conscience was restored to all; Protestants were to be eligible to all offices. Two documents, also signed by Henry IV., were joined to the Edict. By the first, his Majesty promised to pay an annual sum of 140,000 livres toward the support of the Calvinist ministers. By the second, he engaged to entrust the Huguenots, for eight years, with the garrisoning of all the places that they then occupied; the sovereign was to pay these garrisons and to appoint Calvinist governors. Among these places thus rendered practically independent were La Rochelle and Montauban, destined to become the last centres of Huguenot arrogance and rebellion. But the Calvinists refused to abide by their engagements, and it required a long and sanguinary struggle to ensure the enforcement of that

dition with the revolutionary exigencies, and the guillotine or exile punished them for not having accomplished a labor of Hercules; but the three last Valois knew nothing about France, wished and tried nothing for France, and did nothing for France. When public opinion emitted its indecisive and obstreperous voice, the Valois neither obeyed nor commanded; and therefore they were fatal for both liberty and authority. A century of efforts had with difficulty given to loyalty an ascendency over a turbulent nobility; and in thirty years the work was so nearly annihilated, that it required seventy-two years of the genius of Henry IV., Richelieu, and Mazarin, to restore it, and to furnish the young Louis XIV. with a crown which was respected, and a sceptre which meant power." PELLISSIER; loc. cit., p. 244.

article of the Edict of Nantes which stipulated for the restoration of the stolen churches and for the freedom of Catholic worship. In 1685, Louis XIV. revoked the Edict of
Nantes, and until the Revolution of 1789 the public exercise of
the "Reformed" worship was thereafter forbidden in France.

Historical and religious prejudice too frequently represents the early Protestants of France as members of a purely
religious sect, desirous of but one thing—a respectful toleration of their mode of worshipping the Almighty and Eternal
God. Race prejudice also leads many to ignore the political
and social side of the struggle between ancient tradition and
their real or presumed ancestors of the sixteenth century ;
once at least in every year our ears are deafened by praises
of the lamblike innocence of the original Huguenots, as
sounded by persons, the French or Dutch smack of whose
names is asserted in proof of their presumedly glorious genealogical claims. At every reunion of our American Huguenot Societies a cry is raised in deprecation of the cruelties
which French Catholics are said to have perpetrated in the
name of the God of Peace; but not a word is ever uttered
concerning the atrocities committed by a rebellious faction,
or of the agony experienced by a nation which was compelled to witness the violation of all the human and divine
laws which it had venerated for more than ten centuries.
On these occasions much is naturally said of St. Bartholomew's Day ; and when we come to treat of that sad episode,
we also shall utter some bitter words of condemnation. But
here we would remind our Protestant friends of a fact which
they are prone to forget, but which the coryphees of the Reformation thoroughly realized. The men of the sixteenth
century, whether orthodox or heretical, had no conception of
two contrary religious systems mutually tolerant; that is a
modern idea. To a man of that day, Christianity was not a
mere fashion of worship ; it was a truth, the very word of
God, the soul of the social order. Two words of God, two
souls of the social order, the man of the sixteenth century
could not perceive ; and hence it was that when the innovators insisted that the traditional Christianity was a mass of
superstition and a foul idolatry, they felt it to be their mis-

sion to subvert an edifice which " reeked with slime." That
mission they undertook ; but they acted with fire and sword,
not as envoys of the God of Peace.   We have not the will, even
though our space permitted, to give many details of the Huguenot procedures against all that was weak, noble, and
sacred ; we hesitate to narrate many instances of the bestial
fury of the Calvinists against priests and women, and to de-
pict all the monstrously obscene tortures which their diabol-
ical malice invented.   But since these pages may be perused
by some whose ideas on this matter have been drawn from
such authorities as the *Calvinist Martyrology*, we would submit for their consideration a very few of the features which
characterized the birth of what French revolutionists regard as
the forerunner of their modern " liberties."   In 1587, while the
contest between Catholicism and " the religion " was still raging, there was published at Antwerp a work entitled *A Spectacle of the Cruelties of the Heretics of Our Time* (1); and its details are given with a minuteness as to time, place, and personalities, which would have rendered fraud easily detec-
table.   According to this work, the heretics of the city of
Angouleme, in the presence of Gaspard de Coligny and his
entire suite, after having sworn to preserve the peace, hung
to death Michael Grellet, a Franciscan, amid shouts of : " *Vive
l'Evangile !*".   Then they massacred another friar, John Vir-
oleau, after having mutilated him—*præcisis prius pudendis.*
In the same city, Friar John Avril, an octogenarian, was despatched with a hatchet, and his corpse was thrown into a
sewer ; while Friar Peter Bonneau was hung outside the
walls.   In the residence of one Papin, also in Angouleme,
thirty Catholics, chained in pairs, were left to starve, the
murderers hoping that their agonies would force them to kill
and devour each other ; but afterward, some of these unfortunates were put out of their misery by slow fires which were
kindled under them.   In the city of Montbrun, some of the
Huguenot garrison often took their meals at the house of a
widow, named Marendat ; and one day, they threw her on her
bed, and applied heated knife-blades to the soles of her feet,

(1) *Theatrum Crudelitatum Hæreticorum Nostri Temporis (Antuerpiæ, apud Adri-
anum Huberti, 1587).*

finally stripping the flesh from her limbs in fillets. Master
John Arnould, a lieutenant-general, taken prisoner when Angouleme was captured, was mutilated and strangled; and on
the same occasion, the sexagenarian widow of an officer was
dragged by the hair through the city. At Chasseneuil a
priest named Fayard was seized, his hands steeped in boiling oil until the flesh dropped off, and the liquid was then
poured down his throat. Another priest, Colin Guillebaut,
vicar of Saint-Auzanne, suffered that species of mutilation in
which the Huguenots so delighted in the case of his order—
absectis pudendis ; and then he was murdered with boiling
oil. Simon Sicot, vicar of Saint-Hilaire de Moutiers, a sexagenarian, was forced to buy his life with a heavy ransom ;
and then, as he was on his way to his parsonage, a Huguenot tore out his eyes and his tongue. Master Peter, parish-
priest of Beaulieu, was buried up to the head, and left to die.
Arnold Durandeau, vicar of Fleix, eighty years old, was
strangled ; and a Franciscan of that place was thrown from
the walls. Octavian Ronier, vicar of Saint-Cybard d'Angouleme, had horse-shoes nailed to his bare feet before he was
killed. Francis Raboteau, vicar of Foucquebrune, was dragged
from the yoke of a pair of oxen, and during the journey
was scourged until he died. By order of an officer named
Piles, the surgeon Philip Dumont, and the merchant Nicholas Guiréc, were tied to a tree, and were pierced by arrows ;
loudly proclaiming themselves Catholics until they died. All
these cases occurred in the diocese of Angouleme ; and we are
assured that in that diocese, during two years, 120 persons of
every age, sex, and condition, suffered martyrdom. In Hou-
dan, in the diocese of Chartres, a priest was compelled to celebrate Mass amid the derisions of the Huguenots, and while
many struck him with their gauntlets, and others pricked him
with their daggers. With his face and entire body bathed in
his blood, the martyr continued the Sacrifice ; but when the
moment of Communion had arrived, the murderers threw the
Sacred Host to the pavement, and crushed it to atoms under
their mailed feet. They then performed similar sacrilege
with the precious Blood ; and finally, they crucified the cele-
brant, mercifully ending his tortures with their arquebuses.

In the burg of Fleurus, near Sainte-Menehould, the troops of the Sieur de Béthune lacerated a priest with horse-whips; but his death was caused by the much admired mutilation—*pudendis amputatis*, the work being done by the surgeon of the squadron, who boasted that he had already served sixteen priests in the same manner. In the village of Pat, about seven miles from Orleans, twenty-five Catholics, pursued by Huguenots, took refuge in the steeple of a church; but fire was applied, and all perished in the flames. In the same village, several priests were dragged to death at the tails of horses. At Saint-Macaire, in Gascony, the abdomens of several priests were opened; and their bowels were taken out by degrees, being rolled around a staff. Here also several priests were buried alive, and many Catholic children cut into pieces. At Bazas, in Gascony, while Ducasse was governing the place in the name of the king of Navarre, his soldiers violated a widow; and then, having filled her matrix with powder, they blew her body to pieces (1). The captain de Gohas, the lord of Sainte-Colombe, and a large number of other nobles, having capitulated to the count of Montgommery, that Calvinist gentleman received their ransom, and then invited them to dinner, saying that he "must treat them as friends." When they had retired to their couches about midnight, he sent his men to their rooms, and all were murdered. The reader is probably familiar with Briquemaut's necklace, which was composed of ears of slaughtered priests; but that was not an isolated case, many priests having lost their ears while officiating at the altar. At Nimes, in Languedoc, many priests who had not died from their wounds were thrown alive into a deep well. James Souris, who bore the title of admiral for Queen Jeanne d'Albret of Navarre, captured a Portuguese ship which was bearing forty Jesuits to the pagans of Brazil; and after having chopped off either their arms or legs, he pitched all the missionaries into the sea. But the horrible monotony of these scenes warns us to drop the curtain. Protestants can indicate many juridical executions for heresy and attendant

(1) "*Milites ejus duo stupratæ viduæ et resupinatæ verendas partes pulvere tormentario replerunt, quamobrem admoto igne disruptus venter et diffusa viscera sunt.*"

crimes, enforced by Catholics according to the laws of the time ; but the persecutions by the Huguenots were not only unauthorized by proper authority, but they exceeded in horror, not only those by pagan China and Japan, but even those enforced by Protestant England.

We shall have more to say about the events which accompanied the attempt to Protestantize the Land of the Lilies, when we treat of Pope Sixtus V., of Henry IV., of the Massacre of St. Bartholomew's Day, and of the Revocation of the Edict of Nantes. Now we shall merely remark, in conclusion of this dissertation on the first efforts of Calvinism to found a French National Church, that there were both political and moral reasons for the failure of a design which succeeded in Scandinavia, in Germany and Switzerland, in England, and in the Low Countries. The "liberal" principles of the Reformation may have had attractions for a few, so long as the matter remained in the clouds of theory ; but when a descent into practical life demonstrated the real despotism of Protestant doctrine, and its tendency to social destruction and communism, there was no danger of its becoming popular. By the mass of the people, Protestantism came to be regarded as unrefined, ferocious, and sacrilegious. As we have already observed, royalty in France had few temptations to favor the Reformation. The most that this movement could promise it was the disposal of ecclesiastical dignities ; and the Concordat of Leo X. had already placed nearly all benefices in the royal hands. Royalty had experienced too much difficulty in subduing feudal independence, to willingly furnish an arm like the Protestant idea of freedom of word and deed to men like Dubourg, Coligny, and d'Aubigné. As to the world of thought in France, it was represented by the Universities, and all of these were traditionally hostile to novelty. "But if the Reformation failed to destroy the religious unity of the French nation, nevertheless it started in the moral world a fermentation which was dangerous to the happiness, glory, and morality of France. The personal conflicts of the nobles, the sterile agitations of the cities and the rural districts, the popular insurrections, and the numerous pillages and assassinations, all these gave a taste for disorder and anarchy.

So much for the practical ; but in theory, the evil was graver, deeper, more incurable. In order to attract the crowd, the Reformers had drawn from the *Voluntary Servitude* of Boetius, from the *Franco-Gallia* of Hotmann, from the *Pleas Against Tyrants* of Hubert Longuet, certain principles concerning the sovereignty of reason, from which the spirit of the Revolution issued. Here is a morsel. 'Magistrates are not to be obeyed when they command irreligious or wicked things ; and this means that they must not be obeyed when they order that to which one cannot submit without violating his vocation, whether public or private.' Here is another : 'Instead of excommunicating tyrannicides, the ancients raised altars to them.' And hear this one : 'The people may at any time depose their king, and choose another.' As an antidote against the passionate application of such principles, there can be only respect for a superior authority, that of God ; but the revolutionary spirit places man above God, makes him God, regarding God as an obsolete word, and consequently leaving nothing for the world but the brutal caprice of force" (1).

CHAPTER XXIII.

THE MASSACRE OF ST. BARTHOLOMEW'S DAY.*

"*Excidat illa dies ævo, nec postera credant sæcula.*—Let this day be lost from time, and let posterity ignore the event." Whether these words of Statius were applied to this fatal day by the chancellor de l'Hopital, as Voltaire asserts, or by the president de Thou, as some contend, no Catholic will refuse to re-echo them ; but, if well informed, he will not deem himself obliged to add with the poet, "*Nos certe taceamus.*" And nevertheless, it is comparatively but a short time since Catholic polemics essayed to answer the allegations of Protestant writers concerning this event, so fearful were they lest they might be suspected of a wish to apologize for a horrible crime. We hear much of La Barthélemy ; but nothing of La Michelade, that frightful massacre at Nimes on St.

(1) PELLISSIER ; *loc. cit.*, page 275.
* Most of this chapter appeared as an article in the *Ave Maria*, vol. XXXIII.

Michael's Day of 1567, when the Protestants anticipated by more than two centuries the horrors of the Carmes and of the Abbaye (September 2, 1792). Now we propose to demonstrate, firstly, that religion had nothing to do with this massacre; secondly, that it was a matter of mere worldly policy; thirdly, that it was not intended that it should extend beyond Paris; fourthly, that it was not long premeditated, but was the effect of impulse; and fifthly, that the number of its victims has been enormously exaggerated. But before we enter upon this task, we must devote some attention to an alleged fact which is presented by most Protestant historians as intimately connected with the massacre—having been, they assert, part and parcel of the original plan.

They who have derived their knowledge of French history from the charming pages of the elder Dumas, or who have been sufficiently distrustful of such sources of historical information as to recur to the rank and file of English Protestant historians, or perhaps even to consult the more respectable works of Sismondi, d'Aubigné, and Henri Martin, are now impressed with the idea that the idol of the Huguenots, Queen Jane d'Albret of Navarre, was murdered by order of Queen Catharine dei Medici, shortly before the Barthélemy. Sismondi says : "Master René, one of Catharine's creatures and a Florentine perfumer, tendered his services to the queen, promising to rid her of Jane d'Albret by poisoning her with perfumery. It is said that the poison was administered by means of scented gloves, and that she died four days afterward. The king expressed a pretended grief with much ostentation, and in order that so sudden a death might not excite suspicion, he commanded that the corpse should be opened ; *but care was taken that the brain, the sole organ which was affected by the poison*, should not be examined. René, the perfumer, who distinguished himself afterward among the perpetrators of the Barthélemy, boasted at that time of the deed he had performed" (1). Henri Martin, willing though he is to receive this yarn as gospel-truth, hesitatingly avows that "Even the historians who speak of the poisoning

(1) *History of the French*, edit. 1835, vol. XIX., p. 140.

admit that the patient had a disease of the chest" (1). And the same Martin admits that Jane, writing to her son (2), says that she fears that she will have, ere long, a severe illness, since she is far from well even now (some weeks before the alleged poisoning). Guizot is willing to admit that the death of Queen Jane gave occasion to accusations which were *probably unfounded* (3). We shall show that the austere Guizot should have said that the charge was *certainly* unfounded. Of course d'Aubigné, whose work (4) is at best a woeful exaggeration whenever he speaks of the French so-called religious wars, helped to propagate this story. Just like Sismondi, the historians Serres and Mezeray are particular in noting the alleged care of Charles IX. in preventing any examination of the brain of the supposed victim. Now all of these writers have simply copied the assertion of Etienne, the author of an obscene libel against Catharine dei Medici (5); and the reader will remember that the great Mezeray often avowed to his friends that when preparing his *History*, he had examined no original documents (6). De Thou treats the matter as dubious (7).

In refutation of this accusation against Catharine dei Medici and her son Charles IX., we might cite the *Journal* of Claude Regin, one of the counsellors of Jane d'Albret, a document which is generally regarded as a faithful and exact narrative of the life of the author's sovereign, and which gives no inkling of a rumor of empoisonment, but simply states that the queen of Navarre died on June 9, having contracted a pleurisy on the 6th. But we draw the reader's attention to the words of Palma Cayet, who, as a Calvinist minister, had been one of the suite of Catharine de Bourbon, sister of Henry IV.; and who expressly states that they lied who declared that the brain of Queen Jane had not been examined, lest the murder should have been proved. "What lies and impostures! There are still living (in 1608) several

---

(1) *History of France*, edit. 1857, vol. IX., p. 297.
(2) *Bulletin of the Society for the History of France* (1838), vol. II., no. 5.
(3) *History of France Narrated to My Grandchildren*, 1874, vol. III., p. 337.
(4) *Universal History*, vol. II., b. I., ch. ii.
(5) *A Marvellous Narrative of the Life of Queen Catharine dei Medici*, 1574.
(6) So says Huet, the celebrated bishop of Avranches.
(7) *Histories*, b. XL.

of the household officers of that queen, who were also mem:
bers of the pretendedly reformed religion, and were present
at the examination made of her body by the surgeon Desneux, assisted by Caillart, her physician-in-ordinary. These
officers know that those learned physicians and surgeons
found that the death was due to an aposteme in the lungs,
which had burst. And they know, also, that Caillart said to
them : 'Gentlemen, you are all aware that the late queen, our
royal mistress, often ordered me, in case I should be with
her when she came to die, to have no hesitation in opening
her body, so that it might be known what had caused the
trouble in the upper part of her head with which she was
ordinarily afflicted, and so that if the same malady should
ever afflict the prince, her son, and the princess, her daughter, a remedy might be applied.' *Then Desneux sawed open
the skull,* and all saw that the queen's pain in the head had
been caused by certain small water pimples which had formed
between the skull and the film of the brain. Then looking
fixedly at them all, Desneux said : 'Gentlemen, if the queen's
death had been caused by smelling some poison, there would
be evidence of it on the film of the brain; *but you see that
the brain is as free as any one could wish.* And again, if her
Majesty had died from poison taken into the stomach,
signs of its presence would be seen in the stomach ; but
there are none. *Therefore her death has been caused by the
aposteme in the lungs'*" (1). Four years after Palma Cayet
wrote this narrative, Andrew Favyn, who had been a preceptor of Henry IV. and in the suite of his sister, corroborated
the testimony (2). It is refreshing to note that Voltaire, in
one of those lucid moments when the truth conquered the
prejudices of the philosophaster, rejects the Huguenot tale :
"Jane d'Albret died after five days of a malignant fever.
There was reason to suspect that her death was due to poison, when one considered the time of its occurrence, as well
as the massacres which followed it, the fear of her courage felt
by the court, and the fact that her illness began after her
purchase of some scented gloves and collars from a perfumer.

(1) *History of the War under Henry IV.,* by Palma Cayet, Paris, 1608.
(2) In his *History of Navarre,* b. XIV.

named René who had come from Florence with the queen
(Catharine), and who was thought to be a professional poi-
soner. It was even asserted that René had boasted of his
crime. ... In his great *History* Mezeray appears to favor
this opinion, when he says that the physicians did not touch
the head when they opened the queen's body. ... It is but
proper to mistrust the notions which always attribute the
deaths of the great to other than natural causes. The people,
thinking always shallowly, lay the death of a prince at the
door of those to whom the death would be a gain. Such wild
suspicions prompted the accusation that Catharine dei Medici caused the murder of her own children; but there were
never any proofs that either these princes or Jane d'Albret
died of poison. It is not true, as Mezeray pretends, that the
skull of the queen of Navarre was not opened; she herself
had ordered expressly that the brain should be carefully examined, after her death. ... And it is noteworthy that *they
who opened it were Huguenots ; and certainly they would have
spoken of poison, had there been any probability of its presence.*
We may be told that these surgeons were bribed by the court;
but we know that Desneux, the body-physician of Jane d'Albret, was a fierce Huguenot, and that afterward he wrote
savage diatribes against the court—which he would not have
written, had he been bought—and in these libels he never
asserted that Jane d'Albret had been murdered. Finally, it
is incredible that so able a person as Catharine dei Medici
would have entrusted such a task to a miserable perfumer
who, as they say he did, would be capable of bragging about
his deed " (1).

L.

Religion had nothing to do with this massacre. In this
matter historians have erred in espousing the cause of either
Protestants or Catholics. To use the words of Cantù, " Varillas and Voltaire, equally unjust, have provoked the judgment of impartial posterity, which weighs them in the same
scale, and which sees on both sides swords dripping with
blood; recognizing in this deadly struggle not the crimes of

(1) In a Note to the Chant II. of his *Henriade*, dated 1723.

a sect or the follies of a court or the instigations of fanati. cism, but the constant passions of humanity." In the first place, one would be led to suspect that zeal for the Catholic faith was not the motive for the Barthélemy, from the fact that many Catholics were numbered among the victims, having succumbed to personal hate or to avarice. "The possession of wealth," says Mézeray, "an envied position, or the existence of greedy heirs, stamped a man as a Huguenot." The governor of Bordeaux systematically ransomed wealthy Catholics, as well as Protestants. And we must not forget that the characters of Catharine dei Medici and of her son, Charles IX., were not exactly those of zealots in the cause of the faith. Hearken to the critical and impartial opinion of Cantù on the celebrated queen of France. "Catharine dei Medici, a woman on whom weighs all the hatred of the French, who saw incarnated in her Italian cunning and ferocity, calculated corruption, cold cruelty, and an egotistic policy, had been raised among the factions of Tuscany ; married for policy, unloved by a husband who preferred his mistress to her ; suddenly exalted above her long debasement ; beautiful, majestic, in the vigor of life ; instructed by misfortune, irritated by humiliation ; absolutely ruling, yet loved by her children ; unequalled in the art of fascinating the souls of men. She did not study the good of a kingdom to which she was foreign, nor the preservation of a faith which she had not in her heart, but only her own power. Nevertheless, she preserved France from falling to pieces, or from succumbing to a tyranny which afflicted Spain. She always wore the widow's weeds ; and although she tolerated immorality in others, not even the calumnious Brantôme ever reproaches her on this score. She was so little hostile to the reformed doctrines that during her meals she often listened to Calvinist sermons. (See Letter of the Nuncio Santa Croce, November 13, 1561.) But since Philip II., the great enemy of France, was head of the Catholic party, France should be allied with the Protestants—a policy adopted, in fact, by the last few French monarchs. But the Calvinists ceased to be a school, and became a dangerous faction ; hence Catharine felt that she could save the country only by siding with the

Catholic majority. Although she hated the Guises, she joined hands with them to supplant the constable Anne and Diana. The latter was banished; Anne went over to the Bourbons; the king of Navarre received a cool treatment which his weakness deserved, and the Guises obtained the highest posts " (1). Certainly zeal for religion could not have been the impelling motive of the massacre, in the mind of a woman who caused the sermons of Calvinist preachers to be read to her while she was taking her meals—of a woman who, as Cantù elsewhere admits, would have declared herself a Protestant, had such a course been dictated by her desire to recover power. But there is more than mere suspicion to warrant the assertion that religious zeal was not the prime motive of La Barthélemy. The motive which impelled the murderers is revealed by the Calvinists themselves in their own historico-religious text-book, their discursive but mendacious *Martyrology*, the author of which often unwittingly furnishes us with facts which completely neutralize the effects of his venom. He informs us that the perpetrators of the massacre, in their joy of success, would show the corpses of their victims, saying, " These are they who would have killed the king." And " the courtiers laughed exultantly, saying that at length the war was ended, and they could live in peace." The same author tells us that after the massacre, " the parliament of Toulouse published the will of the king that no one should molest those of the religion, but should rather favor them"; and we know that on August 26 a similar edict was issued in Paris. Again, Charles IX. needed no religious motive to render him furious against the Huguenots. They had plotted to kidnap him; they had drawn entire provinces into rebellion, and they had introduced foreign troops into France. Not content, as presumed apostles of religious liberty, with calling upon the king to " exterminate idolatry and to pull down the images of Christ "; with insisting upon his abandonment of " the impious, the besotted firebrands of purgatory "; the Huguenots had subjected France to disorders such as had not been seen since the fourteenth century, during the insanity of Charles

(1) *Universal History*, b. **XV.**

VI. Among other proceedings which were odious to French-men, the Huguenots had summoned the aid of the foreigner who, as Lanoue said, " was wriggling to enter France;" Co-ligny maintained himself in Normandy only by the gold of Elizabeth, and at the battle of Dreux the misguided Condé had vainly availed himself of German troops. In 1563, the Calvinists had so far succeeded in enamoring the peasants with the worldly profitableness of Protestantism, that the rus-tics began to refuse to pay taxes. " Show us," they pleaded, " a page of the Bible wherein we are taught to pay taxes ; we are not asses, even though our ancestors were." At the Peace of Amboise, the queen-mother had been forced to sell large pieces of church property in order to pay the German dragoons of Condé. In fine, after the murder of Francis de Guise, the Huguenots had so thoroughly abolished the au-thority of Charles IX. in the south of France, that Condé alone played the king, confiscating, endowering, negotiating with foreign sovereigns, and coining money which bore his own effigy with the inscription, " Louis XIII., First Christian King of France." Were not these things sufficient to enrage Charles IX. against the Huguenots ?

But it is said that Roman cardinals prepared the massa-cre ; the names of Birague and De Retz are mentioned. The Roman purple is easily cleared of this stain. The former prelate was made a cardinal six, and the latter fifteen years after the Barthélemy. The poet Chenier, of the school of Voltaire, represents, on the operatic stage, the cardinal of Lorraine as blessing the poniards destined for the massacre; but at that time this prelate was in Rome, having been one of the Conclave which had chosen a successor to St. Pius V. Perhaps the reader is one of those who have been deeply im-pressed by the libretto of Scribe, furnished by that clever manipulator of historical facts in the service of the operatic stage, to Meyerbeer's grand but mendacious opera of *The Huguenots*. The chief scenes of this libretto are taken from the famous play of *Charles IX.* written by Chenier, and first presented in that disastrous year 1789 on the stage of the Théâtre-Français. This play of Chenier effected more for the diffusion of false ideas concerning the Barthélemy than had been effected by the lies of Etienne, L'Etoile, and Voltaire. In his *Dedicatory Epistle to the French Nation*, Chenier tells his audience that now, before the Revolution, he has conceived and written a tragedy which the Revolution alone can represent, and then he says : "Those whom our Revolution opposes, and who even now lift their heads with an audacity which is too ridiculous, think that it is atrocious to lay the Barthélemy before the eyes of the French people. But Voltaire, whose authority is as great as theirs is miserable, delineated this grand and terrible subject, and predicted the *happy days* which would witness its presentation on our national stage." Then the poet's madness causes him to thus apostrophize the unfortunate monarch who has already begun to hear the clamors which are to accompany him to the guillotine. " Louis XVI., come to the theatre of the nation, when *Charles IX.* is represented ! You will hear the plaudits of the French ; you will see their torrents of *tears of tenderness :* and the *author-patriot* will gather the best fruit of his labor." Scribe followed the example of Chenier when, in the Act IV. of *The Huguenots*, he concocted the famous scene of the blessing of the daggers. Chenier thus excuses his falsification of history in a matter of great importance. "At the time of the massacre, the cardinal of Lorraine was in Rome. I do not think that it is right to change history ; but I think it is allowable, in an historical tragedy, to invent certain incidents, providing that the privilege be used with moderation." And we know what ideas of " moderation " Chenier, like his fellow-revolutionists, possessed and actuated. Under the inspiration of these ideas, he makes the cardinal thus address those who were about to undertake the massacre : " A humble and docile son of the immortal Church, and made a priest of the Living God by her hands, I am able to interpret the divine decrees. If your souls are filled with burning zeal to devote themselves to the interests of heaven without reserve ; if you bring to murder religious hearts ; you will accomplish a tremendous task. Serve well the God of nations, all of whose blessings I now shower upon you. His justice delivers your victims to you. Know that in heaven God now breaks the chain of your iniquities ; by the God who inspires me, I declare the forgiveness of whatsoever crimes you have ever committed. When the Church impressed in my soul her ineffaceable mark, she forbade me to shed even the most guilty blood; but I shall follow in your path, and in the name of the avenging God I shall direct your blows. Warriors, whom Divine Providence is about to lead; ministers of justice, chosen by His prudence; it is now time to accomplish the eternal decrees. Bathe yourselves holily in the blood of the wicked! If any one of you dies in this great work, God will place in his hands the palm of martyrdom." The verses of Chenier are fine and impressive; the imitation by Scribe lends force to the music of Meyerbeer; the ignorant hearer goes home to dream of those sweet and angelic Huguenots so foully murdered by the Church; and all the ado is made by a lie. Again, much stress is laid upon the conduct of the Roman court when it heard of the catastrophe. Gregory XIII. proceeded processionally to the church of St. Louis, and rendered thanks to Heaven; he proclaimed a Jubilee, and struck medals commemorative of the event; and the famous Latinist, Mureto, pronounced an encomium on the slaughter in the presence of the Sovereign Pontiff. But the words of Pope Gregory writing to the king in congratulation for his escape, as well as the words of Mureto, show that the Roman court thanked Almighty God merely for the escape of the royal family from a Huguenot conspiracy.

Finally, throughout France and in Paris itself, the Catholic masses acted on this occasion in a manner which showed that their religion was not a prime agent in the affair. On the very night of the massacre, Charles IX. sent orders to all the governors of provinces and of cities, to take measures to prevent any occurrences like those which had just stained the capital. At Lyons, as even the Calvinist *Martyrology* informs us, many of the Huguenots were sent for safety to the archiepiscopal prison and to the Celestine and Franciscan convents. And if we are told that some of those who were consigned to the archiepiscopal prison fell victims to their enemies, we reply, with the same Calvinist author, that this outrage was committed during the absence and without the knowledge of the governer; that on his return he put a stop to it, and offered a reward of a hundred *scudi* for the names of the criminals. This author also tells us that "the Calvinists of Toulouse found safety in the convents." At Lisieux the bishop saved many, as the martyrologist admits (1); and he also says that "the more peaceable Catholics saved forty out of sixty who had been seized at the town of Romans; of the twenty others, thirteen were afterward freed, and only seven perished, they having many enemies, and having borne arms." Even at Nimes, where the Huguenots had twice massacred the Catholics in cold blood (in 1567 and 1569), the latter abstained from revenge (2). Paris also furnished many examples of compassion. The Calvinist historian, La Popelinière, a contemporary author, records that "among the French nobles who distinguished themselves in saving the lives of many of the confederates, the greatest good was effected by the dukes of Guise, Aumale, Biron, Bellièvre. ... When the people had been told that the Huguenots, in order to kill the king, had attacked his body-guards and killed over twenty, a further slaughter would have been perpetrated, had not many nobles, content with the death of the leaders, prevented it; even many Italians, armed and mounted, scoured the city and suburbs, and gathered many fortunates into the security of their own houses" (3). In fine, instead of religion having caused this massacre, we may conclude with Count Alfred de Falloux that, considering the state of men's minds at that time, religion alone could have prevented it. "Instead of a court full of intrigues and adulteries, suppose that then there was one influenced by the Gospel; that the law of God guided the powerful; that instead of a Catharine and a Charles IX., there had reigned a Blanche and a St. Louis; in such a case let us ask our consciences whether this slaughter would have been possible" (4).

II.

The massacre of St. Bartholomew's Day was an affair of worldly policy. The Huguenots had certainly been guilty of

(1) Cf. also M. de Falloux, in the *Correspondant* of 1843, pp. 166-168.
(2) MÉNARD; *Civil, Ecclesiastical, and Literary History of Nîmes*; vol. V., p. 9.
(3) *History of France from 1550 to 1557*; edit. 1581; b. XXIV., p. 67.
(4) Discourse at a scientific congress held at Angers in 1843.

high-treason. As to Coligny, the journal of his receipts and expenses, laid before the royal council and the parliament, and his other papers seized after his death, revealed deeds and projects which would have ensured his capital condemnation in any country of Christendom. Concerning these papers Bellièvre said to the deputies of the Thirteen Cantons: "The king learned from them that the admiral had established, in sixteen provinces, governors, military commanders, and a number of counsellors charged with the task of keeping the people armed, and of assembling them together at his first sign." Charles IX. wrote to Schomberg, his ambassador to Germany: "Coligny had more power, and was better obeyed by those of the new religion than I was. By the great authority he had usurped over them, he could raise them in arms against me whenever he wished, as indeed he often proved. Recently he ordered the new religionists to meet in arms at Melun, near Fontainebleau, where I was to be at that time, the third of August. He had arrogated so much power to himself that I could not call myself a king, but merely a ruler of part of my dominions. Therefore, since it has pleased God to deliver me from him, I may well thank Him for the just punishment He has inflicted upon the admiral and his accomplices. I could not tolerate him any longer, and I determined to give rein to a justice which was indeed extraordinary, and other than I would have wished, but which was necessary in the case of such a man" (1). Brantôme, Tavannes, and Montluc, all courtiers of Charles, speak of his fear of Coligny; and Bellièvre says: "His Majesty told some of his servants, myself among the number, that when he found himself so threatened, his hair stood on end." Is it likely that any monarch would tamely submit to such dictation as Coligny uttered? "Make war on Spain, sire, or we wage war against you" (2). Tavannes informs us that the king, while talking about the means at his disposal for a campaign in the Netherlands, said that one of his subjects

(1) VILLEROY; *Memoirs Illustrating the History of Our Time*; vol. IV. The letter to Schomberg is of September 13, 1572.

(2) TAVANNES; *Memoirs from the Year 1530 until his Death. Written by his Son*; Paris, 1574.—The quotations that follow are taken from the *Memoirs of Condé, from the Death of Henry II. to the Troubles of 1565*; vol. IV., p. 303; Paris, 1741.

(Coligny) had offered him ten thousand men for that purpose. Then Tavannes replied : " Sire, you ought to cut off the head of any subject who would use such language. How dare he offer you what is your own ? This is a sign that he has corrupted these men ; that he has gained them over to use them, one day, against your Majesty."

Many Protestant writers are prone to dilate on the virtues of Coligny, but they have not freed him from the imputation of having directed the assassin's blow against Duke Francis of Guise. Not merely by the deposition of the wretched Poltrot, but by the very avowals of the admiral, we are led to regard the latter as the instigator of the crime. In a letter to the queen-mother, he admitted that " for the last five or six months he did not strongly " oppose those who showed a wish to kill the duke; and he gave as a reason for his non-opposition, that certain persons had tried to kill himself. He did not name these persons in the course of his justification, but said that he " would indicate them at a fitting time." In his answers he admitted that "Poltrot told him that it would be easy to kill the duke of Guise, but that he (Coligny) made no remark, because he deemed this matter frivolous ; " in fact, he " said nothing as to whether he regarded the design as good or evil." In another letter to Catharine, he spoke of the death of the duke as " the greatest benefit that could accrue to the kingdom and to the Church of God, and a personal advantage to the king and to the whole family of Coligny." And finally, his course in claiming the right of prescription, when he fell back on the privileges of the " Edict of Pacification," would not indicate a consciousness of innocence.

III.

It was not intended that the massacre should extend beyond Paris. We learn from Tavannes that the popular fury rendered the massacre general, " to the great regret of its advisers, they having resolved on the death of only the leaders and the factious." They who hold that orders to slaughter the Huguenots had been sent into the provinces, adduce in proof only two letters: one from Viscount d'Orthez, governor of Bayonne, to Charles IX.; and one from Catharine to Strozzi, who was watching for an opportunity to surprise La Rochelle, one of the four cities accorded to the Calvinists. Now, there is very good reason for regarding both these letters as unauthentic, and no argument can be urged in their favor. The first letter, whatever some authors may say, is not found in De Thou, not even in the Geneva edition of 1620; and this writer's Huguenot proclivities and his aversion to Charles IX. would not have allowed him to overlook it, had he deemed it authentic. It is given only by the malevolent d'Aubigné in these words: "I commence with Bayonne, where a courier arrived with orders to cut in pieces the men, women, and children of Dax, who had sought refuge in the prison. D'Orthez, governor of the frontier, thus replied to the king: 'Sire, I have communicated the order of your Majesty to the inhabitants and soldiers of the garrison; and have found them to be good citizens and brave warriors, but not executioners. Therefore they and I supplicate your Majesty to employ them in any possible, even though hazardous, matters,'" etc. But the Calvinist "martyrologist" furnishes us with reasons for supposing that no such orders as the above were expedited, either to d'Orthez or to any other governors in the provinces. This author, whose work is a veritable *Lives of the Saints* for French Protestants, says nothing, save in one case, of such instructions: and certainly he was interested in chronicling them, had he known of them. But, on the contrary, he tells us that the murderers "at Orleans resolved to put their hands to the work without any orders from the governor, d'Entragues;" that those of Bourges "sent Marueil in haste to the court, but he returned bearing no commands;" that Charles IX. wrote many letters to Bordeaux to the effect that he "had not intended that execution to extend beyond Paris." The exception to which we have alluded is that of Rouen, the governor of which city, says the "martyrologist," received orders "to exterminate those of the religion;" but this assertion is contradicted, by the inactivity of the governor, and by the date of the Rouen murders, which occurred nearly a month after those of Paris.

As for the second letter, that of Catharine to Strozzi, no French contemporary or *quasi*-contemporary historian speaks of it; not even Brantôme, who was then at Brouage with Strozzi; and there are intrinsic arguments for its rejection. It is supposed that six months before the massacre, the queen-mother wrote to Strozzi, enclosed in another to be read at once, a letter which was not to be opened until August 24, the fatal day. In this reserved document Catharine is said to have written: "Strozzi, I inform you that to-day, August 24, the admiral and all the Huguenots here present were killed. I earnestly request you to make yourself master of La Rochelle, and to do as we have done to all the Huguenots who fall into your hands. Beware of backwardness, as you fear to displease the king, my son, and me." Now, he who would regard this letter as genuine must ascribe to Catharine a gift of prophecy such as few of the saints have received. She must have foreseen that Jane d'Albret (1), queen of Navarre, an ardent Huguenot, would consent to the marriage of her son, Henry de Bourbon, with Margaret de Valois. She must have known that Pope St. Pius V., who would not grant the necessary dispensation, would soon die, and that Gregory XIII. would concede it. She must also have seen Coligny and his followers madly confiding in the affectionate disposition of Charles IX.; the admiral ignoring the warnings of the Rochellois and other Huguenots; the crime of Maurevert failing to cause the flight of the future victims; and, finally, the certainty of no imprudence on the part of Strozzi, or perhaps his death, revealing her letter to the Calvinists. We decline, therefore, to accept as authentic either the letter from d'Orthez or that to Strozzi.

In 1579, the Huguenots published at Rheims a pamphlet entitled *A Tocsin against the Murderers and the Authors of Discord in France;* and we read therein a passage which shows that its authors did not accuse Charles IX. of issuing an order for general massacre. "What augments the crime

(1) Jane d'Albret, queen of Navarre, married in 1548 Anthony de Bourbon, duke of Vendome, a lineal descendant of Robert, count of Clermont, son of St. Louis; this latter having married Beatrice, daughter of Archambault de Bourbon. On the death of Anthony, in 1562, Jane embraced Calvinism. Her son, the great Henry of Navarre, becoming Henry IV. of France in 1589, definitively united France and Navarre.

is the fact that the king selected his capital city to shed innocent blood, for which that city already had too great a
thirst; and this he did in order that other cities might follow the example." But if an execution *en masse* had been
ordered by the court for Aug. 24, and had provoked those
many heroic resistances of which we read, in those circumstances such an order could not have remained a secret; and
when success had been attained, there would have been no
reason for keeping it secret. And if public rumor had
charged the king with having commanded a general slaughter,
why did not the authors of the *Tocsin* mention the fact, especially since a knowledge of that royal refinement of cruelty
would have furthered the attainment of the object for which
the pamphlet was written, namely, a coalition of the Protestant sovereigns against France? Finally, since there is no
positive proof that the massacre was intended to be general,
we may be permitted to suppose that the slaughter in Paris
corresponded sufficiently to the views of the court, since it
really decapitated the Huguenot party by the removal of its
principal leaders.

IV.

The massacre was not the result of long premeditation.
The rejection of the aforesaid letters does away with one of
the strongest arguments which militate against this position.
The contemporary historians, Capilupi, Masson, Tavannes,
Castelnau, and others, are said to declare that the massacre
was planned at the conference held at Bayonne in 1565, between Catharine and the duke of Alva. But these authors
speak only of a general agreement as to mutual aid in extir-
pating heresy; when any of them mention any sanguinary
advice on the part of Alva, it is to be noted that they do not
say that he counselled a massacre, but that the Huguenot
leaders should be "arrested and executed." Now listen to
the testimony of Margaret, sister of Charles IX. In her
"Mémoires" she says that the massacre was designed because of the Huguenot resolution to avenge the wounding of
Coligny; and that her brother was with difficulty persuaded
to consent to it, and only when "he had been made to re-

alize that otherwise his crown and life were lost." Then we have the testimony of the duke d'Anjou, the king's brother, drawn from a MS. of the Royal Library by Cavairac. This prince had been elected king of Poland in 1573, and while on his way thither he was often insulted by Huguenot refugees. He was so affected by their curses that he could not sleep, and on one occasion the horrors of St. Bartholomew's Day so oppressed him that he summoned his physician and favorite, Miron, that he might relieve his mind. Then the duke detailed all the circumstances of the massacre, and plainly showed that it was a sudden conception. We give a synopsis of this testimony. "I have called you," said the prince to Miron, "to share my restlessness, which is caused by my remembrance of the Barthélemy, concerning which event perhaps you have never heard the truth." Then the duke narrated how he and the queen-mother had observed that Coligny had prejudiced the king's mind against them; that when, after any audience accorded to the admiral, they approached his Majesty, "to speak of business or even of his own pleasures, they would find his countenance most forbidding," and he would show no respect to his mother and no kindness to Anjou. One day the prince approached the monarch just as Coligny had withdrawn; and Charles would not speak to him, but walked furiously up and down with his hand upon his dagger, looking askance at the prince, so that the latter feared for his life, "and deemed himself lucky to get safely out of the room." Anjou now consulted Catharine, and "they resolved to rid themselves of the admiral." They took Mme. de Nemours into their confidence, "on account of her hatred for Coligny;" and they sent at once for a certain Gascon captain, but did not make use of him, because he assured them too readily of his good-will, "and without any reservation of persons." Then they thought of Maurevert, as "one experienced in assassination;" but they could influence him only by representing that the admiral was bent on avenging the death of Moul, whom Maurevert had lately murdered. Mme. de Nemours put one of her houses at their disposal; and when the attempt failed, "they were compelled to look to their own safety." When Charles wished to see the admiral, they determined to be present at the interview; and the wounded man having been admitted to a private conference with the king, "they retired to a distance, and became very suspicious, especially since they saw themselves in the midst of over two hundred of the admiral's followers, who, with ferocious countenances, constantly passed them with little show of respect." Catharine soon put an end to the colloquy under the specious pretext of care for Coligny's health, and then tried to learn from her son the purport of the admiral's remarks. At first Charles refused; but, being pressed, he swore "by death," and brusquely declared that "all Coligny had said was true," and that he had reproached the king with being a mere cipher in the hands of his mother. "This touched them to the quick," and the queen-mother "feared some change in the government of the kingdom;" but "for some hours they could come to no determination." The next day Anjou and his mother deliberated "as to the means of getting rid of the admiral." After dinner they waited on Charles, and Catharine "told the king that the Huguenots were rising in arms; that the leaders were enrolling troops in the provinces; that Coligny had procured ten thousand cavalry from Germany and as many Swiss; that these dangers could be obviated only by the death of the admiral and of the chief leaders of the Huguenot faction." Tavannes, Birague, and Nevers corroborated these assertions; and the king "became furious, but nevertheless would not at first hear of any injury to Coligny." He asked each one for his individual opinion; and all agreed with Catharine "except the marshal de Retz, who deceived our hopes," saying that "if any one ought to hate the admiral, he was one, since Coligny had defamed his race throughout Europe; but that he would not revenge himself by means dishonorable to the king and country." But no one seconded De Retz, and "we soon observed a sudden change in the king." The rest of the day was devoted to the details of the terrible enterprise. Guise was entrusted with the death of Coligny. Toward the dawn of day, the king, Catharine, and Anjou were standing at a window, when they heard the report of a pistol, and fell back in horror. They sent to revoke the order given to Guise, but it was too late (1).

Such, according to the duke of Anjou, is the inner history of the Barthélemy; and although the prince was brother to Charles IX., we hold that his testimony is valuable. No one will deny that he knew all the circumstances of the massacre; and what had he to gain by deceiving Miron? Certainly not self-justification; for he painted himself in the darkest colors. And he could not have wished to conciliate the Poles, his future subjects; for Miron could not effect such conciliation; and, again, the Polish representatives had already shown by their unanimous vote that such a course was superfluous. And now to the testimonies of Margaret and Henry de Valois add those of three celebrated contemporary historians—the hostile Brantôme, the Protestant La Popelinière, and Mathieu. Brantôme, when treating of Catharine dei Medici, says of Coligny's aspersions against that queen: "Behold the cause of his death, and of that of his followers, as I learned it from those who knew it well; although many believe that the fuse was laid sometime previous to the catastrophe." La Popelinière gives the arguments for and against the supposition of premeditation, and inclines to the latter view. Mathieu says that he understood from Henry IV. that Catharine informed Villeroy, her confidant, that the massacre was unpremeditated. And it may be observed with Cavairac that, if long prepared, this tragedy would have been executed simultaneously, or nearly so, throughout France; and most Protestants believe that it was so effected. But at Meaux the slaughter happened on August 25, at La Charité on the 26th, at Orleans on the 27th, at Saumur and Angers on the 29th, at Lyons on the 30th, at Troyes on September 2, at Bruges on the 14th, at Rouen on the 17th, at Romans on the 20th, at Toulouse on the 25th, at Bordeaux not until October 23. Finally, no one has charged the Machiavellian queen-mother with a want of dexterity in executing a plan, or with a proneness to forget circumstances which would interfere with its actuation. But if the massacre was the result of a long deliberated plot, Catharine erred sadly by procuring the assassination of Coligny before the

(1) CAVAIRAC; *Dissertation on St. Bartholomew's Day*; 1758.

moment destined for the grand and general stroke. She should have dreaded lest the fate of the admiral would precipitate a flight of all the Huguenots out of Paris, and not improbably their general recourse to arms.

But in reply to all the proofs of the non-premeditation of the massacre, it has been alleged that Sir Henry Austin Layard, president of the London Huguenot Society, discovered facts which caused him to come to the conclusion that "there cannot be a doubt that Pius V. had instigated Charles and the queen-mother to exterminate the Huguenots, and that Salviati had been instructed to press the matter upon them." Thus says the Hon. John Jay, addressing the American Huguenot Society in its annual meeting on April 13, 1888. But long before Layard was heard of, Lingard had investigated the real connection of the nuncio Salviati with the massacre, and had judged that the event was not premeditated. While Chateaubriand was ambassador at the papal court (1828–30) he procured a copy of the correspondence of Pope Gregory XIII. with his nuncio Salviati, and sent it to Mackintosh, who used it in his *History of England*. This correspondence proves that at the time of the massacre Salviati knew nothing of the designs of the French court. We transcribe Lingard's synopsis of these letters : " On August 24 he (Salviati) wrote an account of the occurrence in ordinary characters (evidently under the notion that in such circumstances his despatch would probably be intercepted and opened on the road): but to this he added another and real statement of the case in cipher : that the queen-regent, in consequence of the ascendency which gave to Coligny in a manner the government of the kingdom (*quasi governava*), consulted with the duchess of Nemours, and resolved to rid herself of his control by the assassination of the admiral. The duke of Guise provided the assassin ; the duke of Anjou, but not the king, was privy to the attempt. The queen, however, when she saw that the admiral would not die of his wound, and considered the danger to which she was now exposed ; alarmed also by her own consciousness, and by the threatening speeches of the whole body of the Huguenots, who would not believe that the arquebuse had been discharged by an assassin employed by the duke of Alva, as she had persuaded herself that she could make them believe; had recourse to the king, and exhorted him to adopt the plan of the general (1) massacre which followed. It appears that the cardinal-secretary, in his answer to this despatch, probably on account of the different reports current in Rome, put to the nuncio several questions respecting the cause, the authors, and the circumstances of the massacre. Salviati, in reply, wrote two notes on September 22. In the first he says: 'With regard to the three points: 1) who it was that caused, and for what reason that person caused, the arquebuse to be discharged at the admiral; 2) and who it was to whom the subsequent resolution of so numerous a massacre must be ascribed; 3) and who were the executors of the massacre, with the names of the principal leaders; I know that I have already sent you an account, and that in that account I have not fallen into the least error. If I have omitted to mention some other particulars, the chief reason is the difficulty of coming at the truth in this country.' This passage was written in ordinary characters; but he wrote the same day in cipher the following repetition of his former statement: 'Time will show whether there be any truth in all the other accounts which you may have read, of the wounding and death of the admiral, that differ from what I wrote to you. The queen-regent having grown jealous of him, came to a resolution *a few days before*, and caused the arquebuse to be discharged at him *without the knowledge of the king*, but with the participation of the duke of Anjou, of the duchess of Nemours, and of her son, the duke of Guise. Had he died immediately, no one else would have perished. But he did not die, and they began to expect some great evil; wherefore, closeting themselves in consultation with the king, they determined to throw shame aside, and to cause him (Coligny) to be assassinated with the others; a determination which was carried into execution that very night.' Evidence more satisfactory than this we cannot desire, if we consider the situation of the writer, the object for which he wrote, and the

(1) The words of Salviati do not necessarily imply, as Lingard would infer, that the slaughter was to be " general."

time and opportunity which he possessed of correcting any error which might have crept into his previous communication ; and from this evidence it plainly follows that the general massacre was not originally contemplated, but grew out of the unexpected failure of the attempt already made on the life of the admiral."

Mr. Jay introduces his arguments under the auspices of Lord Acton, whom he carefully notes as "a very distinguished Roman Catholic historian, who so admirably represents the honorable members of that faith who reject the doctrines and methods of the Jesuits." Since many very good Catholics have rejected certain teachings of certain Jesuits, just as other good Catholics have rejected certain teachings of other schools, this remark might be allowed to pass. But coming from Mr. Jay, this sentence would indicate, even to those who are unacquainted with Acton's career, that his "liberal Catholicism" was impatient of all control. And at the time of his letter to the London paper, the quondam Catholic editor had thrown off his allegiance to the centre of unity, had joined the "Old Catholic" heresy, and was no more of a Catholic than Mr. Jay himself. Mr. Jay tells us that Acton furnished the London *Times* of November 26, 1874, with a translation of some Italian letters from Salviati to his Roman superiors, which prove that religion had very much to do with the massacre. On September 22, 1572, a month after the tragedy, the nuncio is represented as communicating to the king the desire of his Holiness, "for the great glory of God, and the greatest welfare of France, to see all the heretics of the kingdom exterminated." And on October 11 the same Salviati is said to have declared that the Pope had experienced "an infinite joy and great consolation in learning that his Majesty had commanded him (Salviati) to write that he hoped that in a little while France would have no more Huguenots." Well, what does all this prove? One who is acquainted with the epistolary style of the Roman Curia will not be frightened at the use, in the first despatch, of a word which Acton translated into "exterminated." Every bishop is sworn to "extirpate heresy;" but who believes that the American hierarchy is ready, if it had the power, to inaugurate another Barthélemy? We, too, sincerely pray that the day will soon come when this Republic will have no more Protestants; but is not the American priesthood full of that material out of which the Catholic Church forms a St. Vincent de Paul, a St. Philip Neri, and a Don Bosco?

V.

The number of the victims of the massacre has been greatly exaggerated. It is remarkable that in proportion to their distance in time from this event, authors increase the number of the slaughtered. Thus, Masson gives it as 10,000; the Calvinist "martyrologist" as about 15,000; the Calvinist, La Popelinière, as more than 20,000; De Thou, the apologist of the Huguenots, as 30,000 "or a little less;" the Huguenot Sully as 70,000; Péréfixe, a Catholic bishop, as 100,000. From this last number to 2,000, the figures established by Cavairac, the difference is immense. Now, if we will compare the authority, in this particular matter, of Masson with that of Péréfixe, we shall opine that the former's estimate is to be preferred. Masson did not wish to hide from posterity the true number of the slain; he openly laments that Calvinism was not destroyed by this great blow; he labors much in gathering apparent proofs that the massacre was long premeditated. Therefore he would have cheerfully recorded a larger number of victims, if truth had allowed him. Péréfixe, however, had an interest in exaggerating the effects of a policy of cruelty; preceptor to the young Louis XIV., he might have too readily accorded credence to the largest estimate of the victims of an event which he offered to the execration of his pupil. But our attention is principally claimed by the calculations of the Calvinist "martyrologist." When this interested author speaks in general terms, he puts the victims at 30,000; when he goes into details, he presents us 15,168; when he gives their names, he can furnish only 786. Now, we must suppose that this writer, engaged upon the pious work of perpetuating the memory of those whom he regarded as martyrs for "the religion," as his title-page announces, took every care to discover their names; and the zeal and vanity of their friends would have helped him. Nevertheless, he could name only 786. We ourselves do not believe that this number includes all the victims of the massacre ; but we do contend that this author's estimate by cities and villages, 15,168, is an exaggeration. He designates the victims in Paris as 10,000, but his details show only 468 ; it is not unlikely therefore that a zero slipped into his Paris total, and that it should be made 1,000. This, indeed, is the opinion of the Calvinist La Popelinière, and it is confirmed by a bill at the Hôtel de Ville of Paris, which indicates that 1,100 were buried in the suburbs. We regard, therefore, as nearly correct the assertion of La Popelinière that the victims in Paris were about 1,000 in number ; and since it is generally conceded that the slain in all the other parts of France together were less numerous than in Paris, it would appear that Cavairac did not err when he declared that all the victims of St. Bartholomew's Day amounted to about 2,000 persons.

The reader will doubtless expect us to allude to the charge made against Charles IX., of having taken an actively personal part in the massacre. Voltaire makes much of the accusation that the monarch fired on the Huguenots from a balcony in the Louvre (1). Prudhomme represents Charles as leaving a game of billiards for this purpose (2). This charge is founded only on the assertions of Brantôme, who, according to his own admission, was a hundred leagues from Paris on the day of the massacre (3) ; and of d'Aubigné, who says that he left the capital three days before the event (4). Sully, a Calvinist who was present and barely saved his life, says nothing in his *Mémoires* of the king's intervention. Again, that part of the Louvre from which Charles is said to have fired an arquebuse, and to mark which with infamy the Commune of 1793 erected "*un poteau infamant*," was not built until nearly the end of the reign of Henry IV., over thirty years after the Barthélemy. Finally, the accusation against Charles IX. is refuted by a Huguenot pamphlet of 1579—that is, written twenty-five years before the narrative of Brantôme, and thirty-seven before that of d'Aubigné. In

---

(1) *Essay on the Civil Wars.—Henriade*, in the Notes.   (2) *Revolutions of Paris.*
(3) *Works* ; edit. 1779, vol. I., p. 62.   (4) *Mémoires*, edit. Lalanne, p. 23.

this work, the *Tocsin* (1) which we have already quoted, we read : "Although one might suppose that so great a carnage would have satiated the cruelty of the young king, of a woman, and of many of their courtiers, they seem to have grown more savage as the work approached their own eyes. The king showed no diminution of zeal; for although *he did not use his own hands in the massacre,* nevertheless, being at the Louvre, he ordered that according as the work advanced in the city, the names of the killed and of the prisoners should be brought to him, that he might decide as to whom to spare." And Brantôme himself shows the small value of his assertions concerning the massacre, when he tells us that the king " wished only Ambrose Paré, his chief surgeon, to be spared " (2). We know from the *Mémoires* of Margaret de Valois that Charles wished to spare La Noue, Teligny, La Rochefoucauld, and even Coligny; and the writings of Paré show that this surgeon was a devout Catholic, and that, therefore, there was no need for anxiety in his regard on the part of the king. The Catholicism of Paré is also proved by the fact of the interment of his body in the church of St. André-des-Arts, of which the famous leaguer Aubry was pastor (3).

In conclusion, we would say with Louis Veuillot that Catholics generally adduce the extenuating circumstances of the Barthélemy with too great timidity. Catharine dei Medici was a free thinker of the Machiavellian school, provoked by Calvinist sedition ; and since she could not otherwise preserve her power, or even save her head, she adopted the policy of assassination. In the whole affair the Catholic faith was conspicuous for its absence ; the executioners were no more influenced by it than the victims. God, says Bossuet, often chastises crimes by other crimes. The ninth Thermidor, says M. de Maistre, witnessed the slaughter of certain monsters by others of the same sort. Just like the ninth Thermidor, the Barthélemy was a human wickedness and a divine justice.

And now for a few words concerning one of the customary

(1) Published in the " Archives " of Cimber and Danjou.
(2) *Illustrious Men*; in the Discourses on Coligny and Charles IX.
(3) See the Introduction of Malgaigne to the *Works* of Paré.

ornaments of the popular version of the Barthélemy, the
generally current story of the horrible death of Charles IX.
Those persons of taste who visited the Universal Exposition
at Paris, in 1855, were surprised at the interest shown by so
many in a painting exhibited by Henry Scheffer—a picture
which was only fairly well executed. But those artistic natures should have known that in art, just as in literature, it is
the loud that attracts the crowd. The subject chosen by the
Dutch artist was the *Vision of Charles IX.*, and his method of
treatment was as loud as his conception was historically false.
A sea of blood was approaching the monarch, and in its waves
was seen Coligny, whose breast was pierced by a Catholic
sword. Goujon, the sculptor, was also there; although it is
far from certain that he perished in the Barthélemy (1). Then
there were women, holding their slaughtered babes; old men
pointing to their white hairs; and victims of every condition.
The pallid and trembling king in vain interposes a crucifix to
ward off the apparitions, and one of them throws the infamous arquebuse at the royal feet. The critics of the day were
right when they declared that the Hollander had put on canvas an epitome of the "histories" of the Massacre and of
the terrible remorse of Charles IX. How much value is possessed by those narratives we have shown; but what are we
to say about the death of Charles IX.? Sismondi, Lavallée,
Guizot, and Henri Martin all compose their narratives on the
basis of a mixture of the sayings of l'Etoile, d'Aubigné, and
Sully; these suspicious authorities being cited by each author as the sole supports of his allegations. If we are to credit
these Huguenots, Charles IX. had so miserable an end, that
even the Huguenots felt some pity for him. His sleep was
constantly interrupted, they said, by visions of those whom
he and his mother had murdered; he often sweated blood, so
tremendous were his fears of eternal punishment. Now Sis-

---

(1) Jean Goujon, the sculptor, was one of the most famous men of his day; and it would
have been the interest of the Calvinist Martyrologist to mention him in that presumedly
correct list which he compiled. But he is silent. Longperier says, in his *French Plutarch,*
that he read in an olden MS. that Catharine dei Medici had forewarned Goujon not to leave
his house on the fatal day. For years after the massacre the Huguenots used to say that the
sculptor was shot while working at his beautiful nymphs of the Fountain of the Innocents;
but it is certain that this production of his chisel was completed twenty-two years before
the Barthélemy.

mondi is fond of quoting the *Curious Archives of the History of France*, a collection which is indeed precious to the lovers of interesting details in historical matters ; and in the very same Series of the eighth volume, to which he often refers when treating of this subject, he must have met a testimony which he ignores, because of its explosion of his theories. In 1574, immediately after the death of Charles IX., Sorbin de Sainte-Foy, preacher-in-ordinary to the king, and also a historian and a poet (1), published a *Life* of the monarch, whose confessor he had been, and at whose last illness and death he had assisted. Sorbin speaks, of course, of his penitent's contrition ; but he says nothing of those horrible effects of remorse, those bloody sweats, those yells for mercy, on which d'Aubigné dilates, and which Sismondi and Henri Martin credit. As for the causes of the death, Sorbin says : "I leave these to the surgeons who attended him during his sickness, and who opened his body." If it be alleged that Sorbin was a courtier, and interested in hiding the crimes of his master, he answers the objection : "I know well that the heretic and misbeliever will charge me with flattery, and with silence as to the imperfections of my master. ... I will hear that before the king was married, he had a child by Marie Touchet, a young girl of Orleans. This is a fact which I would wish never to have happened ; and in this matter I must speak evil of my king. But if thou, heretic, couldst have seen, as I often saw, this sinner weeping because of his sins, and if thou hadst known his gentleness, thou wouldst never have spoken of him as thou hast been accustomed to speak." As to the death of Charles IX. having been produced by the bloody sweats wrung from him by his remorse for the Barthélemy, medical science testifies that the monarch succumbed to disease of the lungs. In 1876, A. Leyert published an article on *The Bloody Sweat of Charles IX.* (2), in which he cited a work by Dr. Corlieu on *The Deaths of the French Kings from Francis I. to the Revolution*, which proves

(1) He finally became bishop of Nevers. He was the author of thirty works in both prose and poetry. The title of the cited work is *A History Containing an Abridgment of the Life of the Very Christian and Gentle King, Charles IX., Truly Pious, A Defender of the Catholic Faith, and A Lover of Right-minded Persons.*

(2) In the Paris *Foyer* of Feb. 12, p. 191.

that in the *Mémoires of Cheverny* (1579), it was made evident
that King Charles was suffering, in 1573, from disease of the
lungs.   And Corlieu proved, after analyzing the report of
the autopsy, that pulmonary disease caused the death of the
royal patient; and he added : " As to the bloody sweats
mentioned by d'Aubigné alone, ignored by all the historians
and physicians of the day, we believe that it was merely a
purpura hemorrhagica. ... If we remember that Charles IX.
was ill with pulmonary trouble for eight months ; if we consider the influence of respiration on the cardiac and hepatic
circulation ; and if we reflect on the state of flacidity and va-
cuity of the heart and on the bloodlessness of the liver ; we
will be convinced that the patient was profoundly anemic, and
that the pretended sweats of blood were merely speckles of
the *purpura*, which were simple after-symptoms (*epiphéno-
mène*), and not a cause of death."   It is noteworthy that the
Venetian ambassador, Cavalli, informed his government of
all the phases of the king's malady, and always found them
perfectly natural; and he says that "the recent conspiracies
(of the Huguenots) plunged his soul in torment, and prevented him from enjoying one instant of rest."   The fact is that
Charles IX. died of a disease produced by anxiety.   As Sorbin
said : " The chief cause of his death was the sadness which
had begun its work in his childhood, through the treasons
and multifold impieties of many of his subjects, and of many
even of his own familiars.   He had been dying by inches, for
thirteen or fourteen years."

CHAPTER XXIV.

THE CONVERSION OF HENRY IV. OF FRANCE.

The death of Henry III., the last of the Valois, on Aug. 1,
1589, at the hands of the fanatical Clement (1), made Henry
of Navarre legitimate king of France, if right of birth was
sufficient, of itself, to establish a right to the crown.   There
being no heir in the line of the Valois, the royal claims naturally fell to Henry de Bourbon, the head of the line which

(1) Two Dominican writers, Frederick Steill and Matthew Dolmans, have tried to prove
that Clement was not the assassin of Henry ; that the real murderer was a Huguenot who
had killed Clement, and donned his garments.

was derived from the marriage of the count of Clermont, the youngest son of St. Louis, with the daughter and heiress of Archambault de Bourbon. In his last moments, which were spent in a manner becoming to his faith, though never augured by his method of life, Henry III. had recognized the Bourbon as his heir, but had thus warned him: " My dear brother-in-law (1), you will never be king of France, unless you become a Catholic " (2). However, Henry de Bourbon was soon deserted by most of the Catholic lords who had followed Henry III. when he abandoned the Leaguers for the camp of the Navarrese ; and they proclaimed the cardinal de Bourbon, an uncle of Henry IV., as king under the name of Charles X., the real authority being understood to belong to the duke de Mayenne, the second son of the late Francis de Guise. The reader must bear in mind that in Sept., 1585, Pope Sixtus V. had issued a Bull (*Ab immensa*) wherein he declared Henry de Bourbon and his cousin, Henry de Condé, relapsed heretics, because of their having violated their abjuration, made after the Barthélemy; and in that Bull the Pontiff had pronounced, as a natural consequence of the heresy of the princes, " them both deprived of all their dignities, and both, together with their posterity, incapable of succeeding to the throne of France." We shall speak of this document at some length, when we treat of the Pontificate of Sixtus V. Henry IV., for as such he was now recognized by very many even of those who had no intention to disobey the Holy See, was constrained, on beholding the smallness of his following, to forward to the Holy See a document wherein he promised, as clearly as he could do so without alienating the sympathies of the Huguenots, to become a Catholic ; and wherein he implicitly admitted that a profession of heresy was incompatible with the royalty of France (3). This paper reads as follows : " We, Henry, by the grace of

(1) Henry's sister Margaret had been married to the Bourbon prince, four days before the Barthélemy.

(2) DAVILA: *History of the Civil Wars in France*, vol. I., p. 48, edit. Rocolet, Paris, 1657. This author was a son of that Davila who had been constable of Cyprus, and having been defeated by the Turks, had been protected by Catharine dei Medici. The son grew up in the court ; and his narratives of its doings may be considered as fairly accurate.

(3) We translate the Italian text of Tempesti, who had translated the original which had been placed in the hands of Sixtus V. by the duke of Luxembourg, Henry's envoy, on Jan. 13, 1590.

God, king of France and of Navarre, do promise and swear by
the faith and word of a king, and by these presents signed
with our own hand, to all our good and faithful subjects, to
maintain and preserve faithfully in our kingdom the Catholic,
Apostolic, and Roman religion, innovating or changing nothing as to its free exercise, or as regards ecclesiastical persons,
leaving to them all of their goods and governments, just as
they have hitherto possessed. We shall also be disposed,
conformably to our letters-patent which were published before our accession to the throne, to receive instruction from a
general or national Council; promising to follow and observe
all its decisions, and to procure its convocation and reunion
within six months, and sooner, if that is possible. In the
meantime, in all the cities and places of our kingdom in
which the Catholic religion is practiced there shall be no
practice of any other religion, as was arranged in the treaty
made on the last 16th of April between us and the late king,
Henry III. of happy memory, our very honored lord and cousin whom may God absolve; that is, until it shall have been
otherwise decided, either after the general pacification of the
kingdom, or by the Estates General which will be convoked
and assembled within six months. We also promise that in
all the districts, places, and fortresses, which we may take
from the rebels (the Leaguers) and reduce to our obedience
by force or otherwise, we shall establish as governors no other
persons than good Catholic subjects; reserving, however, those
places which, according to the treaty just cited, were assigned
by the late king to the professors of the reformed religion in
each bailliage or seneschalship. We also promise that within six months capable and faithful Catholics shall be appointed to all the governorships and other offices which may
become vacant in other places, excepting in those in the
hands of persons of the reformed religion." When Luxembourg, who was a Catholic, handed this declaration to Sixtus
V., he remarked: "When giving me his final instructions,
his Majesty said to me: 'Tell his Holiness, on my royal
word, that facts will show that I wish to live and die as the
Eldest Son of the Holy, Catholic, and Roman Church'" (1).

(1) TEMPESTI; *Life of Sixtus V.*, vol. II., p. 279. Rome, 1754

Having read the document, the Pontiff replied : " Not long ago we wrote to the Catholic King (Philip II. of Spain) that so long as we reigned in Rome, no heretical prince should reign over France. Now we are pleased with the conditions imposed on the Bearnese at his election, and also with his protestations ; but before there are any negotiations in regard to his reconciliation with the Church, let him free his uncle, the cardinal de Bourbon (the so-called Charles X., then in the hands of Henry). When that is done, we shall consider carefully as to what ought to be done for the reception of the prince as a penitent and converted son; let him put away his obstinacy and give us this proof of his obedient spirit. Then we shall press him to our heart; for it is only his sin that we detest. But be assured that all negotiation is futile, until he has complied with our injunctions." If the reader thinks that Sixtus V. asked too much when he required the liberation of the pretender, he must remember that Henry could very easily have sent the aged cardinal to Rome, where he would have been no longer a rival for the French throne ; and even if the liberated prelate had placed himself at the head of the Leaguers, Henry would have soon realized that he had little to fear from the pretensions of an aged celibate.

The reception of Luxembourg by the Pontiff was a thorn in the side of Philip II., as well as in that of the League. In Paris and Madrid the ultra zealots raged because of what they termed moderation in regard to one whose relapses merited the stake ; and on March 11 the cardinal Cajetan, papal legate to the League (1), received from the leaders, in the church of St. Augustine, an oath that they would never recognize Henry de Bourbon as their king. In Spain, opposition to the pontifical moderation took the form of insolence ; one preacher declared that Sixtus should be deposed as a protector of heretics. The count of Olivarez, ambassador of Philip II. at Rome, wrote to the viceroy of Naples to encourage brigandage in the Papal States, so as to create

(1) Although accredited to the League, Cajetan had been instructed to not commit himself irrevocably to its objects ; but the legate's Spanish sympathies revolted at this restriction. If it appears strange that the Holy See should send a nuncio to a government which had no legitimate head, we must remember that Rome could not accredit a legate to a prince who was cut off from the Catholic communion, and there was a need of a nuncio somewhere in France.

embarrassments for Sixtus; and in the name of his sovereign he demanded that the Pontiff should excommunicate all the adherents of the Bearnese. When the cardinal-pretender died at Fontenay, and the Pope refused to allow a royal funeral at Rome, Olivarez publicly denounced his conduct; whereupon Sixtus thought seriously of excommunicating the madman, and of expelling him from the Eternal City. In public consistory the Pontiff thus expressed his resolution not to yield to Philip II.: "If the Spanish envoy has not invented these demands, and if they really emanate from his master, we shall never yield to such pretensions. Nor would we yield to such demands, if urged by all the princes of Christendom; for this matter concerns only us and this Holy See." When the subject of this discord heard of the stand assumed by Sixtus in his favor, he remarked to one of the princes of the blood: "The world shall see whether I am sincere in swearing to preserve the Catholic religion in France; and if the Pontiff needs my sword to defend him, I shall draw it" (1). Meanwhile many of the Catholic partisans of Henry constantly wrote to Rome, complaining of the conduct of Cajetan, guaranteeing the ultimate success of their prince, and urging the Pope to make certain peace with the child of destiny. At this time Cajetan had held no other relation with Henry than to request the prince not to intercept the despatches which arrived for him from Rome; and Henry had replied that he was necessarily obliged to treat the legate as an enemy. When the envoy, Mocenigo, urged that the attitude of Cajetan would change as soon as the prince returned to the Church, and thereby attracted all Frenchmen to his banner, Henry replied: "If I am in error, I wish to be instructed; but not with lances and arquebuses, as the legate would teach me. Hitherto these have failed to convince me, because I am more a master of the art of war than Cajetan is; I have been in the school of war for twenty years, and all that time has been passed by the legate in reading his Breviary." Very soon Sixtus complained of the policy of Cajetan in full consistory; and he wrote to the unlucky man that he would be obliged to punish him severely if he did not show himself the envoy of the Apostolic See, rather than one of Philip II. (1). However, it was by no means the intention of the Pontiff to be caught in the meshes of the diplomatic processes of Henry, which were just as tortuous as those of his Catholic Majesty ; the Holy See could not entertain the pretension of the king of Navarre that a papal legate should be accredited to one who was under ecclesiastical censure.

The fortunes of war were unfavorable to the League. Defeated at Ivry, March 30, 1590, Mayenne became embittered not only toward Philip II., whose game of dynastic aggrandizement he began to perceive, but against the Pontiff, whom he charged with a calculated coolness in regard to the League. As though he felt that his innumerable defeats would have been obviated by such small succors of men and money as the Pope might have afforded, he wrote to Sixtus a caustic letter which should be read by those historians who represent the Roman court of that day as the train-bearer of his Catholic Majesty. "As head of the Church, your Holiness ought not to listen to the arguments of those who assert that if we (the League) wax strong, our prosperity will help to augment the power of the Catholic king, of whom every one is so jealous. Religion should pass over all other considerations. However, the king of Spain does not dream of acquiring another crown, and we have never thought that he had any design other than the preservation of the faith in this kingdom. ... But if we ought to suspect Philip, your Holiness will increase the danger by abandoning us, and thus making us owe to that monarch our altars, our goods, and our lives " (2). When this letter was read to Sixtus in the presence of several cardinals, he observed : " That man would tell the truth, if he said some more ;" and certainly Mayenne did not expose the entire situation. The great object of the Holy See was not to further any particular pretensions ; it was to maintain Catholic rule in France. "If the League, a wonderful and noble instrument for so grand a work, failed to actuate it because the chiefs of the party were impotent, or because they were too occupied with triv-

---

(1) *Ibid.*, p. 313   (2) *Ubi supra*, p. 290.

ial interests, it was proper for the successor of St. Peter to modify his course. But in doing so, did Sixtus abandon the League, ignore its devotion, or renounce its aid? His political perspicacity led him to discern in Henry the victor destined by Providence to put an end to sixty years of civil war; and to realize that the Church ought not to repel him if he proposed to return to her bosom as a prodigal son. That same perspicacity revealed to Sixtus the projects of him who had inherited a part of the dominions of Charles V. and all of that emperor's dream of universal monarchy. Thenceforth, faithful to his mission of vicar of that Christ whose Gospel gave notions of liberty to the world, the attitude of the Pope gave notice of the danger, and he moderated a movement which was dragging the defenders of a noble cause to unknown extremes, preparing by his action, as far as possible, the road for a better future " (1). In this entire matter of the Pontiff, the League, and Henry of Navarre, the real question was not one of the miserable interests of Bourbons, Lorrains, or Spaniards; it was whether Catholic civilization was to be preserved, as well as a proper equilibrium between the powers who remained faithful to the Church. The triumphant excursion of the great Italian captain, Farnese, contributed much to this result. Henry beheld his capital snatched from his grasp; and when he saw Farnese renewing his prodigies before Rouen, he realized that his sole hope was in a reconciliation with Rome.

Gregory XIV., the successor of Sixtus V., was more partial than Sixtus had been to Spain; but he was no more subservient to the policy of Philip II. He sent succors to Mayenne; but that did not please the Spaniard, who feared a prompt and complete victory of the League as an obstacle to his own plan of either acquiring the French throne for himself, or of seating on it a Spanish Infanta. Innocent IX., who reigned for two months after the six months of pontificate of Gregory XIV., endeavored to force Philip II. to put an end to his temporizing policy, but without success. One of the first acts of Clement VIII., who mounted the papal throne on Feb. 11, 1592, was to order Mayenne to place be-

(1) SEGRETAIN: *Sixtus V. et Henry IV*. Paris, 1861.

fore the States General the question of the succession to the
French crown ; and Henry felt the significance of this step
so deeply, that he resolved to improve his position by showing himself publicly at Mass at Saint-Denis. The States
General met on Jan. 26, 1593 ; and their evident desire to respect the right of hereditary descent in their monarch, only
on condition that the prince did not violate the religious traditions of France, showed Henry that the day of temporiza-
tion had passed. He suddenly yielded to the solicitations of
Renaud de Beaune, archbishop of Bourges ; and after some
conferences with the celebrated convert, Du Perron (1) and
other able theologians, he demanded to be received again
into the communion of the Church. As we shall show, the
suddenness of this resolution ought not to lead us to doubt
the reality of Henry's religious convictions, and therefore the
sincerity of his too long delayed conversion. Having taken
this resolution, common sense and honor, to say nothing of
religion, demanded that Henry should ask from the Pontiff
absolution from those censures which the Holy See had pronounced against him. But Renaud de Beaune, an easy going
ecclesiastic (2), and one of those schismatics *in posse* who
ever combat an effective and active Papacy, persuaded the
not very theological mind of the convert that an absolution
by the French bishops, subject to the future ratification of
the Pontiff, would be perfectly regular. Henry was too willing to take this view of the matter ; for he knew that the
Pope would grant his absolution only on condition that the
Bearnese would promise to observe the ancient public law of
France, and to repair the damages caused by the Huguenots.
It was natural for a prince who was a consummate master in
diplomatic trickery, and whose soul was as yet strange to the
real spirit of Catholicism, to avail himself of the counsels of
courtier-bishops ; but when Renaud de Beaune and his accomplices proclaimed Henry of Navarre a Catholic, and by that
act placed the crown of France on his brow, without demanding any guarantees in return for it, they assumed a great responsibility before their contemporaries and before posterity.

(1) Afterward bishop of Evreux, and finally cardinal.
(2) He used to take seven meals a day, and two of them lasted an hour each.

Never until that day had a successor of Clovis been hailed as Most Christian King without the consent and blessing of the Roman Pontiff; but on July 25, 1593, certain French bishops, with his Grace of Bourges at their head, presumed to receive into the society of Christian sovereigns a prince who labored under the censures of the Vicar of Christ (1). Had the papal legate to France, at that time the cardinal of Piacenza, been ever so disposed to a lenient interpretation of the mind of the Holy See, he could not have ignored this contempt of the authority of the keys. Accordingly, as soon as he heard of the project of Renaud de Beaune, he issued a monitory wherein he launched excommunication against each and every person who would take any part in a pretence of according to Henry de Bourbon an absolution which he could receive only from the Roman Pontiff. Notwithstanding this decree, on the third day after its appearance, Henry was pronounced, in the abbatial church of Saint-Denis, a member of the Catholic Church, no other forms having been observed than those used in the case of private individuals. It is well for the reader to reflect upon this anarchical procedure of Henry and his courtier-bishops ; for too many historians are utterly silent as to the matter, and therefore they find it easy to convey the impression that Rome, by her delay of two years before a final absolution of the Bearnese, was guilty of a blind and inexplicable obstinacy in the assertion of her prerogatives.

(1) "Some have affected to see in this matter a purely theological difficulty, a point of Canon-Law to be debated, with closed doors, between the Holy See and the episcopate. To so regard it is a sign of ignorance or of prejudice, both of which fail to recognize the real conditions of society in the sixteenth century, and which do not perceive that then all religious questions were necessarily political questions of the highest order. It may be said with truth that this usurpation by the royalist bishops, this contempt of the most certain laws of the sacred hierarchy, was sadder and more dangerous in the civil, than in the ecclesiastical order. ... The Bearnese knew well that it was no vain complacency in his own prerogatives which caused the Holy Father to reserve the absolution in question to himself. Had the case been one concerning only the royal soul, any priest could have received its avowal of repentance, and a mitre would have given enough of solemnity to the public abjuration. But here the interest of the whole of society was involved. Was Catholicism to be the end regarded by the State, as it was by the individual? Was the ancient magistracy of the Pope, the guardian of the temporal effects of the divine law, to be abolished, as the Protestants wished ; or was it to be maintained, as Catholics desired, and for which maintenance they had shed their blood ? Was heresy a political, as well as a spiritual crime? Such were the questions involved in the reservation of Henry's absolution to the Pope." SEGRETAIN ; loc. cit., p. 232.

When Henry sent the duke of Nevers to inform Pope Clement VIII. of his absolution, practically he asked the Pontiff to recognize as a member of the Church a prince who had just trampled under his feet the document wherein that Pope's predecessor had excommunicated him. His submission to the Holy See was apparent; but in reality, he was prolonging his rebellion. Therefore the Pontiff refused his homage. In a very short space of time Henry realized that he was in a false position. By declaring his wish to be of the same religion as his subjects, he had imbued the people with a desire for peace; but so long as his right to the crown was not sanctioned by Rome, he could not but expect to have enemies who would find strength in an illegitimacy which he himself was perpetuating. He endeavored to obviate the danger by separate treaties with the leaders of the League; but the attitude of the Holy See impeded his success, Mayenne even joining the Spaniards with a determination to prevent, with their aid, a movement for Catholic unity from becoming hostile to the supreme authority of the head of the Church. The eyes of Henry were finally opened; and through the medium of D'Ossat (afterward cardinal) he besought Pope Clement VIII. to receive him into the Church. The Pontiff declared that certain guarantees would be necessary, before he could remove the censures inflicted by Sixtus V.; and accordingly Du Perron was joined to D'Ossat for the purpose of negotiation. Du Perron himself gives us the result of the labors of himself and his colleague in the articles which the ambassadors signed in the name of their master; and we must admire the prudence and perspicacity with which Clement VIII. protected the essential principles of Catholic society, even though the defection of Henry's courtier-bishops had much weakened his power. The articles read as follows : I. The procurators will take the customary oath to obey the commands of the Holy See and of the Church. II. They will abjure Calvinism and all other heresies, and they will make their Profession of Faith, in the presence of the Pope. III. The king will restore the exercise of the Catholic religion in the principality of Bearn, and will nominate Catholic bishops therein, as soon as possible; and until their property is restored to those churches, the king will provide proper support for the bishops out of his own revenues. IV. Within a year the king will withdraw the prince of Condé from the hands of the heretics, and will consign the said prince to Catholic persons, that he may be raised in the Catholic religion. (The reader must know that Henry had no children by his first wife, and that at this time his cousin, the young prince de Condé, was his presumptive heir. The imposition of this obligation upon Henry was a justification of the deprivatory Bull of Sixtus V., and also a measure destined to forestall any necessity for a similar Bull in the future.) V. The Concordats shall be observed in regard to the collation of benefices, and all other things. VI. The king will never nominate heretics, or persons suspected of heresy, to any bishopric, abbacy, or other benefice to which he has a right to nominate. VII. The king will cause the Council of Trent to be published and observed, excepting in such things, if any are found, which cannot be enforced without disturbance of the tranquillity of the realm. VIII. The king will specially protect the sacerdotal order, and he will see that ecclesiastics are not oppressed by military persons or others. IX. If the king has enfiefed any castles or other church property, either to Catholics or to heretics, he will revoke the concessions. X. The king will prove, by word and deed, and in his appointments to the dignities and honors of the kingdom, that Catholics are dear to him ; so that all may know clearly that he desires only one religion, namely, the Catholic, Apostolic, and Roman, which he professes, to flourish in France. XI. The king, unless he is legitimately impeded, will recite, every day, the Rosary of Our Lady ; on Wednesday, he will recite the Litanies ; on Saturday, he will again recite the Rosary ; every day he will attend at Mass, and on feasts he will attend at High Mass ; and he will observe all the fasts and all the commandments of the Church. XII. The king will confess, and also receive Communion in public, at least four times every year. XIII. In each province of the kingdom and in Bearn the king will build a monastery. XIV. The king will ratify the abjuration, the Profession of Faith, and the promises made by his procurators, in France,

in the hands of the legate or some other representative of
the Holy See; and he will send to the Pope the said ratification. XV. The king will write to all Catholic sovereigns,
expressing his joy on having been received into the favor
of the Roman Church, in whose communion he professes
himself resolved to remain. XVI. The king will order that
throughout his kingdom thanks be given to God for the great
grace he has received.

On Sept. 19, 1595, the throne of the Pope was placed in
the vestibule of the Basilica of the Apostles; for the Vicar
of Christ was about to perform an act which would open the
doors of the Church to Henry de Bourbon, and thereby sanction that prince's title of King of France and Navarre. At a
given signal a master of ceremonies conducted the procurators of the penitent, James Davy du Perron and Arnald d'Ossat, to the feet of the Pontiff, which they humbly kissed.
Then Du Perron read aloud the title of procuration which his
royal master had given to him and his colleague, following
with a prayer that the Father of the Faithful would pardon
all the irregularities of his master's reception into the Church
at Saint-Denis, and grant to the said prince full absolution
for his past errors, especially for his grievous relapse into
heresy. Pope Clement now ordered the reading of the following decree, whereby he declared null the illicit absolution
at Saint-Denis: "We, Clement, eighth of that name, Pope,
having invoked the name of Our Lord and Saviour, Jesus
Christ, from whom all just judgments come, and sitting on
our throne of justice as in a tribunal; having God alone in
our mind; and after a consideration of everything which
ought to be considered; we decide and declare that the pretended absolution of Henry, king of France and Navarre, by
a certain prelate of the kingdom of France, whether administered by the advice of certain other French prelates or
from any other motive, is null, and without any effect or validity, and that it ought to be annulled, as we do now annul
and invalidate it. Nevertheless, we will that such religious
acts, otherwise Catholic and worthy of approval, which have
been performed in consequence of that absolution, and which
could not have been done unless by an absolved person

and by virtue of the absolution, be valid and firm, just as
though the king had been absolved by us. And now because
of motives which worthily influence our mind, we decree
and declare that the said King Henry, who has long and humbly requested the favor from us, ought to be and is relieved
from the greater excommunication and other ecclesiastical
censures which he incurred by adhesion to heresy and by
overt heretical acts, and which were fulminated against him
by Sixtus V. of happy memory and our predecessor in his
letters of the Fifth of the Ides of September of the year 1585,
because Henry had relapsed into heresy after he had abjured
his errors at Paris in the year 1572. We declare that Henry
ought to be absolved and relieved, received into the fold of
his mother, our Holy Church, allowed to share in the Sacraments ; but after having supplicated according to the legitimate rites, and after having, according to the canonical regulations, abjured and anathematized every species of Calvinism,
Calvinistic error, and all other doctrines which are hostile
to the Holy Catholic and Apostolic Roman Church; and also
after having made a Profession of Catholic Faith according
to a form to be prescribed by us, and having confirmed his
profession by a solemn oath. He must also promise, also by
oath, to observe the commandments of the Holy Church, his
mother ; to obey her and all of our injunctions ; and to do all
these things in good faith and in the customary ecclesiastical ·
manner, to the praise and glory of Almighty God and of His
Holy Church. So we have pronounced." After the reading
of this decree the royal procurators humbly accepted it; and
then, with their hands on the Gospels, they read a detailed
formula whereby Henry abjured all his heresies, and professed explicitly the Catholic faith. Then a papal notary
promulgated the conditions of absolution which we have already given ; and then, the Pontiff solemnly relieved Henry
of his excommunication, and consigned the procurators to the
care of the grand-penitentiary, Cardinal Santa Severina, to
be led through the now opened portals of the basilica—thus
symbolizing, according to the Roman Liturgy, the return of
their royal master to the bosom of the Church.

We now approach the subject of Henry's sincerity when.

he definitively abjured the errors of Protestantism. Men naturally suspect the sincerity of a religious conversion when it is accompanied by the acquisition of temporal advantages ; and certainly they are inclined to question the single-mindedness of the convert when a royal crown rewards his change of religion. Therefore we need not wonder that Protestant and rationalistic. historians have represented Henry of Navarre as uttering the flippant phrase, "Paris is well worth a Mass," as an excuse to his former co-sectarians for his change of religious profession. But did Henry XIV. ever pronounce such a sentiment? Must it not be ranked among the many more or less brilliant verbal scintillations which imaginative biographers have placed, without any historical foundation, in the mouths of their heroes—or their victims—as indicative of a fancied *rôle* on the stage of history? In fine, is not this moderately smart effusion, which might run trippingly on the tongue of a truculent trooper as one of the salacious sallies appropriate at the fire of a bivouac, to be stamped as entirely foreign to the taste and probable language of an adroit diplomat like Henry of Navarre? We have little sympathy with that school of French royalists who would represent the first of the Bourbon royal line as a sort of demigod. Nor do we even agree with those who fancied, a few years ago, and with good reason during a moment or two, that a 'fifth Henry was about to be evolved from the noble Chambord ; and who therefore, in order to clear the path of that prince to the throne of the Bourbons, endeavored to convince the French nation that his dashing ancestor was the consummately great one among its sovereigns (1). No; we find that though the conscience of Henry IV. became Catholic, some of his policy retained a Protestant tendency ; and that Louis XIV. was by far a greater king, if indeed, he was not the sole truly grand monarch of the Bourbon family. But it is due to the memory of Henry IV., and due to historical truth, to prove that he could not have spoken as Protestant polemics, in order to convict him of hypocrisy, would have us believe. We must show, in fine, that he was sincerely con-

(1) See, for instance. the over-enthusiastic, but otherwise valuable, *Life of Henry IV.*, by M. de Lescure.

verted to Catholicism.   With this end in view, we shall rely
upon the narratives of Palma Cayet, an ex-preacher who could
say of the disputants summoned to controversial debate by
Henry : " *Quorum pars magna fui* ;" of Péréfixe, preceptor
of the young Louis XIV.; of De Bury, a reliable Catholic author ; but principally upon one whom, in this matter, we regard as the most trustworthy historian of King Henry, namely, Henry himself, as he is manifested in his correspondence, the publication of which was confided to M. Berger de
Xivrey (1), and who has thus effected more for the reputation
of the gallant monarch than all his panegyrists.

Born of Catholic parents in 1553, Henry of Navarre was
baptized by the cardinal d'Armagnac, bishop of Rodez and
vice-legate of Avignon ; his sponsors, King Henry II. of
France, King Henry d'Albret, and Madame Claude de France,
being, of course, Catholics.   His father dying in 1562, his
mother, Queen Jane d'Albret, returned to Bearn, where she
apostatized ; leaving her son, however, at the court of France,
under the guidance of a sage Catholic tutor named La Gau-
cherie.   This preceptor died when the young prince was thirteen years old ; and his mother summoning him to Bearn, his
further education was entrusted to a Huguenot, and he was
trained in the Calvinist system.   Unlike most of his co-sectarians, the young Henry displayed no fanaticism ; and when,
in 1577, the Estates of Blois urged him to abjure his heresy,
he replied to their spokesman that " he was not obstinate in
matters of religion ; that he had believed in the doctrines
taught him in his youth ; and that the surest way to convert
him from them was not to threaten a war which would desolate the kingdom."   A few years afterward, Pope Sixtus V.,
an excellent judge of character, opined that " the head of that
prince was expressly fitted for the crown of France " (2).   On
August 2, 1589, Henry of Navarre claimed the French throne
by hereditary right, and as the designated heir of the assassinated Henry III.   For the first time in its history, the crown
of the Most Christian King seemed destined to be worn by
a heretic.   Now, in the France of that day, as in the France

(1) *Correspondence of Henry IV.*, in the *Collection of Unedited Documents Concerning the History of France*, vol. I.
(2) GREGORIO LETI : *Life of Sixtus V.*, Amsterdam, 1686.

of all post-Clovis times down to her fell upheaval in 1789, there was something more appreciated by the people than hereditary monarchical right,—something which entered into the very constitution of the monarchy, and consecrated it. From the coronation of Clovis by St. Remigius, the incumbent of the French monarchy incurred the obligation, *sine qua non*, of being a Catholic in name and in fact. Therefore the contest menacing France on the death of Henry III. was not an ordinary war of succession, but one for religious right, which was outraged in a society religiously constituted in its very origin,—a society which was bent on preserving its ancient constitution at any cost, even at that of hereditary royalty. The royalists of the school of Voltaire, of the Regent d'Orléans, and of the Encyclopedists, were quite sentimental and *courtisanesque;* they loyally professed " the religion of the king ; " and, nevertheless, they could not perceive all the grandeur of the Christian kinghood. Modern royalists have perhaps rivalled the republicans in making a noise, but too few of them have grasped the symbolic meaning of that ceremony of the Church at the consecration of a Catholic monarch, when she administers to the newly-anointed the Communion under both species, uniting, in a way, the priest with the king. When the spirit of Catholicism permeated the body politic, royalism was not merely sentimental ; it was religious and social. This fact was well understood by Henry of Navarre ; and on the very day of his accession he proclaimed, in a circular letter to the principal cities of France, that " he would preserve the Holy Roman and Apostolic Church with all his power." Finally, in 1593, he resolved to investigate the claims of that Church, and wrote to several bishops to meet him on July 15 at Suresne near Paris.

On May 18 he thus opened his heart to the bishop of Chartres : " I have determined to receive, at the earliest possible moment, instructions concerning the differences which cause schism in the Church, and I have always declared that I would not decline this instruction ; in fact, I would have received it long ago, had I not been impeded by well-known obstacles. Perhaps circumstances might excuse me now from attending to this matter, but I have resolved to defer it no longer. Therefore I have summoned some Catholic prelates and doctors, by whose teachings I may be enlightened as to the difficulties which separate us in religious matters. ... Having the glory of God for my sole object, I shall act in all sincerity." Writing to the archbishop of Bourges, he says: "I trust that God will grant me the grace to bring to this conference a mind bent only on His glory, and the grace of seeking only my own salvation and the good of the state." Palma Cayet tells us that about this time Henry remarked to one of his household: "I can perceive neither system nor devotion in Protestantism. It consists merely of sermons in fairly good language; whereas, in short, I suspect that we ought to admit the real presence of the Body of Our Lord in the Sacrament. Otherwise, all that 'the religion' effects is a mere ceremony." Péréfixe informs us that at one of the conferences, a Calvinist minister having admitted that a Catholic would be saved if he led a blameless life, the king exclaimed: "Then prudence impels me to enter the Catholic Church; for as a Catholic I may, according to both priests and ministers, attain salvation; whereas if I remain a Protestant, the priests contend that I shall be lost." After a long course of debate, the religious doubts of Henry were dissipated; and in July, 1593, he abjured his errors, emitted a solemn profession of his faith in Catholic doctrine, and received absolution, as we have seen, at the hands of Renaud de Beaune, archbishop of Bourges. From that time the Parisians, who hitherto had styled Henry "the Bearnais," hailed him by the royal title. On the 25th he sent to all his subjects a letter, from which we take the following passages: "Remembering the promise made on our accession to the throne—a promise which we ardently desired to keep, but which the artifices of our enemies prevented our fulfilling,—we conferred with certain prelates and doctors upon the points concerning which we desired enlightenment; and having been satisfied thereupon by arguments deduced from the Scriptures, from the Fathers, and from doctors recognized by the Church, we have acknowledged the Roman Apostolic Church as the true Catholic Church of God, as full of truth, and as incapable of error. Therefore we have entered into her pale, and are determined to live and die therein. And, that we might begin the good work at once, we have attended at the Holy Mass this morning, joining our prayers with those of the said Church ; ... and we request that public thanks be tendered to God by processions and prayers, and that God may be entreated to maintain us in our holy resolution." Announcing his conversion to the Pope, he said : " Most Holy Father, having recognized, through the inspiration which God has vouchsafed to grant to me, that the Catholic, Apostolic, and Roman Church is the true Church, ... I have resolved to render to your Holiness and to the Holy See my entire obedience and respect. ... I have wished to send you this first token of my filial devotion in lines drawn up by my own hand. ... And I hope to merit your holy blessing by my actions." From the first day of his conversion, Henry IV. evinced such sincerity that St. Francis de Sales, whose sublime truthfulness would permit no flattery for any purpose, did not hesitate to thus eulogize him : " In your conduct toward Holy Church I discern rare qualities which reveal in you the blood and the heart of Charlemagne and of St. Louis, the most prominent invigorators the Church has known." When his son and heir, who afterward became Louis XIII., was born, Henry laid his glorious sword in the little hand, praying God that the prince " might draw it only for His glory and in defence of the French nation." The faith of Henry in the Real Presence was most vivid. Among many instances of his manifestation of this faith, Péréfixe records the following : One day, while promenading with Sully, who was a Huguenot, he met a priest bearing the Holy Viaticum. Henry at once fell upon his knees in adoration ; whereupon Sully remarked : " Can your Majesty believe in that ? " Henry replied : " Yes, by the life of God, I do believe in it; and I would give a finger from my hand were you also to believe in it." Péréfixe says that Henry used every legitimate exertion to propagate the faith, and that he was, under God, the direct cause of sixty thousand conversions. " But he would allow no coercion, and he despised one who could be affected in this matter by worldly interest."

At the time of which we write France exercised a veritable

magistracy of thought over all Europe; and Henry IV. availed himself of this and her other ascendencies in favor of persecuted Catholics, wherever the children of the Reformation had obtained the upper-hand. Very little appears to have been known concerning this phase of Henry's foreign policy, until M. Ferrière-Percy drew attention to it in a careful study on M. de la Boderie, ambassador of France at the court of James I., and who was one of the noblest characters of that time (1). La Boderie was unable to ameliorate greatly the lot of the English Catholics, owing to the craze that afflicted the Protestant majority after the collapse of the Gunpowder Plot; and also because of the indifference of the English monarch, who was, according to the zealous ambassador, "nearly always engaged in cock-fighting or in gluttonous pleasures, and gave the smallest portion of his time to affairs of state." But La Boderie effected all that man could effect in the circumstances, and Ferrière-Percy could write: "If we have dwelt with some complacency upon a life which never belied itself, it is because we thought that a more marked significance would be attached to the intervention of Henry IV. in favor of the English Catholics, when viewed under the management of an ambassador whose convictions were so absolute. The choice of the servant reveals the inmost thought of the master." Nor ought this intervention of Henry in behalf of the English Catholics be regarded as an isolated fact, prompted by passing circumstances. From the moment when he assumed that proudest and peculiar title borne by a French monarch, "the Eldest Son of the Church," he continued the most glorious tradition of his crown—a tradition which even the degenerate France of our day is unwilling to ignore,—and he claimed the privilege of protecting the children of the Catholic Church in every quarter of the globe. He evinced his claim to this privilege in a most vigorous manner in his instructions to Jeannin, his envoy to Holland, insisting that such a course was "due to his religion, and to that charity which should be a characteristic of a Most Christian King, as God had constituted him." This phase of the foreign policy of Henry IV. undoubtedly forms another argument in

(1) The Embassies of Antoine de la Boderie, in the Correspondant for 1857, p. 237.

evidence of the sincerity of his abjuration of sectarian error, and of his vow of obedience to the One Holy Catholic Apostolic Roman Church. Had he been actuated by such sentiments as the utterance of the flippant phrase, "Paris is well worth a Mass," would imply, nothing would have been more easy or more natural than for him to have followed a policy of indifference in regard to his foreign religious brethren.

Not content with the protection of foreign Catholics, Henry IV. devised a project truly worthy of a French monarch, and the mere conception of which would almost vindicate his right to the title of "the Great" which his ultra admirers bestow on him. Certainly so sublime a design was not born in the brain of a hypocrite. With the possible sole exception of the question of the Papal temporal dominion, the most "vexing" political problem of our time is that which turns on the future fate of the "sick man of the East." In the days of Henry IV., a more evident vitality of religious ideas made the cruel fate of the Oriental Christians more poignant to the sympathies of their Western brethren than that fate is to us of the nineteenth century. Well, the hero of Ivry nearly arranged the affairs of the Grand Turk for all time. The *Mémoires* of Sully, who knew the secret mind of his royal master, give the details of the grand idea. Henry had sent to the Levant a few gentlemen, who, under the pretence of visiting the Holy Places, obtained accurate information as to the disposition of the people, the strength of the Mahometan forces, etc. He then resolved to undertake the conquest of Palestine; he endeavored to secure the co-operation of the other powers of Christendom, offering to them the temporal fruits of the enterprise, he coveting no other dominion than that of France. He began by trying to enlist the sympathy of those countries which were the more friendly to France; such as the Netherlands, Venice, and Switzerland. He then sought to placate England, Denmark, and Sweden; endeavoring to procure their recognition of the Supreme Pontiff as at least the first prince of Christendom in temporal matters. Then, taking special interest in that Holy Roman Empire which had begun its career under the ægis of his royal predecessors, he consulted the emperor and

the imperial cities ; and sought to know whether the rulers of
Poland, Hungary, and Bohemia would concur with him in
doing away forever with every cause of discord in Christendom.   Finally, he treated with the Pontiff, who promised to
aid his design in every legitimate manner.   His main hope of
uniting the powers of Europe resided in the constitution of
a Christian Republic—in the revival of the *Populus Christianus* of the Middle Age.   The Pope was to have, in addition to
the states he already governed, the kingdom of Naples and
the suzerainties of Sicily and of an Italian Republic.   In order
to regulate possible differences, each domination was to del-
egate four members to a general assembly which would meet
in some place convenient to the majority.   We cannot enter
into the details of this vast project, which certainly was not
above the strength of Henry IV.   The enterprising hero intended to start on his Eastern expedition in 1610, but Providence had otherwise decreed.

We need not wonder at the readiness with which men have
accepted as authentic the phrase with which many historians
associate the name of Henry IV.   His good naturedness has
detracted from his grandeur, at least in the eyes of the
masses ; and he had so much of the usual weakness of fallen
humanity that the undiscerning—who compose, after all, the
majority of even those who try to think—have readily fancied
him capable of worse than weakness.   Few men have spoken
the language of sincerity more plainly than it was spoken by
Henry IV., and his loyal utterances captivated the affections of
all who knew him; nevertheless, he does not produce that
effect upon a sane imagination which the English James II.,
a less striking character, excites by preferring the Mass to
the crown of three kingdoms.   And although the verses of
Voltaire would lead us to believe that the French of his day
" cherished the memory of Henry," it is certain that now
there is not enough of popular tradition concerning that
memory to form even an inconsistent myth.   If you ask the
first man whom you meet in the streets of Paris, what he
thinks of Ivry, you will find that the newly-fledged republican knows not whether you allude to a man, a place, or a dish ;
although it is probable that, thanks to a tavern-song, he will

hazily remember the *vert galant;* and that, thanks to the theatre, he may know that some French king wished that " every peasant had a chicken in the pot." Is it any wonder, then, that the authenticity of the absurd phrase has been so generally credited?

CHAPTER XXV.

RELIGIOUS INNOVATORS IN ITALY.

It is a great mistake to suppose that the Lutheran movement in Germany had no important religious and civil consequences for Italy; and it is certain that the first signs of an agitation against the then existing order of religious things manifested themselves among the Italians long before the rash Augustinian began his innovations. Many of the peninsulars were actuated by a spirit of true piety in their denunciations of too evident abuses; and like the disciples of Savonarola, they never dreamed of disputing the dogmatic decisions of the Spouse of Christ. And the very freedom which all the Italian governments—even the Papal—then allowed to almost any criticism of the methods and conduct of the *Curia*, served as a safety-valve for an effervescence which repression, in other lands, caused to eventuate in an explosion. Nor should it be forgotten that the superiority of Italian logic over that of the northern nations, and the thorough acquaintance of the people with the jeopardized institutions, prevented their fall into that error of confounding principles with individuals, which was the bane of the less judicial minds of the Germans and English. And another fact contributed to reduce to a comparative minimum the results of the Protestant propaganda in Italy. Nations do not easily abandon the cult of their glorious traditions. Hence the Italians remembered that the influence of their country over the rest of the civilized world, and even their material wealth, were results of the residence of the Pope-Kings in their land. The prime object of Protestantism was war upon that Pontiff, who represented Italian liberty and Italian culture; and therefore the Italians rejected it with disdain. Again, Prot-estantism was the work of a "barbarian," and it was a par-venu. *Noblesse oblige.* Scarcely one of the great families was unable to boast of its connection with the grandest and the sole unadulterated aristocracy in the universe—that of Heav-en. How could the scions of such houses welcome a system which tore the halo from the brows of their ancestors, pro-faned their tombs, and scattered their holy relics to the winds ? Look at Tuscany alone. There were the houses from which came the Seven Founders of the Servites : Buon-figliuolo Monaldi, Buonagiunta Manetti, Manetto dell'An-tella, Amadio Amadei, Uguccione Uguccioni, Sostegno Sos-tegui, Alessio Falconieri. The Ricci gloried in their St. Cath-arine ; the Orsini lauded their St. Andrew ; the Falconieri told of their Blessed Juliana and Carissima ; the Pazzi point-ed to their St. Magdalen ; the Guidi narrated the won-drous deeds of their Blessed Charles ; the Soderini descanted on the graciousness of their Blessed Jane ; the Vespignani presented their Blessed John; the Adimari indicated their St. Ubaldo ; the Della Rena di Certaldo prayed to their Blessed Julia ; the Gambacurta of Pisa sought the interces-sion of their Blessed Peter. And so on ; throughout Italy the praise of innumerable Italian saints was daily chanted by Italian voices, and it is not likely that those blessed ones ne-glected to pray for those who were bone of their bone and flesh of their flesh. Undoubtedly there were a few who fol-lowed the Will-o'-the-Wisp of the day ; and these came from the lettered circles, rather than from the nobles, as was the case in France, or from the sovereign princes, as happened in Germany—at least at the outset.

VALDEZ. In Naples the first seeds of Protestantism were sowed by the German troops of Charles V. who, after their sacking of Rome in 1527, entered the kingdom to expel the French ; but the real "Triumvirs of the Satanic Republic," as Anthony Caracciolo termed them, were Valdez, Ochino, and Peter Martyr (Vermiglio). John Valdez was a courtier of Charles V., and having been denounced as a heretic by the papal nuncio at Madrid, he deemed it prudent to move to Naples, where the national privileges restrained Charles from intro-

ducing the Spanish Inquisition. His learning obtained for
Valdez admittance into the most refined circles of Naples,
and he became secretary to the viceroy, Toledo. Commenting on one of the works of Valdez (1), a famous innovator of
that time, Celio Secondo Roterio (2), terms the author "the
most solid writer on religious matters that the world has
seen, since the Evangelists handled pen." Vergerio says
that Valdez was assigned by God as teacher to many of the
most illustrious personages of Naples, and that the most
worthy of the Italian Reformers owed their enlightenment to
him. We are not certain as to what doctrines Valdez professed : but we know that the Socinians claimed him. Beza
says that this innovator's *Considerations* effected "much
harm to the Reformed Church in Naples," and that the
Lyonnese publisher of that book asked the pardon of Calvin for having issued it (3). Balbani, a minister of the Italian Protestants in Geneva, asserts that most of the converts
of Valdez continued to attend at Mass, and that they generally backslided.

OCHINO. Bernardine Tommasini, generally known as Ochino, from the district of Oca, near Siena, where he was born,
was in his youth a Franciscan of the "Strict Observance";
but he entered the Capuchin family, and in 1538, in the third
General Chapter of that then new branch of the Minor Friars, he was chosen as General. He acquired a reputation
for successful preaching, and Sadoleto—a good judge—used
to say that he was the equal of any of the ancient orators.
Charles V. declared that Ochino could wring tears from
stones ; and even Bembo, who cared little for the preaching
of his day, wrote to the marchioness of Pescara in 1536, that
he deemed himself blessed in having heard an orator so
truly unctuous. Boverius, the Annalist of the Capuchins, is
quite extravagant in his praise of Fra Bernardino's austerity, modesty, sagacity, and spirituality. Certainly, if epistolary evidence can be considered as enabling one to form a
judgment of a writer's character, Ochino was, at one period,

(1) *One Hundred and Ten Divine Considerations by John Valdez, wherein are Dis-*
cussed Things most Useful, Necessary, and Perfect, to Christian Perfection. Basel, 1550.
(2) Called "Curione," from Chieri, his birthplace.
(3) *Works* of Beza, vol. III., ep. iv.

a markedly holy religious. But as early as 1539, there were whispers derogatory of his orthodoxy; and when he preached in Naples, in that same year, he broached several errors concerning justification, purgatory, and indulgences. In one of his discourses, he audaciously falsified a passage of St. Augustine, in order to show that the great Doctor denied the necessity of good works. The saint had written: "He who created thee without thyself, will not save thee without thyself." But the friar read the words: "Will not He who created thee without thyself, save thee without thyself?" And about this time, the brethren of Ochino perceived that their superior was becoming careless, if not disgusted, with the devotional exercises of the community; and even with the Holy Sacrifice. However, he continued to preach with the usual signs of sincerity; and when a certain wise friar warned him that preaching without previous prayer was like riding without stirrups, the poor man was informed that he who does good constantly, is always at prayer. He tried to impress this sophism on the mind of the Pontiff; for he asked for a dispensation from the Office, because of his many engagements for the pulpit. The crisis came. Pope Paul III. had signified his intention to enroll the famous Capuchin in the Sacred College; and he was invited to visit the Eternal City. The uneasy conscience of the unfortunate must have led him to fear that a trap had been set for him; for he visited Peter Martyr Vermiglio at Florence, and asked his advice. Vermiglio had already crossed the Rubicon; and he counselled the Capuchin to do likewise—to give up everything, red hat and all, for God's sake. Ochino yielded to the arguments of Martyr, and taking from Renée of France, duchess of Ferrara, letters of introduction to Calvin, he bade farewell to Italy in Sept., 1542; and proceeding to Geneva, made the first step in the path of renunciation of all creature comforts in the cause of "the Gospel," by taking to himself a wife. It is needless to say that Calvin received the convert with open arms, and aided him in founding, in the Rome of the Reformation, a conventicle for Italian Protestant refugees. From the pen of Ochino there now began to issue a number of onslaughts on Catholic doctrine and practice, the chief of

which (1), even Sleidan, the panegyrist of the Reformers,
termed a shameless production. But this work was less nau-
seating than the diatribe which he published concerning the
character of Pope Paul III., and which decency will not allow
us to quote (2). Ochino saw very little good in human reason. He regarded it as utterly incapable in all endeavors to
arrive at truth in religious matters; there divine revelation
is necessary; and an infallible interpreter of that revelation,
he insisted, is also needed And since he had rejected the
Church as this interpreter, he was constrained to invoke the
aid of immediate divine inspiration for each individual. Of
course he discovered that divine inspiration told diametrically opposite things to Calvin and himself; and the discovery
was emphasized when the former excommunicated him as a
pestilent heretic, and forced him to flee for his life. Proceeding to England with Vermiglio and their respective wives, he
helped in the Protestantization of that kingdom until the accession of Mary, when he settled in Zurich. Here his Unitarian notions brought him to grief, and he signed a Profession of Faith, whereby he swore to live and die in the faith
of Zwingle. Nevertheless, he soon attacked the Zwinglian
theories in the pulpit; and in his *Labyrinths* he denied nearly every Christian tenet. In the depth of winter, and in his
seventy-seventh year, he was expelled from Zurich; and betook himself to Cracow. Neither age nor persecution had
diminished his vanity; for we hear him thus descanting on
himself to the Italian refugees in Poland: " Know that you
are here to-day to behold no less than an apostle of God;
for no man has ever suffered as I have, for the name and
glory of Christ, and for the manifestation of truth regarding
heavenly things. And even though it may not be granted to
me to perform miracles, you ought t , have as much faith in
me as you would have in the Apostles; for I teach the very
truths that they taught, and my sufferings are certainly mir-

---

(1) *A Hundred Apologies, in which are Revealed the Abuses, Superstitions, Errors,
Idolatries, and Impieties of the Pope's Synagogue, and especially of His Priests, Monks,
and Friars.*

(2) It is preserved in the Laurentian Library of Florence, with a tag directing that no
copy shall ever be taken of it. But in 1581, Crispin, a disciple of Calvin, was not deterred
by its filth from printing it in his *Condition of the Church.*

aculous enough for you." During the residence of Ochino in Poland, he gave a signal proof of his condescendence to worldly power. Like Luther in the case of the landgrave of Hesse, he advised King Sigismund to practice simultaneous bigamy; contending that when a man's wife is unhealthy or, in any way, distasteful to him, he should pray to God for the grace of continence; but that if he finds that gift not granted to him, "he need not fear that he will commit sin, if he follows his *divine instinct*, since obedience to God cannot be sinful" (1). When Bullinger styled Ochino "a man learned in a reprobate sense, an impious and malicious person, and an unmitigated liar," the ex-friar retorted: "I did not know that Bullinger was Pope in Zurich." Beza called him "a most libidinous wretch, an Arianizer, and a scoffer at Christ and his Church"; and this opinion of Beza caused Basel and Mulhausen to close their gates to Ochino when he sought their hospitality in his old age. He finally died in Moravia, in 1564. The Capuchin annalist, Boverius, contends that Ochino died in Geneva; that some days before the dread event, he confessed sacramentally to a priest, and avowed his repentance to many; that the Genevan magistrates ordered his assassination, in case of his persistence in his retractation; and that the sentence was executed with a dagger. Boverius adduces many witnesses, but their testimonies are not direct.

PETER MARTYR VERMIGLIO. In the year 1500, a devout Florentine gentleman, formerly a disciple of Savonarola, having lost all his boys in their infancy, made a vow to St. Peter Martyr (2), that if another were granted to him, he would dedicate the child to the saint. The prayer was heard; the young Vermiglio received the baptismal name of Peter Mar-

(1) In the Twenty-first of his *Thirty Dialogues*, he represents Sigismund under the name of Telipoligamus, and thus converses with him on the matter of a new wife:

T. *Quid vero mihi das consilia?*

O. *Ut plures uxores non ducas, sed Deum ores ut tibi continentem esse det.*

T. *Quid si nec donum mihi, nec ad se petendum fidem dabit?*

O. *Tum, si id feceris ad quod te Deus impellet, dummodo divinum esse instinctum exploratum habeas, non peccabis. Siquidem in obediendo Deo errari non potest.*

(2) Peter of Verona was martyred by the Lombard Patarines in 1252, and was venerated thereafter under the name of St. Peter Martyr. The epitaph on his tomb in the church of St. Eustorgius in Milan was written by St. Thomas of Aquino. Another famous Peter Martyr, a litterateur of Anghiera, was a contemporary of Vermiglio.

tyr; and by that name his memory is now revered by sincere Protestants. His mother was a highly educated woman, and under her care and that of Marcello Vergilio, secretary of the Republic, he developed into a most promising lad. In his seventeenth year he joined the Regular Canons of St. Augustine; and for ten years applied himself assiduously to the study of every branch of sacred and profane science. His first essay as a preacher was made at Brescia in 1527, and for some time he distinguished himself as a professor of Scripture in Padua, Ravenna, Bologna, and Vercelli. In 1541, while giving a course of Biblical interpretations in Naples, he explained certain passages of St. Paul's Epistles to the Corinthians in a manner which the Theatines and many others denounced as unorthodox; and the viceroy, Toledo, prohibited his preaching. Upheld by his own Order and by many influential civilians, Vermiglio refused to obey, and appealed successfully to the Holy See. Appointed to the priory of San Frediano in Lucca, his expressions became noted for rashness, even when he discoursed in the cathedral; and when, in 1542, instead of attending a General Chapter of his Order—which he probably dreaded, he fled to Zurich, few were surprised. Of course he now married, and in 1547 Cranmer invited him and Ochino to contribute to the diffusion of spiritual light in England. He was made Regius professor of theology at Oxford, and from that time until his death, even when he was residing abroad, the course of the Reformation in England revolves around the name of Peter Martyr. When Mary ascended the throne, Vermiglio proceeded to Strasburg (1); then to Zurich, where he taught Biblical science for several years. At the famous Colloquy of Poissy he played a prominent part; and when he described the occurrences to Bullinger, he declared that Catharine dei Medici was blind, if she thought that the Church would ever be reformed by the bishops. During this Colloquy, Cardinal Commendone wrote to St. Charles Borromeo: "Friar Martyr

(1) The first wife of Vermiglio died in England, and was buried in the cathedral of Oxford, next to the body of St. Frideswidda. When Catholicism was restored by Mary, the corpse of Mrs. Peter Martyr was removed to a more appropriate spot; but Elizabeth again located it next to the holy remains; the ceremonial oration concluding with the words, "Here religion and superstition lie side by side."

has free access to the queen, and although I do not doubt the good will of her Majesty, I fear that this intimacy will prejudice the good cause, since it disconcerts the Catholics, and encourages the Protestants." When Vermiglio was at the point of death, he was attended by Bullinger; and in his delirium, he confuted the Ubiquitists (1). Protestant polemics are prone to dilate upon the conciliatory tendencies of Peter Martyr; but they do not ask attention to one very eloquent instance of his exhibition of these estimable proclivities. We have seen how Ochino imitated his spiritual father in allowing a man to commit simultaneous bigamy. Vermiglio's conciliatory inclinations led him to a similar act of kindness. Among the conquests of Valdez in the kingdom of Naples, was Galeazzo Caracciolo, only son of Colantonio Caracciolo, chamberlain to Charles V., and one of the first personages of the realm. Galeazzo was married to a daughter of the powerful duke of Nocera; the couple were devoted to each other; and several children had blessed their union. When the sophisms of Valdez had obscured the brain of Galeazzo, he tried in vain to shake the faith of his wife, and therefore joined the Reformers in Germany, unaccompanied by his family. In his loneliness he applied to Peter Martyr to learn whether he could take another spouse, one of "the religion," who would help him to save his soul. Calvin also, and Zanchi, an apostate Canon from Bergamo, were consulted. Scriptural passages certainly proclaimed the indissolubility of consummated Christian matrimony; but the three conciliatory theologians found that Galeazzo was justified in marrying again, for did not Our Lord say: "Every one that hath left house ... or wife, ... for my name's sake, *shall receive an hundredfold*"? (2) By this conclusive argument the tender conscience of the convert was satisfied; and on Jan. 10, 1560, he was united to one Anna Fremery of Rouen.

VERGERIO. The Vergerii, or rather Verzerii, were among

(1) When Luther was told that the Body of Christ cannot be in the Eucharist because it is at the right hand of the Father, he replied that the Redeemer is present everywhere, even as man. This opinion was inserted in the Lutheran Creed in the *Book of Harmony*. The opinion of the Ubiquitists coincides with that of the ancient Eutychians, who held that the humanity of Christ, like his divinity, is everywhere, even in hell. Most Lutherans are Ubiquitists.

(2) MATT. XIX. 29.

the noblest families of Dalmatia, and since the day when that
territory became a Venetian possession, they had been far
more Italian than Croatian. Peter Paul, like all noble Dal-
matians of his day, made his studies in Padua; and when he
had taken his degrees, he filled various juridical positions in
Verona and Venice, until he entered the service of Cardinal
Contarini at Rome. His brother Aurelio, afterward a knight
of Malta, was then secretary to Pope Clement VII.; and thus
he was brought to the notice of the Pontiff, who conceived a
favorable opinion of his ability. As legate to King Ferdinand of Germany, he manifested much zeal in opposing the
progress of Protestantism; and his letters during that mission are redolent of contempt for the leading innovators (1).
On Aug. 27, 1534, he writes to their Serenities of Venice to
warn them how much the Republic will suffer, if any leniency is shown toward "the accursed progeny of Luther"; and
he tells them to be alert lest "the poison of heresy and sedition he smuggled among the commodities imported into
that Republic which has ever been known to God and men
as most ready to shed its best blood in evidence of its devotion to the true faith." Three days afterward, he writes to
Mgr. Carnesecchi that "if the Most Serene is lenient toward
the Reformers, woe to all Italy!" At Vienna he talked with
Luther; but the reader must not credit the account of that
interview which Fra Paolo Sarpi invented for the delectation
of the credulous foes of papal Rome. The bribes which Vergerio is said to have offered to the ex-Augustinian in the
name of the Pontiff; the melodramatic scorn with which the
burly heresiarch is said to have repulsed the oily intermediary; all these minutiæ are wanting in the pages of Seckendorf, who would have gladly detailed them, had they existed
in the regions of fact. Vergerio says that he found Luther
"Ugly in features, in dress, and in manners. ... He speaks
Latin so vilely, that I cannot believe that he is the real author of the treatises which bear his name. ... He is arrogance itself, malignant, and impudent. ... It sickened me to
listen to him; and I addressed to him only a couple of words,
and those merely because I did not wish to appear like a

(1) Vatican Archives: *Nunciatures of Germany*, vol. IV.

log " (1). At this time, Vergerio was still a layman; but when he returned to Italy, he was ordained, and soon consecrated as bishop of Madrusc in Croatia. Then he was transferred to the see of Capo d'Istria, his birthplace. At the conference of Worms in 1540, he represented both the Pope and the French monarch; and he delivered an impressive discourse on the unity of the Church. But it would seem that at this very time some parties had insinuated doubts as to his orthodoxy; for on December 26, he wrote to the cardinal of Brindisi in terms of strong indignation concerning the hideous inculpation. He admits that he has corresponded with Bucer, Melancthon, and other heretics, but adds: "If you do not think that the Holy Spirit and my conscience will keep me in the path of duty, you may rely upon the influence of my temporal comfort, my family, my bishopric, and my country, to restrain me." However, it is certain that his entry into the diocese of Capo d'Istria was signalized by many innovations, some of which endangered the purity of dogma. His correspondence with Margaret of Navarre, a fanatical Calvinist, became constant. In Aug., 1544, the famous Mgr. Della Casa arrived in Venice as papal nuncio. Although preconized to the archiepiscopal see of Benevento, this prelate had not yet received even minor orders— a state of things which was but too common at that period. Soon after the arrival of Della Casa, the suspected incumbent of Capo d'Istria was cited to appear before his tribunal, to justify himself of the charge of heresy. Vergerio replying that he would appear before no tribunal other than that of a General Council, the nuncio began to take evidence in the case; and the process dragged its weary length along for several years, during which the criminated prelate was in no way disturbed, unless by ebullitions of his people, who were firmly convinced that their ordinary was a heretic. When Vergerio presented himself at the Council of Trent, the synodals refused to admit him to their sessions, unless he justified himself before the Supreme Pontiff. Finally, as he persistently declined to obey the papal citations, he was declared

(1) Vatican codex 3,914, fol. 263. The letter is dated Nov. 12, 1535, from "The residence of Duke George of Saxony, in Dresden."

contumacious, and deposed from the episcopal dignity, on July 3, 1549. If the Reformers exulted when the one-time-legate entered their ranks, they soon lamented their welcome to a firebrand in their already discordant circles. The convert differed especially with Luther. He never ceased to remind his comrades in revolt that he had received episcopal consecration; and ever tried to exercise a kind of episcopal authority. To the ex-Augustinian this assumption was more than distasteful; for he affected to despise the consecration of "the Beast." When Bullinger reproved Gallicius for discourtesy to Vergerio, he was told that a man could not be tolerated, who thought that the heavens would fall, unless he, like Atlas, supported them on his shoulders. In 1553, Vergerio was made counsellor and preacher to the prince of Wurtemberg, by whom he was supported during the remainder of his days. This curious man knew no such thing as certainty or consistency in religious matters; and his panegyrist, Xist, naively apologizes for his alternations between Calvinism, Lutheranism, Zwinglianism, and Picardism, by the convenient theory that the atmosphere which we breathe must necessarily determine our religious convictions.

GENTILE. Among the members of that Academy of Vicenza concerning which the lettered of the sixteenth century talked so much, but of which we know very little, was an eminent physician of Cosenza named Gentile. Having been illumined by the light of the New Gospel, he took his family out of benighted Italy, and educated them in the progressive school of Geneva. His son Valentine progressed into a denial of the Trinity, and became one of the prominent Unitarian professors who so worried the life of the Genevan Pope. In a book dedicated to the king of Poland, he says: " There are no such words as Trinity, Homoousion, Person, Essence, or Hypostasis, in the Scriptures or in the Catholic Symbols. You find therein only one God, and he is *autotheos*, infusing His divinity into Christ, His Son. Christ is the symbol of the glory of the Father; He is God, but not such *per se*. The Holy Ghost is the divine power in actuation. Father, Son, and Holy Ghost are distinct in person, essence, and degree. Calvin adores a Quaternity, not a Trinity; for he

teaches that if the Hypostasis be removed, the Divinity remains; that each Person is truly God; that, therefore, there
are four Gods" (1). Calvin can find no invectives sufficiently
bitter to indicate his hatred of Gentile; he terms his co-in-
novator a good-for-nothing "who eats the mud which he finds
in the trough of Servetus." And the Genevan despot, who
would brook no rival in his hold on the intellects of the
emancipated, drew up a formulary of "orthodoxy" which
all the Italian Protestants were to sign, under pain of banishment or death. Gentile would not willingly court the fate
of Servetus, and like the immense majority of the "escaped
slaves of the Pope" then in Switzerland, he signed the saving document. But as he continued to teach Unitarianism,
Calvin threw him into prison. Again he retracted; whereupon sentence was pronounced in these terms: "Although
your wickedness and malice are so tremendous that you deserve to be exterminated from among men as a seducer, heretic, and schismatic; nevertheless, since you have come to
your senses, we sentence you to merely the following punishment. You shall be stripped to your shirt; and then, bare-
headed and bare-footed, with a lighted candle in your hand,
you shall come before us your judges, and beg for our forgiveness; and finally, with your own hands, you shall cast
into the flames all of your pernicious and lying writings."
This sentence was carried out on Sept. 2, 1558; and Gentile
was also compelled to swear that he would not leave Geneva
during the remainder of his life. But he availed himself of
an early opportunity to escape to Savoy; from whence he
went to France, and then, for several years he propagated
his tenets in that kingdom, in Poland, Moravia, and even Vienna. When Calvin died, Gentile fancied that he might return to Switzerland with impunity; but the spirit of Calvin
survived, and he was arrested on June 11, 1566, regularly
tried on the charge of relapse into heresy, and beheaded in
Berne. While walking to the block, he vaunted: "Many
have died for the Son; I am the first to die for the supreme
glory of the Father."

SOCINUS. The Anti-Trinitarians of the sixteenth century

(1) GABEREL; *Calvin at Geneva.*—LADERCHI; *Continuation of Baronio.*

boasted of no members so learned and influential as the Sozzini, or, as they are now known, from the Latin form of their name, the Socini. Alberic Socinus taught jurisprudence at Oxford in 1608, and Scipio in Heidelberg. Lelio, who was a member of the Academy of Vicenza, settled in Zurich ; and the catastrophe of Servetus led him to dissimulate his religious theories, while he lived within reach of the clutches of Calvin. But when he migrated to Poland, he openly propagated them. Faustus Socinus, a nephew of Lelio, born in Siena on Dec. 5, 1539, was an elegant writer, an impressive orator, a learned jurisconsult, and a profound general scientist. Educated by Lelio, he naturally became a fervid Unitarian, and after twelve years of honorable service in the grand-ducal court of Tuscany, he migrated to Cracow, where, thanks to the indifferentism of King Sigismund Augustus, the Anti-Trinitarians possessed a college, printing establishment, and all the paraphernalia of a legally recognized sect. Socinus found the Polish Unitarians in sad confusion concerning what was really meant by their cardinal tenets ; and his arrival augmented the discord, for he brought forward a Creed which he had found among the papers of his uncle, which advanced doctrines essentially different from those received in Poland and Transylvania. According to Socinus, the first Reformers effected some good, but their work was very imperfect ; religion, said he, ought to be freed from all dogmas which transcend reason. God is one in essence and in person. Christ is inferior to God in that majesty and power which He acquired by His obedience and death. Conceived by the power of the Holy Ghost, and therefore styled the Son of God, Jesus was carried before the divine throne before He entered upon His teaching career, and at the foot of that throne He learned His sublime doctrines. As a reward for His obedience, Jesus was raised to divine dignity, and received dominion over everything heavenly and earthly ; therefore, concluded Socinus, we may and ought to adore Christ as God. In this last doctrine, the Italian theorizer differed from the Transylvanian Unitarians ; but at the most he made Christ a subaltern God, whom the One, True God had placed over the universe. He differed also from

the Arians, inasmuch as those heretics, although they regarded the Son as a created being, insisted that He was created before all other creatures. Socinus taught that man
was mortal before his fall; otherwise, Christ would have
abolished death, when He conquered sin. Original sin, said
Socinus, is not transmitted. Man has free will; the divine
omnipotence does not cover human actions; Christ did not
satisfy for the sins of men, for God had pardoned man before
Jesus was born. Of his own strength, declared Socinus, man
discerns evil from good; and he obtains the idea of God and
divine things only from instruction. The reader will perceive
that Socinus was a far more resolute heresiarch than Luther
dared to be. Socinus did not openly deny all the supersen-
sible; but he rejected all dogmas, taught unbelief, and was
the progenitor of our modern rationalists. When he died in
1604, his admirers wrote as his epitaph : "Luther destroyed
the roofs of Babylon; Calvin her walls; Socinus her foundations."

BRUNO. This ex-Dominican friar was one of the most famous innovators of his day, but he merits the title of Buddhist as much as he does that of Protestant. He never
claimed to be either Lutheran, Anglican, Calvinist, or
Zwinglian. He tells us that while he resided in Geneva, the
headquarters of Calvinism, he listened to the sermons of the
French and Italian sectarians there assembled, but he adds :
"When I was warned that I could not remain, unless I adopted
the Genevan creed, I departed." The year 1579 found him
lecturing at the Sorbonne in Paris. During his three years in
England, he prudently lauded Elizabeth, "The unique Diana
who is to us all what the sun is to the stars"; but he manifested no leaning toward Anglicanism, and when he taught
the movement of the earth, the Oxford dons forced him to
leave the country. Arrived in Germany, he was pleased with
the toleration accorded to him by the Lutherans, "although
their faith differed from his own " (1). In fact, Bruno taught

---

(1) "*Non vestræ religionis dogmate probatum.*" Thus in his *De Lampade Combina-
toria*—Cantù says of Bruno : " He was in reality a rationalist two centuries before Hegel;
and he furnished to the German the formula of the harmony of contradictories (" That
which is contradictory everywhere else, is one and the same in God ; and everything is the
same in Him." Thus in his *On Cause*, Dial. 3). His mind was solitary and impassioned ;

everywhere the Pythagorean system concerning the world, and an Eleatic pantheism which he clothed in Neo-Platonic forms ; and he advanced both with ridiculous vanity. He announced himself to the Oxford professors as "A teacher of the most sublime philosophy ; professor of the purest and most harmless wisdom ; a doctor recognized by every academy in Europe ; a teacher unknown only to barbarians ; the awakener of sleeping geniuses ; the tamer of presumptuous and recalcitrant ignorance ; a universal philanthropist, as all his actions proclaim ; a man who loves an Italian no more than he does an Englishman, another man no more than he does a woman ; ... he is detested by hypocrites and by the propagators of insanity, but is revered by the upright, and applauded by every noble genius." As to the tragic death of Bruno at the stake on Feb. 17, 1600, it was almost certain until 1891 that the sentence was carried out only in effigy ; but investigation into the archives of the Confraternity of San Giovanni Decollato has proved that the unfortunate perished as his otherwise mendacious Roman monument asserts. We shall devote a special chapter to Bruno, since his nearly extinct memory has been recently revived.

VANINI. This theologaster, also a Neapolitan, was born in 1586, and made his studies at Padua, finally becoming a Regular Canon. He tells us that when he visited Geneva, he feared for his life, because of the Calvinists ; that then he went to Lyons, where also he narrowly escaped death, but at the hands of the Catholics ; that therefore he passed into England, " where the Protestants imprisoned him for forty-nine days, he being ardently desirous of martyrdom" (1). Having returned to Italy, he opened a school in Genoa, but his strange doctrines soon caused another expatriation, and

and his thoughts were like his style, a mixture of the sublime and the trivial, of hymns and imprecations. His genius was grand, vague, and paradoxical. He was melancholy, and as rampant as his own Vesuvius. He knew not what he really desired ; and he possessed none of that sentiment of the real which sacrifices forms for substance. When we see him trying to found a Nolan system of philosophy, and hear him promising to explain everything if he has only the time, we must place him among those who abandon the universal laws of thought, and its harmony with reality, in order to recur to those of sense and self-love." *Heretics of Italy* ; dis. 42.

(1) Thus in his *Divine-Magical, Christian-Physical, and Astrologico-Catholic Amphitheatre of Eternal Providence, against the Ancient Philosophers, Atheists, Epicureans, Peripatetics, and Stoics.*

going to Gascony, he became a monk, and led an apparently
edifying life for some years. But having been detected in
gross immoralities, he was unfrocked, and proceeded to Paris. Here the papal nuncio took pity on him, gave him hospitality, and finally procured a chaplaincy for him. But he
now attracted the attention of the Sorbonne by his atheisti-
cal talk ; and after a vain flight to Toulouse for impunity, he
was arrested, tried, and condemned to the stake. He died
unrepentant on Feb. 19, 1618, boasting that he was more intrepid than Christ, for the Saviour had sweated blood through
fear. Probably Leibnitz judged rightly when he said that
Vanini should have been sent to a lunatic asylum, rather than
to execution. Cousin says that if Vanini had succeeded in
having his case tried by the Roman Inquisition, as he desired,
instead of by the parliament of Toulouse, merely some disciplinary punishment would have been inflicted. According
to Vanini, intelligence has no influence over matter ; the
soul none over the body. Nay, matter gives impulse to intelligence ; the body to the soul. Therefore, God is not the
Author of the universe. Man comes from putrefaction, and
from the successive perfection of the species. Many animals
are stronger than man, and *therefore* his destiny can be no
higher than their destiny. Hence the best thing for man
here on earth, is to enjoy himself ; " Every hour is lost, which
is not devoted to love." In spite of his flagrant materialism,
Vanini was wont to assert : " However, I submit all my teachings to the judgment of the Church." One day, when he
was interrogated as to his candid opinion on the matter of
immortality, he replied : " I have sworn never to tackle that
question, until I am old, rich, and a German." Once an admirer observed to him : " If you were not Vanini, you would
be God " ; whereupon the wretch complacently returned :
" I am Vanini." Certain philosophasters of our day must
have studied Vanini's ideas of social economy : " Just as the
prudent forester annually cuts down dead or otherwise useless
trees, so in all large cities the government ought to rid itself of
the old, the infirm, and all other useless persons, by putting
them to death " (1).

(1) For details concerning Vanini, see VAISSE ; *Lucilio Vanini, His Life, Doctrine, and*

FERRANTE PALLAVICINO was a learned noble of Piacenza, and a Canon Regular. Amorous intrigues in Milan necessitated his departure for Germany, where he fell in love with the "New Gospel." Then he inundated the world with a torrent of lucubrations, would-be sacred and profane—ascetic and erotic songs, moral discourses and novels, panegyrics and diatribes—in all of which the salient feature was obscenity. His most "spiritual" treatise was one on the *Beauties of the Soul*, as illustrated by those of the female bosom. As may be conjectured, his manner of treating such subjects as *Susanna*, as *Joseph*, as *Samson*, was equally prurient. The German and English Protestants gladly acclaimed his lubricious *Celestial Divorce Caused by the Dissoluteness of the Roman Wife; Dedicated to All the Most Famous Courtesans*. Arrested by the papal authorities of Avignon, he was beheaded in 1644.

DE DOMINIS. This apostate archbishop was born in 1546, in Dalmatia, then Venetian territory. He became a Jesuit, but soon secularized himself. In time he was raised to the metropolitan see of Spalatro, thus becoming primate of Dalmatia and Croatia. His early years under the mitre were distinguished by an affectation of apostolical simplicity, and by an inordinate yearning for religious novelties. Called to Rome to vindicate his orthodoxy, he allayed all suspicion; but soon afterward he laid aside his pastoral staff, and proceeding to London, he was received into the Anglican communion in St. Paul's. The royal theologian, James I., made him dean of Windsor; but remorse soon seized him, and he announced from the pulpit that mere jealousy had prompted his apostasy. He then wrote to Pope Gregory XV., who had been one of his pupils: "I have wandered, like a lost lamb. Seek me, Most Blessed Father, for I have not forgotten the commandments of God and of His Church." Returning to Rome, the unfortunate made his abjuration in full Consistory; but Urban VIII., just made Pontiff, having learned that the apparently repentant prodigal continued to correspond with suspicious persons, relegated him to Castel Sant' Angelo, and

ordered an investigation.   While this was in train, the ex-
prelate died, in 1623 ; and when it was afterward proved that
he had recently contended that salvation could be attained
with equal ease in any Christian organization, his remains
were removed from consecrated ground and burned, together
with his work on *The Christian Republic* (1).

At an early period of the Reformation, the foes of the Holy
See anticipated success in the Republic of Venice ; even in
1520, Luther congratulated some of his Venetian correspon-
dents on the " progress made by the word of God " in their
country (2).   In 1538, Melancthon besought the Senate to
allow the erection of a Protestant temple, urging that their
Serenities " should grant, especially to the learned, the right
to express their opinions, and to teach them " (3).   But in
1539, the same Melancthon complained that the Most Serene
was not sufficiently severe in repressing the Anti-Trinitarians,
and he implored the oligarchs not to confound those " heretics "
with himself and the other " pure Reformers of Germany " (4).
With few exceptions, however, the Venetians were not disposed to encourage a movement which was, at its best, a powerful incentive of discord in the state ; and furthermore, as
we shall see when we come to consider the interdict launched
against the Republic by Pope Paul V., the Most Serene was
Catholic to its inmost core.

Of all the Italian states, Lombardy seemed to promise, at
one period, to be a favorable field for the religious despoiler,
despite the fact that the intense aversion of its people for
the German line of the Holy Roman Emperors had ever been
a powerful nutrient of Guelphic sentiment.   The Patarine
and kindred sects of the thirteenth century had left too many
seeds in the Catholic soil.   And Humanistic ideas were quite
the fashion among the Lombards ; the Renaissance had excited a spirit of inquiry, and its worship of antiquity had evolved,
in some minds, a sort of pitying contempt for so comparatively modern a system as Christianity.   Hence the " Gospel
of liberty " was less horrible to the average Lombard than

---

(1) The curious reader will find an account of this trial in the *History of the Inquisition*
by the Protestant Limborch.

(2) *Complete Works*, edit. Walch., XXI., p. 1092.

(3) *Epistles*, edit. Lond., col. 150 and 154.   (4) *Ibid.*, vol. I., p. 100.

to other Italians, and as early as 1521, verses in praise of the unfrocked friar of Wittemberg were current in Milan (1). When Philip II. mounted the Spanish throne, and thereby obtained the Iron Crown of Lombardy, he thought to stem the advancing torrent of heresy by the introduction of the Spanish Inquisition. But the people resisted, and besought Pope Pius II. not to gratify the prince. They insisted that "it would be tyranny to establish in a Christian city, that form of Inquisition which had been designed for Moors and Jews." They sent representatives to the Council of Trent to beg the synodals to remember the abuses of the Spanish tribunal, and to reflect that "Philip might be expected to exercise greater ones in Lombardy, which was not his own country." Cardinal Morone, then presiding legate at the Council, assured the petitioners that the synodal decrees would exempt their land from the dread tribunal, leaving it under the milder jurisdiction of the Roman Inquisition ; and although this promise was not fulfilled, the influence of the Lombard prelates led the duke of Sessa, the royal governor, to suspend his master's decree, and soon it became a dead letter.

We have observed that such influence as the German innovators obtained in Italy was exercised chiefly over the minds of the superlatively lettered class, the too frequently wayward devotees of the Renaissance. But there were some other celebrities, in whose writings there sometimes appear expressions which seem to have been conceived in the atmosphere of Protestantism, but who, nevertheless, remained faithful to Holy Mother Church ; as will be evinced by an examination of not merely the remote, but even the proximate context of the writings which interested criticism would fain criminate. And even though such persons may have wandered temporarily, their intellects, not their wills, were at fault ; for sincere error is not wilful heresy. Nor ought it

(1) One of these poems thus terminated :

" Macte igitur virtute, pater celebrande Luthere,
Communis cujus pendet ab ore salus ;
Gratia cui ablatis debetur maxima monstris,
Alcidis potuit quæ metuisse manus."
—SCHŒLHORN ; *Ecclesiastical Amenities.*

be forgotten that the doctrines on justification had not yet
been precisely explained by the Council of Trent; and it was
precisely because of certain ambiguous notions on such difficult subjects that suspicion fell, in the minds of some, on the
learned and devout princess, Victoria Colonna, on Cardinal
Pole, and on other celebrities of their circle. Let it be noted, also, that in the early years of the sixteenth century,
many very pious Italians were confounded with real heretics,
merely because of their austerity and their frequent theological debates, things which were a kind of protest against an
indifference which was but too prevalent at the time.

Among the more celebrated of those Italians of the sixteenth century, whom Protestants would have us regard as
at least sympathizers with the Reformation, we shall notice
only Marcantonio Flaminio and Michelangelo Buonarroti.
Flaminio was one of the foremost Humanists of the day, a
learned physician, and an elegant Latinist. He did not escape the vigilance of Muzio, an untiring and over-zealous
seeker for heresy, wherever it might lurk (and wherever it
was not); and the result of the investigation was that the
works of Flaminio were regarded by many as dangerous for
Christians. But the reader shall judge whether a heretic
would have written as this scholar wrote to the famous Carnesecchi : " May God deliver you from the arrogance of those
who despise the judgment and the practice of the Universal
Church. ... Let us humble ourselves before God ; and let
us be carried away by no argument, be it ever so specious,
to withdraw from the unity of the Catholic Church. ... We
should not explain divine things by human reasons." When
Cardinal Pole went as papal legate to the Council of Trent,
he made the Humanist one of his secretaries ; and when
death summoned him in 1550, the same zealous prelate
placed his remains in the vaults of the English College at
Rome. As to the orthodoxy of Michelangelo, it was reserved
to a German writer of our day to question it (1). This genius asserts that the great artist and poet denied the existence
of purgatory and the necessity of the Sacraments ; and he
adduces as proof a letter in which, after deploring the death

(1) HERMANN GRIMM : Life of Michael Angelo Bonarotti, 1860.

of his brother, Michelangelo writes : "You inform me that he did not have all the rites of the Church, but that he had great contrition. Well, that was enough for his salvation." Certainly this phrase may be so understood as to imply the truth of the German biographer's supposition. But the reader will note what Grimm carefully ignores ; namely, that in a previous letter to the friend who had told him of the demise of Giovansimone, the artist had so expressed himself as to indicate his own orthodoxy as plainly as he shows the contemptibly bad faith of the historian. He had said : "I would very much like to know what kind of death he met ; whether he confessed and communicated, satisfying all the ordinances of the Church. Were I to learn that he did all this, I would grieve less." So much for Grimm. Again Vasari tells us that he accompanied Michelangelo, in his last days, through all the exercises of the Jubilee, and that the artist showed every mark of ardent faith.

And now a word as to the assertion by Protestant polemics that Italy lost much worldly prosperity by her rejection of the New Gospel. It is not our province to examine here whether worldly prosperity is or not a necessary concomitant of the possession of religious truth. But we would ask whether the modern decadence of Italy—which has been greatly exaggerated (unless we regard the Italy of the last thirty years)—is attributable to Catholicism. That the reply must be negative, is evident from the fact that Catholic institutions once, and for many centuries, were productive of the greatest glories of Italy. The careful student of history discerns very different reasons for the decadence of Italy (1). In their argumentation to the effect that Italy would have retained her commercial and industrial primacy, had she accompanied England and Germany in their revolt against Rome, Protestant polemics fall into an error of logic unworthy of a schoolboy ; they insist that "after that" implies "because of that"—*Post hoc, ergo propter hoc.* At the time of the Reformation, many causes were contributing to the decadence of Italy. The discovery of the New World, due to one of her

___

(1) What we now remark concerning Italy, will apply also, *mutatis mutandis,* to Spain and Portugal.

sons ; and the rounding of the Cape of Good Hope by Vasco
da Gama ; turned commerce from her shores. And then,
remarks Cantù, came " the destruction of her small republics ; the mania of Italians for fighting no longer for country
and their rights, but for the pretensions of princes ; the revival in Europe of ambition for foreign conquests, one of the
sores of pagan Rome which had been healed by feudalism ;
the consequent invasion of Italy by the foreigner ; the general adoption of standing armies by the invaders ; the revival
of classic studies, which substituted a veneration of force
such as the pagan State demanded, instead of Christian
justice." Then came the religious, or rather the irreligious
Thirty Years' War, terminated by the Peace of Westphalia,
the consequence of which was that " Germany lost that primacy which had been hers during the Middle Age. Hence,
the Germans, who had been driven into the Reformation by
their envy of our more brilliant sun, of our more harmonious
language, of our more polished manners, of our more liberal
institutions, of our more advanced civilization ; encountered
their own ruin through their hatred of Italy. They feared
the pre-eminence of the Latin race ; and therefore they warred
against Spain ; that country was Catholic, and therefore they
warred against Catholicism. And all that resulted was the
consolidation of the House of Austria, which thenceforward
retained the German crown and the dominion of Italy. Instead of abolishing the Empire, they abolished the Pope ;
instead of acquiring civil and municipal liberty, they obtained
freedom from going to Mass and Confession, and the right to
sing hymns in German. But Italy suffered much more.
Her fruitful partition into small states disappeared before the
Austro-Spanish supremacy, which was no longer counterbalanced by France, and was held within some sort of bounds
only by the republics of Venice and Genoa " (1). So much
for the decadence of Italy, whose people, until the triumph
of Cavour, Mazzini, and Co.—that is, of the Masonic Lodges—
were in much better economic conditions than those entailed
by the Reformation upon Great Britain (2).

(1) *Heretics of Italy*, discourse 48 ; Turin, 1866.
(2) The following observations of Fergueray are worthy of attention : " The Church should'

CHAPTER XXVI.

THE PROTESTANTIZATION OF ENGLAND.—ANGLICAN "ORDERS."

A detailed account of the laying of the corner-stone of the English Church Establishment is not necessary for our purpose. Probably the reader is acquainted with the first steps in the path of schism taken by the royal lecher who placed the bed of his concubine between England and Rome. Henry VIII. detached England from the unity of the Church; but it was during the reign of his successor, Edward VI., that England was first subjected to the process of Protestantization. So long as Henry lived, no man in his kingdom dared to broach the idea of a subversion of Catholic doctrine, unless in the one, albeit vital, point of Papal Supremacy. Every English Christian, according to his need, still imbibed divine grace from its sacramental fountains; the Sacrifice of Calvary was still repeated on every English altar; and the Sacramental Lord of the Tabernacle still welcomed His devoted visitors. Henry shed torrents of blood in his sacrilegious endeavor to unite the prerogatives of the tiara with those of the crown (1); but he would tolerate an attack on the deposit of faith, only when the onslaught conduced to the gratification of his lust. But in 1547, when the soiled

not be made responsible for the inferiority of certain Catholic countries during the seventeenth and eighteenth centuries. Then she had lost all influence in the civil government of those peoples. The 'external bishop' (the sovereign), encroaching upon the prerogatives of the real bishop, had usurped even purely spiritual functions; and the clergy were (too often, but not always, thank God!) slaves of the monarch. Then, at Madrid as well as at Paris, monarchical supremacy had raised itself on the ruins of all anterior powers, even of the ecclesiastical. Certainly, priests and monks enjoyed wealth and honor; but these were no compensation for lost freedom. *Openly assailed by the Protestant sects, insidiously attacked by the blind ambition of princes, the Catholic Church was forced to allow the world to follow its inclinations. She waited for better days; when, after many disappointments, the world would again hearken to her voice; and she confined herself to her principal function, the preservation of dogmatic truth. She had abdicated as the director of Christian states. Therefore man should not blame her for the evils of the seventeenth and eighteenth centuries. It is not difficult to point out the culprit whom men should blame; that culprit was absolute monarchy."* And we must never forget that absolute monarchy, as experienced in Christian States, was the progeny of Protestantism.

(1) During eight years of his reign, he sent to a traitor's death, because of their fidelity to the Holy See, one cardinal, twenty bishops, thirteen abbots, five hundred monks and friars, thirty-eight secular priests, twelve dukes and earls, one hundred and sixty-four gentlemen, one hundred and twenty-four citizens, and one hundred and ten women.

crown of Britain was placed on the head of Edward **VI.**, the son of Henry by Jane Seymour, the nine-year-old monarch was admonished by Cranmer, archbishop of Canterbury, that it was his royal duty, "*as God's vicegerent and Christ's vicar*, to see that idolatry be destroyed; that the tyranny of the Bishop of Rome be banished, and images be removed; ... let him do this, and he would become a second Josias, whose fame would remain to the end of days" (1). Somerset, the protector of the boy-king, had been a follower of the New Gospel for several years, although fear of Henry had led him to dissemble his notions; and now he and his dependents were but too willing to aid Cranmer in a cause which promised, through additional confiscations of Church property, to augment their private fortunes (2). The first overt measure of the conspirators was a "visitation" throughout the kingdom, during which each diocesan and his clergy, together with several householders of each parish, were summoned to take the oath of royal supremacy in religious matters, and to receive a *Book of Homilies* which was ordered to be read in every church on Sundays and holy-days. Then successive restrictions were issued by which the right to preach was finally accorded only to those who could obtain a license from the lord-protector or from Cranmer; not even a bishop could preach in his own diocese without such permission. Thenceforward, therefore, the people heard no religious doctrine but that set forth in the *Homilies ;* and thus a great advance was made in the Protestantization of the nation (3). Gardiner, bishop of Winchester, was one of the few prelates who resisted the innovations of Cranmer, defying the primate to prove the truth of the Homiletic distinctive doctrines. A commitment to the fleet answered the challenge; and when the courageous man was told that he might enter the royal council in lieu of his cell, if he would yield, he replied that were he to do so, "he would deserve to be whipped in every market-town in the realm, and then to be hanged for an example as the veriest varlet that ever was bishop in any realm christened" (4). In 1548, Cranmer, in conjunction with a

(1) STRYPE; *Cranmer*, 144.   (2) HEYLIN; 33.—GODWIN; 88, 91.

(3) WILKINS; IV., 11, 14, 17.—COLLIER; II., *Records*.

(4) See the correspondence in FOXE, II., 64, 65.

committee of divines, compiled an English Liturgy, based indeed upon the *Roman Missal* and the *Breviary*, but altered here, augmented there, and with omissions everywhere ; all the changes being designed to further the Protestantizing process of their inventors. Thus was born the *Book of Common Prayer ;* but it is to be noted that this original Anglican Liturgy differed considerably from the one now used in the English Establishment. Thus, like all the olden Liturgies, it contained, in the prayers of the Consecration, these words : " Heare us, we beseeche Thee, and with Thy Holy Spirite and worde vouchsafe to bl✠esse and sancti✠fie these Thy gifts and creatures of bread and wyne, that they may be unto us the Bodie and Blood of Thy most dearly beloved Sonne." It contained also the unctions for baptism and for confirmation, the sign of the cross in matrimony, the anointing of the sick, and a prayer for the dead. The little " Head of the Church of England," now advanced to the mature age of ten, at once brought the *Book* before parliament, informing the presumedly devout members that it had been perfected " by the aid of the Holy Ghost, with one uniform agreement" on the part of its framers ; which was false, for eight of the eighteen bishops of the committee voted against the *Book* in the House of Lords (1). If any parson or other " spiritual person" dared thereafter to refuse to use the *Book* or to speak against it, his first offence would entail the loss of a year's revenue and imprisonment for six months ; a second dereliction would cause the loss of his benefice and imprisonment for a year ; a third would be punished by imprisonment for life (2). But in three years from the time when the Holy Ghost was alleged to have inspired the new Liturgy, the whole kingdom was filled with the clamors of the more ultra among the foes of the Scarlet Woman, denouncing the *Book of Common Prayer* as redolent of idolatry. The royal boy-pontiff, now more theologically advanced than when he said that the *Book* gave him " great comfort and quietness of mind," took up the cry, and declared that if his bishops did not reform the obnoxious Liturgy, he would see that others did it (3). Accordingly,

(1) COLLIER ; II., 243.—*Lords' Journals,* 331.   (2) Statutes of the Realm, IV., 37, 38.
(3) BURNET ; II., 155.

a committee hearkened to the suggestions of Peter Martyr Vermiglio and Bucer; a more Protestant *Book* was issued; and after reading it through and through, the presumedly competent parliament confirmed it (1). Immediately after this adoption of the *Common Prayer*, the bishops of the Establishment doffed their wonted episcopal garments, and the prebendaries clipped off their hoods, in accordance with the prescription to wear only the surplice (2). This bit of ecclesiastical millinery craft was seriously welcomed by the evangelicals as a long farewell to Rome; but what chiefly made this farewell an actual fact was the order of Cranmer issued to the wardens of every parish, "to bring in and deliver ... all antiphoners, missals, and ordinals after the use of Sarum, Lincoln, York, or any other private use, and all books of Service; ... that you take the same books into your hands or into the hands of your deputy, and them so deface and abolish, that they never after may serve either to any such use as they were provided for, or be at any time a let (impediment) to that godly and uniform order which by common consent is now set forth." From that day until days which are remembered by persons still living, Catholic literature of every kind was contraband in England; and excepting during the reign of Mary, for two centuries the ban was enforced with barbarity, and often its violation was punished with axe or rope. In the meantime, England was being flooded with Protestant publications; and the people hearing no refutations of the venomous productions, in a few generations they were "reformed." Well might Manning exclaim: "The people of England did not reject the Catholic faith. A thousand times I have said it, for in my soul I believe it, that Englishmen never rejected the Catholic faith—they were robbed of it.

---

(1) Lingard thus explains this parliamentary confirmation: "The book, in its amended form, received the assent of the Convocation. But here a new difficulty arose. It was the province of the clergy to decide on matters of doctrine and worship; how then could they submit a work approved by themselves, to the revision of the lay branches of the legislature? To elude the inconvenience, it was proposed to connect the amended service and the ordinal with a bill which was then in its progress through parliament, to compel by additional penalties attendance at the national worship. The clergy hoped that both forms would thus steal through the two houses without exciting any notice; but their object was detected and defeated. The books were read through, before the Act was permitted to pass; and both without alteration were allowed and confirmed." *Hist. of England*, vol. V., ch. iv

(2) COLLIER; II., 325.

They were robbed of it by force. They rose up to defend it in arms, but they were beaten down."

In 1549, Cranmer introduced into parliament a bill which was very dear to his heart; namely, one countenancing the marriage of the clergy. The primate's first wife had died before he received the priesthood; but after his ordination, and during one of his errands for Henry on the continent, he had "married" a step-niece of Osiander, and had left her in Germany. Naturally he yearned for the society of the lady; therefore on Feb. 19, the complacent parliament declared that though it were to be wished that the clergy would observe perpetual continency, as more becoming their spiritual character, rendering them better able to attend to their duties, and freeing them from worldly cares and embarrassments; yet so many inconveniences had arisen from compulsive chastity, that it was deemed better to allow to those who could not contain, the godly use of marriage. Therefore his Majesty's faithful Lords and Commons enacted that thenceforward, all laws made by man only, and prohibitory of the marriages of spiritual persons, should be void (1).

Notwithstanding these and similar enactments, the immense majority of Englishmen still cherished the hope that the ancient religion would be restored. To crush this yearning, a parliamentary Act now subjected, for a first offence, to a fine; and for a second, to indefinite imprisonment; any person, clerical or lay, who retained any book which contained any portion of the Roman Liturgy (2). Furthermore, since the Protestantizers had adopted a new fashion of administering the Sacraments, the clergy were to be ordained in a new way. Therefore parliament enacted that six prelates, and six other persons learned in God's law, should be appointed by his Majesty to compose a manner of making and consecrating archbishops, bishops, priests, and deacons; and that such manner, being set forth under the great seal before April 1, 1549, should afterward be lawfully used and exercised, and no other (3). But in spite of the new liturgy,

(1) *Statutes of the Realm*, IV., 67.   (2) *Ibid.*, 110.—*Lords' Journal*, 384.

(3) *Statutes*, IV., 112. It is well to note here that as early as 1540, Cranmer had enunciated not only loose, but absolutely heretical opinions concerning Holy Orders. Cromwell, by order of Henry VIII., had announced the appointment of two committees of prelates and

new ordinal, and every new-fangled arrangement of matters
ecclesiastical which fanatical ingenuity could devise; it was
found that in the fourth year of Edward's reign, eleven-twelfths
of the English people still clung to the faith of their fathers (1).
Therefore Cranmer and his associates resolved to rid the Establishment of the most Catholicly inclined prelates. He began with Bonner, bishop of Lincoln; ordering him to preach,
at St. Paul's Cross in London, a written discourse which was
delivered to him, and which was of a nature very unlikely to
prove acceptable to him. As was foreseen, Bonner did not follow the instructions; and he was denounced by two reformed
preachers, Latimer and Hooper. Brought to Cranmer for
sentence, he contended that his real crime was his Catholic
explanation of the Eucharistic doctrine; but he was deposed,
his diocese handed over to Ridley, and he himself imprisoned
in the Marshalsea, where he remained until the death of
Edward. Gardiner, bishop of Winchester, had been a prisoner for two years when he was asked, in July, 1550, to sign an
act of conformity with the new religious system. He replied
that it was unfair to talk to him about submission when he
was not free; and that it should never be said that he had
sacrificed his conscience for his liberty. Brought before the
royal council, his firmness could not be affected; and "on

theologians, for the compilation of a Book of Doctrines and Ceremonies. Three years were
spent in the work, and when it was completed, the *King's Book*, as it was termed, was recognized as the standard of English Orthodoxy. When it was being begun, certain questions
were proposed separately to each collaborator, and the answers were collated and laid before Henry. Some of these have found their way to the public; others are to be seen in the
British Museum (Cleop. E., 5). Now Cranmer, archbishop of Canterbury though he was, expressed his views on orders as follows. The king, said he, must have spiritual as well as
civil officers; and *of course* has a right to appoint them. In the time of the Apostles, observes the subservient innovator, the people appointed, *because they had no Christian
king*, and therefore they occasionally accepted such as might be recommended to them by
the Apostles; but the people accepted such apostolic nominees " of their own voluntary
will, and not for any superiority that the Apostles had over them." In the appointment of
bishops and priests, continues this enterprising discoverer, some ceremonies are to be used
"*not of necessity, but for good order and seemly fashion. ... He who is appointed
bishop or priest, needeth no consecration by the Scripture; for election or appointing thereto is sufficient.*" It is no wonder that, with a view to the safety of his head on
his shoulders, Cranmer added : " This is mine opinion and sentence at this present ; which,
nevertheless, I do not temerariously define, *but refer the judgment thereof to your Majesty.*" See STRYPE, 79 ; App., 45, 50.—BURNET ; 1 Coll, 201.—COLLIER ; *Records* ; II., 159

(1) We find in Strype (*Records*, II., 110) a letter from Paget to Somerset, dated July 7, 1549,
which says : "The use of the old religion is forbidden by a law, and the use of the new is
not yet printed in the stomachs of eleven of twelve parts of the realm, what countenance so-
ever men make outwardly to please them in whom they see the power resteth."

the day of his judgment given againste him, he called his
judges heretiques and sacramentarys, they being there the
kinge's commissioneres, and of his Highnes counsell" (1).
He was deposed, and his diocese was given to Poynet, bishop
of Rochester. He also remained in prison until the accession
of Mary. The next depositions were of Heath of Worcester, and Day of Chichester. The latter's offence was different from those of Gardiner and Heath. These prelates having been in prison when what was termed the "Lord's Supper" was substituted for the Sacrifice of the Mass, they had
no opportunity of resisting the outrage; but Day had nobly
availed himself of the opportunity he enjoyed. Since Sacrifice and Altar are correlatives, it was no sooner resolved by
the Protestantizers to abolish the Mass, than the church
plate, etc., became a choice morsel for the human vultures
who were fattening on the spoils of the olden worship; for
these valuables were all appurtenances of the altar, for which
there was now, of course, no use. The cry went up for the
removal of all altars, and the substitution of "communion
tables"; and after a few unauthorized incursions by certain
rapacious preachers and nobles, and a more formal raid in
the London churches by Ridley, the royal council ordered
every diocesan to banish all altars from his jurisdiction (2).
Day refused; Cranmer and Ridley were commissioned to
convert him, but he would not be converted; and he also was
imprisoned until the next reign (3). The narrative of this
raid upon the sanctuaries of England, of this exhibition of
hellish rage toward every vestige of the sacrificial worship of
their ancestors, cannot be pleasant reading to the Ritualists
who ask the Catholic world to concede that they celebrate
Mass; that the traditions of the English Establishment allow
them to participate in that Unbloody Sacrifice which is daily
offered to God, from the rising to the setting of the sun.
The damning fact remains, that the authoritative commission
instituted by the Head of the English Church ordered that
"all altars in every church or chapel be taken down, and instead of them a table be set up; ... to move the people from

(1) *Council Book*, fol. 152. (2) WILKINS; Councils; IV., 65.
(3) *Council Book*, fol. 140, 141, 200.—STRYPE; II., 391.

the superstitions of the Popish Mass unto the right use of the Lord's supper ; the use of an altar being to sacrifice upon, and the use of a table to eat upon. ... Altars were erected for the sacrifice of the Law, which being now ceased, the form of an altar was to cease together with them." And the Protestantizers were not content with removing the altars ; they must needs gratify their diabolic malice by setting the altar slabs in the pavement of the churches, so that the people, if· they did not run their daggers through the Sacred Body of Christ like the Luciferian Masons of our day, might at least trample upon what had been His resting-place. When Ridley was called upon, during the reign of the Catholic Mary, to answer for his blasphemies, he justified his course toward the altars by alleging that "it was done upon just considerations, for that the altars seemed to come too nigh the Jews' usage." This melancholy fact may well be contemplated by Romanizing Anglicans. It may be placed in the same category with the sneering words of their *Homily on the Sacrament*, about "massing priests" and "mummish massing" ; with Henry's slur on the priestly "*mumpsimus* and *sumpsimus* " ; with the declaration of the quoted Homily that we "need no sacrificing priest, no Mass " ; all of which emphasize the sad words of Cardinal Manning : " The once Catholic, but now Protestant, churches of England stand like the open sepulchre ; and we may believe that the angels are there, ever saying : ' He is not here ; come and see where the Lord was laid ' " (1).

(1) When Elizabeth undid the restoring work of Mary, the "tables" were placed "in the body of the church or in the chancel " (*Rubric*). Bramhall wrote to Laud that "the table used for the administration of the Blessed Sacrament in the midst of the choir is made an ordinary seat for maids and apprentices." And in the *Constitutions and Canons Ecclesiastical*, 1640, *by his Majestic's Authority under the Great Seal of England*, we read that "experience hath showed us how irreverent the behavior of many people is, some leaning, others casting their hats. and some sitting upon, some standing, and others sitting under, the communion-table in time of divine service." But although common decency rebuked these practices, and although an "obeisance " toward the altar was enjoined (Laud, like a child at play, used to bow seven times toward the *unconsecrated* elements, but *never after* what he called the " consecration "), the royal Head of the Establishment was careful to enjoin in the Canons just cited, that " albeit at the time of reforming this church from that gross superstition of Popery, it was carefully provided that all means should be used to root out of the minds of the people both the inclination thereunto, and memory thereof, especially of the idolatry committed in the Mass, for which cause all popish altars were demolished, ... we declare that this situation of the holy table *doth not imply that it is, or ought to be, esteemed a true and proper altar whereon Christ is again really sacrificed.*"

We do not propose to give any detailed account of the terrible sufferings of Catholics while England was being Protestantized; still less can we spare space to notice the inconsistent persecutions visited by the Anglican inquisitors upon such of their comrades in revolt as they thought proper to brand as "heretics." But there are two instances of the latter procedure which ought to be recorded. The first is that of Joan Bocher, a Kentish woman who, during the reign of Henry, had rendered good service to the secret Reformers by the clandestine importation and distribution of prohibited books. Her "heresies" caused the orthodox Cranmer to forget his debt to Joan; and in April, 1549, she was led before him, Latimer, Smith, Cook, and Lyell, to answer the charge of having maintained, in her sermons (for she was a preacher), that "Christ did not take flesh of the outward man of the Virgin, because the outward man was conceived in sin; but by the consent of the inward man, which was undefiled." What this jargon meant, or what the inquisitors understood by it, we are not informed; but Cranmer ordered her to be delivered to the secular power; whereupon she cried: "It is a goodly matter to consider your ignorance. It is not long ago that you burned Ann Askew for a piece of bread; and yet came yourselves soon afterward to believe and profess the same doctrine for which you burned her. And now, forsooth, you will needs burn me for a piece of flesh, and in the end will come to believe this also, when you have read the Scriptures and understand them." Whether or not he appreciated the logic of Bocher, now that he was matured even unto his eleventh year, Edward hesitated to confirm Cranmer's sentence; and it was only when the primate proved by the conduct of Moses in causing blasphemers to be stoned, that his Majesty should sign the death warrant, that Joan was lead to the stake. When the preacher Scory tried, at the pyre, to induce her to recant, she cried: "Thou liest like a rogue, thou shouldst go home and study the Script-

As to the official view of the Altar and the Mass, taken, in modern times, by the highest court of ecclesiastical appeal known to Anglicanism, we need to refer merely to the famous St. Barnabas case (*Westerton vs. Liddell*): wherein it was decided that "The change in the view taken of the Sacrament naturally called for a corresponding change in the altar. *It was no longer to be an altar of sacrifice, but merely a table at which the communicants were to partake of the Lord's supper.*"

ures " (1). Another interesting case of Anglican inquisition
was that of the Dutch surgeon, Von Parris, who had been
excommunicated by the Dutch Consistory in London. Although Cranmer could lawfully have no jurisdiction in
this case, Parris was arraigned before his tribunal on the
charge of having denied the divinity of Christ. Coverdale
acted as interpreter, and sentence of death having been pronounced, the victim was burnt on April 24, 1551 (2). Parris
seems to have been the sole foreign innovator whom Cranmer sent to the stake. As a rule, while he, and all the other
founders of the English Establishment, were cruelly severe
toward all native disturbers of whatever they saw fit to designate as truth, they were most favorable to a horde of foreign
preachers who thronged in the palace of Cranmer and in those
of nearly every Anglican prelate. Choice preferments in the
Establishment, and prompt protection at court, were ever at
their command. Thus Peter Martyr Vermiglio and Bucer
were appointed to chairs of theology in Oxford and Cambridge ; Faggio, Tremelio, and Cavalier gave lectures in Hebrew at Cambridge ; Knox became chaplain to the young king ;
Utenhoff and Peter Alexander received choice prebends in Canterbury ; and many others were richly paid for their arduous
labors in the enlightenment of the stolid British public (3).

We have seen how the new Liturgy was forced upon the
English people. A French translation of the *Book of Common Prayer* was issued for the natives of Jersey and Guern-
sey ; which was but in accordance with the Protestant idea

(1) In 1543, Henry VIII. discovered that many ladies of his court, his own queen, Catharine Parr, in the number, were dallying with the doctrines of the German Reformers. Works
of these innovators had been smuggled into his own palace by the Bucher just mentioned,
and by Ann Askew. Among those implicated with the two women were Latimer, who was
to attain to the dignity of " martyrdom " under " Bloody Mary," after a life of repeated
apostasies and abjurations ; and Shaxton, the deprived bishop of Salisbury. These two wor-
thies escaped the vengeance of Henry by recantation ; Shaxton even delivered the funeral
sermon at the execution of Askew and her associates, pitying their blindness, and exhorting
them to merit the royal grace, as he and Latimer had done. The good man was rewarded
for his zeal with the mastership of St. Giles's Hospital in Norwich. Latimer, who had been
made bishop of Worcester by Henry in 1535, but had been obliged to resign in 1539, because
the king suspected his orthodoxy, saved his life, indeed, by submitting in the affair of Askew ;
but he did not leave his prison until Edward VI. called him to his court, where he distinguished himself by the bitterness and coarseness of his pulpit oratory. See *State Papers in
the Reign of Henry VIII.* : I., 846 850.—FOXE ; III. 379, 383.—WILKINS ; III., 748.

(2) STOWE ; 605.—*Edward's Journal*, 24.

(3) STRYPE ; *Cranmer*, 194, 234, 232.—Idem, *Memorials*, II, 121, 205, 240.

of a vernacular liturgy in every land. But when the Reformers began to think of the claims to enlightenment possessed by the benighted Irish, they were confronted by a serious difficulty. For centuries the English conquerors had been striving, by every means excogitable, to destroy even a memory of the Irish language. Certainly, they had failed; for at the time of the Reformation, not one Irishman in ten knew a word of the invader's language. Principle was at stake; how could the Establishment carry out the grand idea of a vernacular liturgy in Ireland, when it was notorious that nothing contributes so much to the vitality of a language as the habit of praying in it. Therefore it was resolved that the Irishman should be compelled to pray in English; and the requisite proclamation was emitted, and forwarded to all the Irish prelates. The order was enforced, so far as it could be, by Archbishop Browne of Dublin, and four other bishops; it was spurned by Dowdal, the Archbishop of Armagh, and every other prelate (1).

By the time that the new Head of the Church of England had reached his fifteenth year, he, like every Englishman who thought at all of the matter, began to reflect that it was an exceedingly difficult enterprise to try to discover what was, and was not, the faith of the Establishment—an enterprise which, many times since, has been vainly essayed by wiser brains than Edward possessed. An authorized standard of orthodoxy was regarded as imperative, even by those who had been the loudest in their clamors against the teaching authority of the Pope. Accordingly, after much discussion with various divines, Cranmer laid the Forty-Two Articles before the king; his Majesty was pleased to approve them; and a royal order was promulgated, commanding that they should receive the subscriptions of all clergymen, churchwardens, and schoolmasters (2). No one could receive a degree in the universities who did not solemnly swear that he would "always place the authority of Scripture above the decisions of men"; and that he "would always defend the Articles lately issued by royal authority, as true and certain, and as con-

(1) LELAND ; III., ch. viii.
(2) STRYPE ; *Cranmer*, 272, 293.—BURNET; II., 166 ; III., 210-213. WILKINS ; *Councils*, IV., 79.

sonant with the word of God "—two clauses which all the graduate's university training could not enable him to reconcile. After the promulgation of the Forty-Two Articles, it was thought that nothing more was necessary to insure the unity of the Establishment, than a Code of Ecclesiastical Law which would supersede the Canons of papal days. Therefore, in the same year, 1552, a royal commission, with Cranmer at its head, framed a Code in fifty-one articles, treating of all matters which pertain to the cognizance of ecclesiastical courts. It begins with what the designers wished to be considered as an exposition of Christian doctrine; and it enacts that heresy shall be punished by forfeiture and death, regulating, also, how the convicted heretic shall be delivered to the secular power for execution. It is very severe on seducers of women; but it allows divorce, *not only for adultery, but for desertion, protracted absence, danger to health, etc.*, permitting the innocent party to take another partner. It is interesting to note that it asserts that excommunication excludes its object from the society of the faithful, from the protection of God, and from all hope of heaven; *consigning him to the everlasting tyranny of the devil* (1).

When Mary mounted the throne of England in 1553, the Protestantizing process was checked; and the nation once more prayed in the household of Christian faith. We are forced to restrict our task to a tracing of the progress of heresy among the English; but if the reader desires fairly accurate information concerning the reign of Mary Tudor, he will refer to the pages of Lingard, being assured that too favorable a view will not be presented by an otherwise grand historian, whose too eager yearning for a conciliation of the prejudices of a bastard patriotism frequently leads him to an economical presentation of the truth. We are grateful to Lingard for the following concessions. "It was the lot of Mary to live in an age of religious intolerance, when to punish the professors of erroneous doctrine was inculcated as a duty, no less by those who rejected, than by those who asserted the papal authority. It might perhaps have been expected that the Reformers, from their sufferings under Henry

(1) *Reformat. Eccl. Laws*, published in 1571.

VIII., would have learned to respect the rights of conscience. Experience proved the contrary. They had no sooner obtained the ascendency during the short reign of Edward, than they displayed the same persecuting spirit which they had formerly condemned; burning the Anabaptist, and preparing to burn the Catholic at the stake, for no other crime than adherence to religious opinion. The former, by existing law, was already liable to the penalty of death; the latter enjoyed a precarious respite, because his belief had not yet been pronounced heretical by any acknowledged authority. But the zeal of Archbishop Cranmer observed and supplied this deficiency; and in the code of ecclesiastical discipline which he compiled for the government of the Reformed Church, he was careful to class the distinguishing doctrines of the ancient worship with those recently promulgated by Muncer and Socinus. By the new Canon Law of the metropolitan, to believe in Transubstantiation, to admit the papal supremacy, and to deny justification by faith only, were severally made heresy; and it was ordained that individuals accused of holding heretical opinions should be arraigned before the spiritual courts, should be excommunicated on conviction, and after a respite of sixteen days, should, if they continued obstinate, be delivered to the civil magistrate, to suffer the punishment provided by law. Fortunately for the professors of the ancient faith, Edward died before this code had obtained the sanction of the legislature. By the accession of Mary, the power of the sword passed from the hands of one religious party to those of the other; and within a short time Cranmer and his associates perished in the flames which they had prepared to kindle for the destruction of their opponents " (1).

With the accession of Elizabeth to the throne of England, joy entered the hearts of all religious innovators. The daughter of Anne Boleyn could scarcely be expected to harbor much sympathy with the power which had proclaimed her mother's dissoluteness and her own bastardy; and she had given good reason for the supposition that her acquiescence with her half-sister's restoration of the Catholic wor-

(1) *History of England*, vol. V., ch. vi.

ship was a matter of mere policy.   Certainly, when she first
donned the ermine, she continued to assist at the Holy Sacrifice, and even to communicate occasionally ; she buried the
remains of Mary with all the ceremonies of the Catholic ritual ; and she caused to be celebrated a solemn Requiem for
the soul of the emperor Charles V.   But the Protestantizers
were encouraged when they beheld the prison doors opening
for the egress of the religionists whom the Marian edicts had
immured ; when they saw prominent Protestant preachers
welcomed at court ; and when Elizabeth ordered Oglethorpe,
bishop of Carlisle, not to presume to elevate the Sacred Host
after the consecration (1).   They were not surprised when,
on Dec. 27, the queen ordered that " until consultation might
be had in parliament," no other change should be made in
the liturgy, than the recitation in English of the Lord's
Prayer, the Creed, the Epistle, and the Gospel.   Very soon
there was announced a repeal of the Marian statutes which
had restored the ancient faith ; and it was enacted that under pain of death, the *Book of Common Prayer*, with certain
changes in a more Protestant sense, should be used by all
clergymen (2).   Then came the declaration that all ecclesias-

(1) On Christmas morning, 1558, as Oglethorpe was vesting in the royal chapel, he received an order from the queen not to elevate the Host in the royal presence. He replied
that his life belonged to her Highness ; but his conscience was his own. When, therefore, he came to the Offertory of the Mass, the queen left the chapel. CAMDEN. 32.—*Losely
MSS.*, 184.

(2) There is a story current among Anglicans to the effect that either Paul IV. or Pius V.
(they cannot agree as to which) offered to approve the *Book* on condition that Elizabeth
would admit the Papal supremacy.   Estcourt, in his *Anglican Ordinations* (P. 354), says:

"If the argument on the Catholic side has gained a certain advantage by the currency
given to so telling a story as that of the Nag's Head, Anglicans, on the other side, have
availed themselves of a similar opportunity in stating the legend of the Pope having made
an offer to Queen Elizabeth of confirming the *Book of Common Prayer*. It is strange
that, after the indignation excited in them by the former tale, they should put forward as a
matter of importance a story resting on no better foundation than the other, and with no
authority quoted for it but mere verbal tradition. The evidence in each case is precisely of
the same character ; if the names of certain persons are quoted in one case as the authorities from whom the story was derived, names are given with equal confidence in the other.
The current of tradition in each case runs equally clearly. If the Nag's-Head story was
not heard of for upward of forty years after the date of the alleged transaction, no more
was that of the Pope's offer. If the one was not published during the lifetime of those said
to be actors in it, neither was the other. If the difference in the three or four versions of
the Nag's Head is fatal to its credibility, there are at least three versions of the Pope and
Queen.   Notwithstanding all this, Bishop Bull, after calling the Nag's-Head story 'a putrid
fable,' within three pages coolly and unblushingly relates two versions of the other story,
both as undoubted facts, although no one else has even ventured to take credit for more
than one.

"Let, then, no man be a judge in his own cause.   Surely we may hence gather the need

tical jurisdiction was an appanage of the crown; and the promulgation of the consequent penalty of hanging and quartering for all who would presume to assert that the Roman Pontiff had any spiritual jurisdiction in the realms of her gracious Highness. In July, 1559, the queen took measures for the institution of a new hierarchy for the royal Establishment. She caused the oath of belief in the royal supremacy in church matters to be tendered to all the bishops; but she found that they were not of the mould in which the episcopal sycophants of Henry's court had been fashioned. One alone, Kitchin, of Landaff, laid his mitre under her royal feet; all the others were deposed and imprisoned (1). It now became necessary to appoint a kind of superintendent for the royal-liveried lackeys of the new hierarchy. Of course he was to be termed archbishop of Canterbury. For this mitred-butlership Elizabeth selected Matthew Parker, who had been chaplain to Anne Boleyn, and was now dean of Lincoln. But by whom was this worthy to be consecrated? Just then there was only one "lawful" bishop in the kingdom, Kitchin; and the 25th of Henry VIII. prescribed that the consecration of the primate should be by four bishops. And another difficulty arose. How was Parker to be "made a bishop"? Then there was no "lawful" form of consecration available; for the *Ordinal of Edward VI.* had been abolished by the Marian parliament, and the *Catholic Ordinal* by the Elizabethan. However, the royal canonists found a way out of both difficulties. Her gracious Majesty, the Vicar of Christ on earth, was fully competent, as Head

of adopting some such principles or rules of evidence as were laid down at the beginning of this work, in order to have a common test or tribunal by which we may know what facts and circumstances are worth being alleged as arguments. Even supposing that it was the fact that an offer such as described was made to Queen Elizabeth, there is no argument to be drawn from it in the present question; for there is nothing said or pretended, which can show how far the offer was to extend; and whether it was meant to include the forms of ordination under the name of *Book of Common Prayer*."

(1) Tunstall of Durham, Morgan of St. David's, Oglethorpe of Carlisle, White of Winchester, and Baines of Coventry, died that year in prison. Scot of Chester, Goldwell of St. Asaph's, and Pate of Worcester succeeded, somehow, in escaping to the continent. Of the remaining seven, Heath, after several periods of imprisonment, was allowed to reside on his private estates in Surrey. Bonner groaned in the Marshalsea ten years, and then died. Watson of Lincoln remained in prison twenty-three years. Thirlby of Ely remained in the episcopal prison of Parker until his death. Bourne of Bath and Wells was put in the custody of the dean of Exeter. Turberville of Exeter and Pool of Peterborough were forbidden to leave their respective houses for the rest of their days.

of the Church of England, to heal every defect that could
possibly arise in the premises. Therefore an apposite sana-
tory clause was inserted in the royal commission for Parker's consecration; and the duty of confirming the election of
the new primate, and of consecrating him, was delegated to
Barlowe, Hodgkins, Scorey, and Coverdale. Barlowe had
been bishop of Bath until he was deposed by Mary, and was
supposed to have been consecrated during the reign of Henry
according to the *Catholic Ordinal.* Hodgkins, suffragan of
Bedford under Henry, had certainly been consecrated according to the Catholic rite. Scorey of Chichester and Coverdale of Exeter had been consecrated according to the *Reformed Ordinal.* These four prelates, Barlowe officiating,
went through with what they and theirs termed the "consecration" of Parker, using the *Ordinal* which had been adopted toward the close of the reign of Edward VI.; and since
all subsequent Anglican prelates derived their claims to consecration from this Parker, upon the validity or non-validity
of his consecration turns the solution of what certain parties
are pleased to term the "vexed" question of Anglican Orders—a matter in which the reader will find, in all probability, very little reason for doubt.

When Parker had initiated all the royally-appointed in-
cumbents of the Elizabethan hierarchy into their future
careers, all proceeded to further the progress of English
Protestantism by tendering the Oath of Supremacy to their
respective clergy. The immense majority of the deans and
prebendaries sacrificed their benefices, and very often their
personal liberty, rather than proffer what was equivalent to
a renunciation of their Catholic faith; but many of the inferior clergy yielded (1). In 1563, the obligation to take the

(1) Some of the uses to which the Elizabethan clergy, as well as their successors under the
Stuarts, were put, are caustically noted by Brooks Adams, in his *Law of Civilization and
Decay* (New York, 1895). Strictly speaking, the Church of England never had a faith in
Tudor times, but vibrated between the orthodoxy of the "Six Articles" and the Calvinism
of the "Lambeth Articles." Within a single generation, the relation that Christ's Flesh and
Blood bore to the bread and wine was changed five times by royal proclamation or act of
Parliament. But the new economic aristocracy understood the value of the pulpit as a
branch of the police of the kingdom, and from the outset it used the clergy as part of the
secular administration. On this point Cranmer was explicit. Elizabeth told her bishops
plainly that *she cared little for doctrines,* but *wanted clerks to keep order.* It was with a
rod of iron that she ruled her clergy. No priest was allowed to marry without the approbation of two justices of the peace. When the dean of St. Paul's offended the queen in a ser-

Oath was extended to persons not contemplated in the original Act; and this severity, said the parliament, was for the purpose of "restraining and correcting the marvellous outrages and licentious boldness of the fautors of the Bishop of Rome." Hitherto, the Oath had been taken necessarily only by an heir holding of the crown, who wished to sue out the livery of his lands; by all who sought ecclesiastical preferment; by aspirants to office under the crown; and by all members of the Universities of Oxford and Cambridge. By an Act of March 3, parliament extended the obligation, under pain of perpetual imprisonment, to members of the House of Commons, schoolmasters, private tutors, and attorneys. Under pain of death for a second refusal, the Oath was demanded also from all who had held ecclesiastical office during the last three reigns; and to all who presumed to celebrate or to hear Mass. Speaking of these provisions, Cecil said: "Such be the humours of the Commons house, as they thynke nothing sharp ynough ageynst papists." We have now dwelt at sufficient length upon the measures which were taken to rob the English people of their faith; and we would say a few words in refutation of the assertion that the Church of England reformed herself in Elizabeth's time, and that only 189 of the old clergy refused to conform. It is certain that the English bishops protested against any change of religion, when, having seen that Elizabeth did not intend

mon, she told him "to retire from that ungodly digression and return to his text"; and Archbishop Grindall was suspended for disobedience to her orders. In Catholic times, the sovereign had drawn his supernatural qualities from his consecration by the priesthood; in the seventeenth century money had already come to represent a force so predominant that the process had become reversed, and the clergy attributed their prerogative to speak in the name of the Deity to the interposition of the king. This was the substance of the Reformation in England. Cranmer taught that God committed to Christian princes "the whole cure of their subjects, as well concerning the administration of God's word, as of things political"; therefore, bishops, parsons, and vicars were ministers of the temporal ruler, to whom he confided the ecclesiastical office precisely as he confided the enforcement of order to a chief of police. As a part of the secular administration, the main function of the Anglican ministers under the Tudors and the Stuarts was to preach obedience to their patrons. Elizabeth bluntly told her bishops that they must get her sober, respectable preachers, *but men who should be cheap.* In fine, the Anglican clergy under the Tudors and Stuarts were not so much ministers, as hired political retainers. Mr. Adams reproduces a part of Macaulay's description: "The coarse and ignorant squire could hire a young Levite for his board, a small garret, and ten pounds a year. This clergyman might not only be the most patient of butts and of listeners, might not only be always ready in fine weather for bowls and in rainy weather for shuffleboard, but might also save the expense of a gardener or of a groom. Sometimes the reverend man nailed up the apricots, and sometimes he curried the coach horses."

to keep the oath which she would have to take at her coronation, they resolved to take no part in the ceremony. Certainly, Oglethorpe finally consented to perform the coronation ceremony, on the express condition that she should take the usual oath to maintain the Catholic faith. This protest was repeated equivalently when, while parliament was debating on the Bill of Supremacy, both bishops and priests met in Convocation, and adopted a solemn declaration of their belief in the Real Presence, in Transubstantiation, in the Sacrifice of the Mass, in the Papal Supremacy, and in the exclusion of all laymen from the government of the Church. Even Froude recognizes this protest as that of the entire "spiritualty" of England, adding that "the clergy never consented, as a body, to any measure of reformation whatever, except under the judicious compulsion of Henry the Eighth" (1). A third protest was made when Archbishop Heath, as primate of the English Church, denounced the Bill of Supremacy in the House of Lords on March 22, 1559, saying, according to Strype, " that by forsaking and fleeing from the See of Rome they must first forsake and flee from all General Councils; secondly, all canonical and ecclesiastical law; thirdly, the judgment of all other Christian princes; and fourthly, the *unity* of Christ's Church; and by falling out of Peter's ship, hazard themselves to be drowned in the waters of schism, sects, and divisions." A fourth protest was entered when, a division having been called, all the bishops voted against any religious change. A fifth protest was made on May 15 at Greenwich, when Heath, in the name of the English Church, told the queen "to remember what her real duty was and the policy she was bound to adopt; to follow in the steps of her sister who had brought back the country to the ancient religion, which had flourished in it for so many centuries; that Rome was the mother of all churches; that history and tradition, and the writings of the Fathers and the great Councils of the Church, all proclaimed Rome as the Head of that Church which their Divine Master had founded." And certainly there was a sixth protest when their twenty-one days' grace having expired, the bish-

(1) *History of England*, VI., p. 165.

ops still refused to acknowledge the female Anti-Pope, and preferred to be thrown into the Tower or the Fleet, to be afterward, all except Kitchin, deprived of their sees. So much for the attitude of the English bishops; but how was it with the priests? The egregious failure of the royal Visitors to cow the clergy into a submission to her Majesty's usurpation of pontifical jurisdiction is evinced by the fact that most of the priests refused even to appear before the Visitors, so that out of 9,400 beneficed clergy, the zealous commissioners, according to their report in the *Domestic State Papers*, were able to give the names of only 806 as having subscribed. In the visitation of the province of York in August and September, 1559, according to Simpson's investigation of the State Papers (1), out of 90 priests summoned, 21 took the oath, 36 refused it, 7 were absent and furnished no procurators, and 16 were absent but sent procurators. As regards the province of Canterbury, Simpson says: "We hear of the dean and canons of Winchester cathedral, the warden and fellows of the college, and the master of Holy Cross, all refusing the oath. Yet only four of them are in Bridgewater's list. And for the whole country, the visitors returned the total of 49 recusants and 786 conformists, significantly omitting the absentees. Thus, out of the 8,911 parishes and 9,400 beneficed clergymen, we find only 806 subscribers; while all the bishops and 85 others expressly refused to subscribe, and the rest were absentees. The assertion, then, of Camden, that only 189 clergymen were deprived in this visitation, proves nothing. Archbishop Parker had orders 'not to push any one to extremities on account of his oath.' But Sanders and Bridgewater give many more names." Camden puts the number as 189, and Collier 243; "but this included, as a rule, the bishops, deans, archdeacons, prebendaries, and heads of colleges,—in fact, the pick of the clergy. Out of this grain of fact church defenders have built up a mountain of fable. Some have even gone so far as to say that all the old clergy of the Church of England conformed to the new order of things with this exception. But this estimate includes only those *deprived* of their livings in the visitation of 1559, which,

(1) Detailed in his *Life of Blessed Campion*, pp. 139 *et seqq.*

beginning in May and ending in December, lasted only six
months. No attempt has been made to estimate the total
number of clergy who resigned rather than face persecution,
who refused to take the oath and were not deprived in the
visitation of 1559, who were deprived in subsequent visita-
tions, who were ejected to make room for the married clergy
removed in Mary's reign. That the number was very great
we have abundant evidence" (1). As to those who resigned,
Cox, writing to Peter Martyr after the visitation of 1559 was
over, says: "The popish priests among us are daily relin-
quishing their ministry, lest, as they say, they should be compelled to give their sanction to heresies." Lever writes to
Bullingham, July 10, 1560, six months after, stating the result to be: "Many of our parishes have no clergymen, and
some dioceses are without a bishop. And out of that very
small number who administer the sacraments throughout
this great country, there is scarcely one in a hundred who
is both able and willing to preach the word of God." And
Collier says : "Upon the Catholic clergy throwing up their
preferments, the necessities of the Church required the admitting of some mechanics into orders." We are justified,
therefore, in declaring with Froude that the entire "spiritualty" of England protested against the Elizabethan foundation of the English Church Establishment which she destined
to supplant the Catholic Church in England. The entire
bench of bishops, Kitchin excepted, preferred imprisonment
or even death to a recognition of royal supremacy in religious
matters. And Collier shows that 12 deans, 14 archdeacons,
60 canons, 15 heads of colleges at Oxford and Cambridge,
20 doctors, and 100 of the well-preferred clergy shared the
fate of the bishops. Of the lesser clergy, besides those deprived in the visitation of 1559, spoken of by Camden and others, a large number, according to Burnet 3,000, were expelled
to make room for the married clergy removed in the previous
reign. Finally, a fresh visitation, that of 1561, was ordered ;
and as this, too, was ineffectual, the statute of 1562, which
visited recusancy with the penalty of death, was passed, "a
fact which demonstrates how absurd it is to say that with

(1) The 18⁰ ; or, The Church of Old England Protests ; by J. D. Breen, O. S. B.

the exception of between one and two hundred, the English clergy consented to conform to the new gospel."

In January, 1563, the Protestantization of England was completed by the adoption, in the two Houses of Convocation, of the Thirty-Nine Articles, as they now stand. The publication of these Thirty-Nine Articles was certainly regarded by their framers as the seal of the Reformation upon their work; and had they been told that the day would arrive when certain Anglicans would venture a belief that these tests of Protestantism were capable of a Catholic interpretation, they would have suspected the sanity of such imaginative prophets. As the torrent of Protestantism has raged, during three centuries, around the monuments of England's Catholic past, ever and anon certain of its victims have thrust a hand into the ruins, and plucking out a robe, or a rubric, or a candle, or a thurible, or a chalice, or mayhap a confessional, have pressed the article to their hearts, and fancied—or feigned to believe—that they were really incorporated with what the admired monuments represented and preached; in fine, that they were Catholics. When John Henry Newman, as yet a Protestant, wrote his famous Tract No. 90, he certainly believed that no Anglican was bound to subscribe to the Thirty-Nine in a Protestant sense. Was not the *Book of Common Prayer* often almost Catholic in tone? (1) But the world

(1) In his *Oxford Movement in America*, Rev. C. A. Walworth writes as follows:

" Queen Elizabeth must be considered as really the founder and really the head of the Anglican church. She herself and a large body of her subjects were, so far as concerned doctrine, strongly biased in favor of the doctrines of the ancient Church. She would gladly have had her church purely Catholic and united in one faith. She would have no Pope, however, but herself to cement that union. On the other hand, a large part of her subjects were not Catholic. Nothing but a compromise could bridge over this great difference between her subjects, and she bridged it with such a compromise. All Englishmen who were prominent enough to be reached by persecution were forced by their fears into this compromise. This compromise is to be found in the *Book of Common Prayer*. In it the catechism is, so far as it goes, Catholic. ... On the other hand, the Englishmen of Protestant proclivities were propitiated by the *Thirty-Nine Articles*, which always thunder, or seem to thunder, against Roman Catholic doctrine. To hold these opposing factions in harmony, both Articles and Liturgy are so skilfully hammered out, that all parties, both Catholics and Protestants, by using the large latitude always practically allowed them, may arrange their consciences comfortably upon the same liturgies and formulas. ... The English church was constituted as a department under the British Constitution. ... Unity in a church so constituted could never mean a unity in point of faith ; apostolicity could never mean the faith of the Apostles remaining unchanged in all ages; Catholicity could never mean a common belief in all nations and in all countries ; no standard of holiness could be maintained which should interfere with appointments to offices and livings, or the right of communion to any loyal British subject, whatever he might do, or whatever he might believe. Out of the

soon beheld the logical consequences of this playing at Catholic.   Those who were sincere, and who corresponded to the
grace which had planted the Catholic sentiment in their
hearts, soon found that no amount of mere man-millinery,
no mere clutching at candles and incense, could ordain a
priest, restore the Sacramental Lord to the sanctuary, or obtain the forgiveness of sin.   Hence they "went over to Rome."
But we will let the reader judge as to the Catholicity of the
Articles, from the following synopsis.   I.–V.   Acknowledg-
ment is made of a belief in the Trinity, the Incarnation, the
Descent of Christ into hell, His Resurrection, and in the Divinity of the Holy Ghost.   VI.–VII.   All the Books of the New
Testament are received as canonical.   From the Old are rejected the Books of Tobias, Judith, a part of that of Esther,
all of Wisdom, Ecclesiasticus, and Baruch ; certain chapters
of Daniel, and both Books of the Macchabees.   VIII.   The
Apostles' Creed, that of Nice, as well as that of St. Athanasius, are received.   IX.–XV.   It is declared that all men
are born in original sin ; that they have free will ; that they
can perform no good works without the aid of grace; that.
man is justified by faith alone.   Works of supererogation
are impieties (1).   XVI.   Sin may be forgiven through re-

compromise, so strange to reason, but which a long experience has shown to be practically
successful, has grown very naturally a certain principle, or at least motto, among Anglicans, for finding the truth in religious doctrine which is known by the name of the *via
media*.   Every Anglican that is really and thoroughly a typical man in his church is a *via
media* man.   For a preacher to confine himself too much to the *Thirty-Nine Articles*, and
to insist upon the most literal acceptation of their wording, shows an inclination to ultra-
Protestantism.   To make too much of the strong flavor of old Catholic doctrines, which is
found in the ritual of the *Book of Common Prayer*, and especially to evince a pleasure in
finding this to conform in so many respects to the sentiments and worship of Catholics, is
thought by Low Churchmen to show an inclination toward Rome, a thing which they hold
to be utterly abominable.   Yet in their peculiarly constructed system, it is a thing to be necessarily tolerated.   Their church is a religious society in the civil order.   It is a state church,
and as such must stand or fall. ... In point of fact, the *via media*, as a way of arriving at
any positive truth, in the religious or moral order, is always absurd, if not ridiculous."

(1) Like the Lutherans in the Confession of Faith which the duke of Wurtemberg sent
to the Council of Trent in 1552, the Anglicans use maliciously, falsely, and absurdly, these
words, "works of supererogation."   In Art. 14 they say that these works cannot be admitted without arrogance and impiety ; because, they say, men pretend that by these works
they give to God more than His due.   Having thus erected a house of cards, the theological babies proceed to demolish it with the text in which Christ calls us useless servants, even
though we do all that is commanded.   Any Catholic *muliercula* or instructed child knows
that we never pretend, by supererogatory works, to give more than His due to God ; but
that we acknowledge that we owe everything to Him.   When Catholics speak of works of
supererogation, or of works performed in following the Counsels, they simply mean works
which are not positively commanded by God.   Certainly our Lord advised a work of super-

pentance; and the Calvinistic doctrine of inamissability of justice is false. XVII. Predestination is admitted; but man should not think of the matter, lest he may either presume or despair. XVIII. Without a knowledge of Jesus Christ, salvation is impossible. XIX. The Church is an assembly of the faithful where the pure word of God is preached, and the sacraments are well administered; therefore the Roman Church is in error, as to dogmas, morals, and worship. XX.- XXI. The Church can decide only as to matters contained in the Scriptures. General Councils can err, and have erred in matters of faith. XXII. The doctrines of the Roman Church on purgatory, indulgences, the veneration of images, and the invocation of saints, are rejected. XXIII. A mission is necessary for preaching, and for the administration of the sacraments; and the mission is legitimate when it is granted by those who have the power. But the Article carefully abstains from any mention as to where that power resides; whether in the civil ruler or in the clergy. XXIV. The liturgy must be celebrated in the vernacular. XXV.-XXVI. The sacraments are efficacious signs of grace, by which God excites and confirms our faith in Him. There are only two: Baptism and the Lord's Supper. The other five are not visible signs instituted by God; although some are imitations of what the Apostles operated. XXVII. Baptism is not only a sign of our profession of Christianity, but a sign of regeneration, and the seal of our adoption, by which our faith is confirmed, and grace augmented. Infants are to be baptized. XXVIII.-XXXI. In the Eucharist the Body of Christ is given, taken, and eaten, only in a "heavenly and spiritual manner." The doctrine of Transubstantiation cannot be proved by Scripture. The Communion ought to be administered in both kinds to the laity, according to the institution and command of Christ. The Mass is a blasphemous forgery (1). XXXII. Bishops, priests, and deacons can marry.

erogation when He told the young man that if he wished to be perfect, he should give all his wealth to the poor, and follow the Master. Do Anglicans suppose that Christ here enjoined an act to be performed under pain of damnation? Another act, clearly of supererogation, is that of renunciation of marriage, for the sake of Heaven (*Matt.* xix. 12). But it is quite evident that the original Anglicans affected to regard the Counsels as impious, simply because those supererogatory works were incentives to mortification.

(1) The Protestant Episcopal General Convention of 1871 condemned unqualifiedly the

XXXIII. Excommunications are valid. XXXIV. Rites
and ceremonies can be instituted and abolished by every
church at its own good pleasure. XXXV.–XXXVI. Sanction is given to the *Homilies* published in the reign of Edward VI., and also to his *Ordinal.* XXXVII. The English
sovereign enjoys supreme authority over all his subjects, and
in all causes, even ecclesiastical. XXXVIII.–XXXIX. The
Anabaptist doctrines on capital punishment, war, community
of property, oaths, etc., are condemned.

Although the Establishment is exceedingly elastic in all
doctrinal matters; so elastic, in fact, that the idea that it possesses any authoritative teaching whatever is merely a play
of the imagination; nevertheless, it is certain that the framers of the Thirty-Nine Articles meant them to be the official Creed of their organization. Therefore it is well to note
the chief doctrinal differences between the Catholic and the
English Creeds; so far, at least, as our historical province
permits. When the Establishment cut loose entirely from
Catholic authority, it did not officially revolutionize the Catholic doctrines which concerned the Trinity and the Incarnation; that enterprise was reserved for certain of its later
members. Neither did it attack the Apostolic, Nicene, or
Athanasian Symbols; nevertheless, the last is rejected by
the American Episcopalians. But when the Elizabethan theologians took the Bible in hand, they entered upon an entirely new departure by branding as apocryphal several of the
Jewish Scriptures, and by insisting that the Bible records all
the teachings of Christ and his Apostles. The Church tells
us that the Bible is silent as to many things taught by our
Lord, but which have been handed down by tradition; *e. g.*,
infant baptism, the observance of Sunday instead of Saturday, which, nevertheless, are admitted by Anglicans. Again,
while the Articles admit that "the Church hath authority in

Ritualistic attempts to simulate the Catholic adoration of the Eucharist. The pastoral issued by the prelates says: "The doctrine which chiefly attempts to express itself by ritual,
in questionable and dangerous ways, is connected with the Holy Eucharist. *That doctrine
is emphatically a novelty in theology!* What is known as eucharistical adoration is undoubtedly inculcated and encouraged by that ritual of posture lately introduced among us,
which *finds no warrant in our Office for the Administration of Holy Communion.*"
Then the pastoral declares that the presence of Christ, whatever there may be in the Eucharist, is such as does not permit of His being worshipped there; and that to do so, is "an
awful error." But of course, the Ritualists are able to "explain away" this declaration

controversies of faith," they nullify this authority to a great
extent by insisting that the Church can decide only on matters contained in the Bible; that the Church cannot assemble
Councils without the consent of the civil rulers; and that
such Councils can err, and have erred, in matters of faith.
The Articles consider the sovereign as supreme in all ecclesiastical affairs; whereas the Church has never recognized
any spiritual authority in any civil ruler, but has always regarded the Roman Pontiff as enjoying the primacy of order
and of jurisdiction over all Christendom. The Articles in-
culcate justification by faith alone; the Church requires also
hope and charity. The Church teaches that there are seven
divinely-instituted sacraments; the Articles admit only two,
Baptism and the Eucharist. The Church pronounces that in
the Blessed Sacrament of the Altar, we take and eat the Body
of Christ "in a real, though spiritual and Sacramental manner"; while the Articles discern "only a heavenly and spiritual manner." The Articles say that Transubstantiation
cannot be evinced from the Bible; whereas the Church teaches that the doctrine follows necessarily from the words of
the Saviour. The Articles also contend that communion for
the laity under both species is of divine institution; whereas
the Church teaches that she can accord the chalice to the
laity, or withhold it, according as she may judge proper in the
circumstances. As to the sacrificial nature of the Mass, the
Catholic doctrine has always been that there is offered to
God a true and propitiatory sacrifice on the altar; and that
it is commemorative of the Sacrifice of Calvary; but the Articles pronounce the Mass a blasphemous forgery (1). Finally, the Articles condemn the doctrines of purgatory, indulgences, the veneration of images and relics, and the invocation of saints; while the Church has always taught that a
soul which is found, at the judgment-seat of God, to be not
so wicked as to deserve hell, but yet too stained to enter
where nothing defiled can enter, is placed at once in purga-

---

(1) Jewel, a contemporary of Parker, and Anglican bishop of Salisbury, must have known
the intent of the Articles. Now he said of the Mass: "They talk much of an unbloody Sacrifice. It is not theirs to offer. Queen Elizabeth shall offer it up to God, *even her unbloody hands and her unbloody sword*; an unbloody people and an unbloody government.
This is an unbloody sacrifice; this sacrifice is acceptable to God."

tory, a place of expiation; that indulgences, remissions of the temporal punishment due to sin, are useful; that an inferior veneration is due to images of the saints and to holy relics; and that it is lawful and recommendable for us to beg the saints to intercede for us at the throne of God. Such are the salient differences between the Creed of the Establishment, so far as it has any Creed, and that of the Catholic Church. Such are the Articles to which every Anglican clergyman subscribes, whether he be High, Low, or Broad; Neo-Catholic or Calvinist; and the reflection justifies the saying of Gibbon: "The clergy of the Church of England preserve the name of religion without the substance, and subscribe the articles of their belief with a sigh or a smile." The Articles are bitterly Protestant; and nevertheless, as Macaulay complained in the House of Lords, he who subscribes to them "may hold the worst doctrines of the Church of Rome, and may hold with them the best benefice of the Church of England." Gladstone once had the temerity to say that unity was the characteristic of the Establishment; whereupon Macaulay replied: "Unity she most certainly has not, and never has had. It is a matter of perfect notoriety that her formularies are framed in such a manner as to admit to her highest offices men who differ from each other more widely than a very High Churchman differs from a Catholic, or a very Low Churchman from a Presbyterian; and that the general leaning of the Church, with respect to some important questions, has been sometimes one way and sometimes another. Take, for example, the questions agitated between the Calvinists and the Arminians. *Do we find in the Church of England*, with respect to those questions, *that unity which is essential to truth?* Is it not certain that at the end of the sixteenth century, the rulers of the church held doctrines as Calvinistic as ever were held by any Cameronian, and not only held them, but persecuted everybody who did not hold them? And is it not equally certain that the rulers of the church have, in very recent times, considered Calvinism as a disqualification for high preferment, if not for orders?" (1)

It is now a little more than half a century since a number of enterprising, painstaking, and generally sincere members of the English Establishment conceived the whimsical idea that their system was identical with that of the primitive Christians. To convince their countrymen of the truth of their theory, they began to translate into English the works of the early Fathers of the Church. "Judge of their dismay, when, according to the Arabian tale, on their striking their anchors into the supposed soil, lighting their fires on it, and fixing in it the poles of their tents, suddenly their island began to move, to heave, to splash, to frisk to and fro, to dive, and at last to swim away spouting out inhospitable jets of water upon the credulous mariners who had made it their home. ... They saw distinctly, in the reasonings of the fathers, the justification of what they had been accustomed to consider the corruption of Rome. ... Time went on, and there was no mistaking or denying the misfortune which was impending over them. They had reared a goodly house, but their foundations were falling in. The soil and the masonry were both bad. The fathers *would* protect Romanists. The Anglican divines *would* misquote the fathers, and shrink from the very doctors to whom they appealed. The bishops of the seventeenth century were shy of the bishops of the fourth "(1). The leader of this movement, Dr. Pusey, had not the slightest intention or desire to bring about the submission of the Establishment to the papal authority ; he wished to furnish his co-religionists with sound weapons against the "wiles of Rome," especially by flaunting audaciously the banner of a presumed Catholicity (2). As we have traced the progress

aulay, "framed in the very spirit of William Huntington, S. S." One was as to whether God had from eternity reprobated certain persons. The prelate was pleased with the reply : " Yes : and because He so willed."

(1) NEWMAN ; *Anglican Difficulties*, p. 121.

(2) In 1842, the Puseyite Camden Society carried its sublime impudence so far as to elect the Count de Montalembert an honorary member. In his repudiation of the honor, the great publicist said : " It is easy to take up a name ; but it is not so easy to get it recognized by the world and by competent authority. ... The attempt to steal away from us, and appropriate to the use of a fraction of the Church of England, the glorious title of Catholic, is proved to be an usurpation by every monument of the past and present, by the coronation oath of your sovereign, by all the laws that have established your church, even by the answer of your own University of Oxford to the lay address against Dr. Pusey, etc., where the Church of England is justly called the Protestant Reformed Church. The name itself is spurned at with indignation by the greater half, at least, of those who belong to the Church

made in the Protestantization of the English Church, it may interest the reader if we devote a moment to this attempt at what its authors would have styled, a re-Catholicization of that church. William Palmer, who, after many years of kicking against the spur, finally "went over" to Rome, knew Puseyism well; and according to his experience, the would-be Neo-Catholicism consisted in hurling an anathema against the Protestant principle; and in abandoning, one by one, the very bases of the English Reformation. It saw in the Establishment a wretched slave of the civil power; it discerned in the teachings of this reformed church only equivocal formulas. It declared that the Anglican Liturgy was the condemnation of Anglicanism; whereas the Roman Missal and Ritual were, it acknowledged, precious treasures of apostolic antiquity. It contended, in defiance of the Articles, that the Bible was not the sole rule of faith; that the Church is the depositary of the divine revelations handed down by Tradition. It taught, again in defiance of the Articles, that in the Eucharist, under the appearances of bread and wine, Christ is personally and corporeally present; and that priests possess the sublime and mysterious power to change the bread and wine into the very Body and Blood of their Lord and Saviour. It upheld the legitimacy and propriety of prayers for the dead, and recognized the existence of Purgatory. It venerated seven divinely-instituted sacraments; and it invoked the aid of the saints, and honored their relics. It advised priests to lead a celebitic life; and it praised and actuated, as far as it could, the monastic state. And nevertheless, it contended that one might conscientiously receive the Thirty-Nine Ar-

of England, just as the Church of England itself is rejected with scorn and detestation by the greater half of the inhabitants of the United Kingdom. ... Even the debased Russian Church,—that church where lay despotism has closed the church's mouth and turned her into a slave,—disdains to recognize the Anglicans as Catholics. Even the Eastern heretics, although so sweetly courted by Puseyite missionaries, sneer at this new and fictitious Catholicism. ... Consistent Protestants and rationalists are more catholic, in the *etymological* sense of the word, than the Anglicans; for they, at least, can look upon themselves as belonging to the same communion as those who, in every country, deny the existence of Church authority or of revealed religion—they have, at least, a negative bond to link them one with another. But that the so-called Anglo-Catholics, whose very name betrays their usurpation and their contradiction; whose doctrinal articles, whose liturgy, whose whole history, are such as to disconnect them from all mankind except those who are born English and speak English,—that they should pretend, on the strength of their private judgment alone, to be what the rest of mankind deny them to be, will assuredly be ranked among the first follies of the nineteenth century."

ticles. Innumerable minds, remarks Palmer, realized the fla-
grancy of this contradiction ; and seeing that if Rome was
right (as Pusey seemed to admit), he did not go far enough;
and that if Rome was in the wrong, he went too far ; abandoned his makeshift theory, and entered the Fold of Christ.
As to the modern representatives of Puseyism, those nonde-
scripts who pose as Ritualists, neither time nor inclination allows us to detail their vagaries. But if, perchance, one of
them should scan these pages, we would ask him to reflect
upon these remarks of W. H. Anderdon:

" Ritual, not Ritualism, is a most honest congruous thing,
where it is at home. It is only when you import it into a
place foreign to it and incongruous, that it becomes dishonest ; as poetry, under the like conditions, may become untrue.
Thus, a chasuble is a sacrificial vestment, quite in place on
the shoulders of a true sacrificing priest. But on a minister,
whom the bishop that made him a minister had no intention
of making a sacrificing priest in any true sense of the word,
it is incongruous in the last degree : it is an untruth, and (in
the sense I have explained) a dishonesty. Lights and flowers on a true altar are honest and in place : on a communion-
table they are meaningless, and, when thus made to enforce
a doctrine inadmissible where they stand, they are a sham.
To stand before an altar, as making intercession for the sins
of the people, is honest and congruous in a priest, whose office
pledges him to do it. His ancestors in the faith have done
it for centuries ; it is the principal function of his life, and
interprets his very name. But to stand in an ' eastward position ' before a table, which is defined by authority to be, of
necessity, ' an honest, movable table,' from which the idea of
sacrifice is excluded,—this must ever be incongruous in a
minister ; it contradicts all received traditions ; it is opposed
to the wish of his bishop, it is not done when that bishop is
present, but *is* done when he is away : and so (still in the
above sense of the word) is dishonest. To stretch a rubric,
to ignore a canon, to go against the plain sense of an article,
to act contumaciously against the obligations one has taken,
and against the living authority before whom one has taken
them,—if all this is honest, if it is genuine, conscientious deal-

ing, then we shall have to go to school again, and learn our English language afresh." The famous Dr. Arnold once said that a Catholic reminded him of a Frenchman waving his flag, while a Ritualist was like the same French soldier disguised in the red coat of her Majesty's service. In the first case, he said, he respected his enemy; but he would hang the pretender. The Catholic reader will not deem Dr. Arnold's criticism severe, unless perchance he is more amused than offended by the pretensions of these Protestant "Catholics." Among these pretensions the most glaring, and one which is also put forth by one of the sections of those Anglicans who scorn the Ritualists, is the assertion that the clergy of the English Establishment and those of the Protestant Episcopal Church in the United States are not mere "ministers" of congregations which can unmake as they make them, but rather true priests of God according to the order of Melchisedech. Much more has been written upon this subject than has been at all necessary. The voluminous pleas with which Anglican sacerdotalists try to fortify their position do no more, even in the minds of their authors, than evince a shadowy possibility that their "orders" may be valid; and even if this possibility were made a certainty, they would no more be members of the Holy Catholic Church than are the schismatic churches of the Orient or the Reinkens, Loysons, Dollingers, Gavazzis, and Chinniquys of the West. Indeed, if it were shown that the Anglican Church and her American daughter were in the enjoyment of an Apostolic Succession, their clergy would incur, before God, a tremendous responsibility for a sacrilege of which they are now innocent (1).

(1) Speaking of the suggestion made by Lord Halifax, that if Anglican Orders were recognized by Rome, then the cause of reunion would be furthered, inasmuch as the Anglicans would then be on the same level as the Oriental schismatics, Rivington says :

" To this, however, we feel bound to demur. The recognition of its Orders would not place the Anglican body on the same level with the Greeks, except in the mere possession of Orders, for these reasons. The Gleeks have never faltered in their hold on the dogma of Transubstantiation. Their habits of thought consequently differ *toto cœlo* from those of the great mass of Anglicans. Witness their invariable repugnance to the idea of a priest marrying—a repugnance which flows from their sense of the dignity of the priesthood and their firm hold of ecclesiastical tradition. The Anglicans, as a body, lost both of these in the sixteenth century. The persistent way in which, as a body, during the past centuries, they have cast the idea of a sacrificing priesthood to the winds, has led to the spectacle, unknown to the Christian Church since the day of Pentecost, of those who call themselves bishops marrying *after* entering upon the Episcopal Office, and of those whom Lord Hali-

When an Anglican minister presents himself for admission into the Catholic Church, and has abjured his errors, he is baptized *conditionally*. His baptism in the Anglican communion may have been valid, for it is certain that if the proper form and *materia* be used in the administration of this sacrament, the baptism is valid, even though its minister be a pagan or a Jew. But the Church must be sure that X., as we will call our convert, is really incorporated into her visible body ; and since too frequent experience teaches her that even among Anglicans, clerical as well as lay, loose notions about baptism are often prevalent, she now confers conditional baptism on our friend X. (1)   But if X. desires

fax and others consider to be priests, marrying a *second time* after their ordination, in violation of the Catholic interpretation of St. Paul's injunction as to bishops, that they must not even have been twice married in their heathen life. Supposing, then, that Anglican Orders were discovered to be valid, we should have the existence of a priesthood which has suffered a degradation unknown to the rest of the Church, and which means to continue that same reversal of the respective order in which alone the Sacraments of Matrimony and of Holy Orders should be received, *viz.*, Matrimony (if at all) before Holy Orders, and never *vice versa*. But that is not all. Supposing Anglican Orders to be valid, what are we to say of the Anglican guardianship of other Sacraments? ... The Episcopate, as a whole, and, we fear, the greater number of the clergy in the Church of England, have not yet been induced to treat the outward elements in Holy Communion as if they were consecrated, except for use. They are, *such amount as is not used in the service*, subjected up and down the land at this moment to indignities which, if Anglican Orders were valid, ought to be stopped at once. A crusade against the careless neglect, to say nothing more, of these outward elements—of what, if those Orders were valid, would be the veritable Body and Blood of our Divine Lord—when not required in the administration of Holy Communion, ought to be inaugurated to-morrow. This would show a Catholic instinct, a practical belief in these Orders. But what would such a crusade bring to light? ... The peculiar attitude of mind toward the unseen world which is fostered by the constant use of this elevating devotion (to the Blessed Virgin) has been steadily suppressed in the Anglican body for the last three centuries and a half. It is a loss in many ways, and influences even their historical sense, lowering it, and lessening the power of appreciating certain crucial passages in the history of the early Church, as has been seen lately in the way in which even the character of St. Leo the Great has been attacked by such writers as Canon Bright and Canon Gore. If ever Greek and Anglican come sufficiently close to contemplate real reunion, one of two things must happen, *viz.*, either the Greek must condemn his entire past and relegate the invocation of saints, and devotion to our Blessed Lady, to the region of opinion, or Greek and Anglican must consent to remain in a state of religious separation. ... Any encouragement of the idea that Anglican Orders are valid, would only help to build higher that wall of separation which the Anglican has erected between himself and Rome by denying the divine institution of that centre of unity. Of course, this is no reason for denying Anglican Orders. If it be true that those Orders are valid, by all means let us work on that truth, and the sooner the better. But such recognition would not make it easier for the Anglican to yield submission to the truth of the *kingdom-feature* of the Church's life. It would not make for reunion. The gulf that, alas! separates the Anglican and the Roman would yawn as wide as ever." *Anglican Fallacies*, by Rev. Luke Rivington ; London, 1895.

(1) The culpable neglect of Anglicans in the matter of baptism is more than exceptional. We request the reader to note these remarks of A. F. Marshall :

" Catholic theologians have taught, from the earliest days, that, for the validity of baptism,

to become a priest, and the authorities of the Church are convinced that he is a fit subject for that dignity, he must receive the sacrament of Holy Orders ; and unlike in the case of his baptism, the ordination is not given conditionally, but *absolutely.* The Anglican baptism of X. may have been valid ; but the Church holds that his Anglican "ordination" was of no more efficacy in segregating him from among laymen, in giving him power over the Real Body of Christ and in conferring upon him the other prerogatives of the priesthood, than if it had been effected by a llama of Thibet. In this difference between the conditionality of X.'s baptism and the absoluteness of his ordination, the reader discerns the mind of the Catholic Church in regard to the value of what the Anglican minister terms his "orders"; and this difference shows plainly to the Catholic that the Church rejects as untenable the theory which a couple of French clergymen have advanced in our day, to the effect that Anglican orders *may possibly* be valid, and that the Holy See should order another investigation into the matter. Never, since the institution of the Elizabethan hierarchy, has an Anglican minister been recognized as a Christian priest by Rome ; unless in the beginning, in the case of those clergymen who

---

the water must be made to 'flow on the head,' and that if the water only falls on the hair, or if only a few drops (which do not flow) touch the infant, the baptism, to say the least, is uncertain ; while, if the water simply falls on the clothes, the baptism is certainly invalid. Now what has been the general practice among Anglicans ? Wheatly tells us, that during the time when the *Directory* was in force (from 1645 to 1660), ' a basin was brought to the minister in his reading desk, and the child being held below him, he dipped in his fingers, and so took up water enough just to let a drop or two fall on the child's face.' Nor did the re-establishment of Anglicanism decrease the carelessness. Mr. Bennet, Vicar of Frome, when writing of sixty years ago, said, ' Baptism as a sacrament was well-nigh lost amongst the English people. ... It is very questionable whether the water, when used, really did touch the person of the child meant to be baptized.' Dr. Lee also, in one of his books, quotes the *Reunion Magazine* as showing that Bishop Alford ' openly baptized fourteen adults by once flicking his wetted fingers in the air over all of them.' While, as to the form and the matter of baptism—up to the time, say, of the *Tracts for the Times*—it was not unusual for a clergyman to dip his finger in the font, and then to go round to each child in silence, touching each child on the head ; in which cases the baptisms were invalid. The writer of the present paper has frequently seen Anglican clergymen—from the year 1845 to 1855—simply ' spirt ' a drop of water at a row of infants ; thus omitting both the matter and the form. Indeed, there is no exaggeration in the statement that Anglican baptisms, before the time of the High Church movement, were purely apologetic and perfunctory ; being retained as a traditional compliment to orthodoxy, but without the slightest idea of regeneration. ... It is morally certain that an immense number of Anglican bishops and clergymen were never effectually baptized, and therefore could not possibly be ordained." *American Catholic Quarterly Review,* vol. XXI.

had been ordained by bishops of the outlawed Church. The mind of the Holy See as to this matter is sometimes unfolded by a citation of a decree of Pope Clement XI., given in 1704, in connection with the desire for ordination expressed by the converted Anglican bishop of Galloway, Dr. John Clement Gordon ; but at as early a date as 1555, Pope Paul IV. set the matter at rest when he approved, by apposite Briefs, the decision of Cardinal Pole ordering the ordination *de novo* of those who had been ordained according to the new Ordinal, and who therefore were *non in forma ecclesiæ ordinati et consecrati* (1). No sane Catholic will contend that for more than three centuries the Holy See has ordered the absolute reiteration of a possibly valid character-impressing ordinance ; that the Roman Pontiffs have enjoined the performance of a rite which their own Canons stamp as downright sacrilege. Rome has not as yet, *totidem verbis*, pronounced the invalidity of Anglican orders ; and perhaps she will never deem it necessary to so pronounce, since her mind has been manifested sufficiently by her practice. But it cannot be held that Rome will never give a decision in the premises, on the ground that herein there is a question of a historical fact, and that the Church does not dogmatize on merely historical facts. The fact at issue is not a simple fact ; it is a Dog-

(1) These Bulls were discovered by the erudite and indefatigable Benedictine, Dom Aidan Gasquet, in the Vatican Archives, and were published in the *Civilta Cattolica* for June 1, 1895. The first of these is a Bull, the general purport of which is to permit of the rehabilitation of those clerics who, by lapsing into schism under Henry VIII. and Edward VI., had been thereby disqualified from the exercise of their orders. All may be rehabilitated according to the orders they possess, yet " so that those who have been promoted to orders, whether sacred or not sacred, by any bishop or archbishop other than such as have been duly and rightly ordained, shall be bound to receive the same orders again (*de novo*) from their Ordinary, and meanwhile must not minister in those orders " (*Arch. Segret. Vatic.* Paul IV., tom. i., n. 1850, f. 55). This Bull is dated June 20, 1555. On October 30th of the same year a Brief was issued explanatory of this clause : " Since, as we have been recently informed, it is doubted by many persons what bishops and archbishops, during the period of the schism in that kingdom, can be considered duly and rightly ordained, desiring to remove this doubt by more clearly explaining the mind and intention which we had in the previous letter, and to afford reasonable relief to the consciences of those who were advanced to orders during the aforesaid schism, we decree that only those bishops and archbishops, who were not ordained and consecrated in the form of the Church, cannot be called duly and rightly ordained, and that it is those who have been promoted by these to their orders, who have not received orders, but must and are bound to receive the same orders afresh (*de novo*) from their Ordinary according to the tenor and contents of our aforesaid letters " (*Ibid.*, t. i., n. 301). There cannot be any possible doubt that the distinction thus drawn between prelates consecrated by the rite of the Church and those not so consecrated is a distinction between those consecrated by the Pontifical and those consecrated by Cranmer's Ordinal.

matic Fact, a *factum cum jure conjunctum*, and as we shall show when we come to the subject of Jansenism, such facts are properly objects of the infallible judgments of the Church.

Having reflected on the mind of the Church in reference to the value of what he has fondly regarded as his priestly ordination (for we suppose him to be an "advanced church-man"), X. is about to present himself for the real reception of Orders, when a Protestant friend urges him not to stultify himself by pretending to receive what he already possesses. He reminds X. that when he stood before the Anglican bishop to be enrolled among the Anglican clergy, he intended to become a "sacrificing priest," and the bishop intended to make him one. And this insistence of the officious friend is very specious, if X. was "ordained" within the last three or four decades ; for in that time a large number of Anglicans have come to disbelieve that sacrificing priests are mere mummers and that the Mass is a filthiness. But if X. considers that although Y., who "ordained" him, may have intended to confer upon him all the prerogatives with which the Church endows her priests, nevertheless Y. himself may not have had the power to do this ; then X. faces a serious issue. Who ordained and consecrated Y.? Z., most assuredly. But is X. sure that Z., or some one of the consecrating prelates who connected Z. with the Elizabethan hierarchy, was not deficient in at least the intention to make real priests, "Massing priests," of his *ordinandi*? If X. finds that even one link in the chain between Z. and an undoubted bishop was defective in what is essential to effecting a valid ordination of a sacrificing priest, he will decide that he is, as yet, a mere layman. And what does history show him, concerning the belief of the immense majority of the clerics of the Establishment, from Cranmer's day to our own, in regard to the essentials for ordination, or in regard to even any necessity whatever for an ordination other than that conferred by a royal or a parliamentary commission? Even to-day, when Ritualists are widening their stoles, elongating or squaring their mitres, bedizzening themselves with crosses, prating about the beauties of solemn vows to observe the three great Counsels, wondering whether a thurible should be swung once or sixty-three times, and so on through a dense paraphernalia of senseless mystification, how many Anglican prelates are there who do not avow among their familiars what some of them boldly declare when about to perform an " ordination," namely, that in the ensuing ceremony, they intend expressly to make no sacrificing priest? If X. thinks that in our day the absence of necessary intention is not very clearly indicated (forgetting that it ought to be expressly announced), let him consider the liturgical surroundings of those prelates of the seventeenth and eighteenth centuries whom he would fain regard as connecting him with the ancient and Catholic Church of England. Is a belief in the sacrificial character of the priesthood consistent with the location of the venerable altar slabs in the pavement of the churches, so that the people may contemn those whilom resting-places of the Body of Christ by trampling upon them; with the ostentatious substitution of a simple table for the altar ; with the rejection of the time-honored Liturgy, and an adoption of that Communion Service which excludes every idea of a substantial Real Presence and of a sacrificial act? Unless X. can satisfy himself on these points, he must apply to the Catholic bishop, if he wishes to be a priest. Indeed, so evident is this necessity to those who have studied the matter with any degree of profundity, and with some measure of sincerity, that a few years ago, Dr. Lee, the Protestant vicar of the parish of All Saints, Lambeth, had himself and some other mistaken zealots baptized, confirmed, ordained, and consecrated as bishops, by some impecunious oriental schismatical prelate (in Malabar, we believe) ; and since the Establishment saw fit to demonstrate its elasticity by allowing the contemner of its dignity to retain his benefice, it is strange that many of the Anglican clergy have not applied to this really full-fledged (albeit schismatical) bishop for the Apostolic Succession (1).

(1) Dr. Lee and his companions resolved themselves into a society for the promotion of reunion with Rome ; and on Sept. 8, 1877, they issued an appeal, commencing : " Thomas, by the favor of God, Rector of the Order of Corporate Reunion and Pro-Provincial of Canterbury ; Joseph, by the favor of God, Provincial of York, in the Kingdom of England ; and Laurence, by the favor of God, Provincial of Caerleon, in the principality of Wales, with the provosts and members of the synod of the order, to the faithful in Christ Jesus, health and benediction in the Lord." The document proceeds to assert that the existing bishops have,

But let us return to a consideration of the quandary in which X. finds himself. If he has come to the conclusion that there is no defective link in the chain which connects Y. with the ancient English Church, a Catholic friend may ask him to explain the nature of the tie which he regards as binding the Elizabethan hierarchy to that Church. We have seen how Elizabeth, in her capacity of head of the new Church of England, dispensed with all irregularities and even invalidating impediments in the "consecration" of Parker, from whom all the prelates and ministers of the Anglican Church and her American daughter are compelled to derive their claims to episcopal or sacerdotal authority. Whether the royal lady had any more right or power to effect the famous

by their conduct, forfeited all claims to canonical obedience ; and that Thomas, Joseph, and Laurence intend to supplant them, representing "three distinct and independent lines of a new episcopal succession." (See Appleton's *Annual Cyclopædia*, 1877, p. 21.)—The following reflections of A. F. Marshall, on the intention of Anglican bishops when conferring orders, are apposite to our position : "From the time of St. Augustine, in the sixth century, to that of Archbishop Warham, in the sixteenth, there was never any doubt about form or intention in regard to the conferring of orders, nor any dispute as to legitimate succession ; while as to jurisdiction—a very different question, indeed—the Holy See was always acknowledged to be its sole source or fountain, in the sense of the ' plenitude of jurisdiction.' But at the time of the Reformation all this was changed. Form was changed ; intention was changed ; while as to spiritual jurisdiction, it was transferred from the Pope to the lay king or queen of the island. Nor was there so much as one aspect in which the essentials of priesthood, as they had always been regarded for a thousand years, were not changed in a revolutionary sense. Thus, to speak of two priestly functions only : For a thousand years every Catholic deacon had been ' made a priest,' that he might offer the holy Sacrifice of the Mass, and hear Confessions in the Sacrament of Penance ; but, after the Reformation, every Protestant deacon was ' made a priest ' that he might *not* offer the holy Sacrifice of the Mass, and might *not* hear Sacramental Confessions." The following remarks by the same polemic are also appropriate. "From the period of this great change to about the year 1850, no Anglican clergyman was ever known to ' say Mass,' or to hear a ' Sacramental Confession.' Thus, the very soul of the institution, ' Catholic priesthood,' was taken out of the Protestant body, the Church of England ; and three centuries were devoted to reviling those priestly powers which are now claimed by the Ritualists as their heritage. Is it probable that an Anglican ministry, which for three centuries has swept the tabernacle from the altar, can have the same orders as a priesthood which, for eighteen centuries, has bent the knee to the Adorable Presence ? Is it probable that an Anglican ministry, which has always placed the consecrated bread in the hand of the unconfessed sinner, can have the same orders as the priesthood which has reverently placed the Adorable Host on the tongue of the confessed and absolved penitent ? Is it probable that an Anglican ministry which has left the consecrated crumbs to be scattered on the floor around the communion rails ; and has allowed the parish clerk to cast away the remnant, or the church cleaner to sweep the remnant into her shovel, can have the same orders as a priesthood whose very care and priestly exactness have been mocked for three centuries by most Protestants? And, finally, is it probable that an Anglican ministry which has always preached against the Roman Catholic doctrine ; has always warned its congregations against the soul-destroying error of the Roman Catholic dogma of Transubstantiation, can have the same orders as a priesthood whose insistence on the Catholic doctrine has exposed it to three centuries of vituperation ?" *Loc. cit.*

dispensation, than a squire of Mud Hill Pond would have in the appointing, instituting, and "making" of a Protestant Episcopal "primus" in our land, is for Anglicans to determine. At any rate, X. feels that he must inquire into the value of the presumed "consecration" which ensued after the healing document had been graciously accorded; and we now proceed to detail the results of his investigations. For many years after the installation of Parker, the English Catholics were wont to object to the innovators that no consecratory ceremony had preceded that act; that, in fact, the sole pretense of a " consecration" had occurred in the Nag's-Head tavern in Cheapside, when Scorey bade Parker and the other bishops-elect kneel down, and then put a Bible on the head of each, saying : " Receive the power of preaching the word of God sincerely." This story, however, is rejected as a fable by Catholic writers such as Lingard, Tierney, Estcourt, and Raynal; chiefly because the *Acts* of Parker's " consecration,". preserved in Lambeth palace, arè presumably authentic (1). But Anglican writers show bad faith when they proclaim their cause as gained by the mere dissipation of the Nag's-Head yarn. Even though there be no ground for the fable ; even though the "consecrators" of Parker had journeyed to Rome, and there in the Lateran Basilica—the *mater et caput omnium ecclesiarum in universo mundo*—in the presence of all the Catholic sovereigns of Europe, with the Supreme Pontiff blessing the act from his high throne, they had performed their famous function, we contend that their act would not have made Parker a bishop. For this assertion there are two reasons; one which seems to be well sustained by cold history, and the other founded in the teachings of Catholic theology. In the first place, we shall examine the historical reason. Barlow, the prelate who " consecrated" Parker, was very probably not a bishop, although he had been elected bishop

(1) In his admirable letters on the consecration of Barlow, written in 1847 while he was still a Protestant, Mr. Serjeant Bellasis says that while he believes the Lambeth *Acts* to be genuine, the Catholics had good grounds to suspect them, especially this : " When, at the time, the Catholics objected to Archbishop Parker that he had not been duly consecrated, he did not reply by producing the register of his consecration, which would have put the fact beyond dispute, but applied for and obtained an Act of Parliament to remedy any defects there might have been therein ; and the register itself was not produced or specifically alluded to for more than fifty years after, and not until every one named in it was dead."

of St. Asaph's in January, 1536; had received a mandate for his consecration on Feb. 2, 1536; had been translated in the same year to St. David's; had been again translated to Bath and Wells in 1548; and had resigned this last see on the accession of Queen Mary. Of Barlow's consecration there is no record whatsoever. Nor is this a merely negative argument; for if the existing records concerning him are true, he could not have been consecrated, since these documents represent his successor at St. Asaph's as succeeding an unconsecrated bishop, and they speak of him after his removal to St. David's as simply the "late bishop of St. Asaph's." I. We must show that Barlow was not consecrated as bishop of St. Asaph's. Now it is certain that while the mandate to Cranmer to consecrate him is dated Feb. 2, 1536, the bishop of St. David's died on the 18th, and Barlow was appointed to fill the vacancy. Was he consecrated before he was transferred? Having examined the *congé d' élire*, or license to the Chapter of St. Asaph's to elect another bishop in the place of Barlow, Mr. Serjeant Bellasis wrote: "Now these licenses to elect always specify the cause of the vacancy; it is always, if the previous bishop is dead, '*vacante per mortem naturalem ultimi Episcopi*'; if he is translated to another See, it is '*per translationem ultimi Episcopi*'; if he has been deprived '*per deprivationem ultimi Episcopi.*' Also a bishop who has been elected and not consecrated is always, in all formal documents, called 'bishop-elect' only. Now, in the '*congé d'élire*' to the Dean and Chapter of St. Asaph's to elect a bishop in the room of Barlow, he (Barlow) is called 'bishop-elect,' and the cause of the vacancy is said to be his *exchange*. The words are '*vacante per liberam transmutationem Wilhelmi Barlow, ultimi Episcopi electi,*' and he is so described throughout the whole of the formal documents relating to the election of his successor. There is no other instance in which a *translation* is described by any other word than '*translationem,*' nor in which a *consecrated* bishop to any See is called a 'bishop-*elect.*' The conclusion is, therefore, I think, not an improbable one, that in consequence of the bishopric of St. David's falling vacant when Barlow was about to be consecrated to St. Asaph's, the consecration did not take place;

but the 'bishop-elect' of St. Asaph's—*viz.*, Barlow—was 'ex-changed to St. David's.'" When Bellasis wrote these words he was still hoping to be able to prove that Barlow was a bishop; else he would not have described the Catholic con-clusion as merely a "not improbable one." And is it not strange that no record of this consecration has ever been found, in spite of the researches of Mason, employed by the archbishop of Canterbury in 1613; in spite of the labors of Bramhall about 1657; in spite of the exertions of Burnet, spurred on by the parliament; and in spite of the energy of the indefatigable Wharton? (1) II. Was Barlow consecrat-ed as bishop of St. David's? Cranmer's *Register* (p. 205, b.) contains all the documents concerning the transfer of Barlow to St. David's, but has not a word implying his consecration. The sole document on which Mason relied to prove that Bar-low must have been a consecrated bishop at this time is a "restitution" of the temporalities of St. David's to him, which document, said Mason, was found in the "Rolls Chapel in Chancery." But Estcourt does justice to this instrument: "It struck the writer as worth while to examine the origi-nal document which was printed by Mason as the restitution to Barlow of the temporalities of St. David's taken (as he states) 'out of the Rolls Chapel in Chancery.' It is printed from Mason, under that title, by Dr. Elrington and Dr. Lee, though Mr. Haddon has accurately noticed that it is not in the usual form. Mason's reference designates the Patent Rolls; but after a most careful search no such document could be found enrolled upon them. Its non-appearance on those rolls of course stimulated curiosity to find it, and, after fur-ther search, it was found on the Memoranda Rolls of the Re-membrancer of the Lord Treasurer of the Exchequer. As these latter rolls belong to the Exchequer and not to the Chancery, and were not kept in the Rolls Chapel, Mason has given a wrong reference to the record. An error in the ref-erence would have been of little consequence, if it had given a correct description of the document, or if he had printed it so as to show its real nature and operation, instead of

(1) This question was asked in the last century by the Rev. Mr. Stephens, Anglican rec-tor of Cherrington.

passing it off as the restitution usually made to a bishop after consecration, and printing only so much as would not betray the deception he was practising. So far from being the restitution in its usual form, it is a grant of the custody of temporalities on account of the vacancy of the see, but with the extraordinary addition of, 'to hold to him and his assigns during his life.' So far from giving any evidence of his consecration, it rather implies the probability that he had not been consecrated, and that he was made and entitled bishop without consecration. And the enrolment was made in the office of the Exchequer, as if the matter were purely secular, instead of on the Patent Rolls in Chancery" (1). Concerning the probability of the consecration of Barlow having occurred while he was the incumbent of Bath and Wells, we can only repeat that the Register preserved at Lambeth is silent. But it may be said, that as it appears that Barlow himself was one of the assistant bishops at the consecration of Bulkeley, bishop of Bangor, in 1541, it is very improbable that he would have allowed so important a cere-mony to have remained unperformed in his own case, and also that it is improbable that Cranmer, whose duty it was to consecrate him, would have neglected to do so. This would be a very important argument if it should appear that Cran-mer and Barlow were at the time convinced of the necessity of consecration to the valid making of a bishop.

But it is certain that neither Cranmer nor Barlow differed from the majority of their comrades in the opinion that the episcopate is a very unessential matter (2). We have already

---

(1) *Questions on Anglican Ordinations*, p. 71.

(2) "The founders of the Anglican Church had retained episcopacy as an ancient, a de-cent, and a convenient ecclesiastical polity, but had not declared that form of church gov-ernment to be of divine institution. We have already seen how low an estimate Cranmer had formed of the office of a bishop. In the reign of Elizabeth, Jewel, Cooper, Whitgift, and oth-er eminent doctors, defended prelacy as innocent, as useful, as what the state might lawful-ly establish, as what, when established by the state, was entitled to the respect of every citi-zen. But they never denied that a Christian community without a bishop might be a true church. On the contrary, they regarded the Protestants of the Continent as of the same household of faith with themselves. Englishmen in England were indeed bound to acknowl-edge the authority of the bishop, as they were bound to acknowledge the authority of the sheriff or of the coroner; but the obligation was purely local. An English churchman, nay, even an English prelate, if he went to Holland, conformed without scruple to the established religion of Holland. Abroad the ambassadors of Elizabeth and James went in state to the very worship which Elizabeth and James persecuted at home, and carefully abstained from decorating their private chapels Anglican-fashion, lest scandal be given to weaker

heard the former expressing his opinion that " he who is appointed bishop or priest needeth no consecration, for election or appointing thereto is sufficient." And the opinion of Barlow, while he was occupying the see of St. David's, is evinced from a letter to the chancellor Cromwell, written on Jan. 15, 1537, by Bishop Rowland Lee, the lord-president of the Marches of Wales. "He affirmed and said that if the King's Grace,. being supreme Head of the Church of England, did choose or denominate and elect any layman, being learned, to be a bishop, he so chosen, without mention of any orders, should be as good a bishop as he is, or the best in England" (1). This enunciation of opinion as to the non-necessity of Orders for valid episcopal or sacerdotal acts was emitted by Barlow in November, 1536; and in 1540, one year before the objected assistance at the "consecration" of Bulkeley, when replying to the *Seventeen Questions on the Sacraments* drawn up by Cranmer, he again declared that at the beginning priests and bishops were all one, that bishops have no power to make priests without authority from Christian princes, and that no consecration, but only appointment, is necessary (2). But hearken to these apposite *Questions* and *Answers*, as given by Burnet. *Question :* " Whether the Apostles, lacking a higher power, as in not having a Christian King among them, made bishops by that necessity, or by authority given of God?" CRANMER: "The civil ministers under the King be Lord Chancel-

brethren. In 1603 the convocation of the province of Canterbury solemnly recognized the Church of Scotland,—a church in which episcopal control and episcopal ordination were then unknown, as a branch of the holy Catholic Church of Christ. It was even held that Presbyterian ministers were entitled to place and voice in œcumenical councils. When the States General of the United Provinces convoked at Dort a synod of doctors not episcopally ordained, an English bishop and an English dean, commissioned by the head of the English Church, sat with those doctors, preached to them, and voted with them on the gravest questions of theology. One of these commissioners was Joseph Hall, then dean of Worcester, and afterward bishop of Norwich. In his life of himself, he says : ' My unworthiness was named for one of the assistants of that honorable, grave, and reverend meeting.' To High Churchmen this humility will seem not a little out of place,—nay, many English benefices were held by divines who had been admitted to the ministry in the Calvinistic form used on the Continent; nor was reordination by a bishop in such cases then thought necessary or even lawful. But a new race of divines was already rising in the Church of England. In their view, the episcopal office was essential to the welfare of a Christian society and to the efficacy of some of the most solemn ordinances of religion." MACAULAY, *History of England*, pp. 74-76.

(1) Strype's *Memorials*, vol. I., App. no. 77.
(2) Burnet's *Collection*, pt. I., bk. III., no. 21.

lor, Lord Treasurer, Admirals, Sheriffs, &c; the ministers of God's Word under his Majesty be Bishops, Parsons, Vicars, and such other Priests as be appointed by his Highness to that ministration—as, for example, the Bishop of Canterbury, the Bishop of Durham, the Parson of Winwick, &c. All the said offices be appointed, assigned, and elected in every place by the laws and orders of Kings and Princes. In the admission of many of these offices be divers comely ceremonies and solemnities, and which be not of necessity, but only for a good order and seemly fashion; for if such offices and ministrations were committed without such solemnity, they were nevertheless duly committed, and there is no more promise of God that grace is given in the committing of the ecclesiastical office than it is in the committing of the civil office." BARLOW: "Because they lacked a Christian Prince, by that necessity they ordained other Bishops. *Question:* "Whether Bishops or Priests were first; and if the Priest was first, then the Priest made the Bishop?" CRANMER: "The Bishops and Priests were at one time, and were no two things, but both one office, at the beginning of Christ's religion." BARLOW: "At the beginning they were all one." *Question:* "Whether in the New Testament *he required any consecration* of a Bishop or Priest, or only appointing to the office be sufficient?" CRANMER: "In the New Testament he that is appointed to be a Bishop or a Priest *needeth no consecration* by the Scripture, for *election or appointment thereto is sufficient.*" BARLOW: "Only the appointing" (1). After reading

(1) "It is said, on the other side, that Cranmer's Erastian opinions were not firmly fixed even in 1540, and probably not held at all in 1536; not fixed in 1540, because in subscribing his name to his *Answers* he wrote: 'This is mine opinion and sentence at this present, which, however, I do not temerariously define, but do remit the Judgment wholly unto your Majesty': and not held in 1536, because between the two dates came the publication of the *Bishop's Book,* in all probability composed largely by Cranmer himself, and certainly subscribed by him. But, in a person like Cranmer, the proviso in his subscription is a mark, not of mental hesitation, but of readiness to subscribe to any doctrine the king should require; and we must interpret his subscriptions, and even his labors of composition over the *Bishop's Book*—not that that book really contradicts his Erastian sentiments—and the *King's Book,* on the same principles. He, and indeed all of them, were prepared and expected to sign what the majority voted, whether it represented their true personal belief or not. In fact, it was on this very ground that some years later (1551) Heath was sent to the Fleet because he would not subscribe to the Edwardine Ordinal; the government, of which Cranmer himself was the ecclesiastical leader, said that when the other commissioners approved it as sound, it was unbecoming of him not to conform his judgment to theirs. Besides, the Erastian doctrine in question is only the logical outcome of Cranmer's undoubted belief in the Royal source of all ecclesiastical jurisdiction, and this belief he expressed as early

these replies expressing that consecration is not necessary ; after reflecting that such an admission would have been specially · gratifying to the royal Henry, then in the first exultation born of his lately assumed headship of the English Church ; after pondering on the fact that there is extant no record of any consecration of Barlow by Cranmer or by any one else ; and after noting particularly that Barlow is spoken of as a "bishop-elect" in the documents relating to the election of his successor at St. Asaph's, and that their phraseology implies something different from a regular "translation"; in all probability our convert X. will come to the conclusion that he is no priest, because his Anglican "ordination" is mediately derived from Parker, who was no bishop, since he received only a pretended "consecration" at the hands of one who had no episcopal power.   Of course, we do not pretend to have furnished any apodictical evidence that Barlow never received episcopal consecration, but we have made out a *prima facie* case of *non-consecration*, and therefore, although our adversaries assert that consecration must be presumed until disproved, jurists will say that the burden of proving it now rests on Z., the Anglican mentor of our converted friend X.   In conclusion, however, we would remark that interesting and important as is the historical question which we have been discussing, it has had but a comparatively small share in determining the practice of the Holy See in reference to the so-called Anglican Orders.   Had Barlow been

as 1536 or 1537, when on the Commission to draw up the Ten Articles : 'You ... are to agree ... whether such ceremonies as Confirmation, *Orders*, or Annealing, *which cannot be proved to be instituted of Christ*, or to certify us of remission of sins, ought to be called Sacraments.'   It is also urged (DENNY ; *Anglican Orders and Jurisdiction*, p. 72), I. that Cranmer's signature is attached to Dr. Leighton's Answers to the Seventeen Questions, evidently to signify his agreement with their doctrine, which is slightly more orthodox than Cranmer's own.   But it is futile to suppose that Cranmer *simultaneously* sent in his own most unorthodox Answers and gave his adhesion to others of a different complexion.   His signature is obviously merely to authenticate the document.   II. That the author of another set of Answers to these Questions, whom Strype (*Life of Cranmer*, b. I., c. xx.) supposes to have been Thirlby (but see DIXON ; *History of the Church of England*, II., p. 305), and who approximates much more to orthodoxy than Leighton, has set down Cranmer's and Barlow's names (with Cox's) in the margin opposite several of his statements, those on Orders included.   It is argued that here again the names are thus written in the margin to mark the agreement of these persons with the doctrine in the text.   But, again, it is futile to suppose that Cranmer *simultaneously* affirmed and denied the same doctrines.   It would be truer to say the names are written in the margin to mark that the statements in the text are directed against these men."   *Reasons for Rejecting Anglican Orders*, by Rev. Sydney Smith, S. J., London, 1895.

consecrated by the Roman Pontiff, and the record been deposited in the Vatican Archives, there could be, on the part of the Catholic Church, no recognition of the Anglican claims to Apostolic Succession and to a true priesthood, simply because Parker was "consecrated" according to an *Ordinal* which, to use the words of Lingard, "was as fit a form for the ordination of a parish-clerk, as of the spiritual ruler of a diocese." But the treatment of this branch of the question pertains to the province of the theologian, rather than to that of the historian. We shall merely observe that in the *Ordinal of Edward VI.*, which was used in all Anglican " ordinations" and " consecrations " down to the time of the Restoration, the rites, both as interpreted by the context and by the expressed opinions of the framers (Cranmer at their head), were intended to exclude the sole sense which could make them vehicles of valid Orders. In 1662 the Convocation made that addition to the rite of episcopal " consecration " which is now used by the Anglicans, and which certainly indicates a wish to bestow an episcopal character which the Edwardine *Ordinal* had ignored (1). Parliament deigned to allow the change, but it came too late ; the men who began to use the improved ritual were not reordained by undoubted bishops, but continued to transmit that phantasm of succession which they had received through Parker, so that no more effect was produced by the revised *Ordinal* of the Restoration than would be produced by a school-girl reciting its prayers over her dolls.

Justice demands that we notice, so far as our historical province permits, the chief objections which Anglican polemics urge against our contention. For replies to the minor historical objections, and for a solution of the Anglican difficulties which are based on liturgical and dogmatic grounds, we refer the reader to the Catholic authors whom we have already mentioned. The most important Anglican objection is to the effect that during the reign of Queen Mary, the Roman

(1) The new form for making a bishop reads : " Receive the Holy Ghost for the office and work of a bishop in the Church of God, committed unto thee by the imposition of our hands, in the name of the Father, and of the Son, and of the Holy Ghost : and remember that thou stir up the grace of God which is given to thee by this imposition of our hands, for God hath not given us the spirit of fear, but of power, love, and soberness."

authorities admitted the validity of Anglican "orders." In our day this assertion has been reiterated by the eccentric Dr. (we ought to say "bishop") Lee, of whom we have already spoken. In a book which he entitled *Roman Catholic Testimonies to the Validity of Anglican Orders*, this schismatic and lone-star prelate says : "In the reign of Queen Mary, those clergy who had actively sided with the innovating school during her half-brother's reign were certainly not reordained, but were formally confirmed in their orders—and this, though they had received them by the revised form of Edward VI. ... In the breve of Pope Julius III. to Cardinal Pole, Archbishop of Canterbury, dated March 8th, 1554, as well as in the commissions consequently issued by his Eminence to the dean and chapter of his cathedral church, as likewise to the several English bishops, the latter are ordered to confirm the clergy in their respective orders ; no distinction whatever being made between those who had been ordered by the ancient rite and by the revised ordinal. This may be seen from the exact words of the pope's breve. ... Pope Julius III., in his bull to Cardinal Pole, orders the legate to confirm all the clergy in their respective orders ; no distinction whatever being made between those who had been ordained by the ancient rite and by the revised ordinal. This may be seen from the exact terms of the pope's bull." Canon Raynal thus replied to Lee : "Tournely, the once famous Doctor of the Sorbonne, has culled from 'these exact words of the Pontiff,' certain terms that classify the holy orders of the schismatical clergy of England. These terms are—*1. 'Rite et legitime';* *2. 'male' ; 3. 'minus rite'; 4. 'nunquam.'* If we would thoroughly understand the true force of these expressions, we must bear in mind the history of the schism, and the heretical notions then held by many on the very subject of the Sacrament of Orders. The English Church had been separated from the Apostolic See for the space of twenty years only, and many of the clergy must have received their Holy Orders before the separation had taken place. These ecclesiastics would, therefore, be regarded as ordained, *'rite et legitime.'* On repentance and satisfaction they would be absolved, and then confirmed in the office they held in the Church. Diff-

culties would begin to arise with those who had been ordained
during the thirteen schismatical years of Henry's reign, for
such were 'male ordinati' and needed a special dispensation.
The accession of the youthful Edward, and the triumph of
the Calvinistic party, only tended to complicate the evil. It
is true that the ancient rite was obligatory in law till March,
1549, but it is no less true that its ceremonies and holy form
were blasphemed and ridiculed by those who then stood foremost in the ranks of the clergy. The delivery of the instruments, the sacred anointings, and the spiritual powers bestowed in the sacramental form of Holy Orders, were rejected
and despised by the Reformers. It is not a mere conjecture,
therefore, to say that, during the two first years of Edward
VI., many must either have avoided ordination altogether, or
have been guilty of such omissions in the sacred rite as rendered their Orders wanting in integrity. Hence they would be
considered as, 'male et minus rite ordinati.' The publication
and legal enforcement of the revised ordinal, in 1549, created
a new and more pronounced difficulty. This ordinal totally
changed the rites of ordination and episcopal consecration, and
their sacramental forms had been altered to suit the peculiar
views of its framers. Neither the Holy See nor the legate could
have closed their eyes to such an unparalleled innovation.
The forms, if altered in their substance, would be held null
and void. All those ordained according to them would, in
very deed, be 'nunquam ordinati.' Could such phantom
priests be recognized and confirmed? Would they not need
reordination? Why, then, do you assert so confidently that
the exact terms of the Pontiff draw no distinction whatsoever
between the Holy Orders that had been received during the
twenty years of the schism? These distinctions not only existed in the papal Bull, but were also practically enforced by
the cardinal-legate and the bishops who acted as his sub-del-
egates. You say that Pole ordered his cathedral chapter and
several bishops to confirm all the schismatical clergy in their
respective orders, no distinction whatever being made as to
the rite used at ordination. In juxtaposition with your statement I shall place that of Collier, the Church of England's
great historian. That writer tells us that the legate granted

a commission to the dean and chapter of Canterbury for reconciling the clergy and laity of that province. 'The instrument,' he says, 'extends to the absolving of all persons who repent their miscarriages, and desire to be restored from all heresies, schism, apostasies, from all excommunications, suspensions, and other ecclesiastical censures: and more particularly the clergy who had received orders from any schismatical or heretical bishops, officiated in virtue of that character, and complied with any unallowed ceremonies and forms of prayer, are absolved, provided the form and intention of the Church was not omitted in their ordination.' These words prove that the legate did not acknowledge the validity of Holy Orders conferred during the schism, without carefully investigating the rite that had been used, and the intention of those who were concerned in the ordination. And if these important words do not especially refer to the revised ordinal, I am, indeed, at a loss to know why they should have been inserted at all." Perhaps it is unnecessary to remark that the refutation of Lee's assertion was not answered.

Anglican polemics are fond of asserting that the absence of any record of Barlow's consecration forms the sole reason for our questioning it; and then they assert that if we are logical, we will deny the validity of Pole's consecration, since the cardinal's consecrator was Heath, who was consecrated by Gardiner, whose record of consecration is wanting in the archbishop's *Register*. We reply, firstly, that we do not question Anglican "orders" solely because there is no record of Barlow's consecration; our belief, as we have already shown, is founded on other omissions as well, and on many facts which all indicate the non-consecration. Secondly, it is true that the consecration of Gardiner is not recorded in Warham's *Register;* but the commission to consecrate him is, according to Archbishop Wake (1), under date November 27, 1531, and the consecration itself is entered in Gardiner's *Register* as having taken place on December 3, 1531. The consecrations of Fox of Hereford, Sampson of Chichester, and Reppes of Norwich, are not recorded at Lambeth; but that of Fox

(1) COURAYER; *Dissertation on Anglican Orders*, App. art. ix., p. 348. Oxford Edition of 1844.

is certified as intended in the *Significavit* (1), and as accomplished, in Fox's own *Register* and in his *Writ of Restitution;* that of Sampson in his *Writ of Restitution;* and that of Reppes is recited as accomplished in his *Writ of Restitution,* and in Cranmer's *Certificate to the King.* On the other hand, in Barlow's case, and his alone, none of these sources supplies evidence of a consecration (2).

(1) Before the rupture of Henry VIII. with Rome, almost every episcopal appointment having for more than two centuries been made directly by the Pope, the procedure was for the Pope to signify his appointment to the king, with a view to the Restitution of Temporalities and to the elect with a permission to choose for his consecrators any three bishops in communion with the Holy See. Henry VIII. in 1534, the better to interrupt all communication with Rome, caused the passing of an Act (25 *Henry VIII.*, c. xx.) by which an entirely new procedure was substituted. According to this, the dean and chapter of the vacant see, on receiving the *congé d'élire* and the letters missive indicating the candidate whom the king desired, were to elect the latter without delay and certify the fact to the crown. On receiving this certificate, the king, if he approved, issued a document called the *Royal Assent,* and another called the *Significavit,* both directed to the archbishop. Both the *Royal Assent* and the *Significavit* were to be entered in the archbishop's *Register.*

(2) The following remarks of Rev. Luke Rivington *(loc. cit.)* will appositely conclude our dissertation :

" A curious impression just now prevails in some circles to the effect that our Holy Father Leo XIII. in some way differs from His Holiness' predecessor, Pius IX., in his attitude toward the Anglican body. It is thought that Leo XIII. looks more kindly on the claims of that body to be part of the Catholic Church. This impression has been partly produced (however unintentionally) by a public utterance of Lord Halifax, giving an account of his lordship's visit to Rome in the spring of 1895. It is also in part based on the idea that our Holy Father's letter to those of the English people 'who seek the kingdom of God in the unity of faith,' urging them to pray for the reunion of Christendom, in some way contradicts the decree of the Holy Office in 1865, condemning the Association for the Promotion of the Unity of Christendom. But this is not the case. That Association was forbidden to Roman Catholics, because on the one hand it was supposed to include them in an Association *under the direction of Anglicans,* and because, on the other hand, it was based on a theory of unity which the Holy Office declared to be heretical. Leo XIII. does not, in his letter to the English people, suggest the formation of any association or confraternity for the purpose of prayer ; his Holiness merely urges the English people to pray in their own way, whilst he supplies his own subjects with a prayer which is obviously meant directly for them only—for it is addressed to our Lady, and it speaks of the rest of the English people (including members of the Church of England) in the third person *(fratres dissidentes)* ; and it is put forth with indulgences attached to it, which, of course, can only be gained by those in communion with the Holy See. This is not at all the same thing as recommending association in prayer in the sense condemned in the decree of 1865. As Archbishop Ullathorne observes *(The Anglican Theory of Union,* p. 7),' it is one of the conservative features of the Church's unity and integrity that her members do not communicate in prayer with those beyond her pale.'

" But the other and more serious count on which the A. P. U. C. was condemned at Rome was its adoption of a certain theory of unity, according to which the Church would be considered to have lost her note of visible unity. As Archbishop Ullathorne said of that Association, 'the spirit which animates it, which it expressly professes, is this—that the three Christian communions, namely, the Roman Catholic, the Greek Schismatic, the Anglican, however separated and divided from each other, have an equal title to claim for themselves the name of Catholic.' It was, in fact, the idea that the Church can consist of three ' branches ' so utterly separate as those three communions, which was condemned. The condemnation was formal and decided. 'The decree,' writes Archbishop Ullathorne, although officially signed by Cardinal Patrizzi, as Secretary, was not a mere letter coming from that

CHAPTER XXVII.

THE COUNCIL OF TRENT (EIGHTEENTH GENERAL).

When treating of the commencements of Protestantism, we noted that in 1520 Luther replied to the censures of Pope Leo X. by appealing to a future General Council. The same appeal was urged in 1530 by the Lutheran princes of Germany in their *Confession of Faith* presented to the Diet of Augsbourg; and these same princes continued until 1540 to denounce the Roman Pontiff for what they alleged to be either fear or supine negligence in not convoking the seemingly desired assembly which might put an end to the woes of Christendom. But when, in 1542, the Papal Bull for the convocation of the Council was issued, the ex-Augustinian used both voice and pen to propagate a distrust, in the minds of his followers, of everything that the Council might effect. And when Luther had gone to his dread account, and seven sessions had been held by the synodals, the other archheresiarch, Calvin, issued an *Antidote against the Council of Trent,* in 1547—a diatribe in which virulence and indecency struggled for predominance. Then, in 1549, in a second Diet of Augsbourg, when the Lutheran princes had again been asked whether they would submit to the conciliar decrees, Maurice, elector of Saxony, procured an assent qualified by such conditions as clearly implied a formal refusal of submission. These conditions were: 1st, the doctrinal points which had been already decided were to be again discussed;

---

distinguished Prelate, but a formal act of the Supreme Congregation, which is submitted to the Supreme Pontiff before its promulgation.' This, however, is not the same as a document signed by His Holiness, or as an *ex cathedra* pronouncement. Leo XIII. in no way contradicts this utterance of the Sacred Congregation. His Holiness, in his letter to the English people, does not give the slightest countenance to the idea that those who are not in communion with the Holy See form part of the visible Church of Christ. The centre of unity is, according to His Holiness, ' divinely constituted in the Roman Bishops,' and from this divinely constituted centre the English were ' wrenched ' in the sixteenth century, so that Father Spencer is praised by the Pope for having instituted ' a society of pious people to pray for the return of the English nation to the Church.' Lord Halifax and others are praised because they ' sincerely labor much for reunion with the Catholic Church,' whilst His Holiness calls his own subjects ' the Catholics of England.' It cannot, therefore, be said with any truth that Leo XIII. regards the Church of England in any other light than did His Holiness' predecessor, Pius IX."

2d, Lutheran representatives were to have a voice in the conciliar deliberations, and their votes were to have a value equal to those of the Catholic prelates; 3d, the Pope should no longer preside over the synodal sessions, either personally or by means of his legates. Such being the state of mind of the Lutheran leaders in regard to the Council of Trent, the Catholic world was prepared for the appearance, in 1560, of the famous collection of complaints (1) which have been, to this day, the stock in trade of all malevolent critics of the great Council (2). One alone of these anti-Tridentine polemics shall be noticed by us to any great extent; Paul Sarpi merits this distinction, for all the others, whether Lutheran, Anglican, Calvinist, or nondescript, are merely his copyists.

The Bull for the convocation of the Council of Trent was promulgated by Pope Paul III. on June 29, 1542. Ranke affects to believe that "the private relations of Paul III. would have induced him to impede the assembling of the Council." The German historian must allude to the fact of Paul III. having children; but it is certain that these were born of legitimate matrimony, before the Pontiff entered into the ecclesiastical state. It is also certain that the "private relations" of Pope Paul did not interfere with his encouragement of the Council in remedying abuses, wherever they were found. The fathers met at Trent in the Tyrol, on Dec. 13, 1545; and during the pontificate of Paul III., they held eleven sessions, three of which were celebrated in Bologna, the Papal legates having yielded to the prayers of the synodals to free them from the dangers of a plague which had appeared in Trent. This transfer was displeasing to the Spanish prelates; and they remained at Trent, sympathizing with the "orators" of the emperor Charles V., who protested against the "Bolognese convention," as they presumed to style the assembly of the majority, headed even though it was by the pontifical representatives. Paul III. therefore suspended the proceedings, and summoned both parties to

---

(1) *Concilii Tridentini Decretis* Opposita *Gravamina.*

(2) Chief among these are to be ranked the *History of the Council of Trent,* by Fra Paolo Sarpi; the *History of the Church* (b. VII., ch. v.), by Basnage; the *History of the Church* (16th cent., 3d sect., pt. 1), by Mosheim; and the *Notes* to the work of Sarpi, by Le Courayer.

Rome in 1549 ; but that Pontiff having died in November of the same year, his successor, Julius III., reconvened the Council at Trent by a diploma issued in December, 1550. The synodals assembled again in May, 1551; and during this pontificate five more sessions were held, namely, the twelfth to the sixteenth. In April, 1552, war caused another adjournment, and not before January, 1562, did Pope Pius IV. succeed in reuniting the fathers. This pontificate witnessed nine more sessions of the Council, and then the assembly was dissolved on Dec. 4, 1563.

We shall give a succinct account of the Sessions of this memorable Council. SESS. I. (Dec. 13, 1545). After the solemn opening, various Congregations were instituted. SESS. II. (Jan. 7, 1546). A sermon exhorting the synodals to personal sanctification was preached ; an order of treatment of all questions was prepared for the particular and general Congregations ; and a decree concerning the conduct of the synodals was issued. SESS. III. (Feb. 4). Each synodal subscribed to the Profession of Faith. It was ordered that the Nicene and Constantinopolitan *Creeds* should be prefixed to the Acts of the Council. SESS. IV. (April 8). In refutation of the Protestants who rejected certain books of the Holy Scriptures, as well as the entirety of Sacred Tradition, the Bible and Tradition were proclaimed as Sources of Faith. At the initiative of the Pope, the fathers discussed measures for the reformation of morals ; and very great liberty of thought and speech was observed in all the debates. SESS. V. (June 17). The debates on reformation continued ; and questions of faith were considered. Concerning original sin, the fathers made no pronouncement as to its nature ; but they were careful to add to their decree a clause which implicitly declared the doctrine of Mary's exemption from the common inheritance of the children of Adam. "In this decree concerning original sin it is not the intention of the Holy Synod to include the Blessed and Immaculate Virgin Mary, the Mother of God." SESS. VI. (Jan. 12, 1547). A decree on justification was issued, together with 33 Canons anathematizing contrary errors. The work of reformation was also prosecuted. SESS. VII. (March 3). There were promulgated

13 Canons on Sacraments in General; 14 on Baptism; and 3 on Confirmation. Then was published a decree on plurality of benefices. SESS. VIII. (March 11). An epidemic having broken out in Trent, the synodals resolved to transfer their sessions to Bologna. SESS. IX. and X. These were held in Bologna, the fathers occupying themselves with abuses in administration of the Sacraments. and with the episcopal obligation of residence. Certain bishops, fourteen in number, having obeyed the orders of Charles V. to remain in Trent, the Pope, in order to obviate possible danger of schism, dissolved the Council. On Nov. 10 Pope Paul III. died; and on Feb. 7, 1548, the cardinal De Monte ascended the pontifical throne as Julius III. On Nov. 14, 1550, the new Pontiff issued a Bull which reconvoked the Council in the city of Trent. SESS. XI. (May 1, 1551). The synodals reconvened, under the presidency of Cardinal Crescenzo, papal legate; but the assembly adjourned until Sept. 1, and then until Oct. 11. SESS. XII. The question of the *materia* of the Holy Eucharist was considered; and eight Dogmatic Chapters concerning it were published. By authorization of the Pontiff, a safe-conduct was accorded to such Protestants as might wish to visit the Council. SESS. XIII. (Oct. 11). A decree on the Holy Eucharist was read, containing 8 apposite Chapters and Canons; and then was issued a decree of reformation in the matter of episcopal jurisdiction. Two serious incidents disturbed this session. Amyot, the French ambassador, in a discourse filled with complaints against the Pope, declared that his royal master refused to recognize the œcumenicity of the Council; and the Protestants put forward an inadmissible demand for the nullification of the already emitted conciliar decisions. SESS. XIV. (Nov. 29). The Catholic teaching on Penance was explained in 9 Chapters and 15 Canons; that on Extreme Unction in 9 Chapters and 4 Canons; and then was read a decree on reformation. SESS. XV. (Jan. 25, 1552). At this time the Protestant princes, Maurice of Saxony and Albert of Brandenburg, instead of keeping their promise to send some of their theologians to Trent, made a treaty with the king of France, and simultaneously declared war on the emperor. The synodals therefore deemed it

prudent to suspend their sittings. SESS. XVI. (April 28). A proclamation, suspending the Council for two years, was issued; but with the provision that if circumstances warranted, the sessions should be resumed at an earlier date. But without any fault of either Pontiff or bishops, the suspension lasted for ten years; and during this period many events of world-wide importance happened. Charles V. abdicated his power, and retired to the monastic seclusion of San Yuste. Pope Julius III. died on March 21, 1555, and had for successors Marcellus II., Paul IV., and Pius IV.; the last of whom was to put the finishing touches to the work of the Council. The civil and religious wars desolating France and Germany long prevented a reconvocation of the assembly; but at length Pius IV., by a Bull dated Nov. 29, 1560, ordered the synodals to meet on the following Easter, at the same time, but in vain, inviting the Protestants to send representatives. SESS. XVII. Owing to delays on the part of many prelates, the reunion did not occur until Jan, 18, 1562, and then the time of the synodals was vainly spent in efforts to conciliate the Protestants. SESS. XVIII. (Feb. 20). A decree of the *Index* concerning prohibited books was published. The first four articles of a decree on reformation were examined; but the first, which treated of the obligation of episcopal residence, led to such vivid discussions that the matter was postponed. SESS. XIX. (May 14). Ambassadors from France, bearing instructions to act in accordance with the imperial agents, arrived. Many grave questions involving the supreme authority of the Pope were raised. SESS. XX. (June 4). The imperial "orators" presented twenty *desiderata* on discipline, and the "orators" of Bavaria imitated them; so that, as Pallavicino remarks, the German princes seemed to think that the Council had been convoked, not to condemn heretics, but to yield to them. SESS. XXI. (July 16). Four Chapters and 4 Canons on the Holy Eucharist were promulgated. In the decree on reformation which followed, it was ordered that no bishop should ordain persons who did not possess either a title to a benefice, or one of patrimony, or one of *mensa*. The abuses of sales of Indulgences were severely condemned. SESS. XXII. (Sept. 17). In regard to the Holy

Sacrifice of the Mass there were promulgated 9 Chapters and 9 Canons; and then was issued a decree concerning things to be done or omitted during the celebration. Then followed a decree, in 9 Chapters, on the life and morals of clerics. As to the question of the use of the chalice by the laity, the matter was referred to the Pope. On Nov. 15, the cardinal of Lorraine, accompanied by fourteen French bishops and eighteen theologians, appeared in the Council, and eloquently represented his royal master's desire for clerical reformation. Before the close of this session, the Pope gave a good example to the synodals by abolishing many grave abuses in his court. SESS. XXIII. (July 15, 1563). There were read 4 Chapters and 8 Canons on the Sacrament of Holy Orders; and also some passages of the decree on reformation, notably that on espiscopal residence. In the 18th Chapter of this decree the Council plied the axe at the very root of the evil of ecclesiastical demoralization by insisting on the establishment of clerical seminaries. The synodals now began the preparation of a Chapter on the reformation of sovereigns; but of course this project excited a unanimous protest on the part of all the imperial and royal "orators" who had been so zealous in reforming the clergy. The princes of the day certainly had reason for their complaints; but in most cases the corruption of the clergy was due to these very princes, who persisted in appointing unworthy men to ecclesiastical preferments. And assuredly the Church had the right to complain of the tyranny, avarice, and ambition of the princes in her regard; and of the ease and indifference with which they, nearly all, violated her most solemn laws. SESS. XXIV. (Nov. 11). There were now published Decrees on the Sacrament of Matrimony, by which were condemned, for all future time, what are known as clandestine marriages, that is, unions undertaken without the intervention of the parish-priest of one of the parties. SESS. XXV. (Dec. 3). The imminent termination of the Council was announced, in face of the strong opposition of the Spanish "orator." Then ensued the promulgation of decrees on Purgatory, the Veneration and Invocation of Saints, the Devotion toward Relics, Images, etc. A decree of reformation, embracing special prescriptions for religious of both sexes, was also published, together with several provisions concerning the morals, etc., of temporal princes. A decree on Indulgences was issued; and finally, on Dec. 4, 1563, Cardinal Morone, the papal legate, declared the termination of the Council of Trent. The fathers subscribing to the decrees numbered 255; that is, papal legates, 4; cardinals, 2; patriarchs, 3; archbishops, 25; bishops, 168; procurators of absent bishops, 39; abbots, 7; generals of religious orders, 7. In a consistory held on Jan. 26, 1564, Pope Pius IV. confirmed the conciliar decrees, ordering that on the next May 1 they should have the force of law.

Just as Protestantism is a synthesis of all the heresies which ever tormented the Christian body, from the outburst of Simon Magus to that of Luther, so the Council of Trent was a synthesis of all the preceding general assemblies of the teaching Church. Concerning the essence of God, the so-called "orthodox" Protestants agreed, at that time, with the Catholic Church; but in the matter of God's relations with man, an impassable gulf separated the heretics from the Mystic Body of Christ. It was a doctrine of Christian faith that man is born with free will, so that he is responsible for his sins. The Council condemned those who denied the existence of original sin; but subjoined that it did not include the Blessed Mother of God among the "all men" whom it pronounced infected with the guilt of Adam's fall. This exception was made, out of reverence for the Bull of Sixtus IV. in regard to the doctrine of the Immaculate Conception, then controverted by the Thomists and Scotists (1). The Church taught that by original sin, man loses his primitive sanctity; that the unregenerate man is an object of the ire of God, degraded in body and soul, and subject to death. Both this original sin and its consequences, said the Church, are transmitted to every child of Adam (Mary excepted); so that no man can perform an act acceptable to God, or become justified, unless through the mediation of Jesus Christ. But man's free will, insisted the Church, is not destroyed, al-

(1) The chief defenders of the Immaculate Conception at Trent were the cardinals Pole and Paceccc.

though it is weakened; therefore although human actions are not perfect, they are not all sinful. In fine, according to the Church, and as is proved by each one's experience, man enjoys moral liberty; he is free to enter into the designs of his Redeemer, just as the first man was free to cut himself aloof from the primitive designs of his Creator. Just the contrary of this doctrine was the teaching of Protestantism. According to the innovators, man is predestined, either to heaven or hell; such words as "the free will of man" are found nowhere in the Bible, but were invented by the Scholastics; it is God who works everything, evil as well as good; men are born in sin and concupiscence, with a positive hatred for God and His law, without any confidence in Him or any desire for His kingdom; and all of man's actual sins are merely so many manifestations of the hereditary guilt. Then the Church taught that the sinner is restored to grace by purely divine mercy, through the merits of Our Redeemer, and by means of the evangelical revelation; the Holy Ghost arousing his dormant faculties, and inspiring him to yield to the divine impulses. If the sinner hearkens to the Spirit, the first blessing he receives is faith in the word of God, and in the fact that God so loved the world as to give His Son for its redemption. Then the sinner turns to the mercy of God, and appreciating God's infinite charity, he finds in his own heart an abomination of sin and sorrow for having committed it. In this entire process, the sinner's free will has co-operated; he becomes justified through sanctifying grace; and the regenerated man produces good and meritorious works. According to the Church, therefore, God and man co-operate in the process of justification; God wakens the sinner before he even desires the wakening; if then the sinner corresponds to the divine impulse, his restoration is complete. In all this, the Holy Ghost does not necessitate man's action; He respects in man that free will which original sin did not destroy. But according to Luther, Christ nullifies the sins of the world, and faith alone justifies man; let man trust in the merits of Christ, because of which God declares him just, even though he is not such, and even though he still bears the original stain and his own actual guilt. However, added Luther, justifying faith is accompanied by sanctification, which manifests itself in good works; but justification and sanctification must not be confused. The work of regeneration, concludes Luther, is entirely that of the Holy Ghost; all of the glory is God's, none belongs to man. Calvin thought differently from Luther in this matter. He found an intimate connection between justification and sanctification; and he asserted that God operates in those only whom He has predestined from all eternity. Calvin having found that original sin had destroyed entirely the faculties of man, he could discern in man not only no free will, but no capability of receiving a divine impulse; therefore, pronounced Calvin, justification is a judgment whereby God frees man, not from sin, but from its punishment. In its decisions on this matter of justification, the Council of Trent declared that our sins are forgiven gratuitously by the divine mercy; that they are not merely " covered," but cancelled by the blood of Jesus; that the justice of the Redeemer is not merely "imputed," but actually communicated to the faithful by the Holy Ghost. As to good works, the Council warns the Christian that although our Lord promised to reward him who would give a drink of water in His name, and although St. Paul says that one moment of earthly suffering may be rewarded by an eternity of glory, nevertheless we must not glory in our good actions, but rather in the goodness of our Lord who has made His own gifts meritorious for us. In fine, our sins are remitted by the pure mercy of God, through the merits of His Son; our justification is a free gift of God; and our good works are so many gifts of grace. But it is not our province to detail the dogmatic decisions rendered at Trent; we have merely alluded to the matter of justification because it was one of the prime points of difference between the early Reformers and the Church.

If every General Council were not of such tremendous import, that it would scarcely be proper to assert that any one of these nineteen assemblies of the collected wisdom of the Church pre-eminently challenges our respectful admiration, we would feel justified in saying that the Council of Trent can claim such qualification. Every previous Œcumenical

Council had been called for the consideration of some particular error or errors; but the Tridentine Fathers were called to consider and confirm nearly every point of Catholic dogma. The pretended Reformers of that day had attacked nearly every Catholic teaching, and had established—as far as they could establish anything—a conglomeration of doctrinal errors. It would certainly be an interesting task to carefully examine the one hundred and twenty-seven Canons issued by this Council. For instance, the Canon establishing the authenticity of the Latin Vulgate, and enjoining its acceptation, "with all its parts," would demand consideration at a time when learned and virtuous scholars deny the authenticity of some of the passages in that Vulgate; e. g., the celebrated text of verse 7 of chap. i. of St. John's Epistle, "*Et sunt tres qui dant testimonium; ... et hi tres unum sunt.*" And then there is the Canon concerning clandestine marriages, and also the one proclaiming the indissolubility of matrimony, even in the case of adultery. This latter decree is of special interest to the Catholics of the United States, now that the increasing flood of European emigration has landed upon our shores thousands of those Greek and other Oriental "Uniates," who, while clinging to their own respected and venerable liturgies, acknowledge the supremacy of the Roman Pontiff. Anathema had been pronounced against him who would say that marriage could be dissolved because of adultery. The orators of Venice here took the floor, and begged the synodals to word their decree in other fashion, for they greatly feared that the already expressed terminology would cause trouble among the Greek subjects of the Most Serene Republic in Corfu, Crete, Cyprus, Zante, Cephalonia, Dalmatia, etc. These Greeks were passionately fond of their own rite and discipline, although they were in communion with the Holy See. The ambassadors reminded the fathers that these United Greeks had been accustomed, from time immemorial, to dissolve marriage in case of adultery; and they drew attention to the fact that for this dissolution the said Greeks had not been condemned by any General Council or by any Roman Pontiff, although their custom was well known to Rome. In deference to this request of the Venetian orators, the synodals mollified the Canon so that it would read : "If any one says that the Church errs in her teaching that the matrimonial tie cannot be dissolved by the adultery of one of the spouses, ... let him be anathema." The judicious Perrone essays a comment on this Canon, but he can only say : "If the Greeks so act, *ipsi viderint.*" But the consideration of these enactments pertains to the province of the theologian, rather than to that of the historian.

Chief among all the historians who have attacked the value and character of the Council of Trent, whether we consider the talent, the force, or the venom of these writers, stands forth Friar Paul Sarpi, a member of the Order of Servites of Mary. When we come to treat of the pontificate of Paul V. and of the Interdict of Venice, we shall dwell at some length upon the career of this curious man ; now our attention is claimed only by his *History* of the Tridentine assembly—a history which he styled "the Iliad of our century." When he was yet a child, he had heard much of the famous Council from men who had taken part in it ; in his youth he became intimate with Olivo, secretary to Cardinal Gonzaga, one of the Papal legates ; and in his early manhood he frequently met, at Venice, men who had represented their sovereigns in the assembly. These associations convinced him that a correct history of the Council had not yet been put forth ; even that by John Sleidan, which he esteemed the most, was very imperfect, from his point of view. Therefore he proposed to narrate, for the edification of mankind, " The causes and the intrigues of an ecclesiastical convocation, which, desired and procured for various ends and with various means, and for eighteen years now assembled and then adjourned—but always for various purposes, attained to a form and a completion diametrically opposed to the designs of those who had furthered it, and thus became a lesson to us to be resigned to the divine will, and not to rely too much on human prudence. For this Council, designed and procured by pious men for a reunion of the Church then commencing to be divided, so firmly fixed the schism and rendered the parties so obstinate, that now they are irreconcilable ; and although princes depended on it for a reformation

of ecclesiastical matters, it caused the worst deformation that
the world has seen since the first sounding of the Christian
name." The friar displayed great patience in his task, but
too often he merely translated Sleidan and Chemnitz, writers
bitterly hostile to the Papacy. He draws much upon contemporary documents, especially upon the *Relations* of the
Venetian "orators." But he systematically invents ha-
rangues which were never delivered; he puts other discourses
in the mouths of men who did not pronounce them—a fault
not to be pardoned even in a profane history, but which cannot be too severely characterized when committed by one who
pretends to weigh discussions bearing upon sacred subjects.
It is strange indeed that this friar, ostensibly, at least, a
Catholic, should so cavalierly and persistently ignore any
presence of the Holy Spirit in the Tridentine debates; that
he should seem to view things as we would view them, if we
were listening to the manœuvring squabbles of a modern parliament. He constantly finds the motive factor of the most
sublime decisions to have been an eloquent speech, or a cardinalitial trick, or some cunning artifice of a Machiavellian
papal legate. Indeed Fra Paolo presents the papal legates as
a laughing-stock to the world, for presuming that "they carried the Holy Ghost from Rome to Trent in their trunks." In
his conceptions of the hierarchy, of ecclesiastical jurisdiction,
of the pontifical supremacy, of monasticism, etc., he is neither
a historian nor a churchman; for he either ignores or travesties the facts of history in their regard, and if we did not
know the contrary, we would think that he had as much knowledge of their true condition as might have been found in the
Chinese of that day. He tells us that the hierarchy was established by papal ambition, and through the ignorance and
weakness of sovereigns; that the priesthood were never of any
good to the people, but were rather oppressors of the lowly;
that if the clergy favored the arts and sciences in the Middle
Age, it was only for their own aggrandizement. The precious
work of the Servite religious first appeared in England, by
care of the apostate archbishop of Spalatro, De Dominis, and
it bore the title "*A History of the Tridentine Council by Peter
Suavis Polanus, in which are Manifested the Artifices of the*

Roman Court to Prevent a Discovery of the Truth and the Reformation of the Papacy and of the Church." In his dedication to the royal theologian and head of the Anglican persuasion, James I., the perverted prelate wonders how so grand a work "could have come from the hand of one born and trained under obedience to the Roman Pontiff"; he praises the author's erudition and good intentions; and he compares the book to Moses, saved from the waters to which, out of reverence to the Papacy, the author had destined it—to Moses, because the *History* would help to free mankind from the Pharaoh who "by means of so false and irregular a Council, holds the peoples in cruel slavery." Immediately after the publication of the book, Sarpi—with what measure of sincerity we cannot tell—caused his friend, Fra Fulgenzio, to reprove, under date of Nov. 11, 1619, the Dalmatian for having abused the confidence of Fra Paolo, "by taking a copy of, and publishing a work, the manuscript of which had been loaned to him for perusal." Fulgenzio also blamed the episcopal apostate for having given to the work "that most improper title," and for having subjected it to "so terrible and scandalous a dedication, and merely for motives of self-interest, not for the honor of the modest author." Here we must note that Pope Pius IV. had prohibited, under pain of excommunication, all unauthorized annotations and commentaries on the Tridentine decrees; that therefore Fra Paolo was presumed to have incurred censure by the London publication. Perhaps this was the reason for the Servite's disclaimer of any complicity in that act. We should not omit to record that several attempts were made against the life of Sarpi. One, which was nearly successful, was headed by a certain Poma, a fanatic who believed everything licit for the good of religion. It is said that when the friar felt the wound, he cried out: "*Conosco lo stile della curia Romana*—I know the style (the dagger) of the Roman court." The play on words was not bad, and Rome was at once blamed by many for the crime. But where were the assassins arrested? In the Papal States, and a papal tribunal condemned one of them to decapitation, and the others to perpetual imprisonment.

In order to repel the attacks of Fra Paolo, influence was

brought to bear upon a Roman Jesuit named Pallavicino Sforza (b. 1607) to compose another *History of the Council of Trent.* Already many had refuted the friar's allegations ; *e. g.,* Bernardine Florio, archbishop of Zara, in eight volumes had convicted Sarpi of unfaithfulness in the use of documents, and of misinterpretation of decisions ; but this work remained unpublished. In the preparation of his book, Pallavicino (as he is generally styled) had recourse, as Sarpi, either intentionally or otherwise, did not have recourse, to the Roman Archives ; and, again unlike Fra Paolo, he carefully indicates the nature and the titles of all the documents proffered by him. He notices three hundred and sixty-one " errors of fact " in Sarpi's work, and an infinite number of recklessnesses. Comparing these two *Histories* together, Cantù says that the book of the Servite is the first historical work which purposely aims at calumny, by the use of a quantity of presumed facts "which the author does not weigh, but accumulates." The great historian finds that Sarpi always " supposes truth to be distinct from probity, and hence he everywhere discovers meannesses and hypocrisies, manœuvres and underhandedness " ; whereas Pallavicino finds " noble characters, sound convictions, and generous resistances." But Cantù, while admitting that Pallavicino elevates the souls of his readers and instructs their intellects, finds in Fra Paolo, " the quick movement of one who attacks and wounds," while his adversary, " reduced to continual defence, wearies one with his constant efforts against his enemy's opinions." Rome condemned the work of Sarpi, and the Venetian oligarchs that of Pallavicino ; and yet the latter never dissimulates any blameable things in the pontifical court. When he was reproved for this candor, he replied : " A historian is not a panegyrist ; when he praises the least, he praises more than any panegyrist." Ranke took care to compare the assertions of Pallavicino with the documents on which this writer relied, and he credited him with scrupulous exactness.

Let us now examine the most important objections which have been urged against the character and the authority of the Council of Trent. Quite naturally all hostile polemics begin their onslaught with an outcry against the Catholic claim of œcumenicity for this assembly. But is it not strange that Protestants should advance such an assertion, when they contend that the Scriptures alone are the rule of faith; that a Council has no right to impose its decision upon the individual conscience? General or not, the children of the Reformation could not claim, in accordance with their prime principle, any part in such an assembly. And it is precisely because a definitive voice was denied to them at Trent, that they decry the œcumenical character of the Council. Just as much a right to that definitive voice in the proceedings of a Catholic Council was possessed by the Oriental schismatics, or even by the heathen savages of then newly-discovered America. The Council of Trent was supposed to represent those children of Christendom who held the same religious belief, and subsisted under the same religious organization, as were in force at the time when the apostate German friar raised the standard of revolt. What part in that belief and in that organization did the partisans of Luther, Calvin, Zwingle, etc., evince or even claim? Well, then, could the Church have answered the Protestant insistence for a definitive voice in her assemblies, with the words of Tertullian : "Who are you? When and whence came ye? What seek you in my affairs, you who are not mine? By what right do you devastate my garden? Why do you defile my fountains? Why do you interfere with my frontiers? I am in possession; I possessed what I have of old; I possessed all this before your names were known; the origin of my claims is from the very Author of the things themselves. I am the heir of the Apostles; I hold my possessions by their last will and testament. They disinherited you, foreigners and enemies that you are " (1). Again, we must remember that the fathers of Trent offered a hearing to the Protestants. In Sessions 13, 15, and 18, they tendered permission and an invitation to the recalcitrants to come to Trent, there to expose their alleged grievances, to defend their opinion by tongue and pen, and " to dispute with the chosen champions of the Council " (2). Certainly, this invitation was acknowledged; and as

(1) *Prescript. Heret.*
(2) " *Tridentum veniendi, ibidemque manendi, standi, morandi, proponendi, loquen-*

an excuse for its non-acceptance, the Protestants urged that they could not trust their lives to the honor of the Papists, since it was one of the Roman maxims that faith was not to be kept with heretics. We have said enough on this matter of papistical Punic faith when treating of the affair of John Huss ; but hearken to Didacus Payva d'Andrade, one of the Portuguese theologians at the Council, as he urges the famous Chemnitz : "Do you assert that you and yours could not attend the Tridentine Council with safety, and that you could not have confidently and freely expressed your views in that assembly ? Now I can testify that the fathers desired nothing more, and that the legates labored for nothing more than that all the transactions of the Council should be conducted in freedom, with calm, and by use of convincing argument. Or do you think that because you refused to attend the Council, we were to desert the cause of the Universal Church, to neglect her needs, to think nothing of her many wounds, and to permit you to propagate your commentitious 'Gospel'? But lest you may say that the conciliar proceedings were not conducted prudently and considerately, listen to an account of things as they happened. ... When we had given up all hope of your coming, the fathers caused to be brought to Trent the writings of that impure man, Luther, as well as the books composed by the other unfortunates who had left the bosom of the Roman Church ; so that these productions might defend the cause which you had cunningly deserted. Nor do I think that you could have urged your cause better than it was defended in those writings. Now I can testify that the legates frequently admonished us to weigh every one of your arguments with as much care as we would give to the sayings of the fathers of the Church. I was often told by the most reverend Cardinal Seripandus, a man of great virtue and erudition, that I could do no better work for the Church, than by collecting your arguments with the utmost fidelity and diligence ; ... for thus the truth and your insincerity would be made to appear in a more striking manner."

di, una cum ipsa Synodo de quibuscumque negotiis tractandi, examinandi, discutiendi; ... et etiam ad objecta Concilii Generalis respondendi, et cum iis qui a Concilto delecti fuerint, disputandi."

There is no need of our replying to the Protestant objection that the Council of Trent was improperly convoked ; that it was the province of the emperor, not of the Pope, to issue a Bull for that purpose. The gentry who are always the first to refuse obedience to legitimate civil authority, can readily discern a little god in their earthly monarch when their temporal interest prompts such recognition. And we have abundantly satisfied this objection when treating of the Councils of Nice and of Chalcedon.

In order that he may lead his readers to believe that the synodals of Trent enjoyed no real liberty, and that therefore no respect is due to the conciliar enactments, Sarpi asserts that every procedure was presented to the fathers, already " cut and dried " by the Papal legates. We constantly meet the phrase, " at the instance of the legates—*proponentibus legatis* " ; and it is notorious that many of the synodals, especially among the Spaniards, protested against this usurpation. But Sarpi and all his imitators refute this very objection, when they so frequently harp on the alleged scandalous disturbances which, they insist, often marred the symmetry of the Tridentine sessions. How could these quarrels, these noisy recriminations, these all but pugilistic encounters, have taken place, if no freedom of discussion was allowed to the fathers ? But was not some one to have, of necessity and to prevent confusion, the right and duty of presenting to the Council the subjects which merited consideration ? And who could perform this task with greater propriety and with more accurate judgment than the Supreme Pontiff, either personally or through his legates ? We have already seen that such was the case in all the early General Councils. The emperor Marcian wrote to Pope St. Leo I. that in the coming œcumenical Council of Chalcedon, the bishops would establish " what would profit the Christian religion and Catholic faith, according as his Holiness would define." And the empress Pulcheria wrote to the same Pope that the fathers of Chalcedon would profess what he should decree—" *te auctore decernunt.*" We have shown that whatever concerning faith was defined at Chalcedon, was so effected simply in accordance with the *Dogmatic Epistle* of Pope St. Leo I. to Flavian.

Similar arguments are presented by all the early Councils. But there are innumerable proofs that the fathers of Trent enjoyed perfect liberty. Thus, Cardinal Farnese wrote to the legates in the name of Paul III., on May 25, 1546, that during that session (the 5th) they should communicate the sentiments of the Pontiff to the synodals, " but not as though a command were being given, but rather so that the opinion of the majority having been found, a wise decision be reached." And the Council itself declares, Sess. 24, in its decree *On Reformation*, ch. 21, the significance of that phrase which so displeased Sarpi : "*proponentibus legatis*" : " Since the Holy Synod desires that its decrees furnish no occasion for doubt in times to come, ... it declares that in its use of those words, ' the legates proposing,' it does not intend that any change be effected in the manner of treating affairs which has ever obtained in General Councils." Therefore as our adversaries willingly admit that in preceding Councils there was sufficient discussion to satisfy the most litigious minds, they should conclude that the Tridentine fathers had every opportunity of manifesting their sentiments. If the interest of the Popes ever led them to wish to intimidate the synodals of Trent, it could have been only in matters of discipline, in which they naturally wished to preserve their pristine authority ; and it is proved by the *Acts* of the Council, by the narratives of the ambassadors, and by the admissions of Fra Paolo and his commentator (Le Courayer), that the bishops of France and Spain often expressed themselves on such matters in a manner very displeasing to the court of Rome. Sarpi asserts that in the Council of Trent the Italians, all devoted to the Pontiff, tyrannized over the other bishops, and that the prelates nearly always emitted their wishes by the simple *placet*. Now this assertion of tyranny on the part of the Italians is mere assertion, and nothing more ; as to the *placet ne vobis ?*, propounded by the legates, that was never used unless in the arrangement of the date of the next session, in a proposition to adjourn, or in some such case of minor importance. Never was this question put when a case of doctrine was to be decided.

Very little need be said in reply to the charges of wicked-

ness and ignorance brought against the synodals of Trent.
The dogmatic value of the conciliar doctrinal decisions, as
well as the respect due to the disciplinary Canons, would be
in no way impaired, were history to show indeed that Protestant writers have been guilty of no exaggeration in the premises. This mine has been worked for all it is worth; and
nevertheless, its yield has been very small. We know the
names of all the synodals, and of nearly all the officials; the
biographies of nearly all the notables are known, but the
wicked and the ignorant seem to have formed a very insignif-
icant minority. It is quite natural for us to suppose, knowing, as we do, that there was a lamentable relaxation of ecclesiastical discipline at that period, that the Council of Trent
should have numbered among its members some of those
who made a Reformation necessary. But the accusations of
our opponents are to be charily credited; it is always to be
expected that a criminal shall calumniate his judge.

It is said that the Papal legates at Trent antagonized many
efforts to reform abuses, and that of those abuses which were
condemned, many are still rampant. It is much easier to declaim against abuses, than it is to prevent their remedies from
suscitating worse ones. And no one will deny that the regulations issued at Trent did abolish many abuses; some of
the enactments would have been better observed, remarks
Bergier, "If powerful men had not found their interest in
preventing it. It is absurd to insist, on the one hand, that
the Church has no right to make laws, and on the other, to
reprove her for being unable to effect their execution. In
throwing off the yoke of the Church, Protestants have appeared to put themselves under that of the civil government;
but they always revolt against that, whenever it weighs heav-
ily. To hear them talk, one would suppose that there are
no abuses among themselves; but is there a greater one than
the liberty to form a new schism whenever a preacher is able
to find partisans?"

We are told that the Council of Trent was a failure; inas-
much as, instead of putting an end to the dissensions among
Christians, its decrees gave rise to new ones. How many
Bulls have been necessary since the famous Synod was dis-

solved, in order to decide questions which the Tridentines dared not to handle ; *e. g.*, on matters of grace. Even in our day, a Congregation periodically meets at Rome for the express and sole purpose of explaining the meaning of the decrees at Trent. And does it not seem that the obscurity of many of the Tridentine decrees is affected, owing to the unwillingness, or perhaps impotence of the synodals, to condemn certain prominent theologians? No Catholic pretends that a General Council will, or can, put an end to disputes or to cavilling. Be a decision ever so clear, there will always arise subtle spirits who, by forced interpretations, will give to them even fantastic meanings; witness, the disputes of Protestants as to the meaning of the Scriptures, even though they contend that the simple and the ignorant can find in the Sacred Text their rule of faith. But there can be no comparison between the disputes of Protestants in Biblical matters and the controversies obtaining among Catholic theologians in regard to undecided doctrinal points. The disputations of these latter entail no schism between the adversaries ; you never hear them anathematizing each other as heretics ; each one is ever ready to renounce his pet theory, if the Church deems proper to decide in the premises, and he will do so *quamprimum*. As to the many papal Bulls rendered necessary by the contentions on divine grace which troubled the fold of Christ during the last century, there would have been no need of those documents, had all the disputants been sincerely submissive to the Tridentine enactments. It is but too true that many of those gentry spoke of those decrees with as little respect as would have been fitting on the tongues of Protestants ; that they gave a Protestant interpretation to the scriptural and patristic passages which seemed to favor their own theories ; and that they even accused the orthodox of semi-pelagianism. just as Protestants accuse the fathers of Trent. Could the Council have foreseen these troubles, its condemnatory decrees would have been more numerous.

But the authority of the Council of Trent, it is urged, is regarded as null by many very good Catholics, as is evident from the fact that the decrees were not received in France :

that Spain and the Netherlands received them only with restrictions. If this objection is meant to cover matters of faith, the reply is that any Catholic country which would have rejected the Tridentine doctrinal decisions, would have been stamped, by the very fact, as heretical; and it matters little that in some lands the decrees of Trent were not confirmed by royal letters-patent or registered in the Acts of parliament. Among the twenty-three articles which the French jurisconsults, speaking to Henry III. in 1579, pronounced contrary to the Gallican "maxims and liberties," not one regarded doctrine. Le Courayer, the Sarpian commentator who adduces this objection, himself admits that the Tridentine decrees have always been the rule of faith in France; that the French bishops all adopted the *Profession of Faith* of Pope Pius IV.; and that even in the opposition of the Estates or parliaments to the acceptation of the Council, it was always declared that the French embraced the faith as contained in its definitions. However, some Protestant polemics have held that France never received the Council of Trent, either as to dogma or discipline. Thus Leibnitz, who, when trying, in very good faith, to compass some efficacious means for the actuation of a reunion of all Christians in one fold, assumed as a preliminary that the Tridentine assembly should be regarded as not having had existence. But in reply to the sanguine philosopher, Bossuet showed that all Catholic bishops were unanimous in upholding the œcumenicity of the Council of Trent, and its consequent infallibility in matters of faith; and that, in France as everywhere else, any pretense of deliberation as to an acceptation of the conciliary doctrinal decrees would be a simple question as to whether the nation would be Catholic or heretical (1). Concerning the question of fact, it is certain that in Italy, the Holy Roman Empire, and Poland, the Council of Trent was received without any reservation. In the Spanish dominions, it was received " without prejudice to the rights and prerogatives of the king " ; and certainly it has never been reckoned among said rights, etc., that the monarch of most Catholic Spain should reject, at his will or ca-

(1) Cf. *The Spirit of Leibnitz*, vol. II.

price, the decisions of a General Council in matters of doctrine. The clergy of distant Mexico realized this truth, when, in their provincial synod of 1585, under the presidency of their arch-bishop, Peter Moya de Contreras, they ordered the promulga-tion and execution of the Tridentine enactments, whether they concerned faith or discipline. As to Portugal, the letter of King Sebastian to Pope Pius IV., dated Oct. 2, 1564, proves that the decrees were all, without exception, promulgated in that kingdom and in its colonies. That Poland willingly, and at once, received all the decrees, is evinced by the *Acts* of the General Estates of 1564, held under the auspices of King Sigismund III., and by the letter of Cardinal Commendoni, nuncio at the Polish court, to Cardinal Borromeo.

Ranke would have us believe that when the synodals of Trent convened, " the great question was to determine, from among those opinions which leaned toward the Protestant system, which one could be received as concordant with the Catholic Gospel." Such was certainly the " great question " for the rebels to Church authority ; but the Tridentine fa-thers saw before themselves only the great question of main-taining the dogmas of Catholicism in their integrity. The German historian affects to see "Pole, present in this Coun-cil, defending with energy" those opinions which leaned toward the Protestant system ; and he coolly informs us that " many of the members of the Council held views which agreed *completely* with those of the Protestants." When treating of the Innovators in Italy, we disculpated Cardinal Pole, as well as Vittoria Colonna, Michelangelo, and other devoted Catholics, of this charge ; and here we need add merely the remark that among the 255 Tridentine fathers, only six or seven expressed opinions of a slightly unorthodox tendency, and every one of these withdrew their assertions by signing the conciliar decrees. Ranke is ever anxious to claim the zealous relative of Henry VIII. as a sympathizer with the Reformers ; and he finds it very " singular" that Pole should have been seized with sickness, and forced to leave the Council, " pre-occupied only with the personal disquiet caused by the condemnation of his opinion." The singularity of Pole's case was shared by scores of the synodals who, either from age, infirmity, or anxiety, succumbed during the Council. Ranke accuses Pope Paul III. of low chicanery in transferring the Council to Bologna, because of an epidemic raging in Trent. "The true reason is found in the fact that the temporal interests of the Papacy were again in opposition to its spiritual interests." The German historian, like all Protestant critics of the Pope-Kings, can never discern any other than thoughts of temporal aggrandizement, or at least of temporal comfort, in all the designs of the successors of St. Peter. But Ranke studiously omits to say that only fourteen of the synodals opposed the transfer; and thirteen of these were subjects of the emperor, who wished the assembly to remain at Trent, in accordance with his thinly-veiled imperialistic pretensions to direct the synodal actions. After his success against the Protestant League of Smalkald, Charles V. had begun to pose in the usual attitude of a German emperor toward the Holy See; and it was to secure the full liberty of the Council, that Paul III. transferred its sessions to a city within his own territories. In reference to this matter of the transfer Ranke also forgets, quite conveniently, to note that it was of their own will that the immense majority of the prelates moved to Bologna, while those who remained at Trent were compelled by the emperor to their course. It is futile for Ranke to allege the comparative innocuousness of the malady then rampant in Trent; for we know from letters of the French bishops, impartial witnesses in the premises, that the epidemic was very dangerous, and that many, even of the household of the legates, had succumbed (1). Ranke tells us that the Tridentine prelates, at one time, were ready to " overwhelm the court of Rome with a reformation which had hovered over it for many a year"; that certain Spanish bishops proposed, " under the form of censures, several articles which had for their object the diminution of the papal authority." But these prelates were those who remained at Trent under the hand of the emperor; and the mentioned articles, while manifesting the imperial mind of Charles V., were never considered in conciliar session, the imperialistic prelates never

(1) These letters were published by Ribier, in the *Letters and State Memoires*, vol. I., p. 622.

having held such a reunion, although Ranke affects to discern a species of schism in the Council itself, between the partisans of the Pontiff and those of the emperor. Ranke says that the Council " condescended to ask the Pope for a confirmation of its Canons " ; but how can that be styled a condescension which is a formality whereby a Council simply actuates the chief condition of its own œcumenicity ? It is not a condescension to ask for that which alone can render synodal decrees obligatory on the faithful. Ranke thinks that the Tridentine fathers "refounded the hierarchy; theoretically by their Canons on ordination, and practically by their Canons on reformation." Does the German historian imply that the Middle Age knew nothing of either the theory or the practice of Canon Law? Certainly the rights and duties of each class of the hierarchy, both in essential and in variable matters, were fully determined many centuries before the Council of Trent. It is a pity that Ranke does not inform us, either explicitly or implicitly, as to his meaning in this sentence : " In the Catholicism of previous ages there was an element of Protestantism, which was now (in the Council of Trent) forever excluded." Ranke often implies that the Church ought to be ashamed of the negotiations which accompanied the celebration of the Council of Trent; but the Church has been so little ashamed of them that historians like Rinaldi and Pallavicino give us, with the utmost ingenuousness, most copious details of all their ramifications. The German historian, with a naiveté that has since become the fashion with a certain class of writers, wishes us to rely especially upon his presentations, because of the new documents which, according to himself, he has unearthed; as though the Vatican and other valuable Archives were unknown lands before his advent. It is certain that Ranke does not give any document of note concerning the Council of Trent which Pallavicino has not adduced, and with more truth of detail; and it is also certain that all of the correspondence in regard to the negotiations on which Ranke dilates was published long before by Mansi, whereas Ranke frequently copies, and often *verbatim*, Paolo Sarpi, in strange disregard of his own admissions as to this writer's veracity.

The theologian will probably, for many years to come, have recourse to the pages of Pallavicino, Alexandre, Mansi, Fleury, and Bergier, for his necessary researches in regard to the Council of Trent. The general reader will be satisfied with the information afforded by Darras, Rohrbacher, Pastor, and other Catholic historians of merit; and if he wishes to apprehend the spirit of the Tridentine fathers, and to appreciate thoroughly the difficulties under which they labored, he can do no better than assimilate the reflections made by Cantù (1). Our heterodox friends, whether Protestant or rationalistic, will probably continue to rely upon Sarpi, or upon such verbal variations of that writer's lucubration as their pet historians may see fit to present; for since no Protestant or rationalistic commentator on the Council of Trent has yet disembarrassed himself from the Sarpian chains, we are justified in supposing that men of that ilk will ever regard the fetters as sources of strength. And nevertheless, Ranke, whom many Catholics praise as comparatively impartial, but who constantly seeks for some little inexactness of detail which may warrant his diffidence toward Pallavicino, is often compelled to judge of Sarpi with a severity which is seldom exceeded by the comments of any Catholic polemic (2). Thus the German historian admits that Sarpi is addicted to the mutilation and malquotation of documents " in order to put bishops in an odious light; he is full of gall and hate; his entire *History* is inspired by a systematic opposition and a violent hatred toward the court of Rome." Ranke tells us that Sarpi takes care, when copying documents concerning the Council, to reject everything which might give one a good impression regarding it; "he exerts himself to produce an unfavorable impression." Ranke says that Sarpi changes the words of the papal instructions; "because he does not wish to admit that the Pontiff ever showed any inclination" for a reconciliation with the Protestants. We are also told that Sarpi puts words into the mouth of the Pope which his Holiness never uttered; and although Ranke represents the embittered Venetian as "the head of the Cath-

(1) *Heretics of Italy.* Discourses 18 and 47.

(2) In the *Appendix* to the vol. I. of his *Papacy During the Sixteenth and Seventeenth Centuries.*

olic (l) opposition," he declares that the Sarpian *History* is
" the first instance of such a work written with a predeter-
mination to vilify, applying the system to all facts—things
which are the object of historical study."

CHAPTER XXVIII.

THE PONTIFICATE OF SIXTUS V.

To the rank and file of the heterodox the name of Pope
Sixtus V., if known at all, recalls certain fantastic tales which
lack any historical foundation, but which have become popular because nearly all Protestant and philosophistic historians have derived their notions of this great Pontiff from a
charlatanesque effusion which would have been buried in oblivion with its author, were it not a mass of lubricity and of
vomitings against the See of Rome. Gregorio Leti, historiographer to Charles II. of England, was born in Milan in 1630,
and he resided in Italy until riotous living and consequent
poverty tempted him to better his fortunes by apostasy at
Lucerne. That Protestants should look on him as an authority in matters which regard the Papacy, is one of the curiosi-
ties of literature ; for the Swiss Calvinists deemed it their duty
to order their hangman to burn his works at the place of execution. By order of the Genevan Council, which Leti styled
"an Inquisition more horrible than that of Rome " (1), the
Itinerary, the *Languishing Vatican*, and the *Political Balance*
were cast into the flames, being pronounced " contrary to faith,
and dangerous to morality and to the State " ; and their author
was deprived of the Genevan citizenship which his diatribes
against the Scarlet Woman had merited for him. Leti himself did not dare to insist upon the truth of his allegations
against Sixtus V.; when the dauphin of France asked him
concerning the matter, he replied that when a thing was well

(1) Leti says that Pope Paul IV. derived his idea of establishing the Holy Office from a
perusal of Calvin's book against Servetus ; and that the Pontiff so informed the Sacred College in a public consistory. Leti gives as his authority for this assertion a book by Mendi,
entitled *The Revolutions in Rome against the Tribunal of the Inquisition* ; but since
Cantù was unable to unearth that work, we may safely refuse to accept such an account of
the origin of the Roman Inquisition.

imagined, it was as good as truth. Certainly the little Felix Peretti, clothed in rags and taking care of pigs, forms a poetical picture for one who afterward beholds him under the light emitted by the triple crown, and who would seize an opportunity to moralize on the mutability of human fortunes ; but the annals of his times show that the boy came from a family which, though humble, was not plunged in abject poverty. His father was chief magistrate—*priore* of Montalto, his native commune. As for Leti's narrative of the election of the cardinal of Montalto (so Peretti had been generally styled) to the tiara, we ask the good sense of the reader to decide whether the Sacred College, after only five days of Conclave, would have elected a man who was capable of playing *Puncinello* as Leti represents him as having played it. And we must remember that Peretti and all his characteristics were very well known by his fellow cardinals, and that therefore we cannot avoid regarding them as fools, if they were deceived in the manner described by the Milanese apostate, in a work written a century after the event. Having told us how Peretti had gone among the electors to urge his own candidacy, coughing and tottering so as to appear more dead than alive, Leti thus describes the final scene. " As soon as he saw that he was sure of the tiara, Montalto rose to his feet, and without waiting until the counting was finished, he threw out into the centre of the hall the staff which he had always used when walking, and stood perfectly erect, so that he appeared to be a foot taller than he had been. But what was much more astonishing, he spat up to the ceiling (1) with a strength such as a man of thirty would scarcely have shown. Perceiving this, the cardinals exchanged glances, and the cardinal-dean seeing that the cardinals of San Sisto and Alessandria made gestures of repentance, exclaimed : ' Wait a moment. There is an error in the votes ; the count is wrong.' But Montalto intrepidly cried ' It is correct' ; and immediately chanted the *Te Deum Laudamus* in so high and sonorous a tone that his voice rang through the hall, although two hours previously he could not utter a word without coughing two or three

(1) We leave to the reader other reflections as to the probability of this exhibition, and merely ask him to remember the height of the rooms in the Vatican, and to note that Leti does not say that Sixtus spat toward the ceiling, but up to it—*sputò nella sofitta.*

times. ... When a master of ceremonies asked him, as is
customary, whether he accepted the Popedom, he turned
upon the questioner a grave and majestic countenance, and
replied : ' We cannot accept what we have already accepted ;
but nevertheless we would accept still another, because we
feel that we have sufficient vigor and talent to rule, with the
divine help, two worlds, to say nothing of one Popedom.'
These words were pronounced so loudly that all heard them,
and Farnese turned to Santa Severina, and said : ' These gentlemen thought to elect a gudgeon, whom they could rule at
will ; but I see that we have a Pope who will hold us all as
gudgeons.' ... While the masters of ceremonies were vesting
him with the pontifical robes, they were thunderstruck on
seeing the agility which he displayed in donning the robes,
moving his arms with incredible ease and vigor, just as
though, as it was observed by one who was present, there
were danger in delay.   Then Cardinal Rusticucci, who was at
his side, and remarked the wonderful change, whispered in
his ear : ' Holy Father, the Pontificate is an excellent medicine ; it makes aged cardinals grow young, and sick ones
healthy.'   And the Pope replied : ' So we have learned by
experience.'"   But let us leave the phantasmagorias of
Leti, and study the real Sixtus V., as he is depicted by Cicarelli (1), a contemporary and reliable author ; by Novaez,
Tempesti, Segretain, and Cautù (2).

Felix Peretti was born at Montalto, near Ascoli, in 1521.
In his eleventh year an uncle, a Franciscan Conventual, having observed the boy's talent and piety, encouraged him to
join the disciples of St. Francis ; and in time he arrived at
the highest dignities of the order.   It is recorded that in 1552,
while he was preaching in the church of Santi Apostoli in
Rome, there was handed to him a paper containing the points
on which he had been dilating, with the assertion " Thou

(1) *Life of Sixtus V.*, Foligno, 1610.

(2) The reader will scarcely look to Don Pasquino for information concerning Sixtus V.;
but some of that worthy's effusions are peculiarly pungent. Thus, when the Pontiff revived
certain indictments which Gregory XIII., his too lenient predecessor, had disregarded,
Pasquino described a dialogue between the statues of Sts. Peter and Paul in front of the
Vatican Basilica. St. Peter is leaving the square ; and St. Paul asks him why he is going.
Peter replies : " I am in danger. I may be arrested for having denied my Master. " Then
Paul reflected : " Then I also must flee ; for Sixtus will charge me with my persecutions of
the Christians."

diest " placed opposite each section. As most of the points were on the all-important matter of justification, then so fearfully travestied by Protestantism, Peretti deemed it prudent to forestall any possible charge of heresy by sending the letter to the grand-inquisitor, Michael Ghislieri, afterward Pope St. Pius V. Ghislieri, calm but inexorable, came to the friar's cell to examine him on the alleged misrepresentations of Catholic doctrine ; and Peretti never forgot the terrible impression which the interview produced in his soul. But Ghislieri was both charmed with the manner of the friar, and pleased with his theological ability and accuracy ; from that day the warmest friendship united them. Peretti was a bosom friend of St. Philip Neri, St. Ignatius Loyola, and many other zealous persons who were then resident in Rome; and as he rivalled them all in a desire to banish all scandals from the sanctuary, he made many enemies. When he undertook the duties of inquisitor in the Venetian dominions, the jealousy of the Most Serene endangered his life on two occasions ; and in later years men were wont to say that when he departed from Venice, he had given as a reason that he had vowed to become Pope, and that therefore he could not remain to be strangled. Pius IV. appointed Peretti one of his theologians at the Council of Trent ; and afterward sent him as legate to Spain in the matter of the celebrated Carranza (1). Raised to the Sacred College in 1570, and made archbishop of Fermo, he resigned his diocese in 1577, that he might devote all his time to an edition of the Fathers which Pius IV. had ordered him to prepare. While engaged in this task, he was encouraged by the admiring friendship of St. Charles Borromeo, and he was supervising the publication of the *Works of St. Ambrose* when he heard of the death of Gregory XIII., which had occurred on April 10, 1585. In the ensuing Conclave, there were six parties among the forty-two cardinals who were present. The first was headed by Farnese ; the second by d'Este ; the third by the cardinal of Alessandria ; the fourth by the cardinal dei Medici ; the fifth by d'Altemps ; the sixth by the cardinal of St. Sixtus, a nephew of the late Pontiff. Fourteen of the cardinals seemed

(1) See our Vol. II., p. 400.

to their brethren to be worthy of the tiara ; and among them was Peretti, now generally styled the cardinal of Montalto. Cicarelli says : " Montalto was a learned man, quiet and amiable to all. He depended on no one, having few relations ; his nearest of kin were two sons of his sister, who were too young to aspire to any office or dignity. His zeal for religion was ardent, and his nature was benign. During the course of his reign, the effects of his goodness pleased many, and enraged others. His election was facilitated by his great dexterity in honoring the cardinals, in lauding them, in amplifying their authority, and in auguring for them every happiness. He had led a tranquil life, far from the tumults of the world in a little villa near St. Mary Major's, where he dwelled in great humility and with a small household. When he sometimes joined the other cardinals to discuss difficult matters, he was never contentious, and he tried little to bring them to his way of thinking ; on the contrary, he yielded easily to others. He sustained injury and outrage without bitterness ; sometimes, in the consistory, he heard himself styled ' the ass of the March of Ancona,' but either he feigned not to have heard the remark, or he affected to regard it as a bit of pleasantry. Nay, more ; the morning after his nephew was assassinated, he manifested in the consistory no sign of trouble, nor did he demand any satisfaction ; in fact, had it not been known that he loved his relatives tenderly, he would have been deemed without feeling. But he bore such things, so as not to make himself odious. When there was question of princes and their affairs, he excused and defended them, unless the dignity and jurisdiction of the Holy See were involved ; of these he was always a protector. He was ever polite, not only to his own, but to strangers. Owing to these and other virtues, the way of the Pontificate was easily open to him. And he was greatly aided by the fact that all the cardinals knew that the king of Spain loved him, and esteemed him as a very learned and very virtuous cardinal. And his cause was served no less by his having never shown any sign of ambition, and by his having been ever ready to conciliate the other cardinals by every kind of good service." It was testimony like this that forced

Ranke to reject the tale of Leti, and to say of that romancer's imputations : "It is not by such means that the highest dignities are obtained " (1). And Sismondi, who would have but too gladly pronounced another verdict, after having reviewed our Pontiff's career, declared : " He occupied a glorious place in the midst of a series of Pontiffs who were celebrated alike for the purity of their morals, for the sincerity of their religious zeal, and for forgetfulness of their personal interests " (2).

From the day of his coronation, May 1, 1585, Sixtus V. seemed to realize that his reign was to be of short duration, for he entered upon it with impetuous zeal, and continued in that course until his death. Although his contemporaries agree in stating that he was exceedingly amiable in private life, still he was never known to. laugh; and they say that when indignant, his language cut to the quick (3). Sixtus V. was certainly severe ; but probably such a temperament was providential after the reign of the gentle Gregory XIII. Gregory (Buoncompagni) was a wise and irreproachable administrator in theory ; but the view of crime excited only his tears, and the wicked could always count on his clemency. During his reign assassinations were of hourly occurrence ; each noble was at least suspected of keeping a troop of *bravi* in his pay. Sixtus determined that his justice should be inexorable ; he renewed the edict of Gregory against the carrying of fire-arms, and unlike that Pontiff, a few days after his installation he caused two brothers, who had violated the law, to be hung at the bridge of San Angelo. Thirty years previously, Attilio Braschi had murdered his cousin, together with that relative's wife and two children. The trial had begun, but influence had caused its proceedings to be quashed. Sixtus ordered the trial to be resumed, and justice to be administered; whereupon Rome read the pasquinade which we have mentioned. The enemies of the Pope-Kings are prone to dwell upon this side of the character of Sixtus V.; and

---

(1) *Papacy in the Sixteenth and Seventeenth Centuries*, b. IV., no. 4.
(2) *History of the Italian Republics*, vol. XVI., p. 188.
(3) " *Radevano il pelo.*" TEMPESTI : *Life of Sixtus V.*, vol. I., p. 123. Rome, 1754.— *Sixtus V. Supreme Pontiff*, MS. in the Altieri Library in Rome.—*Life of Sixtus V., Corrected by His Own Hand*, MS. in the same Library, cited by Ranke and Cantù.

they leave their hearers possessed with the idea that severi--
ty was his most salient characteristic. But our Pontiff actuated many beneficent projects for the temporal welfare of
his subjects ; and death alone prevented the actuation of others which he had devised. Thus, he endeavored to increase
both wool and silk industries among his people. To give
an impetus to the latter, he decreed that in every acre of land
at least five mulberry trees should be planted immediately,
the Papal treasury bearing the expense ; he devoted a large
portion of his own villa, now the Villa dei Massimi, to the
raising of silk worms ; he established weaving looms in the
houses surrounding the Piazza di Termini ; and when a Venetian Jew, Magino di Gabriele, promised to furnish the secret of producing two yields of silk a year, Sixtus allowed to
him the monopoly for sixty years, permitted him and his
family to reside outside the Ghetto, and gave him a royalty of an ounce of gold for each pound of silk, besides five
per cent. of all the profits which the pontifical treasury might
gain by his invention (1). Sixtus V. effected much for artistic and antiquarian Rome. He raised the great obelisk
in the Square of the Vatican ; he completed the dome of St.
Peter's ; he made many new streets ; the number of beautiful
improvements which he made in the churches of the city is·
marvellous ; he designed and began the palace of Monte Ca-
vallo (the Quirinal), and he built that of the Lateran ; among
the many works of antiquity which he restored, we mention
only the horses of Praxiteles and Phydias now admired on
the hill of the Quirinal. By the fostering care of the Popes·
the ancient Roman aqueducts had been kept in constant repair, and the Eternal City had always been the envy of all
European capitals on account of its superabundance of the
purest water ; but Sixtus V. brought an additional supply in
the Acqua Felice, at an enormous expense and in defiance of
the opinion of the best engineers, and the main outlet of this
aqueduct (near the Baths of Diocletian) is one of the ornaments of Rome. But we must refer the reader to the pages
of Cicarelli, if he desires to know all that Sixtus V. effected, in
five years, for the culture and comfort of his temporal subjects.

(1) CANTU ; *Heretics of Italy*, Discourse XXXIX.

Sixtus V. found the financial affairs of the Holy See in an evil condition. After the lavish expenditures of Leo X., all undertaken for worthy, and some for holy purposes, Adrian VI. had succeeded to an empty treasury, and with great difficulty he managed to send 40,000 ducats to help the Hungarians in their fight against the Turks, and he was scarcely able to equip three ships of war to aid the gallant Hospitalers in their defence of Rhodes. Clement VII., after seeing his capital sacked by the troops of Charles V., had been obliged, in his efforts to succor that same Charles V. when trying to resist the Islamites, to levy unusual taxes and make heavy indebtedness for his successors. Paul III. had been forced to demand a general subsidy from his subjects; and when St. Pius V. was obliged to bear far more than his share in the prosecution of the triumphant campaign of Lepanto, it seemed a miracle that he should have been able to aid the French court, to succor the persecuted Catholics of England, to help Mary Stuart, and to give two millions of golden scudi to the poor of his States. "Sixtus V. did not introduce a good system of finance; but, at that period, who· knew such a one? Nevertheless, after having spent 600,000 scudi in warring against the Turks, 50,000 on the obelisks, 200,000 on the aqueduct of the Acqua Felice, 800,000 in provisioning Rome, he left in his treasury four millions which were mentioned, to our surprise, in the Treaty of Tolentino" (1). One of the most important acts of this Pontificate was the institution of several new Roman Congregations. Already there were the Congregations of the Index, that of the Inquisition, one for the Execution and Interpretation of the Tridentine Decrees, another of Bishops and Regulars, the. Segnatura, and the Consulta; and Sixtus V. added greatly to the importance of these. He instituted the Congregation for the foundation of new dioceses; that of Rites and Ceremonies; and several for the consideration of cases brought for decision by the Holy See. The temporal policy of Sixtus V. rivalled that of the grandest of the Roman Pontiffs. He intended to crush the Turk by an alliance of Poland with Persia, a conquest of Egypt, and a piercing of the Isthmus of Suez in order to re-

(1) CANTU ; *loc. cit.*

store the commercial primacy of the Italians. His chief
motive, one which animated his every political act, was the
preservation of the faith; therefore he excited Philip II. to
undertake the invasion of England and a vindication of Mary
Stuart, and he meditated an attack on Geneva. All of these
points would merit our consideration; but our limits force
us to treat chiefly of the relations between Sixtus V. and
Henry of Navarre.

Sixtus V. understood thoroughly the *Gesta Dei per Francos:* the prominent and, we may say it, the necessary part
which Providence has assigned to France in the movement of
civilization. It was his influence which counterbalanced
that of Philip II. over the League, and prevented the triumph of that monarch's egotistic policy, thus assuring the
political and religious unity of France. The first great demonstration of the reign of Sixtus V. was the Bull of Excommunication and Deposition pronounced against Henry IV.
When treating of the attempted Protestantization of France,
and of the conversion of Henry IV., we traced the events
which compelled Sixtus to issue this decree; and it ought not
be necessary to prove that in this act the Pontiff was not the
servile instrument of the interested anger of Philip II. In
pronouncing Henry of Navarre excommunicated, and therefore incapable of wearing the crown of France, Sixtus V.
simply applied a principle of the Canon Law and of the funda-
mental law of France. At that time the laws of all Christian
nations condemned the relapsed heretic to the stake ; Henry
of Navarre was civilly dead, as the humblest Catholic magistrate would have declared, but the Pontiff alone was sufficiently high-placed to pronounce definitive sentence in the
case of a sovereign. If the reader will read the Bull *Ab immer-
sa,* he will perceive that it was not an ebullition of passion, a
mere satisfaction of obstinate prejudice; but rather a pronouncement by the head of Christian society, insisting upon
the right of that society to protect its dearest interests. Nor
did Sixtus propose, as Philip II. would have had him propose, to do any more than vindicate the principle which was
involved; he did not intend to obstinately refuse all future
compromises which the march of events might necessitate.

As we have seen, when considering the conduct of Henry IV. after his excommunication, this very Bull was no obstacle to an understanding between the prince and the Pope, once that the former showed an inclination to follow the path of duty. The following are the principal passages of the Bull *Ab immensa*. "Sixtus, Bishop, Servant of the servants of God, in perpetual remembrance of this Act. The authority accorded to the Blessed Peter and his successors, by the immense power of the Eternal King, exceeds all the powers of the kings and princes of the earth. Resting on the immovable rock, never deviating from what is just, neither in adversity nor in prosperity, it emits its infallible judgments over all. It watches with particular care that the divine laws be not violated; and if it finds men resisting the ordinances of God, it visits them with severe punishment. Be they ever so powerful, it expels them from their thrones, as so many ministers of the haughty Lucifer, and it humbles them in the dust. Therefore, in accordance with the care imposed upon us for all the churches, peoples, and nations; and in order that the destruction of impious and detestable monstrosities may contribute to the salvation of souls, both during our pontificate and for all time to come, and bring repose to all parts of Christendom, and especially to that great kingdom of France where the Christian religion has so flourished, and the faith and devotion of whose kings have been so grand, leading them to perform so many services to the Roman Church that they have merited the glorious surname of Most Christian; and finally, that we may not be charged by God with having neglected our duty; we are now compelled to use our weapons, spiritual indeed, but stronger than any ramparts, against those two children of ire, Henry of Bourbon, once king of Navarre, and Henry of Bourbon, once prince of Condé. This Henry, once a king, from the early days of his youth, followed the heresies and errors of Calvin, and gave to them his constant support, down to the time when he yielded to the pious and frequent exhortations of the illustrious Charles IX., king of France, and of our dear daughter in Christ, Queen Catharine, and also of his uncle and our dear son, the cardinal Charles of Bourbon, as well as to the prayers

of the duke Louis of Montpensier; when, after having examined the demonstrations of many eminent and virtuous theologians, he was converted, as was believed, to the Catholic
Apostolic Roman faith, and publicly abjured and anathematized in Paris all opinions which are contrary to the Catholic
faith, formally professing that same Catholic faith. ... But a
short time afterward, this vacillating prince renounced the
Catholic faith, his obedience to this Apostolic See, and all that
he had sworn to observe. ... We, compelled by our duty to
employ the sword of punishment against these men, and
grieving because their many crimes force us to severity
against the degenerate descendants of the illustrious family of
Bourbon, which has ever been distinguished for virtue and
for its veneration of this Apostolic See; do now pronounce
from this sublime throne, in virtue of the power given to us
by the King of kings, and by the authority of Sts. Peter and
Paul and our own, that Henry, once king, and also Henry of
Condé, are relapsed and impenitent heretics, guilty of high-
treason to the Divine Majesty, and enemies of Christian orthodoxy; and that they have incurred the censures contained
in the sacred Canons and Apostolic Constitutions against relapsed and impenitent heretics, and that by this fact they and
their descendants are incapable of succeeding to any duchy,
principality, domain, or kingdom whatsoever, and especially to
the kingdom of France. ... Over and above all this, and in
so far as it is necessary, we deprive forever Henry, once king
of Navarre, and the other Henry, of all their principalities
and fiefs; and we declare them and their descendants forever
incapable of possessing or succeeding to any principality,
duchies, fiefs, or kingdoms whatsoever, and especially to the
kingdom of France. ... We forbid all persons to obey their
laws and orders; and declare that all who disregard this interdict are excommunicated, by the very fact." This Bull is
dated the 5th of the Ides of Sept., 1585.

Elsewhere we have descanted sufficiently on the principle,
universally acknowledged in Catholic times, that a heretic
could not wear a Christian crown (1). Here we shall remark
merely that, so far as France is concerned, if there was no

(1) Vol. II., ch. xv.

precise text of civil legislation, as there was in other countries, which declared that the Roman Pontiff could and ought
depose a heretical prince ; if in France the kings were slow to
proclaim a supremacy which threatened their omnipotence ;
it is certain that even there the deposing power was expressly recognized as possessed by the French bishops (1), and
that French kings so often invoked the deposing power of
the Pope in their quarrels with others, that they equivalently proclaimed the supreme political magistracy of the Holy
See. This fact was well understood by the League ; and
therefore it had solicited the Bull *Ab immensa*, and Sixtus
knew that he could not refuse it. But the Pontiff differed
from the League on one very important point. So horrible
was the idea of a Protestant king to the great Catholic heart
of France, that it could not suppose the possibility of the culprit being ever cleansed from his stain. Here was an opportunity for the House of Lorraine; and Guise and his partisans availed themselves of the stepping-stone for their vaulting
ambition. Loudly proclaiming the theory that religious contumacy was so terrible a crime that its consequent inability
for office could not be removed, they influenced the Faculty
of Paris, too often subservient to the powerful of the nonce, to
decree excommunication against all who would presume to say
that a relapsed heretic could be received to penance, and then
reinstated in his dignities. Sixtus V. was not the man to wait
a moment in rebuking this appeal to anarchy in an absurd
and illogical defiance of his supreme authority. Hence he
ordered the secretary of the Consistory to write to the arrogant Faculty : "His Holiness has condemned most strongly
the audacity of the Sorbonne in daring to usurp a power
which belongs only to this Holy See and to Councils" (2).
The partisans of the League could not, or would not see, for
a long time, that while it was necessary to the maintenance
of Catholicism in France that the relapsed Bourbon should
be denounced juridically as incapable of reigning over the
Land of the Lilies, it might be advisable for the supreme judge
of Christendom to exempt the culprit, if really repentant, from

(1) *Ibid.*, p. 216.

(2) "*Detestata est Sanctitas Sua Sorbonæ temeritatem, quæ sibi vindicare audeat
quæ hujus Sanctæ Sedis opera sunt, et ad eam et Concilia spectant.*"

the perpetual duration of his punishment. Sixtus V. was ever willing to make this exception; for he felt that the interests of France demanded such a mitigation of the canonical penalty. Undoubtedly the Guises had attained great popularity in France; and when the last of the Valois would be summoned to his dread account, the proximity of the Guises to the throne would be considered in conjunction with their sacrifices for the faith and their country, and would form a good title to the crown. And certainly Catholicism had nothing but good to expect from the House of Lorraine. But Sixtus V. could not forget that Henry of Navarre was in possession, before his excommunication, of a direct hereditary right; and this right of heredity was then regarded as a guarantee of stability in a government. Therefore the Pontiff reflected that if he wished to foil the schemes of Philip II., who was aiming to secure the French crown for himself or for one of his family; and if he desired to avoid the danger to France of having her crown perpetually disputed by one who was strong in his right of blood; he must direct his policy so as to effect the return of Henry de Bourbon to the Church. In this design he was greatly encouraged by the knowledge that, although Henry had been addicted to dissimulation; and although he had shown that religious dogmas had as yet but little hold on his mind or heart; it was certain that the prince shared none of the Huguenot animosities toward Rome, and that he also realized very well that a French monarch must, of necessity, be a Catholic. Animated by these considerations, when the time came that Sixtus applied to himself, in reference to Henry III., the words of God in regard to Saul (repenting for having made Saul king), the Pontiff would not aid the Lorraines when they attacked the "king of the *mignons*," and he refused to give his niece in marriage to the duke de Guise.

On Dec. 22, 1588, Henry III. procured the murder of Duke Henry de Guise (1); the cardinal de Guise was impris-

(1) The more exalted of the Leaguers had resolved to change the Law of Succession, even during the lifetime of Henry III., in favor of Henry de Guise. Henry III. prohibited Guise from entering the capital, but the order was disregarded; the bourgeois took arms to defend his claim; barricades were erected, the royal guard disarmed, and the king was a prisoner in his palace. Those who defend Guise from the charge of criminal ambition point

oued, and then murdered ; and the archbishop of Lyons, the dukes de Nemours and d'Elbeuf, the marquis de Joinville, and the president de Neuilly were imprisoned. When the Papal legate, Cardinal Morosini, presented himself for an audience with the wretched monarch, he was refused admittance, and received the following letter. "My lord legate, now I am a king, and I have resolved to suffer no more outrages. I shall keep this resolution, strengthened by the example of our Holy Father the Pope, remembering well that he is wont to say that we must make men obey us, and that we must punish those who offend us. I shall see you to-morrow, if so you desire. Adieu. Henry." The crimes of Henry III. had long previously deprived him of the respect of his people ; and now, incapable of leading the League in a defence of Catholicism and France, he had struck down its head. Thus he broke the last tie which bound his subjects to him, and he forced the League into revolutionary courses. The murder of the cardinal de Guise drew upon him the sentence of excommunication, launched by our Pontiff on May 5, 1589. When Pope Sixtus heard of the assassination of Henry III. by the fanatical Clement, he refused the request of the pious widow, Louise de Vaudemont,.to order the solemn requiem which the Papal court always celebrates for the sovereigns who have died in the communion of the Church. Some writers have concluded from this fact that the Pontiff believed those who said that the wretched Henry died before he had an opportunity to confess. But it is certain that the

---

to the fact of the non-seizure of the royal person. While Catharine was negotiating for the preservation of some shadow of authority for her son, he escaped to Chartres ; but he soon made a treaty with the League, which rendered that body master of the government, Guise being made lieutenant-general of the kingdom. Henry de Guise, however, was not enough of a revolutionist to receive the crown from a seditious mob, though he might have accepted it from the deputies of the nation. Surprised at his moderation, the Parisians assented to his making a treaty with Henry III. (the Edict of Union, July 21, 1588) by which the king again declared himself the head of the League, accorded a general amnesty for the past, gave to the League several cities as "places of surety," and convoked the States-General at Bloix. This assembly declared the Edict of Union the law of the state, and added clauses which further weakened the royal authority. Henry III. now resolved the death of Guise ; and the rash soldier despised the warnings which he received in reference to the design. He entered the royal council, as was his custom : ten assassins attacked him ; he fought to the death ; and died, exclaiming, "God, have mercy !" This murder only increased the determination of the Leaguers ; the victim's brother, the duke de Mayenne, took his place ; the Sorbonne declared all Frenchmen free from allegiance to Henry III.; and this prince had no resource but to throw himself into the arms of Henry of Navarre.

royal widow sent Montmort to the Pope with an attestation as to all the circumstances of her husband's demise; and that this document (1) told of Henry's repentance, of his submission to the excommunication, and of the piety with which he received the last Sacraments. The real reason for the rigor of Sixtus is found in a letter which d'Ossat, French envoy at the Vatican, wrote to the queen-dowager, on Aug. 7, 1590. D'Ossat gives a conversation which he held with Cardinal Santa Severina, in which his Eminence told him that the Bull of Excommunication mentioned as its cause not only the murder of the cardinal de Guise, but also the incarceration of the cardinal de Bourbon and of the archbishop of Lyons; and that since the wounded monarch, although he had time, had not, by ordering the liberation of the prelate, furnished the really efficacious proof of his repentance, the Holy See could not glorify a sovereign who was execrated by his people, both because of his personal immorality, and because he had assured the progress of heresy, so far as his power permitted. We shall say no more about the policy of Sixtus V. in reference to Henry of Navarre; as to the consequences of that policy, we have noted them when treating of Henry's conversion.

CHAPTER XXIX.

THE PONTIFICATE OF CLEMENT VIII. CAMPANELLA.

On Jan. 8, 1592, fifty-two cardinals entered into Conclave to elect a successor to Pope Innocent IX., who had occupied the Chair of Peter during only two months. In many previous Conclaves the electors had been beset by difficulties growing out of the pretensions of this or that sovereign to a controlling voice in their selection of an incumbent of the primatial See of Christendom; but in the present case their Eminences were confronted by a threat, on the part of a prince who had frequently merited well of the Church, to

(1) This certificate was signed by Charles d'Orleans. grand prior of France; the duke d'Epernon; the marshal de Biron; the grand ecuyer Roger de Bellegarde; the captain of the body guards, Chateauvieux; by d'O, governor of Paris; and by five others.

refuse obedience to a Pontiff who would not have been chosen from among those whom he had designated as acceptable to himself. Philip II. of Spain, ever intent on his projects for Spanish aggrandizement at the expense of France, was playing the League against Henry IV.; and he felt that his success depended on the attitude of the Holy See toward the French monarch. In his endeavor to secure the election of a Pope whom he might expect to favor his views, Philip relied upon the efforts of the cardinal of Montalto, who, although a nephew of Sixtus V. and therefore naturally favorable to Henry, was nevertheless the head of the Spanish faction in the Sacred College. Montalto proposed to his colleagues the name of Cardinal Santorio, the most esteemed of the five candidates urged by the Spanish king. Immediately it became evident that Santorio had the probabilities in his favor; for thirty-six cardinals, the necessary two-thirds, appeared disposed to vote for him, when the *scrutinium* should be held, Madruzzi (the head of the Austrian party) having brought over his followers to an alliance with the pro-Spaniards. Then occurred an incident both sad and amusing. Montalto and Madruzzi, deeming the election as good as made, proceeded to the cell of Santorio with their news. The tidings were overheard by some of Santorio's attendants; and in accordance with an old custom which gave to the domestics of a Pope-elect all of his former household trappings, they began to sack the cell, as an earnest of what they were to have when they would pillage their master's palace. In the meantime, Santorio was informing the cardinals who were assembled in the Pauline Chapel, that he would assume the name of Clement; but it was soon found that although the next Pope would indeed be a Clement, Santorio would not be the man. When the ballot was announced, it appeared that some of the electors had changed their minds as to the propriety of electing one of King Philip's favored five; for there were not thirty-six votes for Santorio. Again and again their Eminences tried to agree, but in vain; and finally, Cardinal Ascanio Colonna insisting that " it seemed to be the will of God that Santorio should not be Pope," attention was turned to other candidates. It was soon demonstrated that one of the pro-Spanish five could not be elected; and then the name of Ippolito Aldobrandini, whom Philip had designated as the least obnoxious of his non-partisans, was brought forward. Aldobrandini was universally respected as learned, prudent, and above all, holy. On Jan. 20 he was elected, and assumed the name of Clement VIII. (1)

Ippolito Aldobrandini was a son of a patrician jurisconsult of Florence who had fled from his native city on account of difficulties with the Medici, and had settled in Urbino. The young Ippolito won the friendship of Alexander Farnese, bishop of Spoleto; and the prelate accorded him a pension which enabled him to study at first in Rome, and finally in Bologna, where he took his degrees. Attached to the papal nunciature in Spain, he so distinguished himself that on his return to Rome he was made an auditor of the *Ruota*. Sixtus V. raised him to the Sacred College, and sent him as legate to Poland, where he contributed to the liberation of Maximilian of Austria, then a prisoner in that country. This action greatly pleased Philip of Spain, and therefore he afterward designated Aldobrandini as his choice for the tiara, if no one of his five candidates could secure it. The contemporary Cicarelli says of the election of Clement VIII. that all Rome rejoiced at the elevation of one in whom were united "integrity of life, great learning, and diplomatic skill." The most anxious hours of Pope Clement VIII. were those which were occupied with the affairs of Henry IV.; but we have seen already his success in inducing that monarch to ignore the invalid absolution at Saint-Denis, and to be really reconciled with the Church by that Papal authority which had censured him. As a souvenir of this happy event, the Pontiff ordered medals to be struck off, bearing his own portrait on one side, and that of Henry on the other; and on his part the king decreed that ever after the French monarchs should address a cardinal as "Dear Cousin," instead of "Dear Friend," as had hitherto been customary. But three months after the reconciliation of Henry, there happened an event which, had the king not been en-

(1) In his autobiography, Santorio says of this incident of his life: "That was the most painful moment I ever experienced. Shall I dare to admit it? Yes; I was so oppressed by anxiety, that drops of blood oozed from every part of my body."

dowed with more than an ordinary measure of good sense, would have caused a serious rupture between the newly-made friends. On Dec. 27, 1595, an attempt on the life of Henry was made by one Jean Châtel, the son of a Parisian woollen draper. Fortunately, at the instant when the blow was given, the king had bent his body in order to raise two officers who had knelt before him; and the dagger merely broke one of his teeth. When the wretched Châtel was questioned, he declared that he was a Parisian; that he had studied under the Jesuits; and that he had learned from those teachers, as well as from other priests, that it was a duty to use every means for the defence of religion against impious tyranny. The magistrates of Paris immediately searched the Jesuit college; and in the room of Guignard, the librarian, they found some writings which contained very bitter denunciations of both Henry **IV.** and his predecessor. The unlucky librarian was arrested; and although he claimed rightly the benefit of the general amnesty proclaimed by Henry, he was condemned to be hung because he had not destroyed the obnoxious papers. All the members of the Society were expelled from the kingdom, excepting in a few provinces, where the parliaments showed a knowledge of logic and an appreciation of justice. When Clement VIII. heard of these outrages, he protested most vigorously to d'Ossat, the French ambassador, that it would have been but just to punish any individuals of the Society, had they been proved guilty; but that every principle of right and equity was violated by the expulsion of all the members of an order which had merited well of the Church (1). One of the curious features of this parliamentary persecution was the fact that the pretendedly zealous magistrates of Paris had themselves been guilty, and to a much greater degree, of the crime which they condemned in Guignard. They had made war against Henry the Huguenot with guns and bayonets, not with mere pen and ink; and by what right did they refuse to Guignard the benefit of an amnesty behind which they sheltered themselves? No one will ever charge Sismondi with partiality for the Society of Jesus; but he says of this

(1) BÉRAULT-BERCASTEL; *History of the Church*, vol. III.

parliamentary madness: "We know not which is the most condemnable ; a fanaticism which armed an assassin against the king, or the cruelty, undue haste, and cowardly servility of the magistracy, a body which was not content with putting the young culprit to death amid atrocious torments, but punished even innocent men whose olden offences had been forgiven, taking no time for investigation, and exiling in forty-eight hours a religious society which had not been heard in its own defence, and for an attempt at regicide in which it had no share.   And this was not only a scandalous iniquity, but an act of political cowardice ; for this parliament which condemned the entire Jesuit order because of certain writings against the royal authority which had been penned by some of those religious, was the same parliament which, only in the previous year, had sanctioned rebellion, and had at least tacitly approved the murderous deed of James Clement. In reality, all this severity tended simply to excuse the parliament's own preceding opposition to the royal authority " (1).   It is not strange that Pope Clement VIII. should have insisted, whenever he gave audience to d'Ossat, upon the necessity of reparation being made to the Jesuits, so far as it could be made, by his Majesty of France ; and it is to the honor of Henry IV. that he recognized the guilt of the Parisian parliament.   In vain did Sully urge upon the royal consideration the well-known predilection of the Jesuits for the Spanish monarch, and the consequent theory that the Society could not be friendly to Henry ; the king shrewdly replied : " I know very well that the Jesuits are much more interested in the grandeur of the House of Austria-Spain than in that of the House of Bourbon ; but the reason of that fact is patent.   In Spain the Jesuits are honored ; but in France they experience only contradictions and affronts. And then remember that if the king of Spain has won them by benefits, they must be capable of gratitude ; therefore I too have it in my power to attach them to my interests.   Finally, if the Jesuits are as obstinately perverse as they are said to be, prudence bids me to conquer them by generosity, rather than drive them to desperation."   A royal decree was

(1) *History of the French* ; vol. XXI.

issued, recalling the Society to France; but the parliament refused to register the document, and deputed its president to lay a protest at the feet of Henry. The parliamentary discourse was artfully prepared; but the monarch's improvised reply was a thorough refutation of its arguments; it was as strong in its logic as it was moderate in its terminology. "Gentlemen, I am grateful to you for the anxiety which you display for the safety of my royal person. But I know your sentiments thoroughly; whereas you are ignorant of mine. When I began to think of recalling the Jesuits, I reflected that two sorts of persons would oppose me; namely, the followers of the pretended Reformation, and certain ecclesiastics of not very edifying life. The Jesuits are reproached with drawing unto themselves men of talent; but I esteem them for that very reason, for when I levy an army, I want good soldiers, and with all my heart I wish that you would admit only the worthy into your body. Men say that the Jesuits enter into every city, as best they can; but did I not enter into my kingdom in the same manner? You would implicate them in the affair of Châtel; but Châtel himself did not implicate them. And even if a Jesuit had struck that blow, of which I only think in order to thank God for my humiliation and for my escape, would it be just to punish all the Jesuits? Must all the Apostles suffer for the act of one Judas? You cast up the League to the Jesuits; but that association was a contagion of the time. The Jesuits thought that they were doing right; and many others were likewise deceived. You say that the king of Spain makes use of the Jesuits; and I reply that I desire to do the same thing. Since the whole world deems the Jesuits useful, I want them in my dominions; and since heretofore they were merely tolerated, I wish that hereafter they be authorized. You may leave this matter in my hands, for I have managed more difficult business." The parliament registered the royal decree.

One of the objects nearest to the heart of Clement VIII. was the conclusion of a treaty of peace between France and Spain; and his efforts were seconded energetically by his legate to Henry, the cardinal Alexander dei Medici, arch-

bishop of Florence, a pious and moderate, but very perspicacious prelate. After many unsuccessful negotiations, during
which the skill and affability of the legate had full scope
for their exercise, peace was finally proclaimed in the Treaty
of Vervins, May 2, 1598; the contracting parties, with the
cardinal as mediator, agreeing to restore matters to the condition in which they had been before the war. But our Pontiff soon found reason for grief in the preparations of Henry
IV. to actuate what had been always the chief aim of his policy, the destruction of the power of Austria. In 1610 the
king was about to head the army for an invasion of the Empire, when the dagger of Ravaillac cut short his career. The
reader may be interested in the following letter which was
written, shortly after this catastrophe, by St. Francis de Sales
to his friend, M. Deshayes. "No death in Europe could be
more lamented than that of the great Henry. But who will
not wonder with you at the vanity and deceitfulness of all the
grandeurs of this world? Here was a prince who was grand
in his ancestry, in his personal valor and victories, in fine,
in every earthly quality; and who would not have thought
that this grandeur had sworn an inviolable fidelity to him, so
that even his last moment would have been enlivened by the
applause of all, as he met a glorious death? One would certainly have thought that so grand a life would terminate amid
the spoils of the Orient, after a final overthrow of heresy and
of Islamism. For this enterprise there would have been an
abundance of time in the fifteen or twenty years which seemed
to be guaranteed to him by his rugged constitution. But
no; this long series of grandeurs finishes in a death which
has no grandeur whatsoever; and he who would almost have
been termed immortal, because of his having escaped from so
many great risks, falls under the ignoble stroke of a dagger
wielded by a nameless youth. The best fortune of this great
monarch was his becoming a son of the Church, and therefore the father of France; his becoming a sheep of the Great
Shepherd, and therefore himself the shepherd of all his
people; the conversion of his heart to God, and thereby con-
verting unto himself the hearts of all good Catholics. This
felicity alone leads me to hope that the sweet mercy of

·Our Heavenly Father moved the royal heart of Henry, in his last moments, to that contrition which is necessary for a happy death " (1).

The eminent prudence of Clement VIII. manifested itself in his attitude during the dispute on the harmony of grace with the free will of man, a dispute which the Dominicans and Jesuits prosecuted with so much violence of language, that their war of words caused as much clamor in Europe as had been produced by the swords of the Huguenots. We shall treat of this matter when we arrive at the subject of Jansenism; here we merely note that by a Brief of Jan. 10, 1595, our Pontiff imposed silence on the vituperative religious, and appointed the celebrated Congregation *de Auxiliis*, composed of eight of the best theologians in Rome, to examine the question. The zeal of Clement VIII. for the propagation of the faith was manifested in his defiance of the wishes of the king of Spain by opening the missionary field of Japan to all the Religious Orders; that monarch having pretended that none but Jesuits, and none of them save his own subjects, should preach the faith to the Japanese. The apostolic labors of St. Francis Xavier and his successors had converted millions of these pagans to the religion of Christ, when, in 1579, the visitor of the Society of Jesus for Japan, Valegnani, was impressed by the fact that his brethren were not sufficiently numerous for the needs of the awaiting harvest. On his return to Rome, he proposed that other religious should be invited to aid in the good work; but many of the Society rejecting the idea, the general laid the matter before the Pontiff, then Gregory XIII. The Holy See did not wish to decide, before consulting the king of Portugal, as the Japanese missions were then under his protection. Perhaps the Portuguese decided against the employment of other religious, and perhaps he returned no reply; at any rate, the affair remained in abeyance until 1585, when, Philip II. having become also king of Portugal, the facile Pope Gregory XIII. was induced to prohibit all religious who were not Jesuits from laboring in Japan. Rohrbacher makes some very pertinent remarks on this decision. "The system of evangelizing and

(1) *Works of St. Francis de Sales*, vol. III.

governing the Christians of Japan through members of only
one Religious Congregation who were all subjects of the same
temporal sovereign, had the advantage of a greater uniformity in administration, so long as that sovereign sustained and
aided that Congregation.   But were discords to arise, terrible
consequences would ensue ; any day the Japanese Christians
might be abandoned like sheep without a shepherd.   And
that is not all.   Let us suppose that the king of Spain and
Portugal will always love and help the Society of Jesus.
May not the English and Dutch merchants suggest to the
Japanese emperor that the Spanish and Portuguese Jesuits
are only the advance guard of the king of Spain, who seeks
to seize on Japan; that for this purpose he names the bishops of Japan, and sends only Jesuits, and Jesuits who are
his subjects, into Japan ; that, in fine, it is for this purpose
that a native Japanese clergy is not formed ?   These Dutchmen and Englishmen know the policy of the Spanish monarch ; and they have dared, the former in order to preserve
their rights, the latter for their national independence, to war
upon him, to expel or kill the Jesuits, and to trample on the
Cross.   Japan should do the same ; or like America, it will
become a Spanish province.   Let us suppose that the heretical merchants of Holland and England said all this to the emperor of Japan.   Would not reasons of State prompt him to
expel the Jesuits, and to exterminate the Christians ?" (1)
The time did come when these Dutchmen and Englishmen
adopted the measures here supposed by the French historian.   Having incited a persecution of the Japanese Christians,
the Dutch loaned their artillery to the sovereign against
whom the converts, in self protection, had revolted ; and the
progeny of Calvin had the satisfaction of seeing the name of
Christ almost ignored in Japan.   Then for years they enjoyed
the privilege of trading with Japan, but only on condition
that they always performed, before landing, what the Japanese called the *ye fumi*, that is, they trampled on the crucifix (2).

(1) *Universal History of the Church*, vol. XXV.

(2) Protestant writers have thought to palliate this sacrilege of the Dutch by saying that
they did not believe in honoring images ; but was that fact an excuse for defiling them?
And the Hollanders knew well that the Japanese pagans regarded the trampling on the Cross
as equivalent to a renunciation of Christianity.   These gentry, however little they knew of

But before the then flourishing infant Church of Japan was visited with dire persecution, the Jesuit missionaries were reinforced by many other apostles; firstly, because of a false report that they had all been expelled from the empire, and secondly, because of the prudent foresight of Clement VIII. In 1592, a rumor reached the Philippine Islands that the Japanese sovereign had banished the Jesuits; and immediately the governor asked Father Pedro Baptista and three other Franciscans to proceed to the care of the young church. Baptista thought of the prohibition of Gregory XIII., and consulted with the best theologians in the Philippines. It was decided unanimously that it was the duty of Baptista, in the circumstances, to go to the aid of Christians who were in danger of suffering a shipwreck of faith; and to strengthen their position, the theologians cited a Bull of Sixtus V. which, they said, revoked that of his predecessor, inasmuch as it allowed the Franciscans to act as missionaries "in all the Indies." The little band of Franciscans went to Japan, and found that the Jesuits were still at their posts. When Pope Clement heard of the state of affairs, he issued a brief permitting the members of all Religious Orders to labor in Japan. Many rushed to the field of toil and martyrdom; and from that day the sons of St. Francis, especially, rivalled the Jesuits in their noble labors.

It was Pope Clement VIII. who decreed the laureate to Torquato Tasso. In 1594, the poet learned that our Pontiff, at the instance of his nephew, the cardinal Aldobrandini, had decreed him the honors of a triumph at the Capitol. "They are preparing my coffin," he replied; but as no poet would dream of declining the laureate, he set out for the Eternal City. On the way from Naples, where he had been residing for some time, he stopped three days with his beloved Benedictines of Montecasino. "If misfortune come to you," said the abbot, "come to us. This monastery is used to giving hospitality to the unhappy." Tasso answered: "I go to Rome to be crowned laureate on the Capitol, taking as companions

the New Testament, had, like most Protestants of to-day, a certain superficial acquaintance with the Old; and they must have remembered the story of Eleazar and the food offered to the idols, even though they might not have known that Christ reprobates those who are ashamed of Him.

of my triumph sickness and poverty. However, I go willing. ly; for I love the Eternal City as the centre of the faith. My refuge has always been the Church,—the Church, my mother, more tender than any mother." Arriving at the gates of the Catholic metropolis, Tasso found an immense multitude—prelates, nobles, knights, and citizens—waiting to salute him and to escort him to the Vatican. Cardinal Aldobrandini took him in his own carriage to the palace, where the Pontiff welcomed him, saying, "We are about to confer upon you the crown of laurel, which you will honor, whereas hitherto it has honored those who have worn it." His reception over, his cardinal protector would have taken Tasso to his own palace to wait for the coronation ceremonies; but the poet felt that his end was drawing near, and begged to be allowed to lodge in the Hieronymite convent of Sant' Onofrio on the Janiculum. In this home of peace, and often reposing under the branches of the oak which, only a few days before (1), had sheltered St. Philip Neri and his class of little Romans, the wearied genius hearkened to the gentle Hieronymites as they prepared him for his last journey. Toward the end he wrote to a friend : "The world has so far conquered as to lead me, a beggar, to the grave; whereas I had thought to have had some profit from that glory which, in spite of those who wish it not, will attend my writings." He made a holy death, in his fifty-second year, on April 25, 1595. During his magnificent funeral ceremonies, which were attended by the entire pontifical court, the laurel crown was placed on his brow. The monument which Cardinal Aldobrandini had designed to erect over the remains of his *protégé* was, for some reason, never undertaken; but Cardinal Bevilacqua, of Ferrara, disinterred the body, and placed it in a small mausoleum in Sant' Onofrio. Afterward, Pius IX., at his private expense, erected a magnificent monument, and placed the remains therein (1857), in a beautifully renovated chapel of the same church.

We have mentioned the name of St. Philip Neri. A firm and tender friendship had united the youths Ippolito Aldobrandini and Philip dei Neri in the year 1535, when they were

---

(1) St. Philip died just one month before Tasso.

making their studies for the priesthood; and when the former was raised to the Supreme Pontificate, he wished to enrol his saintly friend in the Sacred College. But whenever the project was mentioned, Philip affected to regard it as a joke; and the Pontiff soon realized that honors were painful to his humility. The duties of the Popedom and Philip's own preoccupations with his Oratory prevented frequent meetings of the friends; but their correspondence was regular, and its tenor is uniquely interesting. We subjoin two letters which were written while the saint was suffering from a dangerous illness. "Most Holy Father, who am I that cardinals, especially their Eminences of Cusa and Medici, should visit me? I needed a little manna; and therefore the latter procured for me two ounces from the Hospital of Santo Spirito, to which institution he had presented a quantity. He remained with me until the second hour of the night, telling me so many nice things about your Holiness; but I do think that he exaggerated, because I am of opinion that a Supreme Pontiff ought to be transformed into humility itself. At the seventh hour of the night Christ came to me, strengthening me with the Sacrament of His Body. But you have not deigned to come even once to our church; while Christ, who is both God and Man, comes whenever I wish for Him. And you are only a man. Your father was a saintly man; His Father is God. Your mother was the Lady Agnesina, a most holy woman; His mother is the Virgin of virgins. I would say much more, were I willing to yield to my displeasure. Now I command your Holiness to condescend to grant me a favor. I want you to allow me to place among the nuns of the Torre degli Specchi the daughter of Claudio Neri, of whose children you promised, long ago, to take care. Remember that a Supreme Pontiff must keep his promises. Therefore leave this affair to me, allowing me to use your authority, if it be necesary. You will do so, I am sure, especially since I am certain of the girl's vocation; and now I prostrate myself at the feet of your Holiness." Pope Clement replied: "The Pontiff observes that the first part of your letter betrays somewhat of a spirit of ambition, since you make great boast of the visits that cardinals pay you. If you mean to

insinuate that their Eminences are pious men, no one doubts
the fact. Now you know that if the Pontiff has not called
upon you, it is your own fault; for you have frequently refused to allow him to make you a cardinal. As to your commands, I yield; you may scold those good nuns in your
usual fashion, severely and with my authority, if they do not
obey you immediately. On the other hand, the Pontiff again
orders you to look after your health, and to not resume hearing confessions without his permission. Finally, the Pontiff
orders you to pray for him and for the welfare of the Universal Church, whenever you receive Our Lord."

In 1598, Clement VIII. reunited the duchy of Ferrara to
the Papal States, Duke Alfonso II. having died without issue, and the Holy See having repeatedly declared that it
would not accord the investiture to any prince who did not
belong to the elder branch of the House of Este (1). Alfonso II. was thrice married; and when he abandoned hope of
having a direct heir, he vainly tried to induce the Holy See
to confer the future investiture on the person of his family
whom he would name. In his will it was found that he had
named as his heir Cesare d'Este, his cousin; and this prince
immediately notified the sovereigns of Europe of his accession to the throne of Ferrara. Clement VIII. ordered the
usurper to abandon his pretensions; and when he refused,
the Pontiff sent an army against him. Cesare finally yielded;
Ferrara became Pontifical territory; and Cesare was recognized as duke of Modena and of Reggio. In 1599 our Pontiff
was greatly afflicted by the political aberrations of certain
Dominican friars, headed by the celebrated Thomas Campanella, in the kingdom of Naples. This scandal is worthy of
our attention both because of the scientific reputation of
Campanella, and because of the revival of his memory effected in 1889 by the erection of the mendacious monument to

(1) In the eighth century Ferrara, following the fortunes of the exarchate of Ravenna,
was seized by the Lombard Astolphus. When Pepin defeated Astolphus, he gave the duchy
to the Holy See. In 986 Pope John XV. enfiefed Ferrara to the marquis Tedaldo, who was
also count of Modena and of Reggio. In 1185, Azzolino d'Este received the fief from Pope
Urban III., and in 1243 Pope Innocent IV. confirmed the House of Este in its possession,
conferring on Azzo Novello d'Este the title of Defender of the Church, but requiring that
every succeeding duke should receive the investiture from the Pope-King. This law was
observed until the definitive annexation of Ferrara to the States of the Church.

Giordano Bruno in the Eternal City. We shall devote a chapter to Bruno, but here we must afford a little space to his enforced associate in the Roman monument, which places Huss, Arnold of Brescia, Servetus, and Campanella in the same category with the philosopher of Nola. There may be some general reason for so treating the Bohemian fanatic and the cut-throat of Brescia. The comparison of Bruno with Servetus, the victim of Calvin, may be tolerated, with a smile at the designer's ungrateful disregard of the feeling of Protestants. But Campanella and Bruno! "Hyperion to a satyr!" Bruno was a Christian only by baptism; Campanella was ever a devout Catholic. Campanella, a martyr to science! His devotion to science caused him no trouble more annoying than some cloister squabbles; politics, mere politics, involved him in serious difficulty. As well ascribe the fate of Savonarola to his zeal for morals. Campanella, a victim of the Inquisition! His only relations with that tribunal came from its interposition to save him from the Neapolitan courts, which would have consigned him to the scaffold for high treason to the Spanish crown. Campanella was born at Stilo, in the kingdom of Naples, in 1568. At the age of fourteen he entered the Dominican Order, and in the course of time became very distinguished in the public disputes on philosophical questions, which were then the fashion of the day in Italy. But his attacks on the peripatetics (1) procured him many enemies in his own Order, and in 1590 he sought the protection of the Marquis Lavello, one of his Neapolitan admirers. During the next eight years we find him disputing at Rome and Florence, and teaching in the Universities of Pisa and Padua. In 1598 he returned to Stilo, and it was soon rumored that he was occupied in projects for the subversion of the Spanish domination. He frequently preached, and wrote that the year 1600 would unfold great changes in the kingdom; that recent extraordinary inundations, earthquakes, and volcanic eruptions prognosticated a

(1) "Italy produced the first school of philosophy of a modern character; for the school of Telesius soon followed that of the platonist Marsilio Ficino, and that of the peripatetic Pomponazzi. ... How is it that the names of Campanella and Bacon are so diversely regarded: the latter as of one who opened the modern era, and the former scarcely remembered? Campanella devoted himself to all the knowable; Bacon confined himself to the natural sciences." CANTU, *Modern Philosophy*, § 1.

coming reformation in both civil and ecclesiastical matters ;
that he was to be an instrument of Providence in all this, for
he " was born to abolish three great evils—tyranny, sophism,
and hypocrisy ; everything was in darkness when he struck
the light " (1). He reasoned on several recent astronomical
discoveries, and announced that his studies showed him the
near advent of the reign of eternal reason in the life of humanity (2). Great revolutions, he said, generally occur every
eight centuries ; the latest previous one was the Incarnation
of the Word. Whether Campanella was the instigator or a
tool was never made known ; but a conspiracy was formed
against Spanish rule, and four bishops and three hundred
friars of various orders were the leading spirits. Of the three
processes of the trial now extant, one tends to show that the
design was to establish a republic in Calabria; the second
insists that the kingdom was to be given to the Holy See ;
and the third indicates a wish to hand the country over to
the Turks ; but it is noteworthy that in the process finally
finished in the Holy Office at Rome nearly all the previous
witnesses retracted. When the conspiracy was discovered,
the viceroy's forces captured nearly all the leaders. The laics
were hung, and the " *privilegium fori* " consigned the ecclesiastics, Campanella excepted, to the Inquisition (3) ; the viceroy insisting on this exception, probably at the instigation
of Campanella's private enemies. Confined in Castel Sant'
Elmo for twenty-seven years, the Holy See again and again
vainly endeavored to procure his release ; but Pope Paul V.,
who sent Schoppe to Naples for that purpose, succeeded in
obtaining permission for him to correspond with his friends,
and to receive every convenience for literary work. Finally,
Pope Urban VIII. availed himself of the accusation of magical practices made against the philosopher, insisting that
such a charge placed the case within the sole jurisdiction of
the Inquisition ; and he succeeded in obtaining the friar's
extradition. Campanella was at once enrolled in the Papal

(1) *Philosophical Poems.*   (2) *On the Meaning of Things and on Magic,* IV., 20.

(3) Writing to Cardinal Farnese, Campanella says that his clerical comrades pleaded guilty
to the charge of " rebelling in order to be free to become heretics." Had they answered
only to the charge of treason, he says, " all would have been executed, without any appeal
to the Pope."

household, and an annual pension was assigned to him.
Caressed by all that was learned in Rome, he passed several
years in happy study; but in 1634 the Spanish residents,
who continued to detest his name, made an open attack on
the French Embassy where he was visiting, and tried to obtain possession of his person. He was saved by the Papal
police, but by the advice of the Pontiff he at once betook
himself to France. Cardinal Richelieu received him with
open arms, and made him a counsellor of state. He was also
elected president of the French Academy, lately founded by
Richelieu. To the day of his death, on May 21, 1639, he continually corresponded with Pope Urban VIII. What is there
in this career to indicate the martyr to science, the victim of
papal tyranny; in fine, the fit companion of Bruno as that
unfortunate receives the ignorant or diabolic homage of so-
called liberalism? Campanella was a profound Catholic, albeit an exceedingly intolerant one. He would have no dispute with an innovator. He would ask: "Who $_s$en$_t$ you to
preach, God or the devil? If God, prove it by miracles."
And if he fails, said Campanella, "let the heretic burn. ...
The first error committed (during the Lutheran movement)
was in allowing Luther to live after the Diets of Worms and
Augsburg; and if Charles V. did so, as they say, in order to
keep the Pope in apprehension, and thus oblige him to succor Charles in his aspirations to universal monarchy, he acted against every reason of state policy; for to weaken the
Pontiff is to weaken all Christianity, the people soon revolting
under pretext of freedom of conscience" (1). He counselled
the king of Spain to have always two or three religious
—Dominicans, Jesuits, or Franciscans,—in his supreme council; and every commanding general, he said, should have a
religious adviser (2). Such sentiments must sound strange
to the *Italianissimi* of to-day; but they came naturally from
Campanella, who thought that "the same constellation which
drew fetid effluvia from the cadaverous minds of heretics,
brought forth balsamic exhalations from the exact minds of
the founders of the Minims, Jesuits, Capuchins, etc." (3)

(1) *City of the Sun*, ch. xvii.—*Spanish Monarchy*, ch. xvii.
(2) *Political Aphorisms*, passim.   (3) *Ibid.*, 70.

He advises all governments to allow no Lutherans within their limits ; because, he contends, these sectarians deny the free-will of man, and can excuse crime by the plea that they are fated to sin (1). As for the Calvinist dogma of predestination, "it renders all princes wicked, the peoples seditious, and theologians traitors " (2). The following passage (3), if read by the committee before it accepted Ferrari's design for Bruno's statue, would probably have caused its rejection : " The Papacy belongs to no one in particular, but to all Christendom, and whatever the Church possesses is common to all. The Italians ought to encourage the wealth of religious corporations, because it belongs to them all, and lessens the strength of Italy's rivals. ... No Italian sovereign should aspire to a rule over the others, but all, whenever the direct line of succession becomes extinct, should proclaim the Roman Church heir to their dominions. Thus in course of time an Italian monarchy would be established. The Italian republics ought to make a law that whenever they fall under the rule of tyrants, their government devolves on the Roman Church." In reality, Campanella aimed at a reformation of the world, and by means of Catholicism. His enthusiasm descried a near conversion of the nations, as prophesied by St. Bridget of Sweden, the Abbot Joachim, Dionysius the Carthusian, St. Vincent Ferrer, and St. Catherine of Siena, the last of whom had predicted that the sons of St. Dominic would carry the olive of peace to the Turks (4). He declared that the day of Antichrist was near, if not already come,— " it is now here, or will come in 1630 "; and he " was born to combat the schools of Antichrist," which schools were everywhere active ; for "where Mohammed and Luther do not rule, there dominate Machiavelli and politicians "(5).

When Clement VIII. died, on March 5, 1605, he left to his successor two precious legacies, a pacified France and an Italy freed from Spanish preponderance. The character of this Pontiff must have been admirable, since even Ranke thus describes it. "The new Pope showed the most exemplary

---

(1) *Ibid.*, 84, 87.　　(2) *Letters*, passim.　　(3) *Discourse II. on the Papacy*.

(4) Campanella's words as given in a contemporary account of the Calabrese conspiracy, published in 1845 by Capialbi.

(5) *Letter to the Pope and Cardinals*.

activity in the exercise of his dignity.   From early morn he
was busy ; at mid-day audiences began, all reports were read
and examined, all despatches discussed, legal questions were
investigated, precedents were compared.   Frequently the
Pope showed himself better informed than the referendaries
charged with the reports.   He labored as assiduously as when
he was a simple auditor of the *Ruota*.   He paid no less attention to the details of the internal administration of his government than to European politics, or to the great interests
of the spiritual power. ... Every evening Baronius heard
his confession ; every morning he celebrated Mass.   During
the first years of his Pontificate twelve poor persons dined with
him each day.   He thought nothing of the pleasures of the
table, and he fasted every Friday and Saturday.   After the
week's labor, his Sunday recreation was found in the company
of some pious monks or of the fathers of the Vallicella, with
whom he discoursed on profound religious subjects.   These
austere habits, continued under the tiara, increased the reputation of virtue, piety, and exemplary life which he had hitherto enjoyed. ... In his person were always observed those
sentiments and manners which agree with the idea of a good,
pious, and wise man."   Such was the view of the character
of Clement VIII. taken by all the authors of the seventeenth
and eighteenth centuries.   But in our day the enemies of the
Papacy have represented this Pontiff as a cruel tyrant, who,
because of an abominable thirst for gold, and a desire to
enrich his relatives, did not scruple to shed the blood of an
entire innocent family.   Naturally this accusation has been
re-echoed by the virulent school which has obtained almost
absolute control of the Italian unitarian movement—a school
which adopts any means to injure the Holy See (1) ; but the
subject-matter of the charge is of sufficient importance to demand a special chapter for its treatment.

(1) Among the most distinguished of the propagators of incredulity and anarchy, pre-eminence must be assigned to Bianchi-Giovini, author of a *History of the Popes*; to Mistrali,
a revealer of *The Mysteries of the Vatican* ; and to Petruccelli della Gattina, who furnished
the world with *Memoirs of Judas Iscariot.*

CHAPTER XXX.

THE TRAGEDY OF BEATRICE CENCI.[*]

In 1854 the famous Tuscan revolutionist, Francis Dominick Guerrazzi, published in Pisa a so-called history of *Beatrice Cenci*, which, being a tissue of historical falsehoods, of
obscenities, ribaldries, and blasphemies, was well calculated
to further the work of the secret societies in Italy. Having
issued his romance as a "history," it was but consistent in
Guerrazzi to declare that, in order to give the world a true
account of Pope Clement's atrocious conduct in the Cenci
matter, he had "searched the records of the past; read the
accusations and the defence; compared narratives, writings,
and memoirs; hearkened to distant tradition; ... opened
ancient tombs, and questioned the ashes, for if one knows
how to interrogate them, even ashes will speak." Guerrazzi
certainly caused the ashes of the Cenci to flatter his own
political passions; but, as we shall see, he elicited from them
no advantage for history. He himself admits that the reader
will try in vain to find any honey in his book; alluding to
the fact of its having been composed in prison, he says that
"the anguish of a prisoner produces poison, not honey" (1),
and he convinces us of the fact when we arrive at this passage: "Beatrice Cenci, a maiden of sixteen, was condemned
by Clement VIII., vicar of Christ, to an ignominious death,
because of a parricide not committed by her. ... The avaricious cruelty of the priests drank the blood, and devoured
the goods of the victim." In 1872 the government of Victor
Emmanuel allowed a "Roman" committee to place a memorial tablet in the Roman Capitol, to perpetuate the remembrance of the priestly iniquity toward the Cenci family, and
the task of composing the inscription was assigned to Guer-

---

* This chapter appeared as an article in the *Amer. Cath. Quarterly Review*, vol. XII.

(1) During the Tuscan revolution of 1848, Guerrazzi, then a celebrated lawyer, became
Minister of the Interior, and in March, 1849, was made head of the provisional government.
On the restoration of the Grand-Duke, in April, Guerrazzi was imprisoned for four years.
He was a man of undoubted genius and a fine romancer, but the term "historical" would
ill befit any of his plays or tales.

razzi. Owing to the peculiarities of epigraphic style, the effusion does not readily bear translation : *Beatrice Cenci—Morte acerba—Fiore di giovinezza perduto—Gioie d' amore negate—Censo, unica colpa, rapito—Sepolcro disperso—Tanto non me dolsero—Quanto la fama per longo secolo contaminta—Ora che per voi si può—Sorelle Romane—Rendete alle ossa il sepolcro—Alla memoria la fama—Cio facendo gioverete—Alla giustizia eterna—Alla patria—A me ed anco a voi.* This inscription is consistent with Guerrazzi's presentation of the Cenci tragedy, and with the view of it which is held by those whose ignorant sympathies have been excited by the lovely portrait of Beatrice by Guido Reni (1).

Desirous of discovering whether the charges made by Guerrazzi, and also by the poet Niccolini, were supported by evidence, Philip Scolari diligently sought for information among the Italian libraries and archives, especially among those of the city of Venice, and published the result of his investigations—a thorough confutation of the ex-dictator (2). But before we recur to Scolari's vindication of Pope Clement VIII., it may be well to lay before the reader Muratori's account of the Cenci matter : "In this year (1599) a rare instance of ribaldry and of justice caused much comment in Rome and in all Italy. Francis Cenci, a Roman noble, abounded in riches, for he had inherited from his father an annual income of more than 80,000 scudi; but much more did he abound in iniquity. His least vice was that of the most degrading kind of lust; his greatest, the utter absence of all sense of religion. His first marriage brought him five sons and two daughters; his second, no children. Toward his sons he was incredibly cruel, and to his daughters he was bestial. The elder daughter appealed to the Pope, and thus escaped from trouble, for the Pontiff compelled her father to bestow her in marriage. Beatrice, the younger, remained at home; and when she had matured into beauty, she succumbed to the disordered inclinations of her father, he having taught her that so wicked an act was not sinful. The

(1) Paul Delaroche also exercised his genius on a tableau of *Beatrice Cenci Walking to the Scaffold.* The two tragedies by Custine and Bysshe Shelley are justly celebrated.

(2) *Beatrice Cenci, a Criminal Case of the Sixteenth Century; an Historical Memoir by Philip Scolari.* Milan, 1856.

perverted man even dared to abuse his daughter in the presence of his wife, the girl's stepmother. But finally the child, realizing the brutality of her parent, commenced to revolt, and then he compelled by violence what he had previously obtained by fraud. In vain did the girl appeal to her relations. Then, being unable to endure such a miserable life, she imitated her sister, and sent to the Pontiff a memorial, written also in the name of her stepmother. Perhaps this was not presented ; it certainly effected nothing, and was not afterward found in the secretariate when it would have served to some purpose. The father discovered this appeal, and increased his cruelty, placing both his wife and daughter under lock and key. Reduced to desperation, they now planned his death, and easily secured the aid of James, the eldest son and a married man, who had felt his father's tyranny. One night, while the old man was sleeping, he was killed by two hired assassins, and the body was so disposed in an orchard that it appeared that death had ensued from an accidental fall. But God did not permit the enormous crime of parricide to remain undiscovered. The criminals were arrested, and they yielded to torture. When Pope Clement had read the whole process, he ordered the wretches to be dragged at the tails of horses. Then the principal lawyers of Rome interceded for the guilty ones. At first the Pontiff refused to hear them ; but the celebrated Farinaccio having obtained an audience, he so dilated, during an interview of four hours, upon the wickedness of the murdered man, and upon the extraordinary wrongs of the children—not to excuse the crime, but to procure a lesser punishment—that the Holy Father relented, and suspended the course of justice. Then there was hope for the lives, at least, of the delinquents ; but just at that time a matricide was perpetrated in another noble family, and the Pope became so exacerbated that he ordered the immediate execution of the Cenci. On September 11th a high scaffold was erected in the Piazza di Ponte, and the two women and the brothers, James and Bernard, were led to it. Bernard, however, was pardoned and set at liberty, he being only fifteen years old, and being proved innocent of complicity in the murder. The women were beheaded, and James received death from the strokes of the mace. All the spectators were filled with compassion, for they remembered the iniquity of the father, the cause of so much woe; and they especially admired the youth and beauty of Beatrice, and her wonderful courage when she mounted the scaffold and laid her head on the block. Many persons fainted, and owing to the great crowd, not a few were trampled upon, or injured by the vehicles. The narrative of this horrible event spread throughout Italy, and various judgments were passed upon it. Farinaccio left an authentic memorial in *Quest. 120, No. 172,* and in *Book I., Cons. 66,* where he says: 'If we could have furnished proof of the violence offered by Francis to his daughter, she would not have been condemned to death, because he who commits such brutality ceases to be a father.'" In the main, this narrative of Muratori is correct, and it agrees with that of Moroni, in his *Dictionary.* But, notwithstanding the assertion of Muratori to the contrary, it is certain that the young Bernard was cognizant of, and consentient to, the murder of his father. The lawyer Farinaccio, in his appeal to the Pope, admits that the boy "confesses his assent to the work of the assassin Olimpio," and he quotes these words of the confession: "Olimpio spoke with James and my brother Paul, and said that he wished to kill our father, because our father had dishonored him, and had expelled him from the fortress. He also said that our sister Beatrice was discontented with our father, because he kept her imprisoned, and she could no longer endure such a life; he also said that Beatrice wished our father's death, and desired Olimpio to effect it with the consent of James, Paul, and myself; ... and James, Paul, and I told him to do what he deemed best."

And now for the documentary evidence concerning the trial of the Cenci. The first document found by Scolari is a "Note" of John Mocenigo, Venetian ambassador to the Holy See, addressed to the Senate under date of September 11th, 1599, and in it we read: "This morning the Cenci, convicted of the murder of their father, were executed." Throughout the report there is not the slightest insinuation that the trial had not been conducted according to the Ro-

man jurisprudence of the day. There is expressed no doubt
of the guilt of the unfortunates, not a hint as to any unworthy motive on the part of the judges or of the sovereign.
But let us come to the process. Scolari drew it from two
authentic codices, which he carefully compared, and found to
be substantially alike. The first belonged to the library of
Thomas Farsetti, a Venetian patrician, and it is Codex No. 79,
Class 6, of the Appendix to the Italian MSS., now preserved
in the Library of St. Mark. Ten of its pages are devoted to
the narrative of the Cenci horror, and the writer, a Bolognese
named Charles Ricci, entitles his work : "Death of James and
Beatrice Cenci, brother and sister, and of Lucretia, their
stepmother, parricides, in Rome, on Saturday, September 11th, 1599." The other codex, numbered 1771, now belonging to the Cicogna family, has a narration entitled : "The
ignominious and memorable death of James and Beatrice
Cenci, parricides of Francis Cenci, and of his second wife,
Lucretia, in the year 1599." From this process we gather :

I. *The Causes of the Murder.*—It appears that Francis
Cenci, only son of the treasurer of Pope Pius V., had an annual income of 80,000 scudi, and was, by his most abominable life, the cause of his own ruin, of that of his family, and
of many strangers. ... That his least vice was the sin against
nature ; his greatest, disbelief in God. That he had already
been fined 200 scudi for the above sin against nature. The
only good he ever performed in his life was the erection of
the church of St. Thomas in the courtyard of his palace ; and
this he did, with the intention of burying therein all his sons,
whom, even in their infancy, he hated. ... That Francis was
again imprisoned for new sensualities, and his sons besought
the Pope to order the execution of one who was a disgrace to
the house of Cenci ; but that the Pontiff repelled them as
rebels against their parent. That the count was liberated
with a fine of 500,000 scudi, and he thereafter hated his sons
more blindly than ever. That the elder daughter influenced
the Pope, by means of a memorial, to order her marriage
with the Count Gabbriello di Gubbio, and her father could
not avoid the payment of a magnificent dowry. That in order to preclude a similar stroke of policy on the part of Be-

atrice, he confined her in apartments into which he alone entered, and where he loaded her with blows. That meanwhile, his sons Rocco and Christopher having been killed, he would not give even one cent for their funerals, and declared that he would not be happy until all his sons were dead; that then he would joyfully burn all his possessions. That this infamous man committed actions, and used language, which ought not to be mentioned. That when she had grown mature and beautiful, Beatrice began to prize her honor, whereupon her father cruelly beat her. That being unable to endure the bestial scandals of her opprobrious and miserable life, she sent a memorial to the Pontiff, but it was lost, and when most needed, it could not be found.

II. *The Plot.*—That one of the frequenters of the Cenci palace was a young, handsome, and lively gentleman named Guerra, who had fallen in love with Beatrice, and was much hated by Count Francis, because he was a friend of the sons. That owing to this hatred, Guerra visited the ladies only when the Count was away from home. That Guerra learned, and showed his will to effect, the desires of the women; that when he delayed, Beatrice urged him to the deed. That he opened his mind to James, the elder brother, who willingly joined in the plot against a father who never gave him any money, although he had a family to support. That James, in the apartments of Guerra, and according to the wishes of his sister and stepmother, arranged his father's murder, selecting for the purpose two of the father's vassals who were most hostile to him,—one called Marzio, a friend of the sons, and another named Olimpio, who had been castellan for the Colonna at Rocca Petrella. ... Guerra agreed with these assassins to pay them 2,000 scudi for the killing of Francis Cenci—that is, he would pay one third of the sum in Rome, and the two women would pay the balance in Rocca Petrella (1), when the deed was accomplished.

III. *The Parricide.*—That during the night of September 9th, 1598, opium having been given to the old man by the two women, and he having, therefore, fallen into a deep sleep,

---

(1) Count Francis had signified his intention of passing the warm season in this castle, and the plotters resolved to there execute their design.

Marzio and Olimpio were led to his apartment by said women, who caressed them in encouragement to their work. That said Marzio and Olimpio returned from the Count's chamber, declaring that they pitied an old man in his sleep. That Beatrice, indignant, upbraided them as cowards and breakers of their word, and cried out: "Very well—since your cowardice demands it, I myself will kill my father, and you will get little by it." After this fulminating reproach, the two vassals returned to the Count's chamber. That they plunged a nail into one of his eyes, and drove it deep with a mallet; they drove another nail into his neck, and thus was that miserable soul seized by the devil (*sic*). That the deed being accomplished, the young girl gave a full purse to the murderers, and a gold-trimmed cloak to Marzio for himself. Then both the assassins departed. That then the two women wrapped the corpse in a sheet, and threw it from an old balcony which looked over an orchard, allowing it to fall among the limbs of a tree, so that in the morning it would be believed that the Count had started for a necessary near the balcony, and had fallen over and been caught in the branches of the tree— an idea which was readily accepted.

IV. *The Accusation.*—That the death becoming known in the morning, the wife and daughter wept for the loss of the husband and father. ... That the Neapolitan Court deemed it its duty, since Rocca Petrella was in the kingdom of Naples, to inform the Court of Rome of the event; but some months passed, during which the youngest of the Cenci family died, and thus there remained in the castle only the stepmother, Beatrice, James and a third brother, Bernard, only fourteen years old. That Guerra, hearing of the investigations of justice, sent assassins to kill Marzio and Olimpio, that they might not testify against the Cenci, but Olimpio alone perished. That Marzio was arrested in Naples and confessed everything. That in Rome James and Bernard Cenci were imprisoned in Corte Savella, while Lucretia and Beatrice were confined in their own palace, whence, on the arrival of Marzio from Naples, they were transferred to prison, and confronted by his depositions.

V. *The Trial.*—That the process having been commenced, all the Cenci rested their case on a denial, and so firm was

Beatrice in refusing to recognize the gold-trimmed mantle given by her to Marzio, that she so filled him with admiration that he withdrew the deposition made at Naples, and died under the torture rather than recede from his retractation. That, therefore, the legal justification for torturing the Cenci being wanting, the Court left them in quiet in the castle for some months. That perchance, however, the murderer of Olimpio was arrested, and he revealed everything, whereupon Guerra fled from Rome disguised as a charcoal burner. That this flight, joined to the confessions of the prisoners, warranted the application of torture to the Cenci; that James, Bernard, and Lucretia did not face the trial, but at once confirmed the avowals. That Beatrice, however, whether under the influence of sweet words, of threats, or of the cord, would admit nothing, so that even the judge, Ulysses Moscati, was confounded. That Moscati, having referred everything to the Pontiff, His Holiness relieved him of the case, fearing that he might be influenced into excessive tenderness by the beauty of Beatrice. That the Pope ordered that while the girl was attached to the cord, and before she should be subjected to further torment, her stepmother and brothers should be brought before her. That James and the others besought her not to persist in a denial which would only expose her to suffering, and would injure her soul instead of saving it. That then Beatrice answered them: "You wish, then, to disgrace our house?" Then turning to the attendants, she said: "Unbind me. Let me be examined and what I ought to deny, I will deny." That then she confessed that she had procured the murder of her father. That immediately all were accorded more liberty, and the whole family were allowed each other's society after a separation of five months. That they dined together, and were then led to the prison of the Tor di Nona. That in consequence of the avowal of the parricide, the Pope ordered that the horrid crime should be punished by drawing at the tails of horses; but this severe sentence so affected many cardinals and princes, that they interceded for the Cenci, whereupon the Pontiff remarked: "I would not have thought that Rome could furnish people to defend parricides." That, however, the Pope listened.

for four consecutive hours, to the arguments of the defenders, and then took their writings ; that he was so concerned about the case that he remained up all night, closeted with Cardinal Zacchia dei Nobili, studying the papers ; that he seemed so satisfied with the arguments that many hoped for a commutation of the sentence. That the Pope finally ordered a suspension of execution in order that he might more fully consider the case. When reflecting on this process, the reader should note particularly that during the trial the violation of Beatrice was not proved, for the unfortunate persisted in silence on that point, remaining firm in the intention she had announced in prison : " Unbind me, and what I ought to deny, I will deny," which meant : "I will avow my crime, but not its cause ; I will die sooner than publish my own dishonor." Had she revealed her provocation, she would, in all probability, have at least escaped death.

VI. *The Punishment.*—That meanwhile a horrid matricide occurred in Rome, namely, the murder of Constance, marchioness-dowager of Oriolo, by her younger son, Paul Santacroce ; that this event so affected the Pontiff that on the morning of September 10th, 1599, he summoned Mgr. Taverna, governor of Rome, and placing the case of the Cenci in his hands, ordered that justice should be satisfied as soon as possible. That the culprits were executed on the following morning, and that Beatrice, especially, died like a Christian penitent, even blessing the cord which bound her arms, saying in a loud voice : "Oh! sweet cord, bind this body to chastisement and corruption, that my soul may obtain eternal glory !"

The process shows us, therefore, that Count Francis Cenci was deliberately assassinated by counsel and procuration of his wife and children ; that the accused confessed their guilt; that Clement VIII. patiently listened to the intercessory arguments of the best advocates of Rome ; that he devoted the vigils of the entire night to a consideration of these reasonings ; that the occurrence of a similar crime caused him to give rein to justice. Nevertheless, Guerrazzi says that " Beatrice Cenci, a virgin of sixteen years, was condemned by Clement VIII., the vicar of Christ, to an ignominious death, for a crime not committed by her," and he asserts that the reason for this outrage was the desire of the Pontiff to appropriate the wealth of the Cenci—"the avaricious cruelty of the priests drank the blood, and devoured the goods of the victim." Now, even if we disregard the value of the process as a synchronous, authentic, and, therefore, an incontestably conclusive piece of evidence, how comes it that the powerful connections of the Cenci raised no cry of horror, emitted no protest, because of the Papal injustice? How comes it that all Rome, all Italy, seems to have entertained no suspicions in the matter? Perhaps fear was the cause of this silence. But we know that just as in ancient Rome there were never wanting writers to register the cruelties of those emperors who caused the world to tremble, so, in mediæval and modern Papal Rome there were always men willing not only to note the real vices and crimes of guilty Popes, but even to do as Guerrazzi has done—to accuse all Popes, even without reason. Was it only in the sixteenth century, and during the reign of a Pontiff whom history does not present as ever having inspired anybody with fear, that Papal crimes were covered by the trembling veil of silence? And we should remember that in the time of Clement VIII., the war excited by Luther against the Papacy was at its height, that even Italy was overrun by the emissaries of heresy. What was to restrain these virulent enemies of Rome from penning such a narrative as Guerrazzi excogitated, had there been the slightest foundation for it? There, too, were the foreign ambassadors to the Roman Court; there especially those Venetian agents whose *Relations* to their Senate always gave even the minutest of gossipy details of the hour. But Guerrazzi's accusation of murderous robbery falls to the ground, if we reflect that the criminal jurisprudence of Rome contained the maxim that the crime of parricide did not entail confiscation of property. "*Singulariter in hoc crimine non habet locum pœna confiscationis bonorum; sed ista deferuntur venientibus ab intestato*"—a maxim which corresponds with that of the Roman law, that "the assassin of him to whom he was to succeed, is admitted to the succession, even though he be unworthy of it" (1). Neither Clement nor his nephews

(1) Commentary of Carpanus *In Cap. Omnium Novell. Tit. De Jure Fisci.* Milan, 1583.

could hope for any inheritance *ab intestato* from the Cenci, for their families, the Aldobrandini and Barberini, were not connected with the house of Cenci. Again, before her death, Beatrice was allowed to make her will, and, according to this instrument, the Archconfraternity *delle Stimate* received 15,000 scudi, and fifty poor girls received dowries ; therefore, the property of Beatrice was not confiscated. Finally, the great lawyer Farinaccio made the greatest effort of his professional career in his defence of the Cenci, and in his works, published after the death of Clement VIII., he dwells much and earnestly upon the tragic affair. Now, had there been any foundation for Guerrazzi's accusation, the advocate would certainly have known of it; and what an excellent opportunity of adding to his reputation it would have afforded him. He needed only to declare that he had lost his case simply because of the covetousness of the sovereign, who was determined to effect the ruin of his clients. But, on the contrary, he says: "This crime was so horrible, so unheard-of—a daughter and a wife plotting, and paying for, the murder of a father and husband—that we may say that only the great magnanimity of the most holy Pontiff freed the young Bernard from the penalty of death. And we trusted to obtain the same pardon for Beatrice, if she had furnished— which she would not—proof of that provocation which we alleged in her favor."

CHAPTER XXXI.

GIORDANO BRUNO.

There is little in the character, career, or teachings of Giordano Bruno which would induce the serious historian to accord to him more than a passing notice. His notoriety is merely adventitious. The contemporaries of the unfortunate, his very few friends and his many opponents, gave to posterity scarcely more than a bare mention of his name ; so far were they from entertaining the notion advanced by a noisy school of our modern free-thinkers, to the effect that the philosopher of Nola was "the herald of a new civilization, and the innocent martyr of clerical intolerance." For more

than a century after the death of this man whom we are asked
to salute as " the hero of thought," and to whom the further-
ers of his mendacious Roman monument ask us to extend
" a tardy tribute of gratitude and admiration," the literary
world preserved an almost absolute silence in regard to him.
Bruno perished in 1600 ; and the first notable reflections upon
his career were emitted in 1702 by Bayle. Had Bruno been
indeed the demigod whom the votaries of the Dark Lantern
offer to our veneration, this eloquent silence would have been
broken; the friends of the Papacy would have paid some attention to the memory of one who had so foully calumniated
the revered institution, were it only by way of defending the
Holy See from his aspersions; but we find not a word about
this supposedly grand genius in the pages of Baronio, Orsi,
or Rinaldi; and when Quetif and Echard mention him, it is
after a coolly academical fashion. The foes of the Pope-
Kings, who were never wanting, would not have been reticent
in regard to the alleged " light of the universe "; but until
the time of Bayle and Grosley, they thought it prudent " not
to disturb Camerina." However, in our day the enemies of
the Church have brought to light a legendary Bruno ; and
they seem to be ignorant or careless of the fact that the archives of Venice and of Rome render their conspiracy futile.
It is because of the sublime effrontery of the Brethren of the
Three Points, and in order that the reader may appreciate
the hideousness of the studied insult to the Holy See which
is covered by the monument in the Campo dei Fiori, that
we devote a chapter to the life and doctrines of Giordano
Bruno. In March, 1885, the following document was circulated throughout the civilized world by the Masonic Lodges
now encamped in the City of the Popes :

'INTERNATIONAL SUBSCRIPTION FOR A MONUMENT TO GIORDANO BRUNO IN
THE CAMPO DEI FIORI.

> At nos quantumvis fatis versemur iniquis,
> Propositum tamen invicti servamus et ausus,
> ... ut mortem minime exhorrescimus ipsam.
> Viribus ergo animi haud mortali subdimur ulli.
> (G. BRUNO, De Monade, Num. et Fig. c. 1.)

" If no name were attached to these verses, every man of intellect would say that they breathed of Bruno and the Renais-

sance. Those *fati iniqui* speak of the tragic combat which
the Middle Age waged against thought at the time of the
Renaissance; that *propositum* and that *ausus* show how
thought realized its own temerity; the phrase *mortem minime exhorrescimus* is a presentiment; the *viribus*, etc., show the
mission of a philosopher. To conceive and to accomplish
this mission, and to die—behold the energy which results in
determination, character, death, and triumph. In two Italians, Dante and Bruno, the resolve to prefer truth to life approached the sublime, and therefore these two will always be
the beacons of Italian genius; the former in art, the latter in
science. In some measure, we have paid our debt to Dante,
as men and as Italians ; but to Bruno ? The historian of the
Roman empire regarded fifteen years—the period we have
passed in Rome—as a long space in a man's life. We were
brought hither by the heroes of the national resurrection, who
were themselves preceded by the heroes of the intellectual
resurrection, the greatest of whom was Bruno. And on the
spot where he was burnt, as yet there is nothing to remind
us of his grand personality. The monument which we propose to raise in memory of Bruno will have, above all else,
a profound moral significance : Gratitude to the hero of
thought, to the herald of the New Philosophy, which allows
us to think and speak with freedom. It will have also a deep
civil significance : The proclamation of our resolution, and a
determination to keep it unconquerably, as befits men who
wish to make that country great which they have created with
great sacrifices. And our aspirations will be echoed by
every cultured people in Europe ; for the Nolan carried the
word of the new civilization to Switzerland, to France, to
Germany, to England, to Bohemia. He was the exquisite
voice of the world, or as he styled himself, *the awakener of
sleeping souls*, declaring that to the proclaimer of truth every
land is his country. And nevertheless, a return to Italy and
a death in Rome appeared to Bruno to form a necessary
climax for his opposition of the Renaissance to the Middle
Age, and to constitute an obedience to the call of the Most
High *who had destined him to be a foremost and extraordinary
minister to the better Age which was at hand.* That better Age

now erects a monument in his honor, and hails him as THE
AWAKENER OF SLEEPING SOULS. This monument is a grand
reparation, and a tribute of gratitude and admiration ; and
*it is not and cannot be an instrument of religious or political pas-
sions.* The erection of a monument to Bruno, the martyr to
freedom of conscience, proves that this freedom shall be found
everywhere, and that it must be respected by all. Inspired
by these sentiments, we have placed our work under the protection of the illustrious personages here mentioned, who
have agreed to form an Honorary International Committee " (1).
It shall be our task to show that the new philosophy of
which Bruno is represented as the " herald," was a denial of
God, and an assimilàtion of man to the beasts of the field ;
that it would have been hard to find a subject more fit than
Bruno for the idolatry of the sect which now flatters itself
that it has nearly attained the object of its long and pertinacious struggles—the enthronization of atheism (or is it devil-
worship ?) in the seat of revealed truth.

Before we sketch the salient features of the career of
Bruno, we shall note briefly the impressions which that career has produced in the minds of his principal biographers.

(1) It may be well to contribute to the notoriety which these "illustrious personages"
have coveted. They are : FRANCE—Victor Hugo, Ernest Renan, Paul Bert, Th. Ribot, A.
Espinas, G. de Mortillet. ENGLAND—Herbert Spencer, Algernon Swinburne, Charles Brad-
laugh. GERMANY—E. Hæckel, L. Büchner, E. Erdmann, R. Jhering, K. Fischer, E. Zeller.
SPAIN—Emil Castelar, N. Salmeron, F. Giner, M. Morayta, E. Chao. AUSTRIA-HUNGARY—
R. Hamerling, Louis Kossuth, J. Nordmann, C. Thaler. PORTUGAL—T. Braga, T. Bastos.
ROUMANIA—C. A. Rosetti. SWEDEN-NORWAY—H. Ibsen, E. Meyer. BELGIUM—E. de Lavel-
eye, P. Janson. HOLLAND—S. V. Honten, W. H. Zouteveen. SWITZERLAND—M. Mon-
nier, Th. Dufour. GREECE—S. Lambros. RUSSIA—N. Grot. UNITED STATES OF AMERI-
CA—H. E. Wright, Col. (*sic*) Robert Ingersoll. ITALY—M. Amadel, R. Ardigò, A. Bertani,
D. Berti, R. Bonghi, G. Bovio, O. Gaetani di Sermoneta, B. Cairoli, G. Carducci, F. Cavallotti,
L. Cremona, E. Ferrari, L. Ferri, G. Giovi, A. Lemmi, T. Mamiani, T. Masserani, M. Min-
ghetti, J. Moleschott, G. Nicotera, G. Petroni, L. Pianciani, M. Rapisardi, G. Rosa, A. Saffi,
S. Spaventa, G. Trezza, Pasquale Villari, A. Vera, G. Zanardelli.—It is morally certain that
nearly all of the Italian members of this committee knew that they were falsifying history
when they adhered to the terms of this circular. Of course the intellect of Italy is but scant-
ily represented in the list ; Berti, Mamiani, and Villari being the only scholars of great reputation. But all the others, although merely of that calibre which is possessed by men whom
the accidents of revolution send to the surface, are educated sufficiently to justify us in
charging them with bad faith. It is gratifying to observe that in this list, as well as in that
of the "adhesions" to the scandalous project, there are only two or three names of Romans
of any social standing. As to the foreign members of the International Honorary Committee,
bad faith must be ascribed to Spencer, Hugo, Renan, Kossuth, De Laveleye ; ignorance
may excuse the others. It is noteworthy that among the many professors, military men,
nobles, and academical laureates, who figure in this Masonic dance, the sole flaunter of a
title is the would-be doughty champion of infidelity in our country.

As we have remarked already, the contemporaries of the
Nolan speculativist give us very little information concerning
him. Avidalius Valens, the Wechel brothers, Henry Alstedt,
and the famous convert from Lutheranism, Schopp, all but the
last of whom either edited or commentated certain of his writings, are the sole authors of the sixteenth century who treat
of him in any way, and their combined information would
scarcely fill three of our pages. In the seventeenth century,
and in the early eighteenth, Bayle, the prince of the philosophistic sceptics of that day, has no words of praise for the
Nolan. "The hypothesis of Bruno," says this rival of Voltaire in his peculiar talent, "is really the same as that of
Spinoza. Between these two atheists the sole difference is
one of method; Bruno adopting that of the rhetoricians, and
Spinoza that of the geometricians. Each hypothesis exceeds
in extravagance all that others have ever advanced; each is
the most monstrous that could be excogitated; and each is
diametrically contradicted by the most evident conceptions
of the human mind" (1). Brucker, whom Protestants term
"the father of the history of philosophy," says of the Brunonian system : "I defy the most acute genius to understand
it, and the most patient of men to read it. Everything is
wrapped in clouds and in mysterious expressions, the meaning of which probably Bruno himself did not know " (2). Bail-
ly avers that "Bruno knew only enough of astronomy to explain the sphere" (3). Barbieri says : "Bruno destroyed
philosophy, under the pretext of freeing it from Peripateti-
cism. His powerful imagination veiled his intelligence, and
he reasoned like a person in hysterics " (4). Berti, the latest
notable panegyrist of the Nolan, blames Giannone, the Jose-
phist historian of Naples, for giving only a few words to the
career of Bruno, and for admitting that he discredited the endeavor to renovate philosophical science ; " observing no law
or just medium, and thus fixing more firmly the errors of the
schools " (5). Nor does Carlo Botta wish to trouble himself

(1) *Critical Dictionary*, art. *Bruno*.
(2) *Critical History of Philosophy*, vol. **V.**, p. 12.
(3) *History of Modern Astronomy*, vol. **V.**, p. 531. Parma, 1794.
(4) *Neapolitan Mathematicians and Philosophers*, p. 110.
(5) *Civil History of the Kingdom of Naples*, bk. **XXXIV.**, ch. **viii.**

about Bruno. "I shall not pause to talk about him who taught that Moses was an impostor and a sorcerer; that the Scriptures smack of the fabulous; and many other worse blasphemies. He was burnt at Rome—an abominable antidote for crazy opinions" (1). The ever impartial and judicious Cantù says : "Intolerant and sarcastic, Bruno praises himself as much as he despises all others. He insists dogmatically upon opinions which are more than contested. He is wanting in gravity when he treats of the most serious problems, repeatedly jesting on sacred matters. He attacks the Immaculate Conception, and of course, Transubstantiation, which is logically incompatible with his notion of a one, sole substance. Whenever he finds religious doctrine at variance with reason, he relies on the latter. He often puts the most extravagant opinions on the tongues of his interlocutors; and then neglects to refute them. He undertakes 'to abolish the puerile fear of death,' because his philosophy 'tears away the gloomy veil of a crazy sentiment concerning Orcus and the avaricious Charon, which poisons the best part of our lives' (2). Bruno was a rationalist two centuries before Hegel, to whom he gave the formula of the concord of contradictories" (3). Gioberti mentions the name of Bruno only three times in the course of his four volumes of *Introduction to the Study of Philosophy ;* and although he eulogizes Campanella, whom the Roman monument unhistorically and wickedly forces into comradeship with the Nolan, the great ontologist charges the latter with having discredited, rather than promoted the study of philosophy. "The license and extravagance of philosophers like Pomponazzio, Bruno, and Cardano discredited totally the speculative sciences, and excited a reasonable fear in men of piety and of common sense, who did not possess that exquisite wisdom of certain moderns which deems it not unworthy of religion to be the laughing-stock of bad philosophers" (4). Fiorentino, although pronouncing Bruno a "supreme philosopher," nevertheless admits : "It would be futile labor to seek in the works of Bruno any rigid and mathematical demonstration" (5). It is for Fiorentino to explain

(1) *History of Italy,* bk. XV. (2) *The Supper of Ash-Wednesday.*
(3) *Heretics of Italy,* vol. III., p. 153. (4) *Loc. cit.,* vol. I., p. 156.
(5) *Telesio ;* vol. II., p. 50. Florence, 1874.

this inconsistency. Another admirer of Bruno, Spaventa, while also pronouncing the "supremacy" of his hero, naively admits that it is impossible to make a satisfactory extract from his ethical works. " His notions," says Spaventa, " are so enveloped in allegories and fantastic figures, that only a love of science, and a love of this supremely unfortunate philosopher, can induce one to endure the ennui produced by his writings " (1). Balan, one of the calmest of Bruno's critics,. finds in his speculations : " Neither order, nor precision, nor lucidity. So verbose is he, so obscure and confused, that often we doubt whether he understands what he is penning. His reasons are intricate and disconnected ; he continually wanders around the circumference, without knowing the position of the centre ; but worst of all, he is always vituperating those from whom he has stolen the theory which he proclaims as his own" (2). Previti, a Jesuit author, the latest of the notable explorers in the Brunonian hazes, arrives at the necessary conclusion that if the Roman monument rightly proclaims the Nolan theorizer as the supreme philosopher of Italy, then Italian philosophy has been, during the last few centuries, wretchedly degraded (3).

Filippo Bruno was born in Nola, one of the most ancient cities of the kingdom of Naples, in 1548. In his writings he frequently boasts of his connection with an imaginary noble family *dei Bruni;* and he tells how his father was an intimate friend of the poet Tansillo, and of many other illustrious personages. But he speaks of his mother's people with very little respect. However, the truth, as derived from such of his writings as were penned in his more lucid moments, seems to be that his father was a plebeian, a common soldier, with no revenue other than his miserable pay and his precarious booty ; and that the boy was indebted for his early education to a maternal uncle. This relative took Filippo to Naples when he was eleven years old, in order that his already manifested talents might be cultivated in the University of the capital. In his sixteenth year the lad resolved to enter the Dominican Order ; and he received the habit in

(1) *Essays on Philosophy;* vol. I., p. 142. Naples, 1867.
(2) *Giordano Bruno ;* Bologna, 1886.
(3) *Giordano Bruno and His Times;* Prato, 1887.

that famous convent of San Domenico Maggiore, which had been the seat of the University in the time of St. Thomas of Aquino, who was one of its professors, and which was one of the chief glories of Naples until the revolution of 1860 turned its venerable halls to profane uses. Whether he himself selected the name of Giordano which he now assumed, we do not know ; but the name should have been a harbinger of a happy life in religion, for it was that of the successor of St. Dominic, a fine mind and a great heart, who thought of nothing else on earth but the glorification of the Church and of his Order. Some writers contend that the novitiate of Fra Giordano was redolent of a spirit of insubordination ; and that his superiors should not have received his solemn profession. Be this as it may, Bruno himself tells us that he was, at this period, " a restive and disgusted man, content with nothing, and as fantastic as a dog who has received a thousand scoldings" (1). In 1572 he was raised to the priesthood, and was transferred to a convent in Campagna, the chief town of the district of that name in the province of Salerno. The locality was delicious ; but he soon complained of the climate, and was transferred to another establishment. For three years he wandered from one convent to another, now complaining of the food, then lamenting because of uncongenial brethren, or growling at some superior's presumed injustice. Finally he was sent back to San Domenico Maggiore ; but he soon frightened his fellow-religious by frequent manifestations of sympathy with the Arian and Semiarian doctrines which had lately been introduced into the kingdom. The nature of his doubts concerning the Blessed Trinity may be learned from his *Cause, Principle, and One*, which he published at London in 1584, and from his replies to the Venetian inquisitors in 1592. He professed to doubt that there is any real distinction between the three Divine Persons ; he could discern only the rational and logical distinction of the attributes. He declared that the Son figures the intellect of the Father; the Holy Ghost figures the soul of the universe. Then, perverting the sense of the Scriptures, he insisted that his theory was consonant with the text in *Wisdom*, ch. i., v. 7,

(1) Thus in the Prologue to his comedy of the *Candelajo.*

"For the Spirit of the Lord hath filled the whole world, and that which containeth all things hath knowledge of the voice." He traced an agreement between his own and the Pythagorean idea ; and the more readily, because he had already conceived a hatred for all things Aristotelian. He proudly quoted these lines of Virgil's *Æneid*, bk. VI., v. 724, etc., as illustrative of his position:

> *Principio cœlum ac terras camposque liquentes*
> *Lucentemque globum lunæ titaniaque astra*
> *Spiritus intus alit, totamque infusa per artus*
> *Mens agitat molem, et toto se corpore miscet.*

Of course he rejected the Catholic doctrine of the Incarnation. " *He could not understand* how the Divinity, infinite in its nature, could form one *suppositum* with the Humanity, which is finite by nature." In vain did Bruno's superiors strive to confirm the tottering faith of their arrogant subject ; and finally the Neapolitan provincial perceived that his duty commanded him to denounce the recalcitrant to the Inquisition. While the indictment was being prepared, Bruno fled to Rome, taking refuge in the Minerva, the mother-house of his Order, and the residence of its master-general. He was received kindly by the head of the Preaching Friars, although he had incurred censure by his flight from his convent. But in a few days he learned that his provincial had sent the documents in his case to Rome ; and as he knew that if he stood trial, he must either retract or be condignly punished, he fled from the Eternal City in secular dress, and he had cast the die. Some years afterward, while he was residing in Venice, Bruno told Giovanni Mocenigo that he had fled from Rome because he had been accused of having thrown into the Tiber the man who had denounced him to the Holy Office (1). That this was one of the innumerable lies fabricated by Bruno in order to make himself an object of interest, is evident from the utter absence of any such charge in either the Venetian or the Roman trial.

Our limits preclude a minute narrative of the wanderings of Bruno from the time he cast off the Dominican habit, and

(1) See the second Denunciation by Mocenigo, in the *Venetian Process.*

with it all connection with the Church of God. After a short
stay in Genoa and Venice, where he supported himself by
pedagogy, the year 1577 found him in Geneva, the "Rome of
the Reformation." It is strange that Brucker should represent the apostate as attending lectures and sermons by Calvin in this city (1); that heresiarch had been in his grave for
thirteen years when Bruno entered Geneva. As he approached the city, the Nolan donned his Dominican robes,
and then betook himself to an inn. Why he put on his olden
religious habit can be only a matter of conjecture. Certainly
the dress was most offensive to the Calvinists of Geneva, who
were more bitter toward everything savoring of monasticism
than were any other progeny of the Reformation; and it
was also obnoxious to the colony of Italian apostates who
had formed in Geneva what they styled the "Italian Church,"
for it reminded them of the dread tribunal of the Inquisition,
to escape which they had exiled themselves. Previti may
have penetrated the reason of the comedy, when he ascribed
it to a fond hope of gaining credit with both the Genevans
and the Italian exiles, by a presentation of himself as a victim
of the tyranny of Rome and of the friars. "And he was a
stainless victim, as was indicated by the white tunic which was
for him, as well as for his olden brethren, a symbol of purity.
It may be urged that such conduct would have been hypocrisy;
but Bruno was always a hypocrite, whether facing his judges,
or in the company of his protectors" (2). The Italian Consistory of Geneva deputed Caracciolo, who was a species of little Pope for his companions in apostasy, to investigate the
strange apparition; and when the envoy found that the
Dominican tunic and scapular covered a "martyr to truth"
like himself, he advised the wearer to doff the insignia of
Satan. His arguments prevailed, and Bruno appeared in
public in the guise of a cavalier, sword and all. The name
of Filippo Bruno was recorded in the Register of the Italian conventicle (3); but it is untrue that a series of dispu-

(1) "*Docebant tunc magna auctoritate in schola Genevensi Calvinus et Beza.*"—
Loc. cit., p. 18.

(2) *Loc. cit.*, p. 81.

(3) In the Archives of Geneva (Historical Portfolio, No. 1477 *bis*) there is preserved a list
of the names of the Italians resident in the city from 1550 to 1607; and at the year 1578 oc-
curs the record, "Filippo Bruno of the Kingdom of Naples."

tations with the Genevan ministers converted the Nolan to their creed. A man who dreamed of founding a philosophy without Christianity would not have accepted a Calvinist travesty of Christianity; and we know that Bruno told Caracciolo that he had come to Geneva with the object of finding security, and not in order to profess a new religion (1). Again, the Calvinian yoke was the most intolerable of all despotisms, and Bruno could endure no subjection. He remembered the fate of Servetus, Gentile, Biandrata, Ochino, Castalion, and innumerable others who had presumed to question the infallibility of Protestant creeds. Too many of the Calvinist disputations led to the dungeon or to the scaffold; and Bruno possessed a certain kind of prudence. Nor did the theology of the "Italian Church" attract him. According to the Italian exiles, our Lord was a mere man, although a mediator with God. "He had been announced by the Prophets, was born of the race of David, was raised by the Father to the dignity of the Christ, and he was the most invincible of kings, for whom God created a new and regenerated world" (2). But if Bruno joined neither the Arianizing Italians of Geneva nor the Calvinists; if he regarded both systems as mere transitory symbols of that natural religion in which he foresaw all religious forms disappearing; how was he to procure food and clothing? During two months and a half he labored at the poorly-recompensed task of a proof-reader; and then he proceeded to France, in which land, then agitated by the throes of politico-religious discord, he fancied that better prospects awaited him.

Bruno spent about a month in Lyons; and then he went to Toulouse, because, if we are to credit his assertion, "there was a famous University in that city." It was here that he first announced himself as a professor of philosophy; and some authors contend that he passed a successful examination in the University, and received the doctorate. Berti, his latest panegyrist, thought to prove that the second University in France had thus honored him; and M. Pont, librarian of Toulouse, was requested by the librarian of the Uni-

(1) Venet. Trial, *Allegation* IX.
(2) SCHOMANN; *Catechism*, cited by Cantù, *Univ. Hist.*, vol. IX., p. 559.

versity of Turin, Sig. Goresio, to furnish any corroborative testimony afforded by the Toulousan archives. But Berti acknowledges that the reply was returned that there was no trace of Bruno's connection with the University of Toulouse in the archives of the establishment (1). Bruno seems to have found enough of pedagogical employment in Toulouse to secure him a comfortable living; but in 1579 he sought in Paris a wider stage for the exhibition of his talents. He obtained the good will of Henry III. by dedicating to that imbecile "king of the mignons" a theory of mnemonics which he had developed from the *Art of Memorizing*, written by Lullo. To show his appreciation of Bruno's work, the monarch offered him a chair in the Sorbonne; and when the philosopher demurred to the rule which obliged every lecturer in the University to assist at Mass each morning, he was appointed to an "extraordinary" professorship, a position to which the unpleasant duty was not attached. For a time the teachings of Bruno in Paris were harmless extravagancies; but when his *Shadows of Ideas* appeared, it was evident that he had thrown off his mask, and was bent on war against all revealed truth. In this first of his avowedly heterodox writings, the Nolan formulates his rationalistic and pantheistic sentiments. He terms Christianity a sect; he insists that all mysteries must disappear before the growth of human intelligence, declaring that they were instituted only for eyes which had not been so strengthened as to endure safely the full light of reason. If the reader is acquainted with the character of Henry III., he will experience mental nausea when he peruses Bruno's fulsome dedication of the *Shadows* to that prince. We give a specimen passage as an illustration of the calibre of the man whom the projectors of the Roman monument extolled as modest and independent. "Who does not know that great gifts must be presented to great personages, and the greatest to the greatest of men? It is clear, therefore, that this work of mine, which must be numbered among the very greatest ones, because of the grandeur of its subject, because of the singular power of invention which has produced it, and because of the accuracy

(1) *Loc. cit.,* p. 113.

of its demonstrations, should be dedicated to your Majesty, the brilliant light of your people, a most shining mirror of virtue, and a most profound genius. It remains for you who are so generous, powerful, and wise, to accept it graciously, and to examine it with mature judgment." In the summer of 1583, love of change, which was one of Bruno's characteristics, prompted him to visit England, then under the sway of Elizabeth. King Henry furnished him with recommendatory letters to his ambassador at the court of St. James's, Michel de Castelnau, Sieur de Mauvissier ; and undoubtedly it was because of these credentials that Castelnau, a fervent Catholic, sheltered the wanderer in his mansion.

One of the first acts of Bruno, after his arrival in London,. was the publication of his *Explanation of the Thirty Seals*, dedicated to Castelnau, and preceded by a letter to the doctors of Oxford. He announced himself to these presumedly grave and reverend gentlemen as a " Doctor of the most elaborate philosophy ; professor of the purest and most harmless wisdom ; recognized by all the principal Academies of Europe ; unknown only to barbarians ; the awakener of sleeping geniuses ; the tamer of presumptuous and recalcitrant ignorance ; a universal philanthropist ; as all his actions proclaim. One who loves an Italian no more than an Englishman, a man no more than a woman, a mitre no more than a crown,. a lawyer no more than a soldier, the hooded no more than the hoodless ; but who loves that man the most whose conversation is the most peaceful, civil, and useful ; one who. cares not for an anointed head, or marked forehead, or clean hands, but only for the mind and for the cultured intellect ; one who is detested by hypocrites and by the propagators of insanity, but who is revered by the upright, and applauded by every noble genius." Lamentable indeed must have been the decadence of Oxford, when the reading of this effusion, than which Cagliostro could not have devised a more flashy advertisement, did not prevent the promotion of Bruno to a chair in the University. During three months " the herald of the New Philosophy " discoursed on the Immortality of the Soul and on the Quintuple Sphere. In regard to the first subject, he taught that after death the body " agglomerates" atoms upon atoms unto itself, thus fabricating a new body ; and that this process will be repeated *ad infinitum*. He averred that the human soul is the same, in specifical and generical essence, as that of a fly, of an oyster, or of any animated thing ; that it is the same spirit which animates and moves a plant, a beast, or a man ; that the effects of this spirit are different, inasmuch as it makes use of different bodily instruments ; that now the soul, a most simple monad, draws to itself a multitude of atoms by "agglomeration," and then it abandons them by "exglomeration." In his *Cabal of the Steed Pegasus*, published in London in 1585, the Nolan gives an exquisite development of his idea on "transformism." "Were the head of a serpent to assume the form of a human head, were the snake to develop a bust, were its tongue to become wider, were its shoulders to become more pronounced, were it to put forth hands and feet ; it would breathe, walk, understand, and talk like a man, because then it would be nothing else than a man. On the contrary, a man would be only a serpent, were he to draw into himself his arms and legs, were all his bones to unite in forming a spine ; he would have more or less vivid an intellect ; instead of talking, he would hiss ; instead of walking, he would glide ; instead of building a house for himself, he would bore a hole for a dwelling. From this you can understand how it is that many animals may have much more intellect than man possesses." After edifying the dons of Oxford with these ebullitions of genius, he dismissed his opponents with :

"*I nunc, stulte, minas mortis fatumque timeto.*"

The lectures on the *Quintuple Sphere* also excited the indignation of the Oxonians ; for the "apostle of free thought" taught that the "flaming bodies" in the heavens are "real ambassadors of God," since they show "an infinite effect of an infinite cause." He insisted that his New Philosophy frees the soul of man from its prison, enables man to inspect the "infinite universe," and overthrows the power of "the sophists and asses who force philosophy to return to heaven, if it wishes to recover its lost ascendency" (1). These and simi-

(1) *Italian Works of G. Bruno* ; vol. I., p. 129. Leipsic, 1830.

lar insanities caused his expulsion from Oxford, despite what
he called his victory over Dr. Leyson, " who was as discour-
teous as a hog, while the patience and politeness of the other
(Bruno) plainly indicated that he was a Neapolitan, born and
educated in a more refined atmosphere." Bruno dwells with
much complacency on the splendid reception and respectful
attention accorded to him by "the virgin-queen"; and he
may tell the truth here, for Italian renegades were ever welcome to the head of the English Church Establishment, and
at that time the " language of *si* " was greatly affected by the
courtiers and by all Englishmen who were at all cultured,
while Italian artists and scientists were extravagantly admired. It is not improbable, therefore, that it was some
special graciousness extended toward him that led the Nolan
to term Queen Elizabeth "the unique Diana, who is to us all
what the sun is to the stars." Wharton asserts that during
his residence in London, our wanderer became a member of
a secret society of atheists; but there is no reason to suppose that any such body existed in the England of that day;
and if there was such a society, it is very improbable that it
would have given fellowship to so loose-tongued a person as
Bruno. It has been said that Bruno was a Mason; and that
Wharton alluded to the adepts of the Square and Triangle.
Had the Nolan lived in our day, undoubtedly he would have
been a brilliant light in the Lodges; but there was nothing
in the Masonry of the sixteenth century to attract a man of
his character. Indeed, it is certain that he would not have
been initiated; it was not until Bruno had been dead for
more than a century, that Masonry fell under the ban of the
Church, and became the natural home for men of his ilk (1).
Before we accompany Bruno out of England, we must observe that he has no words of praise for the men of that
country, unless in the case of those, few in number, who
petted him. The dons of Oxford, he says, "are more like
hogs and ploughmen than like anything else " (2). He declares that he was the sole wise man in the University; and

---

(1) Pope Clement XII., the first Pontiff to condemn Masonry, issued his Constitution *In Eminenti* on April 24, 1738.
(2) *Supper of Ash-Wednesday*, p. 18.

he congratulates himself, because "such a man, even if alone, can easily triumph over the general ignorance; for entire worlds are worth less than one discerning person, and all the fools combined cannot equal one sage. ... What shall I say of the Nolan? Is it improper for me to praise him, when he is is as near to me as I am to myself? No reasonable man will blame me, since such a course is sometimes necessary. Who blames Phydias for avowing that such and such works are his? If in our day men glorify Columbus because he was the one of whom it had been predicted: '*Novos detegat orbes, nec sit terris ultima Thule,*' what should men do to Bruno, who has discovered the way to mount to heaven, to walk along the circumference of the stars, to turn one's back to the convex surface of the firmament? Human reason, so long oppressed, has sometimes deplored its terrible debasement; and in a moment of lucidity it has cried to the divine mind which often communicates with the soul: 'Who will ascend to heaven, and recover for me my lost genius?' *And who but Bruno could go?*" (1) If Bruno found the "asininity and hoggishness" of the Oxonians brought into fuller evidence by their velvet robes and golden necklaces, their twelve rings on two fingers (2), he could scarcely be expected to find any charms in the society of the English knights and gentry. He was disgusted with their manners at table; especially with their habit of passing a drinking vessel from mouth to mouth. "When one guest has drunk from it, he passes it on, smeared with grease; and each succeeding drinker deposits on the rim a lot of bread-crumbs or bits of meat or whatever remnants of food may have been clinging to his mustaches" (3). He describes the streets of London as reeking with filth, the houses as utterly wanting in the sanitary conveniences which were common in Italy. The manners of the lower orders, whom he terms half-savages, terrify him; he says that the blow of an English fist, which he often felt, is "worse than the kick of an ox or of a mule." But he salaciously smacks his lips at the thought of the charms of English women. "They are gracious, polite, pulpy, tender, soft, blond-haired, with red and white cheeks, lips of sugar,

(1) *Italian Works of Bruno*, vol. I., p. 137.   (2) *Ibid.*, p. 22.   (3) *Ibid.*, p. 150.

and divine eyes. ... They are made of some celestial substance " (1).

In 1586 Bruno departed from England, and after a short stay in France, he went to Germany. His first resting-place was Marburg; and he registered his name on the roll of the University as "Giordano of Nola, Neapolitan, Doctor in Roman Theology." However, permission to lecture was denied to him; and he proceeded to Wittemberg, which he styled the "Athens of Protestantism." In order to recruit his drooping finances, he laid aside his wonted arrogance for a time, and announced himself to the academical senate as "a student in the halls of the Muses"; whereupon he was licensed to lecture on metaphysics in their relation to astronomy, physics, and mathematics, and also to explain the *Organon* of Aristotle. His metaphysico-astronomical lectures were published at Wittemberg in 1588, preceded by a dedication to King Henry III. of France, and by a letter to Filesac, rector of the Sorbonne. These discourses, substantially the same ones which he had delivered in Paris, were comparatively harmless, so long as he taught that "there are myriads of worlds, and a synod of stars, all inhabited; that our earth is a small atom launched into space, having no special importance and no pre-eminence over the innumerable other earths which move in the infinite ætherial regions; and that all nature is determined and produced by equal and invariable laws." But he soon ventured to proclaim: "Science is contradicted by the doctrine which, like the Christian system, regards our earth as the scene of a redemption of the human race, and which sees on the earth a supernatural order which had its beginning in Adam, and its complement in Christ." He drew from the Copernican system the necessity of a new philosophy, and of a new religion which would agree with that philosophy. He avowed that he had come to Wittemberg with the determination to destroy the philosophy which men had received for centuries, and to also destroy Christianity, because that religion could not be made to agree with the latest discoveries and criterions of science. His theories produced no

(1) *Ibid.*, p. 125.

great excitement in the stolid Wittembergers, probably because they were familiar with the equally insane ravings of their Lutheran teachers. In fact, Bruno felt that he was justified in congratulating his auditors, because "they did not turn up their noses at him, nor grind their teeth, nor puff out their cheeks, nor hammer on the benches" (1). Of course the Nolan affected to think, and perhaps he did think, that the Wittemberg authorities tolerated him because of his immense reputation ; and therefore he flattered them by declaring that he had never met any pupils who knew so well how to preserve intact their philosophical liberty (2). During his second year in Wittemberg, Bruno lectured on the *Organon* of Aristotle ; but ere the course was finished, he bade an "affectionate" farewell to the birthplace of the Reformation. He tells us why he abandoned a city which furnished him with ample means of living, and with full liberty to spout his vagaries. "I found in Wittemberg two factions, Calvinist philosophers and Lutheran theologians ; and among the latter was Alberico Gentile, whom I had known in England as a professor of jurisprudence. This gentleman favored me greatly, and procured for me a chair from which I dictated lectures ; but when death came to the old duke, a Lutheran, and he was succeeded by his Calvinist son, the Lutheran party was persecuted, and therefore I proceeded to Prague" (3). It is evident, therefore, that it was a sort of gratitude which impelled Bruno to eulogize Luther, the spiritual father of his protectors, styling him "the liberator of genius, the sole Reformer who prepared the way for the triumph of reason, the new Hercules who battered down the adamantine gates of hell."

In Bohemia our wanderer followed a line of conduct very different from that which he had pursued in Switzerland, France, England, and Germany. Since the emperor Rudolph II., although forced to tolerate heresy in Germany, was determined to prevent that pest from desolating his kingdom of Bohemia, the Nolan deemed it prudent to abstain from his ordinary tenor of language ; and he avoided care-

---

(1) "*Non nasum intortistis, non sannas exacuistis, buccæ non sunt inflatæ, pulpita non strepuerunt, in me non est furor scholasticus incitatus.*"—*Latin Works*, p. 624.
(2) *Ibid.*   (3) Venetian Trial, *Allegation IX.*

fully the society of all whose orthodoxy was questioned. Being unable to teach, he tried to obtain funds by publishing one hundred and sixty *Theses Against the Mathematicians and Philosophers of the Day*, dedicating the work to the emperor, and naturally eschewing many of his real sentiments. But in spite of his care, the general tone of the book was such that Rudolph, while sending to him a present of 300 thalers, requested him to leave the country. The duchy of Brunswick next received the honor of a visit from Bruno; but he tried in vain to obtain an introduction to court circles. Bartholmess and some other biographers of the Nolan say that he was charged with the education of the duke Henry Julius; but Bruno would have mentioned that fact in some one of his works, had it really happened. He never omitted the slightest opportunity of drawing attention to anything which would indicate his importance. Again, the duke Henry Julius was twenty-five years old when Bruno arrived in Helmstaedt, the capital of Brunswick. In the spring of 1590 he saw himself menaced with persecution by the Evangelico-Lutherans of Helmstaedt; and he proceeded to Frankfort, where religious animosities were then less rampant than in any other city of Germany. During his trial at Venice, Bruno stated that his object in visiting Frankfort was the publication of his work entitled *Number, Monad, and Figure*. Having given this book to the press, he paid a short visit to Zurich, where he replenished his purse by giving private lessons in philosophy, and also busied himself in the preparation of a work which, according to him, was to have been a complete development of every human science (1). He had scarcely returned to Frankfort, when he abandoned the comparative comfort which he was enjoying; and went to Venice, the land of The Ten and a hot-bed of the Inquisition. Some writers discern a trick of the Holy Office in this risky proceeding; others ascribe it to an irresistible longing to breathe again the air of beautiful Italy. It appears, however, that the sole cause of this journey to Venice, which was to entail the catastrophe of Bruno's life, was his consummate and

---

(1) So he told Bertano, a bookseller of Antwerp, whom he met in Zurich, and who thus testified in the Venetian trial. See *Allegation* VI.

irrepressible vanity, his overpowering desire of being an object of interest. A bookseller, Ciotto by name, returning in 1591 from the Lenten Fair of Frankfort, brought to Venice a copy of the book just published by Bruno. The work fell into the hands of Giovanni Mocenigo, an influential patrician; and it filled him with such raptures, that he sent a highly complimentary letter to the author, and begged him to come to Venice, tendering him the hospitality of the Mocenigo palace, and expressing his desire to study sublime philosophy under so consummate a master. Confident that the protection of so powerful a patrician as Mocenigo would ward off any annoyance on the part of the orthodox Most Serene Republic (1), Bruno hastened to the shores ot the Adriatic. So long as he restricted his teachings to an explanation of his "Art of Memory," of which Mocenigo was especially enamored, his protector continued to esteem him; but the poor man could not avoid, for any length of time, a satisfaction of his animosity against Christianity. The true character of his guest was made evident to the patrician by declamations like the following: "The system presented by the Church is not that which the Apostles advanced. ... The assertion that God is triune is a display of ignorance and a blasphemy against the Divine Majesty. ... All friars are asses. ... I am very fond of women; but as yet I have not enjoyed as many as Solomon enjoyed. Certainly the Church errs egregiously when she condemns as sin that which is perfectly natural, and which I hold to be a very meritorious thing." Mocenigo rebuked Bruno for these and similar utterances. "I told him that he was worse than a Lutheran, and that I was a good Catholic; that he should confine himself to the subjects that I wished him to explain, when I invited him to my house. He laughed, and replied: 'When you rise from the grave, you will see how much of a reward

(1) The Mocenigo family was one of the most conspicuous among the Venetian aristocracy. It had already given four doges to the republic; Tommaso in 1414, Pietro in 1474, Giovanni in 1478, and Alvise in 1570. The denouncer of Bruno should not be confounded with that Giovanni who went as ambassador to France in 1558, nor with that one who was commissary in Candia some years later. The Giovanni of Bruno's acquaintance was one of the *Savii in Eresia* (Experts in Heresy)—three nobles who were chosen annually to report to the doge every movement of the Inquisition, and whose presence at trials was necessary for the validity of all the acts of the tribunal. See the *Familiar Letters of Giov. Battista Leoni*; Venice, 1592.

you will have merited by your goodness ' " (1). Shortly after this ebullition Bruno visited Padua ; " for what would his contemporaries have thought of the reformer of the heavenly and sublunary worlds, if he had never cut any figure at Padua ? " (2) But the "herald of modern thought" was not appreciated in the home of the great University ; he obtained very few pupils, and they were foreigners. After a stay of two months, the emptiness of his purse forced him to return to Venice ; and during the night of May 23, 1592, emissaries of the Holy Office took him from the palace of Mocenigo, and lodged him in the prison of the Inquisition.

Six days after his arrest, Bruno was led before the tribunal which, according to the laws of Venice, was to decide whether he was a pertinacious heretic, and therefore subject to the penalty provided for such enemies of both Church and State. The members of the court were Mgr. Taberna, the Apostolic nuncio ; Mgr. Lorenzo Priuli, patriarch of Venice, who had been Venetian ambassador in France, while Bruno was lecturing in Paris ; the inquisitor, Fra Giovanni Gabriele da Saluzzo, a most virtuous and erudite Dominican ; and the three "experts in heresy," Luigi Foscari, Sebastiano Barbarigo, and Tommaso Morosini—all, as their names indicate, members of the first families of the republic. The charges formulated in the denunciation of Bruno by Mocenigo were that the accused had repeatedly taught : I. That Catholics blaspheme when they say that in the Mass the bread and wine are transubstantiated into the Body and Blood of our Saviour. II. That the Holy Mass is an imposture. III. That all religions are false. IV. That Christ was a wretch, and a worker of evil deeds. V. That a distinction of three Persons in God would be an imperfection. VI. That our world is eternal, and that there is an infinity of worlds. VII. That God is continually making an infinite number of worlds. VIII. That Christ's miracles were only apparent ones, and that Christ was a magician. The Apostles were also magicians. He (Bruno) could work as many miracles as Christ, and more. Christ did not die voluntarily, and He fled whenever He was able. IX. That there is no

---

(1) Venetian trial, *Allegation* VIII. (2) PREVITI ; *loc. cit.*, bk. I., ch. xiii.

punishment for sin ; that the soul, the work of nature and not of God, passes from one animal into another; and that men are born of corruption, like the brutes. X. That the Blessed Virgin could not, if a virgin, have given birth to Christ. XI. That the Catholic Faith is full of blasphemies against the Majesty of God. XII. That it cannot be proved that our faith merits anything before God. XIII. That in order to live properly, it is enough to do as we would have others do to us ; and that God laughs at all sins other than the violation of this principle. To this summary of Bruno's teachings, Mocenigo added that the accused had asserted that in comparison with his knowledge, that of St. Thomas and of all the other Doctors of the Church was nothing.

At the very outset of his trial, Bruno strove to ingratiate himself with his judges, protesting that he desired to be re-admitted into the pale of the Church, and avowing repentance for having spoken and written "too philosophically, too rash-ly, and not sufficiently like a Christian." They who hold that the Nolan philosopher was ever determined to lay down his life in the cause of "truth," so violently oppressed by the Roman Church, should reflect on this appeal to the Venetian inquisitors : "I detest, abhor, and repent of having fallen into all the heresies and errors of which I have been guilty; as well as all the doubts which I have expressed in regard to matters of Catholic faith. And I beseech this holy tribunal, which knows my weakness, to receive me into the bosom of the Holy Church, providing me with the opportune means for my salvation " (1). Two months were now allowed to Bruno for the consideration of his miserable position ; and when he was brought again into court, he repeated his avowal of repentance, finally falling on his knees, and exclaiming : "I humbly beg pardon from God, and from your lordships, for all my errors ; and I declare myself ready to comply with all that your prudence may order as expedient for my soul. And I beg you to punish me severely, so that by a public demon-stration of penance I may cleanse my monastic habit from the stain I have put upon it; but if, through the mercy of God and of your lordships, my life is spared, I shall so re-

(1) Venetian Trial, *Allegation* XIII.

form it that its tenor will be as edifying as it has hitherto been scandalous " (1). Had this protestation been sincere, the Roman catastrophe would not have occurred; but the event proved that the unfortunate was only aiming at a dismissal, with a view to a return to Frankfort, and to his vomit. The Venetian tribunal pronounced no judgment in the case; but on June 12, Cardinal Sanseverino demanded, on the part of the Holy See, the extradition of Bruno, that he might be tried by the Roman Inquisition. The request was granted on January 15, 1593 (not 1598, as asserted by Schopp and some biographers); and on Feb. 27, the unfortunate was lodged in the prison of the Holy Office in Rome (2).

After seven years of patient and charitable effort to induce Bruno to make a sincere retractation of his heresies, and when it had become evident that the recantation at Venice had been a mere mockery of truth, the Holy Office proceeded to the solemn degradation of the culprit, and to his condemnation to the stake. The sentence seems to have been executed; the unfortunate dying in his obstinacy, and, according to Schopp, contemptuously turning his gaze away from the crucifix which was held in encouragement before him. We say that the sentence "seems" to have been executed; for until 1891 the arguments showing that the execution was merely in effigy were more conclusive than were those which indicated its reality. A letter purporting to be from Gaspar Schopp, who was then residing in Rome (3), describes the execution; but many good critics have denied the authenticity of this epistle. Again, Schopp is alone in his assertion. The Vatican Archives contain documents of the trial, but not of

(1) *Ibid., Allegation* XVII.

(2) The decree for the extradition of Bruno was signed by the doge Pasquale Cicogna, the same who had, a few months previously, appointed Galileo to a chair of mathematics in the University of Padua. Berti finds inconsistency in the ducal action ; but it was rather an indication of impartiality and good judgment.

(3) Convinced of his errors by the study of Baronio's *Annals*, this Lutheran scholar became a Catholic. Invited to Rome by Clement VIII., he wrote many pamphlets in defence of Catholicism, the Papacy, etc. But he was very litigious, and was given to paradoxes. In his presumed letter he says of Bruno's errors: "The Inquisition did not impute Lutheran doctrines to him. He was charged with having compared the Holy Ghost to the soul of the world; Moses, the prophets, the apostles, and even Christ, to the pagan hierophants. He admitted many Adams and many Hercules. He believed in magic, or at least he upheld it, and taught that Moses and Christ practised it. Whatever errors have been taught by the ancient pagans or by the most recent heretics were all advanced by this Bruno." (CANTU, *Illustrious Italians*, art. *Bruno*.)

the condemnation, nor is there any account of the execution; whereas, in every similar case, both of these are detailed. Again, the *Relations* of the foreign ambassadors resident at the Holy See, which never omitted any such items, say nothing of this event. Not even in the correspondence of the Venetian ambassador, the agent of that Government which must have felt an especial interest in the fate of Bruno, since it had initiated his downfall, do we find any allusion to the alleged catastrophe (1). Cantù cites a MS. of the Medicean Archives (No. 1608), dated at Rome on the very day of Bruno's trial, which narrates the burning of an apostate friar a few days before. Here some mention of Bruno's catastrophe would naturally occur, but there is not a word. Finally, the celebrated Servite, Friar Paul Sarpi, who never missed an opportunity of attacking what he feigned to regard as Roman intolerance, Roman treachery, etc., although he continued this course for many years after the trial of Bruno (2), and although his own position of antagonism with the Roman *Curia* perforce kept him on the lookout for instances which might inculpate Rome and justify the recent rebellious conduct of Venice toward the Holy See, never alludes to the alleged fate of Bruno. The same silence is found in Ciaconio, Sandrini, Alfani, Manno, and d'Ossat, all of whom would scarcely have omitted to notice so important an event, had it really occurred. And how is it that the *Martyrology* of the Protestants is also silent on this matter? Truly, Bruno was no more a Protestant than he was a Buddhist; but in those days, just as in our own, any person of Christian ancestry who antagonized Rome, and did not avow himself a Jew or a pagan, was claimed as their own by all the progeny of Luther. Such are the arguments which, until quite recently, appeared to justify the belief that Bruno was burnt in effigy, not in person. But in 1891 a document was

(1) The *Relations* of the Venetian ambassadors to the home government are rightly regarded by historians as the most precious, both for detail and accuracy, of all available sources for a knowledge of the events of the time.

(2) As late as December 6, 1611, we find Sarpi describing the execution at Rome (by strangling) of the French Abbé Dubois, for libels against the Jesuits, and claiming that the unfortunate had received a safe-conduct before journeying to Rome. At the same time he greatly decries Schopp, whom he describes as "meriting a greater punishment than burning in effigy."

unearthed, which leads us to believe that the philosopher of Nola did perish at the stake. Among the many institutions of mercy which have, for centuries, formed one of the chief glories of the Eternal City, one of the most interesting is that of the Confraternity of San Giovanni Decollato, the members of which devote themselves to the preparation of the capitally condemned for a happy death. For centuries this society has kept an exact record of all its unfortunate clients. Now, in the *Journal* of the " provisor " of the confraternity, which contains an account of the executions attended by the brethren from May 14, 1598 to Sept. 1, 1602, certain investigators appointed by the Crispi administration found, on page 87, the following narrative : " On Thursday, Feb. 16, 1600, at two hours of the night, it was intimated to our Company that in the morning justice was to be vindicated on an impenitent friar. Therefore, at six hours of the night the chaplain and the consolers, having assembled in Sant' Orsola, and having gone to the prison of Torre del Nona, and entered our chapel, and having made the accustomed prayers, the condemned apostate friar, Giordano Bruni (*sic*), a native of Nola in Naples, an impenitent heretic, was introduced. He having been exhorted by our brethren with all charity, we having also called to the work two Dominican priests, two from the Gesù, two Oratorians, and a Hieronymite. With every mark of affection and with much erudition, these priests showed the miserable man his many errors, but he remained fixed in his accursed obstinacy, confusing his intellect with a thousand perversities. His determination proving invincible, he was led by the officers of justice to the Campo di Fiori, and there having been stripped and bound to a stake, he was burned alive, our Company constantly chanting the Litanies, and the comforters exhorting him to the very last moment to abandon his obstinacy. But he finished his miserable life in it." Thus the question of the fate of the Philosopher of Nola appears to be finally settled. There need be no suspicion cast, great though be the temptation to do so, upon the authenticity of the decisive document; for although the unscrupulous Crispi presided at its delivery from the bowels of oblivion, the members of the Confraternity of San Giovanni Decollato admitted that it was transcribed from their records.

We are not disposed to apologize for the Inquisition in the matter of its treatment of Bruno; undoubtedly the ends of justice and the interests of society would have been met most amply, had he been kept in rigid seclusion during the term of his natural life. As to the rights of the Holy Office in the premises, they have been vindicated by us in an apposite dissertation (1). Concerning the philosophy of the Nolan, the scope of our work forbids our saying more than we have said; however, we may observe with Previti that " Bruno had all the weaknesses of the pagan philosophers, all the hypocrisies of the Byzantine heretics, all the impudence of the innovators of his day, all the unbridledness of the sophists of the eighteenth century, and all the intolerance of our modern free-thinkers " (2). Some have regarded him as a heretic, others as an atheist; the fact is that he was each in turn, for in one and the same treatise you will find him a pantheist and a materialist, a sceptic and an incredulist, a Lutheranizer and an Arian. His admirers have affected to compare him with the Angelic Doctor; but in the sketch of his life and doctrines which we have given—a sketch which is brief indeed, but wanting in no important feature—where is the indication that he ever effected anything great, advanced anything new, opened up any new horizon for modern thought, or gave any impulse to his age? There have been hundreds of Italian speculativists whose intellects were more brilliant, their erudition more profound and exact, than those of Bruno; but the modern mania for "statuefication" has never been excited in their regard. In truth, it is not the genius of Bruno that is apotheosized in the Campo dei Fiori; it is the renegade from Catholicism, the deserter from the cloister, the foe of the Roman Pontiff, the contemner of Catholic philosophy, the hater of " everything which is called God."

(1) Vol. II., ch. xxxi.　　　(2) *Loc. cit.*, p. 6.

APPENDIX.

CHRONOLOGICAL TABLE

Of the Roman Pontiffs, Rulers of Principal Nations, Principal Councils, Ecclesiastical Writers, and Heretics.

FIFTEENTH CENTURY.

Popes. Date of Election.	Holy Rom. Emp'rs. Date of Death.	Eastern Emperors. Date of Death.	Eccl. Writers.
Innocent VII., 1404	Wenceslaus(dep.),1400	Manuel, 1425	Peter d'Ailly.
Gregory XII., 1406	Robert, 1410	John Paleologus	St. Vincent Ferrer.
Alexander V., 1409	Sigismund, 1437	II., 1448	John Gerson.
John XXIII., 1410	Albert II., 1439		Thomas De Walden.
Martin V., 1417	Frederick III., 1493	*Kings of England.*	St. Bernadine of Siena.
Eugene IV., 1431		*Date of Death.*	Nicholas Tudeschi.
Nicholas V., 1447	*Kings of France.*	Henry IV., 1413	Alphonsus Tostat.
Calixtus III., 1455	*Date of Death.*	Henry V., 1422	St. Lawrence Justinian.
Pius II., 1458		Henry VI., 1471	St. John Capistrano.
Paul II., 1464	Charles VI., 1422	Edward IV., 1483	St. Antonine of Florence.
Sixtus IV., 1471	Charles VII., 1461	Edward V., 1483	Nicholas Cusanus.
Innocent VIII., 1484	Louis XI., 1483	Richard III., 1485	John Torquemada.
Alexander VI., 1492	Charles VIII., 1498		Denis the Carthusian.
			Thomas à Kempis.
			Bessarion.
			Platina.
			Gabriel Biel.

COUNCILS:

About 150: Pisa, Constance, Basel, and the Sixteenth General (of Florence).

HERETICS:

John Huss, Jerome of Prague, Adamites, Peter De Osma, Fossarii.

SIXTEENTH CENTURY.

Popes. Date of Election.	Holy Rom. Emp'rs. Date of Death.	Kings of Spain. *(After the Union of the Various Kingdoms.)* Date of Death.	Eccl. Writers.
Pius III., 1503	Maximilian I., 1519		Nicholas Tudeschi.
Julius II., 1503	Charles V., 1558	Ferdinand the	Tostat.
Leo X., 1513	Ferdinand I., 1564	Catholic, 1516	St. Lawrence Justinian.
Adrian VI., 1522	Maximilian II., 1576	Charles V. (abd.), 1556	St. John Capistrano.
Clement VII., 1522		Philip II., 1598	St. Antoninus.
Paul III., 1534	*Kings of France.*		Nicholas Cusanus.
Julius III., 1550	*Date of Death.*	*Kings of England.*	John Torquemada.
Marcellus II., 1555		*Date of Death.*	Thomas à Kempis.
Paul IV., 1555	Louis XII., 1515	Henry VIII., 1547	Denis the Carthusian.
Pius IV., 1559	Francis I., 1547	Edward VI., 1553	Bessarion.
St. Pius V., 1566	Henry II., 1559	Mary, 1558	Cajetan.
Gregory XIII., 1572	Francis II., 1560	Elizabeth, 1603	Blessed John Fisher.
Sixtus V., 1585	Charles IX., 1574		Erasmus.
Urban VII., 1590	Henry III., 1589		Sadoleto.
Gregory XIV., 1590			Pole.
Innocent IX., 1591			Melchior Canus.
Clement VIII., 1592			Soto.
			Louis de Blois.
			St. Charles Borromeo.
			Louis of Granada.
			Toledo.

COUNCILS:

About 100. Seventeenth General (of Trent).

HERETICS:

Luther, Zwingle, Calvin, Anabaptists, Anglicans, Anti-Trinitarians.

CONTENTS OF VOLUME III.

CENT. XV.-XVI.

Lightning Source UK Ltd.
Milton Keynes UK
UKHW051226090119
334855UK00010BB/1817/P